Beowulf at Kalamazoo

Medieval Institute Publications is a program of
The Medieval Institute, College of Arts and Sciences

 WESTERN MICHIGAN UNIVERSITY

Beowulf at Kalamazoo
Essays on Translation and Performance

Edited by Jana K. Schulman and Paul E. Szarmach

Studies in Medieval Culture L

MEDIEVAL INSTITUTE PUBLICATIONS
Western Michigan University
Kalamazoo

Library of Congress Cataloging-in-Publication Data

Beowulf at Kalamazoo : essays on translation and performance / edited by Jana
K. Schulman and Paul E. Szarmach.
    p. cm. -- (Studies in medieval culture ; 50)
  Includes bibliographical references and index.
  ISBN 978-1-58044-152-0 (clothbound : alk. paper)
  1. Beowulf--Translations--History and criticism. 2. Epic poetry, English
(Old)--Translations--History and criticism. I. Schulman, Jana K., 1959- II.
Szarmach, Paul E.
  PR1587.T7B46 2012
  829'.3--dc22

                                      2011040793

Contents

Part 2. Essays on Performance

Part 3. Reviews of Heaney's *Beowulf*

Acknowledgments

The editors, Jana K. Schulman and Paul E. Szarmach, would like to thank the contributors to this volume and are particularly grateful to those who revised their essays at the eleventh hour. Publications on *Beowulf* appear in journals and essay collections at an amazing pace, one difficult to keep up with. We also owe a special debt of thanks to Georgina Kleege for allowing us to publish Nicholas Howe's essay. Finally, thanks are due to Paul from Jana and to Jana from Paul. It's been an adventure.

Introduction

Jana K. Schulman and Paul E. Szarmach

"Beowulf" at Kalamazoo: Essays on Translation and Performance is a collection of essays designed to capitalize on the success of Seamus Heaney's prize-winning translation of *Beowulf* (1999). Heaney's translation bridges the gap between the ivory tower where most who study *Beowulf* reside and the lay readers drawn to the poem because of Heaney's reputation, the review in the *New York Times Book Review*, the Whitbread Prize for poetry in 1999, and even perhaps, the attractive and eye-catching cover. The reality is that Heaney's *Beowulf*—no matter the response—did something that few other translations have done: cause people to read the poem. At the same time, the last half-generation of scholars has shown a noteworthy interest in the performance aspects of the text, influenced by oral-formulaic theory to a significant degree. Scholars have sought to replicate the context and style of *Beowulf*, which has led, in turn, to readings, recordings, performances, and even inspired a rock opera.

Although we argue that Seamus Heaney's translation of *Beowulf* brought the poem out of the ivory tower and to many more and varied readers, the poem, its characters and settings, have long fascinated many, prompting these readers to render their own stories and/or to incorporate aspects of the poem into their own work. Tracking *Beowulf* through popular culture reveals movies, a rock opera, an opera based on John Gardner's book *Grendel*, comic books, graphic novels, classical music (an orchestral piece by Howard Hanson called "A Lament for Beowulf"), video games, and fan literature. For a thorough bibliography of *Beowulf* adaptations, see John William Sutton's website, Beowulfiana: Modern Adaptations of *Beowulf*, which is twenty-four pages long. With recognition of the popular and scholarly reception, we offer this collection.

We have conceived this book in three parts. The first, essays on translation, is subdivided into three sections: one on translations of *Beowulf* into English, responding specifically to Heaney; one on translation issues pertinent to the poem; one on translations of *Beowulf* into languages other than English. The second part explores issues of oral theory and performance. The third part collects all the reviews of Heaney's *Beowulf* written by Anglo-Saxonists. Finally, the book comes with a CD that provides readings of the first fifty-two lines from *Beowulf* in Old English and other languages as well as selections from Turkish and Asian epics, giving its readers a glimpse of old and modern epic singers.[1]

Part 1

Daniel Donoghue opens the book by analyzing Heaney's translation of *Beowulf* against the criticisms raised by Anglo-Saxonists who have reviewed the poem. Donoghue argues that Heaney's language does succeed as a medium for translating *Beowulf* precisely because he has created an idiolect that belongs to no one. Heaney's language is not elevated, not derived from Klaeber's glossary, not always Standard English, and not an Ulster dialect. Donoghue's apologia for Heaney's diction goes behind the appearances to suggest that in the deep structure of any response to Heaney is the glossary that Klaeber so brilliantly created for his edition. This "Klaeber consensus" lurks everywhere for, after all, there is no native speaker to guide readers differently. Heaney's idiolect disorients and disquiets the reader, forestalling any illusion that the translation is a transparent medium to the authentic *Beowulf* and creating a special place for *Beowulf*-in-translation. Donoghue thus offers a reconceptualized framework of understanding well beyond the usual scoring of hits and misses, which mark the reviewer's trade in a review of a translation. It is evident that Donoghue has such a high regard for Heaney and his translation that he can even voice the concern that Heaney will usurp the place of the *Beowulf*-poet with the result that *Beowulf*, as known through Heaney, could replace the original!

Nicholas Howe follows another direction altogether, as he considers the translation of *Beowulf* as a literary project per se and also with reference to Heaney's translation.[2] In a functional prologue Howe considers general relations between translator and original text, citing such successes as Richmond Lattimore's *Iliad* or Allen Mandelbaum's *The Divine Comedy*, or apparent mismatches as Charles Scott Moncrieff, who gave the English-speaking world Proust, but who impaled himself on the caesura of *Beowulf*'s mighty line. In short, "we should all be afraid of translating *Beowulf*. Very afraid." Anyone who steps forward to translate should fear three things: alliteration, diction, and variation. With witty aside ever-ready, Howe explores the snares and traps that these three fatal sisters can lay. He describes the obvious consequences of too insistent alliteration in several examples that make the translation incomprehensible or fog other verbal faults such as slackness. Problems with diction reflect the "ye olde" school of translation, where English appears as a historical thesaurus and Old English appears as a hotchpotch of archaisms and colloquialisms mixed together. Variation is the most difficult feature of Old English poetics to reproduce. When badly rendered, variation can appear as redundancy or as an obstacle to smooth syntax. For Howe the modern master of variation is Geoffrey Hill in "Mercian Hymns." Heaney's triumph, by contrast, is in the rendering of famous speeches, especially by old Beowulf in the final third of the poem.

The next group of articles focuses more narrowly on issues of translation. Roy M. Liuzza draws attention to the difficulty a translator has in interpreting and reading the tone, the emotional coloration, of the poem. In the nineteenth century, *Beowulf*, as an older poem, was assumed to have a simpler ethos and outlook, to be an unadorned heroic tale, a text taken at face value. These views represent the "iron" in Liuzza's title: iron represents either a gleaming sword, an emblem of heroism, or it is rusted and decayed, an emblem of treasure useless to man. In the twentieth century, critics began to recognize the complexities of the poem. Instead of viewing the author/narrator as merely a reporter, critics now recognized him as an artist. With the recognition of artistry came possibilities previously denied to the poem: one, in particular, is irony. Yet how do we understand irony in early literature where we lack verbal cues? Liuzza argues that just as we have to assess the context, our values, our attitudes in our own society to understand irony, so too must we do in reading and evaluating *Beowulf*. We have to judge whether irony is appropriate in the situation described, whether it enhances or confuses the provisional meaning, and whether or not the speaker might have intended it. In fact, it is our very openness to tonal ambiguities, to the possibility of irony that may make our reading of the poem more complex, but also more satisfying.

Just as Liuzza calls for the poem's audience to be open so too does Jana K. Schulman. While Liuzza calls for readers' openness to tonal ambiguities, Schulman calls upon readers to reconsider their initial views of and reactions to the words used to introduce Grendel and his mother. She investigates the introductory words for Grendel (*ellengæst*) and his mother (*āglǣcwīf*) first as defined by lexicographers, then by editors, and then by translators. Lexicographers in England and Germany codified the interpretation of the two characters by identifying Grendel as supernatural (a demon or spirit) and his mother as a monster or crone. Editors (from 1833 to 2010) and translators (from 1837 to 2010) vary somewhat their choices but few significantly. All three are complicit in influencing how readers of *Beowulf* react to Grendel and his mother, their definitions and translation choices succeeding in marginalizing Grendel and his mother even before the latter have proven their mettle. Schulman then engages in a thorough philological analysis of both compounds, concluding that *ellengæst* should be translated as "powerful guest" and that *āglǣcwīf* should be translated as "female warrior, fearsome woman." Reconsidering the definitions and translations of these words will affect the interpretations of the characters of Grendel and his mother, letting the readers of the poem form their own opinions.

While the translations considered in this volume follow any number of recognizable general paths, Henry Sweet's *Beowulfes sið* is one of a kind in that it is a rendition of the Old English poem into Old English prose. Displaying ultimately a concern for students that won him their admiration, Sweet sought a pedagogical *Beowulf* that introduced the language as well as broader cultural issues to them. The practical instructor speaks when Sweet says elsewhere: "Useful texts may be constructed by retelling the story of some literary composition in simple language." This path is the same taken by basic Latin primers that offer a "Dick and Jane" approach to the story of Troy in lesson 1. Sweet would undoubtedly be offended by this comparison, but he has to make choices that do not even create a "translated" or "paraphrased" *Beowulf*; thus, the dragon disappears from smoky view and the splendid oral style, the understanding of which just begins some two generations after Sweet, is no factor. The contra-position is too easy to assert, viz., it is a cruel kindness to offer students substitutes when for "a little extra effort" the genuine article, so to speak, can be had. In the two-course sequence that is typical in many curricula where "Intro" in the fall precedes *Beowulf* in the spring, Sweet's approach could be the teaser that tips the enrollment scale for the second course. As Paul E. Szarmach suggests, Sweet can still offer practical, pedagogical value in a classroom exercise where his take on the poem, compared to the *Beowulf*-poet's actual words, throws a special early light on the text that illuminates our own take on it and discloses the development of the subject. In this special way the present can join the past as part of the community of understanding.

Heaney's translation of *Beowulf* has definitely increased the poem's access for readers of modern English. But those of us who can read the poem either in Old English or modern English often do not realize or think about the significance of the poem for students of English literature and language in non-English-speaking countries. In what language do non-native speakers of English read the poem? In fact, *Beowulf* has been translated into at least twenty-three languages other than English in the last two centuries.[3] The poem itself is taught in English departments throughout the world, in Old English, modern English, and in translation. So readers can begin to appreciate and understand the issues involved with translating *Beowulf* into languages other than English, the third group of essays in part 1 presents five essays on translations of the poem into Czech, Spanish, Icelandic, Hungarian, and Italian respectively.[4]

Jan Čermák translated *Beowulf* into Czech, bringing the Old English epic into being in a country and language with little previous engagement with either that text or others of the English Middle Ages. His translation came out in 2003, and in 2004 Čermák was awarded the Josef Jungmann Prize, an award for translation given by the Czech Association of Translators and Interpreters. In addition, since the publication of his translation, more and more Old English texts have been or are being translated into Czech. Čermák's essay focuses on translation from the point of view of the translator himself. He identifies four key problems that beset him: (1) the lack of an epic register comparable to *Beowulf*, forcing him to draw from the idiom of thirteenth- and fourteenth-century Czech romances; (2) the need to avoid the romantic lexical layer coined during the Czech National Revival; (3) the dependence on verbs for sentence structure as opposed to nouns in Czech; and (4) the recognition that alliteration is not an organizing principle of Czech verse and that he would have to determine another way to orchestrate a sound pattern. Focusing on a key passage, provided in Old English and in Czech with an interlinear translation, Čermák then analyzes the choices that he has had to make, resultant losses in meaning, and the need to find synonyms, among other dilemmas facing a translator.

María José Gómez-Calderón discusses and evaluates the translations of the poem into Spanish and later Catalan. *Beowulf* has been translated more than any other Old English text, but the first translation, one for children, did not appear until 1934. In fact, the first few translations were intended to instruct their audience of young boys in the moral values of loyalty to one's kin and lord, comradeship, and courage and often did not even identify the poem as Old English, but merely presented it among other Nordic legends. The first literary sampling of the poem, a verse translation of several sections, appeared in 1947. Marià Manent opted to use the traditional, Spanish line for narrative and epic poetry, the *alejandrino*, an unrhymed sequence of fourteen syllables with some variation. Orestes Vera Pérez published the first complete prose translation in 1959 and provided a comprehensible text for a wide community of readers on both sides of the Atlantic. When this translation was done, *Beowulf* had been acclaimed as the foundational piece of the English Canon, an equivalent to the *Cid*, and Vera deemed access to the poem most important. The second stage of *Beowulf* translations included three—Luis Lerate's 1974 in verse, Antonio Bravo's 1981 in prose, and Ángel Cañete Álvarez-Torrijos's 1991 in prose—all translated as a direct consequence of the stabilization of the English Studies curriculum in Hispanic universities and all invested in presenting *Beowulf* to Spanish readers in the most effective way possible.

While *Beowulf* was translated into Spanish in 1934, the first complete translation of the poem into Hungarian did not appear until 1994. Just as Old English had a more linguistic significance for scholars in Czechoslovakia, so too was there a dearth of Anglo-Saxon literary studies in Hungary. The first anthology that included a selection of Old English poetry did not appear until 1986 and Old English was not taught at universities until well into the second half of the twentieth century. It is against this background that Katalin Halácsy Scholz situates and evaluates György Szegő's translation of *Beowulf.* Translation issues that Szegő had to deal with are similar to those faced by Jan Čermák: variation is possible in Hungarian and with the verse form that Szegő opted to use, but it often required him to rearrange lines; compounding is easy and Szegő was able both to use already existing compounds and generate new ones. On the other hand, kennings do not exist in Hungarian, but Szegő tried to re-create them whenever possible, with varying success. Scholz provides examples of some of Szegő's lines and demonstrates what works and what works less well. She concludes that regardless of the occasional infelicitous word choice or a loss of meaning, the translation of *Beowulf* successfully opens a window to the Germanic heroic world and conveys in Hungarian the spirit of the original.

Italian has the honor of being the first Romance language to have produced (an admittedly partial) translation of the poem (1833). The first complete translation of *Beowulf* appeared in 1883. Claudia Di Sciacca and Loredana Teresi introduce the six translations of *Beowulf* done in the twentieth century and then analyze them in terms of the prosodic, metrical, and lexical solutions adopted by the respective translators. In the introduction to each, the authors assess each translation for what it provides for its readers—notes, bibliography, division of sections, basic information provided, among other things—and offer a brief evaluation of the quality of the translation and the success of the translator. Next, Di Sciacca and Teresi provide examples of how the translators deal with alliteration and enjambment in the Old English. All six translators try to imitate the aural effects of the Old English by using looser alliteration and enhanced assonance and rhyme, even in prose. Turning to the lexical issues facing the translators, the authors focus on how they approach the kennings, compounds, and variation. The earliest two translators tend to a more archaic general lexicon; the latter four are closer to standard Italian. The earliest three pay little attention to kennings, compounds, and variation, while the latest three try to reproduce the poetic artistry of the original, with varied success.

Unlike the other four essays that focus on the problems besetting translators who translate from one language into a very different one, Pétur Knútsson offers us a glimpse into an intimate translation, one from Old English into modern Icelandic, that allows for a unique fidelity. While considering many of the same issues—problems with conveying archaic words, formulas, meter, kennings, rhythm, and compounds—Knútsson focuses on the similarities between the two Germanic languages and how these may influence a translator. He argues that disparity between two languages often causes a translator to put aside, quite consciously, the shapes and sounds of the original to search for an underlying content. Yet an intimate translation—one between closely related languages— makes apparent the dichotomy of translation, a denial of the essential role of form couched in language made up of forms. Halldóra B. Björnsson's translation of *Beowulf* has a fidelity arising not from her knowledge of Old English, since she had little prior knowledge of it before she began, but born of her familiarity with the idiom and with medieval Icelandic. This translation is unusual in many ways, not least because many of the problems that face translators who must consider language issues do not obtain: Old English and modern Icelandic are so closely related that Björnsson can not only echo and evoke other Icelandic texts with ease by incorporating some of their very vocabulary, but she can also use some of the exact words (OE: *cyning*/OI: *konung*).

Part 2

What Seamus Heaney has done for translation studies and *Beowulf*, Benjamin Bagby has done for oral theory and performance. His performance of the first 852 lines of *Beowulf* at the Thirty-eighth International Congress on Medieval Studies (2003) as well as other venues over the last several years has sparked debate, controversy, and delight. He has recorded a DVD of his performance of the first third of the poem (2006). Only now, with the ability to record the entire performance—including the interaction of the audience with the performer, the performer, and the supertitles themselves as opposed to just the audio—does the medium succeed in capturing the orality and the synergy of such a performance.

The second part of this volume focuses on oral theory and performance, responding to Bagby's *Beowulf* but also on comparative performance of epic in Turkey and Asia today. After Bagby's performance, a roundtable, chaired by Mark Amodio, followed the next morning at the Congress. The panelists were Bagby, who talks about how he moved away from conservatory performance to think about performing *Beowulf* and what exactly that entails, Karl Reichl, and John Miles Foley. The latter two, both specialists in oral epic and performance, comment on their own experiences as audience members—listening to Bagby's *Beowulf* and also respectively to performers of Kirghiz epic and South Slavic oral epics. What the transcript of the roundtable reminds us of is the relationship between audience and text.

For so many of us, *Beowulf* is a text we read, either in translation or in Old English. We do not perform it. It is a fixed text that we read into to find meaning, occasionally declaiming lines aloud to impress upon ourselves or upon our students the alliteration and the stress and the meter. But what Bagby's performance revealed and the discussion at the roundtable centered upon is that the poem is more than that. Music is linked to stories, to the transmission of history and the creation of myth. The performance of the poem requires not just the performer, but also the audience. The relationship between the two is a continuum that creates energy and even synergy. Reichl notes about the Kirghiz singers he has observed that "it's almost as if the singer is only a medium for the text, allowing the poetry to pass from him to the audience" (p. 215). Bagby's answer to a question about the authenticity of his performance echoes this comment by Reichl: authenticity comes from the fact that the audience, the listeners and the viewers, are caught up in the story. The audience for both Bagby's performance and the roundtable confirmed this energy as both audiences responded vigorously with applause and questions. The edited transcript of the roundtable is the first section of this part. The second section contains essays by Reichl and Foley on their own work with epic performance and what such study reveals or may reveal about performances of *Beowulf*.

Foley's essay, "Why Performance Matters," focuses on the question posed in the title, turning to comparative analysis of South Slavic epic to assist in the investigation. Foley takes as a given that we cannot reconstruct the "true" event of a performance as it really happened, and argues that it is far more important to understand the idiomatic implications of performance event and language. It is these idiomatic cues that connect epic performance and text, no matter when written or performed, transcending the biases of readers and auditors. Foley explores the idea of performance and reperformance, arguing that a credible reperformance is one that connects with a modern-day auditor because it removes the distance between the performance and the auditor by demanding the latter's attention and participation. Foley then analyzes keys or cues in South Slavic oral epic that prompt that audience, turning then to the first few lines of *Beowulf* to assess the cues there. These are, just as in the epic *The Wedding of Mustajbey's Son Bećirbey*: (1) the announcement of a performance by drawing attention—*hwæt*; (2) the linking of the performer and the audience by the use of the pronoun *we*; (3) the stipulation of the oral medium, *we have heard*; (4) the establishment of a mythic context by referring to the time when the retold events originally took place—*in gēardagum*. These four cues announce the telling of a heroic tale.

Reichl's essay, "'Swutol sang scopes': Field Notes on the Performance of *Beowulf*," complements Foley's and supplements his own remarks from the roundtable discussion. Like Foley, Reichl turns to living epic to provide examples for Anglo-Saxonists interested in the performative elements of *Beowulf*. He points out that while such comparisons may seem odd, they are not. *Beowulf* has been compared to the *Iliad*; both are epics and share certain typical traits of epic poetry. The *Iliad* can also be compared with the Kirghiz epic *Manas*, thus extending the comparative approach to allow us to assess a performance of *Manas* and extrapolate about a performance of *Beowulf*. Reichl argues that the scop's performance of poetry for an Anglo-Saxon audience must have been perceived as something like the sound of a musical instrument, something different from speaking. After considering examples of performances of the Kirghiz epic *Manas*, the Uzbek epic *Alpamish*, and the Karakalpak epic *Edige*—focusing on elements of plot, melody, gestures, the singers themselves—Reichl concludes that the study of oral epic contributes to our understanding that Performance (with a capital *P*) is in the foreground, comprised of words and sounds, which in turn comprise meaning and an aesthetic quality. Like Bagby and Foley, then, Reichl believes that a performance of *Beowulf* brings the audience closer to Anglo-Saxon oral poetry than any reading of the text.

Part 3

Since Heaney's translation of *Beowulf* was published in 1999, it has been reviewed at least thirty-five times: in popular magazines such as *Newsweek*, *Time*, *Forbes*, the *Economist*; in poetry journals such as *Poetry*, *Poetry Review*, *Poetry Wales*; and in more academic venues such as the *Times Literary Supplement*, *Arthuriana*, *Medieval Life*, *Notes & Queries*, and the *Kenyon Review*. Just as the venues for these published reviews vary, so too do the backgrounds of the reviewers. For example, the reviews written in poetry journals tend to be written by scholars who are also poets or poets who are also scholars. This essay collection, with its focus on *Beowulf* in English and other languages and particular emphasis on translation theory and performance, takes as a given that Heaney is a prize-winning poet. Therefore, this part of the book is a collection of the reviews written by Anglo-Saxonists who by and large take issue with the diction, alliteration, and meter of the translation as well as with any particular lapses in rendering here and there.[5] Few individual words in recent times, for example, have received such scrutiny as Heaney's "So," his opening word for Old English "Hwæt"!—a word that has tested many a translator of *Beowulf*. G. Storms says outright: "no translation of the poem is possible, only a literary commentary would do it justice." Such a perspective, understandable in a mature scholar, would keep the poem away from students and the general public. Daniel Donoghue's opening essay for this collection and his own review offer counters to the various strands of criticism that find difficulties with the execution or intention of Heaney's translation. One can discern in the longer reviews, which have the scope to introduce the larger subject of Anglo-Saxon literature or to amplify comments on the practical difficulties or to offer observations on translation theory, a consideration of significant issues in the study of literature. Heaney's translation does what all good literature does: force a reconsideration of the ends and means of literary activity. Many, if not most, of the reviews display the tension that sets the work against the audience, forcing a translator to make hard choices. One extraliterary issue in the publication of the Heaney translation is Nortonpower. "Norton I," *The Norton Anthology of English*

Literature—Norton's sophomore-level anthology of earlier British literature—features the Heaney translation of *Beowulf*, as does a new edition of the Norton critical edition of *Beowulf*, thus ensuring a dominant position of Nortonwulf in the college classroom. Heaney has made *Beowulf* new for the general public and for students, turning it into a classic, contemporary then and now. Robin Norris shows the way in her teaching by offering the Heaney translation at the beginning of her survey course as an Old English poem and at the end as a contemporary poem.[6]

So. This book came out of a series of activities and programs: speakers who participated in the "*Beowulf* Extravaganza," a series of lectures at the Medieval Institute; the *Beowulf* seminar that the editors taught in spring 2003; solicited essays; and expanded papers presented at the 2003 Congress. The interest in issues of translation and performance ran high, as attendance at Bagby's performance of *Beowulf* at the Congress and at the subsequent roundtable indicated. For all these reasons, we believe that the intended audience for *"Beowulf" at Kalamazoo: Essays on Translation and Performance*—a group that includes, but is not limited to, Anglo-Saxonists, translation theorists, linguists, oral and performance theorists, and anyone anywhere in an English department who teaches *Beowulf* in translation—will find this collection of essays and reviews informative, insightful, jargon-free, provocative, and useful.

Notes

1. The tracks on the CD are in the following order: 1. Bagby (Old English); 2. Čermák (Czech); 3. Gómez (Spanish); 4. Knútsson (Icelandic); 5. Scholz (Hungarian); 6. Di Sciacca/Teresi (Italian); 7. Reichl (*Manas*); 8. Reichl (*Alpāmish*); 9. Reichl (*Edige*). With the exception of Bagby's recording and Reichl's, the others are listed under the name of the author(s) of the essay and include the language of the recording. Reichl's three tracks are the recitation of three different epics.

2. Nicholas Howe died 27 September 2006, of complications from leukemia. The section on "Memoirs of Fellows" in *Speculum* 82 (2007): 813–15 contains a remembrance of him written by Robert W. Hanning, Anne Middleton, and Roberta Frank (chair).

3. There are complete translations of the poem into Czech, Danish, Dutch, French, Frisian, German, Hungarian, Icelandic, Italian, Japanese, Korean, Latin, Norwegian, Spanish, and Swedish. There are also translations into Arabic, Bengali, Bulgarian, Croatian, Finnish, Polish, Portuguese, and Russian.

4. We have included essays on five different languages into which *Beowulf* has been translated. In order to keep track of *Beowulf* translations, one may consult the following bibliographies and databases. The most recent online bibliography is Marijane Osborn's "Annotated List of *Beowulf* Translations" in which she lists recordings of the poem and various operatic versions, as well as translations. In addition, another online database, the Index Translationum, is available through UNESCO's website and is searchable. The most

recent print bibliography came out in 2005: "Translations, Paraphrases and Adaptations of *Beowulf* 1805–2005: A Preliminary Bibliography" by Hans Sauer, Inge B. Milfull, and Diana Rumrich.

5. In addition to these reviews, two others are worthy of mention: one by Frank Kermode, "The Geat of Geats"; and the other by James Shapiro, "'A Better Beowulf': Seamus Heaney strives for a close translation that is also good poetry in its own right."

6. Norris, "From *Beowulf* to 'Heaneywulf.'"

Part 1
Essays on Translation

The Languages of *Beowulf* between Klaeber and Heaney

Daniel Donoghue

Tom Shippey begins his review of Seamus Heaney's *Beowulf* with a note of exasperation that the poet's status as a Northern Irish Catholic Nobel Laureate trumps any reviewer's chance to question the translation's acceptance as the definitive version of the poem.[1] "Trump" isn't quite the right word, because Shippey turns to another metaphor from the world of card-playing. Heaney's *Beowulf*, he protests, is the equivalent of a straight flush, ace high, in the power-poker of American academic publishing, which makes it an impossible hand for any reviewer to beat. It is a surprising analogy, as if reviewing is a competitive game that depends a good deal on luck, or on the luck of a good deal. Not only is Heaney's hand unbeatable, but Shippey claims his own contains a mere two pairs, black aces and eights, or what is commonly known as the Dead Man's Hand. This part of Shippey's analogy alludes to a historical poker game with the direst consequences, because the loser is not just anyone, but Wild Bill Hickok, who was shot dead holding black aces and eights in a South Dakota town called Deadwood; hence the expression "Dead Man's Hand." What hope can there be for the reviewer as Wild Bill? He may as well fold, get up from the table, and ride off to live another day. Shippey might have done himself a favor by choosing an analogy from *Beowulf* itself and comparing his task to Beowulf's fight against a monster protected by a charm from the sharp edges of human weapons. In this case the reviewer-as-hero at least has a fighting chance, and we all know that Grendel left behind a Dying Monster's Hand. But both comparisons are excessive caricatures. If the poker analogy is unfair to the reviewer-as-desperado, the latter is unfair to Heaney-as-monster. He is not out to devour his reviewers. After all, Grendel started his reign of terror after becoming enraged at the sound of poetry, a response that is the exact opposite of Heaney's in setting his translator's hand to *Beowulf*.

Even though Shippey's playful analogy makes the odds too long, every Anglo-Saxonist can sympathize with the difficulties of reviewing Heaney's translation for a general audience like the readership of the *Times Literary Supplement*.

To give it anything less than glowing praise might seem ungenerous at best, and at worst a display of jealous sniping that would only confirm the unflattering stereotype of philologist-as-geek. The stakes are higher than with other *Beowulf* translations, the audience is wider, and Anglo-Saxonists cannot review it as we would a translation from any lesser luminary. The reviews of non-medievalists, although unengaged with the Old English, have been almost uniformly celebratory. Readers by the thousands catapulted *Beowulf* into best-seller lists. Heaney's translation won the Whitbread Prize in 1999 for Poetry and for Book of the Year. Why should Anglo-Saxonists spoil the party?

These pressures may be enough to motivate dead-hand-wringing by any reviewer, but once Shippey gets on with the task before him, he moves smartly to the language of the poem he knows so well, because here at least he finds firm ground for making comparative judgments. The confrontation with the Danish coast guard early in the poem is often singled out for its rhetorical deftness, and Shippey focuses specifically on the use of the subjunctive mood of several key verbs, such as *lēoge* in the clause *næfne him his wlite lēoge* (line 250), which his review translates as "unless his looks should happen to belie him."[2] In recasting the sentence Heaney puts the verbs in the indicative mood: "unless I am mistaken / he is truly noble" (lines 249–50). This passage is but one example of several instances where Shippey takes exception to Heaney's announced preference for the indicative mood (see below). Shippey's point is that Heaney finds indicatives even where the original has subjunctives, thus diminishing at least one aspect of the poem's rhetorical complexity. Heaney, in other words, finds the *Beowulf* he is looking for, even at the expense of a basic feature of grammar.

Heaney would not be the first to find a *Beowulf* he was looking for, but the syntax of the poem is more equivocal than Shippey allows. For the sake of discussion let us set aside the fact that the interpretation of *lēoge* depends on an emendation of the headword of the clause (*næfre* in the manuscript, emended to *næfne* in Klaeber 3). If we accept *næfne him his wlite lēoge* as the reading, then the use of the subjunctive verb may very well be driven by Old English syntax, because clauses introduced by the conjunction *næfne* quite often, though not always, take a verb in the subjunctive mood. In other words the verb's mood may have little to do with the coast guard's rhetorical skills if the *Beowulf*-poet was responding to syntactic preferences built into the language.[3] In this case, a translation into modern English could choose equally between an indicative verb ("unless his looks belie him") and a more periphrastic construction with "may" or "should," as Shippey has it: "unless his looks should happen to belie him." From a syntactic point of view the choice between Heaney's indicative and Shippey's subjunctive is arbitrary and depends ultimately on the translator's overall sense of drama in the scene.

I mention this passage from Shippey's review not for the sake of the tiresome academic game of "gotcha" or to rehearse a lesson of syntax. Any Anglo-Saxonist in Shippey's place would turn to the language of the original to see if the translation was faithful to it. Instead I am interested in how Heaney's translation has forced to the surface ways that we as Anglo-Saxonists position ourselves as possessors and protectors of *Beowulf*, how we decide what makes a translation acceptable, and how we address a general audience about the poem's interpretation by such a famous interloper. We are anxious that Heaney's translation will eclipse the original to such an extent that generations of students will come to accept his version as the real thing. We are anxious that the "authentic" *Beowulf* will lose out in this competition, whether it is conceived as a poker game or something else. Hence Shippey, who is well-qualified to point out the syntactic subtleties in the Old English, places such weight on a feature of language that may very well escape a nonspecialist like Heaney or the typical *Times Literary Supplement* reader. The turn to Old English is a way of reclaiming the poem.

Each review by an Anglo-Saxonist typically makes a similar turn from the translation to the original *Beowulf* in order to find where Heaney gets it right or falls short.[4] Yet as Shippey's poker analogy suggests (even with its disarming humor) each is engaged in more than a dispassionate compare-and-contrast exercise. The reviews at times convey a sense of urgency, as if they are caught up in a debate for the identity of *Beowulf* itself, so that they feel obliged to pass judgment on whether Heaney will sweep the field of all rivals. On one side of this struggle is the translation by Heaney (with his public stature and the book's positive reception) and on the other is the Old English poem, in the care of scholars with specialized training. The viability of Old English studies depends to a great extent on the reputation of *Beowulf* among nonmedievalists both within and outside the academy, so while the popular reception of Heaney's translation is a vindication of our attention to the poem, that success comes with a danger of replacing the authentic *Beowulf* with another. In addition, for many Anglo-Saxonists the professional stakes are deepened by our aesthetic and emotional attachment to the Old English poem. The danger is that Heaney may not be just an interloper but a usurper.

But just what is this original or authentic *Beowulf* that we set against Heaney's translation? Shippey's *Beowulf* has more syntactic nuance in the dialogue, as his interpretation of the clause with *léoge* and other passages suggests. His critique of Heaney's preference for the indicative mood in such instances is motivated, as he puts it, against the "academic folk narrative" that "Anglo-Saxons were just plain primitive."[5] To insist on the indicative, Shippey suggests, is to reinforce this demeaning folk narrative, whether Heaney intends it or not, because the leveling of subjunctives is a way of dumbing down the original poem. Shippey's sensitivity on this point is one that I and many medievalists can sympathize with, because we have all witnessed those subtle and not-so-subtle moments of condescension from others who, relying uncritically on a master narrative of cultural progress over time, assume that whatever was written at such an early date must lack sophistication. It is a remarkably tenacious if naive assumption, even among people who ought to know better; even among those who can quote approvingly T. S. Eliot's imagined exchange from "Tradition and the Individual Talent": "'The dead writers are remote from us because we *know* so much more than they did.' Precisely, and they are that which we know."[6]

Some of what Heaney writes of the Old English poem in his "Translator's Introduction" seems alarmingly consistent with the "academic folk narrative" that equates Anglo-Saxon with primitive, as for example when he recalls his approach to the poem:

> I came to the task of translating *Beowulf* with a prejudice in favor of forthright delivery. I remembered the voice of the poem as being attractively direct, even though the diction was ornate and the narrative method at times oblique. What I had always loved was a kind of foursquareness about the utterance, a feeling of living inside a constantly indicative mood . . .[7]

It is easy to see how this catalogue of the poem's rhetorical features—"forthright delivery," direct voice, foursquare utterance, "a constantly indicative mood"—could set off warning bells in Shippey and others to be on the alert for a translation that strips away or ignores the poem's various complexities of mood, voice, narrative perspectives, and so on. That is, the terms could be euphemistic substitutes for "crude," "simpleminded," "backward," and the like. But does Heaney's attitude toward the poem really support the "academic folk narrative"? The passage quoted above is cut off in midsentence; it continues,

> . . . in the presence of an understanding that assumes you share an awareness of the perilous nature of life and are yet capable of seeing it steadily and, when necessary, sternly. There is an undeluded quality about the *Beowulf* poet's sense of the world that gives his lines immense emotional credibility and allows him to make general observations about life that are far too grounded in experience and reticence to be called "moralizing."

Rhetorical virtues have now given over to *Beowulf*'s conceptual virtues—an understanding of life, an undeluded sense of the world, a hard-won wisdom, or as Heaney put it more recently, a "facing up to silent things accumulated within a consciousness"[8]—all of which seem to remove the poem from any trace of

condescension and instead elevate its affective and intellectual qualities to a level
that withstands the test of time and cultural difference. A classic, one might say.
On a more pragmatic level, there is no reason Heaney would devote years of his
career to render primitive charms in *Beowulf* or any other poem, no matter how
well W. W. Norton paid him for the job.

So far I have understood "primitive" as at best a backhanded compliment
with connotations of naiveté and ignorance, which I take to be close to Shippey's
understanding of the word. It stands in contrast to "sophisticated." But how useful is this primitive/sophisticated binarism in discussing the merits of a work of
literature? More precisely, can good literature display unsophisticated syntax? In
Old English poetry, at least, the answer is clear. We no longer try, as S. O. Andrew
did over sixty years ago, to find subordinating conjunctions wherever possible, as
if hypotaxis were a necessary condition for good literature. By the same principle,
Fred C. Robinson and others have demonstrated the kinds of complex readings
that can be drawn from clauses and phrases in apposition, which is a construction
that relies on the most basic syntactic repetitions.[9] Heaney makes a similar claim
about what he calls *Beowulf*'s "constantly indicative mood." This phrase alludes
to something beyond verb morphology, because whatever the shortcomings of
Heaney as a translator at the literal level, he was not unaware of the many occurrences of subjunctive verbs in *Beowulf*. In fact Heaney's full wording of the phrase,
"a feeling of living inside a constantly indicative mood," refers to a pervasive narrative attitude with the capacity to gaze steadily upon "the perilous nature of life" in
an "undeluded" way (as if delusion were a condition of contemporary poetry). This
feeling is a positive virtue in *Beowulf*, not the absence of something else. Far from
being a reflex of backwardness, it is a mark of maturity and clear-eyed wisdom,
which Heaney wants his translation to convey to its readers. In an essay on "The
Impact of Translation," Heaney uses similar phrases to discuss his attraction to the
language of poets who came of age in the Soviet Union and Eastern Bloc countries, poets with names such as Tsvetaeva, Akhmatova, and the Mandelstams. "For
these poets, the mood of writing is the indicative mood and for that reason they
constitute a shadow-challenge to poets who dwell in the conditional, the indeterminate mood which has grown characteristic of so much of the poetry one had
grown used to reading in the journals and new books, particularly in the United
States."[10] Here Heaney plays off the two basic meanings of *mood*: the first is the
grammatical feature of a verb; and the second is a state of mind or feeling—what
else can an "indeterminate mood" be? As an Anglo-Saxonist I am tempted to gloss
the second of the two meanings with "spirit" or "courage" from the Old English
mōd. In this sense Heaney's turn to the constantly indicative *mōd* in *Beowulf* is a
corrective, almost therapeutic in providing a healthy alternative to the language of
contemporary poetry.

The aspect of language in Heaney's translation that has excited the most searching comments from all reviewers, however, is not syntax but diction. Indeed that diction would be hard to ignore, not because of the modest number of "Ulsterisms" sprinkled throughout the text, but because of the attention given the topic in his "Translator's Introduction," where Heaney gives us two intertwined narratives. One concerns his personal coming-to-terms with English as an acquired language, a language imposed by the colonizers of Ireland and thus somehow alien even to those who speak it as a first language. As an undergraduate at Queens University, Belfast, he was struck by the sudden realization that a word used by some of his older relatives, *thole*, was a dialectal survival of the Old English *þolian*, which he found in the glossary of his student edition of *Beowulf*. This nugget of etymology had an effect on him far beyond the desultory curiosity it might arouse in many college students. It was an epiphany (now well known because it has been repeated about as often as his *Beowulf* has been reviewed). *Thole* became the key for the young Heaney to unlock an English word-hoard much older than the colonization of Ireland in the seventeenth century. It taught him that in some basic way his Ulster dialect is the equivalent of every other in English because it can trace a linguistic history back to the earliest records of the language. Moreover, if all dialects of English are equivalent from the long view of history, then Heaney's own has as much legitimacy as a poetic language and as much claim on the tradition of English literature as any other. This realization was an enabling moment for a young poet struggling to find his voice, and Heaney points to a similar epiphany in Joyce's *Portrait of the Artist as a Young Man*, when Stephen Dedalus discovers that the local word for *funnel*, "tundish," is "good old blunt English."[11] In their immediate contexts the homely epiphanies of *tundish* and *thole* give young Dedalus and Heaney the license they need to turn to their local linguistic resources to forge an artistic voice, which they proceed to do with famously happy results.

The second narrative in the shaping of his poetic language concerns the neo-Anglo-Saxon style Heaney picked up from Gerard Manley Hopkins and, more remotely, from the alliterative phrasings of Old English verse, which had emerged unbidden in his earliest poems. At a later date Heaney noticed "that without any conscious intent on my part certain lines in the first poem in my first book conformed to the requirements of Anglo-Saxon metrics" in their rhythms and alliteration. Other poems throughout his entire career show an inventiveness with compound words, which are a staple of Old English poetic diction. "Part of me, in other words, had been writing Anglo-Saxon from the start."[12]

Taken on their own, however, these two narrative threads that tie him to Old English do not necessarily give Heaney special insights or tools as a translator. Applied directly to the task of translating *Beowulf*, the threads might lead us to expect something that foregrounded the neo-Anglo-Saxon lines he had been writing all along, with its *tholes* and alliterating syllables. Nor do the threads supply him with a motive to take on *Beowulf*, although his estimation of the poem as equivalent to classics by Dante or Sophocles, which he has also translated, might be enough. A more specific motive concerns the now-familiar postcolonial move of a writer to appropriate a foundational text in the literary canon and reinterpret it in subtle ways (as in the case of Heaney's *Beowulf*), or re-create it more radically by defamiliarizing it, inverting hierarchies, and rewriting it for the formerly subject people.[13] One lesson learned from Heaney's encounter with *thole* in a glossary of a student's edition of *Beowulf* is that compared to our immense temporal distance from the poem today, the differences among contemporary dialects are trivial. After the passing of more than a thousand years does any variety of English have a better claim for translating *Beowulf* than another? "Standard English" (though notoriously difficult to define) is the frequent answer to the question, and the fact that *Beowulf* was written in a standard late West Saxon poetic dialect may contribute to a perception of equivalence. But Standard English is a prestige dialect for reasons that have little to do with its linguistic features, and, as this paper argues below, Heaney has his own reasons for turning to a different linguistic register.

Without doubt Heaney goes to some lengths to put an Irish thumbprint on what is, chronologically, the *most* foundational text in the English literary canon. There is almost a sense of a heroic *bēot* that if he can appropriate *Beowulf*, everything else is within reach too. This motive is most obvious in his deliberate use of Hibernicisms and dialectal words, many of which appear nowhere else in his poetry. Heaney and others have noted the irony that these words work against the most basic principle of translation because they require a second layer of translation in the form of a gloss to make them comprehensible to the intended audience.[14] The irony extends in yet another direction if words like *kesh* and *bawn* and *graith* make the diction of his *Beowulf* even *more* Irish than Heaney's many poems that take Ireland as their theme or setting.

This incongruity between the language of the Old English *Beowulf* and Heaney's translation (including but not limited to the Hibernicisms) has attracted the most spirited criticism from Anglo-Saxonists. We know the original poem's language to be formal, elevated, traditional, rich in formulas and apposition, and full of textual ambiguities that can frustrate even the most literal translation. The consensus seems to be that, whatever else can be said about Heaney's translation, it falls short in a number of the linguistic features that constitute the *Beowulf* known to Anglo-Saxonists.

As before, I want to ask: what is this authentic *Beowulf* that makes a fixed point of comparison for any translation? Specifically, how do we Anglo-Saxonists recognize when a translation is faithful to the Old English diction? The answer to this question may not be so obvious for the simple reason that there is no one around who is a native speaker of Old English, despite the number of scholars who have made that language their life's study and who know it with some intimacy—but not with native fluency. In some fundamental sense there is no original *Beowulf* available for comparison because everyone's *Beowulf* is already a translation. So when Anglo-Saxonists compare Heaney's translation to the authentic *Beowulf*, we end up measuring it against another modern translation. The Old English poem drops out of view; or perhaps a better metaphor is that it becomes a platonic shadow on the wall of a cave. We can even Germanicize the cave by reappointing it as a dragon's lair, but the important point is that the *Beowulf* known to the Anglo-Saxons remains behind us, out of our direct sight.

The question becomes not "What is the authentic *Beowulf*?" but "Whose *Beowulf* is the authentic one?" As far as diction is concerned the authentic *Beowulf* begins with the glossary of Friedrich Klaeber's edition. The historical basis for this answer is rather obvious: the current generation of Anglo-Saxonists closely associate *Beowulf* with Klaeber's edition, which has been an imposing and magisterial presence since it first appeared in 1922, although most of us came of age with the third edition of 1950. To single out Klaeber's is not to ignore other editions, such as Wrenn/Bolton, Dobbie's ASPR volume, Mitchell/Robinson, and now Klaeber 4.[15] But Klaeber 3 has been the vade mecum that almost all Anglo-Saxonists used during their training in graduate seminars. We cut our professional teeth on it. Many of us continue to consult our old dog-eared Klaeber 3s even now that a new edition has replaced it. They are not only dog-eared, but when closed and viewed from the side, our Klaebers reveal a clump of pages darkened by repeated thumbing. This part is the 150-page glossary. Beginning with the formative years in our careers, we have come to accept an equivalence between Klaeber's definitions and the Old English headwords so that *ōretmecg*, for example, means "warrior" and nothing else, because the glossary lists no other definition.

When I teach Old English, one of the first bits of advice I give the students is to resist the urge to write their glosses between the lines of text, because no matter how convenient it is for the immediate purpose of in-class translation, it has a deleterious effect on their ability to prepare for an exam. When they return to those glossed passages for review, they may think they are reading the Old English words, but their eyes spend far more time on the interlinear jottings. They become aware of the illusion only when an exam text is put before them and the Old English looks surprisingly and dauntingly unfamiliar. Something similar but on a larger scale has happened with our understanding of the text of *Beowulf*, so that a translation sounds "faithful" or "correct" or "exact" insofar as its language echoes the definitions found in Klaeber's glossary.

The strength of this equivalence between the Old English words and

Klaeber's glosses becomes clear when Anglo-Saxonist reviewers pick out specific instances where Heaney's translation of *Beowulf* is found wanting. In these cases they cannot go into technical detail for the general reader, so they point to other published translations to represent the Old English text. For example, in commenting on the scene in which Æschere's head is discovered, Howell Chickering points to R. M. Liuzza's "very exact translation":

> To all the Danes
> the men of the Scyldings, many a thane,
> it was a sore pain at heart to suffer,
> a grief to every earl, when on the seacliff
> they came upon the head of Æschere

for the Old English

> Denum eallum wæs,
> winum Scyldinga   weorce on mōde
> tō geþolianne,   ðegne monegum,
> oncȳð eorla gehwǣm,   syðþan Æscheres
> on þām holmclife   hafelan mētton.
>   (lines 1417b–21)

Chickering's immediate point is that Heaney's translation does not preserve the artful delay in the Old English, which withholds until the final half-line a crucial detail about just what caused the feeling of shock in the Danes. Describing an emotional reaction before revealing its cause is a narrative technique the *Beowulf*-poet uses here and elsewhere to great effect. Heaney, by contrast, gives away the detail of Æschere's head at the beginning of the last line:

> It was a sore blow
> to all of the Danes, friends of the Shieldings,
> a hurt to each and every one
> of that noble company when they came upon
> Æschere's head at the foot of the cliff.

Part of what makes Liuzza's translation "very exact" is the way each lexical word (as opposed to function words) corresponds to a word in the Old English text, and the translation of almost every such lexeme can be found under that headword in Klaeber 3's glossary, such as *mōd* 'heart', *geþolian* 'to suffer', *ðegn* 'thane', *eorl* 'earl', and *holmclif* 'sea-cliff'. (Exceptions would be Liuzza's use of "men" for *wine* and "sore pain" for *weorc*.) To Anglo-Saxonists Liuzza's translations of these individual words have a self-evidently authentic ring to them, even to the extent that we may not pause to think what a novice reader, for example, might make of "thane" or "earl." To point out the close correlation with Klaeber's glossary is no criticism of this or any translation but merely illustrates the larger point that when specialists reach for a translation to represent the Old English *Beowulf*, it is usually one with diction drawn heavily from Klaeber.[16]

Likewise Nicholas Howe's review turns to E. Talbot Donaldson's prose translation to give readers of the *New Republic* a sense of the Danish coast guard's aphoristic rejoinder to Beowulf and his companions shortly after their arrival: "A sharp-witted shield-warrior who thinks well must be able to judge each of the two things, words and works."[17] The Old English in Klaeber 3 reads:

> Æghwæþres sceal
> scearp scyldwiga   gescād witan,
> worda ond worca,   sē þe wēl þenceð.
> (lines 287b–89)

Again Donaldson's modern English comes straight from Klaeber 3's glossary with few changes—although to be fair words like *word* and *þenceð* could hardly be glossed as anything but "word" and "think." Heaney's translation of these lines in Howe's estimation "misses the original's proverbial tone":[18]

> "Anyone with gumption
> and a sharp mind will take the measure
> of two things: what's said and what's done."

Since Donaldson's prose smoothes over the intricate dance steps of verse syntax and meter, his diction must bear the burden of conveying what makes the tone proverbial. But I am not at all sure a general reader would see what makes Donaldson's more proverbial than Heaney's. The choice of "gumption" marks Heaney's as more folksy, but does that make it less aphoristic? Perhaps it does, but we specialists may not be the right readers to ask. We have internalized Klaeber's glossary so thoroughly that we can read translations like Donaldson's in reverse, as it were, and through its familiar diction sense that we are reaching back to the Old English poem itself. This perception of synonymity can become a comfortable illusion for anyone who accepts Klaeber's glossary uncritically.

Because of its perceived contiguity with the Old English poem, Klaeber's glossary has become a synecdoche, a part of the whole that Anglo-Saxonists call *Beowulf*. How can we characterize this diction? We can begin by noting that it is conservative, not only because it preserves some old fashioned or antiquarian meanings such as "corslet," but also because glossaries are almost always compiled by building on earlier ones. Its conservatism is also apparent in Klaeber's preference for preserving etymons, identified by small capitals in definitions like "GLEE-wood, harp" for *glēo-bēam*. The diction of the glossary is also analytical, literal (not given to metaphors), and formal (the opposite of colloquial).[19] These features are in some measure the product of Klaeber's rigorous academic training, which was undertaken in late nineteenth-century Berlin, and are in no way a flaw in his scholarship. Indeed the reason that his glossary has become synonymous with the language of *Beowulf* is that he did such a superb job. His scholarship is so richly detailed and precise that many Anglo-Saxonists have implicitly conceded that it cannot be gainsaid. Only in recent years has the field begun to move away from what has been called the "Klaeber consensus."[20]

According to his own account, Seamus Heaney first worked out a literal translation of *Beowulf* using Klaeber's edition and only afterwards began to turn it into lines of poetry.[21] One of the most striking results of his versification is how cleanly the language of Klaeber's glossary drops off even while Heaney keeps a roughly line-for-line correspondence to the Old English. For example, he translates a passage summarizing the hardships endured by the Danes while Grendel was occupying Heorot after dark:

> So that troubled time continued, woe
> that never stopped, steady affliction
> for Halfdane's son, too hard an ordeal.
> There was panic after dark, people endured
> raids in the night, riven by the terror.
> (lines 189–93)

Only three of the lexical words in this passage, *woe*, *son*, and *people*, are found in the relevant entries in Klaeber 3's glossary; by contrast Donaldson's translation keeps close to Klaeber, and only about three words (depending on how strict the correspondence must be) are *not* found in the glossary: "So in the cares of his times the son of Healfdene constantly brooded, nor might the wise warrior set aside his woe. Too harsh, hateful, and long-lasting was the hardship that had come upon the people, distress dire and inexorable, worst of night-horrors."[22] The changes introduced by Heaney cannot be called errors because they are at once consistent with the general sense of the passage and not literal enough that one can point to individual mistranslated words. Yet sustained over 3,182 lines this freedom from the glosses in Klaeber 3 can be disorienting to Anglo-Saxonists, who are trained to be literalists.

Largely because Heaney's "Translator's Introduction" contains all the necessary ingredients for identity politics, reviewers of every sort have been quick to impute a political motive to his "Hibernicisms" or "Ulsterisms." But with the exception of the somewhat archaic "riven," the passage from Heaney quoted above has no word that is not part of written Standard English, and the same is true of many passages; the language is merely un-Klaeber-like. Throughout the poem the number of words with an Irish etymology is relatively small (they include *bawn*, *bothy*, *brehon*, *kesh*, *sept*, and *session*), while others like *graith*, *hirpling*, *hoke*, *howe*, *tarn*, *thole*, *wean*, and even *riven* are dialectal or rare words with a non-Celtic etymology. Most of the idioms or syntactic constructions that seem dialectal are not exclusively found in Irish English. *Gumption*, for example, is a colloquialism in Scottish and American English. Tom Shippey singles out "That was one good king" and "They were a right people" as idioms that fit in the English dialects that he knows. Heaney's *tarn* is a northernism also used in Edwin Morgan's translation of *Beowulf*.[23] Without the "Translator's Introduction" tipping us off, just how "political" or "Irish" would Heaney's translation seem?

But the fact is that Heaney did tip us off, and readers and reviewers respond in ways that reveal their ideological preconceptions about *Beowulf*. Howe calls the insertion of words like *bawn* and *hoke* "puzzling and intrusive, for they introduce an element of what one might call political dialect into the modern English version that is not in the Old English version."[24] Chickering calls them "a signal of cultural difference" that can alienate readers who have no acquaintance with Hiberno-English. Chickering goes on to say, "this strange dictional coloration does not accurately represent the language of *Beowulf*."[25] These observations carry an implicit assumption—let's call it a desire—that the language of the Old English poem is apolitical and culturally neutral in ways that a modern translation should reflect in its own neutral language. One obvious place to find such language is in the glossary of Klaeber 3, which as we have already seen is the time-honored touchstone for the diction of *Beowulf*. According to this way of thinking Klaeber's *Beowulf* is apolitical where Heaney's is political. Modern and postmodern criticism has taught us to be suspicious of what presents itself as ideologically neutral, but even without such an admonition it is clear that the late West Saxon poetic koine displayed in our only copy of *Beowulf* had political significance a thousand years ago, even if we may never know just what precise dimensions that significance took. Similarly, we can accept in principle that Klaeber's scholarship was motivated at least in part by political ideals even if he left them unexamined and unarticulated.[26] We may argue the merits of Heaney's politics as they are revealed in his translation, but there is no point in arguing for an ideologically bleached *Beowulf*. Every version of the poem, whether it is the one preserved in London, British Library, MS Cotton Vitellius A. xv or a modern translation, offers itself in a political dialect. Heaney was simply explicit about his.

The way readers respond to the entire poem begins with the now-famous opening word of Heaney's translation, "So." Or more precisely the response begins with the extended discussion in his "Translator's Introduction," in which he describes "So" as coming from "a familiar local voice . . . that had belonged to relatives of my father, people whom I had once described (punning on their surname) as 'big-voiced scullions.'"[27] Heaney's extensive discussion about this remarkably localized voice creates an overdetermined "So" that subtly provokes a response that cannot be politically or culturally disengaged. Like other readers, the reviewers make a choice either to accept or to resist Heaney's self-described "Hiberno-English Scullion-speak." But why did he privilege this particular variety of language when Heaney presumably could have chosen another?

It has become a commonplace for translators of *Beowulf* to speak of the difficulties of finding the right linguistic register to convey the language of the original. Part of the difficulty is that today there is no stylistic equivalent to the formal, artificial, traditional language in *Beowulf*, especially for poetic translations. Nothing comparable to the Miltonic epic style, for example, is available, and it is hard to imagine a poet after Tennyson even attempting a style so self-consciously elevated. Heaney's decision to turn to Scullion-speak has its risks, but there is an interesting logic to it. If an elevated style is unavailable in English prosody today, then (to continue the spatial metaphor) Heaney turned in a horizontal direction for a suitable voice, which he found in a dialect familiar to him. The risk of this sideways move is that the dialect is not literary but oral, and known to very few. In fact it is known only to Seamus Heaney.

I am not an expert on the English spoken in Ulster, nor have I ever listened to one of Heaney's Scullion relatives, although I am willing to believe that they would utter "So" and "We cut the corn today" as Heaney describes it. But I am quite sure his father's relatives never said anything like "Then he who had harrowed the hearts of men with pain and affliction in former times and had given offense also to God found that his bodily powers failed him." While this sentence from lines 808–11 is picked almost at random from Heaney's *Beowulf*, there are scores of others that demonstrate that the dialectal identity frequently attributed to the translation is something of an illusion. It may be an enabling illusion (just as "So" was an enabling note), but in reading Heaney's *Beowulf* we are assuredly not reading the transcription of an Ulster dialect. From a descriptive point of view, the language of his translation has much in common with Standard English, but with an admixture of colloquial idioms and dialectal words. As the sentence quoted above demonstrates, it also has archaic and formal literary properties such as complex syntactic patterns that are part of no one's spoken language today. The language is not elevated, it is not from Klaeber, it is not quite Standard English, and it is not an Ulster dialect.

So, in attending to "the enabling note" of the "big-voiced scullions," Heaney has invented an idiolect for the purpose of translating *Beowulf*. It is important to remember that Heaney himself does not identify the language as an Ulster or

Scullion dialect. He writes that he wanted his translation "to be speakable by one of those relatives,"[28] which is a much different thing from a language spoken by them. The idiolect can still contain syntax and diction never uttered by a Scullion as long as Heaney's poetic ear can hear their voices speaking the lines. If criticism about the presence of ideology is misdirected, another criticism about Heaney's language, inspired by Ben Jonson's memorable quip about Spenser, may be nearer the mark. To paraphrase: Heaney, in affecting the Scullions, writ no language. Like Spenser's faux-archaic English, "Scullion-speak" is not "natural" and reveals its artful contrivance in almost every line. But Jonson's criticism has more wit than sting, because generations of readers have continued to enjoy Spenser's nonlanguage, just as many contemporary readers have been able to enter into the imaginative world of *Beowulf* through Heaney's nondialect. The next clause from Jonson's assessment is no less applicable: "yet I would have him read for his matter."[29]

Much attention has been given to the politics of Heaney's voice, but the artifice of his language has important consequences for the aesthetic reception of his translation. Because the idiolect belongs to no one, it subtly disorients each reader, even those whose personal dialects may be similar to Heaney's own. Augmented by Hibernicisms like *kesh* and *bothy* and even by Heaney's identity politics, this sense of disquiet forestalls any seductive illusion that the translation is a transparent medium through which readers can apprehend the authentic *Beowulf*. Every defamiliarizing touch reminds us that the old poem is the product of a now-distant culture, because neither language is ours. Thus the reader is suspended between the Old English of *Beowulf* and Heaney's nonce creation, between what is no one's native language and one poet's idiolect. This place turns out to be a good *middangeard* for *Beowulf* in translation.

Notes

I would like to thank colleagues and students at Yale and Harvard, whose comments on earlier versions of this essay were invaluable in shaping the argument. I also thank Paul Szarmach for inviting this contribution and Brandon Tilley for research help.

1. Shippey, "*Beowulf* for the Big-Voiced Scullions," p. 9. Shippey reviews the earliest publication of Heaney's *Beowulf* (London: Faber and Faber, 1999), but throughout this article the edition quoted is Donoghue, *Beowulf: A Verse Translation*.

2. All Old English quotations come from Klaeber, *Beowulf and the Fight at Finnsburg*, 3rd ed., hereafter called Klaeber 3. Although the fourth edition (Fulk et al., *Klaeber's Beowulf*, hereafter Klaeber 4) has now been published, Heaney's translation and the subsequent reviews rely on Klaeber 3.

3. See Mitchell, *Old English Syntax*, §877, §§3552–55, and §3658. See also the note to these lines in Klaeber 4, which paraphrases the passage with indicatives: "it is my hope that he is what he appears to be."

4. Besides Shippey's, the other two reviews quoted in this article are Chickering, "*Beowulf* and 'Heaneywulf,'" and Howe, "Scullionspeak," but see the others reprinted in this volume. In this paragraph and elsewhere, I take the liberty of generalizing about opinions of Anglo-Saxonists expressed in various written and oral contexts.

5. Shippey, "*Beowulf* for the Big-Voiced Scullions," p. 9.

6. Eliot, *Sacred Wood*, p. 4. Eliot's validation of the past was anticipated by Bernard of Clairvaux, whose extended simile confirms Eliot's point in the most literal way: "We are like dwarves sitting on the shoulders of giants; we see more things and more distant things than they did, not because our sight is keener or because we are taller, but because they lift us up and add their giant stature to our height" (John of Salisbury, *Metalogicon*, 3. 4).

7. Heaney, "Translator's Introduction," p. xxxvi.

8. Heaney, "Irish Poet," p. 414.

9. Andrew, *Syntax and Style*; Robinson, *"Beowulf" and the Appositive Style*.

10. Heaney, "Impact of Translation," p. 39.

11. Quoted from Heaney, "Drag of the Golden Chain," p. 14.

12. Heaney, "Translator's Introduction," p. xxxiii; see also Heaney, "Drag of the Golden Chain," pp. 14–15.

13. See especially Eagleton, "Hasped and Hooped and Hirpling."

14. The irony is often overstated because archaisms like *mere*, *byrnie*, and *thane* are just as foreign to Standard English though commonplace among *Beowulf* translations.

15. With the arrival of Mitchell/Robinson in 1998 and the revision of Klaeber just published by Robert E. Bjork, John D. Niles, and R. D. Fulk, the exclusive hold of Klaeber's third edition on the current generation of Anglo-Saxonists will give way to something else. But for scholars working today the pervasive influence of Klaeber is hard to overstate.

16. As the author of a rival translation, it is to Chickering's credit that his review cites sparingly from his own *Beowulf: A Dual-Language Edition*, but it is also the case that the diction of his translation corresponds closely to Klaeber's glossary.

17. Howe, "Scullionspeak," p. 34.

18. Howe, "Scullionspeak," p. 34.

19. See the headnote to the glossary in Klaeber 4: "Many archaic or excessively formal items of vocabulary [found in Klaeber 3] have been eliminated from the glosses, but for many OE words, natural-sounding modern equivalents are not to be found, and it should be remembered that the diction of OE poetry is by design formal and elevated" (p. 343).

20. Klaeber's editorial decisions have not gone unchallenged; see, for example, Robinson, "*Beowulf* in the Twentieth Century," which surveys the "Klaeber consensus" and concludes that a new edition is needed to bring the study of *Beowulf* up to date with advances in the field, as the Mitchell/Robinson edition has subsequently done, as has Klaeber 4. See also the superb new prose translation by R. D. Fulk, *The Beowulf Manuscript*. In many passages Fulk's translation shows a refreshing willingness to depart from the glossary of Klaeber 4 (which he co-edited). It is destined to replace Donaldson as the standard prose translation of *Beowulf*.

21. Heaney, "Translator's Introduction," p. xxxiii.

22. Donaldson, *Beowulf: A Prose Translation*, p. 6.

23. Morgan, *Beowulf*, lines 846 and 1426.

24. Howe, "Scullionspeak," p. 35.

25. Chickering, "*Beowulf* and 'Heaneywulf,'" p. 173.

26. See, for example, Bloomfield, "Diminished by Kindness," and "Benevolent Authoritarianism."

27. Heaney, "Translator's Introduction," p. xxxvi.

28. Heaney, "Translator's Introduction," p. xxxvi.

29. Jonson, *Timber*, p. 38.

Who's Afraid of Translating *Beowulf*?

†Nicholas Howe

No one, or so it would seem from the number of *Beowulf* translations that have been done into English and other languages since the early nineteenth century. Leaving aside children's versions, condensations, novelizations, comic-book versions as well as additional exotica and ephemera, focusing only on those translations that are likely to be shelved in the PR 1583 classification of a university library, there are some "sixty-four substantial or complete translations into modern English" of one variety or another and a substantial additional number into such languages as Bulgarian, Serbo-Croatian, Hungarian, Spanish, French, Italian, Arabic, and Japanese, as well as the modern forms of the cognate Germanic languages.[1] This information appears in Marijane Osborn's invaluable survey of the subject in Robert Bjork and John Niles's *Beowulf Handbook* published in 1997, though it must now be supplemented by at least four new versions done into English in the subsequent years.[2]

There are also, I suspect, other versions being completed as I write by those convinced they have found the magic formula to produce that much-desired achievement: a version of *Beowulf* to match those of Homer by Richmond Lattimore, Robert Fitzgerald, or Robert Fagles; or of *The Divine Comedy* (in part or whole) by Allen Mandelbaum, Robert Pinsky, or W. S. Merwin; or of *Gilgamesh* by David Ferry or . . . but there is no need to extend this list. That some would say Seamus Heaney has already done such a *Beowulf* has, I am certain, only confirmed the desire of these closet translators to produce their own versions because (as I have learned) they are more than ready to say that he—Nobel or no Nobel—does not understand the poem. A brief aside about the sensitivities of *Beowulf* translators will illustrate this claim that the work has become a Holy Grail of sorts. After publishing one of the very few mixed reviews of Heaneywulf—that is to say, one that was not entirely a rave—I heard from other translators of the poem.[3] One

Editors' note: Nicholas Howe died on September 27, 2006.

bitterly attacked me for the success of Heaney's version, as if I had somehow manipulated its critical reception in the United Kingdom and the United States, only then to cover my tracks by writing my own less favorable review; and two others sent me their joint translation in typescript with the hope that I would read it and agree that it was proof Heaney's failure to employ regular alliteration throughout his version proved that he did not appreciate the poem.

No doubt some readers reached a very similar conclusion about the translator's failure to understand the poem after the then-famous William Morris turned A. J. Wyatt's prose version of *Beowulf* into alliterative verse in 1895. A hundred years and more later, one can only say that such readers were right. For all of his reputation and prominent role in the late Victorian revival of medieval culture, Morris produced an unreadable *Beowulf* written in a variety of English never used by any human being known to have walked on this planet. Consider, for example, the opening lines of Morris's version:

> What! we of the Spear-Danes of yore days, so was it
> That we learn'd of the fair fame of kings of the folks
> And the athelings a-faring in framing of valour.
> Oft then Scyld the Sheaf-son from the hosts of the scathers,
> From kindreds a many the mead-settles tore;[4]

Put aside for a moment the inaccuracies in this passage, starting with the misreading of *we* in line 1 as referring to the Spear-Danes, and try to imagine yourself fated to hearing all 3,182 lines of this *Beowulf* in a sitting or two, even with all the beer in Heorot.

To name only two *Beowulf* translators would be invidious—though Heaney and Morris are the most famous as literary figures—so here are a few others that frequently appear on library shelves: poets and other writers of reputation such as Edwin Morgan, Burton Raffel, Kevin Crossley-Holland, William Alfred; accomplished scholars such as John R. Clark Hall, E. Talbot Donaldson, Constance Hieatt, Stanley Greenfield, Ruth Lehmann, Marijane Osborn, and R. M. Liuzza; as well as the odd figure of literary fame such as Charles Scott Moncrieff, the first and still wonderfully readable translator of Proust into English.[5] With a cast of characters like these—and many others have been excluded, including a few that could be diagnosed as cranks worthy of cameo roles in any academic novel—we have the makings for a vivid piece of literary history. When one adds the close brushes *Beowulf* has had with figures of true literary greatness, such as passages translated by Tennyson and Longfellow or the first popular paraphrase of the poem published in Charles Dickens's *Household Words*, then this piece of literary history acquires value beyond the merely curious.[6] It gains yet more importance if one considers those poets who have been deeply influenced by their reading of

Old English poetry, sometimes done in the course of translating it while under-graduates: Gerard Manley Hopkins, Ezra Pound, W. H. Auden, Basil Bunting, David Jones, Richard Wilbur, Thom Gunn, Geoffrey Hill, and Susan Howe.[7]

There is, in other words, a history to be written of the influence that Old English poetry has had on nineteenth- and twentieth-century poetry in English. This influence came about partly through reading the poetry in the original language, partly by reading it in published translations, and partly by doing it as interlinear glosses for in-class translation assignments. The present study is not a full rehearsal of that history, though it will refer to many of the translations of *Beowulf* done since Grímur Jónsson Thorkelin published the first one in 1815, in order to suggest a different answer to the question posed in my title: namely, we should all be afraid of translating *Beowulf*. Very afraid.

I offer this answer because the casualty rate among *Beowulf* translators seems inordinately high. Almost all of the translations done of the poem in the past, especially before 1960 or so, are unreadable today and many were probably unreadable when they first appeared. Take the case of Charles Scott Moncrieff whose *Beowulf* appeared in 1921, early in the same decade when he altered the course of modernist fiction in English by translating the first seven parts of Proust's *À la recherche du temps perdu*. On the face of it, anyone who could render Proust's French into compulsively readable English should have stood a reasonable chance of doing *Beowulf* into something that might be considered fluent, if not contemporary English. Here are the first five lines of his version:

> What! We of Spear-Danes / in spent days,
> Of the Folk-Kings' / force have heard,
> How the Athelings / excelled in fight.
> Oft Shield of the Sheaf / from scathing hordes,
> From many meinies / their mead-stools tore.[8]

The slashes that Scott Moncrieff prints in the caesura of each line read less as punctuation marks meant to signal a pause than they do as signs of his inability to write a continuous, flowing version of *Beowulf*. Their use suggests a translator who could not successfully resolve the two half-lines of the Old English poetic line into a single line of modern English poetry. If pressed to the wall, I think I could listen to more of Scott Moncrieff's *Beowulf* than Morris's—but I would infinitely prefer to savor his version of Marcel remembering his need for his mother's kiss as he lies in bed of a summer night or of his desire for the elusive Albertine. Perhaps we should simply say that Scott Moncrieff chose in *Beowulf* the wrong work for his talents. Not all translators of genius are right for all works of greatness, just as we learn from Proust that lovers often torment themselves by choosing the wrong object for their desire.

That acknowledged, we might consider another translator of great abilities, Richmond Lattimore. For those of us in the1960s and 1970s who read the *Iliad* in his translation, done originally in 1951, the work seemed to have found its true exponent, its astonishing ventriloquist.[9] The critical orthodoxy then, and one that still has some validity to it, was that Lattimore was the great *Iliad* translator and Robert Fitzgerald the great *Odyssey* translator. The two were quite different in their techniques and tonalities, but each seemed particularly suited to his chosen epic. Reading their two translations in sequence was a way to register the differences between the original poems and thus to illustrate the case for the two Homers. More urgently, reading Lattimore's *Iliad* during the Vietnam War was to understand its particular claims on our attention after all the centuries: he made it read, in Simone Weil's phrase, as "the poem of force."[10] A translator capable of making the *Iliad* speak to a generation that saw the horrors of war each night on live network television should have been able, on the face of it, to do a memorable *Beowulf*. Lattimore never published a version of the Old English poem and I have no reason to believe he ever tried one; but he did include a version of its closest analogue, *The Fight at Finnsburg*, in his *The Stride of Time: New Poems and Translations* published in 1966.

From reading this translation of *Finnsburg* we can sense why Lattimore never offered a *Beowulf* and, what is more instructive, learn a great deal about the sheer difficulty of translating Old into modern English. A few characteristic lines from his *Finnsburg* will serve to illustrate this claim:

> Then in the hall   was a huge noise of havoc
> And the hard shields held   in the hands of the fighters
> And the bonehelms burst   and the burgfloor echoed,
> Until in his grim fight   Garulf went under,
> first man to fall   of the Frisian people,
> Guthlaf's son with   good men about him,
> many huge bodies.[11]

Lattimore's "Garulf went under" for the Old English "Garulf gecrang" seems to me a boldly colloquial rendition that keeps the energy and force of the original far better than would the literal "Garulf fell in battle." Less successful as translation but also more revealing of the virtual impossibility of the enterprise is Lattimore's "And the bonehelms burst and the burgfloor echoed" for the original Old English. But do I even need to quote the line? We can recover the original from Lattimore's line that is neither Old nor modern English. "And the bonehelms burst and the burgfloor echoed" comes from "bānhelm berstan, buruhðelu dynede."[12] To keep the alliterative pattern of the Old English intact the translator relies on words that may seem to meld Old and modern English but succeed in being neither:

bonehelms and *burgfloor*. Only someone who already knew Old English could define these compounds adequately, though why such a reader would want a translation of *Finnsburg* then becomes an interesting question.

At this moment one is reminded of Ezra Pound's famous dictum, or maybe just his wisecrack, that poetry should be at least as well written as prose. More specifically, this would seem to mean that one should not use words in a poetic translation that one would not use in careful, everyday prose. Or, using words for poetic effect if they need a gloss is cheating. Of using such words, Pound was notoriously guilty in his version of the Old English *Seafarer*. Among his words and phrases neither Old nor modern English one might count: "mere-weary," "hail-scur," "bosque," "breastlock," and "earth-weal."[13] Pound, characteristically, had the brass to omit the footnotes. Not so Heaney, who uses arcane forms in his *Beowulf* that require glosses so that, in its incarnation in the *Norton Anthology of English Literature*, his version footnotes such words as "tholed," "bothies," "graith," "boltered," "bawn," "brehon," "wean," and "hoked."[14] Glossing these words here would only exaggerate my point that no one wants a translation that needs its own moments of translation, however infrequent.

Thinking about the passage from Lattimore's *Finnsburg* as well as the word choices of Pound and Heaney suggests some of the reasons why we should all be afraid of translating Old English poetry and, more immediately, *Beowulf*. In ascending order of importance, these causes for fear seem to me to be: (1) the poem's use of alliteration; (2) its diction; and finally, (3) its brilliance of variation. Indeed, these features are clearly interconnected in the poetry, so much so that my separation of them is nothing more than a matter of convenience.

Just as terza rima is for *The Divine Comedy*, so alliteration seems to be for *Beowulf*: the formal device that orders the poem, that allows the poet to emphasize key words, and that breaks the back of translators. The shape of the Old English line—two half-lines held together most commonly by three alliterating words and yet also kept distinct by a medial caesura—has little if anything in common with the most familiar line of later English poetry, the iambic pentameter and its variants. The translator who relies too heavily on the caesura, as did Scott Moncrieff, seems never to capture the full line as a sense unit and usually ends up underscoring this continual hesitation with a heavy use of alliteration: "Oft Shield of the Sheaf / from scathing hordes" jerks along like a car with a clogged fuel line. The argument for maintaining alliteration in a modern translation, as for maintaining terza rima, is that it is the most audible evidence of the poet's technique and thus should be honored by the translator if he or she is to be worthy of the original. This argument can lead to terrible excesses: alliterating lines that beat on one's ears like a pile driver at a construction site, alliterating lines that echo the technique of advertising jingles and rap lyrics, alliterating lines that make one long for the good gray dullness of prose. Consider, as examples, these two versions done at quite different moments in the history of English-language poetry. The first is by Charles Kennedy in his once widely used translation of 1940 when the major poets in English were figures like T. S. Eliot, W. H. Auden, and Wallace Stevens:

> Lo! we have listened to many a lay
> Of the Spear-Danes' fame, their splendor of old,
> Their mighty princes, and martial deeds!
> Many a mead-hall Scyld, son of Sceaf,
> Snatched from the forces of savage foes.[15]

Kennedy claims in his foreword to have translated "the poem faithfully into authentic modern verse"—a statement that would doubtless have made Eliot, Auden, and Stevens wonder what they were writing. The second example is from Frederick Rebsamen's translation of the poem done in 1991, some twenty years after he published his monologue version, *Beowulf Is My Name*.[16] At that moment, major poets in the United States were figures like John Ashbery, Adrienne Rich, and James Merrill. Here is Rebsamen's version:

> Yes! We have heard   of years long vanished
> how Spear-Danes struck   sang victory-songs
> raised from a wasteland   walls of glory.
> Then Scyld Scefing   startled his neighbors
> measured meadhalls   made them his own.[17]

The need for alliterating words in these modern English translations produces such flat or clichéd phrases as "splendor of old" and "savage foes" in Kennedy or else such unfaithful intrusions as "wasteland" and "measured meadhalls" in Rebsamen. Each reader must decide if the alliteration in these lines compensates for their verbal infelicities. The necessary claim that I will make is that every translator's choice comes with a price that must be weighed to the last penny by readers who care about both the Old English original and the modern English rendition. What seems hardly in need of comment, however, is the distance of each of these two translations from the poetic idiom of its moment.

Translators with ears more attuned to the poetry of their own moment, such as Seamus Heaney and Roy Michael Liuzza, are less likely to rely on regular three-beat alliteration, offering instead a telling use of the technique at moments of emphasis so as not to hammer their readers into a stupor. Thus we find Heaney opening the poem in 2000 with:

> So. The Spear-Danes in days gone by
> And the kings who ruled them had courage and greatness.

> We have heard of those prince's heroic campaigns.
>
> There was Shield Sheafson, scourge of many tribes,
> A wrecker of mead-benches, rampaging among foes.[18]

Even Heaney's fiercest defenders would have to concede that these lines are among the most banal in his version (typed out as prose, they have no poetry in them), but they have the clear virtue of never sacrificing meaning to render alliteration. Liuzza in his translation, also published in 2000, makes the same choice of sense over sound in his version of the poem's opening but does so with greater rhythmic energy:

> Listen! We have heard of the glory in bygone days
> of the folk-kings of the spear-Danes,
> how these noble lords did lofty deeds.
>   Often Scyld Scefing seized the mead-benches
> from many tribes, troops of enemies.[19]

Reading Heaney and Liuzza leads one to ask if alliteration is so important to the Old English original that all should be forsaken in the modern English rendition to do it full honor. Is alliteration, finally, as central to a poem like *Beowulf* as terza rima is to the *Comedy*? The practice of Heaney and Liuzza as translators, and it is among the best we have for the poem, suggests that the answer must be in the negative. I will go on to argue that there is another feature of Old English poetry that is more deeply essential than alliteration, and thus more damaging to a translation when neglected, but for the moment I want to consider the obvious consequences of too insistent alliteration. And here I will, for the sake of argument, grant the alliterating translators their use of the technique for its auditory value. What is harder to grant them is license to ransack the word stock of English to find alliterating words to fill out their lines. Lattimore's "And the bonehelms burst and the burgfloor echoed" is only one example of this license.

For additional examples one can turn to translations of *Beowulf* done at various moments in the twentieth century, though I will avoid those that are so bad that quoting from them seems gratuitous. Nor will I evoke such older versions as that published by Francis B. Gummere in 1909 that might as well have been written, to judge by its use of poetic idiom, sometime in the mid-nineteenth century by someone who had yet to recognize the poetic genius of Tennyson.[20] Consider instead this passage from Michael Alexander's 1973 version that describes Grendel's mere:

> The tarn was troubled; a terrible wave-thrash
> brimmed it, bubbling; black-mingled,

> the warm wound-blood welled upwards.
> He had dived to his doom, he had died miserably;
> here in his fen-lair he had laid aside
> his heathen soul. Hell welcomed it.[21]

After reading these lines it is no surprise to learn that Alexander has written extensively on Ezra Pound, for his method in translating *Beowulf* owes a clear debt to that of Pound's *Seafarer*.[22] In his introduction, Alexander stresses that "[t]he verbal vigour of the epic cannot be separated from the movement of the verses."[23] In principle, one agrees; in practice, one wonders if Alexander's version privileges the movement of the verses, especially their alliteration, to the point that verbal vigor is lost. Or, perhaps more precisely, until verbal clarity is lost. For would a reader of these lines, who did not already know the poem well, make much sense of a "tarn" that was "troubled" or a "wave thrash" that was "terrible" or "wound-blood" that "welled upwards"? I suspect not, though it is hard for me to be an innocent reader of the poem after thirty years and more of reading and teaching it.

This experience suggests that translations of *Beowulf* which strongly evoke the original Old English are usually the least likely to be comprehensible to a first-time reader. These versions exist in a strange world between Old English and modern English that one can enter with one's knowledge of the original as a passport. Thus when I read Alexander's lines I make sense of them not by parsing them into modern English but by hearing through them:

> Ðær wæs on blōde   brim weallende,
> atol ȳða geswing   eal gemenged,
> hāton heolfre,   heorodrēore wēol;
> dēaðfǣge dēog,   siððan drēama lēas
> in fenfreoðo   feorh ālegde,
> hǣþene sāwle;   þær him hel onfēng.
> (lines 847–52)[24]

Put another way, Alexander's technique in the quoted passage is to rely heavily on a certain kind of verbal intensity—that of tight compounds and participial forms—to echo the original. Whether the consequent loss of narrative clarity, that is, of any full sense of what is happening in the passage, is an acceptable price to pay is, again, the reader's choice. But he or she should not for a moment conclude that the narrative in the original Old English lacks clarity.

Using alliteration heavily in a modern translation can cover other verbal faults, such as a slackness of language when rendering some of the less dramatic passages of the poem. This phenomenon becomes more and more troubling as one reads and rereads Heaney's version. Consider, for instance, this passage concerning Wiglaf and the dying Beowulf:

> It was hard then on the young hero,
> having to watch the one he held so dear
> there on the ground, going through
> his death agony. The dragon from underearth,
> his nightmarish destroyer, lay destroyed as well,
> utterly without life. No longer would his snakefolds
> ply themselves to safeguard hidden gold.
> Hard-edged blades, hammered out
> And keenly filed, had finished him
> So that the sky-roamer lay there rigid,
> Brought low beside the treasure-lodge.[25]

This is not one of the heartbreaking moments in the original that characterize the last thousand lines of the poem; it is simply the poet stopping for a moment to maintain narrative coherence in the midst of the great speeches delivered by Beowulf, Wiglaf, the unnamed messenger, and the grieving Geatish woman. It is the kind of passage one reads over quickly in this part of the poem precisely because it is not a speech. And yet without it and others like it, the poet would not have been able to establish the extraordinary shifts of narrative time between the hero's youth, the present moment of the dragon fight, and the future destruction of the Geatish people that are essential to the poem's conclusion.

All this said, one must still observe that Heaney's lines here are utterly flat and sometimes quite slack; the diction oscillates from the prosaic "hard then on the young hero" or "going through his death agony" to the forced and unearned poetic compounds "sky-roamer" and "treasure-lodge." Is it any surprise that Heaney makes greater recourse to alliteration than usual in these lines to give them some energy and swing, to keep his reader awake? It is not easy to enliven a passage such as this piece of narrative summary, and perhaps one does not need to do so. But resorting to two-beat alliteration on a regular basis when one's work as a translator sags does seem to misrepresent the poem's use of that technique.

Translators who strive to do justice to the technical features of the Old English poetic line risk two related dangers: relying on a version of English that is more historical thesaurus than living poetic idiom; and thereby suggesting to the reader without Old English that the language was similarly a hotchpotch of archaisms and colloquialisms all mixed together so that poets could get their three alliterative beats per line. We can call this, for convenience, the "ye olde" school of translation. As an extreme example of this school, all the more valuable for being extreme, consider the opening lines from William Ellery Leonard's version of *Beowulf*, first done in 1923 but more commonly read in the 1939 edition with Lynd Ward's vaguely fascistic illustrations (think of Beowulf as a member of the Hitler Youth):

What ho! We've heard the glory   of Spear-Danes, clansmen-kings,
Their deeds of olden story, —   how fought the aethelings!
Often Scyld Scefing   reft his foemen all,
Reft the tribes at wassail   of bench and mead in hall.
Smote the jarls with terror;   gat good recompense
For that he came a foundling,   a child with no defense:[26]

Leonard's bizarre use of rhyme throughout seems to be an attempt to render the original alliteration by another means: what the Old English emphasizes with alliteration, his translation does with rhyme. Regardless of that choice, these lines as they attempt to be true to the spirit of the original utterly betray its diction. For Old English poetry is not filled with words of wildly discordant registers and historical moments as in this translation. Recognizing that the vocabulary of Old English poetry may not be quite the same as that of Old English prose is very different from imagining it to have been an invented lexicon of intermixed forms from the then current state of the language in the eighth or eleventh century and forms from Proto-Germanic and Indo-European of a sort that we mark today with an asterisk because unattested.[27] But such a mélange is what Leonard's language resembles here.

This argument can be pushed harder. Excessive attention to alliteration often reads as the modern translator's betrayal of the deep structure of Old English poetics in order to honor its surface features. To put it more simply, the insistence on alliteration is the response of a translator who has not read deeply enough in Old English poetics. To say, in rebuttal, that it is the response of a translator who honors the oral, performative, bardic nature of the original poems may perhaps be true—and I can certainly hear some Anglo-Saxonist colleagues saying so—but it is also to convict the translator of the yet more heinous offense of assaulting his audience's ears.

To claim variation as the essence of Old English poetic technique is in 2003 hardly a radical move. Under the influence of such scholars as Arthur G. Brodeur and Fred C. Robinson, Anglo-Saxonists have become far more attentive to the ways in which poets use words and how they combine them into meaningful and subtle runs of variation.[28] What seemed a bold claim in 1975 when I was in graduate school—that an Old English poet could make artfully ambiguous use of words and not just churn out formulaic expressions—now seems so much the orthodoxy that it will soon, no doubt, be challenged. But let us accept that orthodoxy and even go one step further to consider the ways in which variation is the basis of the *Beowulf*-poet's artistry, and thus the necessary challenge for the translator. As a useful working formulation, I would cite Robinson's definition of variation as "syntactically parallel words or word-groups which share a common referent and which occur within a single clause."[29] By which I take Robinson to mean: all the variant expressions that refer to the same person or thing must be parallel in syntax as well as in meaning.

Following Brodeur's example, we can consider these lines from *Beowulf* as providing a classic example of the technique and thus as posing a classic dilemma for the translator faced with rendering them:

> Đā wæs gylden hilt   gamelum rince,
> hārum hildfruman   on hand gyfen,
> enta ærgeweorc;   hit on æht gehwearf
> æfter dēofla hryre   Denigea frean,
> wundorsmiþa geweorc;   ond þā þæs worold ofgeaf
> gromheort guma,   Godes andsaca,
> morðres scyldig,   ond his mōdor ēac;
> on geweald gewearf   woroldcyninga
> ðæm sēlestan   be sæm twēonum
> ðāra þe on Scedenigge   sceattas dælde.
>   (lines 1677–86)[30]

In this passage, as Beowulf gives to Hrothgar the sword hilt he has brought up from the mere of Grendel and his mother, the poet weaves variant terms for all of the figures in the narrative: for Hrothgar, for the sword hilt and its makers, for the Grendelkin. The passing of the artifact to the king of the Danes is eloquent testimony that his land is now free of the Grendelkin. The sequencing of variant forms in this passage, especially in the line and a half that reads "æfter dēofla hryre Denigea frean, wundorsmiþa geweorc," allows these various figures to be woven together, and brilliantly testifies to the value of the technique when well handled. There is nothing repetitious here, nothing to convict the poet of ineptitude or ambivalence. And the true sign of the poet's skill in these lines is that Beowulf is cited neither by name nor by epithet. He is not made the object of variation because he is simply the agent of this extraordinary transfer by which the sword hilt of the monsters and thus their power are passed over to the old king. Using variation at the highest level sometimes means knowing when not to use it. Beowulf is not named or made the object of variation in these lines because he is irrelevant to the poet's purpose of signaling the return of Hrothgar and his people to autonomy and authority.

To a contemporary poet, variation is likely to seem mystifying if not indeed evidence of incompetence. In an aesthetic driven by the use of the inevitable word, the single and only possible form, the stroke that proves genius, variation shows the poet did not get it right. Such a reading is conditioned more by nineteenth- and twentieth-century theories of poetry, however, than by an understanding of Old English poetics. In what seems to me the single most necessary statement about Old English variation, Brodeur observed that it allows the poet "to exhibit the object of his thought in all of its aspects." He cautions as well that it can be "a dangerous instrument in the hands of an inferior poet: it could impart on the one hand an effect of sheer redundancy, on the other an unpleasing jerkiness of pace; it could stiffen the flow of style, and clog the stream of thought."[31] Substituting "translator" for Brodeur's "inferior poet" here will clarify my argument that variation is the most difficult feature of Old English poetics to work with, whether in the original or in translation.

As an accretive technique that puts forward a run of expressions in order to enumerate and in that way anatomize a whole, poetic variation seems very distant from the poetry we know from our own time. A prose translator can thus have it easier when he sets out to render a passage like the one I have just quoted. Here, for example, is E. Talbot Donaldson's version of 1966:

> Then the golden hilt was given into the hand of the old man, the hoary war-chief—the ancient work of giants. Then came into the possession of the prince of the Danes, after the fall of devils, the work of wonder-smiths. And when the hostile-hearted creature, God's enemy, guilty of murder, gave up this world, and his mother too, it passed into the control of the best of worldly kings between the seas, of those who gave treasure in the Northlands.[32]

The meaning here is clear enough, partly because the longer sentences of modern English prose can accommodate the many iterations imposed by variation, and partly because Donaldson has quietly rearranged the half lines of the original to make a more lucid modern version. The problem of course is that the contemporary reader is likely to re-parse Donaldson's sentences yet further so that all the variants for a given referent will appear together. Thus, in this further re-parsing, "Then the golden hilt was given into the hand of the old man, the hoary war-chief—the ancient work of giants" might become "Then the golden hilt, the ancient work of giants, was given into the hand of the old man, the hoary war-chief." And when that happens, the variation of the original is no longer interwoven but instead seems needless repetition.

Here is another translation of this same passage, also done by an estimable scholar, Stanley B. Greenfield:

> Then the golden hilt, the age-old work
> of giants, was handed to Hrothgar,
> the old chief; with the fall of the fiends,
> the well-wrought piece passed into control
> of the Danish prince: when the demon,
> foe to God and man, guilty of murder,
> turned from this world—and his mother, too—

> it passed into the power of the best
> of worldly kings between the seas
> who shared their wealth in the Danish realm.[33]

Notice that Greenfield reorders the variants so that those belonging to the same referent cluster together: those referring to the hilt itself appear in immediate sequence with each other rather than forming an envelope pattern around variants for the other referent (Hrothgar) in the opening lines of the passage. Greenfield also seems to conflate two of the epithets for Hrothgar into one, and employs his proper name (as the poet does not), thereby making the passage seem redundant. His version also makes the passage easier to comprehend, I suspect, than is the original with its shifts between grammatical subjects, direct objects and indirect objects that are not always placed where they would be in a modern English sentence with subject-verb-object order. On the other hand, the gain in clarity comes at the cost of losing the poem's interweaving of figures in these lines.

In a radically different version of this same passage, the poet Edwin Morgan throws narrative continuity aside and plays up the complexity of variation, so much so that one is not always quite certain which terms in the original are being rendered in his translation:

> Then into the hands of the year-worn warrior
> Was the golden hilt given, titan-work of old
> To the grey-haired battle-leader; it came into the possession
> Of the lord of the Danes when the demons fell,
> Master-smiths' wonder-work; when God's adversary,
> The man black of heart, murder-sin-stained
> And his mother with him went from the world,
> It passed into the power of the best of kings
> Ruling on earth from sea to sea
> Who ever distributed treasures in Denmark.[34]

There is no question that Morgan understands the poet's use of variation: he interweaves his forms in close imitation of the original, and he sees the presence of the variants not as a burden to be met by listing pallid synonyms but rather as an incitement to poetic invention and brilliance. Hence he gives us such phrases as "year-worn warrior," "titan-work of old," "the man black of heart," "murder-sin-stained," and the rest. Whether we like them or not as individual forms, the reader without Old English can learn something very necessary about variation from his version: that it is a means to introduce emphasis and dynamics into the poetry. In other words, it is the technique that Brodeur described: one that allows the poet "to exhibit the object of his thought in all of its aspects." And yet—because, of course, in discussing any translation there must be an "and yet"—Morgan's use of variation here clots the narrative and jams up the flow of the original in ways that are likely to make most modern readers skim over the passage because they find it confused or confusing.

That most modern readers would prefer, if forced to choose, a rearranged passage of variation that maintains the narrative rather than preserves the richness of the poet's thought is hardly to be denied or even questioned. For it is very hard for a reader to imaginatively value a poetic technique that has so little currency in his or her own contemporary poetry: that act of appreciation may simply demand too much translation into another aesthetic register. When reviewers of Heaney's *Beowulf* praised it for its narrative directness and fluency, I suspect they had exactly this kind of response in mind: they liked the fact that it moves forward briskly and avoids getting entangled in the thickets of variation, as did the translations they remembered reading as undergraduates. Yet one must also note that most of the reviewers who praised the translation did not demonstrate any convincing knowledge of the poem in the original and thus were hardly able to address what was lost in the act of translation.

Heaney admits in his introduction that he by and large passed over variation as a central feature of *Beowulf*: "The appositional nature of the Old English syntax, for example, is somewhat slighted here, as is the *Beowulf* poet's resource-fulness with synonyms and (to a lesser extent) his genius for compound-making, kennings, and all sorts of variation."[35] The use of the passive voice here is amusing, as if it were not Heaney himself who chose to slight the appositional nature of the poetry. But we can leave that aside and instead consider his version of the sword hilt passage:

> Then the gold hilt was handed over
> to the old lord, a relic from long ago
> for the venerable ruler. That rare smithwork
> was passed on to the prince of the Danes
> when those devils perished; once death removed
> that murdering, guilt-steeped, God-cursed fiend,
> eliminating his unholy life
> and his mother's as well, it was willed to that king
> who of all the lavish gift-lords of the north
> was the best regarded between the two seas.[36]

One immediately understands Heaney's choices as a translator here: group together the variants that belong to the same referent, keep the translated forms of each variant as straightforward or unpoetic as possible (unlike Morgan), and guide the reader along to the next great speech. For that is where the true genius of Heaney's translation lies: in its ventriloquized rendering of the famous speeches, especially of those by the old Beowulf in the final third of the poem. No translator has ever done any aspect of *Beowulf* as well as Heaney does those speeches, or so it seems to me. But the critic in me also notes that those same speeches are the parts of *Beowulf* closest to Heaney's own poetry and to his earlier triumphs as a translator, most transcendently his heartrending version of the Ugolino cantos of Dante's *Inferno*.[37]

Faced with Heaney's decision to slight or (more frankly) to evade the presence of variation and other appositive forms in *Beowulf*, one might very well conclude that he has simply acknowledged the inevitable or, more accurately, the untranslatable. That is, he has chosen to concentrate his gifts on what can be passed over from Old to modern English and thus to let the remainder of the poem fade off in ways that only specialists will notice. And specialists, who by definition have no need for a translation, also have full license to criticize his version and all the others out there, so there is no hope of making us happy. Heaney's decision about how to handle variation in his translation helps to explain its extraordinarily favorable reception. Older reviewers especially praised his *Beowulf* because it did not remind them of the versions they had read as students—many of which were, no doubt, the same ones I have quoted from in this piece. And yet, the critic in me (he appears more and more as we get closer and closer to the end) wants to say that this response betrays not only the Old English of *Beowulf* but also the possibilities of contemporary poetry in modern English. For there was a brilliant example of how to render variation in original modern English poetry available to Heaney and those who reviewed his translation.

I refer to the magisterial poetic cycle published by Geoffrey Hill in 1971 that is evocatively titled (with a nod to Sweet's *Anglo-Saxon Reader*) as *Mercian Hymns*. This cycle appeared in the United States with an introduction by Harold Bloom, who was then the most rigorous and respected American critic of contemporary poetry and who ensured that *Mercian Hymns* received a great deal of attention. Bloom had little to say about the poet's use of Old English poetic technique, but for anyone who had worked through Klaeber's *Beowulf* as a graduate student, that use of technique was everywhere to be seen. Such is immediately evident from the first of the cycle's thirty sections, all of which are poems printed in modern English to evoke the way poems were written in Old English, that is, without ragged lineation but instead full across the page, margin to margin:

> King of the perennial holly-groves: the riven sand-
>   stone: overlord of the M5: architect of the his-
>   toric rampart and ditch, the citadel at Tamworth,
>   the summer hermitage in Holy Cross: guardian of
>   the Welsh Bridge and the Iron Bridge: contractor
>   to the desirable new estates: saltmaster: money-

> changer: commissioner for oaths: martyrologist:
> the friend of Charlemagne.

"I liked that," said Offa, "sing it again."[38]

The sly joke of this poem, of course, is that the same variation I have celebrated as central to Old English poetry here becomes the technique of the sycophantic praise poet. The grimness of Hill's joke would have been most apparent to those scops of Old English poetry, Widsith and Deor, who knew what it meant to make a living and lose a job. But they might also have savored the joke because they would have seen in Hill's *Mercian Hymns* a wonderfully adapted use of their variation, that is, adapted to the times of Hill's own writing and the state of his language. But variation nonetheless.

Hill's *Mercian Hymns* demonstrate that variation can be done successfully by a contemporary poet or translator of *Beowulf*. The technique need not be seen as clotting or redundant or retarding of the narrative. But doing so would mean coming to terms with the fact that variation provides much of the verbal energy in Old English poetry, just as it does in *Mercian Hymns*. For Old English poetic variation relies on the richness of the language's word stock, that is, its full range of technical terms for matters and persons and objects of cultural importance. The point here is not to indulge in naive laments about the penury of the modern English word stock when set against the Old English word stock but rather to admit that we today have relatively limited need for terms involving swords, shields, body armor, ritualistic gift-giving, kings, retainers, dragons, and the like. And that we also have, as a corollary, a very rich word stock for terms involving motor vehicles, firearms, sexual acts, political figures, athletes, aliens, and the like. Every culture has, in other words, the synonyms it needs, if not those it deserves. The successful translator of *Beowulf* must thus understand how we use variation and synonymy and apposition in our own poetry; he or she must know, in other words, the poetry of the moment of translation as well as the poetry being translated. As R. M. Liuzza, accomplished editor and translator of Old English texts, has argued persuasively of *Beowulf*: "our experience of the poem occurs only within the framework of expectations given to us by the literary world in which we live and move."[39]

In this movement from Old to modern English poetry, the translator must also beware of the dangers of proximity: that the very closeness historically speaking of the two stages of the language introduces difficulties that are not faced by the English-language translator rendering the Heian Japanese of *The Tale of Genji* or the Homeric Greek of the *Iliad*. The danger of this proximity between *Beowulf* and us explains the practice that translators have of smuggling in archaic words for weapons, such as "burney" or the like, words which might best be called

"Beowulfese." I sometimes think that if in the future I can read one translation of the poem that scrupulously avoids this kind of smuggled diction, I will die a happy Anglo-Saxonist.

But as a living Anglo-Saxonist, especially one who has to assign a translation for my classes and recommend a version to friends and strangers on airplanes, I have to work in the world of available choices. I stress the word choices in the plural because the translation I would assign or recommend depends entirely on the circumstances in which it will be read.[40] To help make sense of these circumstances, I would suggest that there are now and have been for over one hundred years three types of *Beowulf* translations: (1) high poetic versions that are willing to sacrifice literal accuracy to evoke the spirit of the original and that are very likely to display the presence of their translator (usually done by poets); (2) self-described verse translations that observe some fidelity to the poetic technique of the original but do not stray far into outright invention and that are rarely marked by the personality of their translator (usually done by scholar-critics); and (3) prose translations that remain highly accurate to the narrative of the poem and some of its poetic technique while sacrificing most of its poetic spirit and carefully avoiding any sign of the translator's existence (often done by scholar-editors). As examples of high poetic translation, I would cite versions by William Morris, Edwin Morgan, Burton Raffel, and Seamus Heaney. As examples of verse translation, I would offer those by Charles Kennedy, Marijane Osborn, Stanley Greenfield, and Roy Michael Liuzza. As examples of prose translation, I would designate those by John Earle, John R. Clark Hall, S. A. J. Bradley, and E. Talbot Donaldson.

At the current moment, we are very well served by Heaney for the high poetic version, and Liuzza for the verse version; we are arguably better off in these categories now than readers have been in any other time of *Beowulf* studies. Where the situation seems less happy is with a prose version. The current one of choice remains Donaldson's, first done in 1966 and still in print, most obviously in a Norton Critical Edition that I edited in 2002. It has, however, fallen from grace in that it no longer appears in the *Norton Anthology of English Literature* where it must have been read (if not enjoyed) by hundreds of thousands of undergraduates over the years. Its great virtues were, and remain, a clear rendering of the poem's narrative flow, a use of modern English diction that rarely puzzles or puts off the reader, and a vivid recognition of the poem's tragic portrayal of life in pagan Germania. Its obvious liability is that it is in prose or, more accurately, a prose that is rather uninventively formal and rhythmically uninteresting. Perhaps, then, the time has come for someone to attempt a prose *Beowulf* that is not fiction, such as John Gardner's *Grendel*, but that does compel the attention of the reader who wants accuracy above all else in a translation but also some sense of linguistic and rhythmic energy. How that version would read, I am not certain, though I think a careful study of Hill's *Mercian Hymns* might offer some valuable models for handling the poem's variation.

Other than that, my only suggestion to this putative translator of *Beowulf* would be to say again: Be afraid, be very afraid. For unlike the poetic or verse translators who can pass off their effusions by claiming that they capture the spirit of the poem, you will have the far more difficult burden of writing something that will have to be judged as good prose.

Notes

1. Osborn, "Translations, Versions, Illustrations," p. 350.

2. These include versions done by Heaney, *Beowulf: A New Verse Translation*; Liuzza, *Beowulf*; T. C. Kennedy, *Beowulf*; and Sullivan and Murphy, *Beowulf: A Longman Cultural Edition*.

3. Howe, "Scullionspeak," pp. 32–37.

4. Morris and Wyatt, *Tale of Beowulf* (1895), p. 1.

5. For full bibliographical information on these and many other translations of the poem, see Bjork and Niles, *Beowulf Handbook*, pp. 379–81.

6. For Longfellow and Tennyson, see Tinker, *Translations*, pp. 168 and 175. The ascription to John Earle of the paraphrase of *Beowulf* ("A Primitive Old Epic") that appeared in the 1 May 1858 issue of *Household Words*, as found in Tinker, *Translations*, p. 160, is incorrect. The author of this unsigned piece is identified as Henry Morley, a staff member of *Household Words*, in the records of that magazine; see *Household Words*, p. 178. I discuss this version in my essay "*Beowulf* in the House of Dickens."

7. See further, N. Howe, "Praise and Lament."

8. Scott Moncrieff, *Widsith*, p. 7.

9. Lattimore, *Iliad*.

10. Weil, *Iliad*.

11. Lattimore, *Stride of Time*, pp. 61–62.

12. Quoted from Klaeber, *Beowulf and the Fight at Finnsburg*, 3rd ed., p. 246.

13. See Pound, *Translations*, pp. 207–9.

14. See Heaney, *Beowulf*, in *Norton Anthology*, lines 14, 140, 324, 419, 523, 1457, 2433, and 3026 respectively.

15. C. W. Kennedy, *Beowulf*, p. 3; the quotation from the foreword appears on p. vii.

16. Rebsamen, *Beowulf Is My Name*.

17. Rebsamen, *Beowulf: A Verse Translation*, p. 2.

18. Heaney, *Beowulf*, p. 3.

19. Liuzza, *Beowulf*, p. 53.

20. Gummere, *Oldest English Epic*, p. 22: "Lo, praise of the prowess of people-kings / of spear-armed Danes, in days long sped, / we have heard, and what honor the athelings won! / Oft Scyld the Scefing from squadroned foes, / from many a tribe, the mead-bench tore."

21. Alexander, *Beowulf*, p. 77.

22. See Alexander, *Poetic Achievement*.

23. Alexander, *Beowulf*, p. 47.

24. Klaeber, *Beowulf*, p. 32.

25. Heaney, *Beowulf*, p. 191.

26. Leonard, *Beowulf*, p. 1.

27. In this regard, I differ with the claims advanced by J. R. R. Tolkien in his "Prefatory Remarks," pp. vii–xxv. Anyone interested in the problems of translating *Beowulf* should consult Tolkien's discussion.

28. Brodeur, *Art of "Beowulf"*; and Robinson, *"Beowulf" and the Appositive Style*.

29. Robinson, "Two Aspects of Variation," p. 129.

30. Klaeber, *Beowulf*, p. 63.

31. Brodeur, *Art of "Beowulf,"* p. 39.

32. Donaldson, *Beowulf: A Prose Translation*, p. 29.

33. Greenfield, *Readable Beowulf*, pp. 93–94.

34. Morgan, *Beowulf: A Verse Translation*, p. 46. Morgan's introduction offers a series of quite telling critiques of earlier translations of the poem.

35. Heaney, *Beowulf*, p. xxix.

36. Heaney, *Beowulf*, pp. 115–16.

37. See Heaney, "Ugolino," pp. 178–80.

38. G. Hill, "Mercian Hymn I," from *Selected Poems* (Penguin Books, 2006), p. 61. Copyright © Geoffrey Hill, 2006. Reproduced by permission of Penguin Books Ltd.

39. Liuzza, "Lost in Translation," 294.

40. For discussions of *Beowulf* translations as they might be used in the classroom, see the contributions by Liuzza, *"Beowulf* in Translation," and J. M. Hill, "Translating Social Speech," pp. 23–40 and 67–79, respectively.

Iron and Irony in *Beowulf*

R. M. Liuzza

Translation is a kind of nakedly explicit reading in which all one's faults, biases, secret loves, and wishes are on public display; its potential for embarrassment is virtually unlimited. In the process of translating *Beowulf*, however, I was surprised to find that what gave me the most anxiety was not the language itself—the minefield of bewildering synonyms, odd grammatical constructions, semantic obscurities, and editorial emendations—but the vague thing usually called "tone," the emotional valence of a string of words, the attitude of a narrator or author towards his story: not the text, but the space around the text; not the sense of *Beowulf*, but its sensibility. I realized to my chagrin that I was not at all sure how we are supposed to "feel" about the poem. I knew the text well enough and was finally comfortable, for the most part, with the difficult choices one has to make in translating it, but by the end of my work I found myself far less certain about its intended effect than I was at the beginning. I still had my convictions, of course; what I had lost was the confidence that these were the product of an objective reading of the text and not just a grab bag of hopes and prejudices I had brought with me from the beginning. This essay is the result of that unsettling realization. In what follows I will try to offer a justification for my sense of the tone of *Beowulf*, make a few suggestions for how one might hear and interpret it, and finally consider the implications of the uncertainty I discovered in myself, suggesting that the very things that make the tone of *Beowulf* so difficult to pin down may lead us close to the heart of the poem's meaning.

Defining the poem's tone may in fact be the central problem of its critical history, connecting deep and still-unresolved problems of genre, origin, date, and audience with philosophical uncertainties over the possibility of fully understanding the past and debates on the nature of literary language itself. The importance of this question has not always been recognized, however, nor its ramifications fully appreciated; most early readers of *Beowulf* do not seem to have thought it was the sort of poem whose tone was much worth worrying about.

50

Since its recovery at the beginning of the nineteenth century *Beowulf* has been called many things,[1] but no label has had a more profound influence on its critical history than "epic." When the poem was first read, it was generally assumed that any important national literature must, on the model of Greek and Latin, have a long, serious martial poem at its point of origin. Pressed into this service, *Beowulf* filled the role somewhat uneasily, beginning with J. J. Conybeare's translation of the poem into Miltonic blank verse[2] and culminating in H. M. Chadwick's classic study *The Heroic Age*.[3] Moreover, an anthropomorphic model of literary history encouraged the belief that literatures grew as people do, so an older poem was assumed to have a simpler ethos and outlook than a modern one. For most early readers, *Beowulf* easily confirmed this assumption. In 1807 Sharon Turner characterized Old English poetry in general as "the rude exclamations of a rude people";[4] a century later J. R. Clark Hall commented that *Beowulf* "is the poem of a nation's childhood," and described the poem's repetitions and digressions as "of such a character as we might be led to use ourselves in telling a tale to an audience of rather dull children," though quickly adding, "of intentional obscurity there is none—the poet says what he means with refreshing straightforwardness."[5] These twin assumptions of seriousness and simplicity mark most early studies of the poem. They supply the "iron" of my title, the belief that *Beowulf* is an artless, straightforward heroic tale, a kind of poetry without poetics: sturdy and solid or drafty and riddled with nonsense, full of the manly vigor and honesty or of the crudeness and brutality (depending on one's sympathies) of the northern world, either the bright iron of an ancient sword, emblem of glory and heroic duty, or the rusted iron of the buried treasure of a vanished race, as useless to men as it was before.

Twentieth-century readers with modernist assumptions about poetic language were more willing to linger on the complexities of *Beowulf*, its subtle, ambivalent, even paradoxical elements. This attitude informs the work of such great mid-twentieth-century readers of the poem as Adrien Bonjour,[6] Arthur Brodeur,[7] and John Leyerle,[8] but it might be said to have been made possible by the early twentieth-century German scholar Levin Schücking, who emphasized the poem's deeply retrospective quality, its author looking back on a vanished heroic age—he observed that the poet was "a sort of Old Germanic Walter Scott."[9] Whatever the other merits or defects of Schücking's work, this is a turning point in the study of the poem because it presumes that the author, standing at some distance from his narrative and characters, had a critical perspective on the story and a coherent aesthetic purpose in telling it; he was no transparent reporter, mythographer, or encomiast, but an artist whose "tone" and attitude merited closer examination. It opened the way for an appreciation of *Beowulf* not only as a story but as a poem, and allowed critics to perceive, or imagine, that its author wrote from a more complex point of view than earlier readers had guessed. This shift in critical expectation from honest simplicity to ambiguous complexity is not just an historical curiosity; the assumptions embedded in these two very different approaches to *Beowulf* are still active, underwriting the ways readers draw meaning from the poem, forming the borders beyond which critical interpretation rarely manages to go. The ways readers recognize, avoid, address, and understand ambivalences and paradoxes in *Beowulf* reveals something about our own reading practices; eventually they may tell us something about the meaning of the poem as well.

The most useful term for such moments of apparent tonal complexity is *irony*, a term which in its broad sense, as most modern critics use it, includes any instance in a literary work in which what is said is different from what is meant.[10] The workings of irony have proved notoriously difficult to theorize. Various sorts of irony have been distinguished—rhetorical, situational, romantic, Socratic, dramatic, and so on—but all seem to have in common an appreciation for moments of semantic incongruity, the tension between a statement and its context that signals some intention in excess of expression.[11] This tension may be resolved by erasing the literal sense in favor of the ironic intention, as in a simple reversal of meaning (saying "nice weather" in a thunderstorm, for example, or giving a professional basketball player the nickname "Shorty"); or it may be, as modern theories of irony insist, that none of the competing readings may finally emerge as the authoritative meaning of a statement. The purposes of irony are many, from humor to aggression to moral censure to philosophical inquiry; its scope in literature may range from a word, phrase, or scene to the entire work.

It has been said that irony is the lingua franca of modern and especially postmodern society. Detachment, insinuation, cutting wit or arch cross-reference marks so much of the discourse of current television, film, and even politics.[12] It would have been odd if twentieth-century readers had not gone looking for irony in *Beowulf*, since a number of influential critics made it practically a prerequisite of poetic language;[13] nevertheless, the fluency with which we speak of irony in modern culture should not lead us to forget that understanding irony in early literature is actually a fairly complex problem. Irony, as Linda Hutcheon has pointed out, depends for its effect on our membership in a "discursive community" that is capable of evaluating statements in context, hearing both sides of an ambivalence and seeing through an expression to a presumed intention.[14] The context of *Beowulf* is unknown, and the words by themselves are not always enough to clarify action and speech even at the literal level, let alone in the murky realm of unmet expectations, shared assumptions, and unspoken attitudes that is the lair of irony. The representation of interiority in *Beowulf* is notoriously opaque: what do we know of the poem's expectations for motive, meaning, feeling, response, all the contours of the inner landscape that we automatically rely on when we talk about "character" in fiction? We seldom know what a character is thinking or hoping or wishing; we know more about Grendel's state of mind than we do about Beowulf's. In order to map out the habitat of this elusive literary device, then, it might be best to begin with the most familiar landmarks.

There are moments in the poem when the gap between expression and intention, in the form of *litotes*, or grimly humorous understatement, is impossible to ignore—the first example is lines 43–46, where it is said of those who load treasure into Scyld's funeral ship,

> Nalæs hī hine læssan   lācum tēodan,
> þēodgestrēonum,   þon þā dydon
> þē hine æt frumsceafte   forð onsendon
> ǣnne ofer ȳðe   umborwesende.[15]

—when of course he had been sent forth across the ocean with nothing at all. Another moment occurs when we are told that Beowulf did not consider Grendel's life useful to any people (lines 793–95), when in fact he is strenuously trying to kill him. Still later it is said that Unferth had not been "ārfæst" (1168) [merciful] to his kinsmen, when we have learned elsewhere that he has in fact killed one of them. These examples share a common negative structure—not fewer gifts, not useful, not merciful—and a common simplicity; we must read between the lines if we are going to read at all, and it is a straightforward matter to replace the literal expression with its implied opposite. Ironic litotes in the poem has been widely noted, and is found in the heroic literature of many cultures including our own; it is the kind of battlefield humor that laughs in the face of danger, makes light of hardships and deprivations, and mocks a defeated opponent—the irony of the sagas or of action movies.

What actually happens in these simple moments, however, is not necessarily so simple. To begin with, each requires some prior knowledge of a character, situation, or expected pattern of behavior—like all irony, these phrases depend for their impact on our membership in a discursive community that recognizes the incongruity of the expression in context. We are required first to know what ought to be said, then to react to the narrator's failure to say it. Each also depends, I would argue, on some degree of sympathetic engagement with the story; one requirement for membership in the community that makes irony possible is a shared set of attitudes and values. Surely we are expected, for example, to take grisly pleasure in the sudden reversal of Grendel's expectations as he enters Heorot—three times we are told what the creature "mynte" (lines 712, 731, 762) [intended] to do, but we know better than he what he will actually find in Heorot.[16] The grim punchline is delivered with deadpan understatement: "ne wæs his drohtoð þær / swylce hē on ealderdagum ær gemētte" (lines 756–57).[17] And yet the same sentiment is tragically sad when applied to Beowulf:

> Scyld wēl gebearg
> līfe ond līce   læssan hwīle
> mærum þēodne,   þonne his myne sōhte.
>   (lines 2570–72)[18]

Here heroic understatement evokes pathos, not aggressive laughter, and the tone of the irony is one of deep regret rather than mocking triumph. Our evaluation of this kind of ironic language, in other words, depends on our engagement with the hero and his story—to understand irony means to take sides, to subscribe, at least temporarily, to the values and viewpoints implied by the story. Ironic reversals of meaning like this cannot work without sympathy—we need to know who is pierced by the point of the barbed word.

This should be borne in mind when we encounter more difficult and more critically contested sites of irony in *Beowulf*, such as the incongruity that occurs when characters are described by traditional phrases and expressions which are inappropriate to the action of the story—not irony *in* the heroic mode, one might say, but irony *about* the heroic mode. The fierce old Swedish king Ongentheow, for example, is called "folces hyrde" (line 2981) [shepherd of his people] at the very moment of his death. Is the dissonance between the traditional epithet and its narrative circumstances deliberate? If so, what attitude does it signify?[19] The heart of the problem of literary irony is that it is an evaluative act, a matter of judging intentions, and our reconstruction of such intentions is entirely conjectural. We have no knowledge whatsoever about the author of the poem and what he or she wanted to say, no way of knowing how well *Beowulf* fulfills these intentions, and no general contextualizing knowledge about how poetry was read and received among the Anglo-Saxons. *Beowulf* is the only poem of its kind; we have nothing to which to compare it to help us determine how to read it.[20] We ought to know what the poem means in order to interpret these individual expressions, but of course our sense of the poem's meaning is itself derived from our understanding of expressions like these.

The theory of oral-formulaic composition developed in the middle years of the twentieth century was, among other things, an attempt to discover an *ars legendi* for Old English, to reconstruct the implications of poetic language from the recurrence of words and traditional phrases in different contexts and tabulate a set of expectations for literary meaning. But in its earliest and most extreme manifestations, as in the works of Francis P. Magoun, Jr., or Robert Creed,[21] the theory assumed that meaning in a particular context was subordinate to meaning in general and to the requirements of composition. A formula like *folces hyrde* arose and was applied in accordance with a traditional portrait of idealized kingship and the necessities of meter, not the subtleties of any particular individual meaning. A strict application of oral-formulaic theory required that all ironies were unintended and all incongruities invisible, because formulaic diction was deployed according to a principle of "metrical thrift." Irony, in this view, is simply not possible in an oral poem; the circumstances of composition, the expectations of the audience, and the exigencies of performance all conspired to prevent its occurrence and preclude its recognition.[22] And so the closest thing Anglo-Saxon literary studies had to a hermeneutics was poisonous to any notion of irony, as it was poisonous to any sense of literary history; theories of formulaic composition foreclosed ideas of individual meaning in local contexts just as they precluded the possibility of specific influences between one text and another. Those who believed that the poem arose within a tradition of oral composition were expected to ignore the occasional incongruities in its epithets; Edward B. Irving, a convert to the oral theory late in his life, admitted that "we really cannot be sure how much such formulas are to be weighted," but then supplied the dogmatic assurance that "they are not at all ironic."[23]

Few modern scholars have sufficient faith in any hypotheses of the origins of *Beowulf* to sustain such a rigorous position, and there is little point in adding to the vast chorus of voices which have pointed out the shortcomings and contradictions of this fundamentalist denomination of oral-formulaic theory.[24] Other readers, however, while less invested in questions of origins, are equally convinced of the poem's earnestness of tone and clarity of intention. The most articulate of these is John Hill, whose book *The Cultural World in Beowulf*[25] often treats the poem as a more or less transparent historical document whose point of view is unreservedly positive. This return to historicism is a retreat from irony: Hill maintains that the poem shares and endorses the values of the world it depicts, and there is no room in the brightly lit meadhall for the shadowy paradoxes that modern readers are too apt to find there. Such readings recall something of the longing for a poem without poetics during the "iron" age of *Beowulf* criticism: the poem must mean what it says, even when it seems to say otherwise. There is something to be gained from such assumptions, as Hill's insightful and deeply rewarding work clearly demonstrates, but something lost as well by giving up the kinds of meaning that an openness to irony makes possible. It may be useful to approach the question of irony in the poem by insisting again upon the necessary connection between irony and sympathy, and by paying attention to the processes by which we infer meaning from literary language as well as to the meanings produced by these processes.[26]

Since this is not a paper about the theory of irony, I will proceed on the pragmatic if simplistic assumption that potential ironies in *Beowulf* can be recognized by analogy to the way we recognize irony in everyday life. On any given day a great many things we hear or read may strike us as ironic, but I am concerned here with the cases where we would like to know whether the irony is significant, that is, whether an incongruous expression is *deliberately* ironic. In the absence of nonverbal clues such as intonation or facial expression, we judge this by deciding whether an ascription of irony adds to the meaning of the exchange, whether the ironic meaning and the attitude it implies are appropriate in the situation, and whether the speaker is likely to have intended such added or reversed meaning.[27] We generally do this automatically, of course, because of our lifetime membership in a set of discursive communities—we know the rules, including the rules about how and when to break the rules. A literary text is a special case; we learn the rules of discourse as we go along and apply them somewhat provisionally, step by step from the beginning of the text to its end. But unless the text is damaged, corrupt, or composite, every statement is presumed to be intentional, or at least resolvable to some construct of imagined intention. In a narrative, unlike life, things happens for a reason, even if that reason is to demonstrate the absurdity of language, literature, or life in general; when we read we are fully justified in expecting more meaning rather than less from each statement. Speeches in a work of literature have two contexts, the scene in which they are spoken and the text itself, and two audiences, the characters addressed and the reader; moreover, events in a narrative are themselves statements by the narrative's author, and thus "dramatic ironies"—the incongruities arising from the different situations of characters and audience, or from the gap between expectations and outcomes, or from the juxtaposition of events—can be meaningful in ways that they presumably are not in life. And yet, to repeat, we decode irony in a text much as we do in life, by judging whether irony is appropriate in the situation described, whether it enhances or confuses the provisional meaning we are trying to construct as we read, and whether the speaker or author, as we imagine him or her, might have intended it.

When Beowulf tells the coast guard that he and his companions have come to seek Hrothgar, the "lēodgebyrgean" (line 269) [protector of his people], the honorific epithet is, on a literal level, inappropriate, since Hrothgar has not been protecting his people very well at all. Is this an example of a traditional formula applied automatically, or is Beowulf using the epithet with deliberate irony to remind his listener that the Danes do, in fact, need a protector? Given the choice between more meaning and less here, which do we choose, and how can we justify that choice on any grounds other than our own desire? Applying the pragmatic rules of "ordinary life," one can note that the ironic meaning is at least potentially appropriate, and congruent with the meaning of the poem so far. But an ironic expression at this moment in the narrative might be taken as an act of aggression and invite a hostile reply; since nothing in the story so far suggests that a character in Beowulf's position would want such a thing, it may be better to assume instead that the hero is merely being generous and diplomatic. Similarly, when the Dane Wulfgar announces that Hrothgar will receive Beowulf, he calls the king "sigedryhten mīn" (line 391) [my victorious lord], an almost equally incongruous epithet, but I think no reader who perceives the awkwardness of his position— welcoming a troop of fearsome unknown warriors to do a job none of the Danes has been able to do—can imagine that he would deliberately call attention to his king's impotence; instead, we conclude, he is maintaining Hrothgar's traditional dignity in the face of a potentially humiliating encounter. If the epithet is incongruous, the incongruity is irrelevant to the intention of the speaker Wulfgar. Beowulf soon afterwards addresses Hrothgar as "eodor Scyldinga" (line 428) [protector of the Scyldings] when he asks permission to fight Grendel; it would be difficult to read the expression as intentionally ironic without questioning the character's judgment in a situation which demands a full measure of formality, courtesy, and above all tact.

In these cases, with the reader's sympathies alert to the delicate situations of these characters, the epithets applied to the king can hardly be interpreted as anything but generous-minded positive statements; whatever ironic resonance they possess is presumably unintentional. Later, however, when Beowulf says to Unferth that Grendel has learned that he need not fear the swords of the "Sige-Scyldinga" (line 597) [victorious Scyldings], can we be so sure? Unferth has verbally assaulted Beowulf, and the hero is responding in kind. The rhetorical situation, a *flyting*, or verbal duel, makes the use of irony appropriate, and the ironic sense and the attitude it implies add to the meaning of the scene (revealing another aspect of Beowulf's verbal skill, and reminding his opponent of the weak position of the Danes and their need for his help); it seems appropriate to appreciate the epithet as intentionally ironic, an expression of restrained anger at the hero's rude challenger. If this is so, then we must conclude that the juxtaposition of a traditional epithet and an incongruous context for ironic effect is within the range of possible tonal effects in the poem, since obviously Beowulf's verbal skill is a construct of the poet's own skill. Later, then, when the narrator himself calls Hrothgar "eodur Scyldinga" (line 663) [protector of the Scyldings] at precisely the moment when the king is leaving the hall, handing over his role as protector of his people to Beowulf,[28] should we conclude that the narrator is inviting the audience to pause over the courteous and diplomatic language used earlier, make the judgment that the characters dare not make, and recognize the pathos behind their words of praise?

Our appreciation of the epithet's irony, if that is what it is, depends on our assumptions about the author's attitude towards his characters[29] as well as towards his audience; as always, interpreting irony requires some evaluation of intention, however reluctantly we may use the word.[30] It is here that our uncertainty about the poem's tone becomes urgently troubling. As far as the reader is concerned the poet is the creation of his text, not the creator;[31] the author's intentions are, if anything, even more difficult to imagine than those of his characters, and our labor to discern and define what one of the most powerful authorial presences in twentieth-century literary theory called "the principle of thrift in the proliferation of meaning"[32] leads us deep into the dark heart of all that we do not know about *Beowulf.* One interpretive position with which most readers will agree, however, is that for the poem to make much sense at all, the king's dignity must be maintained. It is, after all, Hrothgar who can bestow glory on Beowulf by his rewards; if the hero is risking his life and the lives of his companions for a foolish, failed old man, then any glory he might gain thereby is tainted at its source. Any lowering of Hrothgar's stature reflects badly on Beowulf; irony at Hrothgar's expense would tarnish the hero as well. This same need to maintain the king's dignity, however, and the unbearable tension it creates between what is said and what is unsaid, may in fact be the very source of the narrator's irony, deployed not at the king's expense but rather in sympathy with him, bringing us to feel, with him, the shame of his situation—it deepens rather than cheapens his character. Hrothgar is a heartbroken old king who has not done what a king should do, yet he is, for all that, still a king, still required to rule and feast and dispense gifts, still responsible for his hall and people, still capable of a kind of redemption by Beowulf's heroic action. Behind every honorific lie the grim facts of the matter, and every word spoken in praise of the king calls to mind his terrible failures and invests him with deeper pathos. Ironic incongruity here is a way of indicating that truth is larger than language, and that sometimes we speak not to express our thoughts but to conceal them.

Hrothgar's dignity is such a precarious thing that any praise of Beowulf is potentially a reproach to the king; after the death of Grendel the narrator must point out that when Beowulf's fame is praised, and many say that there is no better shield-bearer in the world, nor none more worthy of a kingdom, "Nē hīe hūru winedrihten wiht ne lōgodon / glædne Hrōðgār, ac þæt wæs gōd cyning" (lines 862–63) [Indeed they found no fault with their own dear lord, the gracious Hrothgar, but (said) he was a good king]. The implication can only be that we, and perhaps even they, are on the verge of thinking that he is *not* a good king, a fact which Beowulf's success has made starkly obvious, but this must not be said aloud. The delicacy of the Danes' situation requires that many things must remain repressed, and many others expressed indirectly or euphemistically.[33] In conditions like this, where the mounting pressure of what-must-not-be-said presses against every utterance, intentions are always at some distance from expressions and the potential for irony abounds. If our sympathies for the characters in their complex situations are fully engaged, we cannot help but notice the insufficiency of this traditional language of kingship, but we need not assume that it cancels out the king's worthiness or makes him incapable of bestowing honor on another. Though the traditional language of praise deals in absolutes, the poem does not, and neither should its readers.

This need to preserve Hrothgar's dignity in an impossible situation may account for the fact that after the fight with Grendel, the epithets which are used to describe the king generally have more to do with his wisdom than his strength; he is characterized more often as *frōd*, *wīs*, or *snotor*, or simply genealogically as the son of Healfdane—inheriting the glory of a vanished ancestor—and less often as the protector of the Scyldings. Reporting to his own king, Beowulf describes Hrothgar as "wine Scildunga" (line 2101) when he rewards the hero for fighting Grendel, and "rūmheort cyning" (line 2110) when he tells his old and strange stories, "eldo gebunden, / gomel gūðwiga" (lines 2111–12)—hardly the mirror of strength and protection, but no less dignified or honored for that. Finally he is "snotra fengel" (line 2156) as he gives more gifts to Beowulf. If the epithets in the poem were applied mechanically, according to the demands of meter rather than sense, we might expect that honorifics referring to wisdom and strength would be more or less evenly distributed throughout the poem, but this is not the case. Instead the figure of Hrothgar the warrior, protector of his people, gives way to the figure of Hrothgar the wise old man. After Beowulf's dramatic achievements, reminders of Hrothgar's protective role or success in battle would be inescapably and bitterly hollow, but epithets emphasizing his wisdom and age maintain some of his dignity by assigning to him a more appropriate role.[34] The king is wise because he can no longer be bold; when the potential for irony becomes overwhelmingly strong, it is gently avoided.

A recent study of the figure of Hrothgar in *Beowulf* suggests that the incongruity between the traditional poetic language used to describe the king and the action of the narrative creates "a confrontation of perspectives unreconciled by the poem itself," a "poly-perspectival matrix that contributes to the poem's decidedly ambiguous characterization of Hrothgar."[35] The study goes on to suggest that "the ambiguity surrounding Hrothgar is truly ambiguous. . . . [T]here are plural perspectives which remain plural, rather than eventually be[ing] given clarity and unanimity by the poem's structure, theme, surrounding traditions, or any other elucidating framework."[36] Making a case for irony in *Beowulf*, however, may not require this utter derangement of meaning or abandonment of interpretive coherence. We may sense deeply mixed feelings in the poem's portrait of the king of the

Danes, but to say that Hrothgar is a complex and ambivalent character, a dignified but failed protector of his people on whom the traditional panegyric epithets of kingship rest uneasily, is not to say that the poem is a Bakhtinian heteroglossia of competing and eternally unreconciled voices. Irony in *Beowulf* is a tool for expressing the poem's meaning, not a substitute for it; ambivalence is not ambiguity, and complexity is not incoherence. When a literary work ends, our job as readers has always been to make what sense of it we can.[37] If we find tension and complexity in the representation of a character, then that tension and complexity itself must become part of the meaning we negotiate for the work, not a sign of its failure to achieve meaning.

Recognizing the potential for irony in the poem's use of traditional epithets depends upon our ability to look both at and beyond the language of the text, to stand both in and apart from its discourse, and to understand that its characters are both more and less than the exemplary figures defined by such formulas. The ironic incongruity of language and action depends on our recognizing both the power and the poignancy of the lives of these characters, and through it we are encouraged to feel sympathy for them without lapsing into complete identification with them. Moreover the relationship between irony and sympathy—ambivalence acting in concert with an emotional investment in the values and attitudes implied in the story—operates at the poem's deepest levels; this poignant space between expression and intention is the arena in which our experience of *Beowulf* occurs, the indispensable medium for its message. The use of traditional epithets in ironic or ambiguous ways is simply a miniature version of the larger ironies of which the poem is made, a way of attuning our ears and alerting our hearts to broader patterns of meaning in the poem arising out of an analogous gap between expression and intention. The most profound ironies in the poem arise from the difference between the narrator's point of view and that of his characters—he knows what is going to happen and Hrothgar does not, and he knows things about the nature of the world that Beowulf does not. As obscure as *Beowulf* is, much that happens in it is clearer to us than it is to the characters themselves, from the origin of Grendel's evil race to the fate of Heorot, which is revealed to us at the very moment the hall is built (lines 81–85). Just as we learn to hear pathos in the discord between the traditional language of kingship and the character of the king, we learn to recognize the distance between the values of the characters and the values of the poem; the action of the narrative becomes as ironic as the language used to describe its heroes, bound by its tradition to present only one side of a more complex story.

Dramatic irony must be the inevitable mode of *Beowulf* if we assume, as most critics do, that it is a Christian poem about pagans. As Fred Robinson has written, "a poet who, in a deeply Christian age, wants to acknowledge his heroes' damnation while insisting on their dignity must find and exercise in his listeners' minds the powers of inference and the ability to entertain two simultaneous points of view that are necessary for the resolution of poignant cultural tension"[38]—words which might serve as a shorthand description of literary irony. The pattern of appositive meaning, as Robinson calls it, operates throughout the poem at many levels, not only in the double sense of individual words like *gōd* and *ælmihtig* whose semantic complexity is a product of their history but elsewhere as well, in, for example, the juxtaposition of passages of narrative with asides of moral instruction. The use of the expression "swefeþ æfter symle" (line 1008) [sleeps (*in death*) after the feast (*of life*)] just before Hrothgar returns to his hall to "symbel þicgan" (line 1010) [partake in the (*literal*) feast] surely invites, indeed almost begs for, a reading that recognizes the dramatic irony implicit in this scene, celebrating a victory that will prove all too temporary, enjoying a life that is violently and inevitably cut short.[39] We are first alerted to the broader connotations of "feasting," then expected to read them into the scenes that follow; to assume any less is practically to accuse the poem of having no meaning at all beyond a sort of reportorial fidelity.[40] Moments like this open our ears to the implications of the scene's language and action and lead us to consider the evaluative purpose of such juxtapositions; they require us to read ironically, attuned to the drama of the poem's structure, open to the possibility that people and things do not mean, or do not only mean, what they say.

The Finn episode, similarly, is placed with exquisite care to remind us of the distance between characters and readers. It is a story told to two audiences, the Danes in Hrothgar's hall and us;[41] to its audience within the poem the story is a "healgamen" (line 1066) [hall entertainment] about Danish victory and the resilience of the code of loyalty and vengeance, but to the audience outside the poem it is a somber, even horrific, story of violence, loss, and the terrible cost of feud and revenge, a bleak recognition that the same values that create and sustain the warrior band can destroy it. As we recognize this double meaning, the story of Finn becomes a model for reading the story of Beowulf: both celebrate martial victory while mourning its extravagant cost; both simultaneously exalt and condemn the destructive energy of honor and fame; both are complex remembrances of the glory and the tragedy of the heroic life; both, indeed, speak to two audiences, some looking for iron and others for irony. Each audience is inclined to hear only one of the melodies that play in a dissonant counterpoint throughout the stories, their contradictions held in tension as the necessarily opposed parts of a single complex, paradoxical—indeed, ironic—attitude towards a past that is both an exemplary point of origin for the present order and irrevocably separated from it. In the long shadow of the story of Hildeburh and her hall, our sympathies grow progressively more ambivalent and equivocal as the poem unfolds; this ambivalence fractures the poem so deeply and pervasively that one cannot help but regard it as an aspect of its meaning, part of the poem's cultural work.

Admittedly, we have no idea when, where, by whom, or for whom *Beowulf* was written, but perhaps we can imagine Anglo-Saxon audiences coming to the poem from two different directions, with radically different expectations and preferences: the first might enjoy the story as a noble portrait of an exemplary warrior, the other might reject it outright as a pack of damnable and damning pagan lies. Presumably most readers fell somewhere between these two extremes, or came to the story with a typically human set of inarticulately mixed feelings. Alcuin of York, however, was decidedly the second kind of reader; he resented the intrusion of secular heroic tales into the cloister and urged their removal with the memorably borrowed phrase "Quid Hinieldus cum Christo?"[42] Pagans are damned, he insisted, and there is simply nothing a good Christian might gain by hearing their stories. Fewer comments have survived from members of the first kind of audience, but it is tempting to imagine one of them on the receiving end of Alcuin's rebuke, scratching his tonsured head and thinking to himself, What's so bad about Ingeld?

I believe that the ironic and ambivalent tone of *Beowulf* speaks—and is meant to speak—to both kinds of readers, for each by his unexamined certainty is prevented from hearing the more complex wisdom the poem offers; from whichever direction one approaches the poem, whether in open admiration or adamant condemnation, one is forced to suspend judgment as the narrative unfolds. Pagans are indeed damned, we are told explicitly (lines 178–88), but at the same time God watched over the Danes as he watches over us today. Beow son of Scyld was sent by God (lines 12–19), even while his father had a full-scale pagan burial in a treasure ship launched out to sea. The funeral scene ends by *insisting* on our inability to judge these characters:

> Men ne cunnon
> secgan tō sōðe,   selerǣdende,
> hæleð under heofenum,   hwā þǣm hlæste onfēng.
>   (lines 50–52)[43]

This suspension of judgment requires us to read ironically, with sympathy that stops somewhere short of identification, accepting without embracing, listening for incongruities, questioning contexts, attuned to gaps and ambivalences, alert to the double meaning of a word, a phrase, a tale, a life.

By the end of *Beowulf* the poem's dramatic ironies place us fully within this space of suspended judgment. Having been shown the splendor of this vanished world, having been made to see time and again the divinely given virtue of this pagan hero and to feel the connections between "those days" and "this life," we are now drawn past and apart from this communion with the pagan past by the almost unspeakably painful ironies of Beowulf's death scene. As Beowulf lies dying he asks to see the dragon's hoard "þæt ic ðȳ sēft mæge / æfter māððumwelan mīn ālǣtan / līfe ond lēodscipe" (lines 2749–51) [so that I may more easily give up my life and lordship because of the abundance of treasure]. While we may applaud his concern for his people even at the moment of his death, it is hardly possible to read the poem in such a way that this love of treasure becomes another value we are expected to endorse. The poem has shown at great length the effect of treasure distributed, treasure hoarded, treasure passed on—we have seen the sparkling glory of Hrothgar's gifts fade into the rusted heap of the dragon's hoard and must conclude that treasure is no help in sustaining an earthly kingdom or, presumably, procuring one's place in a heavenly one. It does not even, contrary to the assertion in the poem's prologue,[44] guarantee one's safety and support when war comes. As Beowulf takes comfort in the treasure for which he has given his life, we cannot but judge his perspective tragically limited—good on his own terms, perhaps, but woefully inadequate on ours. When he offers thanks to God for this treasure (lines 2794–99), the irony of his words is inescapable; his values and ours cannot be reconciled. In the end, our discursive community is not the same as the hero's, however much they may overlap: we have been brought through and beyond the values of the poem's world.

And yet, before we have time to settle into this new position of detached judgment on the characters, we are told that Beowulf's soul departs this world to seek "sōðfæstra dōm" (line 2820) [the judgment of the righteous], a line which not only shifts the center of gravity of the word *dōm* from the secular "fame" of Beowulf's world to the Christian "judgment" of ours[45] but answers (in a finely ambiguous way, admittedly) the question that has hung over the poem from the very beginning—who received the cargo of Scyld's soul?[46] When we are also told that "heofon rēce swealg" (line 3155) [heaven swallowed the smoke] of Beowulf's funeral pyre, we may read through the pagan sign to the Christian signification behind it: somehow God has accepted Beowulf, ironically signaling His favor by an ambiguous pagan blessing. By whose standards, finally, do we judge the actions of this hero? What is the value of his life? The discomfort we feel in framing an answer to such questions is, I have come to believe, an important part of the meaning of *Beowulf.* The poem carries us beyond the simple acceptance of the values of the heroic creed, and the equally simple rejection of them, into what one critic has called "the very matrix out of which, and from which, our creeds are abstracted."[47] Whatever expectations we bring to the poem, whatever sympathies we might have as we begin, are exposed, interrogated, and refined by our response to this carefully

ambivalent ending and its final moment of irony as, apparently, the noble pagan
Beowulf enters the Kingdom of Heaven.

Our openness to the possibility of irony in the tone of *Beowulf* is autho-
rized by the language, theme, structure, and attitude of the poem itself; a reading
that embraces and emphasizes these tonal ambiguities offers, in the end, not only
a complex and satisfying experience of the poem but a historically plausible one,
because it arises from and helps account for the poem's conjunction of subject and
style within its cultural context. The ironic mode is particularly attuned to express
those moments of historical crisis when universal truths lose their mandate and
language loses its transparency, when literary forms suddenly seem inadequate to
the task of representation; we might say that *Beowulf*, a Christian poem in praise
of a pagan hero, celebrating an exemplary life in a lost and hopeless world, is
naturally, even necessarily, ironic. In some respects it might have been more fitting for early critics of *Beowulf* to classify the poem as tragedy rather than epic;
we come away from *Beowulf* with something of the same horror and pity that
Aristotle ascribed to tragedy, and perhaps something of the same catharsis. We
also gain a deeper and more complex sense, because it is a less certain sense, of the
relation between the past and the present, between strength and grace, between
success and salvation, between fame and divine favor, and between language and
history. In many respects the whole poem is an exercise in learning not to read at
face value, learning not to take words, or lives, or cultures—including our own—at
their own estimation. In the course of translating *Beowulf* I have come to believe
that this is what the poem is for, and why readers who find the poem deeply
moving can still have such trouble agreeing on its tone and meaning; its work
takes place within this space of uncertain sympathy, tentatively proffered, through
our education, line by line and phrase by phrase, in the subtle and sad ironies of
Beowulf's world.

Notes

I am grateful to Paul Szarmach for inviting me to Western Michigan University in 2002 to
present the talk that grew into this essay; I am sorry that the constraints of publication have
not made it possible to acknowledge scholarship that has appeared since then. My debts,
large and small, to the many scholars who have shaped my understanding of *Beowulf* will be
obvious to most readers, and I apologize for any places where I have not properly attributed
particular critical observations.

1. An excellent recent overview of the early critical history of the poem is Shippey
and Haarder, *"Beowulf,"* pp. 1–74. See also Liuzza, "Lost in Translation."

2. Conybeare, *Illustrations of Anglo-Saxon Poetry*, esp. p. 79: "It can hardly have
escaped notice that the Scandinavian bard, in the general style and complexion of his poetry,
approaches much more nearly to the father of the Grecian epic, than to the romancers of

the Middle Ages." In contrast, Turner's second edition of *History of the Manners*, p. 303, had called the poem "a complete metrical romance."

3. Chadwick, *Heroic Age*. The classification of *Beowulf* as an epic led inevitably to the complaint that it was not a very good epic, lacking both epic unity and high seriousness, most famously Ker's observation in *Dark Ages*, pp. 250–54, that the poet had no sense of proportion: he placed the important things in the margins and the "irrelevances" like monsters in the center.

4. Turner, *History of the Anglo-Saxons*, p. 285.

5. Clark Hall, *Beowulf and the Finnsburg Fragment*, pp. xxix, xxx–xxxi, xxxii.

6. Bonjour, *Digressions in "Beowulf."*

7. Brodeur, *Art of "Beowulf."*

8. Leyerle, "Interlace Structure," pp. 146–67. See also Liggens, "Irony and Understatement."

9. Schücking, "Wann Entstand der *Beowulf*: Glossen, Zweifel und Fragen," p. 393; cited in Shippey and Haarder, *"Beowulf,"* p. 536.

10. A traditional definition would specify that one means the *opposite* of what is said; see, e.g., Lanham, *Handlist of Rhetorical Terms*, p. 93. My own definition, if somewhat recklessly inclusive, at least has an honorable pedigree; it is essentially that of Cleanth Brooks, who wrote that "irony is the most general term we have for the kind of qualification which the various elements in a context receive from the context.... Moreover, irony is our most general term for indicating that recognition of incongruities" (*Well-Wrought Urn*, p. 210). One of the more pleasant books on the subject is Muecke, *Compass of Irony*, and a particularly insightful modern reassessment is Hutcheon, *Irony's Edge*. A trenchant interrogation of the history of the term is Dane, *Critical Mythology*. I am grateful to DeGregorio's "Theorizing Irony in *Beowulf*," for these references, and for energizing my own thoughts on the role of irony in the poem.

11. I do not take issue here with critics such as Hutcheon who contend that "the final responsibility for deciding whether irony actually happens in an utterance or not (and what the ironic meaning is) rests, in the end, solely with the interpreter" (*Irony's Edge*, p. 45), though I think it is important to insist that irony in a literary text generally arises from the combined intentions of an author and a reader—an irony that exists solely in our reading of a text makes the reader him- or herself the ironist, not the author.

12. See, among many examples, Wilde, *Horizons of Assent*.

13. See, e.g., Brooks's *Well-Wrought Urn*, and "Irony as a Principle of Structure." Dane is only slightly parodic when he writes that "postromantic critics find in the word irony a convenient evaluative term for what is interesting, moral, or worth study in literature" (*Critical Mythology*, p. 2).

14. Hutcheon, *Irony's Edge*, pp. 89–115.

15. "[B]y no means did they provide him with fewer gifts than those did who in the beginning sent him forth alone across the waves as a child." All quotations from *Beowulf* are taken from Klaeber, *Beowulf and the Fight at Finnsburg*, 3rd ed.; all translations are my own.

16. See Ringler, "*Him sēo wēn gelēah*."

17. "His habit there was nothing like he had ever met before."

18. "The shield defended well the life and body of the famous prince for less time than he might have wished."

19. On intention and irony, see Hutcheon, *Irony's Edge*, pp. 116–40. The agnostic

position that ironies are present in the text, even if not placed there by an author or recognized by a text's early audience (as, for example, implicitly in the arguments posed by DeGregorio, "Theorizing Irony in *Beowulf*," pp. 338–41, and explicitly in Fish, "Short People Got No Reason to Live"), is finally not a very interesting one—it may tell us something we already know about ourselves (that we hear irony in everything) but tells us nothing about *Beowulf*. The ironies that help us understand a literary work as something other than a hall of mirrors are those which arise from the interworkings of an (implied) author, a text, and a reader. Unintentional irony, by its accidental nature, is about as relevant to the meaning of *Beowulf* as the fact that you can sing the first three lines of the poem to the tune of "Red River Valley."

20. The fact that the poem appears in its manuscript (London, British Library, Cotton Vitellius A. xv) with a poem about the biblical Judith and a prose life of St. Christopher offers a tantalizing suggestion—some compiler placed the poem among stories of marvels and wonders, violence and miracles, in biblical and Christian settings, and some early reader who found it there might have thereby been attuned to the inherent paradoxes of heroic language and values in a Christian culture. But this is only one setting in which the poem was read; we have no information about any other.

21. Magoun, "Oral-Formulaic Character"; Creed, "On the Possibility of Criticising Old English Poetry." An excellent bibliography on the oral-formulaic theory is found in Foley, *Oral-Formulaic Theory and Research*, and Olsen, "Oral-Formulaic Research."

22. This position is summarized well by DeGregorio, "Theorizing Irony in *Beowulf*," pp. 335–39.

23. Irving, *Rereading "Beowulf*," p. 50.

24. I do not wish to imply that the theory has been or should be superseded; a far richer and more subtle version of it can be seen, e.g., in works such as Foley, "Texts That Speak to Readers That Hear."

25. Hill, *Cultural World*. See also Hill, "Hrothgar's Noble Rule."

26. I readily acknowledge that this is hardly a new position, but merely a reminder of the critical possibilities that have been well expressed and widely read in the works of scholars like Brodeur, Bonjour, Leyerle, and Fred C. Robinson, *"Beowulf" and the Appositive Style*. Other examples might include Whallon, "Diction of *Beowulf*"; Lewis, "*Beowulf* 992a"; and Taylor, "Epithetical Style in *Beowulf*." One of the earliest critics of the poem to point out the possible irony in these epithets was Arnold, *Beowulf*, p. 43, note to line 597, but the view was in a decided minority at that time.

27. The process described is a homelier version of the one outlined in Booth, *Rhetoric of Irony*.

28. The line in fact is "eodur Scyldinga ūt of healle"; the alliterative link "eodur–ūt" presumably makes the incongruity as obvious as modern italics or a set of quotation marks.

29. A number of critics have argued that the poem portrays the king in a negative light; many of these are listed in DeGregorio, "Theorizing Irony in *Beowulf*," p. 315n21. Among the most prominent of these are Goldsmith, "Christian Perspective in *Beowulf*"; Kaske, "*Sapientia et Fortitudo*"; Irving, "What to Do with Old Kings."

30. I have insisted on using this uncomfortable term because it is, as Hutcheon points out (*Irony's Edge*, pp. 116–40), unfortunately indispensable to the understanding of literary irony—without some assumption of intention, however provisional or qualified, there is no irony. Swift's *Modest Proposal* is ironic; a headline in the newspaper's Food section reading "Kids Make Delicious Snacks" is merely incompetent.

31. I have borrowed this apt phrase from Leicester, "Art of Impersonation," p. 218.

32. Foucault, "What Is an Author?" p. 118.

33. It is one thing for Hrothgar to articulate a sentiment such as "nū sceale hafað / þurh Drihtnes miht dǣd gefremede, / ðē wē ealle ǣr ne meahton / snyttrum besyrwan" (lines 939–42) [now a servant has, through the might of the Lord, brought about the deed that we all could not contrive to do in our cleverness]; it would be quite another thing for Beowulf himself, or one of Hrothgar's men, to point it out.

34. DeGregorio problematizes the king's avowed wisdom—he allows, for example, the "potentially treacherous" figures Unferth and Hrothulf to hold places of prominence in his court ("Theorizing Irony in *Beowulf*," p. 328), and apparently fails in his efforts to settle the Heathobard feud by the marriage of his daughter Freawaru to Ingeld—but these concerns belong, strictly speaking, outside the poem; they refer to events which do not happen onstage. The king's wisdom should probably be taken seriously; among other things, it keeps him from sounding like Polonius when he counsels Beowulf at such length on the dangers of the heroic life.

35. DeGregorio, "Theorizing Irony in *Beowulf*," pp. 333, 342.

36. DeGregorio, "Theorizing Irony in *Beowulf*," p. 342. DeGregorio cites Overing, *Language, Sign and Gender*, perhaps the most cogent and elegant argument yet made for the complexity of the poem's language. To describe the poem Overing employs the metaphor of weaving for its implication "of open-ended movement, of ongoing, multifaceted process, of continuity, and the continual possibility of connection" (p. xv).

37. Here one feels compelled to cite Hirsch's classic *Validity in Interpretation*, as the most lucid and accessible statement of this proposition.

38. Robinson, *"Beowulf" and the Appositive Style*, pp. 13–14.

39. See Kavros, "Feast-Sleep Theme."

40. The juxtaposition of death and feasting appears again when Wealhtheow rewards Beowulf with the great neck-ring; in its description the poet brings together in the same line (1214) a field of dead Geats and the noise of the Danish hall, forcing us to read the one in terms of the other, death and life, the sleep and the feast laid side by side.

41. It is, again in the words of Fred Robinson, "appropriate on one level to the public occasion being celebrated in Heorot and on another to the tragic irony which poet and audience see in the future of the Danes" (*"Beowulf" and the Appositive Style*, p. 26).

42. For Alcuin's use of this expression, and for its literary and historical background, see Bullough, "What Has Ingeld to Do with Lindisfarne?"

43. "Men do not know how to say truly—not trusted counselors, nor heroes under the heavens—who received that cargo."

44. "Swā sceal geong guma gōde gewyrcean, / fromum feohgiftum on fæder bearme, / þæt hine on ylde eft gewunigen / wilgesīþas, þonne wīg cume, / lēode gelǣsten; lofdǣdum sceal / in mǣgþa gehwǣre man geþeon" (lines 20–25) [That is how a young man should bring about good, with thoughtful gifts from his father's possessions, so that later in life loyal comrades will stand beside him again when war comes, the people will support him—praiseworthy deeds make a man prosper among any people]. In light of the behavior of Beowulf's own comrades we may be tempted to reread these lines too as tragically ironic.

45. We are reminded a few lines later (2858–59) that the "dōm Godes" ruled the deeds of men then just as it does today.

46. The ambiguity lies in the genitive plural *sōðfæstra*, which can be taken subjectively

("the judgment that righteous people deserve") or objectively ("the judgment of righteous people upon Beowulf"). The evidence of similar grammatical constructions in the poem is inconclusive, e.g., "hæþenra hyht" (line 179) [the hope of heathens] and "homera lāfe" (line 2829) [the leavings of hammers (*i.e., swords*)], are subjective, but "wīgendra hlēo" (lines 429, 899, etc.) [the protector of warriors] is objective.

    47. Brooks, "Irony as a Principle of Structure," p. 745 (in reference to Randall Jarrell's "The Eighth Air Force").

Monstrous Introductions: *Ellengæst* and *Āglǣcwīf*

Jana K. Schulman

The job of the lexicographer has long been a difficult and thankless task. Lexicographers, editors, and translators of Anglo-Saxon works are quick to point out flaws in previous dictionaries, editions, and translations. Pointing out flaws, though, may be easier than deviating from tradition, especially when words in question refer to the so-called monsters of *Beowulf*. Lexicographers in England and Germany codified the interpretation of Grendel and his mother by defining the words *ellengæst*[1] and *āglǣcwīf*. Readers, in turn, take these definitions and/or interpretations "as if they represent authoritative truth," which can prove problematic. Christine Alfano further notes that "[t]he reader must resist and challenge this tradition, so as to liberate the translated work from its critical baggage."[2] This essay seeks to do just that. By analyzing dictionaries, editions, and translations of *Beowulf* into English, it first provides a critical survey of definitions and choices that inform and color subsequent decisions. These choices, in turn, codify how readers view Grendel and his mother because readers accept these editors' and translators' interpretations as faithful renderings into modern English, rather than the products of perception or interpretation. Future translators should adopt new translations that will allow readers to appreciate the ambiguity of the poem and form their own opinions.

Lexicographers, editors, and translators are all complicit in influencing how readers of *Beowulf* react to Grendel and his mother; for the most part, Grendel and his mother have been marginalized even before we know their capabilities. Because of the definitions provided in various dictionaries for the words *ellengæst* and *āglǣcwīf*, the majority of editors and translators depict Grendel and his mother as "other," as not-human, and as evil. This becomes problematic because of the different readers of the poem: those who read Old English know to turn to dictionaries and editions and can, if they choose, compare the various definitions; they can exercise their own critical faculties. Those who do not read Old English, however, read only what is on the page of a certain translation before them. It is telling that these two words direct so much critical response.

69

Joseph Bosworth, John Clark Hall, and Henry Sweet compiled English dictionaries of the Anglo-Saxon language.[3] They do not differ greatly in how they define *ellengǣst* or *āglǣcwīf*:

	ellengǣst	*āglǣcwīf*
Bosworth-Toller:	a bold or powerful spirit	a wretch of woman, vile crone
Clark Hall:	a powerful demon	a female monster
Sweet:	a bold demon	a wretched, monstrous woman

All three dictionaries identify Grendel as supernatural, a spirit or demon, and his mother as a monster or crone; these definitions are neither neutral nor, in light of recent work, the most accurate. The *Dictionary of Old English*, which began to produce its results in 1986, defines *ellengǣst* as a "powerful spirit [or] bold spirit," following Bosworth-Toller, although the entry goes on to say that the "second element has also been interpreted as a form of *giest* 'visitor, guest', or word-play on both senses."[4] The very entry for this word demonstrates its inherent ambiguity, for the entry notes the possibility of wordplay, but defines the word differently, privileging the traditional reading. The *Dictionary of Old English* defines *āglǣca* as "awesome opponent, ferocious fighter" and *āglǣcwīf* as "female warrior, fearsome woman."[5]

The earliest dictionaries did not allow for this more positive reading or an acknowledgment of wordplay. The editors of the earliest editions relied on the Anglo-Saxon dictionaries available to them and recapitulated their definitions, with one exception.[6] John Kemble (1833) defined *ellengǣst* as "jealous spirit" and *āglǣcwīf* as "a wretched woman."[7] Benjamin Thorpe (1855) varied from Bosworth-Toller, translating *ellengǣst* as "potent guest" and *āglǣcwīf* as "the woman, wretched crone." Thomas Arnold (1876) followed Bosworth-Toller, defining *ellengǣst* as "potent demon," but he may be the first to define *āglǣcwīf* as "monstrous witch." James Harrison based his edition (1883) on the earlier German one by Moritz Heyne (1863), defining *ellengǣst* as "strength-spirit" or "demon with heroic strength" and *āglǣcwīf* as "demon, devil, in the form of a woman." A. J. Wyatt (1894) seems to have followed Harrison in defining *ellengǣst* as "strength-ghost" and also ventured out on his own, suggesting another alternative, "powerful sprite." He also is the first to translate *āglǣcwīf* as "monster wife." W. Sedgefield (1910) rejected the reading of *ellengǣst*, and emended the line to read *ellorgāst*, which he defined as "a spirit living apart, an alien spirit." His decision to emend the line is based on the fact that the manuscript shows that the scribe emended *ellengǣst* to "ellorgǣst" in line 1617 (as the Early English Text Facsimile clearly shows). He defines *āglǣcwīf* as "female monster," following in the tracks of Clark Hall. R. W. Chambers (1914) defined *ellengǣst* as "powerful sprite" and *āglǣcwīf* as "monster wife," following Wyatt.[8] Friedrich Klaeber's own edition of *Beowulf* first appeared in 1922. He follows Clark Hall, choosing "demon" over "spirit" and defining *ellengǣst* as a "powerful or bold demon," but he appears to agree more with Sweet's definition of *āglǣcwīf*; Klaeber defines this word as "wretch, or monster, of a woman."[9]

Both Elliot Van Kirk Dobbie's and C. L. Wrenn's editions appeared in 1953. Dobbie's edition has no glossary, merely notes; the note for *ellengǣst* refers the reader to the one for 102, a lengthy discussion about problems with determining which word, *gǣst* or *gēst*, is intended. Dobbie provides no note for *āglǣcwīf* but would probably translate the word as "formidable woman" since the note for *āglǣca* at line 893 argues for the reading "formidable one." Wrenn, on the other hand, offers several alternatives for *ellengǣst*—"bold demon" or "mighty spirit"— and "monster of a woman" for *āglǣcwīf*. Francis P. Magoun (1959) has neither notes nor glossary. Howell Chickering's dual language edition came out in 1977. Since this edition also provides a translation, it does not have a glossary. Chickering, however, does gloss certain lines specially; *ellen-gēst* is glossed as "strong spirit, demon." He does not, however, gloss *āglǣcwīf*, but translates it as "monster woman."

The next edition to appear—in 1994—was George Jack's student edition of *Beowulf*. His definitions of *ellengǣst* as "fierce creature" and of *āglǣcwīf* as "female warrior" reflect an awareness of the problems of the previous definitions of these terms. The poem makes it clear in line 1352, some 1,266 lines after Grendel's first introduction, that he is "akin to a human being"; he is reported to be "on weres wæstmum" [in the form of a man].[10] Jack's choice of the word *creature* shows Grendel's human connections. With the exception of Thorpe, who defined the second element of the compound *ellengǣst* as "guest," Jack is one of very few editors to allow the reader/translator to draw his/her own conclusions about Grendel. His definition of *āglǣcwīf* as "female warrior" follows from his definition of *āglǣca* as "fierce assailant"; Jack is one of the few editors or translators to recognize that Grendel's mother is, contrary to previous lexicographers or editors, not in and of herself, a monster. The edition of *Beowulf* by Mitchell and Robinson came out in 1998; it has since been revised and reissued in 2006. They define *ellengǣst* as "powerful creature" and *āglǣcwīf* as either "warrior woman" or "female combatant." R. D. Fulk, Robert E. Bjork, and John D. Niles, the editors of *Klaeber's Beowulf* (2008), have not deviated from Klaeber's definition of *ellengǣst* as a "powerful or bold demon," but like more recent editors have redefined *āglǣcwīf* as "troublemaker, female adversary." These editions reveal an awareness of various trends in scholarship, both linguistic and feminist, a turnabout in perception, and bode well for readers of *Beowulf* in the Old English,[11] who will be able to draw their own conclusions about Grendel and his mother. Unfortunately, readers of *Beowulf* in translation will not; the translations that came out in 1999 and 2000, Seamus Heaney's and Roy Liuzza's, as well as those less well known that were published after 2000, perpetuate the idea of Grendel as a demon and his mother as a monster.

If we turn now to the history of *Beowulf* translations in English, we see the influence of the lexicographers there as well. Kemble was the first to translate *Beowulf* in its entirety (1837). Heaney's translation appeared first in 1999. Since then, at least eight other translations have appeared in English.[12] Between 1837 and 2010, there have been sixty-six complete translations into English alone.[13] While there are certain constraints involved for those who translated the poem into alliterative or rhythmic verse, the majority of the translators, like the editors, fall into two main camps. Twenty translators follow Bosworth-Toller and identify Grendel, the *ellengæst*, in his first appearance as some kind of spirit.[14] Another twenty-three follow Clark Hall and Sweet and translate the second part of the compound as "demon."[15] The remaining twenty-three translations can be loosely grouped as follows: A: "sprite" (3) and "ghost" (2), which I would include in the spirit category; B: "hobgoblin" (1), which I would include in the demon category; C: "monster" (3), "fiend" (1), "enemy" (1), "one evil" (1), and "outcast" (1); D: "being" (3), "creature"(2), "beast" (1); E: "behemoth" (1), "immense one" (1): F: "soul" (1); and G: "guest" (1).[16]

While Grendel is characterized as a spirit or demon, his mother is, most often, described as "monstrous." Forty-four translators follow Clark Hall and Sweet, including either the noun, *monster*, or the adjective, *monstrous*, in their renderings of *āglǣcwif*. They differ slightly in their translations of the word *wif*; some treat it separately and translate it as diversely as "woman" (20); "she-monster/female monster" (12); "wife" (5); "hag" (2); "lady" (1); "witch" (1); "ogress" (1); "princess" (1); and "hell-bride" (1).[17] Five translators follow Bosworth-Toller and translate the word as either "wretched crone" or "wretch of a woman."[18] Seventeen other translators ventured further alternatives: "beldam/troll-wife" (3); "terrible woman" (3); "devil-shaped woman" (1); "female horror" (1); "troublemaker, female adversary" (1); "fiend of a woman" (1); "ghastly creature" (1); "both woman and beast" (1); "witch of the sea" (1); "greedy, gloomy mother" (1); "dam of evil" (1); "dim denatured woman, large" (1); and the only truly neutral alternative "woman-like adversary."[19]

Unlike the recent editors, who have recognized Grendel's mother as a woman and a worthy adversary, the best-known translators, Liuzza and Heaney, deny her that. Liuzza follows Clark Hall and calls her a "monster woman," while Heaney one-ups him and refers to her as a "monstrous hell-bride." Considering the alliteration on the *b* of bride, "the monstrous hell-bride, brooded on her wrongs," "monstrous hell-bitch" would be more in keeping with the previous tradition, except for the problem of the *r* (in the *br* alliteration).[20]

Although Mitchell and Robinson's edition allows readers to come to their own conclusions about Grendel and his mother, to judge for themselves the nature of these characters, none of the recent translations do. I would argue, along with Mitchell and Robinson, that neither Grendel nor his mother deserve such introductions, such appellations, and, furthermore, that there is linguistic justification for revising these definitions as well.

Admittedly, the compound, *ellengæst*, occurs only once in Anglo-Saxon. Both parts of the compound occur frequently, however, in both prose and poetry. The first part of the compound does not cause any problems in definition. The noun *ellen* occurs some 121 times in poetry and is always used positively; its meaning, "courage, strength," cannot be used otherwise.[21] There are seven adjectival compounds; in two of them, the second part indicates a loss or diminution in or of strength; four of them occur only once or twice, and one occurs twenty-two times.[22] These latter five compounds are used exclusively positively with one exception; in *Juliana*, the adjective *ellenwōd* is used to describe her father and the *DOE* defines this instance as one of strong negative emotion; her father is "very angry, furious."[23] There are ten compound nouns including *ellengæst*; of these, but not counting *ellengæst*, six are positive;[24] one, *ellenhete* (jealousy or fierce hatred), negative;[25] and two, *ellenwōd* and *ellenwōdnes*, while they can have a negative connotation, are usually translated as "fervour" or "righteous indignation."[26] Careful analysis of all the occurrences of *ellen* does rule out such translations as "brutish" (Crossley-Holland), "horror" (Scott Moncrieff), "sorry" (Lehmann), "evil" (Gummere, Garnett, and C. W. Kennedy), "obdurate" (Bradley), "fell" (Garnett, Child, Wackerbarth), "dread" (Ringler), "outcast" (Earle, Morgan, Roberts), "hostile" (Trask), "jealous" (Kemble), "deadly" (Lumsden), "sorry" (Lehman), and does confirm the translations "bold," "powerful," "mighty," "strong," and "fierce."

The word that causes readers to fear Grendel is the second component of the compound, the word *gæst*. The problem in terms of knowing how to translate the word is exacerbated by the fact that it is not spelled consistently either throughout *Beowulf* or throughout the corpus of Anglo-Saxon texts. There are, after all, neither spelling standards in Anglo-Saxon manuscripts nor are long vowels consistently marked. The word *gēst*, assumed to be *gāst* and to mean "ghost," "demon," or "spirit," appears eight times in *Beowulf* (in lines 102, 133, 1123, 1274, 1357, 1747, 2073, and 2312). Line 1123 refers to fire as the greediest of spirits; line 1747 refers to the devil. The remaining occurrences, with the exception of line 2312, a reference to the dragon, refer to Grendel. The word *gæst*, assumed to be *gist* and to mean "guest," "visitor," "stranger," appears seven times (in lines 1138, 1441, 1522, 1602, 1800, 1893, and 2227). In addition to these simplex occurrences, there are also six compounds: "ellengæst" (line 86);[27] "ellorgāst" (lines 807, 1621) "wælgæst" (lines 1331, 1995); "ellorgæstas/ellorgæst" (lines 1349, 1617);

"inwitgæst" (line 2670); "nīðgæst" (line 2699), which are interpreted in various ways. There are two compounds whose spellings and referents are clear: "selegyst" (*Beowulf*, line 1545) and "gryre-giest" (the dragon, line 2560). Carolyn Anderson has observed that "[l]exicographers from Bosworth and Toller onwards have differentiated in their editing of instances of this word or words, according to whether they see Grendel and his Mother as demonic."[28]

It is the editors of the poem who, based on their predecessors or on their own interpretations, determine the word and its spelling. R. W. Chambers notes in his edition that "vowel length is only rarely marked. Hence difficulties like that of determining whether *gæst* stands for *gæst* 'stranger' or *gēst*, 'spirit.'"[29] It is worth quoting his full discussion of the problems surrounding this word:

> gæst. This ambiguous word may stand for *gāst* 'spirit,' or *giest, gist, gyst*, 'stranger'; *giest* is, of course, akin to the Latin *hostis*, and sometimes acquires the sense of 'hostile stranger,' 'foe' (e.g. ll. 1141 [a misreading for line 1441, corrected in the 1920 reprint], 1522, 1543 *sele-gyst*, 2560 *gryre-giest*).
>
> In ll. 1800, 1893, there can be no doubt that *gæst* stands for *giest*, 'stranger.' In l. 2073 and in *inwit-gæst* (2670), the word is connected with *nēos[i]an* 'to visit,' which makes it highly probable that it means *giest* and is used with grim irony. In the last instance we have confirmation from the fact that *gryre-giest* is applied to the dragon in l. 2560; and I should be inclined also to take *gæst* (2312), *nīð-gæst* (2699) as = *giest, nīð-giest*. The dragon is not regarded as a spirit of hell, but as a strange phenomenon. Grendel and his mother, on the contrary, *are* regarded as diabolic spirits (cf. 1266); and when applied to them I take *gæst* = *gāst* 'spirit' (102: *wæl-gæst*, 1331, 1995; *ellor-gæst*, 1349, 1617). This is confirmed by the fact that ll. 807, 1621 give *(ellor)-gāst*, which can only mean 'spirit.'[30]

In his edition of the poem, Friedrich Klaeber also has commented on the problems with this word: "It is [sometimes] difficult to decide whether (-) *gæst* (*gist*) or (-) *gēst* was intended."[31] Signe Carlson states, perhaps wryly, that

> an arbitrary decision that (-) *gæst* should always be interpreted as (-) *gēst* or that it should be so interpreted when used in reference to Grendel and his mother may be convenient, but it may also interfere with the accurate representation of the characters or creatures described. . . . It would seem that "stranger" or "spirit," depending on the context and not on any fixed formula, might more adequately convey the poet's intended meaning of *gæst* or *gēst* without prejudicing the reader.[32]

Anderson also focuses on the arbitrary determination of this word, especially in light of perception and point of view:

> [F]or Hrothgar, Beowulf is a guest who is also a visitor. For Gren-
> del's Mother, he is a hall-guest who is both a stranger and an enemy.
> Similarly, Grendel is a hall-guest, who is stranger, enemy, and ghost
> as well. If the perception of strangers and enemies, ghosts and guests
> is a social one, depending not only on the actions and attitudes of the
> outsider, but also those of the host, then the cautious ambivalence
> displayed in the words describes both an attempt to explain the world
> and a recognition of worldly reversals which deconstruct those expla-
> nations.[33]

Forms of *gæst* occur in the poetic corpus 170 times.[34] Forms of *gast* occur
190 times.[35] What an analysis of poetic texts and manuscripts reveals is that the
Exeter manuscript, which has the largest and most varied collection of poems,
tends to the spelling *gæst*, even in religious poetry; the riddles are the exceptions as
we find *gast* (1) and *giest* (5) as well as *gæst*. The Junius manuscript has the spelling
gast, almost exclusively—there is one occurrence of *gæst* in *Daniel*, one of *gyst*(*sele*)
in *Exodus*—with the exception of *Genesis* which also includes occurrences of *giest*
(2), *gyst* (2), and *gist* (2). The Vercelli manuscript, without exception, uses *gast*. The
Cotton Vitellius A. xv manuscript's two poems are less easy to quantify. *Judith* has
gæst and *gystern* (1), and *Beowulf* contains all six spelling variants: *gæst* (6), *gast* (4),
giest (1), *gyst* (2), *gist* (4), *gest-sele* (1).[36] It is possible that the reasons for the variants in both *Beowulf* and *Genesis* are the respective lengths of the poems.

According to the *Dictionary of Old English Corpus*, the noun *gast* appears
some 861 times in prose texts.[37] It derives its meaning—whether positive (spirit)
or negative (cursed spirit or devil)—from the adjectives that more often than not
precede it. The texts that *gast* occurs in—most predominantly religious ones—
reveal that their authors did not confuse either their spellings or their understanding of the meaning of the two words.[38] For instance, neither Ælfric nor his scribes
ever spell the word *gæst*, using only *gast* throughout his entire corpus.

Not only do the spellings differ in simplex words, but also in compounds.
In the *Concordance*, Bessinger discusses the second half of compounds that appear
in poetry. He lists twenty different compounds,[39] eight of which occur in *Beowulf*:

> *ellengæst*: Bosworth-Toller: a bold or powerful spirit, Bwf. 1. 86, Grendel
> *ellorgæst*: Bosworth-Toller: a spirit living or going elsewhere, Bwf. 1. 807
>   (Grendel); *ellorgast*: 1. 1349 (Grendel and his mother), 1. 1617 and 1.
>   1621 (Grendel, his mother, or both)
> *geosceaftgæst*: Bosworth-Toller: a fatal, dire spirit (?), Bwf. 1. 1266
> *gryregiest*: Bosworth-Toller: a dreadful guest, 1. 2560, referring to the dragon.
> *inwitgæst*: Bosworth-Toller: guileful, evil guest, Bwf. 1. 2670, referring to the
>   dragon
> *niðgæst*: Bosworth-Toller: malicious, malignant guest, Bwf. 1. 2699, the dragon
> *selegyst*: Bosworth-Toller: a guest in a hall, Bwf. 1. 1545, referring to Beowulf

wælgæst: Bosworth-Toller: a deadly guest, a murderous guest, Bwf. l. 1331
(Grendel's mother), l. 1995 (Grendel)[40]

and five of which Bosworth-Toller read as "guest." In actuality, twelve of these
twenty compounds, regardless of the spelling, are translated as "guest" and only
eight are translated as "spirit"; three of the "spirit" compounds appear in *Beowulf*.
Of the other five "spirit" compounds, one (*heah-gæst*) is found in *Christ* and refers
to the Holy Ghost, two (*ærend-gast* and *wuldor-gast*) appear in *Genesis* and refer
to angels, and two occur in *Guthlac*—one compound (*nyð-gista*) refers to the dev-
ils who persecuted Guthlac, the other (*cear-gest*) to a "spirit of anxiety, a fearful ghost." The remaining compounds all describe different guests: a guest at the
table, that is, an invited guest ("beod-gast," *Andreas*); a sea-guest or sailor ("brim-
gast," R3); a pedestrian guest ("feðe-gast," *Exodus*); a welcome guest ("wil-gest,"
Vainglory); a battle guest or enemy ("hilde-giest," R53); a guest or foe that comes
quickly ("ryne-giest" [used for lightning], R3); a thievish guest ("stæl-giest," R47).
The "spirit" compounds' occurrence, with the exception of *Beowulf*, in religious
texts, suggests that the tendency to call Grendel a spirit or demon is misguided.
As the poem itself tells us, albeit after Grendel is introduced, he is "in the form
of a man." Lexicographers, editors with the exception of Jack and Mitchell and
Robinson, and translators have done, and continue to do, Grendel a disservice. Let
readers draw their own conclusions after having been introduced to Grendel; let
the word *ellengæst* be translated as "powerful guest" or "powerful visitor."

Unlike the word *ellengæst*, which has not been the subject of many articles, the word *āglæcwif* has. Scholars, perhaps motivated by feminism and/or by
monster-theory, have sought to recuperate Grendel's mother from her "monstrous
past," to encourage readers of the poem to see her for herself. In "The Issue of
Female Monstrosity," Alfano wrote of Grendel's mother that

> [her] monstrous imagery does not lie in physical claws or in talons,
> but rather in her alienation, her ties to the Cain-kin, and her defi-
> ance of traditional gender conventions. In fact, a large part of her re-
> puted monstrosity lies not in Grendel's mother, but in Grendel himself.
> Lacking any identity independent of her son's even in name, Grendel's
> mother replicates the historical experience of millions of women who
> were defined through their male relatives. . . . Refusing to differentiate
> between mother and son, . . . translators, lexicographers, and critics
> transform her into an inhuman beast; . . . It is time to relieve Grendel's
> mother from her burden of monstrosity and reinstate her in her de-
> served position as *ides, aglæcwif*: "lady, warrior-woman."[41]

Keith Taylor argues that the stress on the line "ides, āglæcwīf" falls on *ides*,
that the information contained in the word *ides* is new, and that the information

in *āglǣcwīf* is merely a given.[42] He concludes that Grendel's mother has a certain nobility, granted by the word *ides*, and that the conclusions we can draw from the word *āglǣcwīf* are that Grendel's mother must be a woman or she could not have borne a son and that, like her son, she is an *āglǣca*, whatever that may mean.[43] Melinda Menzer has analyzed -*wīf*, the second part of this compound. She concludes that -*wīf* itself does not mark gender in a compound; that "the morpheme *wif* as the second part of a compound does not make the first part feminine"; and that *āglǣcwīf* falls into the *be* pattern of compound nouns, meaning that "Grendel's mother, then, *is* an *aglǣca*, like her son, but she *is* also a woman." Moreover, the word is an attributive compound, denoting status: "Grendel's mother is a woman with the status of an *aglǣca*."[44]

The word *āglǣc* in the compound *āglǣcwīf* is extremely difficult to define. Like *ellengǣst*, *āglǣcwīf* occurs only once in the corpus. The related noun *āglǣca*, however, occurs thirty-five times in poetry;[45] a related adjective, *āglǣca*, occurs once in prose.[46] The word occurs in nine

> different poems [and] refers to characters such as Satan ([Christ and Satan] 446a), assorted demons (Jul 268b, And 1312a), the cannibalistic inhabitants of Mermedonia (And 1131b), Grendel (Beo 159a), Grendel's mother (Beo 1259a), sea monsters (Beo 556a), the dragon (Beo 2520a), Beowulf (Beo 2592a), and Sigemund (Beo 893a), characters who are all extraordinarily powerful and (in one way or another) threatening.[47]

Bosworth-Toller glosses the word *āglǣca* as "a miserable being, wretch, miscreant, monster, fierce combatant,"[48] and almost every editor and translator of *Beowulf* focuses on the meaning "monster" when the word refers to Grendel or the dragon. The word occurs once, however, referring to Sigemund, and once to Beowulf and the dragon together. It is in these instances that we see that there is a linguistic inconsistency as these references have led lexicographers and translators to include the definitions "hero and warrior," thereby further demarcating the differences between good and evil. Yet these demarcated differences come from lexicographers influenced by the expectations of their own cultures[49] and strip the ambiguity created by the poet. In *Pride and Prodigies*, Andy Orchard has observed about the term *āglǣca*, that "[w]hatever the precise connotations of the term, the fact that the poet employs the word to designate not only monsters but monster-slayers clearly underlines the linked contrasts between the worlds of monsters and men which run throughout the poem and the manuscript."[50] Sherman Kuhn, allowing for all referents, has suggested that "we define *āglǣca* as 'a fighter, valiant warrior, dangerous opponent, one who struggles fiercely' and *āglǣcwīf* as a 'female warrior woman.'"[51] Such a redefinition allows the reader to appreciate the fighting skills of all the adversaries in *Beowulf*—as the editions of both Jack and Mitchell and Robinson do—without harping on the monstrosity of any one of them. In fact, the *DOE* has defined the word *āglǣca* as "awesome opponent, ferocious fighter" and *āglǣcwīf* as "female warrior, fearsome woman."[52]

One of the advantages of such a reading is that it frees Grendel's mother from the monstrous behavior of which her son is guilty. Readers tend to associate Grendel's mother with her son's monstrosity, but there is no evidence in the poem that she herself is descended from Cain. She may have married into that family. Edward Irving has observed:

> Since Grendel's mother has no apparent ancestry, she does not seem to be directly involved in the great feud between Cain's descendants and God. When first mentioned (1258b–65b), she is included among the monsters who have lived on in the "cold streams" ever since Cain killed his only brother, but the poet immediately shifts to retelling how Grendel came to Heorot and was defeated by Beowulf. The total effect of this passage, illogical as it may seem, is to suggest that Grendel is a lineal and faithful descendant of Cain in a way that his mother is not.[53]

Another point worth mentioning concerns the word *monster*. The word comes from the Latin *monstrum*, a word originally belonging to religious language: I. "a divine omen indicating misfortune, an evil omen, portent"; II. Transf. "a monster, monstrosity."[54] The Alexandrian version of the Septuagint says that the angels of God have intercourse with the daughters of men, resulting in the birth of giants, "forming the basis of later interpretation that these 'giants' were the result of sexual intercourse between spiritual beings and human women and thus of mixed, or 'monstrous,' nature."[55] In *Deformed Discourse*, David Williams refers to the "commingling of 'natures' that Nature meant to keep apart," as an identification and mark of monstrosity;[56] we can read the term *monster* as merely descriptive, as beyond nature. Working with these definitions of monster—a being that has a mixed parentage and is beyond nature—we can ask ourselves what it is specifically that makes Grendel's mother monstrous.

Doreen Gillam assumes that the older heroic secular use of the term denotes a "monster" and that the meaning, in later, religious "Cynewulfian" poetry denotes "devil"; she argues further for a "semantic transfer."[57] Her analysis is interesting, but her very premise presupposes that *æglæca* means only "monster." That noted, she adduces four implications: IA: an *æglæca* is "a monstrous creature with bestial characteristics," that has great strength and size and a predilection for human flesh; IB: "a monstrous creature with sinister characteristics," that is like a giant, credited with black-magical properties, lonely or alien, living in a strange and dreary place, and possibly indifferent to weapons; IC: "a monstrous creature hostile to man," that when it attacks is intent on "murdering his victim"; ID: "a monstrous creature which is evil."[58]

Of these implications, the majority of them apply to Grendel. Grendel's mother, however, is harder to fit into these categories. We are not told that she eats human flesh, but she does have great strength, as evidenced in the difficulty Beowulf has defeating her. She is not, unlike her son, indifferent to weapons. She does live in the mere, which is described by the poet in such a way as to see it as being strange and dreary. Yet the same poet refers to Grendel's mother's domain as a hall and Beowulf as a hall-guest. Kevin Kiernan argues that the poet depicts her holding court in the land of monsters, surrounded by many retainers (many a race of serpents), in her hall, surrounded by treasures.[59] While Grendel attacks Heorot out of envy and anger, evidence that he is hostile to man, his mother does not attack, but takes vengeance for the death of her son; there is no evidence that she herself is evil.

In fact, the first time the reader becomes aware of her existence is when the poet tells us in line 1256 that a "wrecend" [an avenger] is still about.[60] We know nothing of this avenger's sex or relationship to Grendel. After we learn that this *wrecend* is a woman (*ides*, *-wīf*) and Grendel's mother (*mōdor*), the poet uses the verb *wrecan* (to avenge) five times to refer to Grendel's mother's act. In line 1276b the narrator describes her as a grieving mother, desirous of avenging her son ("galgmōd . . . wolde . . . sunu . . . wrecan") and in line 1546a, he reiterates her desire to avenge her son, her only child ("wolde hire bearn wrecan, āngan eaferan"). Hrothgar, in lines 1333b–34b, also recognizes her desire for vengeance and the righteous nature of her desire when he tells Beowulf that "she avenged the enmity (feud) in which you killed Grendel yesterday night" [Hēo þā fæhðe wræc, þē þū gytsran niht Grendel cwealdest]. Again, in line 1339b, Hrothgar reemphasizes the act of vengeance: "wolde hyre mǣg wrecan." Beowulf, too, comments on her act in line 2120: "The awful woman avenged her son, killed the warrior boldly" [Wīf unhȳre hyre bearn gewræc, beorn ācwealde ellenlīce]. Considering that Beowulf himself says, at lines 1384–85, "Better is the man who avenges his friend than he who mourns much" [Sēlre bið ǣghwǣm, þæt hē his frēond wrece, þonne hē fela murne], it is clear that the Anglo-Saxons regarded vengeance as just. Kiernan has noted that "Grendel's mother accepted and adhered to the heroic ethic of the blood-feud, the main difference between Grendel's feckless feud with the noise at Heorot and his mother's purposeful one exacting retribution for the death of her son."[61] Furthermore, her grief at Grendel's death "seems as real as Hrothgar's [grief for Æschere], and her response, swift life-for-life vengeance is . . . at least as heroic as Beowulf's."[62]

Many critics have discussed Grendel's mother as a woman and mother and tried to discern why or how she is an *āglǣca*, a "monster" (their term, not mine).

Jane Chance observes that Grendel's mother is described in human and social terms.[63] Chance examines her in connection with Hildeburh, who represents past helplessness (to avenge her son) and Wealhtheow, who seeks to avoid future dangers for her sons. Chance argues that Grendel's mother operates in the present by avenging her son, that "her masculine aggression contrast[s] with the feminine passivity of both Hildeburh and Wealhtheow. Indeed, she resembles a grieving human mother."[64] Chance argues further that "such a woman might be wretched or monstrous to an Anglo-Saxon audience because she blurs the sexual and social categories of roles. For example, she arrogates to herself the masculine role of the warrior or lord."[65]

At this moment, Chance's arguments support the idea of Grendel's mother as a woman and mother. The problem is that while convincingly arguing for the centrality and significance of this episode—framed by the story of Hildeburh (a mother) and the entrance of Wealhtheow (another mother)—Chance refers to Grendel's mother as "Grendel's dam" and as a female monster.[66] The word *dam* refers only to animals; Kiernan specifically refers to what he calls "the tendency to translate *modor* in this seemingly bestial context [the word *āglēcwīf*] as 'dam' or 'bitch,'" contrary to Hrothgar's own description of her as "idese onlīcnes," in the form or likeness of a woman.[67] The irony here is that Chance is well aware of the other meanings of *āglēca*: the word "not only means 'monster' . . . but also 'fierce combatant' or 'strong adversary' as when directed at Sigemund," but she does not choose to use either of these terms to refer to Grendel's mother.[68]

Chance goes on to say that "[i]t is monstrous for a mother to 'avenge' her son as if she were a retainer, he her lord, and avenging more important than peace making. . . . If we compare her vendetta to the Virgin's forgiveness, it becomes even more monstrous."[69] Yet Alexandra Olsen, who defines *āglēca* as one who plays or fights with the law (either human or divine), argues that "Grendel's mother is clearly right by human law in carrying on a feud for her son, but since she is a descendant of Cain, who violated God's law, toward her we can be at best ambivalent."[70] Klaeber himself states that

> There is, moreover, an element of justice in representing the combat with Grendel's mother as more formidable and pregnant with danger. Grendel, who has ravaged the hall because of the innate wickedness of his heart, deserves to be overcome without difficulty. His mother, on the contrary, is actuated by the laudable desire for revenge (1256 ff., 1278, 1305 f., 1546 f., cf. Antiq. § 5) and besides, is sought out in her own home; hence a certain amount of sympathy is manifestly due her.[71]

Grendel's mother deserves at best the audience's sympathy and at least its ambivalence and neutrality. As Irving argued, she may not be connected to Cain;

if we agree with his reasoning, then Olsen's second point is rendered moot, leaving the audience with a grieving mother, right by human law, disturbing not because of the deeds of her cannibal son but because of her being an *āglæca*. As Dobbie says in his edition of *Beowulf*, "in the historical period of Anglo-Saxon it [*āglæca*] did not need to have any more specific meaning than 'formidable (one).'"[72] If we understand this word as meaning "formidable one" or "fierce adversary," which she has proved herself to be, then we should not translate *āglæcwif* as "monster wife."

To support this argument further, we can turn to Middle English. Robert of Gloucester refers to Empress Maud (Matilda), the daughter of Henry I and opponent of King Stephen, as *egleche*: the lady was *egleche* and skilled in many wiles ("þe lefdi was egleche & quointe of fale wrenche").[73] The fact that she is the daughter of a king whose only son had died and who had begun proceedings to recognize her as his legal heir makes it difficult to see Maud as "monstrous."[74] "Maud is certainly both bold and daring, but there is nothing about her that links her to the more physically threatening, liminal *āglæcan* we have encountered elsewhere, although we must admit the possibility that in transgressing the accepted code of behavior for women she may have been a rather threatening figure to many men."[75] "Bold" and "daring" do not equal monstrous. Grendel's mother's introduction, unlike her son's, is not contradicted by her actions later on. Instead of introducing her as a "monstrous hell bride," let the readers appreciate her grief, her nobility, and her heroism. She is, after all, a "lady, a warrior-woman."

This essay has sought to bring to the reader's attention the problems associated with the words *ellengæst* and *āglæcwif*. From the earliest lexicographers to the most recent translators, there has been little change in how Grendel and his mother are introduced. The negative words used to introduce the characters deny any positive or neutral potential and color the readers' perceptions from the beginning. It is true that the *DOE* accounts for wordplay and ambiguity in its definition of *ellengæst* and defines *āglæcwif* positively; so too do the most recent editions (Jack and Mitchell and Robinson). Unfortunately, the translators have not followed in their path, retaining the negative, initial impressions of both Grendel and his mother.

Surveying these dictionaries, editions, and translations has allowed for an assessment of the choices made by the people who compiled, edited, or translated the poem. Analyzing how the word *ellen* is used reveals that the word should be translated only in a positive manner; those translators who opt for words such as *brutish* and *sorry* demonstrate their own prejudices about Grendel and not their understanding of Anglo-Saxon. Analyzing the occurrences of the various spellings of the word *gæst* across different genres and manuscripts demonstrates that religious authors knew exactly what they were doing when they wished to refer to a spirit and that the longer the poem, the more potential exists for deliberate ambiguity. Considering the nature of monstrosity in light of recent work on the subject and in light of the original meaning of the word *monstrum* as "beyond nature" allows for a different interpretation of Grendel's mother, confirming the idea that she is not the monster that her son is.

Grendel's mother has the form of a woman, just as Grendel has the form of a man. Here, the likeness ends. While Grendel's actions after he is introduced do reveal him to be an unhappy cannibal, his mother's show her to be as heroic as the poem's hero. It is hard to mount a defense for Grendel, but the poem benefits from a gradual introduction to the evil of which Grendel is capable and which he performs. Translating the word *ellengæst* as "powerful guest" creates an image of someone who has strength and comes from outside Heorot, someone who, theoretically, for a brief moment, sounds like Beowulf himself—an idea that is echoed later in the poem when Beowulf is described as a hall-guest in Grendel's mother's home. After all, both Grendel and Beowulf, both guests who visit Heorot, are uninvited and very strong, a fact that has not eluded translators and scholars. Many have, in fact, commented on the ambiguities that color these two characters, which sometimes, especially as the poet gets caught up in the narrative and the action, makes it hard to distinguish one from the other.[76] Gillam discusses, moreover, how Beowulf and the dragon, referred to in the plural in line 2592 as "āglǣcan," blur:

> Beowulf, the champion of good, the "monster" amongst men, challenges the traditional incarnation of evil, the dragon: *æglæca* meets *æglæcan*. Daringly, the poet allows pejorative emotions—horror, hatred, condemnation—full play, relying on Beowulf's blameless record to divert them from him to the Dragon; . . . to transform these pejorative emotions into admiration for Beowulf, the champion of men and the greatest *æglæca* of them all.[77]

For too long, translators have introduced Grendel as a powerful demon and his mother as a monstrous woman. The word *ellengæst* need not be read as referring to and introducing a demon or spirit, *āglǣcwīf* as referring to or introducing a troll or monster. An analysis of the compounds reveals much more subtlety than that. Let *ellengæst* be translated as "powerful guest" and *āglǣcwīf* as "warrior woman." Given the blurring between foe and hero, the ambiguities embedded in the words *gæst* and *gǣst*, even the problems of what an *āglǣca* is, rendering *ellengæst* as Heaney does, as "powerful demon" and *āglǣcwīf* as "monstrous hell bride" does Grendel, his mother, and the reader an injustice.

Appendix 1

Editions of *Beowulf*

John Kemble. *The Anglo-Saxon Poem of Beowulf.* London: Pickering, 1833.

Benjamin Thorpe. *The Anglo-Saxon Poems of Beowulf, The Scop or Gleeman's Tale, and The Fight at Finnesburg.* Oxford: James Wright, 1855.

Thomas Arnold. *Beowulf.* London: Longmans, Green, 1876.

James Harrison. *Beowulf.* Boston: Ginn, 1883.

A. J. Wyatt. *Beowulf.* Cambridge: Cambridge University Press, 1894.

W. Sedgefield. *Beowulf.* Manchester: Manchester University Press, 1910.

R. W. Chambers. *Beowulf with the Finnsburg Fragment.* Cambridge: Cambridge University Press, 1914.

Friedrich Klaeber. *Beowulf and the Fight at Finnsburg.* Lexington, MA: D. C. Heath, 1922.

Elliot Van Kirk Dobbie. *Beowulf and Judith.* Anglo-Saxon Poetic Records 4. New York: Columbia University Press, 1953.

C. L. Wrenn. *Beowulf.* London: Harrap, 1953.

Francis P. Magoun, Jr. *Béowulf and Judith.* Cambridge, MA: Harvard University Press, 1959.

Howell Chickering. *Beowulf: A Dual-Language Edition.* Garden City, NY: Anchor Books, 1977.

George Jack. *Beowulf: A Student Edition.* Oxford: Clarendon Press, 1994.

Bruce Mitchell and Fred Robinson. *Beowulf: An Edition with Relevant Shorter Texts.* London: Blackwell, 1998.

Seamus Heaney. *Beowulf: A New Verse Translation.* New York: Farrar, Straus and Giroux, 1999.

Kevin Kiernan. *The Electronic Beowulf.* 2 CDs. London and Ann Arbor: The British Library and the University of Michigan Press, 1999.

R. D. Fulk. *The Beowulf Manuscript: Complete Texts and The Fight at Finnsburg.* Dumbarton Oaks Medieval Library. Cambridge, MA: Harvard University Press, 2010.

Appendix 2

Translations of *Beowulf*

John Kemble. *The Anglo-Saxon Poem of Beowulf.* London: Pickering, 1837.

A. Diedrich Wackerbarth. *Beowulf: An Epic Poem.* London: Pickering, 1849.

Benjamin Thorpe. *The Anglo-Saxon Poems of Beowulf, The Scop or Gleeman's Tale, and The Fight at Finnesburg.* Oxford: James Wright, 1855.

Thomas Arnold. *Beowulf: A Heroic Poem of the Eighth Century.* London: Longmans, Green, 1876.

H. W. Lumsden. *Beowulf: An Old English Poem.* London: Kegan Paul, Trench, 1881.

James Garnett. *Beowulf.* Boston: Ginn, 1882.

John Earle. *The Deeds of Beowulf.* Oxford: Clarendon Press, 1892.

John Lesslie Hall. *Beowulf, an Anglo-Saxon Epic Poem.* Boston: D. C. Heath, 1892.

William Morris and A. J. Wyatt. *The Tale of Beowulf.* 2nd ed. London: Longmans, Green, 1895 [1st ed., Hammersmith: Kelmscott, 1895].

John R. Clark Hall. *Beowulf and the Fight at Finnsburg.* London: Swan Sonnenschein, 1901.

Chauncey Tinker. *Beowulf.* New York: Newson, 1902.

Clarence Child. *Beowulf and the Finnesburg Fragment.* Boston: Houghton Mifflin, 1904.

Wentworth Huyshe. *Beowulf, an Old English Epic.* London: Routledge, 1907.

Francis Gummere. *The Oldest English Epic: Beowulf.* New York: Macmillan, 1909.

Ernest Kirtlan. *Story of Beowulf.* New York: Crowell, 1913.

John R. Clark Hall. *Beowulf: A Metrical Translation into Modern English.* Cambridge: Cambridge University Press, 1914.

Charles Scott Moncrieff. *Widsith, Beowulf, Finnsburgh, Waldere, Deor: Done into Common English after the Old Manner.* London: Chapman & Hall, 1921.

R. K. Gordon. *The Song of Beowulf.* London: Dent, 1923.

William E. Leonard. *Beowulf.* New York: Century, 1923.

A. C. Baugh. *Beowulf.* In *English Literature: A Period Anthology*, edited by Albert Baugh and George McClelland, pp. 18–53. New York: Appleton-Century-Crofts, 1954. [Originally published in *Century Types of English Literature*, 1925.]

James B. Munn. *Beowulf.* In *Ideas and Forms in English and American Literature*, edited by Homer A. Watt and James B. Munn, pp. 11–51. New York: Scott, Foresman, 1925.

Archibald Strong. *Beowulf.* London: Constable, 1925.

D. H. Crawford. *Beowulf.* London: Chatto and Windus, 1926.

Gordon H. Gerould. *Beowulf and Sir Gawain and the Green Knight*. New York: Ronald, 1929.

A. Wigfall Green. *Beowulf*. Boston: Humphries, 1935.

Charles W. Kennedy. *Beowulf: The Oldest English Epic*. New York: Oxford University Press, 1940.

B. J. Whiting. *Beowulf*. In *The College Survey of English Literature*, edited by B. J. Whiting et al., pp. 16–50. New York: Harcourt, 1942.

Mary E. Waterhouse. *Beowulf in Modern English: A Translation in Blank Verse*. Cambridge: Bowes and Bowes, 1949.

Edwin Morgan. *Beowulf*. Aldington, Kent: Hand and Flower, 1952.

David Wright. *Beowulf*. London: Penguin, 1957.

William Alfred. *Beowulf*. In *Medieval Epics*, edited by William Alfred, W. S. Mer win, and Helen Mustard, pp. 3–83. New York: Modern Library, 1963.

Burton Raffel. *Beowulf*. New York: New American Library, 1963.

Lucien Pearson. *Beowulf*. Bloomington: Indiana University Press, 1965.

E. Talbot Donaldson. *Beowulf*. New York: Norton, 1966.

Constance B. Hieatt. *Beowulf and Other Old English Poems*. Indianapolis: Odyssey, 1967.

Kevin Crossley-Holland. *Beowulf*. London: Macmillan, 1968.

George Garmonsway and Jacqueline Simpson. *Beowulf and Its Analogues*. London: Dent, 1968.

Thomas J. McLeod. *Beowulf: An Interlinear Translation*. Hillsboro, TX: Medical School of the Southwest Foundation, 1970.

Michael Alexander. *Beowulf: A Verse Translation*. Harmondsworth: Penguin, 1973.

J. L. Brown. *Beowulf*. Campbell, CA: Academy, 1973.

John Porter. *Beowulf*. London: Pirate, 1975.

Howell Chickering. *Beowulf: A Dual-Language Edition*. Garden City, NY: Anchor Books, 1977.

Albert Haley, Jr. *Beowulf*. Boston: Branden, 1978.

S. A. J. Bradley. *Beowulf*. In *Anglo-Saxon Poetry*, edited by S. A. J. Bradley, pp. 408–94. London: Dent, 1982.

Stanley Greenfield. *A Readable Beowulf*. Carbondale: Southern Illinois University Press, 1982.

Marijane Osborn. *Beowulf*. Berkeley and Los Angeles: University of California Press, 1983.

William H. Hull. *The Hull Alliterative Beowulf*. Lake Gardens, Calcutta: Lal, 1984.

Gildas Roberts. *Beowulf: A New Translation into Modern English Verse*. Saint John's, NL: Breakwater, 1984.

Bernard Huppé. *Beowulf*. Binghamton, NY: Medieval and Renaissance Texts & Studies, 1987.

Ruth Lehman. *Beowulf.* Austin: University of Texas Press, 1988.

Marc Hudson. *Beowulf.* Lewisburg, PA: Bucknell University Press, 1990.

Randolph Swearer, Raymond Oliver, Marijane Osborn. *Beowulf: A Likeness.* New Haven, CT: Yale University Press, 1990.

Barry Tharaud. *Beowulf.* Niwot: University Press of Colorado, 1990.

Frederick Rebsamen. *Beowulf.* New York: Icon, 1991.

Michael Swanton. *Beowulf.* New York: St. Martin's, 1997.

Richard M. Trask. *Beowulf and Judith.* Lanham, MD: University Press of America, 1998.

Seamus Heaney. *Beowulf: A New Verse Translation.* New York: Farrar, Straus and Giroux, 1999.

R. M. Liuzza. *Beowulf.* Peterborough, ON: Broadview, 2000.

Bertha Rogers. *Beowulf.* Delhi, NY: Birch, 2000.

Thomas C. Kennedy. *Beowulf.* Overland Park, KS: Leathers, 2001.

Louis J. Rodrigues. *Beowulf.* London: Runetree, 2002.

Alan Sullivan and Timothy Murphy. *Beowulf.* Vol. 1 of *The Longman Anthology of British Literature*, edited by David Damrosch et al. 2nd ed. New York: Longman, 2002. [While this is the second edition of Longman's *Anthology*, it is the first edition of Sullivan and Murphy's translation.]

John McNamara. *Beowulf.* New York: Barnes & Noble Classics, 2005.

Martin Puhvel. *Beowulf: A Verse Translation and Introduction.* Lanham, MD: University Press of America, 2006.

Dick Ringler. *Beowulf: A New Translation for Oral Delivery.* Indianapolis: Hackett, 2007.

R. D. Fulk. *The Beowulf Manuscript: Complete Texts and The Fight at Finnsburg.* Dumbarton Oaks Medieval Library. Cambridge, MA: Harvard University Press, 2010.

Appendix 3

All compounds with some version of *gæst* or *gǣst* in final position.

ASPR

-GǢST "guest" (see also -GAST, -GEST, -GIEST, -GIST, -GYST) [xxii]
inwit-	Beo 2670
nið-	Beo 2699

-GǢST "spirit" (see also -GAST, -GEST) [xxii]
ellen-	Beo 86
ellor-	Beo 1617, 1349
geosceaft-	Beo 1266
heah-	Chr 358
wæl-	Beo 1331, 1995

-GAST "guest" (see also -GǢST, -GEST, -GIEST, -GIST, -GYST) [xxiii]
beod-	And 1088
brim-	R3, 25
feðe-	Exo 476

-GAST "spirit" (see also -GǢST, -GEST) [xxiii]
ærend-	Gen 2298
ellor-	Beo 807
wuldor-	Gen 2913

-GEST "guest" (see also -GǢST, -GAST, -GIEST, -GIST, -GYST) [xxiv]
feðe-	Ele 844, Beo 1976
wil-	Vgl 7

-GEST "spirit" (see also -GǢST, -GAST) [xxiv]
cear-	Glc 393

-GIEST "guest" (see also -GǢST, -GAST, -GEST, -GIST, -GYST) [xxiv]
gryre-	Beo 2560
hilde-	R53, 9
ryne-	R3, 58
stæl-	R47, 5

-GIST "guest" (see also -GÆST, -GAST, -GEST, -GIEST, -GYST) [xxv]
nyð-   Glc 540

-GYST "guest" (see also -GÆST, -GAST, -GEST, -GIEST, -GIST) [xxv]
sele-   Beo 1545

Notes

1. While Klaeber marks the vowel in *gæst* long (as *gēst*), I have opted not to for reasons spelled out in the text.

2. Alfano, "Issue of Female Monstrosity," p. 12.

3. References to Bosworth-Toller in the essay are to *An Anglo-Saxon Dictionary*. References to Clark Hall in the essay are to the third edition of *A Concise Anglo-Saxon Dictionary*, unless noted otherwise. Sweet, *Student's Dictionary of Anglo-Saxon*, s.v. "ellengæst" and "aglæcwīf."

4. *DOE*, s.v. "ellengæst."

5. *DOE*, s.v. "āglæc-wīf" and also "āg-læca."

6. See appendix 1 for a list of editions.

7. The first Anglo-Saxon dictionary in English is Bosworth's; it was published in 1838. The earliest German dictionaries of Anglo-Saxon also postdate Kemble's edition. In his introduction, Kemble acknowledges his debt to Rasmus Rask and James Grimm and refers specifically to Lye's Saxon, Gothic, and Latin dictionary, *Dictionarium saxonico et gothico-latinum*.

8. According to Elliot Van Kirk Dobbie, Chambers's edition is "[n]ominally a revision of Wyatt's edition, but [is] actually an entirely new work" (*Beowulf and Judith*, p. lxxvii).

9. It is worth noting that in the new edition of *Klaeber's Beowulf*, edited by R. D. Fulk, Robert Bjork, and John Niles, the editors have not revised the definition of *ellengæst*. They have, however, changed Klaeber's definition of *āglæcwīf*: "troublemaker, female adversary."

10. Jack, *Beowulf: A Student Edition*, p. 13.

11. Kiernan's *Electronic Beowulf* came out in 1999. I have mentioned it in appendix 1 with other editions, but it is not a traditional edition, providing images of the manuscript and the early transcriptions as well as a glossary. In the glossary, Kiernan defines *ellengæst* as "powerful spirit, bold demon" and *āglæcwīf* as "female warrior, fearsome woman." In addition to Kiernan's edition, Heaney's facing-page edition and translation also appeared. I speak about his translation below; the edition is reprinted from Wrenn/Bolton.

12. Rogers (2000); T. C. Kennedy (2001); Rodrigues (2002); Sullivan and Murphy (2002); McNamara (2005); Puhvel (2006); Ringler (2007); and Fulk (2010).

13. See appendix 2 for a list of all the complete translations in English.

14. Kemble, Garnett, Lesslie Hall, Clark Hall, Tinker, Gummere, Strong, Crawford, Gordon, C. W. Kennedy, Morgan, Pearson, Donaldson, Alexander, Osborn, Roberts, Tharaud, Trask, T. C. Kennedy, Rodrigues. These translators also vary in their translations of *ellen*, which can only be used positively. Not all of them maintain this positive valence, although the majority do: "mighty" (5); "fierce" (3); "powerful" (2); "bold" (2). Others opt for negatively charged words: "evil" (2); "jealous" (1); "hostile" (1); "fell" (1). Three have

chosen other options: the neutral "outcast" (2) and Osborn who does not translate *ellen* at all.

15. Arnold, Child, Huyshe, Baugh, Munn, Green, Whiting, Alfred, Hieatt, Crossley-Holland, McLeod, Brown, Haley, Greenfield, Huppé, Hudson, Swanton, Heaney, Liuzza, McNamara, Puhvel, Ringler, and Fulk. These translators also vary in their choices for *ellen*, but to a lesser degree: "powerful" (8); "mighty" (3); "bold" (4); "daring" (1); "valorous" (1); "brutish" (1); "fell" (1); "dread" (1); "fierce" (2); "potent" (1).

16. (A) SPRITE: Lumsden, Clark Hall (*Metrical*), Kirtlan. GHOST: Morris, Scott Moncrieff. (B) HOBGOBLIN: Leonard. (C) MONSTER: Gerould, Raffel, Chickering. FIEND: Wright. ENEMY: Wackerbarth. ONE EVIL: Sullivan. OUTCAST: Hull. (D) BEING: Waterhouse, Garmonsway, Bradley. CREATURE: Earle, Rebsamen. BEAST: Porter. (E) BEHEMOTH: Rogers. IMMENSE ONE: Swearer. (F) SOUL: Lehman. (G) GUEST: Thorpe.

17. WOMAN: Clark Hall, Tinker, Gummere, Munn, Crawford, Waterhouse, Morgan, Wright, Pearson, Crossley-Holland, Garmonsway, Brown, Chickering, Porter, Greenfield, Tharaud, Rogers, Liuzza, T. C. Kennedy, Puhvel. SHE-MONSTER: Huyshe, Gordon, Baugh, Gerould, Whiting, Hieatt, Bradley, Roberts, Swanton, Rodrigues, McNamara, Ringler. WIFE: Morris, Child, Scott Moncrieff, Donaldson, Rebsamen. HAG: Lumsden, C. W. Kennedy. LADY: Haley. WITCH: Arnold. OGRESS: Alexander. PRINCESS: Alfred. HELL-BRIDE: Heaney.

18. Kemble, Wackerbarth, Thorpe, Green, McLeod.

19. BELDAM/TROLL WIFE: Earle, Hull, Trask. TERRIBLE WOMAN: Garnett, Kirtlan, Sullivan. DEVIL-SHAPED WOMAN: Lesslie Hall. FEMALE HORROR: Raffel. TROUBLEMAKER, FEMALE ADVERSARY: Fulk. FIEND OF A WOMAN: Clark Hall (*Metrical*). GHASTLY CREATURE: Lehman. BOTH WOMAN AND BEAST: Hudson. WITCH OF THE SEA: Osborn. GREEDY, GLOOMY MOTHER: Leonard. DAM OF EVIL: Strong. DIM DENATURED WOMAN, LARGE: Swearer. WOMAN-LIKE ADVERSARY: Huppé.

20. The term *bitch* might be even more appropriate, given some critics' references to Grendel's mother as "dam," another word for a female animal, but only assuming that one buys into the metaphor that she is an animal.

21. Bessinger, *Concordance*, s.v. "ellen," "elne," "elnes" (pp. 267–69).

22. *Ellen-heard* (firm in courage, brave); *ellen-lēas* (lacking courage or strength); *ellen-rōf* (brave, strong); *ellen-sēoc* (feeble in strength); *ellen-þrīst* (daring in courage, brave); *ellen-wōd* (positive meaning: righteously indignant)—these six all occur in poetry. *Ellen-rōf* and *ellen-wōd* occur in both poetry and prose; the seventh compound, *ellen-līc* (courageous, brave) occurs only in prose. *DOE*, s.v. "ellen-heard," "ellen-lēas," "ellen-līc," "ellen-rōf," "ellen-sēoc," "ellen-þrīst," and "ellen-wōd."

23. *DOE*, s.v. "ellen-wōd."

24. *Ellen-cræft* (courageous strength, virtuous power); *ellen-dǣd* (act of strength, vigor; deed of courage); *ellen-lǣca* (glosses champion or martyr); *ellen-mǣrþu* (fame for courage, renown for strength); *ellen-sprǣc* (speech of courage); *ellen-weorc* (courageous deed, work of valor). *Ellen-lǣca* occurs only in prose. *DOE*, s.v. "ellen-cræft," "ellen-dǣd," "ellen-lǣca," "ellen-mǣrþu," "ellen-sprǣc," and "ellen-weorc."

25. *DOE*, s.v. "ellen-hete."

26. *DOE*, s.v. "ellen-wōd" and "ellen-wōdnes."

27. In the following examples, I follow Klaeber's marking of vowel length with the exception of the word *ellengæst*.

28. Anderson, "Gæst, Gender, and Kin in *Beowulf*," p. 10.

29. Chambers, *Beowulf with the Finnsburg Fragment*, p. xiii.

30. Chambers, *Beowulf with the Finnsburg Fragment*, p. 8. Tolkien has also commented on the problems with this word: "Apart, however, from this expression [*wergan gastes*] little can be made of the use of *gast, gæst*. For one thing it is under grave suspicion in many places (both applied to Grendel and otherwise) of being a corruption of *gæst, gest* 'stranger': compare Grendel's title *cwealmcuma* [murderous visitor]" (*"Beowulf": Monsters and the Critics*, p. 90).

31. Klaeber, *Beowulf and the Fight at Finnsburg*, 3rd ed., p. 338. If we look at two debated lines in *Beowulf*, line 2073 (Grendel) and line 2312 (the dragon), we can see that editors are less clear about what exactly Grendel is and much clearer about what the dragon is. Nine out of sixteen agree that the word in line 2073 should be read as *gǣst* 'spirit' (Kemble, Sedgefield, Klaeber, Wrenn, Magoun, Chickering, Jack [who does acknowledge that it might mean "stranger, visitant"], Mitchell and Robinson, and Heaney). Dobbie does not use accents in his edition. Thirteen out of sixteen editors agree that the word in line 2312 should be taken as *gæst* 'stranger, visitor'. Only Kemble and Mitchell and Robinson have *gǣst* 'spirit', 'ghost'.

32. Carlson, "Monsters of *Beowulf*," p. 361.

33. Anderson, "Gæst, Gender, and Kin in *Beowulf*," p. 12.

34. Bessinger, *Concordance*, pp. 375–77. Of those occurrences, 113 (or 66 percent) are found in three poems in the Exeter manuscript, *Christ, Guthlac*, and *Juliana*, in addition to another 44 occurrences (26 percent) in various other poems in that manuscript. The remaining 13 *gæst* spellings can be found in *Beowulf* (6), *Judith* (3), *Solomon and Saturn* (2), *Daniel* (1), and the "Metrical Epilogue to the *Pastoral Care*" (1).

35. Bessinger, *Concordance*, pp. 380–82. Of those, 64 (or 34 percent) are found in the Junius manuscript; 54 (or 28 percent) in the Vercelli manuscript (21 times in *Andreas* and 20 in *Elene*); and 32 (or 17 percent) in the Psalms (Paris Psalter manuscript). The remaining 40 (or 21 percent) *gast* spellings can be found in various other poems, including *Solomon and Saturn* (6), *Beowulf* (4), and *Maxims II* (1).

36. All of these occurrences are to simplex forms of the word unless otherwise noted.

37. This total does not include occurrences of *gast* where the word is modified by any form of the adjective *halig*.

38. Some 40 plus. There are 591 (or 69 percent) occurrences that refer either to good or neutral spirits and 270 (or 31 percent) that refer to bad or evil spirits. Out of all the prose texts listed in the *Dictionary of Old English Corpus* in which the words *gast* or *gæst* appear, only ten of them have instances of the *gæst* spelling. The initial references follow the *Dictionary of Old English Corpus'* citations: Hom S4 (Second Sunday after Epiphany [Vercelli Homilies]); Hom S39 (Tuesday in Rogationtide [Vercelli Homilies]); Hom S40.3 (Tuesday in Rogationtide [Vercelli Homilies]); LS 24 (*Life of St Michael*); LS 25 (*Life of St Michael* [Blickling Homilies]); Sol II (*Solomon and Saturn II*); CP (Gregory the Great, *Pastoral Care*); Bede 1 (Bede, *History of the English Church and Nation*); Lit.4.3.5 (*Confessional Prayers*); and Mart 5 (London, British Library, MS Cotton Julius A. x.); of these ten, seven of them have both spellings (Mart 5; Hom S4; Hom S40.3; LS 25; Sol II; CP; Bede 1).

39. See appendix 3.

40. Bessinger's *Concordance* does not mark vowel length; however, Bosworth-Toller does. Bosworth-Toller, s.v. "ellen-gǣst," "ellor-gāst, -gǣst," "geosceaft-gāst," "gryre-gǣst," "inwit-gǣst," "nīð-gǣst," "sele-gist," "wæl-gǣst."

41. Alfano, "Issue of Female Monstrosity," p. 12. While Alfano seeks to recuperate Grendel's mother from monstrosity, other studies of Grendel's mother view her differently. In her book *"Beowulf"'s Wealhtheow and the Valkyrie Tradition*, Damico argues that Grendel's mother is "an abstract rendering of the battle-demon" or valkyrie and refers to her as a giant (pp. 46–47).

42. Taylor, "*Beowulf* 1259a," pp. 16–18.

43. Taylor, "*Beowulf* 1259a," p. 16.

44. Menzer, "*Aglæcwif* (*Beowulf* 1259a)," pp. 3–4; emphasis added.

45. In the four primary manuscripts that contain the majority of the poetry, we find the word some thirty-five times. In the Junius manuscript, there are five occurrences in "Christ and Satan," one reference to demons, the other four specifically to Satan. In the Vercelli manuscript, there are four occurrences, three in *Andreas*, one in *Elene*. Of the three references in *Andreas*, one is to the tribe of outcast cannibals, one is to Andreas himself, but the speaker is Andreas's enemy, and the third is to Satan. The one in *Elene* refers to the devil. In the Exeter manuscript, there are seven occurrences, one each in *Guthlac*, *The Phoenix*, *The Whale*, and *Riddle 93*, and three in *Juliana*. The references in *Guthlac*, *The Phoenix*, and *Juliana* are to the devil and the one in *The Whale* to the whale itself. The reference in *Riddle 93* is unclear. The occurrence is listed as a variant spelling of the word *āg-lāc* in the *DOE* with the following note: "a. in a crux: 'attack, conflict' if *aglæca* is from *āglāc*, with *aglæca ealle* a partitive genitive; 'awesome opponent' if *aglæca* is from *āglæca* noun." In the Cotton Vitellius manuscript, there are nineteen occurrences, all in *Beowulf*.

46. The prose reference occurs in *Byrhtferth's Manual* and is to Bede: "þæt Beda, se æglæca lareow" [that Bede, the formidable teacher]. The *DOE* defines this adjective as meaning "formidable, awe-inspiring," s.v. "āg-lǣca."

47. Amodio, *Writing the Oral Tradition*, p. 135.

48. Bosworth-Toller, s.v. "āg-lǣca"; *DOE*, s.v. "āg-lǣca."

49. See for instance Bloomfield, "Bourgeois Family in *Beowulf*."

50. Orchard, *Pride and Prodigies*, p. 33.

51. S. Kuhn, "Old English *aglǣca*—Middle Irish *oclach*," p. 218.

52. *DOE*, s.v. "āg-lǣca" and "āglāc-wīf."

53. Irving, *Rereading "Beowulf,"* p. 71.

54. *New Latin Dictionary*, s.v. "monstrum."

55. Williams, *Cain and Beowulf*, p. 19.

56. Williams, *Deformed Discourse*, p. 117.

57. Gillam, "Use of the Term 'æglæca' in *Beowulf*," p. 147.

58. Gillam, "Use of the Term 'æglæca' in *Beowulf*," pp. 149–55; see also Cohen, "Monster Culture (Seven Theses)." Not all of Cohen's categories apply equally well to Grendel—and even less well to Grendel's mother—but they are definitely thought provoking.

59. Kiernan, "Grendel's Heroic Mother," pp. 24–25.

60. Alfano noted about Grendel's mother that "[h]er worst crime before the murder at Heorot is to give birth to a cannibalistic, Cain-like creature such as Grendel" ("Issue of Female Monstrosity," p. 15). I disagree with Alfano's use of the word *murder* to describe Grendel's mother's action; vengeance and murder are not the same, not according to Germanic law and literature.

61. Kiernan, "Grendel's Heroic Mother," pp. 24–25.

62. Kiernan, "Grendel's Heroic Mother," p. 27.

63. Chance, *Woman as Hero*, p. 95.

64. Chance, *Woman as Hero*, pp. 99–100.

65. Chance, *Woman as Hero*, p. 97.

66. Chance, *Woman as Hero*, p. 99. On p. 97, she writes, "The poet constantly highlights the unnatural behavior of Grendel's dam by contrasting it with feminine ideals." Chance is not alone in referring to Grendel's mother in this way. An article by Bonjour that appeared in 1949 which searches for the source of the motif of the fight against Grendel's mother is called "Grendel's Dam and the Composition of *Beowulf*."

67. Kiernan, "Grendel's Heroic Mother," p. 15.

68. Chance, *Woman as Hero*, pp. 95–96.

69. Chance, *Woman as Hero*, p. 101.

70. Olsen, "*Aglæca* and the Law," p. 67.

71. Klaeber, *Beowulf and the Fight at Finnsburg*, p. lii.

72. Dobbie, *Beowulf and Judith*, p. 160.

73. Cited in Amodio, *Writing the Oral Tradition*, p. 146.

74. See Garnett, "Conquered England," p. 82.

75. Amodio, *Writing the Oral Tradition*, p. 146.

76. Both Grendel and Beowulf have exceptional strength, the strength of thirty men; both are described as *gebolgen* (swollen), usually with rage; for both the actual word *āglǣca* is used; and in two instances, it is not clear if the *ǣglǣca* is Grendel or Beowulf (lines 646b, 1269). In her article "Hrothgar's Admirable Courage," Roberts argues that "þǣm āhlǣcan" in line 646b may refer to Beowulf. For line 1269, see Schulman, "Translating *Beowulf*," pp. 13–14. On the blurring of "the distinction between the two adversaries," see O'Brien O'Keeffe, "*Beowulf*, Lines 702b–836," p. 488. See also Gould, "*Beowulf*: A Formulaic Translation," pp. 7–8, 11, 30–31; Clemoes, "Action in *Beowulf*"; and Huffines, who argues in "OE *āglǣce*" that *aglæca* is appropriately used for both Beowulf and Grendel since both inspire fear (p. 72). While I agree that both characters may inspire fear, I do not agree with Huffines' assertion that calling Beowulf an *āglǣca* should be seen as an indication of his moral decline.

77. Gillam, "Use of the Term 'æglæca' in *Beowulf*," p. 169.

Sweet's Prose *Beowulf*

Paul E. Szarmach

Sir James Murray. Good morning, Dr. Sweet.
Henry Sweet. Damn you, Murray.

This casual exchange on the street, reported by C. L. Wrenn in his presidential address to the Philological Society in 1946, marks presumably the personal and emotional decline of Sweet (1845–1912) after years of academic disappointment in the Oxford community.[1] Though he was a Balliol undergraduate when he produced the still-serviceable Early English Text Society edition (with translation *en face*!) of King Alfred's rendering of Gregory the Great's *Regula pastoralis*, and indeed he followed this phenomenal success with many another book including the oft-reprinted and revised (by others over the years) *An Anglo-Saxon Primer* and *An Anglo-Saxon Reader*, Sweet's "rigorous candour which was alike a virtue and defect of his character" did him in with his colleagues and associates.[2] Never elected to the British Academy, and passed over for the Oxford chair (Joseph Wright was elected), he did finally receive appointment as Reader in Phonetics in 1901. It is common belief that Sweet was the model for George Bernard Shaw's irritable phonetician Henry Higgins in *Pygmalion*, who by a form of dramatic displacement became the lovable curmudgeon in *My Fair Lady*. Shaw himself says outright: "Pygmalion Higgins is not a portrait of Sweet, to whom the adventure of Eliza Doolittle would have been impossible; still . . . there are touches of Sweet in the play."[3] Shaw offers many astute observations on Sweet's personality and the reasons for his failures at Oxford, while noting that "the future of phonetics rests probably with his pupils, who all swore by him."[4] (As it turns out, Shaw seems to have been wrong in judging Sweet's "failures," if Eugénie J. A. Henderson's glowing tribute to Sweet as an "'all-round linguist'" is any indication.)[5] Sweet had a "Satanic contempt"[6] for academic dignitaries who should have known better, but evidently he took an altogether different view of students.

H. C. Wyld, who collected Sweet's papers,[7] gives warm testimony to Sweet's special relations with his students. Wyld's appreciation of Sweet, written "by one who set at his feet as a learner, and who considers himself honoured in having been admitted to his friendship," has a hagiographic glow to cast on Shaw's judgments:

> Nothing can be franker and more unconstrained than Sweet's relations
> with his pupils. His interest in their pursuits, his sympathy with their
> difficulties, his readiness to put himself in their position and to tread
> with them the straight path of knowledge, his unfailing resourcefulness
> in illustration, his encouragement of independent thinking in others,
> and his own fruitfulness in clear ideas—all these things inspire his pu-
> pils with confidence and affection. It is impossible to work with Sweet
> and not to feel that one is dealing with a great Master.[8]

Wyld's accumulation of pedagogical virtues recalls Sulpicius Severus and his summary of the personal virtues of Martin of Tours in the rhetoric lavished upon
them! Even Shaw grants that Sweet was "not in the least an illnatured man: very
much the opposite, I should say: but he would not suffer fools gladly."[9]

These biographical and pedagogical preliminaries sketch and suggest the
context for Sweet's *First Steps in Anglo-Saxon* (Oxford: Clarendon Press, 1897),
where Sweet's rendering of *Beowulf* into Old English prose appears.[10] Produced
in the busy 1890s and in the same year as his *The Student's Dictionary of Anglo-
Saxon*, *First Steps* is effectively a reflex of Sweet's *Primer*. Sweet contrasts the two
teaching books in his preface to *First Steps*.[11] The *Primer* is "an introduction to a
scientific as well as a purely practical knowledge of Old English," while *First Steps*
is "a purely practical introduction to the language." The former is "well-suited for
those students who have had some linguistic training—especially those who know
German," while the latter is "for learners who require a less concise and abstract
exposition, one in which the strain on the memory is reduced to a minimum." The
Primer is a more detailed exposition of the systemic grammar, while *First Steps*
offers a simplified grammar "necessary to enable the beginner to recognize the
grammatical forms which occur in the texts he is about to read." Sweet sees *First
Steps* as providing a knowledge that will be "mainly unconscious and instinctive
rather than systematic and analytic" with the result that a "few weeks' work at
the *Primer* will then systematize [the learner's] knowledge and round it off." The
learner will have a "zest" for the elements of historical and comparative grammar
because he will not have had these elements "crammed into him prematurely."
Alternatively, some may use the two books simultaneously, or those who have the
Primer under control may use *First Steps* to test and strengthen their knowledge.

Sweet's previous work created a problem for him. He observes that he
exhausted texts suitable for a beginner in his *Anglo-Saxon Reader* and that for his
Primer he had to rely on biblical material and homilies. For *First Steps* he sought
to make "new texts by free adaptation of existing texts suitable in matter but not in
form." Of course, it is beyond possibility that Sweet meant what Pound did when
he said "make it new," but changes he most certainly made. The three texts are
"Bede's Astronomy," which concerns the sun, the moon, rain, and air, among other

things; the *Colloquy of Ælfric*, normalized and put into idiomatic Old English; and a paraphrase of the first part of *Beowulf* put into "simple prose."[12] It would appear that it is the paraphrase, a "very difficult task," that allows Sweet to give himself some guarded self-congratulation in the observation that he has been "more successful than . . . expected," though not without (possible) errors. The texts not only give an interesting introduction to the language, Sweet feels, but they offer "a brief but comprehensive view of the science, daily life, and epic and mythological traditions of our forefathers." In the body of his texts the three have these respective titles: *Be þissum middangearde*, *Be manna cræftum*, and *Bēowulfes sīþ*, but the table of contents gives the equivalents, *Physiography*, *The occupations of men*, and *Beowulf's expedition*. Nowhere does Sweet indicate if he is specifically adapting any antecedent edited text to his suddenly twin purposes of language training and cultural introduction.

Two years after *First Steps* Sweet produced *The Practical Study of Languages: A Guide for Teachers and Learners*, which gives among other things a generalized rationale for the use of readings and instruction in dead languages.[13] Sweet cites his own practice in *First Steps* as example of how to select a literary text: "Useful texts may be constructed by retelling the story of some literary composition in simple language."[14] The construction is necessary in dead languages, which particularly lack prose texts, and thus Sweet compares *Beowulf* lines 99–125, "which in its metrical form bristles with obscurities and difficulties," to his own "simple Old English prose" by juxtaposing them.[15] Sweet's injunction is to keep such texts in "a simple, colloquial style."[16] With this emphasis on simplicity Sweet seeks to bridge the gap between a grammar and a reader.

Sweet begins *First Steps* with a basic grammar organized primarily according to the parts of speech. Phonetician though he was, Sweet offers only slightly more than three pages on pronunciation. His comments on nouns and their gender illustrate his methods and procedures. Thus, the beginner learns that there are three genders, "most easily remembered by learning each noun with the definite article," that gender is sometimes natural as for "sēo mōdor" (but the exception "þæt wīf" is noted), sometimes grammatical as "se fōt," and that in compounds nouns follow the gender of their last element (para. 11–13). Though there are paradigms here and there, for the most part Sweet prefers to present information in continuous prose rather than abstract patterns in the twenty-five pages devoted to Grammar. Personal pronouns, the demonstrative, and anomalous verbs are among the presentations that recall (now) standard school and reference grammars. The result is in the main a speaking voice that explains rather than a technical, mechanical presence.[17] *Bēowulfes sīþ* is nevertheless the centerpiece of *First Steps*, occupying pages 39–67 (para. 91–247) with notes following at pages 85–107, which are virtually half the book.

Before looking more closely at what Sweet has produced in his rendition, it seems right to say that Sweet cannot be held accountable in any sense for failing to produce an award-winning translation or paraphrase into prose. With so manifest an intention to introduce Anglo-Saxon language forms to the beginning student as his primary aim and yet to include cultural forms as part of that major aim, Sweet is seeking a pedagogical *Beowulf*. How well Sweet succeeded in the two-step approach in language instruction, *First Steps* and *Primer*, would certainly be difficult to judge empirically except by citing the fewer reissues of *First Steps* (two: 1925 and 1936 according to WorldCat) relative to the some nine revisions of the *Primer* as well as nine reprintings of the eighth edition and four of the ninth.[18] Sweet nevertheless did produce a partial *Beowulf* that at least, as an artifact of the nineteenth century, deserves comment. When Sweet ventures into cultural forms, he gives evidence of choices made that shed light on the understanding of *Beowulf* for his time. His *Beowulf* cannot be our *Beowulf*, and at this juncture in the subject it would seem out of the question that anyone would attempt any Old English prose rendering of *Beowulf* for any purpose, pedagogical or otherwise. Yet it is with a sympathetic attitude that the following analysis comes forward.

Bēowulfes sīþ begins with an introduction to Hrothgar and his court, following the main plotline until Beowulf returns home with success to Geatland. No doubt any contemporary teacher of the poem would rush to supply the first fifty-two lines and their stunning account of Scyld Scefing complete with cultural resonance, for example, a discussion of burial practices. It is not readily obvious why Sweet would have suppressed the heroic in so categorical a fashion, but the omission may signal that for him plotline is more important than any other feature of the text. The tableau of Scyld, striking the heroic chord as it does, contributes tone, theme, and meaning, but not much to the narrative line. The dragon episode, the account of Beowulf's defeat, and the emphasis on loss and mourning, would have lengthened this prose *Beowulf* unduly, but the elimination of everything roughly beyond line 2200 makes Sweet's rendition a tighter narrative focused on Denmark and its interactions with the monstrous Grendelkin. This kind of narrative economy probably also explains why the "Fight at Finnsburg" receives but a mention and no exposition, and why Beowulf's return to Hygelac and Geatland, which contains somewhat differing accounts of antecedent events and their meaning, is so spare a closure.

If there is a narrative tendency that Sweet imports into his rendition, it is his habit to fill in those gaps in narrative, or in detail, or in motivation that might challenge a beginning student who seeks to understand them, just as they continue to challenge critics and scholars still. This habit of mind is like the "apocryphalizing" tendency that one readily discerns in the transmission of the Bible; next to nothing, for example, is known about Joseph in the New Testament, and so the apocryphal

History of Joseph the Carpenter comes forward with much to say about Joseph (subsequently considered heterodox) as it attempts to join the biblical canon. No such grand move in literary history is evident in Sweet's *Beowulf*, but there are many places where Sweet fills in. The rise of Hrothgar, the building of Heorot, and the coming of Grendel present a case in point (para. 91–112). Whereas the *Beowulf*-poet deftly traces the Danish royal line of the Scyldings in a few short lines (53–63) and highlights Hrothgar's success in war before going on to present the building of Heorot, Sweet gives more of the "back story" on who Hrothgar was and how he rose to power. In this contrast lies the practical effect of audience knowledge: the *Beowulf*-poet expects his audience to know about the Danish line, while Sweet must make an introduction. Sweet uses an equivalent of "once upon a time" with the opening "hit gelamp gēo þæt ān cyning wæs on Denum" [once upon a time there was a certain king among the Danes]; Hrothgar was a "heretoga" [leader of battles], a word duly explained by Sweet in his notes but not part of the lexicon of *Beowulf*. Hrothgar was so successful that he had victory wherever he went "ægþer on sæ ge on lande" [both on land and sea], a formulaic phrase for hegemony not found in *Beowulf*. Sweet further brings out Hrothgar's apparent ruthlessness in pursuit of power, for Hrothgar sought out his enemies in their own lands, we learn with emphasis, and "forslōg and fordyde" [subjugated and destroyed them], inspiring in them an "ungemetlicne ege" [a fear without measure]. His enemies asked for peace, hostages and oaths were exchanged, and friendship was affirmed "mid worde and mid wedde" [with word[s] and with pledge[s]]. The *Beowulf*-poet simply states that Hrothgar ordered Heorot to be built, but Sweet injects the practical note that Hrothgar ordered "þa betstan wyrhtan" [the best workmen], who began the work when they were all assembled. The *Beowulf*-poet stresses that within the hall everything would be distributed to young and old except "folcscare and feorum gumena" [public land and the lives of men], whereas in Sweet's Heorot "herehȳþ" [booty], which is another vocabulary item not in *Beowulf*, is the object of exchange, and the implicit praise for Hrothgar's liberal and proper reign disappears. Sweet's divergences from the original depict a Hrothgar who is somewhat more aggressive and less beneficent than the original.

Sweet likewise makes important adjustments in his account of the coming of Grendel. The *Beowulf*-poet is allusive and elusive in his description of the Cain connection.[19] The shorthand retelling of the Cain and Abel story, the condemnation of the race of Cain, and the resultant feud with God are compressed to create some ambiguity in the half lines "ne gefeah hē þære fæhðe" (109a) [he took no joy in that feud] (presumably "he" = Grendel/Cain, perhaps God himself) and "hē him ðæs lēan forgeald" (114b) (presumably "he" = God, perhaps Cain). Sweet gives straightforward exposition: "sume menn cwædon þæt Grendel wære of Cāines cynne" [certain people said that Grendel was from the race of Cain]. He goes on to tell that Cain killed Abel and that the Almighty sent Cain into exile to live in the wilderness far from mankind. From Cain sprang "unfæle wihta" [evil creatures] who have struggled with God; Sweet's list shares giants and elves with the *Beowulf*-poet's list, but offers dwarves in place of sea monsters and omits giants. The phrase "unfæle wihta" and its forms occur several times in Sweet but not in the original. In *Beowulf* Grendel attacks Heorot because of the loud joy he hears in the hall where there was the clear song of the scop. The scop sings a Song of Creation, which by implication but hardly by overt statement, is the real point of antagonism for Grendel, who strives with God. But Sweet detaches the Song of Creation, placing it earlier with a description of the joys of Heorot, with the result that it is not possible to connect the Song of Creation as the impetus or cause for Grendel's attack. Perhaps Sweet's boldest move in the matter of Grendel comes when he develops the possible implications of

> Swā rīxode   and wið rihte wan,
> āna wið eallum
>
> (lines 144–45a)
>
> [Thus, one against all lorded it over them and fought against the right]

which becomes

> Wæs þæt micel wundor þæt Grendel āna wiþ hīe ealle winnende wæs!
> On eallum þæm fæce hē rīcsode on Heorote on þæm sweartum nihtum
> swelce hē cyning wære[!] (para. 109)
>
> [It was great marvel that Grendel alone was struggling against them
> all! During that whole time he ruled over Heorot in the dark night as
> if he were king!]

Presumably it is *rīcsode* that inspires Sweet to make Grendel a royal pretender, but there is no real warrant in the original for this leap. The fight is between humankind and the race of monsters, and as such is more fundamental than political.

Surprising to say about a Victorian interpreter of *Beowulf* living among the Pre-Raphaelites with their regard for female pulchritude, Sweet gives his student audience a Wealhtheow who is not terribly different from her major appearances in the original. At the pre-visitation banquet (para. 149–52) Wealhtheow walks among old and young alike, giving the cup to Hrothgar and Beowulf. Her reaction to Beowulf's boast that he will overcome Grendel or die trying meets with Wealhtheow's approval, as both narrators present it. When the social evening is over, the *Beowulf*-poet gives us Hrothgar's somewhat problematical departure from the hall:

wolde wīgfruma [Hrothgar]   Wealhþēo sēcan
cwēn tō gebeddan.

                                     (lines 664–65a)

[the war-leader was intent on seeking out Wealhtheow as a bedmate]

It is an odd time to put apparent connubial bliss ahead of the expected and impending confrontation with Grendel. Sweet solves the problem by leaving Wealhtheow
out of the narration entirely, and Hrothgar leaves the hall apparently alone. The
bizarre possibility in *First Steps* that Wealhtheow is left with the Geats to wrestle
with Grendel could inspire mirth. Sweet heads off this possibility by explicitly
stressing that the Geats are left alone. Victorian *pudor* rather than defective narration per se keeps the bed out of view. Wealhtheow's second major appearance
is at the false victory banquet where she has much to say about Danish politics,
loyalties, and Beowulf's role in all of these things. Sweet gives Wealhtheow three
separate speeches by his paragraphing, breaking the original first speech into two.
By and large the content of both versions remain the same with the result that
Wealhtheow appears a major figure in both the original and its paraphrase. Sweet
retains Wealhtheow and her entourage when he describes the preparations for
the first celebration with an amplifying detail: "manige weras and manig wīf þe
þā healle gearcodon" (para. 181). A few paragraphs earlier (para. 176) Sweet has
Wealhtheow arrive "samod mid hire mægdena hēape" [together with an entourage
of maidens], thus echoing the arrival scene in lines 918b–24b.

The treatment of Grendel's mother forms a relatively self-contained unit in
First Steps, divided into two sections, *Be Grendles mēder* and *Hū Bēowulf ofslōg Grendles
mōdor* (para. 194–218). Recent criticism of *Beowulf* has often sought to find sympathy
for Grendel's mother as a lone revenger of her son. Sweet does not make so fundamental an interpretation in his paraphrase. As with his portrayal of Wealhtheow,
Sweet adjusts some details within the overall account while keeping others. Thus,
at the outset both versions point out that Grendel's mother was less of a threat to
the Geats because she was a woman: "Ac se ege wæs læssa, for þǣm þe hit wīf wæs,
næs wer" (para. 196) [The terror was the less because she was a woman, not a man].
Sweet's formulation introduces a contrast that allows the pedagogic aim to introduce
vocabulary contrast and perhaps some prose assonance for effect in the quadruple *wæs
lēssa*, *wæs*, and *næs*. Whereas in the original the victim of Grendel's mother's attack is
not immediately known, Sweet gives the name Æschere early on and states Æschere's
close relation to Hrothgar at that point too. He also makes it clear that Grendel's
mother took her son's hand and shoulder back with her when she took flight. Sweet
gives the Jungian mere with its dystopic features the name "nicera mere," which con-
verts *Beowulf* 845b, "on nicora mere," from a general description to a place name.
There may be something to his intuition here, which would require further study.

The fight with Beowulf is the major incident, of course. In Sweet's portrayal of the fight Grendel's mother gives as good as she gets, which also always surprises first-time readers of *Beowulf*, while second-time readers, and readers coming back again and again, see Beowulf's prowess here as an indication of the decline of his power or the strength of the monstrous kind or Beowulf's reliance on his own strength (not God's grace) or a reliance on weaponry rather than his own physical strength. Exactly how one might envision this two-person brawl, or stage it in performance, is a question that uncovers problematical issues. There is a lot of knocking about, Beowulf surviving thanks to armor but no thanks to the failed sword Hrunting, and the moment of truth comes when Grendel's mother sits on Beowulf (line 1545)[20] and draws her *seax* to avenge her son. Awkward as this position might be for Beowulf, Sweet too apparently has discomfort, for while his Grendelkin likewise throws Beowulf down and draws her short sword, she neither sits on Beowulf nor otherwise touches him. The sexuality of this position is now a topic fit for scholars and critics to discuss. Is the absence of the sitting position in *Bēowulfes sīþ* an instance of Sweet's *pudor* or sense of decorum? Since Grendel's mother is a fierce fighter in either account, it is more likely the former rather than the latter applies.

The telling of the second fight has one further additional feature unique to its narration. Sweet more or less offers a third-person point of view rather than a bardic point of view, that is, he does not ventriloquize an "ic-teller" anywhere. In para. 212, however, Sweet comments on Beowulf's descent into the mere: "Segþ þæt spell þæt hē ealne dæg niþer swamm ǣr hē mihte þone grund ongietan" [The story says that all day he swam below before he could touch bottom]. The citation of tradition in the received "spell" and the implication that the tale told now continues that tradition in some sense seem out of place here. Perhaps Sweet is trying to offer a realistic alibi for anything that recalls a tall tale. Under metrical constraint the *Beowulf*-poet, on his part, cites God three times ("hālig God," "wītig Drihten," and "rodora Rǣdend" [lines 1553–55]), while Sweet needs only to cite "God" once to make the point. The variation brings forward the theme of divine presence in a more emphatic way.

There is one passage where Sweet may have built better than he knew. Beowulf recapitulates his fight with Grendel before Hrothgar, saying,

> ic hine ne mihte,   þā Metod nolde,
> ganges getwǣman   nō ic him þæs georne ætfealh,
> feorhgenīðlan;   wæs tō foremihtig
> fēond on fēþe.   Hwæþere hē his folme forlēt
> tō līfwraþe   lāst weardian,
> earm ond eaxle
>
> (lines 967–72)

> [I could not prevent him from going, since the Measurer did not will it, nor did I grab him the deadly enemy firmly enough; the enemy was too strong in getting gone. Nevertheless, he left his hand, arm, and shoulder behind as life insurance.]

Beowulf explains how Grendel got away, invoking divine will as a factor and Grendel's powerful attempt to get away. The sense and tone are clear and serious, the content matter-of-fact. Sweet renders the passage thus:

> Ic þohte hine fæste gebindan; ac God ne ūþe mē þæt ic him flēames forwiernde, þēah ic him georne ætfulge: hē wæs mē tō strang on fēþe. He forlēt þēah his earm him behindan. (para. 179)

> [I intended to bind him fast, but God did not grant me that I might refuse his fleeing, though I held him firmly; he was too strong in getting gone. He left his arm behind, however.]

The last sentence cited above can have a sardonic or ironic effect as in the Norse sagas where such quips are in fashion in and around battle scenes. All hinges on how *þeah* (nevertheless/however) falls in its emphasis. The word could mark a change in register as well as a counterpoint to a narrative fact announced immediately preceeding. Thus, one could understand the last sentence to mean something like "Grendel is not here; his arm is here, however." Though *Beowulf* does not generally invite comic interpretations *in magno aut in parvo*, it is possible that Sweet was here ready to show a saga tooth. It is lean and spare prose that sets up the Norse quip for its remarkable effect, and certainly Sweet's prose does tend towards a Norse model in broad terms.

It goes without saying that a prose rendition will necessarily lack the characteristics of poetry. Ælfric and Wulfstan show how Old English can avoid the disjunctive fallacy, viz. a bald choice of either prose or poetry, by offering forms of rhythmical prose that scholars and critics still have failed to describe adequately. It is possible to create something of an inventory of prose features that on their own terms create appropriate aesthetic effects. Sweet's pedagogic purposes, however, clearly could not support a creative move in that direction. And so the kenning and the *kent heiti* disappear because they may prove too extravagant for a beginner. Variation, which is a likely major cause of that "lack of steady advance" that Klaeber criticized, would appear as nothing less than bizarre in the bald prose. Alliteration has no structural role to play in constructing a prose sentence; it is thus relegated to certain phrases that give emphasis. Sweet seems to have a fondness for *w*-alliteration. The maxim or aphorism can appear in both modes. *Beowulf* 455b, "Gæð ā wyrd swā hīo scel!" [Fate goes on ever as it must!] undergoes a slight transformation to "Wyrd gæþ ā swā hēo sceal!" (para. 135). Here Sweet chooses normal subject-verb order instead of the inversion, which arguably is superior. Would any beginner be foxed by the inversion? The brilliant parallelism of *com* found in the approach of Grendel (lines 720ff.) disappears. All in all, Sweet is true to his purpose to construct simple transparent prose to aid instruction.

One further truism, stunningly obvious, is that *Bēowulfes sīþ* is pre-Magoun, which means that Sweet had no way to understand how the oral dimension of poetic composition does not easily translate into the world of the written word.[21] It is no great generalization to point out that repetition is central to oral style and that variation particularly has its brilliant meaningful effects. Repeatedly Beowulf passes muster from the coast guard to Unferth, the same incident is retold as Beowulf recapitulates his fight with Grendel or recapitulates the entire Danish expedition, the story of Cain is repeated, among other matters. These repetitions likewise impede the narrative, but they provide layers and nuances of narrative meaning. In this way *Beowulf* is a twice-told tale. The repetitions have no particular place in a straight-line narrative with a sequence of events. Had Sweet been aware of the more aesthetic view (and of course willing to accept it), his introduction would likely contain a scholar's apology for his diversion of students from the original text. Granted: for the now-contemporary audience that appreciates *Beowulf* the aesthetic object, Sweet appears as the helpful roommate who straightens out the grapefruit knife.

Yet Sweet's attempt to bring a pedagogical *Beowulf* to beginners has value in the contemporary classroom. The pedagogical *Beowulf* can accomplish several objectives. Where enrollment management is a concern and the crossover from an introductory course to the next level a potential problem in the curriculum, the pedagogical *Beowulf* can serve as an enticement to students or a teaser to continue study in Old English. The adjustment to the *Beowulf*-poet's style, that *curiosa felicitas* critics and scholars all praise in unison, does require some extra effort on the part of students, especially if their introductory course is heavy with selections from the prose literature. *Beowulf* in an introductory course might prove daunting to a typical class taking Old English. *First Steps* offers a bridge text in *Bēowulfes sīþ* giving, as Sweet put it, a text "suitable in matter but not in form."[22] How much to do for a beginning student has always been an issue in the teaching of Old English (as it has been elsewhere). The discussions over whether to offer normalized texts or to let stand the sometimes near-chaotic manuscript spelling is a case in point. Some argue that normalized texts are a cruel kindness, while in rebuttal others point out that Latin has been taught with normalized texts for considerably longer than Old English. Why offer *Bēowulfes sīþ* when the genuine *Beowulf* is available? The answer has to be situational relative to the skills and abilities of the students. Good teachers never stand in the way of their students, but like Sweet *per* Wyld give their students confidence.

The foregoing literary analysis of *First Steps* furthermore has meant to define, not to deny, literary value in Sweet's rendition. If translations and comparative studies of translations assist understanding of the original text, then so can Sweet's artifice serve as a point of reference to highlight or uncover issues in the interpretation of *Beowulf*. Sweet's *First Steps* is not quite an inter-text for *Beowulf* because of its transparent closeness to the original, but it can serve as a text for comparison that brings out issues of narration, asking questions and occasionally giving answers to questions of realism that are of no concern in *Beowulf*. A classroom exercise where Sweet is in parallel columns or in juxtaposition with the *Beowulf*-poet can prove to enlighten the original as well as a late nineteenth-century scholar's view of the poem. This exercise would be an immersion in Old English and its possibilities. In his review that may have been more favorable out of self-defense (given Sweet's formidable powers of rebuttal!) than out of conviction Klaeber observed somewhat pointedly: "It is only to be questioned whether this elementary Primer will be appreciated by those for whom it is written."[23] Sweet did not quite envision a use of his paraphrase in literary criticism or literary study, but in the practical adaptation of *Bēowulfes sīþ* we would join that circle of students Wyld so warmly described.

Notes

1. Wrenn, Presidential Address, p. 195. Michael K. C. MacMahon gives an updated biography of Sweet with a useful bibliography of Sweet's works and select secondary sources, "Henry Sweet." H. C. Wyld offers two tributes to Sweet: an appreciative biography, "Henry Sweet," *Modern Language Quarterly*, and the obituary "Henry Sweet," *Archiv*; Wyld's obituary is followed by Alois Brandl's, pp. 8–10. There is now the Henry Sweet Society for the History of Linguistic Ideas, founded in 1984, which aims "to promote and encourage the study of the history of all branches of linguistic thought." The website, formerly maintained at the University of Glasgow, appears now at http://www.henrysweet.org. Dr. Steadman-Jones (University of Sheffield) maintains the website for the society. The main page has a colorized photograph of Sweet, also reproduced as part of Wyld's tribute in *Archiv*, p. 1.

2. Wrenn, Presidential Address, p. 194. See Sweet, *King Alfred's Version of Gregory's "Pastoral Care."*

3. Shaw, "Preface to *Pygmalion*," p. 51.

4. Shaw, "Preface to *Pygmalion*," p. 48. Shaw also observes: "I do not blame Oxford [for the failure to do justice to his eminence] . . . because I think Oxford is quite right in demanding a certain social amenity from its nurslings. . . . if [a man of genius] overwhelms [Oxford] with wrath and disdain, he cannot expect them to heap honors on him" (p. 51).

5. Henderson, *Indispensable Foundation*, p. ix, taken from the glowing first paragraph of her introduction. She says further: "[Sweet] was a brilliant phonetician, a highly distinguished comparative and historical linguist, a perspicacious grammarian, an eminent Anglicist, the inventor of an excellent system of shorthand, and a passionate advocate of spelling reform." Such rows as Sweet had with Henri Logeman over "Junius' Transcripts

of Old English Texts" have naturally faded. See *Academy* 38 (1890): 274, for Logeman's first letter; p. 319 for Sweet's first response; pp. 343–44 for Logeman's rejoinder; p. 366 for Sweet's reply.

6. The phrase is Shaw's ("Preface to *Pygmalion*," p. 48).

7. Wyld, *Collected Papers*.

8. Wyld, "Henry Sweet," *Modern Language Quarterly*, pp. 78–79.

9. Shaw, "Preface to *Pygmalion*," p. 49.

10. Greenfield and Robinson, *Bibliography of Publications on Old English Literature*, item 318, p. 29, report only three reviews. They are: Jantzen, Klaeber, and an anonymous review in *Athenaeum*.

11. Hereafter in this paragraph I summarize the relevant parts of the preface in Sweet's *First Steps*, pp. iii–ix.

12. Sweet observes that a translation of *Beowulf* is out of the question. Presumably he means that a translation, perhaps in modern English and *en face*, would be of no help, which seems to be stunningly obvious.

13. Reissued in 1964 and 1972 by Oxford University Press as the first volume in the series Language and Language Learning. As Henderson does, general editor Ronald Macklin praises Sweet and cites his importance: "The work of many present-day 'methodologists' is derived in large part from the idea adumbrated by Sweet" (p. vi).

14. Sweet, *Practical Study*, p. 180.

15. Sweet, *Practical Study*, p. 180.

16. Sweet, *Practical Study*, p. 182.

17. Mitchell and Robinson, *Guide to Old English*, continue the tradition of the speaking voice begun by Mitchell in his first edition (1964).

18. *Sweet's Anglo-Saxon Primer*, p. iv.

19. Klaeber, *Beowulf and the Fight at Finnsburg*, 3rd ed., pp. 130–31, note to lines 86–114, observes that "the thought of this passage, though proceeding by a circuitous route, is not obscure."

20. See Fred C. Robinson's discussion of the problem of *ofsittan* in "Did Grendel's Mother Sit on Beowulf?"

21. Applying the insights of Milman Parry and Albert Bates Lord, Francis Peabody Magoun, Jr., first argued for the oral roots of Old English verse in his classic article "The Oral-Formulaic Character of Anglo-Saxon Poetry." In this collection the contributions of John Miles Foley, Karl Reichl, and indeed Benjamin Bagby are part of the tradition of interpretation and understanding Magoun began. This "school" has had wide and deep influence in the study of Old English verse, sometimes also inspiring contrary views. See more generally, Ong, *Orality and Literacy*.

22. Sweet, *First Steps*, p. viii.

23. Klaeber, Review of *First Steps in Anglo-Saxon*, p. 94, col. 188. Klaeber observes, more favorably perhaps, "no Old English scholar has ever had the courage for so novel an undertaking" (p. 93, col. 186). Sweet, *Practical Study*, p. 229, observed that Zupitza made students translate Shelley's *Prometheus Unbound* to impress upon them the continuity of the English language.

Behēmas þa Hildlatan:
Beowulf and Its First Translation into Czech

Jan Čermák

"The art of Anglo-Saxon national epic is of little worth. Its structure is mostly frail: every now and then, the main narrative is interrupted by episodes only loosely knit-in. The characters, not clear-cut enough, lack psychological depth. Depiction is patchy and hurried in stark contrast to the tranquility that characterizes true epic; the language, often rough-hewn and awkward, is given to the heaping up of synonyms and abundant use of ornate epithets but it shuns similes,"[1] wrote Václav Emanuel Mourek (1846–1911), a professor of German at Charles University, a specialist in Gothic syntax, and the first Czech academic ever interested in English medieval literature, in his *Přehled dějin literatury anglické* (1890). This assessment, though partly reflecting Mourek's German sources[2] and generally far from unique in the contemporaneous literary criticism of Anglo-Saxon epic, foreshadows the process of the twentieth-century reception by Czech Anglicists of Old English literature that culminated in the project of the *Beowulf* translation—the first full-length rendering of an Old English text into Czech—more than a hundred years later.[3]

However, this culmination is little more than a solitary hill in a gently undulating landscape. Twenty years after Mourek, his pupil Vilém Mathesius (1882–1945), the founder of English Studies in the Czech Republic, redeemed the reputation of Old English literature in his *Dějiny literatury anglické* but, unfortunately, his original observations, based on firsthand reading experience and accurate philological analysis, did not come to be known well enough to arouse the interest of the following generations.[4] His failing eyesight soon made Mathesius devote his scholarly attention almost exclusively to linguistics, which proved to be a perfectly mixed blessing. On the one hand, his founding of the Prague Linguistic Circle in 1926 established a highly influential school of linguistic thought; on the other hand, this vigorous linguistic tradition, thriving to this very day, has mainly worked with modern languages on a synchronic basis. On the small plot of English historical linguistics, texts like *Beowulf*, if not completely ignored, had been quarried for Anglian spellings, manifestations of velar umlaut, and related matters, becoming thus a terror of lecture halls, sure to discourage any future translators and editors. The literary garden of the English Middle Ages therefore soon fell into a state of neglect, so much so that in the latter half of the twentieth century the translators and critics managed to grow there only very few plants (mainly partial translations of Chaucer) while most lecturers in the history of English literature did not venture behind the fence at all. The *Beowulf* research was no exception and so, very typically, the two most significant bibliographic additions came from Bohumil Trnka, a pupil of Mathesius and another outstanding member of the Prague Linguistic Circle.[5]

A total lack of literary precedents and the virtual absence of a receiving context are the two major external circumstances that make the task for a belated translator of *Beowulf* so very challenging. Other factors that predetermine the process of translation are of internal, or functional, nature. They concern Czech literary idiom as well as linguistic structure and can be summarized as follows:

(1) The history of Czech literature knows no epic tradition at least remotely comparable to the complex register of *Beowulf*. The earliest idiom available to the translator is thus that of romance of the thirteenth and fourteenth centuries.

(2) While carefully sifting the chivalrous vocabulary, the translator must also take care to steer clear of the romantic lexical layer, coined during the Czech National Revival in the late eighteenth and nineteenth centuries largely on Slavonic (particularly Russian) and German models in an attempt to fill the lexical gaps created in the preceding period when Czech had been ousted from the position of an official language by German and Latin.[6]

(3) The inflectional sentence structure of Czech depends on the verb as a nuclear component and is ill adapted to nominal condensation. The heavy nominalizations of the Old English poetic register that allow of syntactic openness and implicit semantic marking must therefore in a great number of instances be resolved into concatenated Czech finite verb phrases, thus giving rise to more explicit semantic marking, fewer paratactic junctures, and, generally, somewhat less fluid rhythm of the verse.[7]

(4) Alliteration, though fairly common both in Old Czech lyric and epic as well as in modern poetry, has never functioned as a pervading organizing principle of Czech verse. In contrast to Germanic, it is not structurally linked to strong dynamic stress, and has probably been at all times perceived as a mere artistic, foregrounding device. The translator must therefore maintain alliteration as the central structural principle of the line

without sacrificing philological accuracy to its obtrusive lures. A way out of this difficult dilemma often consists in orchestrating an alternative sound pattern, most often by employing heavy consonant buildup of the word structure, another inherent feature of inflectional languages like Czech.

These and other constraints within which any translator of Old English poetry into Czech is likely to work are best illustrated by collating in the two languages a specific passage, such as the one describing Grendel's approach to Heorot (*Beowulf,* lines 702b–45a)—to some "a hair-raising depiction of death on the march,"[8] and for others a manifestation of a mock approach-to-battle scene.[9] The Old English original printed below follows Klaeber (1950); the Czech rendering is provided with glosses in modern English that are inadequate as translations, but will help in establishing the literal (though not the literary and stylistic) sense of the Czech version:

> Cōm on wanre niht
> scrīðan sceadugenga.   Scēotend swǣfon,
> þā þæt hornreced   healdan scoldon,
> 705   ealle būton ānum.   Þæt wæs yldum cūþ,
> þæt hīe ne mōste,   þā Metod nolde,
> se s[c]ynscaþa   under sceadu bregdan;—
> ac hē wæccende   wrāþum on andan
> bād bolgenmōd   beadwa geþinges.
> 710   Đā cōm of mōre   under misthleoþum
> Grendel gongan,   Godes yrre bær;
> mynte se mānscaða   manna cynnes
> sumne besyrwan   in sele þām hēan.
> Wōd under wolcnum   tō þæs þe hē wīnreced,
> 715   goldsele gumena   gearwost wisse
> fǣttum fāhne.   Ne wæs þæt forma sīð,
> þæt hē Hrōþgāres   hām gesōhte;
> nǣfre hē on aldordagum   ǣr ne siþðan
> heardran hǣle,   healðegnas fand!
> 720   Cōm þā tō recede   rinc sīðian
> drēamum bedǣled.   Duru sōna onarn
> fȳrbendum fæst,   syþðan hē hire folmum æthrān;
> onbrǣd þā bealohȳdig,   ðā hē gebolgen wæs,
> recedes mūþan.   Raþe æfter þon
> 725   on fāgne flōr   fēond treddode,
> ēode yrremōd;   him of ēagum stōd
> ligge gelīcost   lēoht unfǣger.
> Geseah hē in recede   rinca manige,
> swefan sibbegedriht   samod ætgædere,
> 730   magorinca hēap.   Þā his mōd āhlōg;

> mynte þæt hē gedælde, ær þon dæg cwōme,
> atol æglæca ānra gehwylces
> līf wið līce, þā him ālumpen wæs
> wistfylle wēn. Ne wæs þæt wyrd þā gēn,
> 735 þæt hē mā mōste manna cynnes
> ðicgean ofer þā niht. Þrȳðswȳð behēold
> mæg Higelāces, hū se mānscaða
> under fȳrgripum gefaran wolde.
> Nē þæt se æglæca yldan þōhte,
> 740 ac hē gefēng hraðe forman sīðe
> slæpendne rinc, slāt unwearnum,
> bāt bānlocan, blōd ēdrum dranc,
> synsnædum swealh; sōna hæfde
> unlyfigendes eal gefeormod,
> 745 fēt ond folma.

V ponurou noc vyšel
On a dark night set out
ten poutník jak stín. Spali střelci,
the wanderer like a shadow. The shooters were asleep
co hrdou hodovnu měli hájit,
who the proud hall should defend
705 všichni až na jednoho. Lidé věděli,
all but one. (The) people knew
že nesvolí-li Soudce, strašná stvůra
that unless the Judge grant it the grim monster/creature (fem.)
sotva je odvleče dolů ke stínům.
hardly them would drag down to the shadows.
Jeden bděl, že způsobí jí bolest,
One was awake to cause her pain
rozzuřen čekal, co přinese řež.
waiting in anger what would bring the battle.
710 Z mokřin vybředl a pod mlžnými srázy
Out of the moors he came and under misty slopes
Grendel se bral, nes Boží hněv:
Grendel proceeded bearing God's wrath:
zlotřile zamýšlel v znamenité síni
maliciously he intended in the magnificent hall
znovu lapit některého z lidí.
to ensnare again some one of (the) people.
Pod mračny mířil tam, kde medovina
Under the clouds he headed where mead
715 zurčela v číše, k dvoraně zdobené
gurgled into goblets to the hall adorned
planoucím zlatem. Nikoli ponejprv
with glistening gold. Not at all for the first time
chystal se hledat Hróþgárův dům,
was he about to seek Hrothgar's house

leč dřív ani později   potkat jej neměla
but neither before or afterwards   meet him should
lítější sudba   ani síně stráž!
fiercer fortune   or hall-guards!
720   Vzápětí bojovník,   jenž nepoznal blaha,
Next the warrior   who knew no bliss
dorazil k dvoraně.   Dveře ve veřejích
reached the meadhall.   The door in a frame
žárem tvrzených   rozlétly se vráz:
hardened in heat   swung open at once:
rukama zlovolně   rozrazil bránu,
with his hands malevolently   (he) burst through the gate
dusil se vztekem.   Soptící vrah
stifling with anger.   The fuming fiend/murderer
725   pramálo váhal,   když vydal se napříč
little hesitated   when he started across
po pestré podlaze.   Škaredý přísvit,
the variegated floor.   A hideous light
požáru podobný,   planul mu v očích.
like a conflagration   was flaming in his eyes.
V hodovně spatřil   houfec válečníků,
In the hall he spotted   a troop of warriors
jak, krví spřízněni,   spolu tam spí,
how they blood-related   were sleeping there together
730   chrabrá to družina.   Tu zachechtal se v duchu:
a valiant retinue.   Then he laughed in his heart:
doufal, že oddělí,   než vzejde den,
he hoped to separate   before the day broke
těm, kdo tam dřímají,   duši od těla.
of those who were slumbering there   the souls from the bodies.
Strašnému běsu   naděje svitla
For the terrible demon   a hope arose
na skvělý hodokvas,   však stát se nemělo,
of a splendid feast   but it was not destined to happen
735   že lidským stvořením   bude se sytit,
that on human beings   he should feed
až skončí se ta noc.   Synovec Hygelákův,
when the night was over.   The nephew of Hygelac
silák z Géatů,   spatřil, že škůdce
the stalwart one of the Geats   saw the wrongdoer
chystá úskočný,   náhlý útok.
was getting ready for a sly   sudden attack.
Hrozný ten host   nehodlal otálet,
The horrible stranger/guest   was not willing to loiter
740   pustil se do díla   a rychle popadl
he set about his work   and quickly snatched
jednoho spáče.   Snadno jej páral,

> *one of the sleepers.*   *Easily was he tearing him,*
> klouby chroupal,   chlemtal krev,
> *joints munching   lapping blood*
> hříšnými sousty   krmil se a sytil,
> *on sinful morsels   feeding and filling himself*
> až ubožáka pozřel   od hlavy k patě,
> *until the wretch he devoured   from head to heel*
> 745   tělo bez ducha.
> *the body lifeless.*

The Czech line is organized around four lifts, invariably bound to their semantic nuclei and accompanied by a varying and variously placed number of dips. No attempt was made to correlate the metrical patterns of the original half lines to those of the translation. The same holds for the distribution of alliteration in the long line. Alliteration, while also directly linked to the semantically and metrically heavy elements of the line, is not compulsory. Wherever present, it is statistically more numerous in the Czech translation (its relative aesthetic prominence being hard to assess). This method was adopted for two reasons in particular: firstly, to compensate both for the missing link between alliteration and strong expiratory stress and for the lack of an alliterative feeling in Czech; and, secondly, to make up for the lines that contain no alliteration but instead are built on echo patterns employing (mainly consonantal) sounds in other than initial positions of the word-structure. This alternative strategy can be exemplified by line 722, where the echo pattern based on an orchestration of liquids is intended to evoke the sounds accompanying Grendel's forced entry into Heorot and the movement of the door swung open, or by line 709, which captures the tension of the oncoming fight by the peculiar Czech sound, ř. At the same time, philological accuracy took precedence over the alliterative buildup of the verse so that word choice proceeded from sense to form and alliteration could not turn from an eloquent servant into a garrulous master. Vocalic alliteration in Czech can be based on a single vowel only, another linguistic fact documenting how different the respective histories of alliteration are in English and Czech.

"Sceadugenga" in line 703 presents a typical problem of the translation process. As pointed out above, the Old English compound does not have a clear-cut structural counterpart in Czech and any attempt at reproducing its juxtapositional effect[10] in the translation would sound hopelessly strained. In the ensuing dilemma, the translator must reject an easy, economical solution by a single word of an opaque word-formation structure—like *phantom* or *specter* in English—and choose to unfold the dense image rendered by the compound in a circumlocution. Ideally, this circumlocution should not take up too much space and, at the same time, preserve at least some of the rich array of potential meanings submerged in the semantically and syntactically open "sceadugenga." Translation is by its very nature a losing battle and translators must continually take stock of the incurred losses. In this particular case, the association of Grendel the dark walker with the shadowy moors as well as with the realm of shadows has been preserved, but the potential suggestion that he is a creature deprived of God's light has not. That major problems of interpretation are indeed associated with deep structure syntax rather than with the multiple surface meaning of the nominal elements is demonstrated by the relative ease with which polysemous parts of compounds like "synsnædum" in line 743 can be rendered into Czech: the Czech adjective *hříšný* captures both the spiritual ("sinful") and the physical ("huge, excessively large") aspects of the image. The compound in line 704, "hornreced," is typically resolved into a noun phrase consisting of an adjective and a noun (hrdá hodovna 'proud meadhall'). An architectural detail with a potential cultic connotation, expressed by the first element of the compound, whose accurate rendering would require an extended adverbial phrase, is thus replaced with an adjective contributing to the sense of majesty under threat, so prominent in the passage. Translating "wīnreced" of line 714 by means of a compound would in the Czech context conjure up the idea of a wine cellar. Again, the compound must be resolved, this time into a lively verb phrase that maintains both the potential mythical floor of the image by preserving—given the free alliterative choice of drinks at Heorot—mead as part of the scene while keeping up the hypotactic link between the clauses that in the original are centered around the verbs *wōd* and *wisse*. Moreover, the phrase strengthens the idea of the hall as the lit center of safety, social reciprocity, and refinement: emblematic images invested with profound cultural and ethical sense such as that of the "medoheall" must not be lost in the process of translation. At the same time, the verbal circumlocution unfolds the compact nucleus expressed by the compound and the problem of resolution again entails struggling for space, appropriate for the cultural colonization, through translation, of a new literary territory. The used metrical space must therefore be retrieved by suppressing the semantically rather weak b-line of 715, "gearwost wisse." More importantly, this shift brings about a typical change in the syntax of the complex sentence running from line 714 to 715b: the prominence of the finite verb (zurčela 'gurgled') results in a weakening of the variation structure by two items as the other compound, "goldsele," also dissolves into a complex noun phrase—"hodovně zdobené zlatem" [to the hall adorned with glistening gold]—again.

Transformations in the profound association between compounding, varia-tion, and asyndetic nominal syntax can be further illustrated by the ways the Czech translation renders adjectival bahuvrihi[11] compounds, both simple and extended. A typical feature of the Old English nominal diction, the adjective "bolgenmōd" in line 709 is syntactically ambiguous: of the two structural interpretations, Czech prefers taking it not as another subject in a variation on "hē wæccende" in line 708 but rather as an adjectival verbless supplementive clause.[12] "Rozzuřen" functions in the Czech version as a subject complement, turning—once again—a nominal variation of the original into a verbal one. Other structural possibilities of translating bahuvrihis include dissolving the nominal element into an adverb (such is the case of "bealohȳdig"—"zlovolně" [malevolently] in line 723) or interpreting the missing nominal head of the bahuvrihi compound at the surface level. Here, a suitable example must be quoted from a different section of the text: in line 1791, the poet characterizes Hrothgār as "blondenfeax," which has been resolved in the translation as "šedovlasý vládce" [gray-haired ruler]. Solutions of the former type lead again to a decrease in the relative structural importance of variation; the amplifications of the latter type lessen the capacity of the Czech *Beowulf* to suggest rather than portray, lending to it a more graphic air.

Thus, generally speaking, the syntax of the translation, building on explicit predications and resolving the paratactic arrangement of Old English variation chains into hypotactic, contiguous structures of Czech subordinate verb clauses, establishes a less even semantic rhythm of the verse and makes it virtually free from "momentary riddles."

What has been said about the Czech verb as the most powerful tool of syntactic representation also applies to its lexical potential. The fact that the "cinematographic effect"[13] of the analyzed passage, based, among other devices, on the triple *cōm*-sequence of lines 702, 710, and 720 gets lost in the translation, becoming thus a mere semantic parallelism, is simply due to the usurping power of the finite verb (reinforced, naturally, by the demands of the alliteration available). In other words, Czech translators of Old English poetry are much better provided with verbal (near-) synonyms than nouns to furnish its rich variation chains. The generally scarcer nominal items must be carefully retrieved from archaic and etymologically foreign layers of the language. To demonstrate these vocabulary deficiencies, one need not look to lexical fields where gaps are both expected and dramatic, such as the synonyms for "sea" in the language of landlocked Bohemians. A much less conspicuous layer might prove the point as well: Old English words for "man" or "warrior" in whose semantic scope the sense of warfare often interlocks with that of courage and nobleness. One such example from the analyzed passage is "rinc." In line 720, Grendel is described as "bojovník" [warrior, fighter], a sense to be preferred to "man" (*muž*), which is a description hard to associate unequivocally with what Grendel is taken to be primarily—a monster. Other possibilities in Czech are drastically limited, the only other option readily available being "válečník" (warrior), which translates "rinc" in line 728. What else? Vladimír Vařecha, the man who inspired the Czech *Beowulf* project (see below), suggested that "rinca manige" in line 728 should be translated as "trupa bojců."

This captures the literal sense fairly well but gives rise to serious problems: *trupa*, a word corresponding to the English "troop" (both come from French), would strike the very few Czech readers who know it as an unacceptable nineteenth-century archaism. *Bojec*, another nineteenth-century loan (this time from Russian), must be rejected downright on the grounds of (a) its artificiality and (b) its association with the Communist political propaganda (even though this link naturally grows thinner by the year).[14] A borderline case in this respect is the Czech expression *bohatýr* (the brave one). It has been used only once in the translation—to render "se gōda" of line 205—primarily out of dire alliterative need. The word is another nineteenth-century loan from Russian (where it came from Persian via Mongolian) and educated Czech readers will associate it with the genre of the Russian *byliny*. This literary association was a secondary motive for choosing *bohatýr*, at the risk of the Czech *Beowulf* ringing perhaps too strong a Slavonic note in that line.

All in all, loans do not present a problem in the translation if they are sufficiently integrated in the receiving language: "škůdce" [the one who harms], which qualifies Grendel in line 737, corresponds etymologically to the second element of its counterpart, the compound "mānscaða," but it is not perceived as in any way foreign because it is a time-tried loan: the verbal root came as early as the Old Czech period from Old High German. Two other general strategies are available to make up for the lack of synonyms. One consists in activating older senses of modern words: such is the case of "vrah" in line 724 (the corresponding Old English form, "fēond," is part of line 725) in whose semantic scope the contemporary sense "murderer" goes hand in hand with the older meaning "enemy," a sense to which educated readers are still alive. The other strategy, which is the most neutral and therefore the most widely applicable one, consists in adding appropriate stylistic color to one or more of the items immediately linked to the noun that is considered in any way deficient. This can be demonstrated using the case of "rinca manige" ("houfec válečníků") discussed above: while the neutral Czech expression *válečník* lacks some of the poetic force of Old English *rinc*, the balance can be redressed by using the bookish suffix *–ec* with the noun *houf* (itself being another medieval German loan and a cognate of Old English "hēap" in line 730).

In 1991, Vladimír Vařecha (1912–99), an associate professor at the Department of Translation and Interpreting, Charles University, invited me to help him fulfill his life's dream—translate *Beowulf* into Czech. As Vařecha, a man with an exceptional gift for languages who brought his English to perfection as an RAF flight lieutenant in World War II, received little training in Old and Middle English philology, he wanted me to keep an eye on his translation so that it would not stray too far from the original. When I wrote up my first—and fairly critical—commentary on his prologue and the building of Heorot he did not seem annoyed at all but instead asked me to give it a try myself. When I then showed him my First Fit, Vařecha—in an act of noble magnanimity that I will remember forever—suggested that I should take over.

And so I did—a novice to the field who had spent the previous five years after obtaining an MA degree from Charles in English, Czech, and Finnish teaching himself Old and Middle English and who had barely emerged from his first real formative six-month period as an Anglo-Saxonist with Terry Hoad and Bruce Mitchell at Oxford University. Enthusiasm and ignorance were efficient prime movers but I soon realized the structural difficulties outlined above and started feeling the weight of the task. Decided to proceed from E. G. Stanley's principal advice on how one should best set about it ("Read *Beowulf*!"), I quickly memorized large tracts of the text and became more independent from my desk cluttered with half-blank sheets of paper and piles of secondary reading. The translation had thus essentially taken shape by the method of action-cum-meditation, not alien to the structure and pace of the poem itself: I remember getting most verses more or less ready while chopping wood ("hand sweng ne oftēah"!) and, in particular, while pushing the pram with my two little sons "þær mē foldwegas fǣgere þūhton," but most often to the Vyšehrad Hill ("Hēantūnbeorh"), the early seat of the Přemyslids and one of the most dignified Prague localities datable to the period of MS Cotton Vitellius A. xv (London, British Library).

Of the long decade the project needed to germinate, the translation proper took about five years. The rest of the time—substantially prolonged by the demise of a colleague and other problems affecting the editorial team, too sad and personal to receive mention here—went into calibrating the nature of the commentary and notes to meet the requirements of the target readership: from a classical academic format I labored towards a book arranged in layers so that the lay readers could plunge beneath the text of the poem to specific problems of philological analysis as well as those of cultural and literary history in a measure they would please.

"Fēasceaft funden . . . weorðmyndum þāh": in 2004, the Czech *Beowulf* was awarded the Josef Jungmann Prize, the major translation award given by the Czech Association of Translators and Interpreters, and this event may mark the final breakthrough in the integration of English medieval literature into the Czech cultural context. Since the early 1990s, the Department of English and American Studies, Charles University—the only academic Czech institution currently involved in Old and Middle English research—has had more than two dozen MA and PhD theses on various medievalist topics, both literary and linguistic. Students and graduates specializing in medieval studies associate in the English Medieval Studies Group (Skupina pro anglickou medievalistiku) whose major projects involve translations of Old and Middle English poetry and prose. In 2005, the series continued with *The Dream of the Rood*[15] (Prague: Jitro Publishing) and in 2009 *Beowulf* was followed by *Jako když dvoranou proletí pták. Antologie nejstarší anglické poezie a prózy (700–1100)* (Prague: Triáda Publishing), bringing in one volume a fairly comprehensive coverage of Old English texts from the laws of Æthelberht to *Durham*.

The Czechs have given up the woods of ignorance, indifference, and distrust and are back on the battlefield.

Notes

See the accompanying CD to listen to the first fifty-two lines of the poem read in Czech.

1. "Veliké ceny umělecké . . . národní epos anglosaské nemá. Osnova bývá chatrna; hlavní děj přes chvíli přeryvá se episodami jen volně vetkanými. Charaktery jednajících osob nejsou dosti určité a nemají psychologické hloubky. Líčení jest rozervané, chvátavé, pravý opak epického klidu; mluva často drsna, neobratna: souznačná slova ráda hromadí, hojně užívá ozdobných přímětkův a smělých tropů, za to podobenství nemiluje" (Mourek, *Přehled dějin literatury anglické* [A survey of the history of English literature], p. 11).

2. Mourek's primary source was Körting, *Grundriss*.

3. Čermák, *Béowulf*.

4. Mathesius, *Dějiny literatury anglické* [A history of English literature]. See also Čermák, "Vilém Mathesius (1882–1945)."

5. Trnka, "Dnešní stav bádání o *Beowulfovi*." [Current research on *Beowulf*] and Trnka, "*Beowulf* Poem."

6. Epic vocabulary drawn from, or modeled on, Slavonic sources forms a distinct lexical layer in Josef Holeček's translation of *Kalevala*. This translation strategy is in full accord with the spirit of the Finnish national epic, reflecting its romantic conception and Karelian provenance, but presents a telling contrast to the linguistic nature and cultural context of Old English poetry. The innovative lexical processes outlined above are similar to the lexical developments in Early Modern English, the major difference being that English, by then a predominantly analytical language, mainly relied on borrowings, whereas Czech, which had to a large extent preserved its inflectional character, continued using its derivational capacity.

7. A distinct manifestation of this structural difference is the compound: this constitutive feature of Old English poetic diction and a measure of the *Beowulf*-poet's genius tends to be only marginally present in inflectional languages like Czech. Its high productivity in Old English seems to have been partly an inheritance from the more agglutinative prehistoric stages in the development of the language, partly an aspect due to the immediate association of the compound with the nominal tenor and alliterative needs of the poetic register.

8. Brodeur, *Art of Beowulf*, p. 90.

9. Heinemann, "*Beowulf* 665b–738."

10. As an interpretation, the present translation largely works within the framework of F. C. Robinson's idea of the appositive style.

11. A compound word in which the first part describes the second or governs it grammatically, and the second element cannot be substituted for the whole, e.g., "yellowhammer" or "afternoon."

12. For an account of functions performed by bahuvrihi compounds in Old English poetry, see Čermák, "'A Prow in Foam.'"

13. Renoir, "Point of View."

14. Klement Gottwald, the first Communist president of the Czech Republic after World War II, used to talk about "the shed blood of our warriors" [krev . . . našich bojců].

15. *Duch můj* (contains *Battle of Maldon, Phoenix, Wanderer, Wulf and Eadwacer, Ruin*, and a selection of *Riddles*); *Dary krásných stromů* (contains Alfred's prefaces to Augustine's *Soliloquies* and Gregory's *Pastoral Care, Fight at Finnsburg, Waldere, Seafarer, Wulf and Eadwacer, Wife's Lament*, and *Maxims I, Maxims II*); *Sudby lidí* (contains *Fortunes of Men*, a selection of *Charms* and *Leechdoms, Ruin, Rune Poem, Deor, Prayer, Bede's Death Song*, Wulfstan's *Sermo Lupi*, and Leofric's *Visions*); *Sen o kříži*.

Beowulf in Spanish

María José Gómez-Calderón

As the most famous of the Old English poems, *Beowulf* occupies a central position in the curriculum of English studies (Filología Inglesa) in the Spanish-speaking world and has equally deserved much critical attention among scholars, as a glance at bibliographies of Old English studies proves. The number of *Beowulf* translations into Spanish is, however, not a large one if we take into account that Thorkelin's *editio princeps* was issued in 1815 and that several translations into languages other than English appeared in the early nineteenth century, romance languages included.[1] It has certainly been translated into Spanish on more occasions than any other Old English text, verse or prose, but, nevertheless, in spite of the rich tradition of translations of literary works between English and Spanish, and the fact that the Spanish-speaking community is integrated by many nations with remarkable translation productions, it is somewhat striking that the first instance of *Beowulf* in this language did not appear until 1933.[2]

Still, this was not a literary translation from the original based on philological research but a version for children by Manuel Vallvé published in Colección Araluce, whose motto was "las obras maestras al alcance de los niños."[3] It is somewhat ironic that the text is referred to as a "masterpiece," and because of that deserving to be adapted for its diffusion among young readers, when quite surprisingly it had never been translated before into Spanish for an adult audience. The example of Vallvé's *Beowulf* illustrates the common perception of the text among Spanish-speaking audiences as a monster-tale for children set in the fantastic world of the heroic Dark Ages. Very few people in the Hispanic community would identify the poem specifically as an Old English text; indeed, *Beowulf* has reached the Spanish-speaking world through the back door of children's books, a text suitable for their imagination but scarcely recognized as a relevant literary work.

Interestingly, Vallvé's is not the only translation into Spanish especially devised for young readers; to name but a few examples issued during the twentieth century, there are Vicente García de Diego's "La leyenda de Beowulf," included in the section "Norse Legends" of his famous anthology of world literary legends (1953); *Beowulfo*, by J. L. Herrera, with illustrations by Julio Castro (1965); and "El poema de Beowulf," published within the collection *Leyendas nórdicas* (1974), selected and adapted by Antonio Urrutia Raspall.[4] The most recent rendering of *Beowulf* for children is María Fernanda Cano's *Beowulf: La leyenda de las dos criaturas* (1994), with illustrations by Óscar Rojas. As can be observed, these *Beowulf* translations appear as part of fairy tales and legend collections, often included in a volume dealing specifically with the Germanic/Nordic world in the company of stories taken from the Icelandic sagas or the German *Nibelungenlied*, as in the case of García de Diego's and Urrutia's versions. Except for Vallvé and Herrera, the translators do not identify the text as an Old English poem—or English, at least—but present the story as one more "leyenda nórdica," thus emphasizing the pagan aspects of the text for the sake of what we could define as a cultural primitivism inherited from romantic sensibility. Often, the illustrations of these *Beowulf*s re-create a picturesque and colorful Viking world most appealing to the imagination of their intended readers. All the *Beowulf*s for children are guided by an evident didactic purpose, that of teaching their audience, mainly composed of boys, the moral values traditionally attributed to the idealized Germanic peoples of the heroic age: loyalty to one's kin and leader, comradeship, courage, and sacrifice.

All these works depart from the narrative of the original text, which the authors seem to judge difficult to be followed by their young readers. As they are prose translations, they systematically ignore the stylistic features of Old English poetry, features that are in any case quite difficult to translate into a romance language with radically different poetic traditions and conventions. Likewise, the story is reduced to the hero's sea travels and his fights with the monsters; as a consequence, the episodes of the plot are reordered, the passages known as digressions eliminated, the secondary characters and their specific stories suppressed, and, eventually, some new figures are added.[5] The translators seem to assume that the early medieval cultural parameters portrayed may be alien to the modern audience they have in mind, and for that reason we find explanatory passages bringing the story closer to their readers' cultural background. Often they include explanations about the ancient Scandinavian world, both cultural and geographical, long sections describing the uses and customs of the heroic age and, above all, they simplify the treatment of the Germanic heroic ethos and the sophisticated system of social relations in the context of the early Middle Ages. As is stated at the beginning of Vallvé's text, "lo esencial es tener una idea, lo más aproximada y exacta posible, de aquellas época [*sic*], de sus costumbres y del ambiente de los países septentrionales de nuestro continente."[6] In this sense, these *Beowulf*s take more licenses in their rendering of the medieval poem than scholarly translations would but, all in all, their merit lies in the fact that they contributed to bringing

Beowulf into existence for Spanish-speaking readers. What John D. Niles notes about "serious" translations is thus still valid for these ones, as they convey "a powerful work of the literary imagination into terms that, far different from the original poet's, may still be compelling for readers in our own time."[7]

Beowulf in Translation

The earliest example of a literary translation of *Beowulf* into Spanish dates from 1947, when Marià Manent offered some passages in Spanish verse in the first volume of his anthology *La poesía inglesa* (1945–48).[8] The author is concerned with illustrating the section devoted to Anglo-Saxon poetry with some of the fundamental texts of this corpus, and for that purpose he selects fragments from *Beowulf* and other Old English texts, as for example *The Dream of the Rood*. Specifically, Manent translates two short fragments from *Beowulf*, lines 1345–82—Hrothgar's description of Grendel and his mother's wanderings and dwelling place in the marshes, followed by his promise of rewarding Beowulf if he completely eliminates the monsters—and lines 2236b–66—the passage known as "The Last Survivor's Lament." Manent places his translation facing the original text in Old English, but he does not identify the edition he uses; nevertheless, all seems to indicate he worked with Gordon's version (1923).

This translation resorts to unrhymed sequences of fourteen-syllable lines, with some exceptions—seven- and ten-syllable lines. This dominant line—*alejandrino*—has a long tradition in Spanish prosody as the meter for narrative and epic poems, and it was especially popular in the Middle Ages and Renaissance period.[9] Manent takes advantage of this long line and the flexibility of Spanish syntax to reproduce the word order of the original whenever it is possible, as in line 1355b, "nō hīe fæder cunnon," which is rendered as "nada de su padre sabían."[10] However, he prefers clarity to strict syntactic fidelity to the source text. The translator is also particularly careful in conveying the complex Old English compounds into the fixed number of syllables of the *alejandrino* so that the poem can be translated practically line by line. Manent's work was, unfortunately, much neglected by later translators, who seem to ignore this pioneering effort.

The first complete literary translation of *Beowulf* into Spanish was published in 1959 by Chilean professor Orestes Vera Pérez.[11] Vera bases his translation on Wyatt and Chamber's 1920 edition, and renders the poem in prose because of the difficulty of accommodating the Spanish language to the diction of Old English poetry, a most complex task even for the translators of the text into modern English. As the author states,

> Si para los traductores al inglés moderno de este magnífico poema
> épico del inglés antiguo ha sido tarea casi imposible dar a sus versiones

> el tono y pausas apropiados al espíritu de la lengua germánica en la que
> se escribió, fácil será comprender que la traducción que hemos hecho al
> español—lengua latina—no tiene otro mérito que poner al alcance del
> lector corriente o estudioso de habla española uno de los monumentos
> fundamentales de la literatura inglesa.[12]

Vera's aim is thus to fill the gap for the Spanish-speaking audiences even if
this means forsaking verse. By the time this translation was published the status of
Beowulf as a "literary monument" was practically uncontested, hence the necessity
stressed by the author of translating it into foreign languages for the benefit of
the international community.[13] In the same line, in his prologue to this translation
Carlos Sander highlights the centrality of the work in the English canon when he
declares that *Beowulf* is "el *Mío Cid* inglés" (p. 16), that is, equivalent to the most
revered literary monument of the Spanish Middle Ages.[14]

At the same time, we must not obviate the fact that the importance of
Beowulf had already been signaled to the Spanish-speaking audiences some years
earlier by Jorge Luis Borges, one of the most outstanding Hispanic authors and
literary critics. Borges had paid special attention to the poem in *Antiguas literaturas germánicas* (1951), where he presented a survey on Old English literature in
the context of the Germanic literary tradition.[15] The section "La gesta de Beowulf"
provided a summary of the poem along with some general critical appreciations,
completed by a brief discussion of the epic character of the text in reference to W. P.
Ker's discussion of the poem in *Epic and Romance* (1897). Moreover, just two years
after the appearance of Vera's translation Borges published a short poem inspired
by *Beowulf*, "Composición escrita en un ejemplar de la 'Gesta de Beowulf'" (1961).
In it, Borges reflects on the hopelessness the scholar feels at the impossibility of
translating in exact terms the ancient language of Old English poetry.[16]

Vera's translation, which extends over 257 pages, divides the text into forty-
two *cantos* after the fashion of classical epic.[17] The text is annotated in an attempt
to make understandable for his readers questions that cannot be included in the
body of the translation, as for instance clarifications about the speaking voice in
certain passages, comments on the legendary and historical references of the text,
and information on the cultural conventions operative in the heroic world of the
poem. Thus, the poet's anticipation of the collapse of Hrothgar's hall Heorot (lines
81b–85)—"No estaba tampoco lejano el día en el que el padre y el yerno rigieran
y la guerra y el odio despertaran de nuevo"—is explained in a footnote: "Como
quienes escuchaban el poema conocían perfectamente bien la historia danesa, el
poeta se refiere con anticipación a la ruina del palacio, debida a la lucha entre el
yerno de Hrothgar y la familia del rey danés Ingel y Freawaru."[18]

A most curious example of annotation is Vera's assimilation of some
Germanic mythological figures to Graeco-Latin ones, as he assumes that the

Spanish-speaking reader would be more familiar with this cultural tradition. Most editors connect the reference to the weaving of fate by God appearing in line 697, "wīgspēda gewiofu," with the Germanic mythological Norns, which Vera explains in different terms by means of the translational device of adaptation or cultural assimilation: "Elemento pagano mezclado con cristiano. Se refiere a las Parcas de la mitología, que tejían en su telar la tela de la vida de los hombres. Presidían su nacimiento y su vida tres hermanas: Cloto, que hilaba; Laquesis, que devanaba, y Atropos, que cortaba el hilo de la vida de los hombres."[19]

Besides, the translator often resorts to licenses that alter the syntactical structures of the original text, assumedly in order to facilitate its reading in Spanish; however, sometimes these licenses are from a syntactical point of view unnecessary and just respond to Vera's stylistic choice, as the beginning of the text illustrates. Thus, the opening lines are transformed from an assertion—whose character of universal truth is stressed by the inclusive first-person plural *wē* in the original—into a rhetorical question: "¡Escuchad! ¿Quién no ha oído cantar las alabanzas a las proezas de los reyes de los daneses—guerreros armados de lanzas—y a la gloria que en tiempos pasados ganaron sus capitanes?"[20] In the same way, Vera introduces loanwords from the English when the concept does not have an equivalent in the target language, so that this can save him from using a complex periphrasis; for example, he adapts English *thanes* as *tanes*, a term that does not exist in Spanish, in translating lines 43–46 as "este inmenso tesoro real, magnífico regalo de sus tanes (1), no era menor a aquel con el cual en otros tiempos pasados, cuando aún era niño de pecho, lo enviaron abandonándolo a la merced del mar."[21]

The didactic purpose of Vera's work can be clearly appreciated. He uses standard Peninsular Spanish in his translation and avoids all sorts of dialectal terms in order to provide a wide community of readers with a comprehensible text.[22] Vera seems particularly concerned with endowing his prose with an elegant style, and in order to achieve a smooth syntax he renounces any attempt to reproduce the *variatio* that characterizes the medieval text and frequently opts for the translational device of transposition, especially when dealing with the Old English compounds. The choice of a simple prose which follows quite closely the lines of the source text, and the fact that the translation is profusely annotated, make it a suitable vehicle for introducing *Beowulf* to an audience not used to the rhythms, diction, and the conventions of the Old English poetic corpus.

No other translation of *Beowulf* into Spanish was issued after the publication of Vera's for a span of fifteen years until the appearance in 1974 of Luis Lerate's *Beowulf y otros poemas épicos antiguos germánicos*, which is currently the *Beowulf* in Spanish enjoying a greater diffusion.[23] As Vera's work had been out of print for years and was very difficult to find even in the catalogues of the libraries of educational institutions, Lerate's *Beowulf* became the only translation of the poem available. Importantly, this is the first attempt at rendering the complete poem in verse—the only precedents being the short fragments translated by Manent—and in a meter that reproduces in Spanish the stress pattern of the original text. The translator does not refer to Manent's work, probably due to its fragmentary character, but in the 1986 revision of his own translation Lerate credits Vera's and Bravo's.[24] He is well aware of the novelty and the experimental and ambitious nature of a project consisting of a complete verse translation, particularly because Spanish prosody does not have any metrical structure similar to the ancient Germanic meter. Because of that, Lerate resorts to translating *Beowulf* in an imitative verse that reproduces the rhythmical pattern of Old English poetry, that is, a line with a variable number of syllables with two main stresses in each hemistich and separated by a caesura. His purpose is that of achieving a text that may convey a rhythm as close as possible to the original despite the fact that, as he acknowledges, it may sound monotonous and alien to the Spanish ear. As Lerate himself points out, "nada obliga, desde luego, a procurar esta similitud, pero hemos creído preferible hacer el experimento a utilizar formas tradicionales españolas como el octosílabo, que desvirtuarían excesivamente el carácter original de esta poesía."[25]

The Spanish text re-creates quite convincingly the cadences of the Anglo-Saxon line; Lerate's skill to reproduce the dignified, elevated tone of the original is remarkable, as is his ability to constrain the translation of compounds, which would take long periphrastic expressions, to the limits of an acceptable number of syllables fitting in the line. All this produces a *Beowulf* able to convey the stylistic features of the medieval text into modern Spanish. In this sense, the final lines (3178b–82) provide a good example of Lerate's achievement:

> La muerte del príncipe   mucho apenó
> A los gautas que un día   en su sala moraron;
> Afirmaban que fue   de entre todos los reyes
> El más apacible   y amante del pueblo,
> El más amigable   y ansioso de gloria.[26]

Thus, *heorðgenēatas*—literally "hearth-companions"—is rendered through an amplification by means of a relative clause as "(los gautas) que en su sala moraron";[27] *wyruldcyninga*—"among all the kings of the world"—becomes "entre todos los reyes," leaving aside the *wyruld* part as redundant;[28] and the compounds *monðwǣrust* (the kindest to people) and *lofgeornost* (the most eager for fame) are combined with the adjectives preceding them by making them share the *más* particle marking the superlative in order to avoid adding extra syllables.

Another interesting and original aspect of this work is that Lerate offers the reader a dual language edition with the Old English text facing the translation; for this purpose, he follows Klaeber's 1922 and Holthausen's 1948 editions. This bilingual option, however, is not preserved in the 1986 revised edition. What is common to the 1974 and the 1986 versions is Lerate's division of the text into four sections ("Grendel," "Grendel's mother," "Beowulf's return," and "The dragon"); and each one is in turn subdivided into several episodes indicated by short epigraphs that summarize the narration. The text in Spanish is annotated—endnotes in the 1974 edition, footnotes in the 1986 one—in order to solve textual problems as well as to clarify the poet's references to the ancient Scandinavian cultural milieu. Lerate, as Vera did before, keeps in mind the fact that for most readers the text needs cultural and literary contextualization to be conveniently appreciated. Because of that, he includes an appendix with the genealogical tables of the characters along with a glossary of proper names and a map of ancient Scandinavia. In contrast with other translators of the poem, Lerate adapts all the characters' names to Spanish—like Herrera did in his version for children—by applying the pertinent linguistic rules to this conversion, whereas most authors keep them in present-day English; thus, in Lerate's *Beowulf* we find names as Híglak, Ongento, or Ekto for Hygelac, Ongentheow and Ecgtheow.[29]

Chronologically, the following translation of *Beowulf* into Spanish is Antonio Bravo's *"Beowulf": Estudio y traducción* (1981).[30] As in the case of Vera's, it is a prose translation accompanied by a critical study dealing with central issues such as problems of authorship, date, and provenance, the poem's intended audience, and the blending of Christian and pagan elements. Bravo's study comprises about one hundred pages whereas the translation takes approximately eighty. As it happened with Vera's *Beowulf*, the prologizer to Bravo's, Professor Patricia Shaw, praises the effort of the translator and emphasizes the extreme complexity of the project, which she regards as a "tarea tan hermosa, pero a veces tan ardua"; most significantly Shaw qualifies the translation of the text in verse as "empresa prácticamente imposible tratándose de dos lenguas tan alejadas entre sí."[31] Bravo, on his part, explains in detail the features of the poetic language of *Beowulf* in an attempt to help the Spanish reader understand the character of Germanic poetry. He does not make explicit the edition on which he bases his translation, although in the preliminary study he points out the relevance of Zupitza's facsimile (1882) and includes in the final bibliography entries for the editions of Klaeber (1922), Dobbie (1953), and Wrenn (1953). Bravo's translation is also annotated, but less frequently than Vera's, as it is preceded by a long study in which many of the obscure textual and cultural references of the poem are already clarified. In addition, the work is completed with a bibliography on *Beowulf* scholarship.

In general, Bravo resorts more often to a word-to-word translation technique than Vera or Lerate. Also, as a rule, the translator follows the line order of the original whenever it is possible although, in spite of the great flexibility of Spanish syntax, he is often forced to relocate some of the words for the benefit of coherence. This is more evident in the translation of the passages containing long sentences or in those in which *variatio* occurs. At these points Bravo opts for rephrasing and pruning the sentences, which sometimes forces him to overuse subject pronouns in Spanish. This may sound a bit redundant, as in this language that information is already present in the verbal ending, as can be observed, for instance, in the translation of lines 2933–41:

> Después *él* siguió a sus mortales enemigos los géatas hasta que *ellos* pudieron con dificultad escapar sin jefe a Ravenswood. Entonces *él* puso sitio con su poderoso ejército a aquellos que habían escapado de la espada agotados por las heridas. Constantemente durante toda la noche *él* amenazó a la desdichada banda de guerreros y dijo que por la mañana a unos les causaría la muerte con el filo de la espada y a otros los colgaría en la horca para alegría de las aves. [Italics added.][32]

However, this is not the only occasion on which Bravo tried his hand at translating the poem. He reassumed the task in *Literatura anglosajona y antología bilingüe del antiguo inglés* (1982), also published by Universidad de Oviedo. This is a handbook for the class, in which Bravo offers the student valuable information about Old English literature; it includes sections on Anglo-Saxon cultural history and is completed with specific sections on the heroic, the Christian, and explanations of the formal aspects of poetry. This section is followed by an anthology of texts, among which we find *Beowulf*. In contrast with his previous work, here Bravo presents a verse translation following the extracts of the poem in Old English, although no specific edition is indicated. The study of the poem is completed with a bibliography on *Beowulf* scholarship. The lines do not present metrical uniformity, as the author uses Spanish *verso libre*, that is, a line without rhyme or a fixed number of syllables, which however resorts to parallelisms and repetitions of some syntactic and phonic clusters in order to stress the text's musicality. Bravo bases this verse translation on his earlier prose one, from which it presents no significant differences. The purpose of this volume is clearly didactic: a brief introduction precedes the fragments and the passages selected are very representative of the work. Bravo translated about four hundred lines, selecting the fragments 1–127, 194–228, 710–808, 2397–2424, 2538–2604, 2792–2820, and 3137–3182.

A new *Beowulf* in Spanish appeared in 1991, by Professor Ángel Cañete Álvarez-Torrijos. This translation was published in the collection Clásicos, issued by Universidad de Málaga, which includes titles such as Tertullian's *De Cultu Feminarum*, medieval works such as *Mozarabic Lyrics*, *La chanson de Roland*, *Le jeu d'Adam*, *Sir Gawain and the Green Knight*, and one more British text, Walter Scott's *Letters of Malachi Malagrowther*. Cañete's is an annotated edition preceded by a study addressing the most challenging problems of the text, such as its dating and provenance, followed by two sections on "estructura y estilo," and "forma y estructura" respectively. After the body of the text, which comprises sixty pages, we find an appendix including a glossary of proper names, diagrams with the genealogies of the protagonists, and a bibliography. Once more, the translator states the difficulty of his work and justifies himself in the preliminary note for not translating the poem in verse, something he categorically judges an impossibility:

> [H]e desistido de cualquier intento de reflejar las características formales del original anglosajón: ritmo, aliteración, uso continuo de nombres compuestos, estilo elevado y arcaico, etc., pues si resulta poco menos que imposible de alcanzar resultados similares en inglés contemporáneo, pienso que lo sería del todo hacerlo en español o en cualquier otra lengua romance.[33]

In the preliminary note, Cañete also marks out the interest of Bravo's translation among the *Beowulf*s in Spanish, about which he laconically indicates that there exist just a few and acknowledges his debt mainly to the modern English translations.[34] The author annotates the text, which is divided into two parts, "Beowulf y los monstruos" and "Beowulf y el dragón." His prose is smooth, unconstrained by the syntactical order and the repetitive, ornamental character of the original; the translator chooses transposition and transference as his main translational tools, thus avoiding complicated phrasal structures and subordination that we could observe in Vallvé's or Lerate's versions. Cañete's stylistic choice can be illustrated in the same fragment of lines 2933–41 discussed above in Bravo's translation; it is rendered as follows:

> Persiguió después a sus mortales enemigos que, a duras penas, consiguieron escapar a Ravenswood sin su señor. Más tarde, con un poderoso ejército, sitió a los que habían quedado con vida: los hostigó durante toda la noche y dijo que al llegar el día los pasaría a cuchillo y los colgaría para diversión de los buitres.[35]

In the first place, Cañete reorders the initial sentence so that it sounds natural in Spanish as "a verb plus object" sequence, the object being amplified by a relative clause. In the following line there is a substitution; whereas in the original we find "sweorda lāfe / wundum wērge" (lines 2936–37), literally, "the survivors exhausted / wearied by sword wounds," the Spanish text is less specific about the way these warriors were injured. Besides, the threat launched against these survivors is presented as a double punishment for all ("los pasaría a cuchillo y los colgaría" [they would be slain and hanged on the gallows]), whereas in the Old English version it is clear that some of the survivors would be slain by the sword and some others hanged. And finally, although in the original text it is said that this slaughter would serve "fuglum tō gamene" [as sport for the birds], in Cañete's text the unspecific birds are emphatically "buitres" [vultures] feeding on carrion. The vulture is not one of the "beasts of battle" typical of ancient Germanic epic poetry, but it seems the translator has opted for it as a popular image of death; the raven, which is actually part of this animal symbology, is just present in the place name of the setting for this episode. However, Cañete does not translate it into Spanish but keeps it as "Ravenswood," and so the reference may escape those readers who are not knowledgeable of English. This sort of translation license can be more fully appreciated when comparing his text to Lerate's more literal rendering:

> A la gente enemiga   después persiguió
> Y éstos huyeron   con grandes apuros
> Privados de príncipe,   al Bosque del Cuervo.
> Sitió con su tropa   a los hombres heridos
> Que al hierro escaparon;   por toda la noche
> A la hueste vencida   le hizo amenaza,
> Diciendo que al alba   daríales muerte
> A unos el filo   y a otros la horca
> Que al pájaro alegra.[36]

The *Beowulf*s of the New Millennium

One of the later renderings of *Beowulf* into Spanish is not a translation proper but a narrative inspired by the Old English text. Juan Alonso del Real Montes's *Beowulf, el sudor de la guerra* (Beowulf, the sweat of war) is a short novel that re-creates the main plot line of the poem. There are, however, important divergences from the original text. To begin with, it is an adventure narrative rather than an epic work, and in fact at certain stages this novel comes close to the parameters of the "sword and sorcery" genre. Thus, the actions are set in a pagan, pre-Christian Scandinavia where the protagonists are subjected to fate and depend just on their courage and physical strength to survive in a hostile environment. The story starts with Beowulf and Breca's swimming contest; the digressions of the original are eliminated and some episodes—as the slave's stealing from the dragon's treasure—are reformulated as new steps of the adventure plot. Likewise, some new characters are added—Goren the bard, Olaf, and Scardi, Beowulf's retainers—and secondary figures in *Beowulf*, such as Breca, developed. Curiously enough, Beowulf's connection with Hrothgar is altered and the Geat hero is here the direct descendant of Scyld Scefing's own son Beowulf, turning him into one of Hrothgar's loyal relatives. In the same way, in this farfetched tale Beowulf takes a wife and has several daughters and sons. This very imaginative re-creation adapts *Beowulf* to the conventions of popular genres more appreciated by the modern Spanish readers than the texts of Anglo-Saxon poetry: the whole project seems to respond to contemporary interest in the Middle Ages as a time of heroism and fantasy rather than to any scholarly pursuit.

The latest translation of *Beowulf* into Spanish is, like the first full version, the work of a Chilean author, Armando Roa Vial, a college lecturer, poet, and essayist who has also translated the works of Shakespeare, Browning, and Pound.[37] Roa's *Beowulf* was published by Norma simultaneously in Chile and Colombia in 2006 and reissued in Spain by Belacqua in November 2007. The American edition presents a preliminary essay in which the author deals with aspects like the interest of the work in the context of the modern appreciation of literature, the problems of the translation, and the long-lasting influence of one of the capital pieces of Beowulfian scholarship, Tolkien's "Beowulf, the Monsters and the Critics" (1936), whose text is included. This critical section, however, is absent from the European version, as are the helpful chronological lists of the first one; only the list of characters is preserved for the benefit of the reader. These significant changes are probably due to the fact that the latest edition had in mind a different target reader, as it appeared on the market just at the time Robert Zemeckis's film version of *Beowulf* was being released. Apparently, the second edition addressed the wider audiences of the film's fans rather than the learned reader interested in medieval literature. This commercial strategy would also explain why the translator's name does not even appear on the book cover of the Belacqua edition, where it has been replaced by a line announcing the volume as "the epic saga on which the film is based."

Like the previous translators of the text, Roa praises the poem's character as the foundational piece of the postclassical European epic tradition and connects it with the *Eddas*, the *Nibelungenlied*, and the *Chanson de Roland*.[38] His *Beowulf* is a quite free, annotated prose translation in roughly ninety pages, in which, however, alliteration plays an important part. Roa acknowledges the influences that earlier translations had on his own, namely those by Bradley, Donaldson, and Heaney in modern English, as well as Lerate's Spanish translation. Unlike the Spanish of earlier translations, the language selected here is American Spanish.[39] The translator tries to preserve the solemn tone of the text by using a learned vocabulary with numerous Latinisms, and when translating the intricate syntactical structures of the lines, Roa tends to avoid the repeated use of hyperbaton and complex periphrasis observable in, for example, Lerate's work. In general, this rendering of the poem allows itself more drastic alterations of the original than earlier versions had done; the case of lines 50b–52, a rhetorical question that has no parallel in the original, is illustrative: "¿Habrá hombre en este mundo, por poderoso que sea, capaz de soportar pesar tan grande?"[40] Roa's intention is to produce a translation attractive to a wide readership that is not necessarily familiar with Old English poetry but that, nevertheless, has a taste for ancient poetry.

Beowulf and the Other Languages of Spain

Beowulf has also been translated into Catalan, one of the co-official languages of Spain.[41] Xavier Campos Vilanova's *Beowulf: Traducció en prosa d'un poema epic de l'anglés antic* (1998) was published by Societat Castellonenca de Cultura and is included in a collection entitled "Llibres rars i curiosos" (Rare and curious books). This classification of the work is little surprising, as it has been seen how *Beowulf* is not very popular among Hispanic audiences but is accepted as an exotic relic of the Middle Ages, a text for experts rather than as poetry available to the average reader. Once more, the translator defines the poem as an "autèntic 'monument' de la cultura d'Occident," a survivor of the ancient times.[42] A short introduction precedes Campos's translation; in it, he discusses the relevance of the text in the history of English literature and briefly explains some formal aspects of the original verse in connection with Western epic poetry. The poem is contextualized in the tradition of the heroic genre and its particular blending of Christian and pagan Germanic folkloric elements is addressed. Campos qualifies his translation of *Beowulf* as an operation of "metaliteratura," because it is dependent on previous translations of the text, not on the Old English original: "La nostra aproximació a *Beowulf*, cal dir des d'ara, ha estat fonamentalment metaliterària; és a dir, no hi hem traslladat des del *Beowulf* original en Saxó Occidental sinó des d'un 'pacte' que naix de la lectura comparada de diverses traduccions en llengües contemporànies"; because of that, the result is defined as "una reconstrucció."[43]

For this purpose Campos relies on different works, namely Gordon's *Anglo-Saxon Poetry* (1926, 1964), and the *Beowulf*s by Swanton (1978, 1986), Alexander (1973, 1978), and Lerate (1986). He neither lists in his bibliography Vera's or Bravo's prose translations of the poem nor refers to the former children's adaptations that may have also contributed to the re-creation of the poem's legendary universe, which Campos sets as one of his aims when approaching this medieval text: "S'ha perdut la poesia, déiem, i per això proposem una humil lectura cantívolla Durant la qual podrem tenir el privilege de coneixer missatges d'un passat mític i llunyà."[44] As a result, Campos's *Beowulf* depends on other translators' choices, with all the "dangers" this entails because of the differences between Old and present-day English, so that in the end his *Beowulf* is rather a translation from modern English through several source texts than his own reading of the original Old English work.

It is important to notice that Campos insists on the connection of Beowulf, a celebrated monster-slayer, with other proverbial destroyers of dragons, St. George and St. Michael, both very popular saints especially in the Middle Ages: "[Beowulf] té molts punts de semblance amb altres matadors de dracs més casolans, Jordis i Miquels."[45] In the Hispanic world St. George (San Jorge, Sant Jordi) is recognized as the patron saint of Catalonia; his figure has been transformed into an emblem of national identity and his day, 23 April, is commemorated as La Diada, the institutional national feast for the Catalan-speaking community, which comprises the regions of Catalonia, Valencia, and the Balearic Islands.[46] As the first translator of the poem into Catalan, Campos readdresses *Beowulf* in the context of contemporary nationalism issues and, in the same way Vera did with his translation into Spanish years before, he is engaged in the task of translating a classic poem in order to fill the gap in the target language. For this reason Bravo and Mora point out that Campos, like other translators before him, is "appropriating the poem for the national culture."[47] The cultural appropriation of *Beowulf* by this minority national identity is a form of linguistic self-assertion and legitimization, and the parallelism drawn by Campos between Beowulf and Sant Jordi as the national heroes of their respective communities clearly reinforces this perception.

Conclusions

The presence of *Beowulf* in the Hispanic cultural background has experienced several stages. First, the poem was translated in the 1950s because by then it had been sanctioned by the academy as the foundational piece of the English literary canon. The interest in finding the oldest texts is but a constant in the history of national literatures, and the recovering of the Old English poem *Beowulf* by nineteenth-century scholarship perfectly suited the patriotic vindications of the period. The poem was then proclaimed the most ancient relic of the Germanic literatures, celebrated as a monument of the heroic spirit of the Dark Ages and, as such, deemed worthy of being translated into other languages for the benefit of international educated audiences.

The second stage, represented by Lerate's, Bravo's, Cañete's, and lately Roa's works shows how *Beowulf* is translated into Spanish as a direct consequence of the stabilization of the curriculum of English studies within the Hispanic academy and the rising interest in English literature. This interest rose in the late 1970s and culminated in the 1990s, when eventually the degree in English became the most demanded one in the field of humanities. The prestige of the discipline at an international level fostered translations of all sorts of English literary texts into Spanish, a cultural phenomenon from which *Beowulf* could not be excluded. Besides, although in recent years Old English studies have experienced a serious backlash, as Bravo and Mora have explained, still in these adverse conditions *Beowulf* has been one of the few Anglo-Saxon works present in some form or another in the syllabi of literature courses.[48] Beyond these academic concerns, it is also important to notice that in the last decade there has been a revival of the fascination with all things medieval which manifests in the popularization of formulas like the "sword and sorcery" novel, medieval comic books, video or role-playing games, or the medieval theme park. The international release of *The Lord of the Rings* films (2001–3) brought Tolkien's novels back in fashion again and caused new interest in their epigones, and it is in this context that the film versions of *Beowulf* appear.[49] This phenomenon, which has fostered general interest in the original text, is in a certain way a cyclic one that takes us back to the romantic sensibility framing the earlier reception of the poem. As with any other cultural construct, *Beowulf* is subjected to the circumstances of its reception, appropriation, and consumption in different periods and contexts. Within the Hispanic world, it is worth pointing out that, in spite of being a text alien in its poetic standards and at least one millennium old, the work is still able to provoke curiosity among modern audiences and to stimulate so many and varied responses.

Notes

See the accompanying CD to listen to the first fifty-two lines of the poem read in Spanish.

1. The first instance of a complete translation is Thorkelin's one into Latin, also issued in 1815; N. F. S. Grundtvig published a partial translation into Danish verse in 1815, followed by a complete one in 1820. Also in 1814 J. J. Conybeare translated into Latin the Finnsburg passage and accompanied it with an English paraphrase. Gumaeleius's partial translation into Swedish verse dates from 1817, and W. K. Grimm's German translation, also partial, was issued in 1829. Regarding romance languages, Giuseppe Pecchio published a summary in Italian based on Turner's in 1833, but the first complete translations did not appear until 1882 with Giuseppe Schuhmann's *Beovulf* and Giusto Grion's *Beowulf*. In French, the first instance is a paraphrase by H. Taine (1863), followed by a second one by L. Botkine (1877), and the 1912 complete translation by Hubert Pierquin. In Portuguese, the first *Beowulf* is a Brazilian comic book, *O Monstro de Caim* (1955), itself a translation of the Italian one created by Enrico Basari in 1941; as a literary work, the first partial translation dates from 1966, by Navarro Gondim. See Shippey and Haarder, *"Beowulf": The Critical Heritage*; and Osborn, "Annotated List of Beowulf Translations" (ACMRS Online Resources Annotated Beowulf Bibliography).

2. Vallvé, *Beowulf: leyendas históricas*.

3. "Masterpieces for children." The translation of this and the following quotations in Spanish and Catalan are my own. All quotations from the Old English text are taken from Klaeber, *Beowulf and the Fight at Finnsburg*, 3rd ed.

4. Vicente García de Diego was a member of the Real Academia Española de la Lengua; his "Beowulf" appears in *Antología de las leyendas de la literatura universal*.

5. Thus, for example, in Urrutia's rendering the story of *Beowulf* is divided into several chapters reshaping the narrative structure and plot of the medieval text: "El poema de Beowulf," "El Castillo de Heorot se viste de luto," "Beowulf llega al palacio de Heorot," "La lucha con Grendel," "La espada encantada," "Beowulf es coronado rey de los géatas," and "Combate con el dragón y muerte del héroe."

6. Vallvé, *Beowulf*, p. 11: "The essential thing is to have an idea, as approximate and exact as possible, about those times, their customs and the atmosphere of the Nordic countries of our continent."

7. Niles, "Rewriting *Beowulf*," p. 859.

8. Marià Manent (1898–1998) was a most accomplished scholar, critic, and poet; his works, both in Catalan and Spanish, were pioneering in the field of English studies. Manent's translations from the English comprise authors as different as Emily Dickinson, Blake, Tennyson, Keats, Kipling, Chesterton, or Rupert Brooke. He also specialized in Chinese poetry.

9. See Navarro Tomás, *Métrica española*; Quilis, *Métrica española*; Azaustre Galiana and Casas Rigall, *Manual de retórica española*; and Domínguez Caparrós, *Métrica española*.

10. "Nothing about his father they knew."

11. Professor Vera worked for Universidad de Chile and other educational institutions in his country; he got his M.A. from Princeton University.

12. Vera, *Beowulf*, p. 32: "If the translators of this magnificent epic poem in Old English have found it almost impossible to provide their versions in modern English with the tone and pauses appropriate to the spirit of the Germanic language in which it was written, it will be easy to understand that the translation we have carried out into Spanish—a romance language—has no other merit but to make accessible for the Spanish speaking average reader or scholar one of the fundamental monuments of English literature."

13. In contrast, the revision of the English canon, as well as the recession movement experienced by Old English studies in general, have lately placed the text in an uncomfortable position. This phenomenon can explain the scarcity of more recent attempts at translating the poem into Spanish as well as into other languages. Let us keep in mind that the text is no longer a required reading in the syllabi of English studies even at educational institutions which, as in the case of Oxford, were in the past the bastions of Anglo-Saxon scholarship, and that relevant literary critics had launched contemptuous attacks against the poem, as for instance Terry Eagleton's remark that "the archetypal English poem sounded rather like the rumble of a sack of potatoes being emptied." See his opinion on *Beowulf* in his article on Seamus Heaney's translation "Hasped and Hooped and Hirpling." On the polemic of the loss of prestige of Old English literature, see also Frantzen, *Desire for Origins*, and Orchard, *Critical Companion to "Beowulf."*

14. Carlos Sander was the Chilean consul in Spain at the time, but he was also an accomplished poet and journalist. Also, the Spanish critic and diplomat Salvador de Madariaga had already remarked on the interest of the Old English poem in *Ensayos Anglo-Españoles* (1922), where he established a series of parallelisms between *Beowulf* and *El Cantar del Mío Cid*.

15. Borges and Igenieros, *Antiguas literaturas germánicas*.

16. "A veces me pregunto qué razones / Me mueven a estudiar sin esperanza / De precisión, mientras mi noche avanza, / La lengua de los ásperos sajones" (lines 1–4). In a quite literal translation these lines would read: "Sometimes I wonder what reasons / Move me to study hopelessly / for accuracy, as my night advances, / The language of the tough Saxons." In 1964 Borges published another poem, "Fragmento," where he alluded to *Beowulf*: "Una espada para la mano / Que derribará la selva de lanzas. / Una espada para la mano de Beowulf" (lines 24–26) [A sword for the hand / That will bring down the wood of spears. / A sword for Beowulf's hand]. Both poems are included in a collected work, *El otro, el mismo* (1969). Borges's last contribution is a partial prose translation of *Beowulf* written in collaboration with María Kodama, "Fragmento de la Gesta de Beowulf"; the excerpt selected comprises lines 26 to 52, and it was included in *Breve antología anglosajona* (1978). On this topic, see Galván, "Rewriting Anglo-Saxon."

17. The original manuscript indicates the division of the text into forty fits by means of a capital letter and a roman numeral; there are three more sections (XXVIII, XXX, and XXXVIII) where the numeral is omitted.

18. " Sele hlīfade / hēah ond horngēap, heaðowylma bād / lāðan līges; ne wæs hit lenge þā gēn / þæt se ecghete āþumswēoran / æfter wælnīðe wæcnan scolde." In Vera's version: "It was not distant the day on which father and son-in-law would rule and war and hatred would rise again." The footnote reads: "As those listening to the poem knew Danish history perfectly well, the poet refers in anticipation to the ruin of the palace caused by the fight between Hrothgar's son-in-law and the family of the Danish king Ingel(d) and Freawaru" (Vera, *Beowulf*, p. 93).

19. Vera, *Beowulf*, p. 143: "Blending of heathen and Christian elements. It refers to the Fates of mythology, who wove in their loom the fabric of men's lives. Three sisters presided over their births and lives: Clotho, who spun; Lachesis, who twisted fibres into thread; and Atropos, who cut the thread of men's lives."

20. Vera, *Beowulf*, p. 87: "Listen! Who did not hear singing in praise of the deeds of the kings of the Danes—warriors armed with spears—and the glory that in the old times their champions won?"

21. Vera annotates "Tanes" as "*Thane* en inglés antiguo, o sea guerrero noble que acompaña al príncipe" (*Beowulf*, p. 90) [*Thane* in Old English, that is, the noble warrior who accompanies the prince]. The whole section is rendered in Spanish as "this immense royal treasure, a magnificent gift of his thanes, was not inferior to the one with which in the past, when still a suckling baby, he was abandoned at the mercy of the sea." In the original, these lines read: "Nalæs hī hine læssan lācum tēodan, / þēodgestrēonum, þon þā dydon, / þē hine æt frumsceafte forð onsendon / ænne ofer ȳðe umborwesende."

22. For example, after the Peninsular Spanish fashion he uses the second-person plural pronoun *vosotros* and its corresponding verbal form instead of *ustedes*, the dominant form among the American varieties of Spanish. Vera's choice may have been influenced by the fact that his translation was published in Spain.

23. Lerate's *Beowulf y otros poemas épicos antiguos germánicos* appeared in the catalogue of one of the biggest publishing houses in Spain, Seix Barral, based in Barcelona. It was later revised as *Beowulf y otros poemas anglosajones: Siglos VII–X* (1986) and issued by Alianza, another important publisher. Professor Lerate has also translated into Spanish the Icelandic *Eddas—Edda Menor* (Madrid: Alianza, 1984); *Edda Mayor* (Madrid: Alianza, 1986)—and an anthology of Old Norse poetry—*Poesía antiguo-nórdica: ss.IX–XII* (Madrid: Alianza, 1993).

24. See below the discussion of Bravo's translations.

25. Lerate, *Beowulf*, p. 17: "Nothing compels one, of course, to procure this similitude, but we thought that experimenting was preferable to using traditional Spanish forms such as the octosyllabic, which would distort the original character of this poetry in excess."

26. "Swā begnornodon Gēata lēode / hlāfordes hryre, heorðgenēatas; / cwædon þaet hē wære wyruldcyninga / manna mildust ond monðwærust, / lēodum līðost ond lofgeornost."

27. "The Geats who dwelt in his hall."

28. "Among all kings."

29. Vera and Bravo, in turn, oscillate between adapting one name—"Scyld" becomes "Scyldo" at the beginning of the poem—and rendering all the other names in English. On their part, Cañete, Campos, and Del Real use English forms, revealing their dependence on Anglo-American editions. See the discussion of these translations below.

30. Contrary to what happened with Lerate's translation, Bravo's was published by a university press and its diffusion therefore is more limited to academic circles.

31. Shaw, qtd. in Bravo, *Beowulf: Estudio y traducción*, p. 8: Respectively, "such a beautiful task, but such a hard one"; and "a practically impossible project with two so distant languages."

32. Italics added. In the original, "ond ðā folgode feorhgenīðlan, / oð ðæt hī oðēodon earfoðlīce / in Hrefnesholt hlāfordlēase. / Besæt ðā sinherge sweorda lāfe / wundum wērge; wēan oft gehēt / earmre teohhe ondlonge niht, / cwaeð, hē on mergenne mēces ecgum / gētan wolde, sume on galgtrēowum / fuglum tō gamene." The Spanish version (Bravo, *Beowulf: Estudio y traducción*, p. 205) basically reads: "Later he followed his deadly enemies the Geats until they could with difficulty escape without their leader to Ravenswood. Then he sieged with his powerful army those who had escaped, exhausted by their wounds. Throughout the night he constantly threatened the wretched warband and said that in the morning some would be put to death by the edge of the sword and others would hang from the gallows to the birds' joy."

33. Cañete, *Beowulf*, p. 15: "I have renounced any attempt at reflecting the formal features of the Old English original; rhythm, alliteration, the continuous use of compound nouns, lofty and archaic style, etc. as, if it is almost impossible to achieve similar results in contemporary English, I think it would be absolutely impossible trying to do it in Spanish or in any other romance language."

34. Cañete, *Beowulf*, p. 15.

35. Cañete, *Beowulf*, p. 76: "He then pursued his deadly enemies, who could hardly escape to Ravenswood without their lord. Later, with a powerful army, he sieged those still alive: he stormed them all through the night and said that at dawn he would slay and hang them as sport for the vultures."

36. "The enemy people he then pursued / and these ran away with great pains / lordless, to the Raven's Wood. / He sieged with his troops the wounded men / who escaped from the iron; / all the night he threatened the defeated band, / by saying that at dawn they would receive death / some by the edge (of the sword) / some by the gallows, which the bird enjoys."

37. Despite the fact that both are Chilean, in an interview published in the blog of Eugenio Olivares (professor of English medieval literature at the Universidad de Jaén) Roa remarks that he did not read Vera's translation until he had finished his own (http://eugenioolivares.blogspot.com/2009/04/entrevista-con-roa-vidal.html).

38. However, in his interview with Olivares, Roa significantly establishes certain differences with *El Cantar del Mío Cid* on account of the respective histories of the English and the Spanish languages. Whereas the modern Spanish reader can approach *El Mío Cid* with relative ease, the profound changes in English make reading *Beowulf* impossible for those who have not studied Old English.

39. Roa's American Spanish manifests in his choice of verb forms and idioms.

40. "Is there a man in this world, as powerful as he might be, who could endure such a great grief?" In the original, "Men ne cunnon / secgan tō sōðe, selerǣdende, / hæleð under heofenum, hwā þǣm hlæste onfēng."

41. In addition, the preparation of a Galician translation of the poem was announced by Jorge L. Bueno in 2005, in "De Frisia a Fisterra."

42. Campos, *Beowulf*, p. 7: "A true monument of Western culture."

43. Campos, *Beowulf*, p. 11: "Our approach to *Beowulf*, I must say now, has been

fundamentally metaliterary; that is to say, we have not translated *Beowulf* from the original West Saxon but from an 'agreement' born from the comparative reading of diverse translations in contemporary languages"; "una reconstrucció" obviously means "a reconstruction."

44. Campos, *Beowulf*, p. 14: "Poetry is lost, let's say, and for that we propose a humble silent reading through which we will be able to enjoy the privilege of getting to know messages from a mythical and distant past."

45. Campos, *Beowulf*, p. 14: "*Beowulf* presents many similarities with other more familiar dragon-slayers, George and Michael."

46. Castellón de la Plana, the place of publication of this translation, is in the Region of Valencia. The complex political and linguistic relationships among the Catalan/Valencian/Balearic-speaking communities are nowadays very controversial.

47. Bravo and Mora, "Anglo-Saxon Studies in Spain," p. 26.

48. Bravo and Mora, "Anglo-Saxon Studies in Spain," p. 23. In particular, Spanish universities in the last years have been introducing drastic changes in their curricula in order to adapt themselves to the very polemical Bologna Declaration on the European Space for Higher Education, a project of convergence affecting all the countries of the European Union. This has in fact completely redefined the curricula for English studies.

49. Up to this moment, there are Graham Baker's *Beowulf: The Legend* (1999); John McTiernan's *The Thirteenth Warrior* (1999), in turn based on Michael Crichton's novel *Eaters of the Dead* (1976); *Beowulf and Grendel* by Sturla Gunnarsson (2005); *Beowulf, Prince of the Geats*, an independent production directed by Scott Wegener (2005); and Robert Zemeckis's *Beowulf* (2007).

Beowulf in Hungarian

Katalin Halácsy Scholz

Translation of foreign literature into Hungarian has a rather long tradition; still, the entire *Beowulf* rendered in Hungarian verse is a curiosity and a special achievement. György Szegő, a native of Transylvania, who has been translating poetry from modern English, Russian, and a number of other languages had been working on the translation intermittently for over twenty years only for the pleasure of the job until he completed the translation in 1994, when the Department of English Studies of Eötvös Loránd University published it. Szegő used Wrenn's 1958 edition for his translation, which was the only one available to him when he started his work.[1] Because of his failing sight he had not been able to revise the text on the basis of other and more recent editions, translations, and notes when he could have had access to such before the publishing. Still, Beowulf does speak in Hungarian, and the voice is not at all unlike his original dictum.

The first three parts of this essay give the background of the Hungarian *Beowulf* in order to enable the reader not only to accept the writer's analysis of the translation, but also to understand it in context. The first part is a short sketch about epic in Hungarian, and the tradition of translating foreign literary works, Anglo-Saxon in particular. The second is a minimal description of some linguistic features, which have an impact on verse making, and the different kinds of versification systems possible and existing in Hungarian. The third part is a short summary of György Szegő's own description of his translation with my comments. Armed with some information about the language, versification practices, and the translator's decisions and views about his work, in the fourth part I wish to take the reader along with me to see the result of Szegő's great venture. I wish to show examples of how he rendered certain features of the Old English epic into a very different language and culture in the translation, and invite the reader to think about the solutions, and to come into the workshop of the translator rather than pass—necessarily superficial—judgments on the result.

The Epic in Hungarian

Hungarian, unlike other languages in Europe, is a Finno-Ugric language, spoken by about fifteen million people all over the world as their mother tongue; of them, ten million live in Hungary, the rest in the neighboring countries and elsewhere. It is the language of a culture and literature which has been part of Europe, and open to its influences, for over a millennium.

No primary epic poem or any part of one has survived in Hungarian, although some heroic stories, which may have had earlier oral epic versions, survive in later medieval Latin chronicles. These stories are about the origin of the Hungarians, the times of the migration period, and the first kings.[2]

The oldest prose text written down in Hungarian is a funeral sermon and oration, and the first surviving poem is a paraphrase of *Planctus ante nescia*, a Marian hymn of Godofredus de Sancto Victore (ca. 1130–ca. 1194) from the thirteenth century.[3] The quality of both prove that there must have been other literary works in circulation at the time, only they did not survive the stormy history of the country either because they were not written down or because the manuscript has not come down to us.[4]

If a translator of *Beowulf* had wished to rely on the existing later Hungarian epic tradition for a model, he could have studied Miklós Zrínyi's full-scale epic written in 1645–48 celebrating the heroic deeds of the poet's great-grandfather of the same name, when he defended the southern Hungarian fort of Szigetvár against the Ottoman attack to the last man. He shaped the story line and the characters so as to present the small Hungarian army of defenders with all epic grandeur to be equals of the attacking forces of Suleiman II, who died during this battle. As a result of the delay of the Ottoman forces in their march towards Vienna caused by the battle at Szigetvár and the sultan's death, Vienna could not be taken in 1566.[5]

Zrínyi composed his poem relying on the examples of Homer, Virgil, Ariosto, and especially Tasso, but in four-line rhyming stanzas in Hungarian meter. This poem was followed by a number of romantic heroic epic poems in the nineteenth century.

Szegő did not have Zrínyi's epic in mind when considering the translation, but rather saw *Beowulf* as having closer connections with folk tradition and heroes of folk tales than with sixteenth-century military leaders or with seventeenth-century epic. He thought Zrínyi's poem was too late and too different—maybe too literary—to imitate in spirit if he wanted to remain true to *Beowulf*, and too early to imitate in language, because readers nowadays would find imitation seventeenth-century language too artificial. His choices resulted in a different kind of epic, a Hungarian *Beowulf*.

Literary texts from various European languages have been translated into Hungarian large scale since the eighteenth century. This practice already followed the tradition of translating the Bible by Hussites[6] and later by reformers together with other religious literature from Latin. Albert Molnár Szenci's translation of the Psalter[7] needs special mention because, in addition to the literary value of his work as early as the beginning of the seventeenth century, he closely followed the verse form of the original.

As to English literature, the first translations were made not from English, but from German and French versions like the first *Hamlet* in 1790 and Ferenc Kazinczy's *Sentimental Journey*, only a few years after the novel's first appearance in English. Besides Latin, these two languages were far more widely known among educated people than English. Kazinczy wrote about his translation of Sterne in one of his letters: "I do not read in English, but the English text was in front of me right opposite Frené's French translation, and at many places I looked into the English text, and my 'divinatio' and the German text set me on the right track."[8] One has the impression that an educated man of letters well versed in at least four languages could retrieve information from the English text, too. Of course, the danger of misreading it because of analogy was present also.

English was already better known in the nineteenth century, and it was a recognized task, almost an obligation, for the best poets ever since then to translate foreign poetry into Hungarian. Since the language is very flexible, and lends itself to different systems of versification, translation in the true form has been the norm: classical Greek and Latin poems into quantitative Hungarian verse, and English into iambic pentameter.

Frequently used classical and European forms also took root in Hungarian poetry and were used by poets for original compositions, too; consequently they did not sound alien in the translations either. As a result, the 1867 Hungarian *Hamlet* of János Arany, one of the greatest nineteenth-century poets, has become almost as canonical a text in Hungarian literature as his original poems. Discussion about whether new translations of such texts are necessary is also very lively nowadays. New translations are made, especially if the play is put onstage.

From the turn of the twentieth century on, English literature has been regularly translated into Hungarian. Well-known works are available and some poems might exist in five, six, or even more translations, because poets with reputations have felt they had to contribute their own version.[9]

Old English, however, was not taught at universities until much later. Germanic meter was known and has been well described in textbooks, comprehensive manuals of versification like Erika Szepes and István Szerdahelyi's *Verstan* (Metrics),[10] and the multivolume encyclopedia of world literature.[11] Examples, however, were only taken from the *Hildebrandslied* and its translation in 1963, from

Scandinavian poetry, a volume of which was published in 1967 containing a quote from the Rök stone. Cædmon and *Beowulf* are only referred to in a list of poems in the "Germanic meter." "Among Hungarian literary translations there is no well-defined tradition of how to translate Old Germanic verse (or verse based on stress counting in general)."[12] At the same time one has to note that some selections of *Beowulf* appeared in anthologies of world literature earlier.[13]

A large collection of English poetry published in 1986 in two volumes contained some excerpts of Old English pieces, beside a selection from *Beowulf*, *The Seafarer*, *The Dream of the Rood*, *The Battle of Brunanburh*, and a few others, all more or less reproducing the alliterative meter not strictly following the pattern of alliteration, but keeping the four-stress lines and the caesura between half lines.[14]

György Szegő had to decide against this background of tradition what sort of verse form to use in his *Beowulf*. He found the strict rendering of the alliterative meter not viable. As far as the language is concerned, it would have been theoretically possible to make a close parallel of the Old English verse form in Hungarian, and some lines in his translation conform to the main rules, as I shall show later. But no verse form exists in Hungarian in which the rhythmic pattern is solely based on the number of main stresses in the line, disregarding more or less the number of unstressed syllables. Consequently it would have sounded very strange and monotonous if the Anglo-Saxon rules had been followed throughout the poem. So he created a form, which is close enough to the Old English, but sounds also natural to the Hungarian ear, because it is also close to one of the native Hungarian verse forms.

Versification in Hungarian

Before analyzing the Hungarian *Beowulf* in detail, however, let us look at some of the characteristics of the phonology of this Finno-Ugric language, which have enabled poets to adopt different systems of versification alongside the native one with relative ease.[15] Then let us survey the different systems of versification that have grown up on this phonological ground:

> Unquestionably, the Hungarian language is characterized by a combination of certain phonological properties which do not occur together in any other European language (with the exception of Finnish and Estonian, both likewise Finno-Ugric languages—although even in the respective national literatures of these languages one does not find the parallel development of several versification systems equal to one another in rank).[16]

In an article about Hungarian metric research András Kecskés and Andrew Kerek list the following three "metrically relevant" phonological features, which "have determined the character of all Hungarian verse forms, even if in different ways and to different degrees":

> (1) phrase accent, a combination of stress and pitch, on the first syllable of the first (content) word in a phonological phrase (= a sequence of syllables between two strong stresses);
> (2) clear and unambiguous syllabification and countability of syllable peaks (regardless of the position of stress and of the quality of vowels);
> (3) an almost complete short-long oppositional system of phonemes, making possible a clear-cut dichotomy between short and long syllables.[17]

The rhythm of native Hungarian verse is basically defined by what Kecskés and Kerek call phrase accent in a phonological phrase. Other metrists call this unit a beat, or measure the boundaries of which are pauses, the end or the beginning of the line or a caesura.[18] As all Hungarian words are stressed on the first syllable, and the beat is also a syntactical unit, each beat is governed by a main stress on the first syllable of the first content word. A beat is usually two to four syllables long, but might also be longer. If it is longer than five syllables, a secondary stress is likely to occur.

There might naturally be other word-beginning stressed syllables beside the main stress in a beat, as a beat might contain more than one word. But the verse sounds good if these secondary stresses are at various places within consecutive beats, because thus the ear does not feel them as regular, that is, they do not compete with the main stress. No other syllable can take over the main stress if there is not one at the head of the beat. If there is no main stress in a beat, the line is badly constructed.

Several beats can make up a line. Theoretically any number is possible. The number of syllables within a line in a poem, however, is fixed; the most frequent ones are six, eight, or twelve, but others are also possible. Rather complicated stanza structures are common. The number of syllables within beats in a line or group of lines, as well as stanzas, usually follows regular patterns, but the fixed number of syllables alone would not be enough to define this type of verse. The rhythm is created by the combination of the regular occurrence of main stresses and the length of beats.

Verse based on the above principles is called "native Hungarian." A classic example is the so-called "four-beat bisecting twelve-syllabic," which has a caesura after the sixth syllable. As an example let us look at the fifth stanza of part 1 in the *Zrínyiad*, the invocation to the Virgin Mary. The numbers on the right show how many syllables there are in each beat, the single lines mark the beat, the double lines the caesura after the sixth syllable.

Adj pennámnak | erőt, || ugy irhassak, | mint volt,	4|2 || 4|2
Arrol, | ki fiad szent || nevéjért | bátran holt	2|4 || 3|3
Megvetvén | világot, || kiben sok | java volt;	3|3 || 3|3
Kiért él | szent lelke, || ha teste | meg is holt.	3|3 || 3|3

[Give strength to my pen to describe what took place,
to relate his story who has died in God's grace,
having discarded all his earthly possessions
kept his soul alive, though his body became ashes.][19]

It is easy to see what this line has in common with an Anglo-Saxon alliterative line. The strange coincidence of stress fixed on the first syllable of the word, four beats, and a caesura in the middle tempt the poet to use this form for the translation of *Beowulf* and other Old English poems all the more because there have been several long epic poems, for example, the *Zrínyiad* above, Arany's *Buda halála* (The death of Buda) composed in such lines, although they do have rhymes.

The *Iliad*, the *Odyssey*, the *Aeneid*, and other classical Greek and Latin poems exist in Hungarian in the same sort of quantitative verse as the originals. Beside the native Hungarian versification, quantitative verse is also possible. As long and short syllables, based on long or short vowels and consonants between them, can be very clearly defined, Hungarian metric feet, iambs, trochees, etc., unlike English feet, can be based on the same principle of the alternation of linguistically short and long syllables practically irrespective of stress as in Greek and classical Latin poetry. Let us take as an example the first seven lines of the *Aeneid*. "–" above the syllable shows that it is long, "˘" marks short ones.

$$- \; \smallsmile \smallsmile \; | - \smallsmile \smallsmile | - \; - \; | - \; \smallsmile \smallsmile \; | -\smallsmile\smallsmile | - \smallsmile$$
Harcokat énekelek s egy hőst, akit Itáliába

$$- \; \smallsmile\smallsmile | - \; - \; | - \; - | - \; - | - \; \smallsmile \smallsmile \; | - \smallsmile$$
Trója vidékéről lávín partig, legelőször

$$- \; - \; | \; - \; \smallsmile\smallsmile \; | - \; \; - | - \; - \; | - \; \smallsmile \smallsmile \; | - \; - \; |$$
Űzött végzete; sok földet, tengert bebolyongott,

$$- \; \smallsmile\smallsmile \; | - \; - \; | - \; - \; | - \; \; \smallsmile\smallsmile | \smallsmile\smallsmile \; \smallsmile \; | - \; - \; |$$
Égi erők és Júnó nem-feledő dühe folytán

$$- \; \; - \; | - \; \smallsmile\smallsmile \; | - \; - \; \; | - \; \; - | - \; \smallsmile\smallsmile | - \; - \; |$$
És sok háborut is tűrt, míg várost alapított,

$$- \; \smallsmile\smallsmile \; | - \smallsmile\smallsmile \; | - \smallsmile \; \smallsmile | - \; \; - \; | - \; \smallsmile\smallsmile | - \smallsmile \; |$$
Isteneit Latiumba vivén, honnét a latin faj,

$$- \; \smallsmile \; \smallsmile \; | - - \; | - \; \smallsmile \; \smallsmile \; | - \; \; - \; | - \smallsmile\smallsmile | - \smallsmile$$
Alba atyái s Róma magas bástyái erednek.[20]

Although the possibility was inherent in the language earlier, too, this metrical system took root only in the mid-sixteenth century under foreign influences, and became widely used among Hungarian poets not only for translation in the late eighteenth century and later. János Sylvester was the first to compose a Hungarian poem in classical distiches in 1541.[21]

In addition to the so-called native Hungarian and classical quantitative, the third type of versification, which has been more and more frequently used by the poets from the nineteenth century on, is called the simultaneous, bimetric, or Western European form. Poems composed in this system show characteristics of both the native Hungarian (based on phrase accent) and the quantitative metrical systems. These poems can be described in terms of at least two systems; that is, they can be scanned according to two sets of rules. This raises a number of theoretical questions we do not want to enter into at this point, but instead, let us see an example, the first stanza of János Arany's epic poem *Toldi*, the lines of which can be scanned both as bisecting twelve-syllable native ones and six-feet quantitative ones.

$$- \;\; \smile \; | \; - \;\; - \; | - \;\; - \; | - \smile \; | - \smile \; | - \smile$$
Mint ha | pásztor|tűz ég || őszi | éjtsza|kákon,   2 | 4 || 2 | 4

$$- \;\; \smile \; | - \smile \; | - \smile \; | - \;\; - \;\; | - \smile \; | - \smile$$
Messzi|ről lo|bogva || tenger| puszta|ságon: 3 | 3 || 2 | 4

$$- \smile \; | - \;\; - \;\; | - \smile \; | - \;\; \smile \; | - \;\; - \; | - \smile$$
Toldi | Miklós | képe || úgy lo|bog fel | nékem   4 | 2 || 4 | 2

$$- \;\; \smile \; | - \;\; - \; | - \smile \;\; | - \smile \; | - \smile | - \smile$$
Majd ki|lenc tíz | ember-||öltő | régi|ségben.   4 | 2 || 2 | 4

[As on an autumn night a herdsman's fire
across the sea-like prairie flashes higher,
so Nicholas Toldi to my gaze is cast,
out of his time, ten generations past.][22]

In such a twofold system, complex mixed rhythm patterns are also used, and the quantitative principle is mixed with the characteristics of the stress-based one, or the other way round. The pattern based on stress shows quantity-based elements. For example, poets replace long syllables with short but stressed ones, or an unstressed long syllable takes the place of a stressed one.

By way of summary one can establish that versification in Hungarian can be based on both the stress of syllables—or more precisely phrases or beats—and the length of syllables. The number of syllables in a line also plays an important role in combination with the above two features. As words are stressed always on the first syllable, it would be very difficult to compose verse merely based on the alternation of stressed and unstressed syllables like English blank verse, which is then usually translated in quantitative iambs. Versification based only on counting the stressed syllables, as in Old English, is not used either because, in Szepes's and Szerdahelyi's opinion, "our sense of rhythm could not feel its beat much."[23] In my opinion English stress is far stronger than Hungarian, or the difference between stressed and unstressed syllables is greater. A differing number of unstressed syllables can be fitted into the equal spaces between stressed syllables in English, whereas in Hungarian the unstressed syllables cannot be compacted like that, and consequently the stressed syllables in any text do not tend to follow each other at regular beats. A proof of this theory is, however much it is based on the simplification of the intricacies of the two languages, that no vowel loses its character in Hungarian, whereas in English the farther a syllable is from the stressed one in a word, the less clear the vowel becomes.

The counting of syllables disregarding their length or stress has never been used as a sole defining principle in Hungarian. If we tried this, it would almost automatically become a version of the native Hungarian versification because of the word-initial stress. Since pitch is not a distinctive feature of the language, versification based on it is not possible. When translating from Chinese or Vietnamese, poets have to use longer lines, create their own rhythmic pattern, but they can naturally keep the rhyme pattern.

Besides the above-mentioned basic decisive factors that shape the rhythm of verse, that is, the number, stress, and length of syllables, there are three secondary ones: pause, alliteration, and rhyme. Although the latter is widely used in Hungarian poetry, there are even folk songs, which do not have it, in addition to all the translated unrhymed poems, like the ones in English blank verse. In some very early examples, where the repetition of certain phrases, parallelisms, and contrasts seem to be far more important structuring elements than in later poems, there are certainly no rhymes.

Alliteration, considered by some scholars to have been a rather more important structuring element earlier,[24] has clearly become an ornament, although a frequently used one. Out of curiosity, I made a count in the first part of the 102 four-line stanzas of the *Zrínyiad* mentioned above. I found that there were only six stanzas in which there was no line with alliteration, in twenty of them there was only one, and in the other three-quarters more than one line carried this ornament. Although I would not dare to state that this has been characteristic of Hungarian poetry all together, even such a minimal statistic shows that alliteration does not sound strange or alien to Hungarian ears. Needless to say, a lot depends on the time of the composition and genre of the poem, too. The high style and the content of the heroic epic do not let the alliteration sound like a jingle here. To support further the above opinion, let me refer to István Tóth, who called attention to the fact that in the age of Bálint Balassi, the sixteenth century, regularly alliterating the first words of lines in a poem was a fairly widespread custom.[25]

As far as fixed line length is concerned within a poem, Kecskés and Kerck quote a very early example of Hungarian folk poetry, a "half-pagan, half-Christian 'deer song'" going back to the eleventh century in which in addition to the abovementioned characteristics of early verse, line length also varies between nine and twelve syllables.[26] By very strict count a kind of instability can be discerned in the lines of the *Zrínyiad* where 0.5 percent of the lines have eleven or thirteen syllables rather than twelve.[27] Metrists, however, do not feel such irregularity irregular by tradition. It seems to be within the limit of tolerance.

Szegő on His Translation

On the basis of these data the reader might be able to form an opinion of György Szegő's decision about the verse form of his translation. He attached a short "apology"—using his words—to the translation, in which he explains the principles upon which the translation is based. Let me sum this up and quote from it in English where necessary:[28] "In Hungarian the translator has to follow the original verse form very precisely (the number of syllables, rhyme pattern, rhythm) if it is at all possible. If not, he has to use something similar, definitely something *having a similar effect*," Szegő writes. After this he carefully explains the alliterative meter, then he continues: "It is more or less general that long sentences reach over the end of lines and finish at the end of a half line. This kind of break, however, is not compulsory. Loose coordination, marked by semicolons in modern editions, is predominant between clauses. This . . . can be followed in the translation without any difficulty."

Alliteration in his opinion needs more deliberation because it is not a decisive structural feature, only a "well-liked ornament" in Hungarian poetry. It is the main stresses that count as strong alliteration: "It is, however, not obligatory to link half lines with alliteration. It is better if the alliteration occurs within a half line. This is already enough to feel the whole line to alliterate. . . . Hungarian folk poetry prefers alliterating syllables to be close to each other, within one half-line." He writes that threefold alliteration is to be preferred in the translation, but fourfold and even more numerous ones can be composed, too. So Szegő does not follow the Anglo-Saxon pattern of alliteration, but loosens it up to include what is common in Hungarian folk poetry, and did not forbid more than three alliterating syllables per line.

In the translator's opinion the most important issue was rhythm. Szegő is also aware that the number of syllables within lines could differ within certain limits in older Hungarian poetry, especially folk poetry. There are no rhymes in

Beowulf, which is possible in Hungarian versification and folk poetry as well. But to define the line with the number of main stresses and divide them in this way is something not known in Hungarian poetry.

As a solution Szegő suggests trying to create a similar effect in the Hungarian reader to the one that we imagine the Anglo-Saxon poem had on its audience, whatever it was like. As *Beowulf* is a primary epic, in his view this audience effect can be reached with some sort of versification characteristic of Hungarian folk poetry, but as it is clear from the above, he does not strictly follow any existing poetic form.

The four divisions in the alliterative line can be imitated with a four-beat Hungarian line, which also has a caesura in the middle. As to the number of syllables in a line he suggests ten to twelve for the majority within which he can create a great variety of half lines as far as the number of syllables is concerned. The four-beat Hungarian line allows longer lines than twelve syllables, the number in his opinion can go up to as many as sixteen, especially if the content is dynamic or sublime. Big differences in line length between consecutive lines, however, have to be avoided, because then the modern ear does not feel the text to be poetry at such places.

Szegő suggests using present-day vocabulary in his translation and suggests signaling that the text is archaic with the help of some grammatical features of older Hungarian, and with the avoidance of words that eighteenth-century reformers entered into the language. They, somewhat like King Alfred almost a millennium earlier, created new Hungarian words—with the intention of remaining in harmony with the rules of word formation—for especially scholarly and abstract notions for which no word had existed in the language before, but a Latin, German, or a French word was used. Some of these new coinages did not take root, though many did, but anyone with a good feel for the language can still identify them, so they would sound anachronisms in Szegő's opinion.

Old English into Hungarian

After clarifying the facts and thoughts behind the translation, let us now look at the result of this great venture. Szegő voices his hope in a very modest way at the end of his explanatory chapter that the translation will give "some vague idea about the original masterpiece's massive powerful beauty."[29] Generally one can say that the translation closely follows the original both in sense and in length. The Hungarian version has the same number of lines as the English edition. The translator follows the Roman numerals in the manuscript and treats them as divisions, and gives titles to each of the forty-three divisions to make it easier for the reader to follow the story.

Hungarian word order has its rules but gives much room for variation, as both noun and verb endings unambiguously mark the meaning of the word and its role in the sentence. Szegő plays with the variation but does not stretch the boundary of possibilities beyond the naturally acceptable. He usually has to re-arrange the long English sentence when synonyms are located very far from each other in the original.

The basic grammatical structure of Old English does not pose great difficulties, because as a rule we Hungarians turn nominal constructions into clauses, and the complex system of past tenses, which does not have an equivalent in Hungarian, is not often used. Only in the case of the passive voice does the translator have to supply an agent subject, since we do not use this construction in literary language. So in lines 818b–19a, "Bēowulfe wearð gūðhrēð gyfeþe,"[30] Szegő had to name who gave glory in battle to Beowulf, God or *wyrd*, and he decided for the latter.

When reading Old English one has to pay special attention to personal pronouns and the lack of them. As the Hungarian language does not distinguish between either natural or grammatical genders, the sentence construction or the repetition of the noun has to show the referent clearly, but third-person pronouns only have to be used for emphasis or clarity anyway, as conjugation marks person and number.

Translation is an interpretation of the text; it can never re-create the same kind of richness of meaning that the original carries. The translator has to choose between possible solutions especially if the text is ambiguous or corrupt like lines 3070–75. As the Hungarian is not an ambitious critical edition, Szegő only signals in a note if he gave a reconstructed meaning, and he does not discuss further possibilities of interpretation. In the same way he had to decide, for instance, if Hunlafing was a sword or a person, and he sided with the latter opinion.

One might be interested also in what he did with the famous "sōðfæstra dōm" in line 2820b. "His soul flew far from his breast," says the Hungarian, "meglelni a bátrak bíráját" [to find the judge of the righteous]. After our long discussion, the alliteration makes Beowulf's afterlife sound rather more Christian, and the meaning "fame" for *dōm* is lost. A short survey of other occurrences of *dōm* showed that in the lines where it means "fame," the translator almost always rendered it with the same word, *hír* [reputation, renown (as well as "news" and "information," which does not disturb at all)], and found a very good alliterating adjective for it meaning "loud." Where *dōm* means "judgment" or "decree," he did not find a uniform solution, but rather uses something more definite, specific in the context like "God's final *mercy*" in line 441, "the *counsel* of the wise" in line 1098, or "Eofor's *anger*" in line 2964. Where it means "somebody's wish" or "will," Szegő again is consistent in his choice. Most probably he found that the Hungarian word for "judgment" was poorer in overtones than *dōm*.

Another "very Anglo-Saxon" word, *wyrd* caused no such difficulty, because it has a close equivalent: *sors*. Three times, however, Szegő did not feel that *sors* was arbitrary and fatal enough, and chose a more old-fashioned word, and for the two terms "wyrd" and "geōsceaft grimme" (lines 1233b–34a) he uses "bal + végzet," a compound of "left" as in the case of the English "sinister" and "destiny."

This example also shows that compounding is just as easy in Hungarian as in Old English, and Szegő does not hesitate to use accepted ones, and new ones, too. We do not produce as complex and multiple compounds as present-day German can, for instance, although grammatically it would be possible; even piling prefixes and suffixes on a main verb or noun produces meaningful words, but complicated structures beyond measure sound like a tongue twister or a grammar game.

The English prefix *un-*, however, loses its special color with a tint of understatement in this translation. Either the opposite has to be used, for example, "sad" for *unblīð* or "splendidly huge" for *unwāclic* or it has to be explained in several words, for example, *unfǣge* for "who were not fated to die." The same kind of English taste is lost when the very colorful list of evil creatures—no less colorful in Hungarian—born from Cain are simply "punished" in line 114 ("hē him ðæs lēan forgeald").

There are, on the other hand, quite a few successes, where not only the translation is precise, but where it similarly alliterates as well, although on a different sound from the Old English, like the simple phrase in line 507a, "on sīdne sǣ," "tág tengeren" [on the wide sea], or "mǣg ond magoðegn" in line 408a: "vére és vitéze" [his blood relative and brave warrior].

Personal names remain as they are in the original, only the spelling versions are standardized and *th* is used for the dental sound to make printing and reading easier. Geographical names, however, like Hronesnæss, Hrefnesholt, and Earnanæs, are translated. The one least easy to get used to for someone who knows the Old English names is "Szarvasterem" [Hart-hall] for Heorot, but the translator's powerful argument in this case was that a magic hart also appears in Hungarian folk lore, thus the word makes the Hungarian reader associate the place with something more important—different in character, almost magical—than just a large building. Almost the same idea led him to translate the *Weder-* compounds with "Vihar-" [storm-]. Moreover *w*, which only occurs in foreign words, and *v* sound the same in Hungarian.

After such a general description of the translation let me select four important features of Anglo-Saxon poetic style, that is, alliteration, compounding, kennings, and formulae, and describe how György Szegő has been able to render them into Hungarian. Consonant alliteration is basically the same in the two languages, and it has already been mentioned that word-initial syllables are always stressed in Hungarian, so therefore it is very easy to compose lines with an Anglo-Saxon alliterative pattern. Examples for such are

dicsérték dolgait a dánok földjein, (line 19)
[his deeds were praised on the land of the Danes]

pengékkel pompázott, páncéllal tundokolt, (line 39)
[he prided himself on edges and shone with mailcoats,]

Megtudtam mindenütt, hogy munkát rendelt el (line 74)
[I got to know that he ordered work to be done everywhere]

Although the caesura is not typographically marked in the middle of the line, it is there as a phrase boundary. Szegő often uses the *aabb* pattern of alliteration very frequent in Hungarian poetry, for example:

gyötri s gyilkolja dühöngve s dúlva (line 2317)
[the dragon "is torturing and killing raging and furiously" the Geats],

ama gaz Grendel a rettentő rém (line 591)
[the wicked Grendel, the horrible creature]

várni a vérengzőt éjnek évadján (line 528)
[wait for the blood-thirsty one in the dead of the night]

In the off-verse of the last line the *a* vowel alliterates. The translator cannot follow the Anglo-Saxon rule in the case of vowels, as in Hungarian we only hear an alliteration if the same vowel is repeated at the head of two words. Neither does he make *sp-*, *st-*, *sc-* alliterate only with themselves.

Szegő set the aim of creating the same effect, and in a number of passages he manages marvelously. The best example I have found is line 650: "scaduhelma gesceapu scrīðan cwōman" [és suhanva sereglik a sötétség sok rémalakja]. Not only does he manage to have the same *sh* sound alliterate, which so well conveys the idea of the creatures gliding in the dark, but finds a word for "darkness" starting with the same sound ("sötétség"), which has one more *sh* sound in the middle, as well as "sok" [many] for emphasis. After numerals there is no plural in Hungarian. An emphatic plural is constructed of a numeral and a singular of the noun. Here the number of night creatures is made fearfully larger by the contrast of the singular and the emphatic numeral. *Rémalak* is a compound meaning "frightful shape," "fearful person." *Suhanni* means "glide" also in the air, and *seregelni* is "to flock," "to swarm." So the line would translate into English as something like the following: "Many frightful creatures of the dark swarm gliding."

"Sötétben settenkedő" for 703a [scrīðan sceadugenga] can probably be seen and felt by the reader; it means "the one sneaking/stealing in the dark."

In the Old English poem the sound of the fourth stress in the line sometimes is the alliterating sound of the next line, forming a link between them. Szegő uses that quite frequently (e.g., lines 123–24).

Szegő is often tempted to use more than three alliterations, or even use more than two alliterating pairs in a line. Two is common in Hungarian verse, but the pattern of *abbacc* which we see in line 4 or *aabbaaa* in line 213 of the Hungarian translation might sound too much for some readers. I find them acceptable but could not defend them with any theoretical argument. Szegő thinks "the more the better alliteration," and once it is accepted that he does not strictly follow the Old English rules, this is also an acceptable view.

Compounding in Hungarian is just as easy as in Old English as far as grammar is concerned. This does not mean that Szegő could translate all compounds with a compound word, because many would have sounded very strange as a result of the novelty of the combination. Sometimes he found very good equivalents; for example, "sunne sweglwered" in line 606 is "lángköntösű nap" [sun clothed in flames *or* sun in flaming clothes]; "āngenga" in line 165 is "egyedül bolyongó" [lonely roamer], where the rule of breaking up compounds typographically beyond more than five syllables prevents the translator from writing it in one word.

Many times a compound is translated with a phrase, such as the adjectival construction in 509a: "ond for dolgilpe" is "dőre dicsekvésből" [for foolish boasting]—note the alliteration. "Hringedstefna," which is a synecdoche, does not call up a ship in Hungarian; it is translated as "ív-orrú bárka" [ring-prowed ship], as in modern English.

Szegő at times constructs new, unusual, but very meaningful compounds. "Grundwyrgen" (line 1518b) is a "rém-nember" [terror female]. The latter word is a very derogatory one for a woman. Note also how he plays with the sound effect—the first syllables do not alliterate, but rhyme.

When Grendel is described in lines 103–5a, the translator very inventively creates his own compounds:

> Wæs se grimma gǣst   Grendel hāten,
> mǣre mearcstapa,   sē þe mōras hēold,
> fen ond fǣsten;
>
> Grendelnek hívták a gonosz szellemet,
> hírhedt határjárót, mocsarak mesterét,
> lápvár lakóját;

In understandable word-by-word English:

> Grendel was the name of the evil spirit,
> the ill-famed border-trotter, master of the fens,
> dweller of the marshland-fort;

This is what King Alfred would call "andgit of andgite."

Hungarian poetry naturally does not know kennings, a special case of compounds, but this is an image in Old English poetry that one certainly should recreate in a translation because without it so much would be lost. At times creating a kenning is not at all impossible, but one has to look out for the pitfalls.

Some kennings lend themselves to almost easy translation like the "whale's riding," "hronrād," "bálna-birtok," that is, "the whale's estate/possession," where the change of the second element was introduced for the sake of alliteration only, but the meaning is close and clear. "Woruldcandel" became "földünk nagy fáklyája" [the great torch of our earth]—*torch* and not *candle*, *earth* and not *world*—in order to alliterate, but the compound had to be diluted into a possessive construction because, using it for the first time, the relationship between the parts of "earth-torch" is not clear; it might be a torch made of earth, or even the whole earth seen as a torch. "Beadolēoma bītan nolde" (line 1523), "a harc villáma nem akar harapni" [the lightning of the battle does not want to bite], creates another kind of problem. Szegő fell prey to the tempting alliteration of *harc/fight* and *harap/bite*, and although the translation could not be more precise, in Hungarian lightning cannot bite; it is a mixed metaphor. "Ganotes bæð" became "fókafürdő" [the seal's bath] to alliterate, which a creative scop could have invented in Old English, too. If "bānhūs" is translated as simply as possible, it may be misunderstood. The first meaning of "csontház" (bone-house) is an ossuary, so the translator could not avoid attaching "body" to it, although this way the riddle is solved in a near tautology for the reader. Szegő is more daring in the case of "fela lāf" (line 1032) than some English translators, who include the word *sword* here. He found a rather long explanation adequate, "the son of the file, ready to cut," which loses its poetic quality in modern English but works well in Hungarian.

So far I have mentioned kennings where the alliteration was luckily in place. If Szegő did not find synonyms that could somehow fit into the pattern of alliteration, he either left the half line—but only one half line—without alliteration, or inserted something "harmless," as in line 1506a: "Bær þā sēo brimwyl[f], . . . hringa þengel," "A víz vad farkasa vitte a vitézt" [The wild wolf of the water carried the hero], where "vad" [wild] is superfluous before "wolf" but does not disturb the meaning. If no close solution presented itself, Szegő went for the meaning rather than the form, trying to preserve the atmosphere. For example, in lines 499a–501a, "Unferð maþelode . . . onband beadurūne," he finds another metaphor for "battle rune." "Epés szóval szólt, fújva bősz beszédét" [He spoke bily [malicious, full of bile] words, blowing his furious speech].

Last of all I looked at whether the Hungarian translation can reproduce anything like formulae, that is, lines or half lines that can be used with variation in similar situations. Szegő does make an effort, not at all without success. "Beowulf maþelode bearn Ecgþēowes" always occurs like "így beszélt Beowulf, Ecgtheow fia," where a close translation shows that Beowulf alliterates with the word for "speaking": "so spoke Beowulf Ecgtheow's son." A similarly good solution is "futott felhők alatt" for "wōd under wolcnum," where "run" alliterates with "cloud"; "ādl oððe ecg" alliterates on *k*, "kórság vagy kardcsapás" [disease or sword stroke].

Success is not always ensured for the translator. In line 2051 he does not know what to do with "wēoldon wælstōwe," so just writes "victorious Danes," and in line 2984 he misunderstands the situation and does not see the logic that Wulf was put back on his feet in order that they could be victorious on the battlefield. Similarly in line 1214a, where he says, "the Geats guarded the battle field," it is not clear for the Hungarian reader that it means that theirs was the victory. "Eorla dryhten" and "Gēata dryhten," which occur several times, receive different translations each time. Some are very colorful, like "mézsört mérető" in line 1050b, which means "the one who measures out mead." In one instance I have found that he created his own formula where there is nothing similar in the Old English; in line 1312 for the hall he has "a bő kéz terme" [the hall of the abundant/loose [not tight] hand].

It is a difficult task to decide when to stop a descriptive analysis like the present one because there is an endless line of interesting examples one would like to share with the reader. I have selected a few with which I have tried to map out the task of translating *Beowulf* into Hungarian, and to show that although the job was an immense one, because of the size of the poem, it was not at all impossible to do. The translating tradition, the flexibility of the language, and György Szegő's inventive mind and poetic talent made it possible for Hungarians to be able to get to know Beowulf, although his Hungarian contemporaries had not yet arrived in Europe, but were probably no less fierce warriors, although fighting on horseback.

After an attempt to introduce the reader to the intricacies of the Hungarian language and versification, and György Szegő's own description of how he intended to translate *Beowulf* into Hungarian, I have tried to answer questions about details of the job, ones that I myself would find interesting to ask about a new translation of the Anglo-Saxon epic. Thus, I have shown individual pieces of a huge mosaic in the close-ups of translations of Old English and Hungarian expressions into modern English. This enables readers of this essay to judge for themselves, to piece together the small tiles, and build up their own overall impression.

Lengthy general comments on the translation would not make much sense in the present essay because the majority of its expected readers have to take the word of the writer for what is said and cannot confront the writer's opinion with their own about the Hungarian *Beowulf* unless they undertake the difficult task of first learning Hungarian. As a final note suffice it to say that to the best of my knowledge all those who have read Szegő's *Beowulf* found it worth the time spent. It is a window that opens to the Germanic heroic world, and I do not think the glass in it distorts the view.

Notes

See the accompanying CD to listen to the first fifty-two lines of the poem read in Hungarian.

1. Wrenn, *Beowulf with the Finnesburg Fragment*, 3rd ed.

2. See the legend of the "Miraculous Hind" in Makkai, *In Quest of the "Miracle Stag,"* or cf. Simonis de Keza, *Gesta Hungarorum*.

3. English translations of the *Funeral Oration* and *The Lament of Mary* in Makkai, *In Quest of the "Miracle Stag,"* pp. 28–29 and 29–33.

4. For more about Hungarian literature, see: Basa, *Hungarian Literature*; L. Czigány, *Oxford History of Hungarian Literature*; Klaniczay, *History of Hungarian Literature*.

5. The first edition, titled *Adriai tengernek Syrenaia groff Zrini Miklós* [The Syren of the Adriatic Sea, Count Miklós Zrini], was published in Vienna, 1651; extracts are translated in Makkai, *In Quest of the "Miracle Stag,"* pp. 89–92: *Zrinyiad*. I use the English title when referring to the whole work throughout the paper.

6. No complete translation of the Bible into Hungarian has come down to us from the Middle Ages. Among the early manuscripts with translations of the Bible into Hungarian there are ones that contain large sections, others with short quotations, and yet others are based on liturgical texts, e.g., they are gospel pericopes. The so-called Hussite Bible is the earliest member of the first group. Parts of it have survived in three codices copied in the fifteenth century.

7. *Psalterium Ungaricum* (Herborn, 1607), critical edition: Stoll, *Szenci Molnár Albert költői művei* [The poetical works of Albert Szenci Molnár]. For more about this psalm translation, see: Szabó, *Szenci Molnár Albert és a Magyar időmértékes vers* [Albert Szenci Molnár and the quantitative meter], pp. 114–21; Kovács, *Szenczi Molnár Redivivus*.

8. Quoted in the afterword by Wéber of Sterne, *Érzékeny utazások* [Sentimental journey], p. 151.

9. There are nine translations of Poe's *The Raven* (http://www.mek.iif.hu/porta /szint/human/szepirod/kulfoldi/poe/hollo.hun) and seven of Burns's *A Red, Red Rose* in the journal *Nagyvilág* (1959): 239–41.

10. Szepes and Szerdahelyi, *Verstan* [Metrics], pp. 480–82.

11. István et al., *Világirodalmi lexikon* [Encyclopaedia of world literature], 3:511–12.

12. "A magyar műfordítás-irodalomban az ógermán vers (és általában a hangsúlyszámláló vers) tolmácsolásának nincsenek szilárdabban körvonalazott hagyományai" (Szepes and Szerdahelyi, *Verstan*, p. 482).

13. For further details consult M. Czigány, *Hungarian Literature in English Translation*; Keenoy, *Babel Guide to Hungarian Literature*; and Tezla, *Introductory Bibliography to the Study of Hungarian Literature*.

14. *Klasszikus angol költők a középkortól a XX. századig* [Classics of English poetry from the Middle Ages to the twentieth century], Old English poetry, pp. 5–37.

15. For more about the Hungarian language, see Benkő and Samu, *Hungarian Language*.

16. Kecskés and Kerek, "Directions in Hungarian Metric Research," p. 320.

17. Kecskés and Kerek, "Directions in Hungarian Metric Research," p. 320.

18. For example, Szepes and Szerdahelyi, *Verstan*, pp. 19–23.

19. Translation by Kabdebo [and A. M.], in Makkai, *In Quest of the "Miracle Stag,"* p. 90.

20. *Vergilius összes művei* [The complete works of Virgil], p. 109. The word-for-word

translation of the Hungarian is as follows: "I sing battles and a hero, who was driven by his fortune first from the area of Troy to the shores of Lavinia; he roamed over much land and sea, because of the heavenly forces and the non-forgetting anger of Juno, he endured many wars, until he founded a town taking his gods to Latium, where the Latin race, the fathers of Alba and the tall bastions of Rome take their root."

21. Szepes and Szerdahelyi, *Verstan*, p. 224.

22. Translated by Kirkconnell, in Makkai, *In Quest of the "Miracle Stag,"* p. 255.

23. Szepes and Szerdahelyi, *Verstan*, p. 24.

24. Vikár, "Hangsúly és ritmus" [Stress and rhythm].

25. Szepes and Szerdahelyi, *Verstan*, p. 79, quoting István Tóth, "Balassi Bálint és az Árgírus-széphistória szerzősége" (Bálint Balassi and the authorship of the Árgírus romance), pp. 155–94.

26. Kecskés and Kerek, "Direction in Hungarian Metric Research," p. 321.

27. István et al., *Világirodalmi lexikon*, s.v. "Zrínyi-vers" [Zrínyi meter] (18:241–42).

28. All quotations from *Beowulf* in Hungarian are from György Szegő and Katalin Halácsy, *Beowulf*. Szegő's chapter "A fordításról, Önigazolás-féle" is pp. 87–91. The translation is mine.

29. Szegő, "A fordításról, Önigazolás-féle," p. 91.

30. Line numbers follow those of the Old English text if that is mentioned first, and those of the Hungarian, if that comes first. The two might be one or two lines off in comparison because of the changes in sentence structure in the translation.

Italian Translations of *Beowulf*

Claudia Di Sciacca and Loredana Teresi

If one were to judge just from the number and date of publication of the Italian translations of *Beowulf*, it could easily be concluded that the reception of the Anglo-Saxon poem in Italy has been prompt and greatly favorable as well as enduring. From the end of the nineteenth century, no fewer than seven complete translations of *Beowulf* have been published. These are—in chronological order—the versions by Giusto Grion,[1] Anna Benedetti,[2] Federico Olivero,[3] Cesare Cecioni,[4] Ludovica Koch,[5] Caterina Ciuferri and David Murray,[6] and, finally, by Giuseppe Brunetti.[7] While only two of these translations, namely those by Benedetti and Cecioni, are in prose, the rest are all in verse.

Besides these complete translations, however, there are a few partial renditions, both in prose and verse, as well as epitomes and even a comic-strip adaptation of *Beowulf* in Italian. The first partial Italian verse version of our poem dates as early as 1833 and is included in a critical history of English poetry by Giuseppe Pecchio.[8] This version is in fact a summary of *Beowulf*'s plot with extracts translated secondhand from Sharon Turner's notorious English verse rendition of selected passages from the poem.[9] Pecchio renders his flawed original very literally, thereby producing a largely inaccurate account of *Beowulf* in Italian.[10] However, this first introduction of the Old English poem to the Italian public is well worth mentioning insofar as it is also the earliest translation of *Beowulf* into a Romance language and into a modern language other than English and Danish in general.[11]

Nearly half a century later, Giuseppe Schuhmann published a paraphrase of the poem including the Italian rendition of interspersed selections.[12] In the last century, translations of passages from *Beowulf* have been included in anthologies of Old English poetry, such as the verse version of around 1,100 lines by Federico Olivero,[13] the verse translation of a few selected passages by Roberto Sanesi,[14] and most recently extracts from Brunetti's translation have been reprinted in an anthology of medieval English poetry.[15]

Finally, Italy saw the first comic-strip version of *Beowulf* published in a weekly comic book by Enrico Basari in 1941.[16] It is an imaginative retelling, merging genuine *Beowulf* material with Arthurian romance and providing an obvious Catholic interpretation of the (freely altered) story. Basari's adaptation was in turn faithfully rendered into Brazilian Portuguese by an anonymous translator in 1955.[17]

This essay will provide a sketchy introduction to the six complete translations of *Beowulf* published in the last century and then focus on a comparative analysis of selected passages. In particular, we intend to analyze the prosodic and metrical solutions adopted by the translators to render the alliterative Germanic verse as well as comparing the interaction of syntax and meter in the Old English poem and in its Italian renditions. Also, specific traits of the lexicon of the selected translations will be discussed, focusing especially on the different renderings of the most evocative elements of the Old English poetic diction, namely the kennings. Finally, we will examine samples of the so-called appositive style,[18] trying to clarify how variation, one of the most distinctive stylistic and structural devices of the poem, has been rendered into Italian.

> *Benedetti (1915)*: Benedetti's translation is a prose rendition of the *Beowulf* and the *Finnsburg Fragment* based on the edition by Alfred J. Wyatt.[19] The translation is prefaced by a twenty-page-long "Introduction," providing some basic information on the poem, its manuscript witness, its date and place of composition as well as its subject matter, and by an "Appendix" with a scanty index of the proper names and place names occurring in the poem. The information and the assessments given in this preface, however, betray a simplistic handling of the most crucial questions concerning *Beowulf*, if not a bewildering lack of understanding of it, including the comment that the artistic value of the poem is close to nothing.[20] No separate bibliography is provided, but bibliographical references are given in a few footnotes accompanying the introduction. Following the manuscript, the translation is divided into forty-three fits;[21] it does not feature the original text on the facing page and is accompanied by brief explanatory footnotes. In spite of some literary pretence, this translation turns out to be a rather unsatisfactory paraphrase of the poem, which does not seem to take into account the complex issues of style and structure in *Beowulf*. As will be shown in greater detail in the discussion of individual passages, Benedetti's rendition of the Old English is often rather clumsy, if not patently mistaken.
>
> *Olivero (1934)*: Olivero's translation is based on Wyatt's edition revised by Raymond W. Chambers;[22] the Old English text is printed on the facing page and accompanied by a set of endnotes ("Notes to the Text"). The translation is preceded by an extensive and informative "Introduction" which

discusses the dating and origin of the poem, its Christian and mythological elements, its historical and sociocultural background, its descriptions of landscape and natural settings, and its style. This introduction is supplied with a set of "Bibliographical Notes," that is a fairly detailed bibliography, and an "Analytical Index" at the end of the volume. Olivero's translation has no internal subdivisions or captions. It is a rather faithful translation and can be defined as the first scholarly and literary rendition of the Old English poem in a fairly imitative meter, although the rules of alliteration are applied rather sparsely and laxly.

Cecioni (1959): Cecioni's translation is based on the editions by Friedrich Klaeber[23] and Charles L. Wrenn[24] as well as on the original manuscript; the Old English text is, however, not supplied. The translation is preceded by a comprehensive and detailed "Introduction," analyzing the manuscript witness of *Beowulf*, the subject matter of the poem, its structure, its historical, fantastic, and Christian components, as well as the figure of its heroic protagonist. The volume concludes with a set of explanatory "Notes" to the translation, a detailed "Index of Proper Names," and a "Bibliographical Note," which is in fact a fairly lengthy annotated bibliography. The translation itself is a prose version divided into two large sections: the first one, entitled "L'uccisione di Grendel" (The killing of Grendel), corresponds to lines 1–2199 of the original poem; the second one, entitled "La lotta contro il drago" (The fight against the dragon) corresponds to lines 2200–3182. It is an accurate and effective rendition from both the philological and literary point of view and, on the whole, one of the most valuable among those here discussed.

Koch (1987): Koch's translation is based on Wrenn's edition revised by Whitney F. Bolton,[25] which is reprinted on the facing page. The translation is prefaced by an "Introduction," a "Selected Bibliography," a "Note to the Text," and a "Note to the Translation"; the volume concludes with a "Glossary of Proper Names." The introduction is a critical essay touching on a variety of aspects of *Beowulf* and particular emphasis is laid on the parallels and analogues found in Norse literature. The "Note to the Text" addresses general questions, such as the origin and dating of the poem, its subject matter, its formulaic and folkloric elements, and its style. The translation is in imitative verse, alluding to the alliterative rhythm and other sound effects of the original as well as reproducing the caesura between the two half lines. The text is divided into forty-three fits introduced by captions that summarize the contents of the individual fit; in turn, the fits often feature internal subdivisions originally introduced by the translator and signaled by a wider spacing. In the "Note to the Translation," Koch presents her work as a faithful rendition that tries to keep close to the original by imitating its syntactic structure and reproducing its alliteration as well as other sound effects. In fact, this translation can be considered to be a poetic re-creation of the original and is highly interpretative. (For example, the social and military organization described in the poem is anachronistically presented as analogous to the feudal hierarchy.)[26]

Ciuferri and Murray (2000): The translation by Ciuferri and Murray seems to have been conceived as a study tool. It is based on the student edition by George Jack,[27] which is printed on the facing page, and the volume is supplied with a compendium of Old English grammar. The translation is preceded by a descriptive and compact "Introduction" presenting a blueprint to the fundamental aspects of *Beowulf*, that is its manuscript, the time and place of its composition, its historical, mythological, folkloric, and biblical elements, its heroic society, its style and structure, and, finally, its plot. This preface concludes with a paragraph on the translation technique adopted by Ciuferri and Murray, and is followed by a selected "Bibliography." The volume concludes with a set of rather elementary explanatory "Notes to the Text," a "List of Proper Names," and a brief Old English grammar. The translation consists of forty-three sections (*Canti*) followed by the *Finnsburg Fragment*; it is a rendition in imitative verse, trying to reproduce the alliteration and bipartite structure of the original Germanic line. As the translators explain in their "Introduction," their Italian version has been mediated via modern English, insofar as Murray has first translated from the Old English original into modern English and then Ciuferri has translated into Italian. As can be seen from the selected passages, however, the result of this double translation is heavily indebted to Koch's work without having the literary flavor and narrative fluency of the latter.

Brunetti (2003): Brunetti's translation is based on the text edited by Bruce Mitchell and Fred Robinson,[28] which Brunetti has collated with the manuscript as reproduced in Kevin Kiernan's electronic edition.[29] The Old English text is printed on the facing page and the punctuation adopted for it is that by Bruce Mitchell and Susan Irvine.[30] This editorial rigor in the reproduction of the Old English original derives from Brunetti's comprehensive project of a translation-edition which would condense the major results of the *Beowulf* scholarship and thereby make the reader aware of the (still largely unresolved) philological and interpretative questions surrounding the poem.[31] For this reason, the text and translation are preceded by a detailed "Introduction," a "Note to the Text," and a wide-ranging "Bibliography," and are followed by a list of relevant "Readings from the

Manuscript" and the corresponding emendations, the most controversial of which are discussed in a thorough set of "Notes" to both the text and the translation. The latter is divided into forty-three fits and is in laxly alliterative verse, which tries to allude to the rhythm of the original thanks to the use of frequent, albeit not insistent or forced, alliteration.[32] In keeping with the native Italian poetical tradition, alliteration consists of consonantal resonances and binds the two sections that tend to make up the line, although such bipartite structure is not formally signaled by a caesura. Finally, the volume concludes with an "Appendix," containing the text and translation of the *Finnesburh Fragment*, and an "Index of Proper Names."

Alliteration, Meter, and Syntax

Rather unsurprisingly, our comparative analysis of the Italian translations of *Beowulf* will begin with the incipit of the poem. As Andy Orchard has recently shown, "these opening lines . . . establish many of the themes of the poem as a whole, and set up resonances which can still be perceived in the closing lines."[33] I quote the first eleven lines of the poem, showing the alliterative pattern identified by Orchard, with structural alliteration highlighted in bold and ornamental interlinear alliteration underlined:

> Hwæt, wē **G**ār-**d**ena   in g̱ear**d**agum,
> **þ**ēodcyninga   **þ**rym gefrūnon,
> hū ḏa **æ**þelingas   **e**llen fremedon!
> Oft **Sc**yld **Sc**ēfing   **sc**eaþena þrēatum,
> 5   **m**onegum **m**ǣgþum   **m**eodosetla oftēah,
> **e**gsode **e**orl[as],   syððan ǣrest wearð
> **f**ēasceaft **f**unden;   hē þæs frōfre gebād,
> **w**ēox under **w**olcnum   **w**eorðmyndum þāh,
> oð þæt him ǣghwylc   ymbsittendra
> 10   ofer **h**ronrāde   **h**ȳran scolde,
> **g**omban **g**yldan;   þæt wæs **g**ōd cyning![34]

We may now compare the rendition of these lines in the four Italian verse translations under discussion. It should be noted that, unlike Old English, in Italian alliteration concerns consonants only and that it applies not only to the same initial consonant or consonant cluster in adjacent or neighboring words, but, in a broader sense, also to the repeated occurrence of a given consonant or consonant cluster in any position within adjacent or neighboring words.[35] In the following quotations, alliteration concerning initial consonants and linking words within the same line is highlighted in bold, while any other kind of relevant consonantal repetition is underlined:[36]

Olivero:

> Udite!—noi abbiamo appreso la gloria dei re della nazione
> dei danesi, branditori di lancia, in antichi tempi,
> abbiamo sentito dire come[37] quei principi compirono atti di valore.
> Spesso Scyld Scefing alle bande dei distruttori,
> 5   a molte tribù tolse le tavole del banchetto,
> atterrì i duci, dopo che egli da prima fu
> trovato d'ogni cosa privo; egli di ciò ebbe consolazione,
> crebbe in potenza sotto i cieli, prospero in onori,
> finché a lui ognuno dei vicini,
> 10   attraverso il mare—la via della balena—dovette ubbidire,
> ed a lui pagar tributo; quello fu un buon re.[38]

Koch:

> Attenzione. Sappiamo   della gloria, in giorni lontani,
> dei Danesi con l'Asta,   dei re della nazione;
> che grandi cose fecero   quei principi nel passato.
> Molte volte Scyld Scefing   strappò, a bande pirate,
> 5   a numerosi popoli,   i seggi dell'idromele.
> Fu il terrore degli Eruli,[39]   lui che era stato trovato,
> bambino, senza niente.   Ma si vide soccorso.
> Salì, sotto le nuvole,   fu coperto di segni
> di prestigio, finché   ogni suo confinante
> 10   oltre la via delle balene   gli dovette ubbidienza
> e gli pagò tributi.   È stato un grande re.[40]

Ciuferri and Murray:

> Ecco. Dei Danesi con Lancia   conosciamo come
>   nei tempi andati,
> i re del popolo,   ricoperti di gloria,
> come quei principi   prodemente si batterono.
> Molte volte Scyld Scefing   a maligne masnade,
> 5   a numerosi popoli   tolse del potere il tavolo.
> Terrore divenne dei guerrieri   giusto colui
> Che senza niente fu trovato.   Tuttavia consolazione ha conosciuto.
> Sotto i cieli cresceva   cinto di onore
> finché ognuno   dei popoli confinanti
> 10   oltre la via delle balene   dovette lui obbedienza
> e gli pagò tributi.   Trattasi di un grande re.[41]

Brunetti:

> Dei Danesi delle Lance in giorni lontani,
> dei re della nazione ci è nota la rinomanza,
> che imprese di coraggio compirono quei principi.
> Spesso Scyld Scefing a schiere nemiche
> 5   strappò a molti popoli le panche dell'idromele,
> terrorizzò guerrieri, dopo che fu trovato
> derelitto, di questo ebbe conforto,

> fu grande sotto il cielo, prospero d'onori
> finché a lui tutt'intorno
> 10 oltre la via della balena dovettero obbedienza,
> pagarono tributo; fu un grande re.[42]

As can be seen, examples of alliteration of initial consonants linking words within any individual line are not very numerous. Out of the eleven lines of this passage, I count three lines featuring such alliteration in Olivero's translation, three in Koch's, and five in Brunetti's translations. An exception is represented by Ciuferri and Murray, who make the most systematic use of initial alliteration (eight lines out of eleven), although this insistence on an imitative verse on the whole generates a rather monotonous rhythm with a taut periodic modulation, and sometimes produces infelicitous renditions. Such is the case with the very last phrase "trattasi di un grande re" [it is about a great king], where the opening verb "trattasi," clearly chosen to alliterate with the preceding "tributi" [tolls], seems to be borrowed from a very prosaic, almost technical register. In contrast, Olivero's translation and those by Koch and Brunetti, in particular, mainly rely on rather free consonantal resonances, which lend phonetic cohesion not only to the individual line but also to subsequent lines. Such consonantal alliteration, on the one hand, sounds congenial to an Italian readership, since it has a tradition in Italian poetry, especially in the contemporary one, although it is also found in medieval poets such as Dante and Petrarch.[43] On the other hand, it enables allusion to the rhythm of the Old English poem, suggesting the distinctiveness of the latter without reproducing it too slavishly or parodistically. The result is a smooth fluency that, especially in Brunetti's translation, favors the progression of the narrative rather than the local effects.[44]

Alliteration is, however, supported and accompanied by other sound effects more congenital to a Romance language, such as assonance and rhyme. These sound effects may link words within one individual line (such as in the noun phrase "**mo**lte **vo**lte" found in both Koch and Ciuferri and Murray's translations, line 4; "po**poli**"/"ta**volo**," in Ciuferri and Murray's line 5; "po**poli**"/"idrom**ele**" in Brunetti's line 5). Assonance and rhyme can also link two subsequent lines or half lines (such is the case with Olivero's lines 3–4: "val**ore**"/"distrut**tori**," and 10–11: "ubbidi**re**"/"**re**"; Koch's lines 3–6: "pass**ato**"/"pir**ate**"/"trov**ato**" and "po**poli**"/"idrom**ele**"/"**E**r**uli**"; Brunetti's, lines 6–7: "trov**ato**"/"confor**to**"). Indeed, it is perhaps worth noting that such assonances and rhymes are concentrated in lines which in the Old English text exhibit double alliteration, that is the lines introducing the crucial figure of Scyld Scefing, the founder of the Danish royal house (lines 4–11).[45] This is especially true of Koch and Brunetti's translations, which precisely in this passage combine assonance with a very dense and varied pattern of consonantal resonances.

In addition to aural effects, the Old English verse achieves cohesion and narrative dynamism also by means of syntactical and metrical devices such as hyperbaton and enjambment. The syntactical and metrical units of the Old English verse are the half lines, which consist of a brief clause (such as lines 7b or 11b), a noun phrase (such as lines 4b and 5a), verb phrase (such as lines 2b, 3b, 5b, 6a, 10b, and 11a), or a prepositional phrase (such as lines 1b or 10a), or sometimes just a compound (such as lines 2a and 9b).[46] These metrical, syntactical as well as semantic units are often connected by means of hyperbaton, especially the hyperbaton between subject and verb, of which we have striking examples in lines 1–2 ("wē . . . gefrūnon"), 4–5 ("Scyld . . . oftēah"), and 9–10 ("ǣgwhylc . . . hȳran scolde"), and between auxiliary and main verb, of which we find again an instance in lines 6–7 ("wearð . . . gefunden"). Unlike modern English, the Italian word order would be flexible enough to replicate the hyperbata of the Old English original to a large extent, and this is indeed the solution adopted by Ciuferri and Murray and, partly, also by Olivero.[47] However, as Brunetti has pointed out,[48] the repeated use of hyperbata in Italian inevitably produces a somehow affected, old-fashioned literary effect and a broken rhythm at the expense of narrative fluency, as is evident in Ciuferri and Murray's translation. In contrast, the verse translation with the most fluent narrative rhythm is that by Koch, who has made very sparse use of hyperbata. Brunetti himself has explained that in his intent to allude to the rhythm of the original, he has indeed employed hyperbata, though reducing their number in the last revisions of his translation,[49] and the result is a judicious compromise functional to the narrative discourse. Interestingly, in his translation of this passage Brunetti independently makes use of a construction typical of the *Beowulf*-poet, that is the *apo koinou*, a grammatical and syntactical element shared by two other elements, may it be an object between two verbs or a verb between two objects, a subordinate clause between two main clauses, etc.[50] Like hyperbaton and enjambment, the *apo koinou* is a device that breaks the boundaries of the individual line, thereby contributing to modulate the narrative discourse. In this case the *koinon*, that is the element in common, is the verb "strappò" (line 5) [took away], which is shared between two datives, that is "a schiere nemiche" (line 4) [from hostile armies], and "a molti popoli" (line 5) [from many nations]. Intriguingly, this particular *apo koinou* is original to Brunetti's translation and has no equivalent in the Old English text, which shows how the translator has assimilated and adopted stylistic devices that are the stock-in-trade of the *Beowulf*-poet, so that he is able to reproduce and re-create them originally in his translation.

Enjambment too is a key device to ensure a welcome variety in the progression and modulation of the poetic discourse, in that the second half-line does not always represent a close, but it projects itself onto the following line, thereby creating effects of rhetorical suspense and artful retardation. In the passage under examination, we find two instances of enjambment. The first, in lines 6–7 ("syððan ǣrest wearð / fēasceaft funden"), significantly marks a central piece of information concerning the life of Scyld Scefing, that is the fact that he was a foundling, and it is noteworthy that the suspense created by the enjambment is further enhanced by the hyperbaton of the auxiliary "wearð" and the past participle "funden." The second, in lines 9–10 ("ymsittendra / ofer hronrāde"), emphasizes the sense of the physical vastness of the domain over which Scyld Scefing managed to exert his authority. All four Italian verse translations reproduce these two enjambments, adopting a practically identical solution for the latter one, while offering different renditions for the former, perhaps more crucial one. In particular, Olivero replicates the strong separation of auxiliary and past participle of the original rendering "wearð / ... funden" with "fu / trovato" [he was found], thereby breaking the line after the auxiliary "fu." In contrast, both Koch and Brunetti have the whole of the verb phrase in the same line (6) and then move to the following line the predicate which defines Scyld's condition of helpless orphan (Brunetti has the simple adjective "derelitto" [wretched], while Koch has the phrase "senza niente" [penniless], significantly separated from the verb by the apposition, "bambino" [as a child].) Finally, in Ciuferri and Murray's translation the enjambment separates the relative pronoun and its antecedent ("colui / che") with a somehow less heightened effect.

The corresponding Italian prose translations of the incipit of the poem by Benedetti and Cecioni read respectively:

Benedetti:
> Attenti! Così fu che noi, Dani da la Lancia, nei giorni andati sentimmo narrare de la potenza dei re di nostra gente e delle gesta compiute dagli Atelinghi.[51] Scilda, figlio di Scefing, con molti de le guerriere tribù, strappò sovente i nemici dal seggio dell'idromele. Temuto Signore egli era, trovato dapprima nudo e miserabile sotto le nubi, colui che tanto conforto diede, e che onorato fu da tutti quei vicini che più spesso battevano i mari; costretti furono essi a pagargli tributi d'oro, finché egli divenne loro buon re.[52]

Cecioni:
> Ascoltate! A tutti è nota la gloria dei re del bellicoso popolo danese in tempi passati. Quali nobili imprese compirono quegli eroi! Spesso Scyld Scefing rapì alle schiere nemiche, in molti paesi, le tavole dell'idromele. Il suo nome ispirava terrore, ma in principio egli non era stato che un trovatello, un fanciullo privo di tutto. Di questo il destino doveva riserbargli compenso: Scyld crebbe sotto la volta del cielo ed ebbe prospera gloria, finché tutti quelli che vivevano intorno a lui, sul mare sentiero della balena, dovettero ubbidirgli e pagargli tributo. Egli fu un buon re![53]

In these two prose translations, especially in Cecioni's, it is possible to identify consonantal resonances too (and again they are underlined), although they sound inevitably looser within the framework of a prose rendition. Only once do such resonances reproduce the sound effects of the original, that is when Scyld is introduced and the "**Sc**yld **Sc**ēfing" alliterating doublet of the original is imitated faithfully. In Cecioni's translation, however, the aural ornamentation is also enhanced by some assonances and rhyme, such as with "trovate**llo**"/"fanciu**llo**," "**cr**e**bbe**"/"**ebbe**," and "ubbidi**rgli**"/"paga**rgli**," and again, these sound effects are significantly concentrated in the passage concerning the circumstances of Scyld's birth and subsequent life. Notably, Cecioni marks the two crucial pieces of information concerning Scyld, that is that he was a foundling but eventually managed to become a powerful king, by consecutive use of negation ("*non* era stato che un trovatello" [he was but a foundling]) and of hyperbaton ("*di questo* il destino doveva riserbargli *compenso*" [of that fate had compensation in store for him]). It is noteworthy that while the negation is an original addition by the translator unparalleled in the original text, it is nonetheless consistent with the *Beowulf*-poet's penchant for negative and litotic expressions.[54] As to the use of hyperbaton in Cecioni's translation of this passage, another example can be found at the very incipit ("a tutti è nota la gloria"), where again a key point in the poem is highlighted by the inversion of the standard syntactical order, that is by placing the dative ("a tutti" [to everybody]) at the very beginning before the verb phrase ("è nota" [it is a well-known fact, it is common knowledge]) and the subject ("la gloria" [the glory]). Otherwise, Cecioni's translation is poor in hyperbata and has instead a rather lively and effective narrative rhythm. In contrast, Benedetti's version abounds in hyperbata, especially those concerning verb and auxiliary or verb and object ("temuto egli era" [feared he was]; "conforto diede" [comfort did he give]; "onorato fu" [honored he was]; "costretti furono" [compelled they were]) and therefore sounds more solemnly literary but less fluent. It should perhaps also be added that Benedetti's rendition of the lines in question strikes one as puzzling if not erroneous at some points.[55]

Another key passage in the poem is represented by the so-called Hrothgar's sermon,[56] which serves as a meditative pause on the dangers of pride after the recount of young Beowulf's victorious enterprises against Grendel and his mother, and, at the same time, as a fitting preface to the second part of the poem, where a fifty-year-older Beowulf will find his death in the ultimate fight against the dragon. In particular, I would like to focus on lines 1761b–68, where Hrothgar reminds Beowulf of the fugacity of any worldly glory and exhorts the young warrior not to take pride in his strength because it is inherently precarious and very soon an enemy on the battlefield or an illness or old age would put an end to it. The inevitable fragility and transience of physical vigor and of the fame that the latter attains are emphasized by a sequence of phrases coordinated by the conjunction *oðða*, each of which concerns one of the dangers constantly threatening youth. In particular, each *oðða*, except the first one ("ādl oðða ecg" [line 1763a]) introduces a noun phrase which consists of a doublet and alliterates with the following one in the same line, according to a rhetoric device typical of homiletic prose.[57] Also, a verb-doublet, that is "forsiteð ond forsworceð,"[58] a hapax occurring uniquely in this passage of *Beowulf* (line 1767), can be said to confer a homiletic flavor to these lines. As has been pointed out, alliterating pairs of finite verbs are rare in *Beowulf*, but are frequently found in Old English homiletic prose.[59] Thus, it can be said that such an alliterating pair as "forsiteð ond forsworceð" helps to modulate the style and diction of the poem in accordance with the explicitly homiletic and hortatory theme and tone of Hrothgar's speech.[60]

The lines in question are quoted below, with the alliterating pairs highlighted in bold:

> 1761   Nū is þīnes mægnes **blǣd**
> āne hwīle;   eft sōna bið,
> þæt þec ādl oðða **ecg**   **ea**foþes getwǣfeð,
> oðða **fȳ**res **f**eng,   oðða **f**lōdes wylm,
> 1765   oðða **g**ripe mēces,   oðða **g**āres fliht,
> oðða **a**tol yldo;   oðða **ēa**gena bearhtm
> **fors**iteð ond **fors**worceð;   **s**emninga bið,
> þæt ðec, **d**ryhtguma,   **d**ēað oferswȳðeð.[61]

The six Italian translations of this passage read:

Benedetti:
> Divulgata è per adesso la fama della tua forza. Presto la malattia, o il fallire di un'arma, o l'abbraccio del fuoco, o l'irrompere de le acque, o un colpo di spada, o il volo di una freccia, o la triste vecchiaia, te da la tua forza separeranno, od anche potrà velarsi la luce degli occhi tuoi, e spegnersi. La morte allora coglierà te pure, o nobilissimo.[62]

Olivero:
> 1761b Ora il fiore della tua forza durerà
> per un certo tempo; ma tosto quindi avverrà
> che morbo o fil di spada,
> o l'assalto del fuoco o il tumulto dei flutti,
> 1765 o il morso di una daga, o il volo del giavellotto,
> o l'orrida vecchiezza ti toglierà il vigore; oppure la luce dei tuoi
> occhi
> se n'andrà e s'oscurerà; subito sarai
> 1768 dalla morte sopraffatto, o nobile guerriero.[63]

Cecioni:
> La pienezza della tua forza non può durare a lungo; ben presto il morbo

o la spada stroncheranno il tuo nobile valore—oppure lo stroncherà
l'abbraccio del fuoco, o i flutti tempestosi, o il morso repentino del
pugnale, o il dardo saettante, o l'orribile vecchiaia. La luce dei tuoi occhi si offuscherà, si spegnerà e sarai infine sopraffatto dalla morte, o
valoroso condottiero![64]

Koch:
1761b   Oggi, la fama
         della tua forza   durerà un certo tempo;
         poi verrà in fretta   la malattia o la lama
         a mutilarti delle tue forze,   o la stretta del fuoco,
1765   o il vortice della marea,   o il morso della spada,
         o il volo della lancia,   o l'orrenda vecchiaia;
         o la luce degli occhi   ti si farà buia e fiacca.
         Arriverà ben presto,   cortigiano,[65] la morte,
1769   che è più forte di te.[66]

Ciuferri and Murray:
1761b   La fama della tua forza
         non durerà che per un po';   poi potrebbe darsi
         che la malattia o la spada   ti privino della forza,
         o l'abbraccio del fuoco   o l'agitazione delle acque,
1765   o l'attacco della spada   o il volo della lancia,
         o l'orrenda vecchiaia   o la luce dei tuoi occhi
         ti si faccia buia e fiacca.   Quanto prima succederà
1768   che te, guerriero,   la morte sopraffarrà.[67]

Brunetti:
1761:   la gloria della tua forza
         durerà ora qualche tempo; ma presto sarà
         che morbo o spada dal vigore ti separi
         o morsa di fuoco o piena di flutti
1765   o assalto di lama o volo di lancia
         od orrenda vecchiaia, o la chiarezza degli occhi
         si farà fioca e scempia; presto sarà,
1768   guerriero, che ti soverchi la morte.[68]

As can be seen, the sound effects of the Italian translations do not often manage
to render the tight pattern of alliterating doublets of the original, but make instead
use of that looser consonantal alliteration which has already been discussed and
examples of which are again underlined in the quotations above. Such consonantal resonances are, however, effective insofar as they succeed in highlighting the
sequence of pitiless threats impending on youth and the fateful consequences they
may have. In particular, it is noteworthy that such a sequence is scanned by the
insistent repetition of velars and rolls (/k/ and /r/). Also, the inevitability of death is
emphasized by some assonances and rhymes involving the verbs, which are in the
simple present in the Old English original but nearly always rendered in the simple

future in Italian, therefore with oxytone forms ending in *–rà*: see, for example, "durerà"/"avverrà" and "se n'andrà e s'oscurerà" (Olivero, lines 1761–62 and 1767); "durerà"/"verrà" (Koch, lines 1762–63); "succederà"/"sopraffarrà" (Ciuferri and Murray, lines 1767–68); "durerà"/"sarà" and "farà"/"sarà" (Brunetti, lines 1762 and 1767). Finally, note also the assonance "velarsi"/"spegnersi" (Benedetti), "flutti"/"giavellotto" (Olivero, lines 1764–65), and the rhyme linking the two crucial final words in Koch's translation, that is "morte"/"forte" (lines 1768–69). Moreover, the Italian translations successfully mirror the patterned rhythms and use of anaphora characteristic of this passage. All translators have maintained the syntactical structure of the long period extending from line 1762b to 1768b, reproducing the sequence of noun phrases with the anaphora of the disjunctive *oððe*, that is *o* or *oppure* in Italian. In some cases, the Italian versions introduce new repetitions, which felicitously allude to the sententious tone of the original. For example, the Old English verb "getwæfeð" (line 1763b), meaning "deprive of," "put an end to," has been doubled by Cecioni and rendered with the Italian verb "stroncare" ("stroncheranno" and "stroncherà"), which has got an equally drastic meaning ("to crush, to destroy"), and thus it effectively emphasizes the utter powerlessness of even the strongest of men in the face of all the perils that fate has in store for him.

The analysis will now focus on Brunetti's translation, as it seems to be the most effective and felicitous of the lines in question. Firstly, from an aural point of view, his rendition is the most evocative and the one that presents the richest texture of alliterating sounds, with some solutions that successfully re-create the pattern of alliteration linking the noun phrases of the original ("fuoco"/"flutti," "lama"/"lancia," "vecchiaia"/"chiarezza"/"occhi"). As far as the verb doublet "forsiteð ond forsworceð" is concerned, the solution adopted by Brunetti to render the anaphora of the prefix *for-* and the alliteration linking the two verbs *sittan* and *sweorcan*, consists in the use of one verb phrase ("si farà fioca e scempia") made up of the reflexive form of the verb *fare*, meaning "to grow, to become," and two synonymous predicative adjectives, that is "fioca" [dim], alliterating with the verb, and "scempia" [feeble, weak]. An analogous rendition is also found in Koch ("ti si farà buia e fiacca" [it will grow dark and dim for you]) and Ciuferri and Murray ("ti si faccia buia e fiacca" [it may grow dark and dim for you]), which also reproduces the alliteration of /f/ of the Old English original. However, in Brunetti's version the two terms making up the alliterating pair, that is "farà" and "fioca," are contiguous, while in the translations by Koch and Ciuferri and Murray the two alliterating terms ("farà" and "fiacca" and "faccia" and "fiacca," respectively) are separated by "buia." In Olivero and Cecioni's translations the sound figure which replaces the Old English alliteration is the assonance produced by the homeoteleuton of the two future forms ("se n'andrà e s'oscurerà" [it will go off and grow dark] in

Olivero's version), as well as the anaphora of the reflexive particle "si" in Cecioni's translation ("**si** offuscherà, **si** spegnerà" [it will grow dim, it will fade away]).

As pointed out above, Brunetti makes a sparing use of hyperbaton and precisely in order to reduce the number of hyperbata, he avoids re-creating the syntactical order of the original too faithfully. Thus, for example, the noun phrases of lines 1764–66, where the genitive always precedes the nominative ("fȳres feng," "flōdes wylm"),[69] are rendered by Brunetti according to a syntactical order more common in Italian, that is with the nominative followed by the genitive ("morsa di fuoco" [the grip of fire], "piena di flutti" [the flood of the waves]). However, hyperbaton is used at least twice in Brunetti's translation of this passage to mark two significant points. The first hyperbaton occurs on line 1763 ("morbo o spada dal vigore ti separi"), and concerns the subject ("morbo o spada" [illness or sword]) and the verb with the direct object ("ti separi" [may separate you]) which are distanced by the indirect object ("dal vigore" [from your vigor]), thus, on the one hand, reproducing the syntactical order of the original ("þec ādl oððe ecg eafoþes getwǣfeð") and, on the other, emphasizing the lethal effects that illness or warfare can have on the physical vigor of the young warrior. The second hyperbaton occurs on line 1768, in the very final clause of this passage, and concerns the verb phrase ("ti soverchi" [it may overwhelm you]) and its subject ("la morte" [death]). Here the inversion of the standard syntactical order clearly aims at highlighting the tragic and inevitable conclusion of any human endeavor, that is death, by moving the key word *morte* to the very end of this passage.

Brunetti also reproduces felicitously the four enjambments of the Old English passage, that is the one between lines 1761 and 1762 ("nū is þīnes mægnes blǣd / āne hwīle," translated as "la gloria della tua forza / durerà ora qualche tempo" [the glory of your strength / will now last for some time]); lines 1762–63 ("eft sōna bið / þæt þec ādl oððe ecg," translated as "presto sarà / che morbo o spada" [soon it will be that illness or sword]); lines 1766–67 ("ēagena bearhtm / forsiteð ond forsworceð," translated as "la chiarezza degli occhi / si farà fioca e scempia" [the brightness of your eyes will grow dim and weak]); and, finally, lines 1767–68 ("semninga bið / þæt," translated as "presto sarà, / guerriero, che" [soon it will be, warrior, that]). It is noteworthy that the two synonymous Old English phrases "sōna bið" (line 1762b) and "semninga bið" (line 1768b) have both been translated by Brunetti with the same Italian phrase, that is, "presto sarà" and, like in the Old English original, they are both followed by a that-clause ("presto sarà / che" [soon it will be that]). Both "sōna bið" and "semninga bið" are given particular emphasis by the key position in which they occur, that is at the beginning of the long sentence enumerating the dangers threatening the young warrior (lines 1762–67), and in the opening of the final sentence announcing the inevitable and precocious advent of death (lines 1767–68), respectively. Also the position of the

Old English phrases "sōna bið" and "semninga bið" and of their Italian rendition "presto sarà" at the end of the line and the resulting enjambment further underscore the sense of impending doom these phrases announce.

Indeed, the lyrical appeal of the passage under consideration capitalizes on the effect of suspense created by the four enjambments listed above, a suspense that ultimately contributes to confirm the inevitable fugacity of the vigor of youth. The first enjambment of the passage ("Nū is þīnes mægnes blæd / āne hwīle" [lines 1761b–62a]) is generally maintained in the Italian verse translations. Olivero, for example, provides a rendition that is both structurally and semantically faithful ("il fiore della tua forza durerà / per un certo tempo" [the bloom of your strength will last / for some time]), with the rather free and felicitous translation of Old English *blæd* with "fiore" [bloom, flower], obviously in an attempt to find an alliterating match to the following "forza" [strength]. In Koch's translation the enjambment divides exactly the two key nouns of the Old English phrase "þīnes mægnes blæd," which is rendered "la fama / della tua forza" [the fame of your strength], with a felicitous alliterating pair, while in Ciuferri and Murray as well as in Brunetti the enjambment separates the noun phrase ("la fama della tua forza" and "la gloria della tua forza" [the fame of your strength; the glory of your strength], respectively) from its verb in the following line ("non durerà" [it won't last] and "durerà" [it will last], respectively). It is interesting to note that Ciuferri and Murray have translated the Old English verb in the negative ("non durerà"), thus making explicit and emphasizing the understood negative meaning of the Old English phrase "is . . . āne hwīle." In this respect an analogous but even more felicitous solution is the one adopted by Cecioni ("non può durare a lungo" [it cannot last long]), where again the use of the negative and of the modal verb *potere* definitely denies any possibility that a man's physical vigor can last long.

The two enjambments introduced by the phrases "sōna bið" and "semninga bið" have also been maintained in Olivero's translation,[70] and in Ciuferri and Murray's,[71] while Koch has maintained only the latter of the two enjambments. However, unlike the Old English original, in her version the line does not break after "semninga bið" ("arriverà ben presto" in her rendition), but after the equivalent of "dēað," that is "morte," which in her translation introduces a relative clause rendering the Old English verb "oferswȳðeð" as "che è più forte di te" [(death) which is stronger than you]. The sententious and irreversible character of this clause, which modifies the crucial noun "morte," represents a very powerful and fitting conclusion to this passage, and again the rhyme linking the two key words "morte" and "forte" only emphasizes the overwhelming power of death and the irrevocable end of any human strength.

Finally, an enjambment also concerns the last item in the list of symptoms of physical decline, that is the brightness of the eyes ("ēagena bearhtm" [line 1766b]), which with age will inevitably fail and grow dim ("forsiteð ond forsworceð" [line 1767a]). The Italian translations have rendered this clause rather faithfully, maintaining the syntactical structure of the Old English original, except the two prose versions by Benedetti and Cecioni. The rendition of this passage is indeed one of the few examples of felicitous translation by Benedetti, who effectively manages to reach a highly lyrical effect and to reproduce the sense of tension and expectancy of the original enjambment by means of the hyperbaton between the subject and verb, the standard succession of which is inverted, so that the verb phrase ("potrà velarsi" [it could veil itself, it could grow dim]) precedes its subject "luce degli occhi tuoi" [the light of the eyes of yours]. It is noteworthy that the occurrence of the possessive adjective "tuoi" after the noun it refers to, "occhi," is a favorite device of Italian lyrical poetry.[72] Also the doublet "forsiteð ond forsworceð" is rendered by the two coordinated verbs "velarsi" [to veil itself] and "spegnersi" [to go off, to fade away], which are linked by assonance but felicitously separated by a long hyperbaton which enhances the melancholic description of blindness advancing on the aging man. Even more intriguing is Cecioni's solution, since he has conflated the clause "ēagena bearhtm forsiteð ond forsworceð" with the last sentence of the passage ("semninga . . . oferswȳðeð") into one sentence where the three Old English verbs "forsiteð," "forsworceð," and "oferswȳðeð" are arranged in a climax ("si offuscherà"; "si spegnerà"; "sarai infine sopraffatto" [it will darken; it will go off; finally, you will be overwhelmed]). Such a solution is very effective not only from a semantic point of view but also insofar as it tries to make explicit in Italian what in the Old English original is an insistent aural link by means of both structural and interlinear alliteration as well as by homeoteleuton between the three verbs of the original, -siteð, -sworceð, and -swȳðeð. This climactic structure requires that in the Italian rendition the sequence of the two Old English verbs making up the doublet "forsiteð ond forsworceð" [it will go off and grow dim] is inverted, so that the equivalent of "forsworceð," that is, "si offuscherà" [it will grow dim], precedes the equivalent of "forsiteð," that is "si spegnerà" [it will go off]. An analogous inversion in the rendition of the two verbs is however adopted also by Benedetti ("velarsi"/"spegnersi" [to veil oneself, to grow dim/to fail, to go off]), so that here too the two verbs are arranged in a climax. In contrast, in Koch's version ("si farà buia e fiacca"), and in Ciuferri and Murray's one ("si faccia buia e fiacca") the succession of the two Old English verbs is rendered faithfully since *buia* means "dark, black" and *fiacca* "dim, weak," thereby creating an anticlimactic effect. Finally, as we have seen, Brunetti's rendition ("si farà fioca e scempia") renders the two Old English verbs with two predicative adjectives that are fundamentally synonymous.

To sum up, it can be said that the Italian translations here examined generally tend to imitate the aural effects of the Old English original, though adapting them to the fundamentally different metrics and prosody of a Romance language.

Such an adaptation implies, on the one hand, a somehow looser use of a kind of alliteration that, unlike the Germanic one, concerns only consonants occurring in whatever position within adjacent and neighboring words, and, on the other, an enhanced use of assonances and rhymes. Moreover, the Italian translators have generally aimed at reproducing the metrical and syntactical rhythm of the Old English poem. The most convincing solutions, however, have avoided a strained search for alliterating effects or a slavish imitation of the many hyperbata of the original and have instead opted for a more allusive kind of translation. Finally, an effective use of the metrical and syntactical enjambment has enabled the translators to reproduce those effects of tensions and retardation that are so crucial in *Beowulf*, thereby achieving an intriguing and varied narrative rhythm.

Lexicon and Kennings

Rendering the lexicon of the *Beowulf* poem in Italian is another serious challenge for translators because of the special nature of part of its vocabulary and the crucial role that lexicon plays in Germanic poetic diction in general.

Beside the various aspects analyzed above, the six translations here under examination also differ in their lexical and stylistic choices, which might be due, to a certain extent, also to their temporal divergences. Benedetti's translation sounds rather "foreign" to a modern reader, partly because of some linguistic aspects of the Italian language which were common in 1915 and have disappeared now (for example, the frequent but not exclusive use of *de li* instead of modern *degli* 'of the', and similar expressions), and partly because of an excessive tendency to use literary, archaic words (see, for example, *secolui*, *ricopersero*, *sovra*, and *melancoliche*, featured in the first fifty-two lines, corresponding respectively to modern *con lui* 'with him', *ricoprirono* 'covered', *sopra* 'above', and *malinconiche* 'melancholic', to name only a few), probably imitating previous Italian poetic traditions and translations. Olivero's rendition of the same fifty-two lines of text also features some literary, remote-sounding words and expressions, such as "alcuno tempo" [some time] (vs. standard Italian *un certo tempo* or *un po' di tempo*), "si dipartì" [passed away] (vs. *morì*), "dispensiero" [distributor] (vs. *distributore* or *donatore*), and "prenci" [princes] (vs. standard modern Italian *principi*), but they sound less remote in his verse translation than in Benedetti's prose one. Cecioni's translation, in contrast, avoids archaisms altogether, leading the way for the later translators, who use literary words sparingly (the passage under examination only features "seggi" [seats] in Koch, "infante" [infant] in Ciuferri and Murray, and "spartitore" [distributor] in Brunetti), and adopt a language that does not sound foreign or remote, thus reducing the distance between the poem and contemporary Italian readers.

A much harder task for the translators is the rendering of the poetic compounds and periphrastic expressions which, barely synonyms, enrich the poem with a variety of images and meaningful shifts of perspective, partly showing multiple aspects of the same referent and partly helping the poet link his half lines through alliteration. The most celebrated of these elements is perhaps the kenning, which, far from being the cryptic figure of Norse skaldic poetry, provides Old English verse with unusual and parallel visions of the same object or concept—often set as variations—delighting the audience with a sophisticated metaphorical or metonymical interplay between the referent and its designation.[73] Transferring this richness to the target language is a very difficult task, especially when the cultural framework of the two linguistic codes is profoundly different, as in the case of Old English and Italian. Translators have to choose between reproducing the kenning as it is in Old English, by means of a literal translation of its elements, or replacing it by a more "intelligible" term to help readers decipher its meaning. Old English kennings are, however, very rarely obscure, as they often appear side by side with the prosaic term they stand for, or other expressions that clarify their semantic value, so that most of the time the choice is actually more stylistic than semantic. The earliest translations under examination appear to be less "daring" in this respect, tending to give prosaic equivalents for many kennings. See, for example, "bānfatu" (line 1116) [vessel of the bones; that is, "body"], which is translated as "corpo"—the Italian word for "body"—by Olivero and Cecioni,[74] or "mægenwudu" (line 236) [wood of strength; that is, "spear"], which Olivero and Cecioni translate as "lancia" [spear] and Benedetti as "asta," which is a poetical term for "spear." Other examples are provided by "sǣwudu" (line 226) [wood of the sea], or "ȳðlida" (line 198) [traveler of the waves], both meaning "ship," which Benedetti and Cecioni translate as "nave" [ship], thereby choosing to ignore the metonymical quality of the two basewords, and consequently obliterating the distinct images that the two kennings suggest, with their load of color, smell, sound, texture, movement, and various connotations. Another consequence of replacing kennings with a more prosaic term for their referents is that the ambiguity which some of them purposefully carry gets lost in the process. Olivero, for example, translates "hringa þengel" (line 1507) [lord of rings] with "ben armato prence" [well-armed prince] and "hringa fengel" (line 2345) [also "lord of rings"] as "il generoso duce" [the generous leader]. Similarly Cecioni translates the former as "il generoso sovrano, il distributore di armille" [the generous sovereign, the distributor of bracelets] and the latter as "l'eroe protetto dalla ferrea armatura" [the hero protected by an iron corslet].[75] Both kennings, however, play with the word *hring*, which refers simultaneously to the coat of mail worn by the warrior and to the gold that the lord shares with his thanes, thus connoting Beowulf as a brave warrior and a generous (and proper) leader at the same time. Olivero's and Cecioni's translations only show one of these two aspects (the former in line 1507 and the latter in line 2345, on the basis of the context), thereby losing the ambivalence.[76]

In several instances Olivero provides a literal translation of both the kenning and the prosaic name of its referent, as in the following examples: "hronrād" (line 10) [road of the whale] as "il mare—la via della balena" [the sea—the road of the whale], "ganotes bæð" (line 1861) [bath of the gannet] as "l'oceano, il bagno della procellaria" [the ocean, the bath of the procellarian], "woruldcandel" (line 1965) [candle of the world] as "il sole, la candela del mondo" [the sun, the candle of the world], "beadolēoma" (line 1523) [light of battle] as "la sua spada—il lampo della battaglia" [his sword, the flash of battle], "ȳðlida" (line 198) as "nave, snella viatrice dell'onde" [ship, slim wayfarer of the waves] or "sǣgenga" (line 1882) [seagoer] as "la nave, la viatrice dei mari" [the ship, the wayfarer of the seas]. Cecioni does the same with "hronrād" and "ganotes bæð" (maybe influenced by Olivero): "mare, sentiero della balena" [sea, path of the whale] and "il mare, regno della procellaria" [the sea, realm of the procellarian], respectively.[77] As Jorge Luis Borges affirms, however, "to explain kennings, reducing them to single words, is to explain them away,"[78] and, although part of the imagery of the kennings gets preserved by these renderings, the fun of the deciphering and recognition process is lost, as well as the feeling of cultural bondage that the process generates.

On other occasions, however, these early translations do imitate the Old English kennings, especially when their meaning is clarified either by the context or by the close presence of the prosaic word for the referent or more transparent circumlocutions. It is the case, for example, of "windgeard" (line 1224), literally translated as "la dimora dei venti" [the house of the winds] by both Olivero and Cecioni, or "swanrād" (line 200), "sentiero dei cigni" [path of the swans] in Olivero and "sentiero del cigno" [path of the swan] in Cecioni, or else "heofones gim" (line 2072), rendered as "la gemma del cielo" [the gem of heaven] in all translations, "homera lāfe" (line 2829), translated as "il prodotto di martelli" [the product of hammers] by Olivero and, with a metonymic shift, "opera del fabbro" [work of the smith] by Cecioni. Another interesting example is given by "wælrāpas" (line 1610), which Benedetti translates as "ghiacciuoli" [icicles], but is rendered as "catene delle acque" [chains of the waters] by Cecioni and, more prosaically but reflecting the original imagery, as "le corde che legavano il profondo mare" [the ropes that were tying the deep sea] by Olivero.[79] In some cases Olivero imitates the kenning but modifies it slightly, presumably trying to make it closer to the Italian poetic tradition and therefore more intelligible to a modern Italian reader, as in the case of "rodores candel" (line 1572), which he renders as "l'eterea fiamma" [the ethereal flame], or "wēgflota" (line 1907), which he translates as "il legno sull'onde fluttante" [the wood floating on the waves].[80]

Koch is the first Italian translator who systematically reproduces the kennings faithfully, thus preserving the complexity of their metaphorical and metonymical games, as well as the variety and abundance of connotations that they reproduce. She does so with the help of a precious set of footnotes which are signaled in the text and clarify the meaning of a particular expression if needs be. Her footnotes leave the reader free to decide whether to read them or not, and in so doing, they avoid spoiling the fun or reducing the poetic value and artistry of the kennings. Her translation opens the way for the later ones—the one by Ciuferri and Murray and the one by Brunetti—which, although not equally systematically, show a much bigger number of literal reproductions of kennings than Benedetti's, Olivero's, or Cecioni's translations.[81] Neither Ciuferri and Murray, nor Brunetti, though, use footnotes: they provide their translations with endnotes not signaled in the text, so that readers do not know which words or expressions are explained and are forced to go back and forth in the book, between text and endnotes, sometimes fruitlessly, if they want to check if further information on a given kenning is available.

Ciuferri and Murray, in particular, are heavily influenced by Koch's renditions and adopt a number of them. See, for example, "ganotes bæð" (line 1861), translated as "la vasca del gabbiano" [the basin of the seagull]; "forstes bend" (line 1609), "i vincoli del gelo" [the bonds of frost]; "wælrāpas" (line 1610), "i ceppi dell'acqua" [the bonds of water]; "hǣðstapa" (line 1368), "il vagabondo della brughiera" [the wanderer of the moor]; "gomen glēobēam" (line 2263), "il diletto del legno sonoro" [the pleasure of the sonorous wood]; "ecgþracu" (line 596), "uragani di lame" [hurricanes of blades]; "ecga gelāc" (line 1168), "giostre di lame"[82] [carousel(s) of blades]; "borda gebræc" (line 2259), "cozzo degli scudi" [clashing of the shields]; "hildelēoma" (line 1143), "lampo della battaglia" [flash of battle]; "fēla lāf" (line 1032), "gli avanzi delle lime" [the leftovers of the files]; "homera lāf" (line 2829), "l'avanzo del martello" [the leftovers of the hammer]; "þrecwudu" (line 1246), "legno d'assalto" [wood for assault]; "bordwudu beorhtan" (line 1243), "le lucide targhe di legno" [the shiny wooden shields];[83] and "friðusibb folca" (line 2017), "patto di pace fra i popoli" [pact of peace between peoples].[84]

An interesting aspect of the translations under examination concerns a group of kennings denoting "warrior" or "battle" and involving a metonymy concerning the material of which weapons are made (*lind* 'linden', *æsc* 'ash'), such as: "lindwiga" (line 2603), "lindplega" (line 2039), and "æscwiga" (line 2042). These are "complex" or "double" kennings, where the limiting word (the first member of the compound) stands for something else: *lind* refers metonymically to "shields" and *æsc* to "spears." Interestingly, most Italian translations seem to have troubles with these complex kennings and simplify them by eliminating the metonymy (the only exception is "æscwiga" in Koch, literally rendered as "combattente col frassino" [fighter with ash], but compare her "guerriero con lo scudo" [warrior with shield] and "gioco degli scudi" [game with shields] for "lindwiga" and "lindplega," respectively). A similar process takes place for complex kennings where the limiting word comprises a synecdoche, designating weapons by means of a part of them (*bord* 'board' for "shields" or *ecg* 'edge' for "swords"), as in "ecghete" (line 1738), "ecgþracu" (line 596), "ecga gelāc" (line 1168), or "borda gebræc" (line 2259).[85] In these instances Brunetti is the only translator rendering consistently *ecg-* with "lame" [blades], but he fails to render *borda* with "tavole" [boards], reducing the kenning to "frangersi di scudi" [breaking of shields]. Koch and Ciuferri and Murray (probably influenced, in turn, by Koch), only venture the Italian *lame* in *ecgþracu* and *ecga gelāc*, avoiding the synecdoche in the other cases, whilst Benedetti, Olivero, and Cecioni avoid the synecdoche in all items. This restraint produces a double negative effect: on the one hand, it reduces the beauty and artistry of the kennings and of poetic diction in general; on the other hand, it deprives readers of that mixture of colors, sounds, and images that the original kennings would have conjured up in their minds.[86]

Another interesting set of kennings are those that are strictly related to Germanic cultural concepts, which might sound foreign and therefore scarcely intelligible to an Italian audience. All the various designations of the king/lord as the "distributor (or guardian) of gold" that appear in the poem (for example, *bēaggyfa, sincgyfa, goldgyfa, bēaga brytta, sinces brytta, goldwine gumena, sinca baldor, bēahhorda weard,* and *hordweard*), or of his retinue as the "drinkers of beer" (*ealodrincende*), or of the queen/woman as the "weaver of peace" (*freoðuwebbe, friðusibb folca*), might be hard to decipher for someone who is not well acquainted with the Germanic *comitatus*, the symbolism of the beer or mead drinking or of the banquet hall in general, or the function of women as a means to establish alliances between different tribes or peoples (although this last concept is not restricted to Germanic society). The various Italian translations under examination admirably tend to reproduce, for the most part, the Old English poetical designations, with their dense meaning. The kennings "bēaga brytta" (lines 35, 352, and 1487) and "sinces brytta" (lines 607, 1170, 1922, and 2071), for example, are consistently translated in a literal way with such expressions as "distributore di tesori" [distributor of treasures], "distributore di armille" [distributor of bracelets], and similar ones, and the same applies to "ealodrincende" (line 1945), which is literally translated as "i bevitori di birra" [the drinkers of beer] (Benedetti and Ciuferri and Murray) or with similar expressions. The origin and meaning of these expressions—and their implications—are explained in the footnotes (Koch) or endnotes (Brunetti, Cecioni, and partly Ciuferri and Murray), when provided, and, as far as Brunetti is concerned, also in the introduction. There are exceptions, however. The compound "bēaggyfa" (line 1102), for example, is translated as "liberale prence" [liberal prince] by Olivero and "generoso sovrano" [generous sovereign] by Cecioni, who both change the sense of the compound in so doing, whilst Brunetti renders it with a generic "signore" [lord], thus canceling the poetic expression altogether.

One last aspect of these translations worth exploring is the way in which the various occurrences of the same expression are treated. Given the formulaic nature of Old English poetry, the tendency to variation features side by side with a tendency to repetition. The expression "goldwine gumena" [gold friend of men], for example, occurs three times in the poem (lines 1171, 1476, 1602), always referring to Hrothgar and to his royal function of "gold-giver." One might reasonably expect translations to reproduce this deliberate repetition; however, only Koch, Ciuferri and Murray, and Brunetti have the same rendition in all three occurrences ("amico d'oro degli uomini" [gold friend of men] in Koch and Ciuferri and Murray, and, less faithfully, "generoso amico d'uomini" [generous friend of men] in Brunetti); Benedetti, Olivero, and Cecioni vary their translations, disregarding the intentional repetition.[87] The same can be said for genuine formulas,[88] as in the case, for example, of "heard under helme" (lines 342, 404, 2539), which is translated consistently only in Koch and Ciuferri and Murray ("ardito sotto l'elmo" [brave under the helmet]) and Brunetti ("forte sotto l'elmo" [strong under the helmet]), while Olivero, Cecioni, and Benedetti translate the three occurrences in differing ways.[89]

In conclusion, the analysis of the way in which Old English poetic lexicon has been treated in the six Italian translations of *Beowulf* under examination shows a progressive chronological differentiation in both the quality of the lexicon used and the way in which poetical compounds are treated. The former, that is to say, the general lexicon, is more archaic in Benedetti's and Olivero's translations, and closer to standard Italian in the later ones. As far as poetical compounds—and kennings in particular—are concerned, the earliest three translations tend to pay little attention to Old English poetical artistry, and either ignore or even modify compounds at times in order to bridge the gap between the original language of the poem and the target language of the translation. Conversely, Koch's translation and the subsequent ones (Ciuferri and Murray's—which is heavily influenced by Koch—and Brunetti's) try to reproduce the lexicon in a way that shows awareness and respect for the artistry of the Old English poet and the poetical devices that he employs, reproducing them more faithfully, powerfully in Koch and more flexibly in Brunetti.

Variation and Appositions

The appositive style is another typical feature of Old English poetry that translators have to face in their renditions of the poem.[90] Once again, the perception of the distance between the two cultural and linguistic (poetic) codes—Old English and Italian—seems to worry the earlier translators much more than the most recent ones, as can be seen from the two passages analyzed here.

The first passage describes the laying of Scyld Scefing's corpse on the funerary ship. The six lines under examination (lines 32–37) contain three examples of variation: the ship is called "hringedstefna" [the one with the ringed prow] in line 32 and "æþelinges fær" [the ship of the atheling] in line 33 (both the subject of "stod"); Scyld Scefing is called "lēofne þēoden" [the beloved chief] in line 34, "bēaga bryttan" [the distributor of rings] in line 35, and "mǣrne" [the famous] in line 36 (all forming the direct object of "ālēdon"); finally the ship is said to be full of many treasures, which are called "mādma" [treasures, precious things] in line 36 and "frætwa" [precious things, decorated weapons] in line 37:[91]

> Þǣr æt hȳðe stōd *hringedstefna*
> īsig ond ūtfūs, *æþelinges fær*;
> ālēdon þā *lēofne þēoden*,
> 35 *bēaga bryttan* on bearm scipes,
> *mǣrne* be mǣste. Þǣr wæs *mādma* fela
> of feorwegum *frætwa* gelǣded;[92]

The Italian translations tend to differ in the way they treat their model. Benedetti partly reproduces the variation pattern in the first two instances (although she misinterprets "mǣrne"), but groups the various denominations together—presumably to make the style sound closer to Italian—thus violating the syntactic pattern of the original. However, she transforms "mādma" and "frætwa" into two distinct elements ("ricchezze" [riches] and "gioielli" [jewels]) joined by the conjunction "e" [and] and followed by a third element ("armi" [weapons]):

> Là, nel porto, stava *la ferrigna inanellata prora*, *la nave de l'Atelingo*, pronta a salpare. E *il diletto lor sire*, *il Distributore de le armille agli eroi*, essi deposero in seno a la nave da l'albero più potente. Era il vascello carico *di ricchezze molte e di gioielli*, e de le armi tolte in lontani combattimenti.[93]

Olivero, in contrast, bravely reproduces the variation pattern rather faithfully, even from the syntactic point of view, signaling the distinct denominations by means of dashes:

> Colà nel porto stava *il vascello dalla prora di anelli adorna*, lucente e pronto al viaggio,—*vascello adatto ad un nobile principe*; essi deposero quindi *il loro amato duce*,
> 35 *di collane dispensiero*, nel grembo della nave,—
> *il loro duce glorioso* presso l'albero. Vi erano molti *tesori*, *cesellati oggetti preziosi* portati da lontane contrade;[94]

His verse translation probably grants him more freedom in terms of syntactic constructions, but nevertheless his choice sets him apart from the other two early translators, as Cecioni, like Benedetti, tends to group the various denominations together, thereby modifying the original syntactic structure. At times he even eliminates them, as in the case of "eroe glorioso" [glorious hero], which becomes the subject of an independent clause, thus violating the original structure, and also in the case of "mādma" and "frætwa," which, again similarly to Benedetti's translation, become two distinct elements joined by "e" [and]:

> Là, all'approdo, stava *la nave dalla prora arcuata, il vascello del principe*, coperto di ghiaccio, ansioso di salpare. Là, nel cuore della nave, essi deposero *il loro amato signore, il distributore di tesori*; *l'eroe glorioso* giacque presso l'albero maestro. Intorno a lui furono ammucchiate *immense ricchezze* e *splendide armature* venute da lontani paesi.[95]

Koch generally mirrors the variation pattern and the syntactic structure of the original, except for "altero" [proud], which departs from the model,[96] becoming an adjective dependent on "il loro frantumanelli" [their breaker of rings]:

> Nel porto lo aspettava   *una prua curva, a anello,*
> impaziente, ghiacciata.   *La nave del principe.*
> E quelli consegnarono   *il re che avevano amato,*
> 35   al grembo della nave,   *il loro frantumanelli,*
> contro l'albero, *altero*.   C'erano molte *gioie,*
> *preziosità* portate   da paesi lontani.[97]

Ciuferri and Murray reproduce the original pattern in the second and third variation set, but erase the first, as they change the first denomination for ship, which is independent in the Old English text, into an adjectival expression ("un anello la sua prua" [her prow [was] a ring]) dependent on "la nave del principe" [the prince's ship]:

> Lo attendeva all'approdo,   *un anello la sua prua,*
> coperta di ghiaccio e già pronta   *la nave del principe;*
> poi lo posarono,   *il tanto amato sovrano,*
> 35   *colui che anelli donava,*   nel grembo della nave,
> *il celebre uomo* contro l'albero;   c'erano molti *gioielli,*
> *preziosi* portati   da paesi lontani.[98]

Brunetti is the translator who reproduces the appositive style of the original passage more faithfully, although he inverts, presumably for metrical reasons, "lo spartitore di anelli" [the distributor of rings] and "l'amato re" [the beloved king], and "ornamenti" [ornaments], and "tesori" [treasures]:

> era nel porto *una prua ricurva*, ghiaccia e pronta
> a prendere il largo, *l'imbarcazione del principe;*

> deposero allora *lo spartitore d'anelli*,
> 35 *l'amato re* in grembo alla nave,
> *il rinomato* presso l'albero; *ornamenti*
> vi portarono molti *tesori* di terre remote[99]

One might object that this state of affairs might be described more correctly in terms of an opposition between prose and verse translations, as Olivero reproduces variation rather faithfully, although being an "early" translator. However, the second passage here analyzed, concerning the passage describing Beowulf's fight with the dragon (lines 2556–64), shows that Olivero's faithfulness to the original appositive style is not consistent. This extract too contains three examples of variation: the breath of the dragon is called "oruð āglǣcean" in line 2557 and "hat hildeswat" in line 2558 (both are the subject of "cwom"); Beowulf is called "biorn under beorge" in line 2559 and "Gēata dryhten" in line 2560 (both are the subject of "onswāf"); and finally Beowulf's sword is called "sweord" in line 2562 and "gomele lāfe" in line 2563 (both are the direct object of "gebrǣd"):

> From ǣrest cwōm
> *oruð āglǣcean*   ūt of stāne,
> *hāt hildeswāt*;   hrūse dynede.
> *Biorn* under beorge   bordrand onswāf
> 2560 wið ðām gryregieste,   *Gēata dryhten*;
> ðā wæs hringbogan   heorte gefȳsed
> sæcce tō sēceanne.   *Sweord* ǣr gebrǣd
> gōd gūðcyning,   *gomele lāfe*,
> ecgum unslāw;[100]

In this passage, the chronological development in the treatment of variation in the translations is more evident. Benedetti, as expected, groups the distinct denominations together (and even completely tranforms the first set, changing the first four half lines into "si sentiva ansare e sbuffare il mostro ardente" [the fiery monster could be heard panting and puffing]):

> Si sentiva ansare e sbuffare il mostro ardente: la terra e le pietre ne erano scosse. *Il guerriero, il signore dei Geti*, entrando nel cavo roccioso, alzò lo scudo, onde meglio difendersi da la terribile creatura. Furiosamente pulsava il cuore del Drago, mentre cercava la zuffa. Il prudente re guerriero aveva già tratta *la spada, l'antica reliquia* bene affilata[101]

In contrast with his treatment of variation in the first passage analyzed, Olivero here echoes Benedetti's example and groups the various denominations together, showing that this trend is not only a feature of prose translations but concerns all three earlier translations:

>   E prima venne
>   fuori della rupe *il soffio del mostro,*
>   *l'ardente alito ostile;* la terra echeggiò.
>   Agitò lo scudo, stando sotto la rupe, *il guerriero,*
> 2560 *il signore dei Geati,* contro l'orrido démone;
>   quindi fu il cuore del drago dalle cerchiate spire incitato
>   a cercar la lotta; e già il bellicoso re
>   brandiva *la spada affilata, antica eredità della sua stirpe,*
>   l'affilato acciaro;[102]

Cecioni's translation shows the same grouping pattern, but transforms "ecgum unslāw" [with edges not blunt] into a noun phrase ("l'acuminato ferro" [the sharp iron], like Olivero's "l'affilato acciaro") and inserts it between the other two denominations for "sword":

> *L'alito del mostro, il soffio ardente della battaglia,* irruppe violento dalla roccia e la terra ne rimbombò. *Il sovrano dei Geati, l'eroe intrepido,* addossato alla rupe, sollevò lo scudo contro l'orribile nemico. L'animo del drago dalle molte spire ardeva nell'ansia della lotta. Già il valoroso principe aveva sguainata *la spada, l'acuminato ferro, antico retaggio della sua stirpe.*[103]

Koch, breaking with the earlier tradition, reproduces the syntactic pattern of the original more faithfully, with the exception of the first set, where the two denominations are brought side by side:

>   Prima di tutto uscì
>   dalla roccia *il fiato del Mostro,   un rovente sudore di guerra:*
>   ne rimbombò la terra.   Sotto il tumulo, scosse
>   *l'eroe* lo scudo tondo   contro l'Ospite orribile,
> 2560 *il signore dei Geati.*   Ravvolto nei suoi anelli,
>   in cuore suo, smaniava   per cercare lo scontro.
>   Aveva già sguainato   *la spada,* il grande re
>   guerriero, *antica reliqua*   dal filo non smussato.[104]

Ciuferri and Murray reproduce the syntactic pattern faithfully, and so does Brunetti:

>   Prima di tutto uscì
>   *il respiro del mostro*   fuori della roccia:
>   *un rovente vapore di battaglia;*   la terra rimbombò.
>   Sotto il tumulo, *l'eroe*   il tondo scudo agitò
> 2560 contro il terribile ospite,   *il signore dei Geati.*
>   Allora la creatura, ravvolta su se stessa,   smaniava in cuor suo
>   per cercare il conflitto.   Già *la spada* avea sguainata
>   l'eccellente re guerriero,   *l'antico cimelio*
>   dalla lama affilata;[105]

venne dapprima
il fiato del nemico fuori della pietra,
torrido vapore di guerra; la terra risuonò;
l'uomo brandì lo scudo sotto il tumulo,

2560   *il signore dei Geati* contro l'orrendo straniero;
       a quell'essere a spire smaniava il cuore
       di cercare la lotta; aveva estratto *la spada*
       il grande re della guerra, *l'antico lascito*
       impotente di lama;[106]

As in the case of kennings, therefore, the six translations seem to show two different trends: a tendency to be less faithful to the original and closer to Italian poetic tradition, which can be observed in the earliest three translations, and a contrasting tendency to reproduce the style of the original more faithfully, which is typical of the three most recent renditions. In this case, however, Oliviero distinguishes himself for a hint of modernity, coming closer to the original at times, though not consistently.

Conclusion

In conclusion, it can be said that the translations discussed above have generally aimed at a compromise between a "domesticating" intent and an imitative one. Unsurprisingly, not all of them have met their target, or not always. The versions by Benedetti and Olivero, for example, are the ones more concerned with meeting the standards of Italian literary style and language, often, especially in the case of Benedetti's translation, to the detriment of the rigor and accuracy of the rendition of the Old English text. On the other hand, being the earliest translations, these two could admittedly not benefit from the greater understanding and appreciation of the poem that nearly a century of vivacious *Beowulf* scholarship has granted to later translators. In this respect, Cecioni's version represents a midpoint between what may be called this "first generation" of Italian translations of *Beowulf*, and the subsequent one represented by Koch and Brunetti (with Ciuferri and Murray being little more than Koch's epigones), since Cecioni combines philological rigor with an effective, at times ingenious, rendition of the Old English original in the target language. However, the translations that show a greater awareness of the highly skillful and multifaceted poetic art of *Beowulf* are the two verse translations by Koch and Brunetti. While the former focuses on the lyrical and evocative potential of the poem and betrays a refined poetic sensitivity on the part of the translator, the latter is noteworthy for the accuracy of its approach to the text and to the historical context therein represented, as well as for its rendition of the narrative scope of *Beowulf* as the greatest, founding epic of the Anglo-Saxons.[107]

Notes

The accompanying CD contains a recording of the first fifty-two lines of the poem from the Italian translation by Giuseppe Brunetti, read by Filippo Marsala.

1. Grion, "*Beowulf:* Poema epico anglosassone del VII secolo."

2. Benedetti, *La canzone di "Beowulf."*

3. Olivero, *Beowulf.* Samples from this translation had already been published in 1915: see below, n. 14. For the reviews of Olivero's translation, see Fry, *"Beowulf" and "The Fight at Finnsburh,"* no. 1582; and Greenfield and Robinson, *Bibliography of Publications on Old English Literature,* no. 1652. Olivero's translation was, in turn, rendered into French by Monnet.

4. Cecioni, *Beowulf.*

5. Koch, *Beowulf.*

6. Ciuferri and Murray, *Beowulf e il Frammento di Finnsburh.*

7. Brunetti, *Beowulf.*

8. Pecchio, *Storia critica della poesia inglese.*

9. Turner, *History of the Anglo-Saxons.* Pecchio's Italian version is based on Turner's third edition (London: Longmans, 1820).

10. See Osborn, "Translations, Versions, Illustrations," p. 346.

11. A number of English versions and paraphrases of *Beowulf* had been published since Turner's 1805 edition of *The History of the Anglo-Saxons.* The first complete Danish verse translation was published in 1820 by Grundtvig, *Bjowulfs drape.* It is also worth remembering that in 1815 Grímur Jónsson Thorkelin published the first complete Latin translation of *Beowulf:* see his *De Danorum rebus gestis secul. III & IV.*

12. Schuhmann, "*Beovulf,* antichissimo poema epico." Fry erroneously labels it as the "first Italian translation," and Greenfield and Robinson present it as a "summary," while in fact it is neither: see Fry, *"Beowulf" and "The Fight at Finnsburh,"* no. 1864, and Greenfield and Robinson, *Bibliography of Publications on Old English Literature,* no. 1680.

13. *Beowulf,* in *Traduzioni dalla poesia anglo-sassone.* The selected passages from *Beowulf* are at pp. 73–119 and relevant notes at pp. 121–26; the translation of the *Finnsburh Fragment* is at pp. 127–29 and relevant notes at pp. 131–32; the Old English original is not provided.

14. Sanesi, *Poemi anglosassoni VI–X secolo,* pp. 3–23.

15. See Teresi, *Poesia medievale.*

16. Basari, "*Beowulf.*"

17. *O Mostro de Caim.* See also Magoun, "Béowulf in Denmark."

18. See Robinson, "Two Aspects of Variation" and *"Beowulf" and the Appositive Style.*

19. Wyatt, *Beowulf.*

20. "Il valore artistico della canzone è quasi nullo" (Benedetti, *La canzone di "Beowulf,"* p. 18).

21. On the fit divisions in *Beowulf,* see Orchard, *Critical Companion to "Beowulf,"* pp. 91–97.

22. Wyatt, *Beowulf: Edited with Textual Footnotes.*

23. Klaeber, *Beowulf and the Fight at Finnsburg,* 3rd ed.

24. Wrenn, *Beowulf with the Finnsburg Fragment.*

25. Wrenn, *Beowulf with the Finnesburg Fragment,* 3rd ed.

26. On this point, see the remarks by Gendre, "Tradurre e altro," esp. pp. 16–17n27.

27. Jack, *Beowulf: A Student Edition*.

28. Mitchell and Robinson, *Beowulf: An Edition with Relevant Shorter Texts*.

29. Kiernan, *Electronic Beowulf*.

30. Mitchell and Irvine, *"Beowulf" Repunctuated*.

31. See Brunetti, "Tradurre *Beowulf*," pp. 68–69; and his "Ritradurre il *Beowulf*," pp. 206–7.

32. See Brunetti, "Tradurre *Beowulf*," p. 70, and "Ritradurre il *Beowulf*," pp. 209–10.

33. Orchard, *Critical Companion to "Beowulf*," pp. 58–61 (p. 59). On the rhetorical structure and highly formulaic character of the incipit of *Beowulf*, see also Campbell, "Adaptation of Classical Rhetoric," and Orchard, "Oral Tradition," esp. pp. 104–5.

34. All quotations from the Old English original are from Klaeber, *Beowulf and the Fight at Finnsburg*, 3rd ed. "So. The Spear-Danes in days gone by / and the kings who ruled them had courage and greatness. / We have heard of those princes' heroic campaigns. / There was Shield Sheafson, scourge of many tribes, / a wrecker of mead-benches, rampaging among foes. / This terror of the hall troops had come far. / A foundling to start with, he would flourish later on / as his powers waxed and his worth was proved. / In the end each clan on the outlying coasts / beyond the whale-road had to yield to him / and begin to pay tribute. That was one good king" (Heaney, *Beowulf: A New Verse Translation*, p. 3).

35. See Bertone, "Allitterazione."

36. In keeping with Germanic alliteration, the alliterating sounds considered mainly belong to verbs and nouns or adjectives, only rarely to adverbs and conjunctions.

37. In Italian the letters *c* and *cc*, *g* and *gg* represent a velar plosive if followed by back vowels such as *a*, *o*, and *u*, and by consonants such as *h*, *r*, and *l*. They represent a palatal affricate if followed by front vowels such as *e* and *i*.

38. Olivero, *Beowulf*, p. 3.

39. It is not clear why Koch translates *eorlas* with "Eruli," which, as she explains in the relevant footnote and also in her "Glossary of Proper Names," apparently were the most ruthless and bloodthirsty of the Germanic nations; eventually, they were probably absorbed by the Danes: see her *Beowulf*, p. 3n6 and p. 272.

40. Koch, *Beowulf*, p. 3.

41. Ciuferri and Murray, *Beowulf e il Frammento di Finnsburh*, p. 57.

42. Brunetti, *Beowulf*, p. 99.

43. See Brunetti, "Tradurre *Beowulf*," p. 70, and "Ritradurre il *Beowulf*," p. 217.

44. Brunetti, "Ritradurre il *Beowulf*," pp. 209–10.

45. See Orchard, *Critical Companion to "Beowulf*," p. 61.

46. See Cassidy, "How Free Was the Anglo-Saxon Scop?"

47. Nearly every sentence in Ciuferri and Murray's translation features a hyperbaton, while Olivero's use of this rhetoric figure is more moderate.

48. Brunetti, "Tradurre *Beowulf*," p. 71.

49. Brunetti, "Ritradurre il *Beowulf*," p. 216.

50. For a definition of *apo koinou*, see Mitchell, "'Apo koinou' in Old English Poetry?" esp. p. 496; but cf. Stanley, "'Apo koinou' Chiefly in *Beowulf*."

51. This noun translates *eorlas* and looks like an ethnonym; however, in the relevant footnote, Benedetti explains that *Atelinghi* means "princes, lords, thanes": see her *La canzone di "Beowulf*," p. 39n1.

52. Benedetti, *La canzone di Beowulf*, p. 39.

53. Cecioni, *Beowulf*, p. 3.

54. For a review of the use of understatement and litotes in *Beowulf*, see Schaefer, "Rhetoric and Style," pp. 113–15.

55. Such is the case with the Old English "hē þæs frōfre gebād," which is rendered as "colui che tanto conforto diede" [he who gave so much comfort]; or with the last three lines of the passage in question which are translated as "onorato fu da tutti quei vicini che più spesso battevano i mari; costretti furono essi a pagargli tributi d'oro, finché egli divenne loro buon re" [he was honored by all those neighboring tribes who most often crossed the sea; they were obliged to pay him tribute until he became their good king]. Also in the phrase "wēox under wolcnum," *wēox* is not translated, or, rather, misinterpreted as "wretched" and the whole phrase is therefore rendered as "miserabile sotto le nubi" [wretched under the clouds].

56. See Orchard, *Critical Companion to "Beowulf,"* pp. 158–62, and relevant bibliography. For a recent discussion of Hrothgar's sermon, see also Gendre, "Coppie di opposti nel *Beowulf*," pp. 62–63, 84–89, and 98–99, and for other homiletic elements in *Beowulf*, see also Tripp, "Bad Breath at the Barrow," pp. 13–14; Tripp, "No Rest for the Wicked"; Tripp, "Homiletic Sense of Time in *Beowulf*"; and Tripp, "Summing Up the Dragon Episode."

57. See Orchard, *Critical Companion to "Beowulf,"* p. 161, esp. n. 153, and Lapidge, "Archetype of *Beowulf*," pp. 38–40.

58. For a recent study on the verb *sweorcan* and its compounds and derivatives, especially in *Beowulf*, see Di Sciacca, "*Sweorcan*."

59. Clemoes, *Interactions of Thought and Language*, pp. 42–46, esp. p. 44, and Orchard, *Critical Companion to "Beowulf,"* p. 161.

60. Cf. above, n. 57.

61. Klaeber, *Beowulf and the Fight at Finnsburg*, p. 66. "For a brief while your strength is in bloom / but it fades quickly; and soon there will follow / illness or the sword to lay you low, / or a sudden fire or surge of water / or jabbing blade or javelin from the air / or repellent age. Your piercing eye / will dim and darken; and death will arrive, / dear warrior, to sweep you away" (Heaney, *Beowulf: A New Verse Translation*, p. 57).

62. Benedetti, *La canzone di "Beowulf,"* p. 94.

63. Olivero, *Beowulf*, p. 121.

64. Cecioni, *Beowulf*, p. 69.

65. On this anachronism, see p. 156, and n. 26 above.

66. Koch, *Beowulf*, p. 157.

67. Ciuferri and Murray, *Beowulf e il Frammento di Finnsburh*, p. 173.

68. Brunetti, *Beowulf*, pp. 189–91.

69. The only exception is represented by the noun phrase "atol yldo" [repellent age], consisting of an adjective and a noun.

70. Olivero's translation of the lines in question reads: "quindi avverrà / che morbo . . ." [then it will happen / that illness . . .] and "subito sarai / dalla morte sopraffatto" [soon you will be / overwhelmed by death].

71. Ciuferri and Murray's translation reads: "potrebbe darsi / che la malattia . . ." [it could happen / that illness . . .] and "Quanto prima succederà / che te guerriero . . ." [very soon it will happen / that you warrior . . .]. Here, however, in the rendition of "sōna bið" as "potrebbe darsi," the use of the modal verb *potere* and the conditional is particularly infelicitous because it definitely weakens the fateful tone of the Old English phrase.

72. Such a use of the possessive pronoun was a favorite with the major poet of Italian Romanticism, Giacomo Leopardi.

73. The term *kenning* derives from the thirteenth-century treatise on skaldic poetical techniques by Snorri Sturluson (*Skáldskaparmál*). As Snorri's definition is rather ambiguous, the term has been interpreted in two contrasting ways, on the basis of the nature of the relationship between the referent and the base word (or second element) of the compound. Some scholars restrict the term *kenning* to the compounds where this relationship is based on a metaphor (e.g., *heafodgimm* 'gem of the head' = "eye"; *woruldcandel* 'candle of the world' = "sun"; *sæhengest* 'horse of the sea' = "ship," etc.), while others extend its realm also to metonymic and synecdochic compounds (e.g., *lindplega* 'play of linden' = "battle"; *bēaggifa* 'giver of rings' = "king, lord," etc.). In the present work the term will be used in its broadest sense. For the "extended" interpretation of the term, see Meißner, *Die Kenningar der Skalden*; and Brinton, "Linguistic Approach." For the contrasting opinion, see Heusler, "Heusler über Meißner"; Brodeur, *Art of "Beowulf"*; and Gardner, "Application of the Term 'Kenning.'" On the kenning in general see Marquardt, *Die ae Kenningar*; Borges, *Las Kénningar*, trans. Di Giovanni, "The Kenning"; Gardner, "OE Kenning"; and Stewart, "Kenning and Riddle in Old English." On the different nature of kennings in Old English and Old Norse, see van der Merwe-Scholtz, *Kenning in Anglo-Saxon and Old Norse Poetry*. On the appositive style see Robinson, *"Beowulf" and the Appositive Style*.

74. Benedetti translates the compound as "ossa" [bones] by using (perhaps unaware?) a synecdoche. Cf also "bānhūs" (lines 2508 and 3147) [house of the bones], which Benedetti translates as "le ossa del suo corpo" [the bones of his body] and "il corpo" [the body], Oliviero as "il corpo" and "il cadavere" [the corpse], and Cecioni as "membra" [limbs] and "corpo."

75. Benedetti renders the two kennings less faithfully as "principe degli eroi" [prince of heroes] and "principe guerriero" [warrior prince].

76. Olivero's translation for "hringa fengel," in particular, misses the point, since the poet is not describing Beowulf as a particularly generous prince but as a proper leader, who fulfills his role of "princeps" within the Germanic "comitatus," distributing gold to his followers. See below.

77. For "ganotes bæð" Benedetti has a less faithful "l'onda, ove si tuffano gli edredoni" [the wave, where the eiders dive].

78. Borges, *Las Kénningar*, trans. Di Giovanni, p. 36.

79. Benedetti's prose translation is rather free compared to the others, and she often skips terms, conflating words and sentences, and changing expressions radically (probably in accordance with her already mentioned opinion that the artistic value of the poem is very limited). See, for example, "swanrād" (line 200), which she renders as "il bianco solco spumoso" [the white foamy crease], "il bagno degli edredoni" [the bath of the eiders], partly basing her translation on "ganotes bæð" (line 1861), and partly adding an imaginative bit which is not in the Old English.

80. Cf. "legno vidi già dritto e veloce / correr lo mar" [I saw a wood journeying on the sea, straight and quick] and "la fiamma del sol" [the flame of the sun] (Dante, *Divina Commedia*, Paradiso, XIII, 136–37, and I, 80, respectively [Petrocchi, *La Commedia secondo l'antica vulgata*]).

81. See, for example, their translations of "hringa þengel" (line 1507) and "hringa fengel" (line 2345), mentioned above: "il signore degli anelli" [the lord of rings] (Koch and Ciuferri and Murray) and "il principe degli anelli" [the prince of rings] (Brunetti). Koch explains the ambivalence in a footnote, and so do Ciuferri and Murray in an endnote.

82. Ciuferri and Murray: "giostra" [sing].

83. In this case Koch is probably influenced in turn by Olivero. *Targa* is a poetic term for "shield," often referring to medieval rectangular light ones, used in carousels.

84. Cf. also "gomenwudu" (line 1065), translated as "il legno dilettoso" [the delighting wood] in Koch and, with inversion, "il dilettuoso legno" in Ciuferri and Murray; and "byrnwiga" (line 2918), "cotta addosso, il guerriero" [with his coat of mail on, the warrior] in Koch, and, in inverted order, "il guerriero, cotta addosso" in Ciuferri and Murray. Other, more obvious, parallelisms are likely to be a matter of coincidence.

85. "Ecghete" can be read as comprising a further metonymy, where weapons stand for warriors. Cf. Olivero, "odio di guerrieri" [hate of warriors].

86. The same can be said for such expressions as "scyldwiga" (line 288), "gārwiga" (lines 2674 and 2811) and "byrnwiga" (line 2918), where the limiting words have the main function of bearing the alliterating sound, as in the examples above, but nevertheless enrich the basewords with the elements and connotations they summon and are associated with, which vanish once the kenning is reduced to a simplex. For some reason the Italian translations reproduce the first element of the compounds only half of the times (when rendering "gārwiga" in line 2811 and "byrnwiga"), and leave it out in the other instances ("scyldwiga"—apart from Cecioni, having "soldato coraggioso che sa maneggiare lo scudo" [brave soldier who knows how to handle a shield]—and "gārwiga" in line 2674).

87. Benedetti has "verace amico deeli [*sic*] uomini" (line 1171) [true friend of men], "amico degli uomini" (line 1476) [friend of men], and "Distributore dei tesori" (line 1602) [distributor of treasures]; Olivero has "generoso amico dei guerrieri" (lines 1171 and 1476) [generous friend of warriors] and "liberal prence" (line 1602) [liberal prince]; whilst Cecioni has "liberale amico dei tuoi sudditi" (line 1171) [liberal friend of your subjects], "generoso amico degli uomini" (line 1476) [generous friend of men], and "generoso sovrano" (line 1602) [generous sovereign].

88. For a list of repeated formulas in *Beowulf*, see Orchard, *Critical Companion to "Beowulf,"* appendix 2, pp. 274–314.

89. Olivero has "ardito era il suo volto sotto il casco" [brave was his face under the helmet], "audace sotto il casco" [courageous under the helmet], and "ardito sotto l'elmo" [brave under the helmet]. Cecioni skips the first occurrence, having then "terribile nell'aspetto sotto l'elmo di guerra" [terrible in his countenance under the war helmet] and "ardito sotto l'elmo" [brave under the helmet]. Finally, Benedetti has "da sotto la visiera dell'elmo" [from under the visor of the helmet] for the first occurrence; she has a loose and inaccurate translation for the second passage, and translates the third occurrence as "l'altero viso aveva nascosto sotto l'elmo" [he had the stern face hidden under the helmet].

90. On variation in Old English, see Robinson, "Two Aspects of Variation" and *"Beowulf" and the Appositive Style.*

91. The relevant words have been italicized.

92. Klaeber, *Beowulf and the Fight at Finnsburg,* p. 2. "A ring-whorled prow rode in the harbor, / ice-clad, outbound, a craft for a prince. / They stretched their beloved lord in his boat, / laid out by the mast, amidships, / the great ring-giver. Far-fetched treasures / were piled upon him, and precious gear" (Heaney, *Beowulf: A New Verse Translation,* p. 4).

93. Benedetti, *La canzone di "Beowulf,"* p. 40.

94. Olivero, *Beowulf,* p. 5.

95. Cecioni, *Beowulf,* p. 4.

96. Her translation of the word also changes the meaning of the original.

97. Koch, *Beowulf,* p. 5.

98. Ciuferri and Murray, *Beowulf e il Frammento di Finnsburh*, p. 57.

99. Brunetti, *Beowulf*, p. 101.

100. Klaeber, *Beowulf and the Fight at Finnsburg*, p. 96. "Pouring forth / in a hot battle-fume, the breath of the monster / burst from the rock. There was a rumble under ground. / Down there in the barrow, Beowulf the warrior / lifted his shield: the outlandish thing / writhed and convulsed and viciously / turned on the king, whose keen-edged sword, an heirloom inherited by ancient right, / was already in his hand" (Heaney, *Beowulf: A New Verse Translation*, p. 81).

101. Benedetti, *La canzone di "Beowulf,"* p. 123.

102. Olivero, *Beowulf*, p. 173.

103. Cecioni, *Beowulf*, p. 101.

104. Koch, *Beowulf*, p. 219.

105. Ciuferri and Murray, *Beowulf e il Frammento di Finnsburh*, p. 221.

106. Brunetti, *Beowulf*, p. 231.

107. Claudia Di Sciacca has written the introduction, the section on alliteration, meter, and syntax, and the conclusion; Loredana Teresi has written the section on lexicon and kennings and on variation and appositions.

The Intimacy of *Bjólfskviða*

Pétur Knútsson

Of all the movements of textuality, the act of translation is the most intimate, the most naked, the most truthful; for both the source text and the translation must disclose their true identities, each to the other. As such it is also invasive, and so may be shocking to some; but if both parties are prepared to put aside their fear of new territories and alien gestures, then the invasion offers solace, the alien will be the loved one. The act itself is a close cohabitation; the two languages exchange their most precious gifts and transact together a third text, a new movement.

Fidelity is not an essential factor in the act: this must be said at the beginning. Insofar as it is a constraint imposed by one of the texts, supposedly the more ancient, the more authoritative, upon the other, it is an unacceptable violence. When it occurs spontaneously, as an act of love, it may be beautiful and enriching in itself, as a mutual bond between the texts; but it has different meanings for different texts, and so often causes frictions and misunderstandings.

Traditionally, the partners are dissimilar, even verging on the incompatible. An oriental language, analytic, tonal, with simple syllabic structure, shares its secrets with an inflected European language of harsh consonant clusters: such unions produce the most strikingly beautiful offspring, citizens of Goethe's "third epoch of translation."[1] From the beginning, translation theory has addressed movements of this type. The European tradition of translation goes back to the literary migrations between Hebrew, Latin, and Greek, starting with the Homeric translations of Livius Andronicus and Ennius in the third and second centuries BC and, in the same era, the translation of the Septuagint. Franz Rosenzweig, for whom translation plays a central role in the history of human thought, sees these movements as seminal in the history not merely of translation but of global culture: "Whatever unity of spirit and purpose exists on the five continents of this earth today derives from the fusion of these two events, and the consequences thereof, events originally related only because in them the Greeks played the double role of giving and taking."[2]

It may be that our planet has shrunk a little in the eighty years since Rosenzweig wrote, and that the so-called West, in thus naming itself and admitting its subglobal identity, has become a little less sure of the centrality of its cultural heritage; although we can probably still agree with Rosenzweig's sense of the enormous import of these beginnings. Crucially, however, we must take account of the set of attitudes towards the activity of translation, which were shaped, from the outset, by the chance linguistic configuration of the languages concerned. Greek, Latin, and Hebrew are linguistically very diverse: Greek and Latin represent two quite different branches of Indo-European, while Hebrew is an unrelated Semitic language. Later, Greek thought was channeled into the European Middle Ages through the medium of Arabic, another Semitic language. This linguistic diversity is also true of the main languages of literature and commerce in the world today. Thus it is not surprising that the burden of translation theory as we know it concerns problems of translation across quite imposing linguistic barriers, and the strategies that have been proposed to negotiate solutions.

Paradoxically, this disparity between the languages draws the discussion away from linguistic form: the translator consciously puts aside the shapes and sounds of the source text, searching for an "underlying" content which alone, it is assumed, will feed the translation. A dual discourse, even a double-talk, arises: while on the one hand form and content are recognized—at least since Saussure—as an indissoluble whole, each entirely informing the other, the quest for "fidelity" to the source text applies itself to content alone, pretending to find there a free spirit without body. Etiquette allows polite discussion of the stylistics of the source text, even strategies for the transfer of discrete formal elements such as meter, assonance, alliteration, and the like; but any more barefaced mention of the limbs and features of language are beyond the pale.

We can take Schopenhauer as a representative voice. Resorting (as we all do) to metaphor based on the technology of his time, he suggests that translation between languages "requires that we melt down our thoughts entirely and recast them in a different form." Nothing of the original dross must remain. "The translation into Latin often requires a breakdown of a sentence into its most refined, elementary components (the pure thought content) from which the sentence is then regenerated in totally different forms."[3]

Schopenhauer's term *regeneration* is disturbingly prophetic: by the middle of the twentieth century the advent of generative grammar provided Nida and Taber with the excuse for a computational model of translation which succeeded at a stroke in erasing linguistic form from the computation.[4] Translation now consists of "back-transformation" to an underlying linguistic layer where "transfer" between the languages occurs, and then "forward-transformation" to the surface form of the language of translation. These movements invoke Schopenhauer's "regeneration" and his terrible unspoken "degeneration," which is surely what "melting down our thoughts entirely" implies.[5] Direct intercourse between the form of the source to the form of the translation is illicit, corrupt; the model is an expressly prescriptive protocol designed to insulate the process of translation from all undesirable—we might say carnal—influence of the original text. The shape of the word is taboo, named only in disparaging terms: false friends, slavish imitation, translatorese. This devaluation of the physical form of language suggests comparison with various other textual and social tensions: the suppression of the feminine, the noncanonical, the peripheral. "Content" receives the privilege of convention, of unspoken acceptance, while "form" is demoted to the subaltern. And here is the root of the misconception of "fidelity" which I noted earlier: "fidelity" becomes a weighted concept, with different meanings for the different partners.

We can see this at work in one of its slippery synonyms, the vexed concept of the "literal translation." Etymologically, the word *literal* means "letter-wise"; but literality in translation has little do with the letters, and in fact not very much with words. The old dichotomy from Cicero and Horace, through Jerome to Alfred and down to Dryden, between word-for-word translation (metaphrase) and sense-by-sense translation (paraphrase) works not in the form or shape of words but in their supposed sememic identity, the slots in the mythical thesaurus of "pure thought." The concept of the "word" is deprived of form. *Dog, chien,* and *Hund* are said to be "literal" translations of each other; *Hund* and *hound* are not—although the literal letters tell us a different story. This recursive discrepancy between the "literal" meaning of "literal" and its indeterminate usage is symptomatic of a wider unease, the difficulty of reconciling the simultaneous arbitrariness and unity of the Saussurean sign, the ineffable link between *signans* and *signatum* in which we see most clearly the fundamental Kantian problem of relation. We are left with a merciless metalinguistic which denies the essential role of form while couched in language made up of forms.

In this essay I shall suggest that while these lapses may pass for the most part unnoticed in "mainstream" translation—translation between dissimilar languages—they become conspicuous in what I shall call "intimate" translation—translation between closely related languages.[6] This does not necessarily imply that linguistic form is *more active* in intimate than in mainstream translation; rather that the nature of intimate translation lays bear its activity. It is *always* active in translation; and we ignore it at our peril.

❖

Shortly before her death in 1968, the Icelandic poet Halldóra B. Björnsson finished her translation into Icelandic of the Old English *Beowulf*, which she called *Bjólfskviða* [The lay of Bjólfur] (1983):[7] the name was already in use by Icelandic scholars to refer to the poem. In the preface to his Icelandic translation of the OE poem *Widsith*, published in *Skírnir* in 1936, Stefán Einarsson remarks that it is high time an Icelandic poet attempt a translation of *Beowulf*,[8] and in an undated letter to Marijane Osborn states his intention to introduce *Beowulf* to Halldóra Björnsson and to suggest that she translate it.[9] Einarsson's own translation of the first sixty-three lines of the poem are kept in his papers (uncatalogued) in the National Archives, National Library of Iceland.

Born on a small upland farm in Borgarfjörður in the West of Iceland in 1907, Björnsson was the second of eight brothers and sisters, six of whom published collections of poetry.[10] She herself had published two books of poetry in 1949 and 1952, a book of translations of Greenlandic and African poetry in 1959, and several prose works before embarking on *Beowulf*. Two further volumes of poetry and a collection of essays were published posthumously.[11] She was well versed in medieval Icelandic literature and some of her published poems were in the Icelandic *ríma* (ballad) tradition which has survived into modern Icelandic from late medieval times.

Halldóra Björnsson's translation of *Beowulf* is an extraordinary work. She had little prior knowledge of Old English, and translated directly from Klaeber's edition of the poem without consulting any translations.[12] However, native competence in Icelandic is probably a better platform from which to learn Old English than any other modern language, since some 90 percent of the Old English poetic vocabulary has close or fairly close Icelandic cognates,[13] and there are significant syntactic and inflectional similarities between the two languages. But Björnsson rarely relies on sustained levels of cognition, and on my count she uses some 53 percent of the original vocabulary.[14] However, while these similarities are not sufficient for sustained word-for-word translation, they allow many present-day Icelanders, with some practice, to read Old English texts without great difficulty. Björnsson's translation is thus *intimate* not only in the sense of the proximity of the languages, but also in her familiarity with the idiom, an almost palpable domesticity, close to her familiarity with medieval Icelandic. Her ear was tuned to the temper of Old English in a distinct fashion, a decidedly, studiedly Icelandic textuality with its roots in medieval poetic diction.

In this essay I shall offer some examples of this "fidelity," examining aspects of Björnsson's concern with the survival of form in defiance of traditional protocols. These occur as relationships that can be traced between phrases, words, or parts of words in both texts, the original and the translation. I have elsewhere used the term *quantum*[15] to refer to the entities in these parcels of text which partake in the relationships, and find that they can be roughly grouped into three types: semantic content or *meaning*, syntactic *function*, and phonological/graphological *form*. These three types are largely independent of one another insofar as they may coincide, forming joint relationships in the same word across the texts, but are also likely to form independent and sometimes multiple relationships with "different" words across the texts.

When all types coincide, the Icelandic translation is "literal" in the strictest sense of the word: it is a *transliteration* of the original. Short stretches of such close correspondence occur throughout the translation. In the following example the original Old English text is given above, followed by Björnsson's translation:

> (1)   Þæt wæs gōd cyning
>   (*Beowulf*, line 11)
>   Það var góður konungur
>   [That was a good king]

For the moment, it will be enough to observe that there is full semantic, syntactic and formal correspondence between the two languages in this passage, given the residue of difference that we would expect: the systematic change of phonemes ("þæt" becomes "það," "cyning" becomes "konung") and the slight inflectional dissimilarity of the Icelandic nominative singular ending *-ur*, representing an original form which the Old English had already lost. And yet, in spite of these close correspondences, there is a remarkable undertow of noncorrespondence and incompatibility; we shall ignore it for the present, but return to it later in this discussion.

This level of close correspondence is however rarely sustained in the translation and never for more than a single line at the most. Stretches of exact correspondence are usually restricted to single words or short collocations. In the following, underlined words are quanta with simultaneous semantic, syntactic, and formal correspondences:

> (2a)   Hæfdon swurd nacod,   þā wit on sund rêon,
>   heard on handa;   wit unc wið hronfixas
>   werian þōhton.
>   (*Beowulf*, lines 539–41)
>   [[We] had swords naked when we into sea rowed
>   hard in hands; we ourselves against hornfish
>   thought to defend.]
>
> (2b)   Höfðum sverð nakin,   er við á sæ runnum
>   í hörðum höndum,   því við hvalfiskum

verjast vildum.
[[We] had swords naked, as we into sea ran
in hard hands, for against whalefish
defend ourselves [we] would.]

In this example there are only minor paradigmatic dissimilarities: the OE preposition "wið" governs the acc. pl. "fixas" (a form of *fiscas*) [fishes] while the Icelandic "við" governs the dative "fiskum"; and the OE reflexive "unc" [us two, ourselves] surfaces in Icelandic as the suffix -*st* on the verb "verjast" [defend oneself]. Analysis of lines 499–606 of *Beowulf*, the so-called "Breca Episode," indicates that 39.4 percent of the translation is made up of these close correspondences.[16]

Other cognate pairs in (2) have lost the syntactic aspect of their correspondence. The OE "hard swords in the hand" appears in Icelandic as "swords in hard hands"; only the semantic and the phonological correspondences remain. Note that I said above that the different quanta were *largely* independent of each other: this does not imply that they do not influence one another, but rather that their independent movements are relatively unconstrained. Thus the reterritorialization (in Deleuze and Guattari's sense)[17] of the semantic concept HARD, relocating it from SWORD to HAND, does indeed change the overall "meaning"—an example of the independent movement of the functional correspondence.

This passage also contains examples of partial rather than full (cognate) phonological correspondence. OE "sund" [sound, sea] becomes "sæ" [sea] (both acc. sg.), while OE "hronfisc" [hornfish] becomes "hvalfisk" [whalefish].[18] The correspondence of these forms is in this case informed by the alliteration of their lines but can often occur without it: the verbs "rêon" [rowed] and "runnum" [ran] also retain a partial similarity, although they are not constrained by alliteration. This illustrates an important aspect of the phonological correspondences in Björnsson's translation: the tendency to retain a measure of phonological form where there are no ready cognate correspondences to hand. This typically appears when a sudden "cognation gap" appears in Icelandic following a stretch of close cognate translation, as in the following:

> (3a)   Ful oft gebēotedon   bēore druncne
>   ofer ealowǣge   ōretmecgas
>   (*Beowulf*, lines 480–81)
>   [Full oft boasted, drunken with beer,
>   over ale-cups, warriors . . .]

Björnsson translates the first line fairly closely, but without any formal correspondences; the second, however, has all the appearance of being a word-for-word cognate rendering:

(3b)   Margir stærðu sig   að staupafulli
        yfir ölveigum   örvameiðar
        [Many boasted, with full cups,
        over ale-drinks, warriors . . .]

OE "ealowæge" [ale-cup] and Icelandic "ölveig" [drink of ale] are full cognates, and although there is a semantic shift between OE "wæge" [cup] and Icelandic "veig" [[intoxicating] drink] the two compounds are very nearly equivalent. However, "öretmecg" [warrior] presents Björnsson with problems. This compound, which occurs three times in *Beowulf*, is formed from *öret* 'battle' and *mecg* 'man', and she finds no immediate cognates in Icelandic. Her solution is to use the kenning "örva-meiðar" which, although it may not occur in this exact form in the medieval Icelandic corpus on which Björnsson models her diction, has many distinct parallels: the element *meiðar*, which may be the plural of either *meiður* 'tree' (as metaphor for "man") or *meiðir* 'harm-doer', combines readily in the sources with terms such as *brynja* 'coat of mail', *stál* 'steel', *málmhríð* 'shower of metal (i.e., arrows)' to make kennings for men or warriors.[19] The formal similarities between the OE and the Icelandic forms are striking: the initial noncognate vowels of *öret* 'battle' and *örva* 'arrows' are graphologically similar although phonetically different (*ö* is a back, *ö* a rounded front vowel); the medial OE -*r*- appears in the Icelandic as the cluster -*rv*-; and the remainder does not correspond. The elements *mecgas* and *meiðar* have the same onsets, the initial consonant being unchanged and the vowel remaining a medium height front vowel. The medial consonants are dissimilar but the inflectional endings are in fact cognate.

I have suggested the term *quasi-cognation* to describe this use of formal noncognate correspondences where "cognation gaps" occur.[20] It is important, however, not to see this as an idiosyncratic tendency of Björnsson's, for it appears to be a recurrent interlinguistic phenomenon. For example, in line 550 Björnsson translates OE "līcsyrce" [body-shirt, coat of mail] with the coinage "lífsserkur," which has the same meaning. *Syrce* and *serkur* 'tunic' are both cognates, but the pair *līc* 'body' and *líf* 'life, belly, body' display a characteristic lexical shift. OE *līc* can refer to a living body, while in Icelandic the term *lík* has narrowed its meaning to "corpse." Thus Björnsson cannot coin the term **líkserkur*, which would mean, if anything, a shroud. It seems that Icelandic *líf* 'life' has acquired the secondary meaning 'body, belly' in order to compensate for the loss of *lík* in the sense 'living body';[21] it would be plausible to suggest that the modern Icelandic collocation *lífs og sálar* '(of) body and soul' looks back to an earlier (unattested) *líks og sálar*, which became unusable as the meaning of *lík* changed. The point I wish to make here is that this is not a peculiarity of this text, but rather the result of an interlingual constraint acting throughout the potential corpus; in other words the formal correspondence—quasi-cognation—is already present in the most "literal" translation. It seems that semantic shifts along the diachronic axis of language change often seek out phonological channels, sliding as it were along the lines of least resistance, like *lík* and *líf*. Thus with Icelandic and Faeroese, languages at least as close to each other as Standard English and Lallands Scots, where Faroese *hyggja* translates as Icelandic *horfa* 'to look', with the same initial consonant; while Faroese *horfa* and Icelandic *hyggja* have other meanings. In the same way these phonological channels often enable interlinguistic loans: many Icelandic neologisms turn out to be formal, noncognate echoes of other languages. We might mention *ímynd* 'image' and Latin *imago*, which dates from the sixteenth century, the use of *ás* 'main rafter, cross-beam' for *axis*, which dates from the nineteenth century,[22] or the current linguistic term *umdæmi*, which corresponds to English *domain*, where -*dæm*- and *dom*- are quite unrelated, and the second vowel of *domain* seems to have colored into the Icelandic form. Between Greek and Latin we may note Cicero's calque of *etumologia* (literally "true wording") as *veriloquium*,[23] where the elements -*logia* and -*loquium* are not cognate. In French, one example of many would be *dérive*, with its associations with English *drive*, *drift*. In English, *day* is unrelated to Latin *dies*, *bridegroom* was associated with *groom* only after the old word *goom* 'man' ceased to be current, and *bastard* is not a cousin to *base*, in spite of Edmund's "Why brand they us / With base? with baseness? bastardy?"[24] Holyrood House in Edinburgh seems to be named after the Holy Rood, while at the same time it echoes the Gaelic *ruigh choille* 'base of the hill'. The list is endless: one example has crept into my crib for passage (3) above, where the verb *bēotian* is necessarily rendered by the formally similar but noncognate "boast."[25]

Björnsson's concern with the phonological—the carnal, or even carnivalesque—aspect of her translation not only insists on the inexorable presence of the original text, but also opens up a complex intertextual environment with threads of connection in both the Old English and Old Icelandic corpora. And as I have already noted, this goes far beyond her own reading: it is as if her text moves freely through the established landscapes of Old English poetic formulae without her knowledge. One short example will have to suffice here: *Beowulf* opens with a memory of the ancient glory of the Danish kings, in which the formula "ellen fremedon" (line 3) [performed deeds of valour] occurs. Björnsson's translation is "örlög drýgðu" [performed/fulfilled [their] fate]. This does not at first sight look very close to the phonological form of the original: admittedly there are affinities in modern Icelandic pronunciation between *ll* and *rl*, but this is hardly distinctive.

If, however, we examine the formulaic sets to which these phrases belong, we find channels of much closer formal correspondence. Björnsson's formula "örlög drýgja" is found in the Icelandic Eddic poem *Völundarkviða* (stanza 3, line 10); exactly the same formula also occurs in Old English as "orleg drēogan" (*Judgment Day I*, line 29). We can trace this formulaic set in Old English as it approaches the form in *Beowulf*:

(4)   orleg drēogan [accomplish deeds of war] (*Judgment Day I*, line 29)
        ellen drēogan [accomplish deeds of valour] (*Riddle 58*, line 1)
        ellen dugan [achieve deeds of valour] (*Andreas*, line 460; *Genesis*, line 1288)
        ellen fremman [execute deeds of valour] (*Beowulf*, line 4)
            (data from Bessinger and Smith, *Concordance*)

Björnsson's association of OE *ellen* with Icelandic *örlög* is thus a correlation that also exists within the OE corpus.

This is one of a number of examples[26] of echoic relationships between formulae in the original Old English texts and in Björnsson's translation that take up or extend formulaic echoic relationships in the Old English corpus—a corpus that she did not have access to. There is no mystique here: the two traditions come together not only in Björnsson's translation, but in the common heritage of alliterative Germanic formulae which can be clearly traced in the literature of both languages, and it illustrates the crucial Barthesian understanding that intertextualities are not the works of the authors: they exist by virtue of the readerly movements of the text. I shall return to this point shortly.

My examples so far have all shown form surviving the translation by virtue of the semantic and/or syntactic support it receives. In the following examples I shall examine what happens when form moves freely, completely abandoning its associations with syntax and semantics.

The first requires some narrative background. At line 1537 the hero Beowulf is grappling with Grendel's mother in the cave at the bottom of the hellish lake. Grendel's mother is not described in the poem, and her son is only indirectly described; we have the impression of a large humanoid creature with claws, living on the "misty moors." Important for our appreciation of the translation here is the fact that the monsters are at least in part aquatic creatures, and the action takes place at this point in an unresolved underwater environment: Beowulf takes "a good part of the day" (line 1495) [hwīl dæges] to dive through the murky waters to reach their cave. The setting is confused, being both under water and apparently in fresh air; there is a fire burning in their dwelling-place (line 1516), and yet when Beowulf hews off the dead Grendel's head, blood wells up immediately and colors the surface of the lake (lines 1591–95). Clearly the long account of Beowulf's swimming contest and his bloody underwater struggles with the monsters of the deep (lines 506–83) have been in part a preparation for the narrative of his exploits in the hellish lake. Grendel and his mother are of much the same perilous kin as the sea monsters.

Thus it is that during his struggle with Grendel's mother, Beowulf—identified in this passage as the "man of the war-Geats"—reaches out and grips her by the shoulder:

> (5a) Gefēng þā be eaxle —nalas for fæhðe mearn—
> Gūð-Gēata lēod Grendles mōdor
> (*Beowulf*, lines 1537–38)
> [Gripped then by shoulder—shrank not from the conflict
> the War-Geats' man—Grendel's mother]

However, in her translation Björnsson explicitly presents Grendel's mother as nonhuman by referring to her shoulder as "bægsli" [flipper] rather than the expected *öxl* 'shoulder':

> (5b) Greip þá í bægsli —glímdi ósmeykur—
> Gautaleiðtogi Grendils móður
> [Gripped then by the *bægsli*—wrestled undismayed
> the Geatish leader—Grendel's mother]

This is a surprising change, since a straightforward cognate translation involving the Icelandic *öxl* for OE *eaxl* would be perfectly in order: "greip þá í öxl" [gripped then by the shoulder] (neither the original "öxl" nor the translation "bægsli" is constrained by the alliteration: the OE alliterates on *f*, with "gefēng . . . fæhðe" and the Icelandic on *g*: "greip . . . glímdi").

The word "bægsli" is a formation from *bógur* 'shoulder of a beast', defined in Cleasby and Vigfússon (under an older form, *bæxl)* as "the shoulder (Lat. *armus*) of a dragon, whale, shark or the like"; in modern Icelandic it may refer to the front limb of aquatic creatures such as seals or penguins. The same root occurs in the verb *bægja frá* 'push away, ward off' (presumably as if with the shoulder) and in the word *bægslagangur* 'commotion'. Björnsson's monster has become a lumbering, fishy creature; perhaps too there are sound-associations with *bæklaður* 'crippled', making her malformed or hunchbacked. However, this is not simply a stylistic embellishment: the word "bægsli" turns out to be a crux, a crossroads where two dissimilar flows are signposted: on the one hand a formal phonological reference to the OE text and on the other a pointer to some remarkable Icelandic counterparts to the *Beowulf* narrative.

The formal correspondence is a striking example of the independence of form. The word "bægsli" is a close formal echo of the Old English text: "be eaxle" [by the shoulder]. Ignoring the word boundary in *be-eaxle*, the vowel undergoes what is essentially an elliptical metathesis (*e-ea* > *æ*), while the medial consonant cluster is in fact identical, since the two spellings *bægsli/bæxli* indicate the same pronunciation (the *g* and *s* of *bægsli* are both unvoiced in Modern Icelandic). The final vowels *-e* and *-i* are (often, although not here) cognates in OE and Icelandic inflections.

It seems that the phonological string has broken free and acquired a completely new significatum in the translation; we are witnessing what Deleuze and Guattari call "no longer an imitation at all, but the capture of a code, the code's surplus value, an increase in valence, a genuine becoming."[27] But Björnsson is not simply signaling the Old English text in a spirit of paronomasia. In calling up the Old Icelandic word *bæxl* she invokes the atmosphere of the later prose romances in which the Icelandic imagination looks back beyond the relatively realistic phase of the Icelandic family sagas to an earlier, more mythical time, where trolls, dragons, and underwater monsters walk freely. In fact she is making an explicit reference to the fourteenth-century *Gull-Þóris saga*, which as it happens figures prominently in scholarly speculations of the relationships between *Beowulf* and Icelandic sources. The fifth chapter of the saga tells of a sally made by the hero and his comrades into a cave of dragons, which, like the dragon fought by the aged Beowulf, are guardians of treasure. Associations with *Beowulf* seem to cluster at this point: the cave is situated in a deep gorge into which Þórir leads the difficult descent by means of a rope suspended from a tree (cf. Beowulf's daylong descent into the lake). The entrance to the cave lies behind a mighty waterfall, and much is made in the saga of the drenching spray and the way the earth quakes under the force of the falling waters (cf. the watery parallel of Grendel's hellish lake). Inside the cave Þórir and his companions conjure up a magic light which causes the dragons to fall asleep, and their way is then lit by the magnificent light that emanates from the treasure and the dragons themselves (cf. the fire burning in Grendel's cave [line 1516] and the great light, like the light of the sun, which flashes from Beowulf's sword after he has killed Grendel's mother [lines 1570–72]). At this point the men see the hilts of swords standing up out of the treasure (Beowulf saves his life by finding a magnificent sword of giants lying in the treasure in Grendel's cave [lines 1557–62]); they snatch up the swords and, running over the sleeping dragons, plunge them "under their *bæxl*." A battle ensues, producing flashes of light which are seen through the great falls so that the men who have remained outside fear for their comrades (blood wells up to the surface of the hellish lake and the watching men fear for Beowulf [lines 1591–99]).[28]

There are further correspondences with Icelandic sources: Beowulf's sword Hrunting (Björnsson's Hrotti), which fails him in the cave (cf. the torches which fail Þórir in the cave) is referred to by the hapax "hæftmēce" [haft-knife] in line 1457, for which Björnsson uses the Icelandic form "heftimækir," which also occurs as a "hapax" in *Grettis saga*. And since we are now deep in the realm of speculation we might allow the phonological similarities between Hrunting and Hyrningur to start us off on another track: Þórir's companion Hyrningur is injured in the foot by contact with poisonous dragon blood; later Þórir heals him by passing his hands, clad in magic gloves, over the foot. One of Beowulf's companions, Hondscio, was killed in the earlier fight with Grendel (lines 2072–82). *Hondscio* means "glove" (hand-shoe): it seems that hands, feet, gloves, and injured or dead retainers come together here in another focus of (readerly) activity.

These correspondences would not have escaped Björnsson; we can safely assume that she knew *Gull-Þóris saga*, which Klaeber mentions, albeit briefly.[29] The striking phonological echo on *be eaxle/bægsli* is a symptom of this readerly environment, a breach in the elusive boundary between Björnsson's text and the other texts it invokes. If texts have edges, as Derrida suggests they do,[30] they must dissolve on intimate contact. Here we see this contact in the act and observe its fertility: the unconstrained association of form between the two texts signals a lateral coupling to a third corpus in what we can best characterize as a *triangulation*.

This tangential intercourse occurs readily in Björnsson's translation. Here is another example: in the Finn episode (lines 1066–1159) Hildeburh, Hōc's daughter, a Danish princess, is married to the Jutish king Finn, who is responsible for the deaths of her kinsmen. The poem goes on to recount the death of Finn at the hands of Hildeburh's Danish kinsmen: the theme of the passage is the grim ethos of the ancient Germanic feud.

> (6a) Nalles hōlinga Hōces dohtor ... bemearn
> (*Beowulf*, lines 1076–77)
> [Not at all without cause did Hōc's daughter bewail]

Björnsson translates:

> (6b) Hló eigi hugur Haka dóttur
> [Laughed not the mind of Haki's daughter]
> (i.e., There was no mirth in her heart)

The striking echoism of the underlined words "hōlinga" [without cause] (related to "hollowly") and the unrelated Icelandic "hló" [laughed] flags for the Icelandic reader a no less striking intertextuality from *Þrymskviða*, the Old Icelandic Eddic poem dealing with Thor and Loki's journey to Jötunheim, the land of the giants, to recapture Thor's stolen hammer. When Thor regains his hammer he rejoices at the prospect of revenge for the theft:

(7)   Hló Hlorriða hugr í briósti
        er harðhugaðr hamar um þecþi[31]
        [Hlorriði's [Thor's] mind laughed in his breast
        as, stern of mind, he recognized his hammer]

The essential quality of the phrase "hló hugr" [laughs the mind, i.e., the mind laughs], is one of mirthless rejoicing at the prospect of feudal revenge, a prospect that Hildeburh is denied. Thus the heroic character of the OE litotes "nalles hōlinga" [not at all without cause] in (6) is perfectly captured by Björnsson's "hló eigi hugur" [laughed not the mind]. Projecting the figure into modern English we might say that Hōc's daughter laughed a *hollow* laugh.

Walter Benjamin, too, has noted this tangential contact, but for him it is formless, occurring at too small a point to admit of physical form: "Just as a tangent glancingly, at a single point only, touches the circle, and as the contact and not the point prescribes the law by which it draws its straight line out to infinity, in the same way, glancingly, and only at the infinitely small point of the sense does the translation touch the original, to follow its personal course, set by the law of fidelity, in the freedom of linguistic growth and movement."[32]

Much as we may admire this metaphor we cannot deny that it also suggests the suppression of form. Even in the final vision of his essay, where he joins with Jerome[33] in claiming for Scripture the possibility of immediate literal translatability, Benjamin is not thinking of the "literal" literalness, the literality of letters: "Where the text belongs immediately, without mediation of sense, in its literalness, to true universal language, to truth and teaching, it is translatable absolutely. . . . The interlinear version of the Scriptures is the archetype or ideal of all translation."[34] And how could he accept linguistic form into this archetype, given the incompatibility of the great languages of Scripture? The austere pairing of Hebrew with Greek or Latin is almost incorporeal in its lack of phonetic grounding: Benjamin's "sense" moves invisibly, without form, breaking free by virtue of its infinite smallness ("the infinitely small point of the sense"). In contrast, in our homely texts of intimate translation, the tangents are solid and readable, consisting of strings of letters, the two texts fusing in a boisterous intercourse. We allow both tangential sense and tangential form their own mutual infidelities, their own independent movements; they embrace and move on. Sometimes, as in (5) and (6), they involve further triangulations, but this is not necessarily the case. Alert readers may have noticed another echo in (5), where "lēod" [man] reappears in

Björnsson's "**leið**togi" [leader, one who leads the way] (*leið* 'way'); this is another example of an independent formal correspondence, but I detect no reference to Icelandic sources (although others may). But the echo is nevertheless not an empty one, even without triangulation: it reaffirms the identity of the Icelandic language, and its intimacy with Old English.

These movements, then, pay no respect to traditional boundaries, those between words, between texts, and between corpora; which like mathematical sets implode on each other and breed Deleuze and Guattari's rhizomic counterflows. Such intertextual flows are thus often perceivable at only certain resolutions, or levels of focus: formal and semantic flows typically appear at levels at which the word is in focus, while wider corpora- or culture-related flows may only appear on the level of discourse, of narrative, of genre, and even display unmistakable traces of extratextuality, effects that originate outside language. I shall return to my first passage to illustrate this point:

> (8) (cf. (1))
> Þæt wæs gōd cyning
> Það var góður konungur
> (line 11)
> [That was a good king]

In spite of the formal similarities discussed above, there is an undertow of incompatibility, a semiotic tension between cultures separated by the lapse of a millennium, although their disparities are belied by a similarity of the language. In this case the concept of the GOOD KING has changed radically over the ensuing centuries. In the context of the original story the king was the focus of social consciousness, an ever-present figure in the Hall, united with many of his people by blood relationship; he was the living repository of much of the tribal wisdom and expertise upon which their existence in a hostile environment depended. More tellingly, the sense of individual identity, which has developed in the West since the Renaissance, was unknown in the feudal hall. Yuri Lotman describes the shared identity of the boyar, his family, his serfs, and villagers under Ivan the Terrible, pointing out that the "notion of collective (in this case, clan) personality, and not individual personality, lies behind the idea of the blood feud, according to which the whole clan of the murderer is perceived to be responsible."[35] This shared identity of lord and subject is manifest in *Beowulf* and in Anglo-Saxon society as late as *The Battle of Maldon*; it also underlies the family feuds in the Icelandic sagas. The modern European concept of royalty has a very different aspect, and it is arguable that, for modern Icelanders, it is even more alien: throughout the history of the Icelandic settlement it has been anomalous at least, if not at times downright suspect. Modern Icelanders tend to be proud of their republican status and a shade derisive of the royal pageantry of the English or Scandinavian thrones.

In other words, there is a lack of correspondence at a wavelength—a domain, shall we say, of analysis—far lower than those we have been working with so far. But it registers nevertheless in the text of (8) in that there occurs a *correspondence between two noncorrespondences* at widely different wavelengths: just as "cyning" and "konungur" refer to different concepts—although we have little choice other than to translate them both as "king"—so *c* differs from *k* and *y* differs from *o*. There is a source of noncorrespondence, which resonates at several different wavelengths.

In order to understand more clearly in what way this source originates beyond the horizons of language, we might compare it to another focus of non-compatibility in the same passage, this time fully intralinguisitic, residing only in linguistic form. It concerns the pronoun "þæt"/"það" [that] at the beginning of the sentence. This time the mismatch occurs between modern English on the one hand and Old English and Icelandic on the other; between Old English and Icelandic there is full agreement. The difficulty becomes apparent if we examine some of the choices made by modern English translators of *Beowulf*:

(9)   A good king was that. (Morris, 1910–15)
        A noble king was he! (Clark Hall, 1911)
        A good king he! (C. W. Kennedy, 1940)
        He was an excellent king. (Wright, 1956)
        . . . : king worth the name! (Morgan, 1964)
        That was a good king. (Hieatt, 1967)
        He was a noble king! (Crossley-Holland, 1968)
        He was a good king! (Alexander, 1973)
        That was a good king. (Donaldson, in Tuso, 1975)
        That was a great king! (Swanton, 1978)
        Yes—a good king! (Osborn, 1983)
        That was one good king. (Heaney, 1999)

Of these, only Hieatt and Donaldson are content with the "literal" translation "that was a good king"; the other translators are uncomfortable with the antecedent of anaphoric *that*. In modern English *that* is not marked for case or gender and refers unequivocally to the king who figures in the discourse: the copula "was" joins "that" and "a good king" in an equation: "that = a good king." But in Old English there is a grammatical mismatch between *þæt*, which is neuter, and *cyning*, which is masculine: the masculine form of the neuter *þæt* is *sē*, and the Old English form for the equation would be "sē wæs gōd cyning." In classical Old English poetry we find that in sentences of the type "that + copula + complement" the form for "that" is sometimes in gender agreement with the complement:

(10)   "sē wæs hēah ond brēd" (*Beowulf*, line 3156)
        [that [= Beowulf's *hlæw* 'burial mound', masc.] was high and
           broad]
        "sē wæs eald genēat" (*Battle of Maldon*, line 309)
        [that was an old retainer [masc.]]
        "sēo is eallum cūð eorðbūendum" (*Riddle 29*, line 8)
        [that [= *wundorlícu wiht* 'wondrous being', fem.] is known to
           all earth-dwellers]

and at other times has the neuter form without agreement:

(11)   "þæt wæs drihten sylf" (*Andreas*, line 248)
        [that was the lord [masc.] himself]
        "þæt wæs egeslic wyrd" (*Dream of the Rood*, line 74)
        [that was a terrible fate [fem.]]

The difference between these two structures seems to be that the form in agreement (*sē*, *sēo*) refers directly to its antecedent, while the neuter form without agreement has a wider scope, referring to the discourse of which the antecedent is the subject. Thus the use of the neuter "þæt" in (8) widens the scope to apply to the whole panoply of Scyld's kingship from the time of his miraculous coming as a foundling: (8) really means "this phenomenon was a good king."

Modern English *that* carries no gender, and so cannot partake in these structures. Many of the translations in (9) attempt to reflect this wider reference, not only by tampering with *that* but also by using a more elaborate adjective than *good*, or rearranging the syntax. Wright responds by substituting "excellent," while Clark Hall's "noble" evokes post-feudal royalty. Swanton's "great" is spoilt by the modern colloquial use of the word. Morgan turns the sentence into an appositive exclamation in order to render the tone and ceremony. Morris, unfettered by the trammels of acceptable English, achieves the weight of affirmative summing-up of the OE sentence with a shift of word order. Osborn manages to achieve the summing-up without unnatural word order and retains a degree of measured but vital ceremony; but this all hangs on the literary register of "yes," which is perilously close to "yeah, man." In contrast, playing with registers is not a danger for Heaney, with his express commitment to the speech patterns of Ulster.

In Icelandic, however, the situation is exactly as in Old English: *það* is the neuter form of masculine *sá* and feminine *sú*, and the usage is the same. These questions simply do not arise: Björnsson has the same choice as the OE poet, between "Sá var góður konungur" and "Það var góður konungur." Her translation does exactly what the original does.

And so the translation problems concerning "that" in this passage are of an entirely different nature from those concerning the "good king." "That" is anaphoric and intralinguistic, an example of textual tension quite unconnected to the cultural backgrounds of the languages concerned, segregating analytic modern English on the one hand from the more synthetic Old English and modern Icelandic together on the other. In contrast, "good king" sets up other tensions that are not confined to the structure of the language but rather involve the historical development of kingship, which occurs outside the immediate text. And yet both these modes of activity, the intra- and the extratextual, occupy the same ground, and resonate in the same phonological form.

The development of the concept of kingship beyond the wildest imaginings of the *Beowulf*-poet is of course only one aspect of the momentous changes that occurred between *Beowulf* and Björnsson's translation. The movement from memory to the manuscript, the advent of writing, was still in progress at the time the *Beowulf* manuscript was written. Franz Rosenzweig identified a later, perhaps even more momentous development, the establishment of Holy Scripture: "So also in the life of a people: a moment comes when writing ceases to be a handmaiden of language and becomes its mistress. This moment comes when a matter encompassing the whole life of a people has been cast into writing."[36] The timescales are very different: *Beowulf* was committed to vellum long before the Bible became a canonical English text, and a good while before Icelandic became a written language. This slippage of contemporaneity, together with a host of other historical changes in the fabric of textuality, sunders our two texts with a far greater mutual incompatibility than we find in the burden of modern translations. In spite of much greater disparities of linguistic structure, today's texts are usually couched in closely related dialects of global culture.

Another radical divide between Björnsson's translation and her exemplar comes with the Bakhtinian proliferation of voices. (Readers may already have been reminded of Bakhtin in this essay; for instance in my use of the term *triangulation* to refer to multiple contacts between texts, *thirdness* being one of his most significant preoccupations.) These many voices that echo in the silence of novelistic discourse, in the midst of the noise in which we conduct our lives, sound no less insistently in our reading of Björnsson's translation, behind closed doors which muffle the accents of the television; in contrast, the chanting of the original poem in a small, noisy hall was surrounded by the silence of the forest. Charles Lock discusses the implications of the fashion of silent reading that grew up in the West in the eighteenth century, a development which coincides nicely with the new plurality of voices in novelistic discourse: only silent reading can elicit the "unspeakable intonation" of the novel.[37] This emancipation of the single word, its diastasis in a plurality of voices, also inevitably ushers into the text a host of gestures from outside, transforming it with multitextual plurality: the explicit reference to another text, the bent finger pointing over the local horizon, demands the same mute intonation.

The original *Beowulf* manuscript is in many respects the archive of a recital, of a single voice, perhaps chanting, perhaps accompanied by a harp; the flow of narrative, the performer's occasional asides, the poem's spectacular digressions, are all strung together in the same monolinear channel, the voice of the Anglo-Saxon scop, the maker and the speaker of the verse. Björnsson's text on the other hand is not limited in this way. By virtue of its epoch alone, the epoch of silent reading and silent writing, it is already infected with the freedom to shift and multiply its references. Both texts, the original and the translation, are woven of intertextualities, as all texts are; but in each text the role of these linkages appears to be radically different. The scop's conventional formulations were elements in the *wordhord*, the treasury of words, the tokens known and understood and expected by the audience. The choice of the formula "ellen fremedon" (line 4) [performed deeds of valour] in *Beowulf* involves no explicit reference to similar formulae in other poems, any more than the choice of the word "æþelingas" [princes] in the same line explicitly invokes the 150-odd occurrences of the word elsewhere in the Anglo-Saxon poetic corpus.[38] In both cases there is of course a close weft of relationships: just as the audience is granted knowledge of the word "æþelingas" by the texts that they already know, so "ellen fremedon" takes its force from its attendant community of formulae. But these relationships are not foregrounded in the text; they are simply features of the machinery of language. In contrast, Björnsson's translation "örlög drýgðu" [performed deeds of fate] for "ellen fremedon" is a multifaceted reference, explicitly linking the Old Norse *Völundarkviða* with the Old English *Beowulf* in an articulate, writerly statement.

In the monologic recital of *Beowulf* in the Anglo Saxon hall, the turns of language that point, index-like, to elements outside the text, and anchor the text in the world of its audience, would be heard in the intonation of the scop, the set of his features, the set of her features, the laughter of the audience, the give and take of the performance. Indexicality would be carried by speakable, audible intonation. But only unspeakable intonation will tell us when Björnsson's finger points beyond her text. The writer cannot speak, for unspeakable intonation can only be heard in the mind of the reader, and in any case much of this pointing is, as we have seen, to texts that Björnsson never knew. In our reading, we have promoted—the ecclesiastical term is *translated*—the original text of *Beowulf* into our own era, putting it on a par with Björnsson's translation; and in our reading the ecclesiastical and literary meanings come together: all reading is translation. We have Bessinger's *Concordance* to hand; and in our computers we can run searches for formulae in our downloaded Old English texts. What was once a pleasing turn of the scop's diction has become for us a silent finger, the memory of another text we have studied. *Beowulf* suddenly teems with indexicality, which feeds back into the textual environment of Björnsson's translation. Both texts, the original *Beowulf* and Björnsson's *Bjólfskviða*, can only be read in translation: translation into our time.

Notes

See the accompanying CD to listen to the first fifty-two lines of the poem read in Icelandic.

1. Goethe, "Translations," p. 62.

2. Glatzer, *Franz Rosenzweig*, p. 272.

3. Schopenhauer, "Language and Words," p. 35.

4. Nida and Taber, *Theory and Practice*, p. 33.

5. I am perhaps unnecessarily harsh on Nida and Taber. Their underlying level of transfer is not in fact Schopenhauer's spectral "pure thought content," shorn of all linguistic form, but a level of "kernel structures," a term also used by the early Chomsky: primitive but recognizable bundles of language. After toying with the idea of transfer at the Chomskyan level of "deep structure," Nida in fact rejects it: "Theoretically and ideally the transfer should take place on the level of the deep structures [although] there are a number of practical reasons for carrying this out in actual practice on the kernel level" (Nida, "Translation," p. 1049). The "depth" of transfer is however beside my point, which is the model's express prohibition of any transfer at "surface level."

6. The term *intimate* is from Knútsson, "Intimations of the Third Text."

7. The 1983 text is an editorial construct from three typescripts left by Björnsson, read and approved by her brother, the poet Sveinbjörn Beinteinsson. It is no longer in print, but can be found at <http:notendur.hi.is/peturk/3T/bjolfskvida.html> (accessed December 2010).

8. "Ekki efast ég um, að hagyrðingar og skáld muni gera hér betur, enda ættu þeir að taka sig til og snara öllum ensku hetjukvæðunum og fyrst og fremst Bjólfskviðu á íslenzku" (Einarsson, "Widsið," p. 184). Stefán Einarsson (1897–1972) was professor of English at Johns Hopkins University, Baltimore, 1945–62.

9. Osborn, "Foreign Studies of *Beowulf*," p. 21.

10. Björnsson et al., *Raddir dalsins*.

11. See the bibliography in the present volume for a full list of her works. Björnsson's life and works are summarized in Einars et al., "Minning."

12. She would of course have read Einarsson's translation of *Widsith*, and among Einarsson's uncatalogued papers in the National Library of Iceland there are two translations of the nineteen lines of the Old English lyric *Wulf and Eadwacer*, one by Einarsson and one by Björnsson. She told me herself of her lack of prior knowledge of Old English and the fact that she did not consult other translations. Einarsson's copy of Klaeber's *Beowulf* remains in Björnsson's library, now in the possession of her daughter Þóra Björnsson.

13. In the first four sentences (nineteen lines) of *Beowulf*, 79 percent of the word stems have full Icelandic cognates with little or no change in meaning; another 14 percent have close but not full Icelandic cognates with minor shifts of meaning, and only the remaining 7 percent have no clear Icelandic cognates.

14. Knútsson, "Intimations of the Third Text," p. 160.

15. Knútsson, "Intertextual Quanta," p. 115.

16. Knútsson, "Intimations of the Third Text" ("Appendices," pp. 269–90). This figure, based on a crude word count, breaks down into 34.7 percent for full cognate correspondence between the source and the translation, and 4.7 percent for closely cognate but not fully cognate forms. It does not register the forms where cognate correspondence is not supported by syntactic and semantic correspondence, nor the number of close but noncognate echoes discussed below.

17. Deleuze and Guattari, *Thousand Plateaus*, p. 10.

18. Klaeber (Björnsson's source) glosses *hron* as "whale"; for *hornfish* the *OED* gives "The garfish, Belone vulgaris," quoting *Andreas*, line 370: "Hornfisc plegode, glad geond garsecg."

19. Egilsson, *Lexicon Poeticum*, s.v. "meiðir, meiðr" (p. 399).

20. Knútsson, "Intertextual Quanta," pp. 112–13.

21. Magnússon, *Íslensk Orðsifjabók*, suggests that the meaning "body" for *lif* is a loan-meaning from German.

22. For *ímynd* and *ás* see my "Learned and Popular Etymology," p. 110. The Icelandic word *ás* 'heathen god', unrelated to *ás* 'beam', has similarly been recycled in the sense of "ace" (in cards).

23. Cicero, *Topica*, line 35.

24. Shakespeare, *King Lear*, act 1, scene 2.

25. The *OED* gives *boast* as having an unknown etymology.

26. I discuss this and other examples in "Intertextual Quanta" and "Intimations of the Third Text" (chap. 3).

27. Deleuze and Guattari, *Thousand Plateaus*, p. 10; here quoted from Johnston's translation in *On the Line*, p. 19.

28. The relevant text of *Gull-Þóris saga* (also known as *Þorskfirðinga saga*) reads: "Þórir var nú kominn í hellinn og dró þá til sín, hvern er ofan kom. Bergsnös nokkur gekk fram við sjóinn allt fyrir fossinn, og fóru þeir Björn Beruson og Hyrningur þar á fram og þaðan upp undir fossinn. Þeir höfðu þar tjald hjá snösinni, því að eign mátti nær vera fossinum fyrir skjálfta og vatnsfalli og regni. Þeir Þórir tendruðu ljós í hellinum og gengu þar til, er vindi laust á móti þeim, og slokknuðu lá login. Þá hét Þórir á Agnar til liðs, og þegar kom elding mikil frá hellisdyrunum og gengu þá um stund við það ljós, þar til er þeir heyrðu blástur til drekanna. En jafnskjótt sem eldingin kom yfir drekana, þá sofna þeir allir. En þá skorti eigi ljós, er lýsti af drekunum og gulli því er þeir lágu á. Þeir sáu, hvar sverð voru, og komu upp hjá þeim meðalkaflarnir. Þeir Þórir þrifu þá skjótt til sverðanna, og síðan hlupu þeir yfir drekana og lögðu undir bægsl þeim, og svo til hjartans" (pp. 292–93).

29. Klaeber, *Beowulf and the Fight at Finnsburg*, 3rd ed., p. xvii. The validity of these correspondences is hotly debated. A recent contribution by Magnús Fjalldal, *The Long Arm of Coincidence*, gives a good overview of scholarly accounts of points of similarity between *Beowulf* and *Grettis saga*, showing how speculation only too easily becomes accepted wisdom. However, in dealing with each point of contention in isolation, Fjalldal fails to account for the combined weight of evidence; he also confines himself to *Grettis saga*, which

is only one of a number of apparent *Beowulf* analogues in medieval Icelandic literature. More tellingly, he is talking solely in terms of historical textuality and the search for specific routes of textual migration, his point being that only what he calls "genetic" relationships bear scrutiny. He is therefore not concerned with lateral thematic movement, and even less with the readerly cross-connections, which I am invoking.

30. "If we are to approach a text, it must have an edge" (Derrida, "Living On," p. 83).

31. *Þrymskviða*, line 30 (p. 113).

32. Benjamin, "Task of the Translator," p. 94.

33. Jerome, *Epistlola 57, Ad Pammachium*.

34. Benjamin, "Task of the Translator," p. 96.

35. Lotman, *Universe of the Mind*, p. 139.

36. Buber and Rosenzweig, *Scripture and Translation*, p. 51.

37. Lock, "Double Voicing."

38. Figures from Bessinger, *Concordance*.

Part 2
Essays on Performance

Performance I:
Beowulf (A Roundtable Discussion)

Mark Amodio, Benjamin Bagby, Karl Reichl,
and John Miles Foley

On the evening of 9 May 2003, a crowd of several hundred medievalists who were in Kalamazoo, Michigan, for the Thirty-eighth International Congress on Medieval Studies filled the chapel on the campus of Kalamazoo College to hear Benjamin Bagby perform the first 850 lines of *Beowulf*. The following morning a roundtable discussion took place in which Ben was joined by Karl Reichl and John Miles Foley. The participants were asked to deliver some brief comments on any aspect of the poem and its performance after which the members of the audience would be invited to join the conversation. I [Mark Amodio] am grateful to Jana K. Schulman of Western Michigan University for arranging to have the session taped and for the careful work she and Leslie Carney did on the initial transcription of the session. I would also like to thank Ulrich Müller of the University of Salzburg, who independently, and quite fortuitously, taped the session and who very generously made a copy of his recording available to us. Working with these two sets of recordings, I have been able to create a record of the entire session. In editing the transcription, I have tried to remain as faithful as possible to the oral nature of the presentations and the discussion that followed.

Mark Amodio: Good morning. Thanks for coming out this morning to the first of two sessions sponsored by *Oral Tradition*. Before we get going today, I'd like to put in a plug for the second of our sessions, which will be held tomorrow at ten o'clock in Valley III, Performance II: Theory and Praxis. For the first part of this morning's roundtable discussion, each speaker will offer some brief comments about performance in *Beowulf* and/or performance of *Beowulf*. Ben Bagby will begin and he'll be followed in turn first by Karl Reichl and then by John Foley. After they finish their remarks, we're going to open this up to a conversation and we hope you'll all join in.

Jana Schulman: Mark, actually, since we're taping this to do a transcription, during the question period would the people who ask questions please identify themselves before asking their questions, so that when we're transcribing we'll know who the speakers are.

Mark Amodio: Good. Okay. Well, then, we'll start with Ben.

Ben Bagby: Thank you, Mark. I thought I would speak very briefly about my own background and what it is that brought me to perform *Beowulf*, and what my values have been, what my agenda has been, and how that's been influenced by the work that many of you have been doing on this text and on the idea of how this story might have been told at one time before it was put into manuscript form. My background is that of a singer and musician. My training is a standard conservatory training in singing art song, which was a kind of rigorous exercise in butchering texts and stories; a very, very systematic dismantling of everything culture in this planet has been trying to do for the last several thousand years. And it took me as a music student a long, long time to realize that the thing, the artifact that we call art song, or the German *Lied*, the French *mélodie française*, or all of these little pockets of art song, all of them represent a tiny blip on the screen of stories and texts and lyrics as they've been performed over the past millennia or so.

What we think of as the main tradition, or as we call it in conservatory, classical music or serious music, is actually a tiny little aberration, which was set in motion during the eighteenth and nineteenth centuries. And what we systematically refuse to recognize is that we're standing on the shoulders of an enormous giant whom we ignore completely. And that giant is, of course, the oral tradition of song and the oral tradition of storytelling, which has made it possible for us singers to stand up in front of the piano in our tails and white tie and sing melodies for paying audiences in concert halls with a stage elevated and the audience sitting lower down in a worshipful stance.

The entire physical structure of the concert as we know it, and here we have it even in this lecture hall, and the structured role of the performer in the performative space, is a very strict and difficult structure to break because we have been indoctrinated with the feeling that a performer is somebody who is interpreting, giving voice to, a work of art which was created by a genius creator, in this case, the composer. We still all suffer, and this is a big debate in music generally, from the myth of the maestro genius; think of Beethoven or Mozart. The word *Mozart* is never uttered without the word *genius* being within four to five words on either side [laughter]. This is an idea which is so deeply rooted in us that we're not even aware of it. That we think of these composers as people who have created masterworks. They have somehow communed with the gods or the muses, they have made sketches in innumerable sketchbooks, they have been tortured and had sleepless nights, and filed away and hammered away at this work of art until finally it emerged in the form of the score, the autograph score. This score then is sent to the printer who prints it and it is then sold to amateur musicians or to symphony orchestras or to string quartets. And it enters into the life stream of the genius interpreter.

And so we have this paradigm of the Bach Suites for Cello being played by Pablo Casals and it's sort of a full circle of gods with gods, and we mortals are outside the circle and are permitted to watch in reverential silence as these gods commune with each other and with something that we call high art.

When, however, you look at the way song is actually performed by singers, especially singers who are coming from a more traditional society, you see that it's a lot more "down and dirty" than the conservatory idea would have us believe, that singers actually do come from families with fathers and uncles and aunts and mothers and sisters and brothers and with all kinds of things happening around them that they are listening to. At some point, they are literally grabbed by the ear and pulled into what is the tradition of their family clan, guild, you name it. And they start to soak it in. They do all this without having an idea that this is high art, that they should be reverentially learning it, and that they should never aspire to enter into the closed circle of the gods. They are simply doing it. They are simply part of the tradition and there's none of this question and answer about "How close am I approaching the truth? How close am I approaching the greatness of this music?" The music is linked to stories. The music is linked to the transmission of history and myth creation, genealogy, and all those things. And the singer is not part of the system of the maestro genius.

There are no schools you can go to in the West, that I know of, where you can escape from the maestro genius paradigm, because it's the dominant one, and it's actually the only one. You would have to learn to sing in another way or by singing a nonclassical, Western music, such as jazz. Although even in the jazz world people now rely more and more on written records than on listening. If you want to learn jazz and it's 1936, you don't go to college, "where we have a very good jazz program and perhaps even a PhD in jazz history." There is none of that. You go to clubs and you sit and listen to your elders, who are themselves not maestro geniuses, they are simply—that's their gig in the club. You sit and listen to them. Once in a while they might let you sit in and play with them and you soak it up. That's one of the closest traditions we can find in our own society. Nowadays, if you want to study jazz you want to have a degree in jazz. And people now—you've heard of the great player Charlie Parker, his improvisations on the saxophone, which were, of course, not improvisations, they were licks that he played in every club, every night, but they seemed to us like improvisations. These solos have, in the meantime, been transcribed by jazz historians or ethnomusicologists, and you can now buy a book with all of Charlie Parker's solos written out in very precise notation. And now what happens is that music students who are working for their master's in jazz performance or whatever will take a copy of this Charlie Parker solo album into a practice room and maybe the person in the next practice room is playing Beethoven and the one on the other side is singing Puccini, and they are sitting in there dutifully learning to play a Charlie Parker solo break from a score. So you can see that learning to play jazz has also entered into the written world in our culture because it belongs to the same system in a way, the same music-training system.

This whole, long preamble is just to say that my work with *Beowulf* was a little bit designed to—as therapy—to cure me from my conservatory training, from the mentality which my voice teachers had instilled in me and to help me find another way to use the voice, because in most conservatory training, and certainly all vocal training, there are very rigorous ideas about vocal usage. And they are accepted worldwide and they have to do with the virtues of singing very loud and very beautifully, and having your voice sound *the same* all the time. In other words, having your voice be unified from the very highest notes to the very lowest notes and whether you're singing in Russian, French, Italian, or German, it's the same beautiful voice because it's vocal *sound* that is the center of attention nowadays.

I think in the time of orally transmitted epics such as *Beowulf*, I can't imagine a scop in an eighth-century or a seventh-century environment, in a place where he might have traveled in his whole life maybe fifteen miles to the left or to the right, I can't imagine that he was participating in a culture that had unified values of vocal usage. I think it's much more likely that his voice was at the service of telling a certain story and that, of course, in his clan or in his group and amongst his masters and those who followed after him, there were some agreements locally linked to language and linked to the way these people spoke and the way they heard rhythm and the way they listened to the sounds of vowels and consonants in their language. I think that that was silently but, of course, very rigorously adhered to. No one had to write it down—well, they didn't write anyway—but no one had to give it any kind of expression; it simply was taken for granted.

My effort was to enter into something that could be of the same fabric as that way of thinking about singing, that way of thinking about how language is given voice in telling a story. How in the given structure, in which you have vowels, you have consonants, you have the evident metrical structure of the text itself and, of course, knowing it was sung and it was vocalized or given vocal utterance, you have that instrument which provides some kind of tonal information so that it's not just random singing on any old note. It has to adhere to some kind of melodic—not melodic, but tonal program. That's a lot of givens.

And so I've been juggling with those givens over the years and it really has been a long process of trial and error in many cases. I did not start out with the theory "This is how it must have sounded; based on this and this and this it sounded like that. Now I will make my instrument and my voice conform to that idea." It was much more a case in which I, without too many preconceptions, other than the tuning of the instrument and what I was taught about the metrics, would sit down and work with all of those issues like a kind of *prima materia*, like a big lump of clay, kneading it and pushing it around. And slowly, slowly, slowly, some kind of primitive shapes began to emerge for me as a singer but also as a storyteller because I had to kind of teach it to myself. There was no one to teach me that. But I did have sources of inspiration in that I could see in other cultures besides our own that this tradition does live on and there are people who do sing stories. They use their voices. They're not opera singers, they're not lieder singers, and they didn't go to conservatory. That's extremely heartening news for someone like me because it shows that it's a powerful tradition, it's viable, it's still managing to survive in our world of instant media transmission and instant documentation. My work with *Beowulf* was really, starting in 1987, a process of working through a very large mass of not very well defined givens, so that I could arrive at something which for me was a precise voice for that text and that story.

You may have noticed if you were at the performance that I seem to be going in and out of singing and speech and it's sort of going through a spectrum of sound from using all the weirdest things that voices do—like screaming and whispering and barking and groaning and so on—through a kind of speech which you could call normal speech, the way you talk to a friend in a café, into a kind of heightened speech, which is what I'm doing now because this is a big room, into a kind of very formal speech which takes on an almost vocal quality of singing, the old style of what we used to call rhetoric, and then into something which is really like spoken song—to the point where you're no longer sure; "Is he singing? Is he speaking? We don't really know"—into something that you would call song, in which you hear one note on a perceivable pitch per syllable of the text, and then into something which you would really call vocalism, which is using long notes, singing more than one note on a given syllable, something we call a melisma, and all the kinds of things you associate with singing. That's an enormous spectrum. It covers a huge range of vocal possibility.

And you may be thinking, "Okay, he sat down and worked all this out and he decided that in line 751a speak, but then in line 751b into 752a gradually shift into song." That is not the case. At no time did I use any notations to read from and observe the rule "Here I have to sing; here I have to speak." That whole process was something that I worked on through a long period of trial and error—and memory. My own personal oral tradition came into being over a period of about fifteen years. And now it's very, very hard for me to change anything. I can, but if I change something I go into a different part of my brain. I noticed that last night when I tried something new, which I had never done before and I thought, "Oh, this is great, I've never tried this and it's working fine." But then it threw me off how it goes into the next part because the doorway had been moved. And in a way I kind of bumped my head going through the door because it was just not where I was expecting it to be. Those are the sorts of strategies that are constantly being worked out in performance, but they can't be fixed beforehand.

I also never wrote down any of the musical notes that I'm singing. There's no score for *Beowulf*; there will never be a score for *Beowulf*. I would hate nothing more than to have to sit down and write this down on music paper. It would be dreadful. It would be something like a seventy-five-page score that would be unusable. Because some day some music student [laughter] might take that into a practice room and I think right there there's a compelling reason to keep these things in oral tradition and not in written tradition, because that music student would certainly do something horrible by very slavishly obeying the written score because we are trained as students of music to think of the musical score as a truly holy artifact. It's really something very much larger than we could ever be. And I think the banishing of those five lines of music staff from our lives as musicians is one of the most important things we could ever hope to accomplish. And one day, if I'm ever given the opportunity to start a music school of my own, it will be a staff-paper-free zone [laughter], especially for singers.

I think I've probably gone over the time limit.

Mark Amodio: No, that's perfect. You'll have more time later.

Ben Bagby: Okay. Thank you.

Karl Reichl: First of all, I would like to express my great admiration for your performance. Also, you have now said so many exciting things, which it would be most tempting to somehow comment upon. I first heard you in Bonn in 1998, and I think I can see some kind of development from the style you had then. So, I suppose that there is material for future study of the development of Benjamin Bagby's *Beowulf* performance [laughter], whether with or without music transcriptions, but that we will leave up to the students.

However, I'm not very good at eulogy, although it is one of the oral genres [laughter], so I thought it might be most useful if I could bring in another perspective. Although I earn my money as a professor of English at the University of Bonn, I do have a different area of research, which is oral epic poetry in Central Asia. My first stay there was in 1981. I think, if I may, I would like to express a few ideas from my experience there and try to ask you, Ben, what you feel about, not changing the first eight hundred lines, but possibly bringing in a few things when you get to the next two thousand or however many lines—whichever is the next portion you are planning to work on.

One question that I find fascinating is the question of gestures. If oral performers in the tradition accompany themselves with musical instruments, they do not use gestures because they are busy playing their instrument while singing—unless it's a prosimetric tradition, i.e., a mixture of verse and prose. When singing the verse portions there are no gestures because the singers are playing their instrument; however, when there is a change from verse to prose, the prose is narrated and gestures are used. However, there is the Kirghiz tradition of *Manas*, the largest epic in Central Asia, which really does compare well to the Homeric epics. These Kirghiz singers use no instruments and they use gestures, and, in fact, they say: "We don't use an instrument so we can use our hands." But what they do with their hands, their gestures, is highly conventionalized. So, for instance, there would be a sort of bow-and-arrow gesture or a way of holding up their hands and so on, but these gestures are not directly related to what the singers are saying.

So my first observation would be, do gestures have to be naturalistic or is there a whole code of gesturing which is also traditional in some ways just as the text and the music are? Another thing I've noticed, just to come back to the Kirghiz singers and also to your style, is that the older the singer (and there are actually singers from eight to eighty; they train them like child prodigies, wunderkinder of epic poetry in Kirghizstan) the less dramatic the performance and the more the text takes over. The younger the singer, the more dramatic the performance. It's almost as if the singer is only a medium for the text, allowing the poetry to pass from him to the audience.

That would be one observation. To remain with the Kirghiz, the other observation is they have different melodic styles when singing, but nevertheless consistently use melodies. However, unfortunately, and this would be a problem to be solved by metricists, the meter of these Turkic epics is syllabic. I mean, this is not unfortunate in itself [laughter], but it's unfortunate when comparing it to *Beowulf* because here we have a completely different meter.

If you have a seven- or eight-syllable line, a Kirghiz singer can sing (I have not been trained in the conservatory): 1-2-3-4-5-6-7 [sung] or 1-2-3-4-5-6-7-8 [sung]. It's always this cadence at the end. This is one melody. But then when an exciting bit comes, and there is some relationship between content and melody, then he would sing 1-2-3-4-5-6-7! [sung] 1-2-3-4-5-6-7-8! [sung]. So there is this kind of change which I think would actually in many ways support your interpretation.

Another question I have, or possibly even suggestion, is the incorporation of genres within the epic. The idea of *Beowulf* as a *summa litterarum* was put into circulation by Joseph Harris, among others. Well, what one can say about *Manas* as a *summa litterarum* is that there is "elegy" when the heroes depart into battle or, in fact, have died. There is a famous elegy of the hero's wife lamenting the death of the hero. And this elegy is actually sung differently. When in the Uzbek epic of *Alpāmish*—which has a return story like the *Odyssey*—the hero returns he tests the fidelity of his wife. In doing this he exchanges wedding songs, improvised wedding songs, with his wife—not only in the Uzbek version, also in the Kazakh and other versions. And these songs are then sung in a different style, namely in the style of wedding songs. There is also a third element, humor, which is also a prominent element in your performance. These wedding songs are contest songs. The hero returns to his wife who is to be remarried but, of course, he returns just in time before she gets remarried. In these wedding songs the future mother-in-law joins in. Now, Central Asiatic mothers-in-law—mothers-in-law in epics not maybe in reality [laughter]—have a particular speech defect [laughter]. They can't pronounce the *r* so instead of "yar, yar"—meaning "love, love"—which is the refrain of these wedding songs, she can only say "ya-i, ya-i," or in Kazakh, "ja-i, ja-i." In the performance the singers do actually make fun of the old crone's speech defect in these wedding songs. This element of humor in your performance is an element which one finds in Central Asiatic epics, although if one's a purist one would say, "Wait a minute, *Beowulf* isn't funny!" That might be so but humor as such wouldn't be extraneous to an epic performance.

A further point is that most singers do accompany themselves with an instrument and do actually sing the epics. And, although I know that Old English *singan* is, as is everything in Old English, ambiguous and can be interpreted in at least a thousand ways [laughter], I was wondering whether when you get to the Finnsburg episode you would consider the possibility of doing one stretch of the epic actually in singing, rather than changing styles or rather than going from speaking, shouting, and so on, to singing. Would you find it possible at all to do this with the particular meter *Beowulf* has, using the harp? I mean, for me it would certainly be an interesting question whether it is possible or whether you believe that singing alliterative meter is just so against any kind of regularity of that kind, despite Tom Cable's book, in which he has, of course, given us the meter and melody of *Beowulf*.

However, I think I am also sort of coming . . .

Mark Amodio: No, no, you're fine.

Karl Reichl: Right. Actually, I thought we'd have a discussion rather than a presentation, so this is why I'm asking, why I'm presenting, what I have to say as questions, because this is in many ways what I feel or what I'm interested in.

There is the other question of how closely should the meaning of the text be mirrored in the performance? We know from music, medieval music, that the idea of expressiveness is fairly late. It's not up to me to tell you anything about medieval music, but the idea is that one wouldn't necessarily try to really bring out textual nuances in the musical performance of a troubadour song. This is a wide and controversial field, but whatever the case might be with medieval lyrics as songs, how does it work with epics? With the Central Asiatic epics, I've often found that there is no direct relationship between the meaning of a word and the way it is performed. There might be a relationship between a passage describing a battle or whatever and the particular melodies used. And some singers use quite a lot of different melodies, which, however, are not dependent on the metrical structure because that stays more or less the same; they are rather dependent on content, at least to a certain degree. But their choice may also be dependent, in a way, on a desire for variety because obviously if you sing for hours, not only does the singer get tired but the audience might get tired as well; so variety is welcome. But there generally isn't any kind of direct semiotic or mimetic relationship. There are, however, some exceptions. In the Uzbek epics, where the singer accompanies himself on a plucked instrument, there are what Parry and Lord call themes, typical scenes, and one of them is the ride of the hero through the desert or through the steppe. This type-scene is highly formulaic. And this particular scene is generally performed somewhat faster and the *dombira* [a two-stringed, lute-like instrument] actually does give a kind of galloping accompaniment. So I must qualify in a way the statement that music and text are not in a mimetic relationship. I think you are probably right when you perform *Beowulf* to us now in the twenty-first century in a way that uses a multiplicity of modes, but I wonder whether the expressive relationship between words and recitation/music is or was originally as close as in your present performance. I don't know, you probably have thought quite a lot about that.

Okay. Well, these are my main questions. And thank you for giving me the time to ask them.

John Miles Foley: Well, I, too, am very grateful to Ben Bagby and also to Mark Amodio and Paul Szarmach—who made last night's performance available to us all. What I have to say this morning is more or less of an evolving reaction to the *Beowulf* that we heard last night. And it's based on three performances that I was able to attend. A couple of weeks ago, at the People's Poetry Gathering in New York City, Ben Bagby performed his section from *Beowulf*, twice. And then at the University in Missouri, in Columbia, he gave us what I think he probably didn't want to give us, and that is the Grendel fight. He had said beforehand to me, "Please don't ask for that because I'm not warmed up." When he later asked the graduate students in the seminar, very generously, "What part would you like to hear?" of course [laughter] that's what they asked for. He was nice enough to do it. And then, of course, last evening.

I also had the advantage of sitting with Ben for some hours in Columbia, and I do want to stress this in his preparation that it took us quite an amount of time, but we went over every last crux in the part that he performed last night. So he's very serious about the scholarly background for what he does.

Now, to start, I'd like to say a word or two about the original basis for my reaction, which I now consider somewhat out of date. My preparation is Homeric epic but then also South Slavic epic, the living analog. And it's on that living analog, I suppose logically enough, that I was basing my reaction originally: the idea that the living epic could, of course, be experienced plurally, directly, without reconstruction, unambiguously. And for this I've brought this morning, if we can make it work, just a small selection from an epic by Halil Bajgorić called *The Wedding of Mustajbey's Son Bećirbey*, which was recorded by Parry and Lord in 1935, in June, actually. Let me try and play a few lines from that; it just may take a half a second. Presumably we'll have some luck with this; we'll see. We're going to have a little bit of instrumental music to begin with [music]. I'll tell you, while this is starting, that he's saying that it's a very early day and the hero gets up. The sun is not yet risen. The morning star has just shown its face. And he goes on then to drink not seven or eight but ten cups of coffee in order to get ready for the day [laughter]. Here he goes. "Djerdjelez Alija got up early. Alija, the tsar's hero. Near Visoko above Sarajevo. Before dawn on the white day. Even two hours before dawn. Before the dawn has happened. When the morning star has shown its face. When he'd gotten up well, he put the coffee pot on the fire. And lit it up and got it ready. When it was ready and he'd had enough" [music ends]—and then he goes on to have his seven or eight or ten cups of coffee.

Now, what you heard there is a very—my students would say, a quite repetitive presentation. The melody doesn't change a great deal. It's a highly stylized presentation, obviously, one musically accompanied both instrumentally and vocally. And it's linked to a present audience as well as to an epic tradition. I'd like to stress a few things about the performance—what it doesn't include—about South Slavic oral performance.

Its idiomatic signals, in short, are outside of our modern frame of reference. There are no visual cues that the singer gives; we know this from working face to face with them. There are no paralinguistics or kinesics of any kind. There is no adoption of different characters' personae or self-presentation, as we heard so memorably with Unferth last night. Although I would quickly add that Plato talks both in his *Ion* and his *Republic* about the rhapsode's adoption of the character identity of the Homeric characters. So there's varying evidence on this.

My students often say, "Where are the signals we're used to?" That would be a short form of their question. And what I usually say to them is I remember a time long ago when Albert Lord was asked to speak opposite a person, a modern poet, who was creating an oral poem in the moment. And he went ahead and did his thing and then Albert played some material from the *guslari* and a very well meaning man stepped up in the audience and said, "Excuse me, Professor Lord, but does the *guslar* gesture meaningfully with his hands as he narrates the song?" And Albert in his modest way said, "Well, he's playing the instrument, you know" [laughter]. And it's that kind of lack of frame of reference, I think, sometimes that we suffer from.

Trying to become an audience for *Beowulf*, then, I think a lot of us have thought in terms of an authentic or original performance as closely as a millennium or so would allow us to get, with success judged only on that criterion, only on whether it is what actually happened, and forsaking any irrelevant—putting that in quotes—"irrelevant" modern cueing.

Penalties for departure? Well, we think of departure as lack of fidelity to the poem in performance, as unprofessional behavior, perhaps. And for myself, I seldom gave a thought in the early going to the anachronism of trying to become such an audience today, which involves not just knowing the language and not just having an acquaintance with the story, but involves knowing an idiom and knowing a tradition. This is something that I think is largely beyond us at this point. There's an inevitable shortfall then in communication, which I think is seldom considered. And then there's also the irony of de-emphasizing the audience's— that is the present audience's—engagement with and role in the performance, all for the sake of, in the name of, a kind of chimera of authenticity. So, in sum, I guess I've been frankly suspicious, up until recently, of what I considered inauthentic modern performances. So that's the confessional part of my presentation.

My mind has been changed on this issue, I'm happy to say. And to admit. Let me characterize the three audiences. What I have to say here, I hope can be theoretically justified, but I'd rather do it empirically on the basis of the three experiences, being a part of three audiences for Ben Bagby's *Beowulf*.

In New York, the People's Poetry Gathering, which happens biennially, is in some ways a perfect audience for him because at it people who are interested, especially in oral poetry, come together literally from around the world. They have no special training and are a complete mélange of an audience. The performance was in some ways very similar to last night's: two large TV display monitors on either side of the stage carried the supertitles rather than a back-lit sort of presentation. There was tremendous enthusiasm during the performance, before it with Mark's introduction, and after it, with the question-and-answer session that Ben was generous enough to do. And, in essence, I had a genuine sense of a performance–performer–audience amalgam being fashioned. And that really was what stayed with me from that first performance, and what I hadn't, frankly, been thinking about before, being so concerned with recovering an authentic presentation.

The second one was in Columbia to my *Beowulf* seminar, eight students who had read at that point, I think, about 90 percent of the poem and who asked for the wrong, as I said, the wrong passage. Not only were they rapt, but for days afterward there were discussions of performance in that seminar that wouldn't have happened unless the connection had been made by the vitality of Ben's performance, irrespective of how closely he adhered to this or that system of meter or whatever else. They were very interested in what was received as well as what was sent. So, again, what came home to me was the formation of the performer–performance–audience amalgam.

And again last night, the same thing. Obviously this was the most knowledgeable, most deeply committed audience, of the three, perhaps because this was the group most used to beer halls, I'm not sure [laughter]. But there was also an obvious pleasure in attending the performance for a lot of people. I noticed the anticipation of favorite passages. People got the jokes or reacted perhaps more readily. They were more quickly reactive, sometimes you could even say prescient, about what Ben was trying to do. And I think people were especially taken with some of the personification or characterization, for a lack of a better word.

The last section of what I have to say on my small handout here is entitled "Choosing a Channel or Speaking and Hearing in Idiom." I'll start with a couple of questions and end with a couple of questions. The one I start with is "Is Ben Bagby's performance the real *Beowulf*?" Or better, "Does his performance convey the real *Beowulf*?" I think there's a slight difference in those questions. As Karl said, we could be here for a long time talking about some features of his method and delivery, but I just enumerate a few. I do appreciate his careful attention to pronunciation, the reconstructive pronunciation, which is beautifully done. His meticulous study of cruces, research behind the instrumentation, which I'm sure he could talk about at great length; it's very interesting. His attention to meter but not for its own sake. And it was included in a special note to the performance last night in the program. His adoption of characters' personalities and variation in voicing and all sorts of vocal effects. Of course, the list could go on.

In the end, I guess, then, and I'm thinking about this for myself and the trajectory of my sense of what he's doing, it's a question of what we mean by "authenticity." Do we answer it by trying to recover a forever-lost moment, doing the equivalent of finding a time machine and going back and conducting fieldwork in Anglo-Saxon England? Should we attempt to re-create an Old English poetic performance, to the extent that we could manage that, even if its signals, its repertoire of signals, might now fall on deaf ears, or do we opt for a communication that can engage a modern audience, that can convey *Beowulf*, if not in light of the original, fully respecting Old English poetics on the one hand, and—*and*—creating an audience, an involved modern audience, on the other? So I am ending with three questions and perhaps the way I tend in the answers is probably obvious, but I'll find out. Which, the original or Ben Bagby's *Beowulf*, is the more effective event? Which is the more effective communication? And finally, and this one I think deserves some thought, which event is truer to *Beowulf*?

Mark Amodio: Okay. Well, thank you Ben, Karl, and John for your stimulating comments and for giving us a good deal to think further upon. Now we'll throw the session open to our audience and invite their questions or conversation. Yes?

Q: Yes, Rick Russom, Brown. I just loved your performance, and I have absolutely no objections, but understand some metrists do have a few to what you do, but I would like to insist on one point that I think is important in terms of interpretation. Meter, as I understand it, has absolutely nothing to do with sound. John Collins Pope thought he was doing meter in a way that told you how to pronounce— how to perform—the poetry; he thought he was doing rhythm, which is musical. And so did Sievers. I hope I never fall prey to the idea that through the study of meter I can know how it originally sounded and I can be the bard. I don't believe that at all. I think meter is the property of the text, the pattern of words, and that what anybody has to do with the text is to realize it. I have a technical question. You wouldn't want to use setting, right? Like song setting or scoring for a performance because those are tricks. Do you just perform it? What you do to a text?

Ben Bagby: I have not really given it a definition.

Rick Russom: Well, as an arranger, say, I take a book out of the American Songbook and prepare the dominants and take out the baby chords, put in seven chords, change it to 4/4, 3/4. What would you call that? Arranging?

Ben Bagby: It's not an arrangement, strictly speaking, because an arrangement is something that is by definition fairly fixed; a given performance, while musically very similar to another, is never exactly the same, although it's functioning under the same kind of performative plan, or arrangement. I think I just set up some performative parameters and remain within them.

Rick Russom: So it would be okay to say you just perform the text?

Ben Bagby: Yes.

Rick Russom: Which is what you do to it. And somebody else could perform it differently?

Ben Bagby: Oh sure.

Rick Russom: So, if I'm right in my theory of meter—you can't help but follow as to whether I'm right or wrong? [laughter]—there cannot be, in my understanding of meter, an unmetrical performance, if you say the words right, which you do. Along with Professor Foley, I heartily congratulate you on your pronunciation. It's up to professional standards and maybe even better. So you were metrical all the way through, as far as I could see, if I'm right. I mean, you had to be metrical if you were pronouncing the words, because it's in the text, is what I'm saying. And performance is a way of realizing meter. I think meter establishes a range of performances that are plausible and also some that are silly but I think you can go right ahead and do whatever you want.

Q: Tom Cable, University of Texas at Austin. I've heard so many good ideas this morning I'd just rather sit and meditate on them. But in an accumulation of a whole week of speaking with Ben in Austin and the performance last night and following up on what Rick Russom said—I am a recovering metrist, like Rick Russom [laughter] and John Foley—I realized in the shower this morning, it was an epiphany, that I've been asking the wrong question, that I had been asking what kind of performance does this text produce? And I should have been asking what kind of performance produces this text? And so I have put myself back into the oral tradition, which I have resisted for thirty years, realizing that Ben's reconstruction is probably as close to a preliterate performance in the seventh or eighth century as we're going to come to in the twenty-first century.

And when the text was recorded, was written down, aspects of the performance were abstracted and the more we find out about the meter, whether we're using Rick's word-lift system or Pope's measured system or Kaluza's law, there are so many elements going on in the meter that I think it would be almost impossible—to turn it around the other way from what Rick was saying—it would be almost impossible to pronounce the text, given the most careful pronunciation, and bring out all of these elements: "Hwæt wē Gārdena"—who would remember that that /a/ was long? or in "in gēardagum þēodcyninga," "at the link, remember: resolution." I think that a very studied performance wouldn't recapitulate all of the intricacies of the text. So it becomes a kind of question of cause and effect. It becomes an ontological question of the status of the text and of priorities. So I think that in turning it into something written we've got something different that has a reality of its own.

Q: My name is Anne Savage, and I work at McMaster University in Ontario. One of the most important things about hearing your performance last night for me as somebody who's been teaching this poem and reading it for many years—and this touches on the question of authenticity as well—is that there's a huge difference between a performance by an academic person reading the text into a tape recorder or somebody who has memorized part of the poem, to somebody who knows the poem; those things are quite different although I'm sure that they occur on a continuum. And therefore we're looking at not one *Beowulf* but any number of *Beowulf*s in performance and what they were like. Or parts of *Beowulf*, anybody's favorite part that they ask for—the fight, the elegies. I bet all of those had perhaps separate existences simply because they were parts that people wanted to hear at different times when they didn't have time to hear the whole thing.

One thing that I wanted to ask is how much of your performance was determined by the sheer physical demands of the length. So this is actually a question for Professor Reichl as well: How do these singers cope with the sheer demands on the voice, which would be ruined if they didn't do it properly? I notice that you used the harp and it seemed a very, very sensible way of using the harp, sometimes as accompaniment, sometimes to make a space for a dramatic pause or a voice rest—I wonder if that's what it was? How do singers cope with the length of the performance? Do they do just do it and therefore to be a singer is it dictated by the fact that you can go on for six hours without collapsing [laughter] or you can do it more than once?

Karl Reichl: Well for one thing, in order to become a singer you really do have to have a good voice. This is a prerequisite, and one finds, for instance, in singers' autobiographies, when singers talk about their own lives, statements like: "I have a voice which carries for five miles." So there is this physical aspect. The way they treat their voice differs from tradition to tradition. In Central Asia, epics, and that includes long epics, are generally performed through the night; if the epic is longer than one night, then it is performed during several nights. The singer does take rests, and he uses the pauses either to drink hot water or tea or, in fact, as one of the Turkic singers I recorded, to smoke hashish [laughter]. By the time he had finished his epic, this singer was so high that—as we all had to sleep in the same room—I couldn't sleep all night because he kept on talking through the night [laughter]. But there are various ways of allowing the voice to rest. There are also various singing styles. The Kirghiz singers use their natural voice when singing, though, of course, in such a way that it carries. But the Karakalpak singers actually use a very strained voice, which must be terrible for the singer. So instead of saying one-two-three [spoken in a normal voice] or something like that, they say one-two-three [spoken in a gravelly voice]. And yet the singer I recorded for the first time in 1981 is still alive and he still has his voice, so I don't know what it is that keeps it intact. I think it would take a speech therapist to really understand, [laughter] but these pauses and rests with drinking or whatever do occur.

John Miles Foley: It's very much similar to what the South Slavic singers do, in fact. During fieldwork, and seeing them pause every once in a while, which we didn't expect, at places we didn't expect, I first began to understand what Old English *wrecan* meant and why the lexicons were not appropriate. The verb "to drive out," or "utter, recite," to have these two senses: not at all. *Turati* in Serbo-Croatian also means "to drive out" but it's concurrently the verb to produce epic song, so there's an idea of impelling, of moving something out of yourself and toward people with tremendous energy—so they can't go more than thirty or forty minutes or so without pausing for a brief rest.

Ben Bagby: To address your question about vocal fatigue, I think the image that we have of singers needing to be rested and of being very delicate creatures is based on, again, this inherited idea that the singer is some kind of precious artifact of genius that has to be pampered: the stories about singers and their backstage antics—having to have things just so—[laughter] are legion.

Mark Amodio: I guess we probably shouldn't mention the green M&M's yesterday.

Ben Bagby: Yes. The riders on contracts are huge. For instance, the things they need to have in order to be in the mood and in voice to sing—but that's also linked to the fact that concert singers today do have to perform flawlessly for one hour, or at the most ninety minutes. They walk out onstage in front of three thousand people who paid a lot of money and their voices have to be just perfect right at that moment. It's an enormously high-pressure situation focused on a tiny moment of time. And then after that they go home and rest for a week before they sing again. It's because of the nature of what concerts are, and the nature of repertoire also, singing high notes that are going to be judged, every one of them, on beauty and perfection. I don't think about those things, or I'm liberated from having to think about those things because I don't see myself as being a part of that tradition; it's not all about high notes. The high notes are in a way just extensions of emotion in a given point in the story, for me, and so I'm not worrying about them. I don't have to practice them. And, indeed, I can't practice *Beowulf*; that's the main problem. I can't sit at home and practice this thing. It's really uniquely linked to the performance. There are many, many places in the text that I have only ever done in performance. It's only with the audience–performer continuum that I have the energy necessary to do that thing.

It's terrifying on one hand, but it's also very reassuring and I think that is one of the reasons I don't experience an enormous amount of vocal fatigue. One of your questions was if the instrument, for instance, was designed to create a moment to breathe, or whatever. That's actually not a factor. Even taking a little drink of water is linked to having to tune the instrument, actually. I do have to stop occasionally and check the tuning of the instrument and I just take a moment there to wet my whistle, really, but I probably could do without it; it's not absolutely essential, barring swallowing a fly or something like that [laughter]. There aren't a lot of vocal fatigue issues for me and I have performed this piece on an intensive schedule. For instance, I think the record is that I once did it nine times in fourteen days. It was okay; I wasn't vocally fatigued so much as I was mentally fatigued, so that after the third night of a three-night run I found myself sliding into that thing I'm sure you all know if you're teachers, that you feel like "They've already heard this. I should try something new because it's boring to them," forgetting that it's not the same audience as the night before. Then trying something new in order to be interesting and getting into trouble. That was a big lesson for me about the need to remain mentally calm, and that that's not linked to vocal fatigue.

Q: My name is Ulrich Müller from the University of Salzburg in Austria. I would like to make some comments. First, I would like to say, Ben, your performance was marvelous yesterday and I think it's the best way you can do it nowadays to present the *Beowulf.* Epic singing still exists in some parts of the world, not only in Central Asia, but I listen to singers in Arab countries and Africa, even in India, even in Europe there is still one small tradition of epic singing at the—the Faroese Islands. And last year I also heard an Amish man who sang part of the medieval *Hildebrandslied,* just one line. But this epic singing is quite different from your style. It must be different because we cannot reconstruct the medieval performance or the performance of epics like Homer or *Beowulf.* We can only present modern interpretations. We also have to reconstruct the audience. We have completely different ways of listening and thoughts. I think there is no real chance to present the medieval epic in the old way. And regarding the voice, a friend of mine tried twice to sing the whole *Nibelungenlied.* It took five hours—five *days,* about thirty-five hours. There was no problem for his voice and I was told also by singers in Arab countries and India that there is no problem for them to sing night after night for hours, ten, twelve, twenty hours.

Ben Bagby: Could I reply to the remark about the audience?

Mark Amodio: Yes.

Ben Bagby: That's something actually I was going to mention after Karl's remarks about the idea of a historical, so-called authentic, no "authentic" is the "*a*-word" of early music [laughter]; you're actually not allowed to utter that word. Let's say I wanted to do a performance where I would say, "We have found a poet living in the jungles of England and his tribe has remained undiscovered all these years [laughter] and I'm going to bring him out onstage and he's going to tell a story." And we would then bring him out, perplexed, terrified, and blinking into the lights, and he would come out and want to know what to do. And we would say, "Sit there, just do your thing and sing." And we would be then treated to the authentic, discovered performer. It would be for us an artifact from some forgotten culture and we would be listening to it principally as such: an artifact from some forgotten culture. I don't think we would be so interested in what was going on with Beowulf and all the rest of the story. We would be more interested in the fact that we were looking at and listening to an authentic artifact from a culture. And if you wanted to say, "Let's be completely authentic," we'd have to have this man with his audience: he would have to bring his whole tribe with him and we'd then have to put them in a room that looked like something that they knew and we would watch from hidden cameras; we would be in some other room spying on them. In other words, the whole idea of the performance that we are comfortable with, the podium-centered, proscenium-oriented performance space, is already so inauthentic that there's no way to come out onstage and tell the *Beowulf* epic in any way, shape, or form that we can say is authentic, because, as you say, we don't have the audience. We don't listen with the right ears. We don't watch with the right eyes. We don't know the codes, we don't know the signals, we don't know the language.

So clearly—you used the phrase modern interpretation—well, in a way those are also words like authentic that we have to be careful with; it's not an interpretation in that I see the correct artifact and I'm now going to interpret it. All I see is a text and I don't think of myself as being modern or not modern. I'm not judging myself in terms of the timeline of how modern I might be. I'm only bringing to it my experience, which I don't identify as modern, and that's the problem with those labels. But this remains a big problem in all performances of medieval music. The motivation—when the motivation is authenticity, in the sense of material things and all the postivistic stuff you can put in place, why don't I then wear an Anglo-Saxon costume? In that case, why do we have electric lights shining? In that case, why are we having video titles? It sets off a whole chain of events as we wrestle with the question of where does the authenticity start and where does it stop? For me the authenticity of a performance, be it a troubadour song or the *Beowulf* epic, the true authenticity is that the audience, the listeners and viewers, are caught up in the story. Or they're thinking about what it's like to be an old king, powerless. Or what it's like to be a brave guy who's bragging all the time. Or what it's like to be drunk and jealous. All of these are authentic experiences that we've all had on one level or another and that's where it begins to resonate. And it's the resonance of the actual content of the story that interests me more than whether I'm going to have soft leather shoes or whether dirty fingernails would make my performance more authentic [laughter].

Mark Amodio: I've had the pleasure of hearing Ben perform the first part of *Beowulf* both with and without supertitles, and I think the performative aspect that you're talking about is really what helps transcend the issue of authenticity, both with academic audiences as last night, and with more general audiences as well. I don't mean just the audiences that came to the Poet's House performances, but the far more general audiences who attended your Lincoln Center performances. With the supertitles, the audience is understandably much more responsive. I don't know if you noticed any change in your own style, how you're reacting to that audience, Ben, because before they would have a printed text which certainly helped to locate them to some extent, but the audience is much more alive now over these last few years since the supertitles have come in. And I think it's raised that performative potential of the presentation and allowed you to forge a different, stronger, and perhaps more vibrant, performer—audience—performance amalgam, to borrow a phrase John used earlier.

Ben Bagby: Yes, using supertitles has also changed the element of timing for me. I used to go to Marx Brothers films in Switzerland [laughter] and you could always tell where the Americans were in the theater because only about 10 percent of the Marx Brothers' gags were actually translated in the subtitles on the screen. And in the laughter patterns in the theater, there was one American laughter pattern and there was a laughter pattern for the people reading the subtitles [laughter]. And in my performances of *Beowulf* it's the subtitles that really feed a lot of the information about the meaning of the text. And it was a change for me in that I realized that sometimes the reaction is not based on what I just said but what they just read. And then I get used to that. And, of course, there's another variable which is that Jon Aaron sitting over there is the person who changes the titles and so he has an enormous amount of power [laughter] to anticipate or to be a little too late and as he's done it many, many times, he's become quite virtuoso at anticipation, where it's necessary.

Mark Amodio: Jana?

Jana Schulman: I'm Jana Schulman, Western Michigan University. I also enjoyed that tremendously, and this ties into something that Dr. Reichl said when he mentioned Joseph Harris's article on incorporating the different genres. And I wanted to ask you because your drunken Unferth was absolutely lovely and very funny. I just finished teaching a *Beowulf* seminar where we read an article by Carol Clover that talks about Unferth and the role of a *þyle*, where he's a very formal orator given the job of grilling, the difficult job of challenging Beowulf, which Hrothgar essentially has to have him do; you just can't let anybody in—you do have to challenge them somewhere. And so I wondered, because you raised the idea of a different style or a different genre—I really liked the drunken Unferth but how could you, how would a performance shift if you started to look at him as more of the challenger, let's say, and not drunk, but performing a rather difficult court function?

Ben Bagby: Yes, it's certainly possible. You know that entire Unferth character is based on two things. One, "bēore druncen": that gave me the license to make him drunk. And the other one was an experience I had: I watched once in the Helsinki airport a drunken man accost a lady who was not drunk and kind of go after her because something about her offended him—I think she was speaking Swedish [laughter]. And the way he did it had something kind of formal about it; it was a formal drunkenness. But it also was unrelenting. He simply couldn't get out of this twisted oration. And I just sat there in complete admiration of the drama [laughter] that I was watching, and that actually was an enormous inspiration for Unferth. It's modeled on something, it's modeled on something which I think is genuine, but I can see your point. Of course, all these options could be tried out—we could have a workshop here. I could have my instrument and someone could say, "Try a more formal Unferth scene" and I could do it: there's absolutely no problem. Also when Karl mentioned the Finnsburg episode, actually he was reading my mind: my plan was to make that a formal piece within a piece that would have a much more formal structure. And in my current performance, Beowulf's recounting of his swimming match with Breca is based on an ostinato pattern played on the harp which never changes, except when he just can't stand it anymore and has to exult about the gold in his chain mail shirt or how he killed sea monsters. It's based on an ostinato pattern that has a very clear beginning and end. And it wasn't always performed like that. In the early days I just sort of sang it somehow. And over the period of years it began to dawn on me that he was actually performing this story. Somebody handed Beowulf the harp and he told the story of how he won the swimming contest, accompanying himself on the harp. So that's for me a big genre piece.

Jana Schulman: Well, and the Unferth thing, if you follow the other genre would be like the flyting, a formal, sort of very Old Norse thing, as in the *Edda*. I know you've worked with that. And so it would be interesting, then, to figure out, how would you present the formal flyting? I mean, would you have musical accompaniment? I have no clue, but it was interesting to me to think about that.

Ben Bagby: Yes. Well, I might have gone in that direction if Beowulf and Unferth had actual exchanges of text; if the one guy went after him about the swimming match and the other responded raising the ante, and he then responded and things escalated. That might have sent me in a completely different direction. But since it was one, long, rambling, bitter [laughter], slightly incoherent speech, "bēore druncen," that's why it ended up the way it had to.

Q: John Niles, University of Wisconsin, Madison. So when do we get to hear the fight in Grendel's mere and the fight against the dragon?

Ben Bagby: Well, I have agreed to perform the Grendel's mother episode in October of 2004, which sends shivers down my spine, because there's not really enough time to learn all of that. That's the plan, if we should all live so long. It's extremely difficult to develop my arrangement, my performance, because these things don't pop out of the ground, although as I mentioned earlier, I have in a way established a personal oral tradition. I have some things sorted out. I have some techniques on the instrument that I didn't have ten years ago. And I'm hoping that as I start to work on the new part of the text, some of it can be ordered according to previously established techniques, but some of it will not be.

Jack Niles: Can I follow up to that question?

Mark Amodio: Go ahead.

Jack Niles: I didn't realize that you were going to do that. But if so, are you worried about the boring parts? [laughter] Even Seamus Heaney, in his whole modern translation, skipped out certain things.

Ben Bagby: Yes, it's true. I'm going to have to face it. I'm going to have to face the boredom issue with modern audiences. But we're hoping supertitles will deal with a lot of that. I'm going to have to see. If I don't try it I won't know. I've gone to some epic performances recently of Korean *pansori* song, and I sat in a performance that lasted five and a half hours of one of the *pansori* epics with an audience that was principally not Korean; and everyone stayed until the end. There was one twenty-minute intermission. It had supertitles but they were quite meager. She would sing for about three minutes and the title would say "she was unhappy and went to the door" [laughter] and there's obviously much more happening here than we know. But it didn't seem to bother anyone. And I'm hoping that also will be possible for the so-called boring parts in *Beowulf*. I'm also wondering if people can listen to that mode on that instrument for what could end up being about six hours for a performance of the entire text. I wouldn't retune the instrument or take another instrument and another tuning just to keep it interesting: that's the tuning of the instrument. And there would probably need to be two intermissions, at the two major breaks. And I don't think vocal fatigue would be an issue. But the vocal fatigue issue, if it comes up, may determine a lot of how I deal with the boring parts [laughter].

Q: Ed Haymes, Cleveland State University. You've said a good deal about performance being—replacing the idea of reproductive performance with a performance that happens each time, and I'm wondering how—I know that there's this need in our society to get these things down on some kind of recording. And if you follow your logic through to the end, you should actually be training a bunch of new Ben Bagbys, and so . . . maybe—

Ben Bagby: Yes, send me your children. [laughter]

Ed Haymes: —maybe you can do both. I'm desperate to have some kind of recording of your work, but at the same time I can see the total contradiction involved in that.

Ben Bagby: It's a big problem for me. I said at the very beginning that I would not record this as an audio recording because every time I've listened to an audio recording of my performance it's horrible. It's not easy listening because when it's divorced from the performance situation, the storytelling, the people in the room together, it's simply not the same thing. So I've kind of had to abandon that idea until the DVD format came along, which allows for a technically high-quality video performance.

Ed Haymes: And you'll have an audience?

Ben Bagby: I hope so. That's a technical problem we have to look at, but the idea would be to tape a live performance or several live performances in the same space with the same audience since the people who make videos are interested in camera angles and they're worried about boredom too. As you know, the MTV generation is used to seeing a different image every 1.6 seconds. It's a very different concept of time. But that's the plan, to make a DVD of a performance. It could be one of many possible performances documented and then a few years later I will probably regret that I had done it. But that's the nature of the thing. At some point you have to just let go. As far as what you mentioned about passing on the tradition, yes—assuming I've created, am in the process of creating, a little one-man oral tradition—if that's not going to die with me then I ought to have some apprentices. But good luck finding a young person in this world who would be willing to sit down every day and rehearse orally, without a text, this story.

Karl Reichl: Just to make a suggestion; this is how it works in traditional societies: in Central Asia, the pupil staying with the singer would help his teacher in the household. Maybe that would solve the problem. [laughter]

Mark Amodio: Send him your children! Yes?

Q: Bruce Blaxton, from the Longship Company and unfortunately the purported translator of the poem "Beowabbit" [laughter] which has been circulating in some odd-stock copies for years. There is a translated one with the copyright. We've spent most of the last thirty years sailing various replica Viking vessels. Sailing is a misnomer. We spend a lot of time rowing various Viking vessels [laughter] and when we're at the oars we don't have a big guy beating the drum, and we don't have somebody yelling "stroke." We don't even have somebody counting 1-2-3-4. We sing. We sing a lot. And we like to sing long songs. Long, interesting songs with lots of things happening. Or extemporized songs. You get a strong chorus and then you just fake the verses as you go along. And this passes the time, which can add up to five days to cover sixty miles at certain times of the year if you're going the wrong way against the wind. Have you all—Professor Reichl had mentioned steppe travel, where the pace changes into something more akin to galloping horses—have you all come across any echoes or analogs of this in the oral tradition, where something that might have been used as a rowing song has now evolved into something else, or nothing at all? I was especially appreciative of the ship verses, of course, in *Beowulf* last night and they described the wide-beam ship, because in a narrow-beam ship, you're hitting the other fellow with the oar. So you want a wide-beam ship. Thank you.

John Miles Foley: The only response I can make would be that in many oral traditions around the world, you have a multiplex of genres that feed off the same mythology but that divide up into a number of different options so that, for instance, the *Siri Epic* in southern India has nine different genres, some of which are as workaday as rice-paddy-picking songs that pass the time until you can get together with someone. And then there's also an Arabic tradition reported recently that's as long as the *Iliad*, so that it's really not a question, in a lot of places anyway, of evolution from one to the other but a suspension or constellation of many different genres.

Mark Amodio: Yes?

Q: [unidentified] Actually, it's a pretty simple question for the gentleman from Bonn, I've missed your name, I'm sorry. It's obvious that they're training people to do this. Are the poets, whatever they are, are the singers—are they recognizing talent as children and taking the children in, sort of fostering them out? Is it a family thing? And at what age do they start training the children? Or do they simply—is there an approximate age? How do they go about perpetuating their craft?

Karl Reichl: My name is Karl Reichl. But anyway, there are quite a number of Turkic peoples in Central Asia and even some of the ethnic groups there have very different traditions. So, in fact, I can't give an answer which covers all the traditions. But one common pattern is that epic singing runs in a family, as in these Arabic traditions that were mentioned, where there is an Arabic singing village or village of singers. The same kind of thing can be found, for instance, in Uzbekistan, where so-called singer schools exist. They are not schools in our sense—what is meant is that the singer trains apprentices. These apprentices are very often his children or nephews or whoever lives in his village. The training starts fairly early, from six years onward; by his teens at the latest a child should have become interested in imitating his father, uncle, or a singer. For instance, the singer I have recorded extensively really started seriously when he was between sixteen and eighteen; he then moved to a singer's household, staying there for three years, and within these three years he learned three epics. Now, when asked "Could you perform this or that?" he says, "Well, performing any of these epics is like eating bread and butter and I can do it just like that." But his art is based on this kind of training. There have also been studies of these so-called singer schools in Uzbekistan. The Kirghiz are different in that according to tradition you have to have a vision, a calling a bit like Cædmon (if you think of Cædmon as an oral poet). You have a vision and in this dream you become a singer—

Q: [unidentified] God gives you the gift.

Karl Reichl: —but in reality training is necessary as well. The Kirghiz are very nationalistic nowadays, as are many of these new republics, and their national heritage is the epic. They have no other great poet. So they are interested in keeping this heritage alive—they have a state agency for this—and in finding young people who are willing to learn this tradition.

Mark Amodio: I hear from the noise out back and see from my watch that we're almost out of time. We have time, I think, for one more question if there's anybody we haven't heard from yet? Yes?

Q: I was wondering—

Mark Amodio: Oh, I'm sorry, not you, Rick, but the gentleman behind you.

Q: Sung-Il Lee. I am from Korea. Last night when I was listening to your reci-tation I was having the illusion of listening to *pansori* performance—earlier you mentioned Korean *pansori*, long epic songs—and I was wondering whether you have ever been exposed to *pansori* performance. You mentioned it a moment ago, so, and might it be a little bit presumptuous, if I ask you whether you wanted to incorporate *pansori* rhythm in your recitation of *Beowulf*. This is kind of, what shall I say, a crossing of two different oral traditions, because when you were reciting *Beowulf*, especially when you were doing very rapid passages, you were using this syncopation rhythm, *da-da-da-da*, and I was, you know, going crazy: "What the . . . ? This guy is doing *pansori* [laughter]; the only difference is the language—he is not doing it in Korean, but in Anglo-Saxon." My question is, were you really incorporating, trying to incorporate, *pansori* rhythm in your *Beowulf* rendition or did you do some very thorough research about the authenticity of that kind of oral interpretation? This is my question. For instance, in *pansori* the performer when he utters his omens very directly can speak very matter of factly, with a sense of distance, like describing Grendel's coming to Heorot—"Ðā cōm of mōre under misthleoþum, / Grendel gongan, Godes yrre bær"—and then he can watch the reaction of the audience, right? But suppose he was reciting the passage of the last survivor's speech, when he throws away all the treasure in the earth saying that he doesn't have anyone left. That is a very sad moment, the sense of doom is there, for the audience and the music would adopt the voice of the last survivor; here it changes form and the music to this speech would naturally be very mournful. But last night when you were performing I was kind of puzzled because some passages are very intense with a sense of doom, a mournful atmosphere, but then you were doing things with it as if you were teasing, playing with, making fun of the form, and I wanted to try to discover some of the thinking behind your way of doing it. That's it. Thank you.

Ben Bagby: Those questions you have posed are good for another hour of discussion. Let me try to answer them very quickly. First of all, I am an enormous fan of *pansori*. Although I'm a big admirer I really know very little about it: I've never studied it seriously. But I resonate with it very much. However, at the time I was developing my performance, that was before my initial introduction to *pansori*, so that I can't say that I'm subliminally lifting anything from listening to *pansori* singers. The fact that you are hearing that is very interesting for me. We would have to go over the exact places where you're hearing that *pansori* sound. It would be interesting to me to see if I am truly being informed subliminally by something I heard. In any case, I'm not making any conscious effort to imitate or replicate some kind of *pansori*. There are all kinds of reasons why that might be the case. As to your other remark about my attitude toward the poem, I never feel that I need to make fun of the poem or make light of something which is serious. But sometimes I sense a storyteller persona who is stepping back from what he's telling and commenting, that some of those remarks are sometimes quite distant and a little bit wry, a little bit ironic. And possibly in a few places that's what you might have heard, a changing of persona from being in the story, which is very horrible at times and very difficult, and then suddenly realizing "Oh, but actually I'm outside of the story just now, and just between you, the listener, and me, the teller, those people in the story didn't know the following thing which I'll tell you now." And there's a constant shift in the play of perception, which is the great thing about storytelling: you are the person you're talking about, one second later you are someone else, and then you are a commentator talking about both of those people. And you're shifting in and out of various levels of perception and focus in the course of telling the story. It's never meant, however, as a comment from *me* about *my* attitude toward the poem, that I think it's something serious but I want to make light of it. I feel that the persona of the storyteller is from time to time offering us a different perspective on what's going on. That's the short answer.

Why Performance Matters

John Miles Foley

Let me begin by stating four assumptions that provide the background for this contribution. First, on the basis of internal and external evidence I assume that *Beowulf* was in fact performed at some point in its history, though I plead realistic agnosticism about the precise nature of that performance.[1] Second, I recognize the fact that our primary guide in all such investigations is a unique manuscript from the latter third of the tenth century, and that its silent, spatialized presentation has undergone a semiotic, phenomenological shift from oral performance. Third, I propose that a comparative perspective from other oral epic traditions—especially well-documented, living witnesses—can assist our investigation; at the same time, comparisons with those other traditions must always remain at the level of parallels or analogies rather than direct genetic proof. Fourth, and most importantly for the present argument, I assume and will try to illustrate that our paramount concern should be understanding the idiomatic implications of the performance event and language, rather than practicing phono-archaeology (reconstructing the "true" event as it really happened). Straightforwardly put, the focus of our inquiry should be "What difference does it make that *Beowulf* was performed?" or, even more simply, "Why does performance matter?"

An Analogue: South Slavic Oral Epic

In order to provide a living, well-studied analogue, I turn to the South Slavic oral epic tradition collected by Milman Parry and Albert Lord.[2] From as early as the eighth through the middle of the twentieth century, this tradition flourished among bards in the lands that constituted the former Yugoslavia, particularly in the region we today call Bosnia. The same stories, often with the very same dramatis personae, existed in Bulgaria, Slovenia, Macedonia, and Albania, and cognate tales have been recorded throughout the Indo-European area, from medieval England to Balochistan.[3] This great and complex tradition was of course

235

the legacy of preliterate epic singers, who transmitted their stories, sometimes at enormous length, without the aid of texts. Parry and Lord were able to sample the South Slavic oral epic at a time when it was still vigorous, even if not at its height, and the archive they compiled (the Milman Parry Collection of Oral Literature) contains many hundreds of oral epic performances, some recorded acoustically and some taken down in writing from dictation.

What are the basic parameters of performance in the *epske pjesme* (epic songs)? In the natural context of everyday performance (and rhetorically in the events staged for investigators), there exists a hair-trigger interactivity between singer (*guslar*) and audience: those listening and reacting have a decided effect upon the transaction, which may as a result be longer or shorter, emphasize one narrative thread or another, include rich or spare description, and in the process be considered more or less successful by those who are its primary constituency. These symptoms are important, but more crucial is the underlying syndrome they indicate—a close cooperation between the performer and audience that bespeaks both a shared fluency in the idiom and a shared knowledge of the traditional story background. Audiences of South Slavic epic comprise many different individuals, each with his or her own predispositions and experience, but the Balkan equivalent of Adrien Bonjour's precious monograph on the episodes and digressions in *Beowulf* could not ever become a best seller for such an audience.[4] Unlike those of us who enter the performance arena from outside, they don't need a handbook to gloss the story content.

Nor do they require a handbook for the specialized vocabulary, which involves what the *guslari* themselves denominate as "words" (*reči*, sg. *reč*). Singers think and express themselves in a particular way as they perform, in an idiom that works quite differently from the language they use for quotidian purposes. One dimension of that special "way of speaking," or *register*, is the deployment of larger units, customarily no smaller than a line or metrically defined line-part and as large as whole scenes or even stories.[5] These "words" correspond to what scholarship has identified as formulas, typical scenes, and story patterns.[6] The singers whom Parry and Lord interviewed were actually quite sophisticated in their linguistic understanding of the specialized epic dialect (more so than many scholars, in fact): on their own terms, they understood both its disparity from other registers and its structural and idiomatic significance. Another dimension of the specialized South Slavic epic diction is its use of multiple dialect forms and archaisms. It is quite normal for a Bosnian singer to employ *ekavski, jekavski,* and *ijekavski* in the same song performance, sometimes in proximate position in the same verse.[7] Likewise, words and grammatical inflections long absent from the conventional, unmarked language are preserved within the epic *Kunstsprache*. Such is the register of South Slavic epic, the dedicated channel for communication between singers and audiences.

As for the prominent place of music in this tradition, we should note both the vocal and instrumental melodies employed by *guslari* as they tell their tales. It has long been appreciated that the melodic underpinning serves a mnemonic and microstructural role in South Slavic oral epic performance, and in recent years scholarship has further established a cueing function for the musical dimension.[8] Narrative shifts, in other words, appear on occasion to be signaled by melodic shifts, as the bard moves from one tune to another in anticipation of a development in the story. Although the lack of acoustic recordings or even musical notation for the performance of *Beowulf* makes it impossible to compare the Old English singer's practice on either of these points, there seems to be evidence of "metrical tunes" in the version of *Beowulf* that has reached us.[9] In the future we might do well to analyze metrical shifts in the poem to determine whether nonlexical signaling is also a property of the Anglo-Saxon epic performance.

An eEdition of South Slavic Oral Epic

Although we scholars seldom admit to the shortfall, there is an intrinsic contradiction and even an irony in using only the textual medium to analyze and report what happens, or is likely to have happened, in oral performance. To write and read about oral performance may be the favored interpretive move within the academic culture, but it necessarily puts distance between the actual performance and those who are seeking to understand it, in effect by reducing a living or once-living experience to a warehousable item. As fine and highly developed a model as the text edition is, it destroys life and presence via silent dismemberment: everything that cannot be contained within the covers of a book is discarded (or at best ostracized to the archive), and what remains is parceled out in academically approved, consumable components suitable for digestion by silent reading. Thus the epitomized text—already a voiceless shadow of the performed event—is prefixed to an apparatus criticus, a glossary, an index, a digest of variants, and other "reading aids." All these parts may indeed physically lie within the single volume, but their very segregation and page-bound spatialization means that one must exit one of them in order to use another. The parts of the prior integral whole are in this way made disparate, and the user of the edition is left to imaginatively extrapolate a dynamic process from a collection of several static products.

In an effort to counter this fundamental problem, I have turned to the creation of the eEdition, an experimental method of representation that seeks to reunite the segregated aspects of the performance and thereby to resynchronize the event. Because the experience of performance (oral or web-based) always speaks more loudly and clearly than any secondhand account of it, at this point I encourage readers of this essay to open their browsers to http://www.oraltradition. org/zbm and to click through the site as I proceed with the description.[10]

This eEdition presents the *guslar* Halil Bajgorić's 12 June 1935 performance of *The Wedding of Mustajbey's Son Bećirbey*, as recorded by Parry, Lord, and their native collaborator, Nikola Vujnović. In addition to the original South Slavic text and an English translation (click on Text Translation), "readers" can access a full audio recording of the entire 1,030 decasyllabic lines of the performance, complete with vocal and instrumental components, and can play it while visually scanning the transcription and translation (click on Play Audio). But the resynchronizing of the event does not end there. By clicking on "Performance by Halil Bajgorić," readers can also consult two kinds of editorial apparatus—and, crucially, they can do so without exiting the main page. The eEdition not only contains everything that the paper edition of *The Wedding* houses, but it also melds the separate sections into a single, uninterrupted, integrated experience on the Internet—complete with the living sounds of the original oral epic performance.

The editorial interventions that the eEdition provides are two: a so-called Apparatus Fabulosus (or story-based apparatus) and a performance-based commentary. For the Apparatus Fabulosus, click on the hot links within the English translation, and a gloss on the idiomatic meaning of the traditional "word" in question immediately appears in a box on the right-hand side of the web page. Likewise, clicking on the orange *C* button brings up the commentary on the given line or passage in that same box. Each reference tool is thus electronically yoked to the rest of the eEdition rather than exiled to an alternate and exclusive location. No need to thumb through the linear length of a conventional book, in other words; readers experience the text, translation, audio, and editorial digests all together as a coordinated unit.

Both editorial aids have pertinence for understanding why performance matters for *Beowulf*. The Apparatus Fabulosus, which glosses traditional units of utterance, amounts to a lexicon of large "words," a guide to the idiomatic meaning of constituent units of utterance. I will have more to say below about the existence and interpretation of such units in the Anglo-Saxon frame of reference. The performance-based commentary focuses on aspects of *The Wedding* best understood by remembering its nature as an event rather than an item, a concern for *Beowulf* as well.[11]

Textual Expectation and the Reality of Performance

Of course, this resynchronizing of the performance event lies well outside our usual experience as readers of texts. Preconditioned throughout our academic lives to rely on textual stimuli and to construct imaginative worlds by building on what we perceive as the rock-solid foundation of the book and its pages, we are trained to reduce dynamic performances to products we can analyze; the living entity best fits our world only after it is "formulated, sprawling on a pin" like the museum specimen that the neurasthenic Prufrock fears he may become. I emphasize this reality because it amounts to an invisible ideology—the ideology of the book—and it lies well below our conscious awareness, embedded in our culture's (especially the academic culture's) cognitive "take" on verbal art. If we struggle to imagine a performance of *Beowulf*, it is not least because we have conditioned ourselves to prefer the museum specimen to the living creature.

Once we do make the leap and ask what sort of performance might be both possible and useful (that is, what kind of event might respect both the original sound-shape of the poem and the realities associated with its modern reception), we encounter a familiar quandary. For the resuscitating of MS Cotton Vitellius A. xv (London, British Library) into an event in some ways very much resembles the problem of translating the Anglo-Saxon original into modern English. Everyone would agree that translation is a good and necessary activity: it has geometrically broadened the audience for *Beowulf*, making it available in more apprehendable form and easing its transit into whatever scholarly or pedagogical canon presents itself. At the same time, we will never universally agree on the "best" translation of the poem. Some will prefer a literal or historically sensitive rendering, others a liberal recasting, still others a poem-in-reflection that closely matches the perceived taste of the period in which it is published. The same will be true of competing reperformances of *Beowulf*, or for that matter any oral-derived work we wish to score for reperformance. While most scholars and students welcome the revivification of the text as an avenue into understanding its art with greater fidelity, they will also quite naturally apply various institutionalized and personal criteria in evaluating whether this or that realization of the Anglo-Saxon epic is more or less acceptable and useful.

My own bias in regard to both translation and re-creation in performance lies decidedly at the audience end of the spectrum. No matter how philologically defensible a translation of *Beowulf* may be, it will not communicate effectively unless it can stand on its own as an engaging textual map, a logical and inspiring script for coherent imagining. The same must be true for effective performances of the poem: reception will not be served by a re-creation that sacrifices intelligibility for a modern audience on the altar of (professed) fidelity to some (postulated) vision of what *Beowulf* must have actually sounded like to Anglo-Saxons in the eighth or ninth century. Instead, I find most credible those reperformances of the poem that connect with modern-day auditors, that speak to both the poem's art and the contemporary sensibility with transparency and grace. Indeed, were we able to stage a completely "genuine" performance of *Beowulf* or any other oral-derived poem, its foreignness (stemming from the present-day audience's lack of knowledge of the tradition as well as the language) might well render it effectively opaque. To put the quandary almost aphoristically, in my opinion the primary challenge for both translation and reperformance is not to practice phono-archaeology but rather to find effective answers to the riddle of reception.[12]

Clarity and availability may seem absolutely self-evident concerns, to be sure, even if they are sometimes submerged in favor of other criteria. But in preparation for the latter section of this essay we need to push the argument further and inquire precisely why—other than the inarguable virtue of intelligibility, of course—these concerns are paramount. It is a slippery topic to discuss (especially in a printed text meant for silent perusal), but only a thorough engagement of the audience will foster the ongoing, involved, in-the-moment experience of *Beowulf*. In a nutshell, we need to remind ourselves that performance is emergent, that it dissolves the distance between performer and audience by demanding continuous attention and response. Performance will not just conveniently stop when an audience member feels he or she needs a break to think about what has just happened, or to consult an article in the library, or to make a cup of tea before resuming text-fueled imagining. The audience and performer are locked—right now—into an ongoing diegesis whose spell cannot be broken without abandoning the performance arena. And just as that virtual arena promotes specialized communication in the designated register or way of speaking, so exiting it means that the dedicated transaction ceases, at least for the foreseeable future or until the intermission is over. Performance is all-consuming in its diegesis.

The Artistic Implications of Performance

I emphasize this last point because the all-consuming experience is the vehicle for a highly idiomatic exchange. Oral traditions around the world and throughout history provide a wealth of data on this point: the performer and audience, having given themselves over to the interactivity of performance, employ a focused, densely coded variety of language to facilitate their transaction. The scenario involves entering the designated performance arena (a virtual rather than physical locus); communicating via a specialized register (the lingua franca or, perhaps more accurately, the indigenous language of that arena); and, as a result, enjoying an increased economy of communication.[13] Within the well-defined performance situation, performer and audience speak a register structurally distinct from everyday language and redolent with idiomatic implications. To a brief exploration and real-life illustration of some of those implications we now turn.

In order to present the oral traditional cues most expeditiously, let me enlist the approach customarily called *performance theory*. According to this method, as Richard Bauman puts it,

> [P]erformance represents a transformation of the basic referential . . . uses of language. In other words, in an artistic performance of this kind, there is something going on in the communicative interchange which says to the auditor, "interpret what I say in some special sense;

do not take it to mean what the words alone, taken literally, would convey." This may lead to the further suggestion that performance sets up,
or represents, an interpretive frame within which the messages being
communicated are to be understood, and that this frame contrasts with
at least one other frame, the literal.[14]

Bauman construes this signaling in performance as a group of *keys*, or cues, that
prompt the audience member to take the interpretive actions outlined above. As
examples of such keys he mentions special codes (such as archaisms), special formulas, figurative language, parallelism, and an appeal to the authority of tradition.
Bauman is careful to stress, however, that each tradition and genre has its own repertoire of keys and that it is always necessary to discover how each form works on
its own terms. Each tradition and each genre signifies idiosyncratically and should
be understood on its own terms rather than through some generalized scheme.

Performance Keys in South Slavic Oral Epic

To illustrate how performance keys work, I will enlist the aid of Halil
Bajgorić's performance of *The Wedding of Mustajbey's Son Bećirbey*, conveniently
available for consultation at http://www.oraltradition.org/zbm. As the event
begins, the instrumental melody functions as a performance key to help designate
what will follow: as the *guslar* bows his *gusle* in increments that match the ten-
syllable rhythm and structure of the epic decasyllable, the audience is drawn into
the arena in which the transaction will take place. After nearly a half-minute of
instrumental cueing, during which the singer clears his throat in preparation for
the arduous task of "driving out" the tale,[15] the vocal articulation begins with the
following line: "Oj! Rano rani Djerdelez Alija" [Oj! Djerdelez Alija arose early].
Even within this single verse a group of coordinated signals serves to mark the
channel for communication. The interjection "Oj!," as explained in the hyperlinked
Apparatus Fabulosus, cues the start of the vocal component of the performance,
commanding the audience's attention and forging a more intimate connection
with the singer and the traditional experience that is now underway. The "large
word" that occurs next—"Rano rani," or "arose early"—may seem like a merely
literal filler, but, as clicking on the link makes plain, it has a traditional valence of
its own as a narrative marker. Clicking on the orange Commentary button will
provide the reader-listener further information about the idiomatic force of this
initial line, such as the typically hypermetric use of the interjection, as well as other
occurrences (both within this performance and in other performances) of the keys
that help to summon a traditional frame of reference for Bajgorić's epic.

At line 19, having brewed and drunk a truly heroic pot of coffee,[16] Djerdelez
Alija, one of the most prominent figures among the pantheon of Turkish heroes,

undertakes what seems a modest, uncomplicated action: "Skoči momak na noge lagane" [The young man jumped to his light feet]. But moving from a presumed sitting position to a standing posture is only literally (nominally) the meaning of this frequently recurring "large word" in South Slavic oral epic, as the link to the Apparatus Fabulosus advises us. For in addition to assuming the new posture, this highly idiomatic line encodes "an honorable response to an unexpected or threatening turn of events that demands the principal's immediate attention"[17] and, by engaging the implications associated with this cue, the poet is adding a gloss on events that have not yet been explicitly prefigured: "Here [the formulaic phrase] keys Djerdelez Alija's preparations of his horse and himself for the journey to Mustajbey and eventual fight for Bećirbey's kidnapped fiancée. Interestingly, this idiomatic marker announces Alija's subsequent actions as a heroic response to a threatening situation long before any reason for his journey is specified. Motivation is cued not by the immediate narrative logic but by traditional implication."[18] When Djerdelez Alija goes on to caparison his horse, arm himself, and travel to the tower of Mustajbey of the Lika, a fluent audience realizes—without being expressly told—that his errand is of a particular, recognizable sort. He will be undertaking a heroic deed or series of deeds with life-or-death ramifications. All this is idiomatically implicit in a single verse-length key.

Performance keys also take the form of larger "words" as well, units like typical scenes and entire story patterns or tale types. In fact, we encounter two common scenes very soon after Alija "jumps to his light feet." The first of these, "Readying the Hero's Horse" (lines 21–49), rehearses an elaborate sequence of actions that starts with the Turkish hero's running to the stable to begin the grooming process and ends with a memorable simile comparing the horse independently prancing around the courtyard to a lonely young shepherdess up on a mountain. The second, "Arming the Hero" (lines 51–99), also presents an involved tapestry of description, focusing on the protagonist's actions from the moment he approaches his clothes-tree until he finishes dressing and arming by strapping on his sword, pouring sequins into his pockets, donning boots and spurs, and throwing on his cloak. Within each unit the *guslar* explores the process of preparation in remarkable and (for the fluent audience) familiar detail.

But the details of these two typical scenes, rich and engaging as they are, are not by any means the whole story. In addition, these "large words" serve as recognizable performance keys that further delineate the generic narrative map: like many other instances of the same units in the audience's experience of the epic tradition, these episodes certify the status of the hero and the nature of his (as yet unspecified) task. In effect, the two typical scenes "slot" him in the familiar role of the protagonist about to journey to battle, and conventionally predict his victory in whatever challenge lies over the horizon.[19]

Likewise with the overall story pattern of *Wedding*, a major subgenre of epic in both the Moslem and Christian varieties of the South Slavic oral epic tradition and the pattern that underlies Bajgorić's performance. The *Apparatus Fabulosus* explains the Wedding Song tale-type in this manner:

> Although the individual characters may change, the generic types and generic events vary only within limits. The broad implications of the story-pattern include, for example, a young man eager to prove himself, a comrade-in-arms who assists him, a young woman eligible for marriage but sought and captured by an enemy, a wedding party invited and assembled by the young man's father that modulates into an armed force to battle for the return of the young woman, and eventually a triumph in battle that ends with an explicit or implied wedding. This large "word" thus lays out a map for the song's action from start to finish, establishing the expectable sequence of actions via idiomatic referral.[20]

Although a title (as the creation of fieldworker and editor) never comes into play, the fluent listener will realize where the song is headed early in the performance, perhaps when Djerdelez Alija sets out on his journey and certainly by the time of Mustajbey's speech at lines 252–77, in which he explains to Alija the debilitating problems associated with his son's fiancée Zlata. As usual in this subgenre of epic, the wedding party sent to accomplish the ritual bride-stealing has been decimated by the enemy, and it now falls to Mustajbey to engineer the recovery of the bride-to-be so that the planned marriage can take place. Soon he will issue letters inviting his Turkish allies to join a force with the double errand of rescuing the maiden and participating in the wedding, and a battle will eventually ensue in which she is won back and during which the bridegroom, his son Bećirbey, comes of age as a hero and leader in his own right. This string of events is keyed idiomatically by audience recognition of the familiar pattern and its implications.

The contract of performance means that all of these traditional implications—from those conventionally linked to the opening interjection "Oj!" through verse- and scene-length "words" to the whole tale-type of *Wedding*—are active, necessary components of the exchange between performer and audience. To the extent we can recover their meaning, whether via an eEdition or in some other way, these performance keys also play a role in the modern reader-listener's experience of the oral epic performance.

Performance Keys in *Beowulf*

Practically speaking, we should start by distinguishing between the full set of keys that are discernible in living performances of South Slavic epic and the smaller set that transfer to (and can be located in) textual transcriptions like the unique manuscript of *Beowulf*.[21] Such features as intonation and vocal and instrumental melody are of course lost to us in the case of an Anglo-Saxon poem that survives only in a tenth-century vellum cenotaph, but performance keys like special formulas and parallelism do survive into text, albeit as merely visual signals until they are revoiced by a modern performer. For present purposes, I will concentrate on a few of the traditional "words"—that is, formulaic phrases and typical scenes— that contribute to the more-than-literal, performance-based meaning of *Beowulf*.

Readers and listeners need go no further than the first few lines of *Beowulf* to encounter a pattern, or collection of cues, that bears more than a literal meaning.[22] The salient elements in the pattern are italicized:

> *Hwæt, wē* Gār-Dena   *in gēardagum,*
> þēodcyninga   þrym *gefrūnon,*
> hū ðā æþelingas   ellen fremedon!
>   (lines 1–3)
>
> *Lo, we* of the Spear-Danes   *in days of yore,*
> of the people-kings   the valor *have heard,*
> how these nobles   performed glory!

Apart from their evident literal value as a prologue, these opening lines carry with them a traditional signification: the composite cue announces the beginning of the performance-event and indicates that what follows will take the form of a heroic tale. The active elements in the pattern are "Hwæt" [Lo!], an interjection or attention-getter;[23] "wē" [we], a pronoun signaling the bond of collectivity linking performer and audience (and, arguably, many performers and audiences over time and space); "in gēardagum" [in days of yore], a phrase that summons the mythic time frame in which the retold events originally took place; and "gefrūnon" [have heard], a verb stipulating transmission via oral tradition. The overall idiomatic effect is to start the performance, involve the audience, designate the mythic context and a rough notion of the ensuing action, and prescribe the medium of oral tradition. With this pattern the knowledge-able audience knows where the tale is headed and which channel to use for reception.

The same pattern signals a performative dynamics in the Old English hagiography *Andreas*, an apocryphal tale of saintly heroism that probably stems ultimately from a Greek source.[24] But even if we assume that this poem was always a written creation and never performed, the rhetorical persistence of the "beginnings" pattern helps to shape reception for whatever reasonably fluent audience it engages.[25] Note the cognate pattern and frame of reference (lines 1–3a), with the active elements italicized:

> *Hwæt, wē gefrūnan   on fyrndagum*
> twelfe under tunglum   tīrēadige hæleð,

þēodnes þegnas.

[*Lo, we have heard in days of old*
of twelve under the stars, glory-blessed heroes,
thanes of the chieftain.]

As with the *Beowulf* proem, the cued announcement of performance ("Hwæt!"
or "Lo!") is accompanied by stipulation of the medium (oral traditional performance), the mythic context ("in days of old"), and the heroic content (in the
present case, St. Andrew's fearless deeds among the cannibals). Interestingly, this
same pattern, which functions as a key to performance, is also deployed across a
wide spectrum of other Old English poetry, notably the biblical *Exodus*, where the
heroic content is identified as "the glories of Moses" (line 2) [Moyses dōmas]; the
saint's life *Juliana*, which also features religious heroism; and *Solomon and Saturn
II*, in which the traditional cue leads to verbal combat between the two principals.
The pattern undergoes variant applications in still other poems like *The Dream
of the Rood*, where the dreamer relates his singular vision of Christ's heroism in
the Crucifixion and Resurrection, as well as the support rendered by the Cross,
or Rood, Christ's companion in battle. Through all of these instances and others,
the illocutionary force of the "beginnings key" announces a performance and prescribes rules for reception, guiding readers or listeners by blazing the interpretive
pathways and idiomatically signaling how what follows should be understood.

Performance is invoked (and reception directed) in *Beowulf* by other keys
as well. One of the more powerful such cues is the simple phrase "That was an
excellent king" [þæt wæs gōd cyning] and its formulaic variants.[26] We discover this
verse-long "word" in cognate forms throughout the Old English poetic corpus,
always as the second half of the alliterative line:

Widsith, line 67b	Næs þæt sǣne cyning!
	[That was not a negligent king!]
Deor, line 23b	þæt wæs grim cyning.
	[That was a savage king.]
Andreas, line 1722b	þæt is æðele cyning!
	[That is a noble king!]
Juliana, line 224b	þæt is sōð cyning.
	[That is a true king.]
Meters, line 24.34b	þæt is wīs cyning.
	[That is a wise king.]
Beowulf, line 11b	þæt wæs gōd cyning!
	[That was an excellent king!]
Beowulf, line 863b	ac þæt wæs gōd cyning.
	[but that was an excellent king.]
Beowulf, line 1885b	þæt wæs ān cyning,
	[That was a peerless king,]

Beowulf, line 2209b	wæs ðā frōd cyning,
	[[he] was then a wise king,]
Beowulf, line 2390b	þæt wæs gōd cyning.
	[That was an excellent king.]

We can the demonstrate this key's morphology by viewing the different instances as variations on the pattern "þæt/þā wæs/is X cyning," or "That/then was/is an X king," where X stands for an adjective bearing the verse alliteration and attributing a traditionally positive value to the king in question.[27] Standing alone syntactically, this phrase idiomatically cues an ideal of kingship that rises above the immediate context and traditionally certifies the designated regent as fulfilling or failing to fulfill the Anglo-Saxon generic character-type of the effective, respected leader of his people.

For example, the itinerant singer-historian Widsith praises the Burgundian king Guthhere for his generosity in rewarding the oral poet's performance, while in *Deor* the eponymous poet extols admirable kingship by imputing its opposite to the tyrannical Eormanric. In the next three instances (in *Andreas*, *Juliana*, and *Meters of Boethius*, meter 24), "That was an excellent king" is transferred anthropomorphically to a religious context, praising God for his all-powerful rule over the kingdom of earth and the *comitatus* of humanity. Within *Beowulf* the phrase invests Scyld Scefing, Hrothgar, and Beowulf himself with its trademark idiomatic implications. At line 11b it closes the brief description of Scyld's paradigmatic behavior as defender of his people, while in the other four instances it serves "the function of legitimation through appeal to the authority of traditional referentiality."[28] In a telling scene that recounts the celebration of Beowulf's victory over the monster Grendel, the poet adds the following couple of lines, capped off by the performance key, that establish Hrothgar's continuing place and authority:

Nē hīe hūru winedrihten   wiht ne lōgon,
glædne Hrōðgar,   *ac þæt wæs gōd cyning.*
        (lines 862–63)
[Nor did they at all blame their friendly lord,
gracious Hrothgar, *but that was an excellent king.*]

Versions of the same phrase certify Beowulf's kingship at appropriate moments, and in each case reveal another diegetic feature of this recurrent cue: marking the conclusion to one narrative increment and signaling a transition to another subject. Thus "[he] was then a wise king" (line 2209b) completes a short notation of Beowulf's reign, after which the poet enters on a description of the challenge represented by the dragon. Likewise, "That was an excellent king" (line 2390b) seals off the brief retrospective of the events of the Swedish wars before the story turns back to the narrative present and Beowulf's preparations for his final battle. In each instance, in *Beowulf* and in the other poems, this performance key invokes idiomatic meaning that gives additional depth to crucial moments in the given poem by glossing the immediate and local through referral to the timeless and traditional. Each usage provides an implied generic context for the particular situation.

As a final example of a performance key and the implications it evokes under the communicative contract of performance, I turn briefly to the celebrated typical scene of the "Beasts of Battle." Defined many years ago by Francis P. Magoun, Jr., as "the mention of the wolf, eagle, and/or raven as beasts attendant on a scene of carnage" and studied by numerous scholars in the intervening period,[29] the description of carrion animals recurs no fewer than twelve times in the Old English poetic corpus. In addition to its appearance in *Beowulf* (lines 3018–30a, with context), this "large word" glosses a variety of events in eight other poems: *The Battle of Brunanburh*, *The Battle of Maldon*, *Elene* (twice), *The Finnsburg Fragment* (twice), *Genesis*, *Exodus*, *Judith* (twice), and *The Wanderer*. The baseline implication of this pattern is clear enough: it follows a description of troops, weapons, or battle and forebodes the onset or continuation of fighting. In simplest form, then, it alerts the audience to imminent combat, as in lines 103b–9 of *Maldon* (active element italicized):

> Þā wæs feohte nēh,
> tīr æt getohte. Wæs sēo tīd cumen
> þæt þær fæge men   feallan sceoldon.
> *Þær wearð hrēam āhafen,   hremmas wundon,*
> *earn æses georn;   wæs on eorðan cyrm.*
> Hī lēton þā of folman   fēolhearde speru,
> grimme gegrundene   gāras flēogan.
>
> [Then the fight was near,
> glory at battle. The time was come
> that men fated to die had to fall there.
> *An outcry was raised there, ravens circled,*
> *the eagle eager for carrion; there was an uproar on earth.*
> Then from their hands they let fly
> file-hard spears, cruelly ground lances.]

In some cases, however, the "Beasts of Battle" key is put to more complex, elegant use by harnessing its conventional performative force to gloss quite unconventional circumstances, and it is in such cases that we can glimpse both its referential power and its remarkable adaptability in the hands of a talented poet. In *The Wanderer*, for example, the "Beasts" appears in the middle of an internal monologue in which the protagonist realizes the ephemeral nature of the world and just before the "Creator of people" is said to have "laid waste this city" (line 85) [Yþde swā þisne eardgeard ælda Scyppend]. In *Beowulf* the same pattern occurs in the messenger's report and prophecy of doom after the fall of Beowulf. Here is the pertinent section of the speech in question (again the active element is italicized):

> " . . . nalles hearpan swēg
> wīgend weccean,   *ac se wonna hrefn*
> *fūs ofer fǣgum   fela reordian,*
> *earne secgan,   hū him æt ǣte spēow,*
> *þenden hē wið wulf   wæl rēafode.*"
>   (lines 3023b–27)

> [. . . not at all will the lyre's sound
> rouse warriors, *but the dark raven*
> *eager over the fated men will have much to say,*
> *to tell the eagle, how he succeeded in his feeding,*
> *while opposite the wolf he plundered the slaughter.*]

When the messenger puts things this way, he is implicitly predicting an inevitable battle with a tragic outcome for the Geats, for he is effectively—via a traditional cue—keying imminent combat. In combination with other signals, the "Beasts of Battle" scene is here forecasting the demise of Beowulf's people. Although the unavoidable conflict will take place beyond the immediate time frame of the text-performance that has reached us, much in the same way that Homer tells us implicitly that Troy will be sacked after the closure of the *Iliad*,[30] this powerful idiomatic signal mandates the eventual outcome. By traditional implication, as also in other ways, we're being advised that Beowulf's death will lead to catastrophe for the Geats.

As with the South Slavic oral epic, then, performance keys enrich the immediate, local narrative action by serving as idiomatic cues for traditional implications. The first few lines of *Beowulf* reverberate with a pattern that opens the channel for composition and reception by prescribing the performance channel: the key, deployed in other Old English poems as well, consists of the attention-getter "Hwæt" [Lo!], the citation of the poet-audience collective ("we"), the stipulation of oral tradition as the medium ("we have heard"), and the encoded promise of heroic action. The simple phrase "That was an excellent king" and its cognate forms offer a freestanding, traditional affirmation of the ideal of kingship that can be pressed into service in a wide variety of situations. Likewise, the "Beasts of Battle" pattern conjures a recurrent frame of reference that implicitly projects an imminent combat, whether it be a simple consequence of the present narrative juncture or a more complex interweaving of traditional signal and immediate context. Value-added keys such as these—and there are of course many more throughout *Beowulf* and the Anglo-Saxon poetic canon[31]—are in my opinion the most important single reason for "reading" *Beowulf* as the performance it once was.

Conclusion

In response to the larger question of why performance matters for *Beowulf*, then, I would emphasize two aspects. The first is the importance of understanding the poem's ultimate roots in performance and of creating and experiencing a modern reperformance that captures the emergent, interactive nature of such oral traditional events. As stated above, the most useful reperformance will not necessarily be the most philologically accurate re-creation; some accommodation needs to be made for the modern audience so that they can participate meaningfully in the ongoing diegesis and thereby understand the all-consuming nature of the cooperative activity. Performance realistically reconfigured will dissolve the distance between performer and audience by facilitating and then demanding continuous attention and response, by creating and maintaining the virtual arena in which a particular species of language is employed for communicative exchange. I have attempted to give some idea of this dynamic by reference to a comparative analogue, the South Slavic oral epic tradition, and to the eEdition of *The Wedding of Mustajbey's Son Bećirbey* that is available online. In the future I plan a similar kind of eEdition for *Beowulf*.

In the final analysis, especially given the mute testimony of Cotton Vitellius A. xv, the most important reason why performance matters in this manuscript-bound, oral-derived poem is nothing more or less than its specialized language and the built-in implications which that register encodes. Using the approach known as performance theory and applying its tenets first to the living South Slavic analogue, I concentrated on showing how *performance keys* of various sizes and sorts—all of them single "words" in the terminology employed by the *guslari* themselves—function to waken idiomatic meanings that complement and enrich the narrative. Within Bajgorić's performance we considered the illocutionary force of the interjection "Oj!" and the phrases "arose early" [Rano rani] and "he jumped to his light feet," the typical scenes of "Readying the Hero's Horse" and "Arming the Hero," and the story pattern of *Wedding*. Within *Beowulf* our inquiry focused on the idiomatic pattern that begins the poem, the imprimatur-like phrase that certifies kingship ("That was an excellent king" and its morphological variants), and the typical scene of the "Beasts of Battle." Many more such cues or "large words" could be summoned as evidence from both traditions, but perhaps this small selection sufficiently illustrates the principle that I am advocating as the central thrust of performance in *Beowulf*: namely, that the performative contract between singer and audience entailed communicating via a specialized language rife with traditional, idiomatic implications. We will read *Beowulf* better—understand the poem more deeply as performance—if we can manage even a partial fluency in that dedicated register.

Parascript: Performing in Text

This brief addendum qualifies as a *para*script because it addresses what happens *alongside* script in a text that derives from oral traditional performance. Although the process may seem counterintuitive to us, the very act of textual inscription can and does entail oral performance in some cases. Once again, a comparison between the Old English and South Slavic poetic traditions demonstrates cognate phenomena.

First, the Old English side of the analogy. In recent years the once-certain assumption of a Great Divide between orality and literacy has weakened and dissolved in most quarters, replaced by a more nuanced awareness of how oral tradition and texts interact in fascinating ways. One of the more intriguing discoveries involves Katherine O'Brien O'Keeffe's demonstration, based primarily on various manuscript copies of *Cædmon's Hymn*, that scribes (re-)composed formulaically, that even during the process of inscription the traditional poetic language retained its ability to morph, to vary within limits. As she puts it, "reception . . . conditioned by formulaic conventions, produces variants which are metrically, syntactically, and semantically appropriate. In such a process, reading and copying have actually become conflated with composing."[32] Against all expectation, Anglo-Saxon scribes were apparently performing in text.

The South Slavic side of the comparison again involves Bajgorić's *Wedding* performance, specifically its journey from audio recording to paper. In preparing the original-language text for my experimental edition-translation, I logically turned first to the prior transcription made by Nikola Vujnović, Parry and Lord's field assistant, who came to Harvard University in the 1940s for the primary purpose of auditing the aluminum-disk recordings and establishing transcribed texts. I assumed that as not only a native speaker of the language but a *guslar* himself he would serve as the best possible guide for my own latter-day transcription. Soon after beginning the checking process, however, I began to realize that Vujnović was committing unexpected errors that, initially at least, I was at a loss to explain. Some of them were attributable to a tacit linguistic policy (transferring forms to his own dialect or eliminating nonlexical hiatus bridges, for example), but others involved wholesale recomposition at various levels. After studying these "errors" carefully, I started to understand that they weren't mistakes at all; instead, Vujnović the *guslar*, fluent in the performative language of the epic tradition, was *resinging* Bajgorić's song even as he wrote it down. Apparently, singers and scribes actually can perform in texts.[33]

Notes

1. In addition to the portraits of oral traditional singers within *Beowulf* and other Old English poems such as *Deor* and *Widsith*, cf. the account of external evidence in Opland, *Anglo-Saxon Oral Poetry*.

2. On the South Slavic oral epic tradition generally, see especially R. Alexander, "South Slavic Traditions"; Bynum, "Collection and Analysis of Oral Epic Tradition"; Coote, "Serbo-Croatian Heroic Songs"; and Foley, "Textualization as Mediation." On the Parry Collection of South Slavic oral performances in particular, see *SCHS* (esp. 1:3–20); Foley, *Immanent Art*, pp. 61–95; Kay, *Index of the Milman Parry Collection*; and the Milman Parry Collection, http://www.chs.harvard.edu/mpc/. For an experimental edition-translation of South Slavic epic to be cited later in this essay, see Foley, *Wedding of Mustajbey's Son*.

3. On the pan-Indo-European story of Return, see Foley, *Homer's Traditional Art*, pp. 115–68.

4. Bonjour, *Digressions in "Beowulf"*; cf. Bjork, "Digressions and Episodes."

5. On the concept of the "word" in South Slavic oral epic, see Foley, *How to Read an Oral Poem*, pp. 11–21.

6. See especially Foley, *Traditional Oral Epic*, chaps. 4–10; Foley, *How to Read an Oral Poem*, pp. 17–21.

7. Thus forms such as *mleko* (ekavski), *mljeko* (jekavski), and *mlijeko* (ijekavski)—all dialectal variants of the word for "milk"—could be used by the same singer in the same performance. See further Foley, *Homer's Traditional Art*, pp. 76–80.

8. See Foster, "Role of Music."

9. See Foley, *Traditional Oral Epic*, pp. 110–19.

10. The eEdition presents the contents of Foley, *Wedding of Mustajbey's Son*, with the various elements and aspects of the performance resynchronized via the electronic medium. For more on the larger Pathways Project, which compares oral tradition and the Internet as media that operate via navigating pathways, see http://www.pathwaysproject.org.

11. See further the "Parascript" in the final section of this essay.

12. For this reason, as stated elsewhere in this volume, I find the reperformance by Benjamin Bagby to be by far the most effective such re-creation I have experienced. Bagby gives us a superb and compelling vocal presentation in Old English against a background of supertitled modern English translation that helps bring those who lack knowledge of Anglo-Saxon into the performance arena.

13. On the theory and practice of the "Immanent Art approach," see Foley, *Immanent Art*, and *How to Read an Oral Poem*, pp. 109–24; as well as Bradbury, "Traditional Referentiality."

14. Bauman, *Verbal Art as Performance*, p. 9. Cf. Foley, *Singer of Tales in Performance*, pp. 7–11, and *How to Read an Oral Poem*, pp. 82–94.

15. The verb that South Slavic singers often use to describe oral performance is *turati* (to impel, drive out). Cf. Old English *wrecan*, which has approximately the same range of meaning and is likewise applied to the performance of oral poetry.

16. This capsule (lines 8–15) is itself a traditional key; see Foley, *Wedding of Mustajbey's Son*, pp. 195–96, or simply click on the eEdition link.

17. See Foley, *Wedding of Mustajbey's Son*, p. 196, or simply click on the eEdition link.

18. See Foley, *Wedding of Mustajbey's Son*, p. 196, or simply click on the eEdition link.

19. On the two typical scenes, see Foley, *Wedding of Mustajbey's Son*, pp. 197 and

198–99, respectively, or simply click on the eEdition links. Cf. Beowulf's preparatory arming and disarming as versions of typical scene involved in a larger narrative pattern (Foley, *Immanent Art*, pp. 231–42).

20. See Foley, *Wedding of Mustajbey's Son*, pp. 203–4, or simply click on the eEdition link.

21. What we have in front of us, it is well to remember, is at most the record of a performance, perhaps some incarnations removed from the event itself. But even if our manuscript represented a written creation by one individual, the roots of its language are firmly imbedded in oral traditional performance and as such mandate our attention to the contract of performance and its idiomatic implications. See further "Rhetorical Persistence of Traditional Forms," in Foley, *Singer of Tales in Performance*, pp. 60–98.

22. For a more detailed analysis, see Foley, *Immanent Art*, pp. 214–23.

23. Here the yield of analogy is particularly helpful. As noted above, the South Slavic oral epic tradition features a parallel signal—the interjection *Oj!* or the equivalent—that also alerts the audience to the onset of the performance. Like *Hwæt*, its lexical value is negligible in relation to its idiomatic, performance-engendering force. Both expletives exist as part of unusual (and therefore meaning-generating) metrical configurations, with the South Slavic particle almost always hypermetric (standing outside the compass of the ten-syllable increment both rhythmically and musically).

24. For an account of the likely relationship between the Old English poem and the Greek *Praxeis*, see Foley, *Singer of Tales in Performance*, pp. 183–84.

25. On the many other traditional signals in *Andreas*, including another *Hwæt* key introducing the poet's interruption at lines 1478–91, see Foley, *Singer of Tales in Performance*, pp. 181–207. On the ontology of oral poetry in textual media, see the categories of "Voices from the Past" and "Written Oral Poetry" as discussed in Foley, *How to Read an Oral Poem*, pp. 45–50 and 50–52, respectively.

26. For a fuller analysis, see Foley, *Immanent Art*, pp. 210–14.

27. The litotes at *Widsith*, line 67b, which portrays the well-regarded king Guthhere, amounts to a positive attribution.

28. Foley, *Immanent Art*, p. 213.

29. For a fuller analysis, see Foley, *Singer of Tales in Performance*, pp. 224–31; based ultimately on Magoun, "Theme of the Beasts of Battle," with a summary of research to date at Foley, *Traditional Oral Epic*, p. 331.

30. See Foley, *Immanent Art*, pp. 174–89.

31. See Foley, *Immanent Art*, pp. 190–242, *Singer of Tales in Performance*, pp. 181–207, and *Homer's Traditional Art*, pp. 263–70; also Amodio, *Writing the Oral Tradition*, and Renoir, *Key to Old Poems*.

32. O'Brien O'Keeffe, *Visible Song*, p. 41. Cf. Doane, "Oral Texts, Intertexts, and Intratexts," and "Performance as a Constitutive Category"; also Zumthor, *Oral Poetry*, and Schaefer, *Vokalität* and "Medial Approach" on "vocality" in medieval documents.

33. For a full explanation and tabulation of the differences between what Bajgorić sang and what Vujnović wrote, see "Nikola Vujnović's Resinging" in Foley, *Wedding of Mustajbey's Son*, pp. 144–91. As I noted there, the amanuensis "does much more than simply reproduce H[alil] B[ajgorić]'s words and syllables with what we like to characterize as verbatim accuracy; instead, he reconstrues the song, remakes it on his own terms" (p. 156).

"Swutol sang scopes": Field Notes on the Performance of *Beowulf*

Karl Reichl

The lights in the auditorium dim, the curtain lifts, the performer walks onto the stage in medieval garb, lyre in hand, plucks a few chords on his instrument and then, with a sweeping movement of his right arm, shouts to the audience: "Hwæt!" This is the beginning of a *Beowulf* recital by Benjamin Bagby, well remembered by all those who have had the opportunity to witness his performance. Philologists agree with the modern bard on the meaning of *hwæt* at the beginning of the epic and have glossed and translated the word accordingly. As translators can neither wave their arm nor shout to an audience they have to seek a way of rendering this call for silence and attention by other means. Seamus Heaney, in his *Beowulf* translation, does this by appealing to another, more immediately accessible tradition than that of Anglo-Saxon England, namely in his case the Irish tradition of storytelling:

> Conventional renderings of *hwæt*, the first word of the poem, tend towards the archaic literary, with 'lo', 'hark', 'behold', 'attend' and—more colloquially—'listen' being some of the solutions offered previously. But in Hiberno-English Scullion-speak, the particle 'so' came naturally to the rescue, because in that idiom 'so' operates as an expression that obliterates all previous discourse and narrative, and at the same time functions as an exclamation calling for immediate attention.[1]

What Heaney seems to say in effect is that a full understanding of the meaning of a performative signal such as *hwæt* presupposes an acquaintance with a world in which such signals still function. If we really want to know what the *Beowulf*-poet means by *hwæt* we must have previously listened to the performance of an oral narrative.

The choice of a rendering of performative signals in a modern language clearly depends on the familiarity of the translator (and the readers) with a particular tradition of storytelling. If *Beowulf* were translated into Tuvan, an appropriate rendering of *hwæt* might presumably be *shiaan am*:

The yurt is full of people, the fire is burning. In the silence setting in
someone says: "Shïaan am." With the invariable *shïaan am*, which can
be translated as 'well then', 'now', 'furthermore', the singer begins. With
his eyes closed and swaying in the rhythm of the tale's melody, he tells
of the mighty heroes of old and their heroic deeds.

No one dared to interrupt the singer during the performance of
a heroic tale. Everybody listened with great attention. People also believed that the life of someone who fell asleep during the telling of tales
would be shortened.

It was not unusual that the oral tale would last for a whole night,
sometimes even for several nights. Therefore the singer would interrupt
his performance from time to time, beginning every time again with
shïaan am.[2]

The Tuvans are a Turkic-speaking people who live in the Tuvan Republic of
the Russian Federation, located in southern Siberia, on the northwestern border
to Mongolia. To the general public they are probably best known for their peculiar singing style, called throat singing or overtone[3] singing (*khöömey* in Tuvan),
which is characterized by two notes being sung simultaneously, the second one a
harmonic, which is produced by modifying the mouth cavity. The Tuvans possess
a rich heritage of traditional oral narratives, among them heroic narratives of epic
form as well as epic dimensions. As is the case in other parts of the world, oral
traditions are rapidly dying out in Tuva, and L. V. Grebnev, from whose study I
have quoted, wrote his description already in 1960 in the past tense.

But, one might ask, "Quid Tuva cum Beowulfo?" Clearly very little; there is
to my knowledge not even a translation of *Beowulf* into Tuvan (though there is a
Russian translation, which Tuvans as Russian citizens can read). What *so* and *shïaan
am* as renderings of *hwæt* tell us is simply that there are various ways of exploring
the performative aspects of *Beowulf*, and one of them is a comparative approach, a
search for parallels in living oral traditions. What this approach has to offer is the
topic of my contribution to this volume. Like Heaney I will base my observations on
personal experience, which in my case is that of research into the epics of the Turkic-
speaking world and, since 1981, regular fieldwork and archival work in Central Asia.

Although there is no evidence that *Beowulf* was ever performed orally, and
although the relationship of the text as we have it to its presumed oral background is unclear and the subject of (as it seems, insoluble) scholarly controversy,
there can be no doubt that narrative poetry on heroes and Germanic legends was
part of the oral lore of the Anglo-Saxons. The *Beowulf*-poet himself tells us that
Hrothgar's scop sang a *gyd* or *lēoð* on Finn and Hnæf, clearly an orally performed
narrative poem and doubtless a version of the independently transmitted "Lay of
Finnsburg." While talk about the performance of *Beowulf* might be problematic,
talk about the performance of Old English heroic poetry is not. Of course, there

are many problems here, too, quite apart from genre questions, that is, questions as to whether terms such as *heroic* or *lay* are appropriate categories for the poetry still extant. In the context of the present discussion the problems concern not so much the type (or genre) of heroic poetry as the manner of its performance. What does "singan" in line 1423 of *Beowulf* or "sang" in line 90 mean? Singing, chanting, reciting, declaiming? What does "swutol" in "swutol sang" mean, or "hādor" in line 497? Clear, loud, high? How does the "hearpe" come in? As an accompanying instrument or played separately, and if accompanying the words, how? And what about gestures, facial expressions, or modulations of the voice's intensity?

More questions could be asked and added to the list. In many cases, no answers can be expected from the texts preserved from Anglo-Saxon England, in some cases answers have been sought in the textual evidence, although never with unambiguous results. The words *singan* and *sang*, for instance, occur in *Beowulf* both in a literal sense, referring to the human voice, and in a figurative sense, as when the iron rings "sing" in the coats of mail of Beowulf and his men approaching Heorot (line 323). In some contexts "song" is used of the human voice but used in a transferred sense ("wail"), as when Grendel shouts a "sigelēasne sang" (line 787) or the unhappy father bewails his son's fate by uttering a "sārigne sang" (line 2447). Specific references to the scop's performance are found three times: when he "sings" about the Creation (line 90), when his "song" is part of the entertainment at Beowulf's arrival in Heorot (line 496), and when he "sings" about Finn and Hnæf ("Lēoð wæs āsungen" [line 1159]). In one instance it is not specified who produced the "song" (line 1063) (possibly the whole company) and in another it is a horn that "sings" (line 1423). The last instance is interesting; here it is not the "singing" of the human voice that is denoted, and we might at first think that a figurative sense is intended, as in the singing out of the iron rings. However, a horn is clearly a musical instrument, so singing here must mean the production of musical sound; this in turn suggests that "singing" when applied to the human voice in a literal sense does mean "sing" in its modern sense and not simply "speaking aloud," "reciting," or "declaiming." There are, of course, many ways of singing and not all types will be thought melodious or musical. This is not the point; the point is that for an Anglo-Saxon audience the scop's performance of poetry was perceived as something like the sound of a musical instrument, in other words as something different from speaking (in however heightened a mode).

Without pursuing the argument any further, it needs no stressing that philological and textual analysis can help to give an answer to some of the questions posed, but, as with the example of *sang* and *singan*, results stay at best in the realm of probability. Sceptics will not be convinced that the scop performed in a way that can be described by modern English *singing*. However, there are other paths that can be followed. Some light on the scop's performance can be cast by looking at other Old Germanic poetry. The most promising candidates are the Old Saxon and Old High German biblical epics. The Old Saxon *Heliand* from the middle of the ninth century contains in one of the manuscripts in which it is transmitted (Munich, Bayerische Staatsbibliothek, cgm 25) staffless neumes, that is, symbols indicating the contour of the melody to which the text was meant to be sung (lines 310–13). This type of notation allows no conclusions as to the precise form of the melody (neither pitch nor rhythm can be established); all we can say is that this epic was performed in singing, whether always and in what context is unknown. A paraliturgical context has been suggested. Although Anglo-Saxonists have placed *Beowulf* in a clerical/monastic milieu, it is not, like the *Heliand*, an overtly religious epic, and there is hence no reason for transposing the possible paraliturgical context of *Heliand* to *Beowulf*.[4] A similar situation characterizes Otfrid von Weißenburg's *Evangelienbuch* from the second half of the ninth century. The Heidelberg manuscript of the *Evangelienbuch* (Universität Heidelberg, cod. Pal. lat. 52) contains two lines with neumes (book 1.5, 3–4); these cannot be musically interpreted with any certainty. However, as a number of Germanists and musicologists have shown, the notation clearly points to a musical performance. As the *Evangelienbuch* is like the *Heliand* a religious epic, it stands to reason that the mode of performance was modeled on that of liturgical narrative (e.g., the readings of the lectionary). On the other hand, as indications about the musical performance of later Middle High German secular epics suggest, there is no reason to suppose that the singing of these two biblical epics is entirely due to clerical and liturgical influence. Such an influence is likely, but the epics also point in form and style to a native tradition of narrative poetry, despite their religious content. And the singing of Old Saxon or Old High German biblical poetry is all the more natural if it builds not only on liturgical models but also on a native tradition.[5]

Much can be said, and has been said, about the possible singing of Old Germanic epic poetry. In view of the fragmentary and problematic form of notation many conclusions must, however, remain speculative. The evidence we have for the singing of Old Germanic as well as of later medieval epic poetry (Middle High German epics, Old French *chansons de geste*) is in need of further interpretation before it can be used as an explanatory model for the performance of Old English epic or heroic poetry. Many observations made by medievalists and musicologists for instance about the singing of the *chansons de geste* make sense when viewed in a broader comparative framework that takes into account epic poetry whose music and performance can still be studied, either because it is still alive or because there is enough unambiguous and detailed documentation available. This means that even if a study of the performative aspects of *Beowulf* attempts to stay within the area of Old Germanic traditional poetry, a wider casting of the net is desirable if not necessary for an understanding of the performance aspects of epic and heroic poetry.[6]

Looking for comparanda much further afield does raise a number of methodological problems. Comparison is only possible if the phenomena to be compared show some similarity. Is Tuvan or other Turkic epic poetry really an appropriate partner for *Beowulf*? We have few problems with comparing *Beowulf* to the Homeric epics. In a famous passage in the *Growth of Literature*, H. M. Chadwick has convincingly shown the similarity of Old English epithets such as *fealu* or *sīdfæðmed* to their counterparts in Homer (πολιός, κοῖλος) and Ann C. Watts has written a stimulating book on *Beowulf* and the Homeric poems at a time when Milman Parry's writings on Homer and Albert B. Lord's seminal book on the "singer of tales" were beginning to make an impact on medieval studies.[7]

However, *Beowulf* is comparable to the *Iliad* not because any influence of the Greek epic on the Old English poem can be assumed (though an influence of the *Aeneid* has been postulated), nor because the two traditions are contiguous in time or place. They are comparable because they both represent a type of poetry that is widespread in world literature, and because as representatives of this type they share certain typical traits. As Wilhelm Radloff, who has edited and translated a large collection of Turkic oral poetry, argued at the end of the nineteenth century, the art of Greek *aoidós* is only fully understandable in the light of the art of the Kirghiz epic singer, and there is hence much that speaks for comparing the Greek *Iliad* with the Kirghiz *Manas*.[8] If *Beowulf* can be profitably compared to the *Iliad* and the *Iliad* to *Manas*, then, according to the law of transitivity, *Beowulf* can also be compared to *Manas*. This is also implied by a comprehensive view of heroic poetry such as Maurice Bowra developed in his wide-ranging study, where the Homeric epics are seen side by side with medieval epics such as *Beowulf* or the *Nibelungenlied* and with Turkic epics such as *Manas* or *Alpāmish*.[9] There are many points in which Old Germanic and Turkic heroic poetry resemble one another.[10] There are probably also old contacts between the narrative traditions of the Germanic peoples and those of the peoples of the inner steppes of Eurasia; at least this is what one might suppose when thinking of their physical, generally warlike, contact in the early Middle Ages. But these are not the points at issue here. What I am trying to suggest is simply that we have among the Turkic peoples (especially of Central Asia) a rich tradition of oral epics and that much of this tradition, which can still be studied, offers us a typologically motivated basis for an evaluation of our textual evidence. It also offers us an "imaginative model" for the missing performative dimensions of Old English heroic poetry and epic.

The world of Turkic-speaking peoples is wide and varied, reaching from Western Europe (with sizable groups of Turkish migrants) to the Yakuts of northeastern Siberia, and from the Chuvash and Tatars south of Moscow to the Turkmens of northern Iraq, northeastern Iran, northern Afghanistan and Turkmenistan, and to the Uighurs of northwestern China. The poetic traditions of these different ethnic groups are equally diverse and manifold. Although some constants can be discerned, which seem to hark back to an older layer of archaic Turkic—first recorded in the eighth-century stone inscription of the Orkhon valley in Mongolia—in their present-day form the differences between the various Turkic traditions are probably more striking at first sight than their similarities. For reasons of space, I will have to restrict my discussion to a few examples. I will choose three heroic epics from three Central Asian Turkic traditions, illustrating each one by a short extract. My comments will be descriptive rather than interpretative, with a minimum of Turcological or musicological technicalities.[11] I will then come back to *Beowulf* and the question of performance in the light of the foregoing discussion.

Despite the variety of poetic and musical styles and traditions among Turkic-speaking peoples, there are many affinities and there is a close interrelationship between the poetry and music of the Islamicized Central Asian Turks: the Turkmens, Uzbeks, Karakalpaks, Kazakhs, and Kirghiz.[12] From these peoples I will take an example from a Kirghiz, an Uzbek, and a Karakalpak epic. My first example comes from the Kirghiz epic *Manas*.[13] To classify *Manas* as an epic is an understatement. It is an epic on a grand scale, in scope and dimension more akin to the Indian Sanskrit epopoeia *Mahābharata* than to the Homeric epics. This Kirghiz epic is more precisely an epic cycle, which in its traditional—one might say, canonical—form consists of three epics, *Manas*, *Semetey*, and *Seytek*. *Semetey* and *Seytek* are continuations of *Manas* into the second and third generations. Further continuations are known and have been recorded.[14] In its barest outline, the main plot of *Manas*, the first part of the trilogy, is in the version of the Kirghiz singer Saghïmbay Orozbaqov (1867–1930), composed of the following building blocks: (1) the birth of the hero and his childhood; the first warlike encounters of young Manas with the enemies of the Kirghiz; his election as khan; (2) the fighting of Manas and his companion Qoshoy against their enemies; (3) Manas's march to the mountains of the Ala-Too to free the land of his forebears; (4) the migration of the Kirghiz under Manas's leadership from the Altay Mountains to the Ala-Too; Manas's victory over Alooke-khan and Shooruq; (5) the history of Almambet, Manas's companion, a Kalmuck who converted to Islam and turned from foe to friend; (6) Manas's marriage to Qanïkey; (7) the complot of the Közqaman brothers against Manas; (8) the funeral feast for Kökötöy, a highly respected Kirghiz elder; (9) the great military campaign of the Kirghiz under Manas's leadership against Beijin; and (10) the birth of Manas's son Semetey; the campaign against Qongurbay, the main foe of the Kirghiz; and Manas's death. As can be seen just from the titles of these episodes, these components are actually full epics within the epic. They are generally performed on their own. "The Funeral Feast for Kökötöy," for instance, was recorded as early as 1856 by the Kazakh prince

Chokan Valikhanov; the poem was critically re-edited and translated into English by Arthur Hatto in 1977.[15] Orozbaqov's version of *Manas* was published (with abbreviations) in four volumes, comprising a total of over 50,000 verse lines.[16] The version of *Manas* written down from the mouth of another famous Kirghiz singer, Sayaqbay Qaralaev (1894–1971), is almost three times as long, with no fewer than over 130,000 verse lines. The whole cycle is much longer; Qaralaev's version is said to run to over 500,000 verse lines.[17] It is true that length alone is no sign of quality; however, the extraordinary gift of memory and invention a talented Kirghiz bard possesses results in an epic performance that is both dramatically varied and poetically powerful. This ability to sing long epics should also allay any doubts as to the unsuitability of longer epics (such as *Beowulf*—a mini-epic by Kirghiz standards) for oral performance.

The epic *Manas* is also known in versions from Kirghiz singers living outside Kyrgyzstan. In Xinjiang, "Chinese Turkestan," the most complete version of *Manas* has been recorded from the Kirghiz singer-collector Jüsüp Mamay (born in 1918). His version comprises 210,000 lines and contains eight branches of the *Manas* cycle.[18] During my first stay in Xinjiang in 1985, Mamay sang the opening passage of his version for me to tape-record in Ürümchi (22 October). I will illustrate both the meter and singing style of *Manas* from this recording. The epic begins with the following lines:

> Ey...!
> Aytayïn bir az qanqordu,
> anïn arbaqtarï qoldoso.
> (Menim) aytqanïm jalghan bolboso.
> 5   Jarïmï tögün, jarïmï chïn,
> jarandardïn köönü üchün.
> Janïnda turghan kishi joq,
> (menim) jalghanï menen ishi(m) joq.
> Kök jalïngday kishi joq,
> 10   (ölümdön ödö ketinche)
> (ötö ele) qorqush menen ishi joq.
>
> [Ey...!
> I will tell a little bit of the hero [Manas]—
> may his spirit give help!
> May what I am telling be no lie!
> 5   Half of it is fabulous, half of it is true,
> [it is told] to please the friends' heart.
> There is nobody who has lived at his side,
> he had (I have) nothing to do with lies.
> There is nobody like our hero,
> 10   (till his death)
> he had nothing to do with fear.][19]

The meter of *Manas* (as of all Turkic folk poetry) is syllabic, comprising either 7/8 syllables, as here, or 11/12 syllables. The shorter line is typical of the heroic epic and always used in Kirghiz epic poetry. As one can see from the text quoted, the lines are generally linked by rhyme (sometimes assonance, sometimes "rich rhymes" or treble rhymes), but they are also linked by alliteration (anaphora), lines 2–4 *a(y)-* and lines 5–8 *j-*. Alliteration is furthermore found horizontally in several lines. The lines are also quite often parallelistically patterned. There is no absolute regularity in the use of these linking devices; some lines might neither rhyme nor alliterate with the preceding or following line. Also, rhyme and alliteration are used independently. Some lines have more than 7/8 syllables or less; however, when performed, the lines become comparatively regular either by lengthening a syllable or adding a pause, if a syllable is missing, or, if there are hypermetrical syllables in a line, by singing two or more syllables to one beat. Although it is possible to study the meter of *Manas* and other Turkic epic poetry on the basis of the text alone, it must nevertheless be stressed that there is a close connection between meter and melody. What looks like a metrical irregularity when considering the words only will generally be resolved into a regular pattern when performed by the singer.

As to the singing of the words, there are several melodies employed in the performance of *Manas*. As every melody, even if it stays the same, is varied continuously, it is perhaps more appropriate to speak of "melodic formulas." A melodic formula corresponds to a metrical line; successive lines are generally sung to the same formula. However, as pointed out, there is constant variation of the formula, and changes also occur from one melodic formula to another. Sometimes a melodic formula extends over two lines, the melody of the second line being a variation of the melody of the first line, with, for instance, a descending phrase in the second line where the first has an ascending phrase. This type of melodic structuring of the words is not unique to Kirghiz epic performance; we will encounter it also in the following examples. What is typical of the performance of *Manas*, however, is (1) the specific melodic shape and rhythm of the formulas and (2) the fact that the singer does not use an instrument to accompany himself. This can be illustrated by the extract quoted above (see CD, track no. 7). After the initial exclamation *Ey!*—corresponding to Old English *Hwæt!*—the following lines are sung to a melodic formula with the following basic shapes:

Typical of this melodic formula (with its variations) is the second bar (measure) with its descending cadence (third-third or third-fourth); this gives a melodious lilt to the line. Widely used for the performance of *Manas* is a second musical formula. Here the syllables of a line are sung on basically the same note, with the last syllable (or the last two or three syllables) raised to a higher note; alternatively the antepenultimate (or an earlier) syllable is sung to a higher note than the preceding and following syllables. The syllables are sung faster than in the melodic formula illustrated above, which gives this type of melody an air of urgency and drama. The epic is divided into passages of irregular length (comparable to the *laisses* of the Old French *chanson de geste*). The end of a passage is marked by a sort of musical flourish and a short rest on the final note, generally preceded by a quick succession of recited syllables. The extract on the CD (track no. 7) consists of eight *laisses*, of these *laisses* 3 and 6 are sung in the second mode (01:06–01:28 and 02:20–02:41, beginning, however, in the first mode), while the others are sung in the first mode.

Russian and Kirghiz musicologists have differentiated between different types of melodies/melodic formulas and commented on the performance of epic singers such as Sayaqbay Qaralaev or Saghïmbay Orozbaqov. This is not the place to go into details; suffice it to say that despite the seeming simplicity of the melodic formulas employed, the analysis of an actual passage performed can become highly complex, revealing a surprising suppleness and subtlety in the interplay between melodic and declamatory formulas on the one hand and words and meter on the other.[20]

The second point concerns the use of gestures. Folk narrators are noted for a lively style of performance, with expressive modulations of the voice, ample gesticulation, and a wide array of facial expressions and gestures. This kind of performance has been studied in a number of oral traditions, as for instance by Harold Scheub with reference to Xhosa storytellers or by Vibeke Børdahl with reference to Chinese professional narrators from Yangzhou, and it is often imitated by modern minstrels performing at medieval fairs or onstage.[21] However, if a narrator plays an instrument, his hands are not free for gesticulation. Also his facial expressions will be controlled by the singing; there is little room for miming and the play of features. A sung performance, with musical accompaniment by the singer, generally implies a lack of gestures and other mimetic elements. The Kirghiz *manaschi*, the singer of *Manas*, is an exception to the rule. It is true that he is singing the epic and that his facial expressions are hence limited in their variability. But as he does not use a musical instrument, he has his hands free for various gestures. These gestures basically comprise movements of the arms and hands into different vertical and horizontal directions, often parallel (lifting the arms, extending the arms, turning the palms upwards, turning the palms downwards) and imitative gestures like drawing a bow or holding the reins of a horse. In addition to these there are gestures such as striking the palm of one hand with the fist of the other or with the extended index finger of the other hand.

An analysis of these gestures reveals that there is not always a one-to-one relationship between a particular gesture and a particular semantic content of the words sung. While some gestures are clearly imitative, the majority are not. Nevertheless, they are not arbitrary but come from a set of traditional gestures that are clearly conventional and an indispensable part of the performance. In some cases the gestures are related to violent action or quick movement (like riding), as when the striking of the palm marks the rhythm of the passage, keeping pace with the accelerated singing. In other cases the gestures seem to be part of the singer's pose as the spokesman of tradition, such as the lifting of the arms with upturned palms, a gesture suggesting prayer and inspiration from above. Many of these gestures have been preserved for posterity in the film *Manaschi* by the Kirghiz film director Bolot Shamshiev, first shown at the film festival in Oberhausen, Germany, in 1966. However lively the gesticulation of a Kirghiz singer, the overall impression is that of a highly regulated, conventional art, not unlike the conventional movements and expressions in other art forms (classical ballet, Japanese Noh plays).[22]

Singing an epic without the accompaniment of a musical instrument is the exception among Turkic traditions. The only other Turkic-speaking group that perform their epics without the accompaniment of an instrument are the Yakuts. They share this manner of performance with other Siberian peoples (Nenets, Nganasan, and others); it might very well be an archaic form of epic singing, preserved only in this remote region of the world. It is to be noted, however, that the Kirghiz epic singer, when he specializes in other epics than *Manas*, sings to the accompaniment of the komuz, a three-stringed, fretless, flat-bodied, plucked lute. The accompaniment by a plucked instrument is by far the most common mode of performance among the Turkic-speaking peoples. It is also typical of the Uzbek *bakhshi*, as the epic singer is called among the Uzbeks and other Turkic peoples; curiously the same word can also denote the shaman or faith healer in some Turkic languages.

My second example was recorded during my first stay in Uzbekistan from the Uzbek singer Chāri-shāir Egamnazarov (b. 1927) in June 1981 on the kolkhoz on which he was working at the time, in the Boka district, about thirty miles south of Tashkent. It comes from the epic of *Alpāmish*, one of the best-known and widely disseminated epics of the Turkic peoples. The most famous Uzbek version was written down from the mouth of the singer Yoldāsh Fāzil-oghli (1872–1955) in the late twenties; it has only recently been published in full, together with a literal Russian translation.[23] This epic is in a mixture of verse and prose; the verse component of the epic comprises 13,715 lines. The prosimetric form is typical not only of Uzbek epic poetry but also of other Turkic traditions. It is to be noted that the verse passages are an important, in fact the most important, part of the epic, and should not be thought of as interspersed verse lines in the manner of the Grimms' fairy tales or the tales of *A Thousand and One Nights*. Although the prosimetric form does not conform to the Aristotelian idea of an epic, it can be argued that these extended narratives are generically identical to what we might consider a heroic epic in the European tradition.[24]

Alpāmish is composed of two parts, the first constructed on the pattern of a bride-winning epic, the second a return story with many similarities to the return of Odysseus and other return narratives.[25] In the following extract Barchin, a beautiful maiden, who had been betrothed to the hero, is wooed by a number of Kalmuck heroes (Kokaman, Qārajān, and their brothers), whose advances she spurns and whom she threatens with the arrival of her lover Alpāmish:

> Āt bāshini saqlab gapir, Kokaman!
> Qahrim kelsa, qāra yerga tiqaman.
> Yā khanjar deya ozimga yā senga suqaman.
> Āt bāshini saqlab gapir, Kokaman, ey Kokaman!
>
> 5 Āt bāshini saqlab gapir, Qārajān!
> Qiz bolsam ham, mening achchighim yāmān.
> Qahrlansam, yā senga yā menga dur āxir zamān.
> Āt bāshini saqlab gapir, Qārajan!
>
> Qirq ming yātgan mening Qongrat elim bār.
> 10 Qongrat elda Hakimbekday yārim bār,
> Sevgili, sevgili, ey dildārim bār.
> Agar kelsa sorab shaharlaringga, qalmāqlar,
> Bolasanmi ani menen baravar?
> Bāshim qilma ming bālaga giriftār!
> 15 Āt bāshini saqlab gapir, ey qalmāqlar!
>
> [Hold firm the horse's head and speak, Kokaman!
> If I get angry, I will throw you down on the black earth.
> I will thrust the dagger either into me or into you.
> Hold firm the horse's head and speak, Kokaman, o Kokaman!
>
> 5 Hold firm the horse's head and speak, Qārajan!
> Although I am only a girl, my anger is deadly.
> If I get angry, life will have come to an end either for me or
>   for you.
> Hold firm the horse's head and speak, Qārajan!
>
> I have my tribe Kongrat of forty thousand peoples.
> 10 In the tribe Kongrat I have my beloved Hakimbek (Alpāmish),
> My darling, my darling sweetheart.
> If he comes and asks for your abode, Kalmucks,
> Will you then be his equal?
> Don't bring over my head a thousand sorrows!
> 15 Hold firm the horse's head and speak, o Kalmucks!]

The extract continues for another seventeen lines; in these Barchin specifies the conditions for accepting a suitor (see CD, track no. 8).

Metrically, some significant differences to the extract from *Manas* can be noticed. The verse line comprises eleven syllables. This at least is the normal length of the second type of line found in Turkic folk poetry, the 11/12-syllable line. As can be seen, however, a number of lines are hypermetric, mostly through the addition of a vocative (lines 4, 12); in line 7 the singer has changed "senga" [to you] into "yā senga yā menga" [either to you or to me], which adds extra syllables and actually corrupts the meaning. However, metrically uneven lines become smoothed over in singing, as can be heard on the CD (track no. 8). Another difference to the *Manas* extract is the formation of the lines into stanzas with a refrain-like last line. As can be seen, the stanzas are irregular, comprising four as well as seven lines.

As to the music, the singer accompanies himself on the *dombra*, a small two-stringed, fretless, pear-shaped lute. The musical patterning corresponds to the stanzaic structure of the words; that means that although the melody or melodic formula is basically repeated for each line, that is, we have once again a stichic melody, there is more musical movement in this verse passage. The singer starts in a lower register and "works himself up" into higher registers in the course of the verse passage, ending with a melismatic flourish. This is a style typical also of other types of Uzbek music; it is found in Turkmen music and in the epic performance of Turkmen bakhshis, but also among Karakalpak epic singers. In classical Uzbek music reaching the musical climax is called *auj* (climax), in epic music *qaynamāq* (boiling). Although the ambitus of the melody is comparatively small, the playing of the instrument, both when accompanying the singing and in the instrumental interludes, adds variety to what might seem a monotonous musical patterning on account of the small ambitus of the sung melody and its constant repetition.[26]

Chāri-shāir is a typical representative of Uzbek epic singing. But this statement does not imply that his style is the only one found among Uzbek bakhshis. Uzbek scholars distinguish different "singer schools"—defined as teacher-pupil relationships, which can be plotted into elaborate singer genealogies—with their respective characteristics; the "school of Bulunghur," for instance, was famous for the cultivation of heroic epics, the "school of Qorghān" for the cultivation of lyrical epics. In addition, every singer tends to develop his own style, however traditional he might be. The musicologist Fayzulla Karāmatli speaks of singers who have only one melody/melodic formula for the performance of an epic and those who have various melodies. Yārkalap Nazar-oghli, a pupil of Fāzil Yoldāsh-oghli's, sings the whole epic of *Alpāmish* to just one melody. Other famous bakhshis sang their epics to different melodies; Jumanbulbul-oghli (1868–1937) used twenty melodies, the Khorezmian singer Bāla-bakhshi (Qurbānnazar Abdulla-oghli, 1904–ca. 1980) even mastered as many as seventy-two melodies. Karāmatli distinguishes three types of melody: a recitative-like, declamatory melody, a songlike, but stichic melody, and a songlike through-composed melody. All three types are found among Uzbek singers; it should be added, however, that it is not always easy to draw a borderline between one and the other type. Also, a through-composed melody is marked by motif repetition and variation and represents therefore only a restricted elaboration of a stichic melody.[27]

My final example comes from a Karakalpak singer. The Karakalpaks (comprising fewer than half a million people) live in northwestern Uzbekistan, on the mouth of the Amu-darya and the southern shore of the Aral Sea in one of the ecologically most damaged regions of the former Soviet Union. They have two types of singers, the *bakhshi* (or *baqsï*) and the *jïrau*. The former accompanies himself on a two-stringed lute, called a *dutar*, and is generally further accompanied by a spike-fiddle player. The latter accompanies himself on a two-stringed bowed fiddle, called a *qobuz*. While the bakhshi specializes in lyrical epics, often based on popular love stories, some of which are found among Turkic peoples and their neighbors from Anatolia to Xinjiang, the jïrau sings heroic epics. These are more restricted in their circulation and generally linked to the epic tradition of speakers of the so-called Kipchak Turkic languages, languages such as Karakalpak, Kazakh, or Noghay (in the northern Caucasus). The singer of my third example, whose repertoire I started recording in 1981, is called Jumabay-jïrau Bazarov (1927–2006). He acquired his repertoire in the traditional way, that is, he stayed with a master singer and learned the epics from him by listening to the master's performances, repeating what he could remember, being corrected and adding step by step to what he had learned. It should be stressed that the apprentice singer does not learn a general technique (say, a list of formulas or themes), but specific epics with a specific plot and specific wording. Of course, the more he learns the better he interiorizes with the text its style and wording and becomes free to sing in the "epic idiom" rather than repeating verbatim again and again the same text. Jumabay-jïrau stayed for three years with the singer Esemurat-jïraw Nurabullaev (1893–1979) and learned three epics from him, *Edige*, *Qoblan*, and *Sharyar*. In addition to these epics, he performed a number of shorter songs (historical songs, didactic songs, and others). The performance time of an epic varies; it can take the singer two to three nights—epics are traditionally performed at night—to sing an epic.[28]

The following extract comes from *Edige*. Edige is a historical figure from around 1400, a commander of the Golden Horde, whose existence and deeds are well attested in contemporary Russian chronicles. The epic offers valuable material for the study of the relationship between history and poetry; it is also interesting for the study of ethnic and national identity, in particular their formation in recent years, when the epic was rescued from enforced oblivion as a symbol of nationhood by the Noghay, Karakalpaks, and Tatars, fifty years after its

performance and publication was banned by Stalin.[29] The epic describes the
miraculous birth of the hero; his exceptional wisdom as a boy; the fear and envy
he awakens in Khan Tokhtamysh, his adoptive father; his flight from Tokhtamysh
to Timur (Tamerlane); Tokhtamysh's defeat at the hands of Edige and his son
Nuraddin; the quarrel between father and son, and their final reconciliation, with
Nuraddin following his father as ruler of the Noghay.[30] The following quotation is
the first sung passage in Jumabay's version, recorded in 1993. In it, Khan Tokhtamysh's vizier Kenjembay urges the khan to expel a man named Tuman-hoja, since
the latter has no children. This enables the khan to confiscate Tuman-hoja's possessions. As it turns out, when Tuman-hoja sets up his yurt on his flight, his servant finds the newly born Edige, with whom Tuman-hoja returns to the khan.
Edige is then adopted by the khan:[31]

> Mïngsan üyli Noghay bar.
> Xalqïmdï biyler adam bar.
> Jaqsï menen jamannïng
> Körki bolghan bendeler
> 5   Härkimnen de tabïlar.
> Mïngsan Noghay ishinde
> Mïna khalqtïng khïzmetkeri
> Keneges ulï Kenjembay-ay
> Toqtamïstïng aldïnda
> 10   Künde arïz etedi,
> Künde qarïz etedi,
> Söz mäniske jetedi.
> Ne qïlar eken Kenjembay,
> Sözdi turïp bejerip-äy?
> 15   Kenjembayday bätshaghar
> Toqtamïstïng aldïnda
> Mïngsan sözdi aytadï.
> Gäp tamamï sol edi:
> Mïna tolghan Noghayda
> 20   Tuman da khoja bar edi(ng)-äy.
> Tuman atlï khojanïng
> Ulï, qïzï joq edi.
> Xangha aytar arzï
> Sol bätshaghardïng tuwghanï
> 25   Kenjembayday bädirek:
> "Taqsïr, khanïm, dat!" dedi.
> "Arïzïng bolsa, ayt!" dedi.
> "Aytar arïzïm shul," dedi,
> "Ay menen kün tutïlïp
> 30   Khïzmeti bolmay tur!" dedi.
> Mänisi munung ne dedi:
> "Här patshanïñ qol astïnda

Ya bes üy, ya jeti üy
Ulsïz, qïzsïz bolsa,
35   Sonnan bolar," dep edi.
Kenjembaydïng sözi edi:
"Häm atam dep, häm qulïm dep
Mïna turghan khojanï
Aqïlgöyge alïpsang.
40   Ïlayïq pa patshagha?
Ulï, qïzï joq edi.
Joq qilmasang usïnï,
Khïzmeting sening jürmeydi.
Däwleting(e)-äy kes," dedi(ng)-aw.

[There are the Noghay with the innumerable yurts,
There are the men who rule my people as biys.
People who have
Good and bad characteristics
5   Are found among everyone.
Among the innumerable Noghay,
Kenjembay, the son of Keneges,
A servant from this people,
Brings a request every day,
10   Makes a plea every day,
Speaks words deep with meaning
Before Tokhtamysh.
What did Kenjembay want to achieve
When he spoke these words?
15   The rogue Kenjembay
Spoke innumerable words
Before Tokhtamysh.
The drift of his speech was the following:
Among the innumerable Noghay
20   There was also a man named Tuman-hoja.
The one who was named Tuman-hoja
Had neither a son nor a daughter.
This son of a rogue told the khan
His complaints,
25   Kenjembay, the son of a slave:
"My lord, my khan, lend me your ears!" he said.
"If you have a wish, speak!" he said.
"The wish that I want to express is this," he said,
"The moon and the sun darken and
30   Do not fulfil their duties," he said.
The meaning of what he said was:
"If five or seven families
Under the rule of any one padishah
Are without a son and without a daughter,
35   This, an eclipse of the moon and the sun, is the result."

Kenjembay's words were:
"You have taken this hoja
As an advisor,
Whom you call 'father' as well as 'slave.'
40   Is this worthy of a padishah?
He has no son and no daughter.
If you do not destroy him,
You will not be served as is befitting.
He impedes your success," he said.]

The musical style employed for this passage (see CD, track no. 9) is typical of the Karakalpak jïrau in general. Once again the melody is predominantly stichic, with the same melody or rather melodic formula repeated each line. It has a clear beat, marking the caesura in the middle of each line. The singer begins the sung passages with a short instrumental introduction. The instrument, the *qobuz*, is an archaic fiddle, played like a small viol on the singer's knees; it has two horsehair strings, which are played in harmonics style, that is, they are not pressed down onto the fingerboard but the fingers, positioned between the strings and touching them simultaneously, exert only a slight pressure on them. Short instrumental interludes, sometimes consisting of only one stroke of the bow, come at the end of some lines (lines 8, 14, 25, 30, 35, 38); they punctuate also the prose parts of the epic. At line 21, the singer changes into a declamatory reciting style, and then ends the passage with a sung last line, characterized by fermatas in the middle and at the end of the line.[32]

There can be no doubt that on first hearing the three examples chosen for my discussion the differences between them will be more noticeable than their similarities. Unaccompanied singing versus accompaniment, plucked instrument versus bowed instrument, natural voice (as with the Kirghiz singers) versus strained voice (typical especially of the Karakalpak singer), all this creates an individual style and differentiates one tradition from the other. On closer analysis, however, all three examples can be seen as representatives of one and the same type of epic singing.

What does this type consist of? Musically, the most salient characteristic is the use of stichic melodies. Singing the epic to stichic melodies is widespread among oral traditions and no peculiarity of Turkic traditions. It is generally considered an archaic type of singing, peculiar to the singing of narrative poetry such as epics, myths, or legends.[33] Better-known examples are the Finnish *runo* and the Russian *bylina*.[34] From what we know about the singing of the medieval *chanson de geste*, this type of epic was also sung to a basically stichic melody.[35] Looking at the melodies, we can see that there is indeed *melody*, but that the melodic features are on the whole fairly simple (small ambitus, small interval steps, singing several syllables on the same note), staying close to a recitative-like speech, to what in music is called "parlando." While more melodic features can be found (such as fermatas and melismas at the end of verse passages), the melody might also turn into a recitativo, as intimated in mode 2 of the *Manas* extract and fully realized in Jumabay's performance of the second half of the verse passage. More florid and musically sophisticated ways of performing the epic can be found among Turkic peoples, in particular for the performance of lyrical epics. But for heroic epics the examples given convey a representative impression of their performance, however varied the styles both within the traditions illustrated here as well as outside them might be.

There can be no doubt that in the traditions discussed above the epic singer is in the first instance considered a narrator. This is self-evident in the case of the Kirghiz manaschi, but it is also true of the Uzbek and Karakalpak epic singers, even if bakhshi and jïrau also sing songs and their musical skill (in particular in the case of the Uzbek bakhshi) is admired and much appreciated. It is not for the music that the audience gathers to hear an epic singer. And yet it is not without music that the epic is performed. Music plays a dual role in the performance of epic. On the one hand, it is, as it were, a heightening of the meter and verse-structure of the poetry, an underscoring of the rhythm and formal patterning of the verse passages. It is like recitation, just one step further. On the other hand, music does take on a life of its own when the songlike elements increase, the musical patterning overlays the verbal patterning, or instrumental interludes embellish the narrative. Even in its most "monotonous" form, there is an aesthetic dimension involved in these melodies. This is most clearly shown by the "Manas melody" with its triadic cadence but otherwise quite simple melodic line.

While the manaschi uses his arms to gesticulate, gestures are rare in the other Turkic traditions. They are only found in the prose recitation of prosimetric epics, and even here narrators use gestures only sparingly. There is something almost impassive about the singing of epics, as if the singer were only the vehicle of the traditional tale, a link in the tradition rather than a shaper, who puts his personality into the foreground. True, many singers have been strong personalities, and they must and do put all their physical and artistic strength into a performance if it is to be successful. However, when it comes to singing, the impression one gathers both from live performances as well as from the sound recordings available is one of "impersonality," of a lack of individual expressiveness. In this respect the Turkic bard seems to be similar to what A. Coupez and T. Kamanzi remark about the court poet of Rwanda: "Contrary to the amateur, who gesticulates with body and voice, the professional performer adopts a calm attitude, a rapid and monotonous flow of speech. During an admiring reaction of the listeners he suspends his voice with indifference until silence is restored."[36]

A dramatic element is as a rule introduced into the performance not by

gestures or expressive interpretations of the words and their melody, but by varying the melody, by using different melodies, by the change between verse and
prose in prosimetric traditions, by adding musical interludes in accompanied performances, even by the use of leitmotif-like melodies (in Yakut epics).[37] Also, there
can be a relationship between a particular melody and a particular passage in the
epic. These melodies have names, and the audience will know that some passage
to be sung will be sung to the tune and in the mode traditionally associated with
it. In *Alpāmish*, for instance, the contest songs at the end of the epic will generally
be sung in the style of wedding songs. In *Manas* elegiac passages known under
the name of *arman* (lit. "unfulfilled wish") are sung to a slow melody. Among
Karakalpak jiraus a number of tune names are known, each linked to specific verse
passages in *Edige* and other epics.[38]

To sum up then, however "monotonous" the music, however much the
words rather than the music might be in the foreground of an epic recital, there is
an aesthetic dimension to the music. The music also brings home the fact that the
oral epic is only alive when it is performed, when the voice of the singer is heard,
in all its richness and resonance.

After this necessarily rapid discussion of some salient traits of the performance of Turkic heroic epics in Central Asia, I would like to return very briefly
to the question of whether any inferences can be drawn from this for the performance of *Beowulf* (or, more neutrally, Old English heroic poetry). Meter seems to
be an insurmountable obstacle for transferring insights from one tradition to the
other. However one might view Old English meter—and there are plenty of possibilities and metrical theories to choose from—the verse is not syllabic in the way
Turkic folk verse is. Even the most "regular" long line with four stressed syllables
will have a varying number of unstressed syllables and varying patterns of the
distribution of stressed and unstressed syllables. Although these patterns might
be scanned along Heusler's "Takttheorie" (and its various later elaborations) into
regular beats, they will not have the comparatively even flow of the Turkic verse
line.[39] As a consequence, measured syllabic melodies like the "Manas melody,"
where each syllable is basically sung to one note and the notes are patterned into
regular bar-type units, are implausible for Old English verse. Recitative melodies
with a more flexible rhythmic structure might be more appropriate for the singing
of the alliterative long-line.

The notational fragments found for Old High German and Old Saxon biblical poetry have led some medievalists to posit a fundamental similarity between
the tunes of Old Germanic poetry and those reconstructed by musicologists and
liturgical scholars for psalmody in Gregorian chant. But this presumed resemblance is a moot point. One might wonder why vernacular poetry should in any
way resemble the liturgical chant of the Christian Church, which has its roots in

the Mediterranean world of the beginning of our era, if not earlier.[40] There is no intrinsic reason why the performance of traditional Old Germanic verse should be modeled on that of the psalms. It does not follow that all vernacular music is like liturgical music simply because it is only the latter that has been written down. When we turn instead to comparative studies, we can learn what types of melodies are used in the singing of epic; we can furthermore recognize the universality of certain types, such as the stichic melodies discussed here. However, comparative studies cannot provide us with a specific melody, as if we were dealing with a *contrafactum* situation, where an existing melody is underlaid with a new text. The "melody" of *Beowulf* can neither be extrapolated from liturgical chant nor from suitable ethnomusicological material, nor can it be mechanically deduced from metrical givens, even if these givens were clearer than they are. Characterizing the presumed melody of Old English oral epic poetry as "stichic, possibly recitative-like" is probably the nearest we can get to the truth.

But was Old English epic poetry actually sung? Above I mentioned the singing of the horn in *Beowulf*, line 1423, as an argument for the sense "emitting a musical sound" of "singan." Of course, for the very same horn also the verb "galan" is used (line 1432), a verb that is generally associated with maybe a loud or harsh or possibly a sad or melancholy sound (in collocations such as "hearmlēoð," "sorhlēoð," "gryrelēoð galan").[41] However we interpret the precise meaning of *singan*, the frequent association of the scop with the *hearpe* in Old English does speak for "singing" in these contexts. Corroboration comes also from Cædmon's story, where both the Latin text and its Old English translation emphasize the musical aspect of Cædmon's gift of turning story in poetry:[42]

> in carmen dulcissimum conuertebat, suauiusque resonando doctores suos uicissim auditores sui faciebat.

> in þæt swēteste lēoð gehwerfde. Ond his song ond his lēoð wæron swā wynsumu tō gehȳranne þætte seolfan þā his lārēowas æt his mūðe wreoton ond leornodon.

This passage is also interesting in that it implies an aesthetic dimension of the performance: the song is "dulcissimum," "swēteste," and melodious in its sound ("suauiusque resonando," "wynsumu tō gehȳranne"). We know from earlier on in the story that the singing was to the accompaniment of the *hearpe* (the Old English text has "be hearpan singan"), and it might not be unreasonable to surmise that Cædmon used the *hearpe* also here.[43] The Old English aesthetic vocabulary connected to the music of epic can be somewhat enlarged if we include this instrument; from collocations in Old English poetry it emerges that the Anglo-Saxons appreciated the resounding sound of the *hearpe*: as the *Riming Poem* puts it, "scyl wæs hearpe, / hlūde hlynede" (27b–28a). This might have been a quality also appreciated in the scop's performance—at least this is what qualifications of his song such as *swutol* or *hādor* suggest.

Neither the accumulation of comparative material nor the semantic (and etymological) analysis of the various terms and collocations connected to the scop and his art result in a score for *Beowulf*. Personally I see evidence for a singing rather than a reciting style (using a stichic melody) and for the use of the *hearpe* as an accompanying instrument to the singing itself, not only for interludes in pauses. However, the most important insight the study of oral epic provides is that Performance (with a capital *P*) is in the foreground. We are confronted not with a text which can be read and interpreted at leisure, but experience an unfolding of poetry in time, in words as sounds, sounds that comprise both meaning and an aesthetic quality: the "sweetness" and "winsomeness" of song. To hear a live performance of *Beowulf*, however speculative, takes us closer to the heart of Anglo-Saxon oral poetry than the most meticulous reading of the text.

A Glossary of Musical Terms

ambitus (of a melody): range of a melody

bar: a group of beats, of which the first generally has an ictus or accent (3/4 bar, 4/4 bar, etc.)

cadence: a melodic or harmonic formula at the end of a composition

contrafactum: in music, the reuse of a melody for a new text

fermata: a sustained note

fourth: interval comprising two whole tones and a semitone (perfect fourth)

fret: strips of material across the fingerboard of plucked or bowed instruments that mark the position of the fingers for playing different notes

harmonics: (1) overtones, the various higher frequencies present in the acoustic composition of a tone of a given pitch; (2) the high flute-like tones produced on a stringed instrument when slightly touching a string at specific points

interval: distance in pitch (or height) between two tones

leitmotif: a recurring melody typical of a character or an idea, as in Wagner's later operas

measure: *see* bar

melisma: several notes sung to one syllable

neumes: an early form of musical notation, as used in the notation of Gregorian chant

overtone (singing): a manner of singing that reinforces in addition to the fundamental of a tone also some of its overtones (or harmonics)

parlando: speechlike singing; singing as if speaking

recitative/recitativo: speechlike singing, as in the singing of the Psalms in Gregorian chant; also various types of speechlike singing in opera

register: range of the voice

staffless (neumes): the earliest form of neumes, without the lines (staff) used for musical notations

stichic (melody): the same melody sung to each verse line

third: interval comprising two whole tones (major third) or a whole tone and a semitone (minor third)

through-composed (melody): a melody consisting of different parts for different verse lines

triadic (cadence): here: succession of three notes that are part of a cadence

Notes

1. Heaney, *Beowulf*, p. xxvii.
2. Grebnev, *Tuvinskij geroicheskij èpos* [The Tuvan heroic epic], p. 8 (my translation).
3. See the glossary of musical terms.
4. See Taeger, "Ein vergessener handschriftlicher Befund."
5. There is a rich literature on this topic, mainly from the 1960s; see in particular Jammers, "Das mittelalterliche deutsche Epos und die Musik"; Hofmann, "Die Frage des musikalischen Vortrags"; Hofmann and Jammers, "Zur Frage des Vortrags der altgermanischen Stabreimdichtung"; Bertau, "Epenrezitation im deutschen Mittelalter"; Kartschoke, *Bibeldichtung*.
6. See Stäblein, *Schriftbild der einstimmigen Musik*; Stevens, *Words and Music in the Middle Ages*, pp. 199–234.
7. See H. M. Chadwick and N. K. Chadwick, *Growth of Literature*, 1:22; Watts, *Lyre and the Harp*; Lord's book has been re-edited with an audio and video CD: Lord, *Singer of Tales*.
8. See Radloff, *Proben der Volkslitteratur der nördlichen türkischen Stämme*, vol. 5, *Der Dialect der Kara-Kirgisen*, pp. xx–xxii (translation volume).
9. Bowra, *Heroic Poetry*.
10. For a comparative study, see Reichl, *Singing the Past*.
11. In order to make reading the Turkic texts easier, I am using a simplified Latin alphabet modeled on the English transliteration of Russian, i.e., <sh>, <ch>, <j>, <y> are to be pronounced as in English (*shut, chicken, jet, yes*); <q> symbolizes a velar *k*-sound; <gh> symbolizes a velar fricative, comparable to the French *r*; <ï> stands for a lax *i*-sound, similar to the schwa-sound in the second syllable of English *bogus*; <ä> corresponds to the vowel sound in English *had*, <ö> and <ü> correspond to the vowel sounds in French *cœur* and *mur*, respectively; <ā> symbolizes a long velar *a* as in English *ball*.
12. For general introductions and surveys of Turkic oral epic poetry, see N. K. Chadwick and Zhirmunsky, *Oral Epics of Central Asia*; Başgöz, "Epic Tradition among Turkic Peoples"; Reichl, *Turkic Oral Epic Poetry*.
13. The Kirghiz (called Kara-Kirghiz in the nineteenth century, while the Kazakh were then called Kirghiz) live in their majority in Kyrgyzstan, with some living in the

neighboring republics, especially in Uzbekistan; there is also a small minority of Kirghiz in the Chinese province of Sinkiang (Xinjiang).

14. On *Manas*, see N. K. Chadwick and Zhirmunsky, *Oral Epics of Central Asia*, pp. 279–80, 304–7; Başgöz, "Epic Tradition among Turkic Peoples," pp. 318–22; Zhirmunsky, "Vvedenie v izuchenie èposa 'Manas'" [Introduction to the study of "Manas"].

15. Hatto, *Memorial Feast for Kökötöy-Khan.*

16. A bilingual (Kirghiz-Russian) edition has appeared in four volumes: Sadykov et al., *Manas: Kirgizskiy geroicheskiy èpos* [Manas: A Kirghiz heroic epic].

17. For a summary of Sayaqbay Qaralaev's version, see Sadykov et al., *Manas*, 1:457–67.

18. See Hu and Dor, "*Manas* chez les Kirghiz du Xinjiang."

19. The singer insisted on singing from his edition but changed the text by adding a line as well as various words, which partly change the meaning and the alliteration (I have put the singer's deviations from the published text in parentheses). For the edited text, see Mamay, *Manas*, 1:1; compare also Hu and Dor, "*Manas* chez les Kirghiz du Xinjiang," p. 31.

20. See Vinogradov, *Kirgizskaya narodnaya muzyka* [Kirghiz folk music] and "Napevy 'Manasa'" [The melodies of "Manas"], in Sadykov et al., *Manas*, 1:492–509; Beliaev, *Central Asian Music*, pp. 16–18; Dyushaliev, *Pesennaya kul'tura kyrgyzskogo naroda* [The song tradition of the Kirghiz people].

21. See Scheub, "Body and Image"; Børdahl and Ross, *Chinese Storytellers*, pp. 81–99.

22. This topic needs further investigation; on the classification of gestures, see also Kendon, "Gesture."

23. *Alpāmish: Ozbek xalq qahramānlik eposi* [Alpāmish: An Uzbek heroic folk epic]. For the edition and translation (into German) of a shorter version of the Uzbek epic, see Reichl, *Das usbekische Heldenepos Alpomish*. The various Turkic versions of this epic have been studied in detail by Zhirmunsky; see his *Skazanie ob Alpamyshe i bogatyrskaya skazka* [The legend of Alpamysh and the heroic tale]. The most informative account of Uzbek epic poetry is still Zhirmunsky and Zarifov, *Uzbekskiy narodny geroicheskiy èpos* [The Uzbek heroic folk epic]; for a shorter account, see Reichl, "Uzbek Epic Poetry."

24. See Reichl, "Mixture of Verse and Prose."

25. See Zhirmunsky, "Epic of 'Alpamysh.'"

26. The literature on the singing of Uzbek epic poetry is very limited and mostly in Uzbek (or Russian); for a characterization of this singer's style, see Reichl, "Oral Tradition and Performance," pp. 616–24; see also Beliaev, *Central Asian Music*, pp. 288–92.

27. See Karāmatli, "O muzyke uzbekskikh dastanov i osobennostyakh eë proyavleniya v 'Alpamyshe'" [On the music of Uzbek epics and its characteristic traits as found in 'Alpamysh'], in *Alpāmish*, pp. 50–63, musical illustrations after p. 816.

28. One of the few publications on Karakalpak folklore in a language other than Karakalpak is Maksetov, *Ocherki po istorii karakalpakskogo fol'klora* [Essays on the history of Karakalpak folklore]; on Jumabay-jïrau, see also Reichl, *Singing the Past*, pp. 37–39 and passim.

29. See Usmanov, "O tragedii èposa i tragediyakh lyudskikh" [On the tragedy of the epic and the human tragedies].

30. See Schmitz, *Die Erzählung von Edige*; Edige and his mythical father, Baba Tükli, have been studied extensively by DeWeese, *Islamization and Native Religion.*

31. For the full text and translation, see Reichl, *Edige.*

32. For a more detailed description of Jumabay-jïrau's musical style, see Reichl, "Performance of the Karakalpak *Zhyrau*."

33. See the examples under the rubric Stichic Tunes in Wiora, *European Folk Song*, pp.18–20.

34. On the music of Finnish *runos*, see Kondrat'eva, *Karel'skaya narodnaya pesnya* [Karelian folk song], pp. 87–96 (nos. 42–45); for sound recordings, see the CD *The Kalevala Heritage*; on the music of Russian *bylinas*, see Dobrovol'skij and Korguzalov, *Byliny: Russkiy muzykal'nyi èpos* [Bylina: The Russian musical epic]; for sound recordings, see the CDs accompanying the *bylina* edition of the series Svod russkogo fol'klora [Collection of Russian folklore], of which the first two volumes are *Byliny Pechory* [The *bylinas* from the (region of the river) Pechora].

35. See Gennrich, *Der musikalische Vortrag der altfranzösischen Chansons de geste*; Chailley, "Autour de la chanson de geste."

36. Coupez and Kamanzi, *Littérature de Cour au Rwanda*, p. 77 (my translation).

37. There is a detailed analysis of Yakut epic singing by A. P. Reshetnikova in the edition of the Yakut epic *Qïïs Debiliye*, an edition accompanied by a small record (pp. 26–69); Dmitriev et al., *Yakutskiy geroicheskiy èpos "Kyys Dèbiliyè"* [The Yakut heroic epic *Qïïs Debiliye*].

38. Needless to say, these remarks can give no more than a sketch of a varied and complex picture. I have tried to assess the musical performance of epic in a wider context in the introduction to Reichl, *Oral Epic*, pp. 1–40.

39. There is no space here to enter into a discussion of the metrics of Old English verse; the question of the singability of alliterative verse is, of course, very much dependent on scansion and hence on the metrical theory one favors.

40. On these questions, see Hoppin, *Medieval Music*, pp. 30–56, 80–91. For an attempt to basically convert Sievers's types into psalmody-like melodies, see Cable, *Meter and Melody*; see also his "Meter and Musical Implications of Old English Poetry." See also above n. 5.

41. See Bessinger, *Concordance*, s.v. "galan."

42. Quoted from Colgrave and Mynors, *Bede's Ecclesiastical History of the English People*, p. 418; Whitelock, *Sweet's Anglo-Saxon Reader*, p. 48.

43. There is no need here to recall the debate on the meaning of the Cædmon story in terms of the calling of an oral poet; for an extensive discussion of the singing of Cædmon's compositions, see Schwab, "Caedmons *carmen*."

Part 3
Reviews of Heaney's *Beowulf*

Michael Alexander

The Sheen on the Mere, or Beowulf in Ulster
Beowulf: A New Translation, by Seamus Heaney. Faber.
[*Agenda* 37.4 (2000): 80–83]

A very famous poet has translated the most famous Old English poem. This is not surprising—poets and scholars have loved the poem since it was published in 1815. In 1830 Tennyson tried his hand at lines in which *Beowulf* 'his word-hoard unlocked.' William Morris did a complete *Beowulf* in 1896. The poem attracted Longfellow, Pound, Tolkien and Auden. There have been complete poetic versions by Edwin Morgan, Kevin Crossley-Holland and myself. On a visit to St Andrews, Jorge Luis Borges asked to be taken down to the pier. There the blind Argentinian recited many of *Beowulf*'s verses at the North Sea. It has been translated into twenty modern languages, and at least sixty-five complete English versions have been published, one by the Scott-Moncrieff who translated Proust. Several are in print. Here comes another tribute to the poem about the man who was 'the kindest to his people, the keenest for fame'.

Composed 700–1000 in England, perhaps in the reign of King Alfred (d. 899), *Beowulf* commemorates the heroic age in majestic style. Generations of students have made cribs to catch its metre, sense and ethical sobriety. But the specialised diction, unfamiliar syntax and allusiveness of *Beowulf* make a full version a formidable task, even for an Irish poet who has learned his trade. This English poem sets its largely unhistorical events among the dynasties of the eastern shores of the North Sea about the year 500. Grendel and his conqueror have become part of English literature. Other names in the poem appear in genealogies giving the ancestors of King Alfred. Yet Hrothgar the Dane and Hygelac the Great are names stranger to us today than Agamemnon. This strangeness can attract poets, rather as the dragon attracts Geat. When Penguin Classics asked me to do a verse *Beowulf*, I declined for some years. Heaney accepted the invitation of the editors of the *Norton Anthology* in the mid 1980s. He has published some good bits in recent volumes. As for the *labor*, the *opus*, the whole thing, the *travail de longue haleine*, he started but stopped, returning to the challenge much later. But the day he accepted was a good one for *Beowulf*.

At Queen's University, Belfast, Heaney studied Anglo-Saxon. His first poetic efforts, he says, mimicked Hopkins, 'a chip off the Old English block'. Heaney returns to sources. He has dug in bogs, Irish and Danish, for heroes, victims and treasure, and has 'set the darkness echoing'. Virgil and Dante open and close his 1991 volume, *Seeing Things*. Like Ezra Pound, he gives blood to the ghosts to make them talk.

Heaney's appreciative Introduction follows Tolkien's tragic projection of the poem. His humane, moral and aesthetic emphases are becoming rare, and will win new readers. He writes persuasively on the role of gold, and on the poem's final phase. The translation itself rides boldly through the reefs of scholarship. Facing his opening lines are some edited lines of the original text. There are no notes, but marginal summaries help the narrative. Inset stories are signalled by italic type. The book is designed, then, for readers of literature, not for examinees.

It has since appeared, however, in vol. 1 of the 7th edition of the *Norton Anthology of English Literature*, the most influential teaching anthology in the English-studying world, a book which has earned millions of dollars. Its new general editor is to be Stephen Greenblatt. It is to be hoped, for other reasons, that the long reign of the Norton, which has colonised UK English departments, will not go unchallenged. Heaney's version replaces Norton's previous (prose) version of Ethelred Talbot Donaldson, and is accompanied by a few notes. It will thus become the version used in many a place of higher education, and will for many be the likeness in which the original poem appears to them. I should report, however, in the spirit of fairness and of commercial competition, that Crossley-Holland's version has been reissued with a good introduction and notes by Heather O'Donoghue, and that my own 1973 verse version will reappear in 2001 in a revised and expanded edition from Penguin Classics. I welcome comparisons—and hope I do not say this in the spirit of Mike Tyson.

It is hard to translate *Beowulf* into prose which can be read aloud. It is far more trouble to put it into verse. Like other verse translators, Heaney imitates Old English alliteration and stress-patterns, though loosely. He breaks the rule, for example, which forbids the fourth stress to alliterate. Heaney is too resourceful to let the imitative metre cramp his movement and idiom. And he avoids the Saxonisms of William Morris, who wrote, of Grendel's mother: 'She sat on her hall-guest and tugged out her sax.' (A sax was a short knife; three of them appear on Essex county cricket caps. The word *sax* is the root of the word Saxon.)

In 'About This Translation', the poet writes that he sees *Beowulf*'s style as direct and indicative. He is in good touch with ships, hawks and horses, physical sensation, texture. He straightens its syntax and diction. At one point Beowulf says:

> And Unferth is to have what I inherited:
> to that far-famed man I bequeath my own
> sharp honed, wave sheened wonderblade.

Those who can read *Beowulf* in the bath will note that alliteration alternates in the first line, and breaks off in the second, and that the stress-pattern of the third is triple rather than balanced. The verse moves well, however, and 'wave-sheened' shows both the blade's appearance and how it was made. What is lost in translation is restored elsewhere, and 'wave-sheened' is in keeping. Heaney can also write, of Grendel's Mere: 'the overhanging bank / Is a maze of tree-roots mirrored in its surface.' Old English is less reflexive. In general, Heaney's rhetorical skills serve his translation.

The declarative speaking voice, he admits, slights some of the poem's reserve. There is life rather than dignity in phrases such as 'a lot was to happen' and 'Away with you!' This last injunction can be heard in Scotland (it is the obverse of 'Haste ye back!'). Those who have never been across the sea to Ireland will find other words seriously unfamiliar: 'bawn' and 'brehon', 'graith' and 'kesh'. Heaney confesses that he 'finally recanted on the word "gilly".' You can't have everything, not in a translation. But Heaney has unmistakably given the poem a new earth in Ulster, and colloquialised it. This is a consequence of making it his own, for his own is Irish, and his Irishness is specifically of the North and of the farm. This (like all translations) is a skewing and a simplification. Those who don't want this should go for the only really good prose version, that of G. N. Garmonsway.

But Heaney's translation is itself a poem. A generous poet has brought back our own, in his own words. Here there is much to be grateful for. *Beowulf*, an elegy for heroism and a critique of feud and fratricide, is once again alive and well. Modern cultural critics will seize on the political dimensions of the search for roots, and the critique of feud in the land of the Red Hand. *Beowulf* scholars, on the other hand, will point out, as Tom Shippey did in the *TLS*, the translation's faults when judged by the criterion of semantic accuracy, the paramount criterion for modern scholarship—if not for John Dryden or Ezra Pound.

But translations are not written for those who know the original language well; where would the Bible, Homer, Tolstoy, Kierkegaard be without translation? Translations are half-way houses in which the host can meet the guest, and the reader can encounter the original, through a glass darkly. In a poet's half-way house there is often a 'hospitality lady' at the door with a friendly smile. The scholar's half-way house is less inviting. Those who know the original personally and do not like inviting smiles do not have to go into the poet's half-way house.

Recently this translation won the Whitbread prize for the best book of the year. It is reported that some judges were worried about giving the prize to a translation rather than to an original work. But a good many of the best poems in English are translations, and some translations are poems. Dr Johnson thought Pope's version of *The Iliad* his greatest achievement. The assumptions behind this Augustan judgement—that men need to be reminded rather than informed— would have been familiar to the poets of Rome, of the Middle Ages and of the Renaissance. Poets have always translated, and their translations can be their best work. This may not prove to be the case with Heaney's *Beowulf*, but it is good to see, as the centuries turn, this generous and popular exponent of the public role of the poet successfully reviving a classic.

Note: a shorter version of this review appeared in *The Observer*.

S A J Bradley

Putting a Bawn into *Beowulf*: some reflections on Heaney's new translation
Beowulf, translated by Seamus Heaney, Faber and Faber, London 1999.
[*Medieval Life* 13 (2000): 3–8]

It proved a controversial decision of the Whitbread judges who awarded the 1999 prize to Seamus Heaney for his new translation of *Beowulf*. None of the detractors was sourer (in print, at least) than A. N. Wilson (*Sunday Telegraph*, 30 January 2000) who scoffed at *Beowulf* as 'a theme-park antique' and at Heaney's translation as 'an Anglo-Saxon dunderhead rendered into Irish blarney.' The double-whammy—*Beowulf* is not significant poetry and Heaney is not a significant poet—might have done damage but for the fact that this is obviously not significant journalism: rather, a seriously over-whipped Sunday soufflé which probably has more to do with the spiteful politics of Oxford than anything else (Wilson resents having 'largely wasted' seven years teaching his opinion of *Beowulf* to undergraduates there). At any rate, Fabers seem far from disappointed at the general public's response as measured by sales figures; and if that witness too is susceptible to cynicism one might note the wider context into which Heaney's publication fits. While the late Ted Hughes works on his re-creation of (Latin-classical) Ovid, Heaney works on his re-creation of (English-classical) *Beowulf*, both classics are acclaimed with prestigious prizes; sales of both reworked classics soar; simultaneously the British Library publishes its electronic *Beowulf*, containing a full examinable facsimile of the codex and its transcriptions plus a great deal more contextual material; and to mark World Book Day the British Library mounts an exhibition giving a priority of place to the thousand-year-old Anglo-Saxon book (designated Cotton Vitellius A xv in the British Library) in which the unique text of *Beowulf* is found. Sunday sages apart, we seem to want to take *Beowulf* with us, as a poem, as a cultural monument as an object for scholarly study, into the twenty-first century.

Heaney's translation serves, of course, to reopen old questions about the accessibility of documents of such antiquity. What does it mean, to 'translate' *Beowulf*? Does one kind of translation afford better access than another kind to the 'originality' of the poem? And even if we are well alert to the fact that 'translation'

comprises a massive pre-emption of the reader's judgment of 'the original', how do
we know whether and when we are reading the original itself 'correctly'? Anglo-
Saxon text, and particularly poetic discourse, is rarely inert objective reportage of
factuality, any more than the contents and disposition of the Sutton Hoo ship-
burial are inert, objective reportage of the material culture of a seventh-century
East Anglian king's household. Of this fact, at least, we can be confident: that
in the construction of texts and ship-burials there is a presumption of an act of
interpretation by the scrutineer.

The translator is a wholesale interpreter, and Heaney's work is better
thought of as a 're-creation' than as a 'translation'. There are Modern English renderings of the poem which have tried to stay close to the standard dictionary
definitions of words, and they have their proper role to play; but they typically fail
to convey at least two fundamental aspects of the text *as poetry*: that words may be
characteristically chosen by poets for their *ambivalence* of meaning; and that very
frequently the *form* of the Anglo-Saxon alliterative line *extends* the meaning contained in the semantic and syntactic aspects of the words distributed within the
line. Unless the translator is lucky enough to find Modern English words conveying the same ambivalence of meaning, or manages to construct an alliterative line
in Modern English which makes the same verbal juxtapositionings and alliterative
paintings as the original, something gets lost and a different nuance may be put
upon the poet's meaning—and the reader is to that extent hostage of the translator's good (or poor) judgment.

But a more radical problem with translating as indeed with reading the
original itself—is that words do not have a strictly definable meaning. Dictionaries will give a kind of core-sense of a word or, better still, will list examples of
the way a word has been used; but words are, as Heaney put it in the 1976 Beckman Lecture (*Englands of the Mind*, published in his *Preoccupations*), 'etymological
occurrences' whose core-sense is surrounded by a nebula of cultural associations.
The word is a 'symptom of human history, memory and attachments.' Thus, for
example, the core-sense of Old English *sciphere* is 'ship-army, fleet' but when King
Alfred uses it in his translation of Boethius's *Consolation of Philosophy*, in his treatment of Boethius's idea of a long-gone golden age of the world when violence and
war were not known and people had never heard of 'ship-armies', we do not catch
Alfred's fuller meaning unless we know that *sciphere* is the word routinely used in
the *Anglo-Saxon Chronicles* for the Viking fleets which were then attacking England. Alfred was apparently intimating that the present afflictions of the English
were to be understood in a broader philosophical perspective, as an aspect of a
fallen world which must look to a providential God for its salvation. How does a
modern translator import this nuance of Anglo-Saxon meaning into a translation,
unless by cumbrous annotation?

Heaney, in his Lecture, uses a metaphor of 'depth-charges' for such words: 'the cultural depth-charges latent in certain words and rhythms, that binding secret between words in poetry ... the energies beating in and between words that the poet brings into half-deliberate play.' How is the translator to replicate this half-deliberate play of the original poet? Heaney's translation of *Beowulf* reveals the alert and resourceful philologist behind the poet. He knows that the phrase *lænan lifes* (*Beowulf* 2845), routinely translated '[of this] transitory life', contains a cultural depth-charge: *lænan* is etymologically related to the Anglo-Saxon verb 'to loan, lend'. It has a linguistic-cultural context in medieval Christian thought, which saw the individual's life and worldly talents as a loan from God (the idea informs the poem *The Gifts of Men* in the Exeter Book), and saw the individual as answerable to God for the stewardship of this loan. In choosing (p. 89) to translate the phrase as 'the life they had been lent' Heaney faithfully conveys into his translation part of the Christian-consistent philosophical superstructure which the poet of *Beowulf* has raised upon the folktale materials of his plot. When Heaney picks the technical term 'anathema' (p. 6) for God's curse upon Cain, he is accurately reflecting the formality of the *Beowulf*-poet's *forscrifen*, itself an imitation of the formal Latin term *proscribere* 'to proscribe'. When Heaney has Grendel gleefully contemplating the 'mayhem' he will create among the sleeping Geats in the hall (p. 24), he is using the word precisely in its full etymological sense: 'the offence of depriving a person by violence of any limb'—though in this case Heaney is extensively recasting the poet's wording where there is no noun corresponding to 'mayhem'. There is much of this academically-informed and carefully-nuanced insight in Heaney's re-creation of the poem.

The problem of finding cultural equivalences which do not diminish or distort also confronts the translator, and the translator's reader, the other way round. Modern English words likewise comprise a nebula of nuances rather than a diamond-hard definitiveness of meaning, and they will bring with them, whether the translator likes it or not, their contemporary and historical cultural associations. 'Æghwæþres sceal / scearp scyld-wiga gescad witan, / worda and worca, se þe wel þenceð' is the coastguard's maxim to Beowulf. 'The sharp shield-warrior must know the difference between words and actions, he who thinks soundly.' Heaney's 'gumption'—'Anyone with gumption / and a sharp mind will take measure / of two things: what's said and what's done' (p. 11)—will have, for some readers, a cloth-capped bluntness about it which communicates the meaning vividly indeed, but might be considered, as idiom, socially a bit below the Danish coastguard in a poetic Denmark where even the doorkeeper is a prince. There are other shifts of tone of this sort, from epic to homely. But 'I consider *Beowulf* to be part of my voice-right,' says Heaney (Introduction, p. xxiii) and therefore, with a calculated risk which has already drawn the inordinate derision of Wilson, he uses the archaic

Ulster-English dialect verb 'thole' for the Anglo-Saxon *polian* ('to suffer') from which it derived. Here, quite categorically, Heaney is choosing 'depth-charges' that are explosive for him personally. This 'thole' was a word in his Irish aunt's vocabulary. He is learnedly conscious of the word having made a journey—north from Anglo-Saxon England into Scotland and so across to Ulster with the planters and so to the locals who had originally spoken Irish; and another journey, with Scots-Irish migrants into America where it turns up in the literary vocabulary of John Crowe Ransom. And so 'The far-flungness of the word, the phenomenological pleasure of finding it variously transformed by Ransom's modernity and Beowulf's venerability' (p. xxv) played their quite essential part in Heaney the poet's response and Heaney the translator's approach to the language of *Beowulf*. On broadly similar grounds he permits himself other Ulster words which will not detonate for his average reader: 'graith' for 'harness', 'hoked' for 'rooted about' and 'bawn' for 'hall'. 'Putting a bawn into *Beowulf*' he calls it, with a light touch amid the autobiographical earnestness. 'Putting a bawn into *Beowulf* seems one way for an Irish poet to come to terms with that complex history of conquest and colony' (p. xxx). Heaney's followers will know that he has often written and spoken of his sense of being in part defined in terms of the linguistic, as well as the wider historical cultural tensions between Irish and English: it is therefore a significant revelation in his Introduction that the long road leading to his linguistic readiness to tackle *Beowulf* was also a road towards a less adversarial perception of the relationship of the Irish with the English language. Here then, clearly, we stand to learn more about Heaney and the conscious, intuitive and complex engagements he makes with language, as a cross-cultural poet, than about the choices and engagements of the Anglo-Saxon poet.

Any modern experiencing of *Beowulf* is of course utterly and irrecoverably remote from the Anglo-Saxon cultural experience of listening to the poem: this we may confidently presume. Even if we listen to an oral delivery before an audience rather than engaging in modernity's strange process of silent treaty with printed words on a page, and even if we equip ourselves with much knowledge of the records of Anglo-Saxon society, we can hardly begin to recreate the complex cultural implications of belonging to, having a real-life stake in, the world and world-view of which *Beowulf* is an expression. That enormous impediment conceded, it can be said that Heaney's translation achieves striking success in replicating some of the most distinctive formal characteristics of the Anglo-Saxon poem.

First and foremost should be acknowledged Heaney's accomplishment in creating a text which works powerfully as an oral-aural experience. It is a text written as though composed orally (which is what many scholars would want to say about the Anglo-Saxon poem itself), a text which ideally one ought to experience by ear rather than by eye. This is to say something more than that it reads well and sounds good. It is to say that, like the original, it relies upon the audience *hearing* the link: (the *alliterative* link, pointing a sense-link) which the poet places on two or more words in any given line, and thereby registering a meaning which may be greater than the sum of the strictly semantic and syntactic content of the words used.

In his Introduction (p. xxi), Heaney offers a fine metaphor of the way in which the poet sustains a concreteness of discourse at the literal level whilst simultaneously suggesting richness of symbolic meaning: 'At these moments of lyric intensity, the keel of the poetry is deeply set in the element of sensation while the mind's lookout sways metrically and far-sightedly in the element of pure comprehension.' It is in part by this means that the poet elicits from the circumstantial plot-material of his legend sources the statement of universal themes and issues: when the poet says of Heorot *lixte se leoma ofer landafela* ('Its light shone over many lands', 311) he is speaking symbolically of the civilized ideal which the community within represented, and he is signalling that it as properly belongs with light, order, creativity and Godwardness as Grendel belongs with darkness, chaos, death and exile from God. And it is in this distinctively poetic art (which, incidentally, is the poetic dimension of text which makes *Beowulf* problematical for those seeking factual information about Anglo-Saxon material culture from it) that Heaney excels. A fine brief example is in Hrothgar's account of Grendel's lake, in a passage which is less a description of Anglo-Saxon landscape than a symbolic image of the adversarial polarization of evil against good in the world of the poem: 'That is no good place. / When wind blows up and stormy weather / makes clouds scud and the sides weep, / out of its depths a dirty surge / is pitched towards heaven' (p. 45).

This poetic symbolism works not only within the longer sequences of 'lyric intensity' but also, often with a high degree of sophistication, within the structure of the individual line. The Anglo-Saxon poetic line is divided about a caesura (actual or notional) into two half lines with (typically) two (sometimes three) metrically-stressed syllables in each. While the caesura notionally separates, the alliteration bridges and binds the two half-fines, thus creating a versatile dynamic for the poet to exploit. A particular one of the metrically-stressed syllables—the first stressed syllable of the second half-line—must always participate in the line's alliterative scheme (and must be the *only* alliterating syllable in the second half-line), whereas *either or both* of the stressed syllables in *the first* half-line may be involved in the alliterative scheme. Thus this first stressed syllable of the second half-line (sometimes called the headstave) is of conspicuously high metrical and alliterative profile. Commonly, therefore, the poet will use this high profile to give prominence to a key *idea-word* in the line. With this range of exploitable options within a line the poet can often *embody in the form* of the line what is also stated in the semantic content of the words in the line. Thus, one of the universal themes in the poet's world-view is the chronic instability of human fortune. Repeatedly, the poet reflects this syndrome of reversal by placing the two states each in their own half-line, ranged about the caesura, and by placing the word defining the reversed condition in the headstave position.

Heaney recreates such lines with masterly skill [# represents the position of the caesura, actual or notional]: when Grendel assailed Heorot 'their *wassail* was over, # they *wept* to heaven' (p. 6); Grendel would rip life from limb and '*feed* on their *flesh*; # but his *fate* that night / was due to change' (p. 24); and of the killing of Hrothgar's counsellor Æschere, 'his *dearest* companion # was *dead* and gone' (p. 43); or, with a more complex patterning, 'Still, what *happened* # was a *hard* reversal / from bliss to *grief*. # *Grendel* struck' (p. 57).

Of course, such artistry depends upon a flexibility of word-order which the syntax of Modern English curtails, having largely dispensed with the inflectional system which in Old English labelled words according to their grammatical function, wherever they were placed within a given stretch of discourse. Modern English syntax relies instead upon the relatively fixed order of words and lots of prepositions, in order to declare syntactic relationships of words within a given stretch of discourse. And modern taste disapproves of that kind of 'poetic diction' which once licensed poets freely to take liberties with the 'natural' word order of English discourse. Consequently, Heaney pleads (p. xxix) a deviance from Anglo-Saxon alliterative rules 'that other translators have allowed themselves': in second half-lines, where in Anglo-Saxon convention the alliteration *must* and must *only* fall upon *the first* stressed syllable (the 'headstave'), he places it instead on the *second* stressed syllable, rather than 'force an artificial shape or an unusual word choice just for the sake of correctness' (p. xxviii). It is not so much the purist in one that may regret this hostile convergence does not set out to be a perfect replica of the original nor could it or any other modern version conceivably succeed in being that, even if such a sterile undertaking were attempted. It is rather that the Anglo-Saxon patterning is such 'natural' rhetoric, responds so truly to some psycho-aesthetic absolute still operative within English discourse, that we still register the one pattern as weaker than the other. The Geats lamenting Beowulf, for example, 'sorrowed for the lord # who had been laid low' (p. 99). If conventions of modern word-order had allowed it, a more powerful rhetoric, matching the Anglo-Saxon, would have been achieved by reordering the words into "sorrowed for the lord # who low had been laid" so as to get 'low' into the headstave position and make the most of the contrast between lordship and lowness—in effect, *embodying* the concept of the fall of lordship in the *form* of the line, in the way the Anglo-Saxon poets so commonly do, and in a way that still answers to our conditioned rhetorical instincts in English.

But these are small and in many cases inescapable deficiencies reminding us of what is unnegotiable between antiquity and modernity. When the call is for straightforward narrative drama, Heaney repeatedly excels in conveying to us the power of the Anglo-Saxon poet—as witness, among so many more major examples, the brilliant cameo of Hygelac's arrival with the dawn to save the Swede-beleaguered Geats at Ravenswood (p. 92). In the magnificent sequences of elegy which distinguish the Anglo-Saxon poet, Heaney also achieves distinction: in the languishing of Hrothgar over the paralysis of Heorot (pp. 6–8), in Hrothgar's lament for the killing of Æschere (p. 44), in the 'lay of the last survivor' (pp. 71–72), and especially in the emotionally complex ending of the poem where Beowulf's will is implemented in the funeral and the building of the tomb on Hronesnæs (pp. 88, 99). The Finn episode (pp. 34–39) which Heaney rightly recognizes as central to the whole poem narrated as entertainment in Heorot on the first night after Grendel's death but yet a dire warning against dropping one's guard in a world cursed by feuding, which is nevertheless disregarded by the audience that night to their terrible cost—is distinguished both by a change of typographical layout and a terse lapidary style rendering almost every statement gnomic in its archetypical force.

As regards the broader interpretation of the his [*sic*] translation itself, appears untempted by the anti-heroic and secular post-Sixties. He acknowledges the religious, Christian-consistent world-view of the poet—first spotted by the poem's first-ever expositor, N. F. S. Grundtvig (who produced his translation of *Beowulf* into Danish, with introductory essay, in 1820), and quarrelled over by the critics ever since. He keeps unobfuscated the evidence of Beowulf's justified clear conscience and integrity of motive. Beowulf is not a hero corrupted by gold, not a king who inappropriately continues to act as though he were still a free-booting hero, not the embodiment of a philosophy which explores the interchangeability between hero and monster. He thanks 'the everlasting Lord of all . . . the King of Glory' that he has been 'allowed to leave my people / so well endowed on the day I die.' At his death, his soul flees from his breast 'to its destined place among the steadfast ones' (*secean soðfæstra dom*, line 2820, p. 88). Beowulf has remained to the end *soðfæst*—steadfast in truth.

There is much to be said for Heaney's (unfashionably) uncomplicated view of Beowulf as a Christian-consistent hero. Nothing in Germanic pagan thought squares with this conceptualization of a man's dying and destiny, whereas the Christian righteous are routinely called the *soðfæste*, and their *dom* (judgment, reward) is described in other Anglo-Saxon poems, such as *Christ III* (*The Judgment*), *Guthlac A* and *The Phoenix* in the Exeter Book, written at roughly the same time as the *Beowulf* codex. That Christ is mentioned nowhere in the poem is not an obstacle to Heaney's espoused reading: 'It has often been observed that all the scriptural references in *Beowulf* are to the Old Testament. The poet is more in sympathy with the tragic, waiting, unredeemed phase of things than with any transcendental promise' (p. xix). But here again we may be up against the problem of understanding, even after we have 'translated' the words of the text, the larger context of ideas into which the poem was launched by the poet and received by its audience, which might have a bearing on what the poem meant to its first audience. The poet links Grendel with God's adversaries, Cain and the giants drowned in Noah's Flood. Bede and other orthodox Christian commentators regarded their counterparts, Abel and Noah, as God's *soðfæste* and, following the lead of *Hebrews* ch. 13, saw them as part of a lineage of righteous men and women (such as Abraham, Sarah, Isaac, Moses) who, amidst all the backsliding and faithlessness of God's people, themselves kept faith with the covenant and lived by a truth glimpsed afar off but not as yet realized, that of a salvation yet to come. Therefore, says *Hebrews*, God is not ashamed to be called their God, and has a city prepared for them. This is a *civitas* not subject to treachery, feud and war or the ravages of time—a *civitas* that St Augustine, in his work well-known to the Anglo-Saxons, called the City of God. In orthodox Christian thought, as in the Anglo-Saxon poems gathered in the codex Junius 11 in the Bodleian Library Oxford, these Old Testament figures who hold steadfastly to the truth prefigure the coming of the one perfectly righteous man, Christ himself, to the whole world's salvation. It is striking, in the world of *Beowulf*, that worthy human communities are shown being saved from the brink of annihilation by the intervention of one worthy man—Scyld Scefing when the Danes are lordless and wretched; Beowulf when no one else can save Heorot. There are other, lesser, reflexes of this pattern (including the rescue of the Geats by Hygelac mentioned above). But regrettably Heaney himself discounts the last and in some ways most important of them. At the end of the poem he says, 'A world is passing away, the Swedes and others are massing on the borders to attack *and there is no lord or hero to rally the defence*' (p. xv). It is true that Wiglaf, who suddenly emerges from the ranks of the fleeing Geats when the dragon seems to be winning the fight, is the last of Beowulf's kin. But the poet habitually contemplates the brink before pulling back from it: Wiglaf intervenes, thereby joins the elite company of dragon-slayers, is dramatically appointed and invested by the dying Beowulf as his successor and—in the 500 or so lines (comprising as much as one-sixth of the whole poem) given by the poet to the establishment of Wiglaf's leadership of the nation—crucially secures what otherwise would have been lost: the remembrance of Beowulf himself, in the burial-mound which henceforth will bear Beowulf's name and guide seafarers journeying upon 'the wide and shrouded waters' of the ocean. The lineage of justified leaders is continued in Wiglaf, however precariously. If such an 'enhanced' version of Heaney's Christian-consistent *Beowulf* is accepted, an alternative is reached to J. R. R. Tolkien's account of a darkly pessimistic world-view in which the wages of heroism is, simply death.

Through all this, through his Introduction as well as in the 'translation' itself, Heaney is saying something quite remarkable about the Anglo-Saxon poem, about the mature vision and articulacy of a text still competent to speak wisdom a thousand years on from its copying down. Categorically, he is not intent upon relaying to historians or archaeologists with all possible accuracy the meaning of each significant term in the Old English text nor upon replicating line by line for the gratification of literary historians the complex alliterative texture of the original poem. Heaney's *Beowulf* is first and last an achievement in contemporary literature. But it is not inconsistent with this to observe that it also testifies to the regenerative potency of the oldest forms of the English language and its poetry over a contemporary poet. It does so in much the same way, one might venture to say, as the remembrance of Cuthbert and Bede on Holy Island and at Durham testifies that, for some people at least, religious tradition is not a matter of scholarly and objective recognition of an inert antiquity but a matter of living within a continuing and ever-accumulating body of testimony and insight relative to an abiding set of perceived truths, constantly recreating a new articulation out of the ancient perceptions and out of the depth-charged language that is the common inheritance.

'Putting a bawn into *Beowulf*' could become a catch phrase for this kind of re-creation which, at its best—however problematical it makes the interdisciplinary collaborations of literature scholars with historians and archaeologists—can yield unique testimony to the articulacy of ancient literature and the mindset of the culture that through it achieved its self-expression.

S. A. J. Bradley

Beowulf translated by Seamus Heaney. Faber & Faber. 1999.
[*Cambridge Quarterly* 30 (2001): 82–86]

It is no more a classical education that has given rise to the finest English literature than it is the flood of Latin loanwords that has given the English language its
beauty and strength, the Danish scholar and *Beowulf* pioneer N. F. S. Grundtvig
declared in 1832. Inspired and provoked by G. J. Thorkelin's heroic but flawed
editio princeps of *Beowulf* (Copenhagen, 1815), Grundtvig had taught himself
Anglo-Saxon and in 1820 produced a Danish translation of the poem with an
interpretative introduction—in order to naturalise into Danish culture a poem so
laden with contemporary relevance for the northern world, so deeply poetic in its
vision and its articulation of guarded optimism for a fallen world, that he wanted
it back in circulation, available to be read by young and old alike. He hoped the
English too would rediscover themselves if, as he proposed to them in 1830, they
undertook the systematic publication of England's oldest vernacular literature,
hitherto shamefully neglected.

Identifying English institutionalisation of Greek and Roman culture as
the main likely impediment to the English themselves ever acting upon a proper
recognition of their Anglo-Saxon heritage, Grundtvig was accurately prophetic.
Repeatedly, English scholars have honoured the antiquity of *Beowulf* while
deploring its non-classical structure, its non-classical monsters which belong in
the nursery or in the childhood of a nation, its unsophisticated Germanic alliteration, its closeness to 'mere' folk-story. When J. R. R. Tolkien in 1936 presented
it to the British Academy as a serious masterpiece of English poetry he had to
proceed by challenging the perceived absoluteness of classical norms.

Now, nearly 200 years after Grundtvig found that 'Beowulf, with a deeply
poetic insight, is conceived and vitally projected as humankind's northern hero
who, finally at the cost of his own life, disarms the power of darkness and by
strength saves the dying life of the people'—during which interval *Beowulf* has
been various things to various causes and generations, for good and for ill—the
British Library publishes an electronic facsimile edition of the manuscript; on the

292

heels of Hughes's Ovid comes Heaney's *Beowulf*; both works win a prestigious prize; on World Book Day a British Library exhibition gives the Anglo-Saxon book containing *Beowulf* a foundational position. There appears to be a spectrum-wide desire to take this poem with us into the twenty-first century. You might almost think the English-speaking world at last recognises that in *Beowulf* it owns a classic of world status. Sadly, the precariousness of the study of Anglo-Saxon literature in UK universities seems to say otherwise, as indeed do one or two of Heaney's reviewers, whose criteria of judgement time-warp us back to the regimes and regrets of Ker and Chambers a century ago.

Heaney for his part makes, like Grundtvig, a *poet's* judgement that this is indeed a classic: because of its serious address to abiding human issues (concerning communality and violence—within kin, community, nation, the family of nations) still painfully with us; because of the visionary character of the poet's insights; because of the poem's structured perspective on history; because of the mythic potency of the telling; because it is poetry of a high order with passages of great lyric intensity; because it is exemplary of the poetic capacity of the English language. A classic not least, we might ourselves add, because it and the whole early poetic culture it represents can still play an acknowledged part in the shaping of one of the most keenly linguistically conscious poets of his generation (again, a parallel with Grundtvig). Certainly it is a remarkable convergence, not lost upon Heaney himself, that this poem pleading the wastefulness of feud has played its part in changing his tendency 'to conceive of English and Irish as adversarial tongues' (p. xxiv). The introduction documents a new stage in the autobiography of a contemporary poet inhabiting the incident-plagued frontiers between two languages and two cultures.

Heaney's 1976 Beckman Lecture, *Englands of the Mind*, showed—and his introduction confirms—his academic and poetic alertness to the Anglo-Saxon resources of the English language, to 'the word as an etymological occurrence, as symptom of human history, memory and attachments'—hence, among a wealth of other examples, the authentic nuance of 'the life they had been lent' for *lænan lifes* (l. 2845) so routinely blurred by translators as 'transitory life', and hence also such calculated risks as his 'thole' for 'suffer' (the personal justification is emphatically worth reading, p. xxv), and his 'storied leader', 'snakefolds', 'graith', 'sept', 'brehon', and 'bawn'—which perhaps regrettably mean that this modern English poem needs annotation from the outset.

'Cædmon too I was lucky to have known', says Heaney in 'Whitby-sur-Moyola' (*The Spirit Level*, 1996). Grundtvig likewise honoured Cædmon—not merely as the hero of English poesy's origin-myth, but as a herder of words and ideas in whose tradition he felt himself to have been shaped. Cædmon's way with words, says Heaney's poem, though the gift of an angel, is as close to the everyday as his cowman's skills, diagnostically sniffing a sick beast's urine on his fingers. What Heaney means there, the reader can discern from his *Beowulf.* A breeze gusts through this translation, laden with the smell of ancient timbers, sweet mead, human sweat, monstrous exhalations, swamp and woodland, salt sea air, smoke, and cremated flesh. The vigour and vividness of the original, often made near-palpable by the structural form of the Old English alliterative line, are here not homogenised, deodorised, or rarefied by translationese but recreated in a poetic idiom graced by a nuance of the antique, yet well in touch with the living language, concrete yet symbolically suggestive. 'At these moments of lyric intensity', says Heaney, 'the keel of the poetry is deeply set in the element of sensation while the mind's lookout sways metrically and far-sightedly in the element of pure comprehension' (p. xxi)—the metaphor holds as good for his translation as for the original. Like the Anglo-Saxon poet, Heaney uses ambivalence to store the text with richness of meaning while sustaining economy of discourse, and sometimes brilliantly replicates the poetic symbolism of the original; thus, of Grendel's lake: 'That is no good place. | When wind blows up and stormy weather | makes clouds scud and the skies weep, | out of its depths a dirty surge | is pitched towards the heavens.' Here Heaney's ear for what rings *aurally* true comes into its own: sound and sound patternings function fundamentally as instruments for conveying meaning—as in the powerful sequence: 'their *wassail* was over, they *wept* to heaven | and *mourned* under *morning.* Their *mighty* prince, | the *storied* leader, sat *stricken* and helpless . . .' (p. 6), where as so often in the Anglo-Saxon, part of the meaning (essentially, the motif of reversal in human fortunes, informing the whole poem) is embodied not solely in the semantic and syntactic sum of the words used but in the patterning of the words' deployment relative to the line's whole metrical-alliterative structure. Examples abound where the terse sense-pointing *heard* so routinely in the original is potently recreated in this strongly oral–aural translation (´ represents the actual or notional caesura between the half-lines): 'fair *reparation* ´ from those *rabid* bands', 'in the *fire's* embrace, ´ *forfeiting* help', 'I suffered a long | *harrowing* by Grendel. ´ But the *Heavenly* Shepherd . . .' It is not the purist alone who might wish for more of this and less use of the licence putting the alliteration on the *second* stress of the second half-line. The line 'sorrowed for the *lord* ´ who had been *laid low*' would have more rhetorical potency if it were acceptable (and not archaic 'poetic diction') to reorder the words as 'sorrowed for the *lord* ´ who *low* had been *laid*' thus more starkly juxtaposing lordship and lowness, embodying more truly in the *form* of the line the poem's motif of reversal. But modern English syntax is often unaccommodating of such flexible word-order.

There are passages to which any jealous lover of the original will turn to test the fidelity of the translator. Tested, Heaney will be found to have risen to them with all his own powers of lyric intensity. The paradigmatic Finn episode (p. 34), narration within narration, warning by way of entertainment, is here distinguished not only by typographical layout but by a terse economy of style vividly suggestive, as the original, of male vengefulness ever smouldering, waiting to erupt in a blaze, devouring the good with the bad and leaving the world in sum impoverished. Where the Anglo-Saxon poetry excels in elegiac lament Heaney also excels: in the grieving of the son-bereft father (p. 77); and in the sequence (p. 44) where Beowulf, unaware of the overnight attack of Grendel's mother, but alarmed at being summoned so early to the hall, asks if the king has enjoyed a comfortable night. To a question offered as a courtesy, the poet gives the king an answer which instantly lifts the discourse to the universal: 'Ne frin þu æfter sælum; sorh is geniwod | Denigea leodum. Dead is Æschere' (Ask you not after happiness; sorrow is renewed | to the Danish peoples. Dead is Æschere). Heaney's 'Rest? What is rest? Sorrow has returned. | Alas for the Danes! Aeschere is dead.' catches the bitter weariness of an old leader of the people, suffering one reversal more than he can bear in a chronically unstable world where, God (explicitly) knows, he has striven his human best to get and hold peace for his people.

Heaney seems not to wish to flirt with ideas that Beowulf is a failed hero, a king corrupted by gold as Hrothgar had warned him not to be, a hero who misguidedly went on behaving like a hero after he had become a king, a hero as monstrous in his heroism as the monsters are heroic in their monstrosity. Key passages presenting Beowulf as an aware agent of God, as a man of justified clear conscience, are kept in all their original lucidity, and when he dies his soul flees from his breast 'to its destined place among the steadfast ones' ('secan soðfæstra dom', l. 2820). The world of the plot, affirms Heaney (p. xix), belongs in 'the tragic, waiting, unredeemed phase of things' parallel to that of the Old Testament—yes, provided one also remembers the Old Testament's lineage of righteous men and women who kept steadfast faith ahead of the revelation of the Messiah (Hebrews 13), whose *soðfæstnes* continued to justify the rainbow covenant after Noah's Flood and defined them as citizens of the City of God.

One hoary romantic misrepresentation of the ending of the poem Heaney does not free himself from: 'A world is passing away, the Swedes and others are massing on the borders to attack and *there is no lord or hero to rally the defence*' (p. xv). Not Wiglaf, then, whose last-moment unanticipated emergence from obscurity to dragon-slaying pre-eminence, directly inspired by Beowulf's example, matches the model established within the providential world-picture of the poem—in the emergence of Scyld Scefing in the poem's opening paradigm and Beowulf himself when no one in the world had seemed capable of saving Heorot? Wiglaf, appointed and invested by the dying Beowulf as his successor (p. 88), to whose assumption of the 'power of words' the poet devotes the final 500 lines (over one-sixth of the whole poem), will give the Swedes a nasty shock if they believe the scholars and attack.

But the measured dignity with which the visionary solemnity of Beowulf's enacted will is recreated by Heaney (pp. 88, 99) speaks for itself. Beowulf's burial-mound here as in the Anglo-Saxon is no mere marker to aid coastal navigation but a monumental landmark for seafarers upon 'the wide and shrouded waters' of the world and the world's history; and *Beowulf* the poem is itself a like monument, a native classic. Bracketing nearly 200 years of *Beowulf* scholarship, Grundtvig's and Heaney's translations give testimony to this. Notwithstanding its quirks, Heaney's remarkable recreation of the poem has a pretty good chance of becoming a classic in its own right.

Beowulf—Dinosaur, Monster or Visionary Poem?
Beowulf: A New Translation, translated by Seamus Heaney. London:
Faber and Faber, 1999; bilingual edition [Old English and Modern English]
New York: Farrar, Straus and Giroux, 2000.
(*The European English Messenger* 10.2 [2001]: 68–70)

Old English studies, we've been hearing for decades, is on its way out of the English curriculum. It's been called 'a dinosauric museum piece' by Valentine Cunningham who considers Latin as being more important to a study of English than Old English. Many consider it the monster at the gate of 'Eng. Lit.', hindering the young from entering into the garden of English poetry. Then along comes Seamus Heaney who talks of the *Beowulf* poet's 'level of insight that approaches the visionary'; it is, he states, 'a work of the greatest imaginative vitality, a masterpiece where the structuring of the tale is as elaborate as the beautiful contrivances of its language.' With his powerful and evocative translation Heaney has done more for Old English than anyone before him. It's not just because it's Heaney the Nobel Laureate, but because he has brought to the translation academic knowledge of the poem and its heritage, an appreciation of the intricacies of Old English verse, and a sensitive and keen ear for the sound of this aural poem. Both original and translation cry out to be heard, not read. Just listen to the sound of Beowulf's arrival in Denmark:

> Guman ut scufon,
> weras on wil-sið   wudu bundenne.
> Gewat þa ofer wæg-holm, winde gefysed,
> flota flami-heals,   fugle gelicost,
> oðþæt ymb an-tid   oþres dogores
> wunden-stefna   gewaden hæfde
> þæt ða liðende   land gesawon,
> brim-clifu blican,   beorgas steape
>   (215–22)

[warriors] then heaved out,
away with a will in their wood-wreathed ship.
Over the waves, with the wind behind her
and foam at her neck, she flew like a bird
until her carved prow had covered the distance

297

> and on the following day, at the due hour
> those seafarers sighted land,
> sunlit cliffs, sheer crags
>   (217–18)

Heaney captures the sound of the boat through the waves and keeps the same images and many of the alliterations that are in the original. 'Wood-wreathed ship' imaginatively conveys the image of 'wudu bundenne', 'the well-bound wood', while the lightness of tone and optimism in this passage, contrasting with the previous, depressing scene of despair and devil-worship, is perfectly captured by Heaney in 'foam at her neck' and 'sunlit cliffs'.

It's gratifying to know that this translation will be in the new Norton Anthology along with Heaney's reading of it on CD and once you hear it, you will never forget the sound of his voice. Perhaps I'm biased, coming from Glasgow University, but only one other person, I feel, has truly captured in translation the sound of *Beowulf* and that's my colleague Edwin Morgan in his masterly 1952 translation.

In the early nineteenth century there was another great translator, the Danish Bishop Grundtvig, who talked of 'the natural, imaginative language of *Beowulf*'. Grundtvig compared the good translator to one who melts and recreates a golden object: 'the original letters have gone', Grundtvig states, 'but the spirit of the spoken word is released anew.' And this is exactly what Seamus Heaney has done. Like the Old English *scop*, a word that means both poet and creator, he has fashioned a work of great beauty while keeping the original sense. Grundtvig saw the work as timeless, 'forever changing yet keeping its essential spirit' through the ages, comparing it to the phoenix which is reborn constantly. Heaney likewise sees the funeral of Beowulf, for example, as 'immemorial and oddly contemporary. The Geat woman who cries out in dread as the flames consume the body of her dead lord could come straight from a late-twentieth-century news report from Rwanda or Kosovo' (p. xxi).

The Introduction to the translation is a brief, but concise, thirteen pages in which he gives an overview of *Beowulf* scholarship, praising Tolkien for revealing 'the poem's integrity and distinction as a work of art' (p. xi). Heaney, again like Grundtvig, brings out the 'mythic potency' of the work and captures the relationship between Christian and heroic value systems by the image of a wheel. The halls and the Germanic ideals form the hub of the wheel, while at the circumference, the rim, we have an English, Christian poet looking back at his heroic heritage and 'conflicting realities find accommodation within a new order' (p. xvii) in this creative work.

Almost as much space in the Introduction is devoted to an explanation of his translating techniques and it is here that one senses his love of the sound of the language and appreciation of the nature of Old English vocabulary as nuclei of meanings clinging to every word. He makes much of his Ulster speech patterns as he considers *Beowulf* 'part of my voice-right'. He lingers over words like fine wine and finds in the language of this poem echoes of his childhood; '*polian*' is not 'to suffer' but 'to thole', a word his aunt used—and one I still use in Scotland. He realised that so many words he thought regional were 'not just a self-enclosed family possession but an historical heritage.' He tellingly calls this realisation 'a little epiphany . . . illumination by philology', and it is reassuring to hear philology these days discussed in spiritual terms. This love of the meaning and sounds of words was what brought Tolkien and many more to a love of Old English. The melody he brings to the translation, he says, is that of his father's relatives who pronounced words with weightiness, solemnity and precision. He could hear them beginning a narrative with a pronounced 'So'—and that's how Heaney translates the initial 'Hwæt' of the poem instead of the traditional 'Lo!' or 'Hark!', that seems stilted today. '"So"', he states, 'is an exclamation calling for immediate attention', and that's just what the poet would do in the noisy meadhall to silence the audience. Heaney sees in Old English an escape from 'the binary thinking about language', as it unites his two languages of standard and Ulster English. Interestingly, this was another reason for Grundtvig's love of *Beowulf*: it was, he said, 'the missing link' between Danish and English, as well as past and present.

Apart from Heaney's work being a faithful translation with which it would be difficult to find inaccuracies, it is amazingly readable. This is a difficult balancing act, as some readers will want it as a 'crib' for their reading of the original, while others wish to read it as the epic poem with an exciting storyline as originally intended. He has a marvellous knack of finding an alternative to an Old English alliterative phrase that doesn't translate directly, e.g., 'heal-ðegnes hete . . . fyr ond fæstor': literally, '[those who escaped] the hall thegn's hate [kept] far away and more secure' (243) is succinctly translated by Heaney as 'that hall watcher's hate . . . they kept a weather-eye open'. In addition to supplying alliteration, Heaney strengthens the sly, silent watchfulness of Grendel and the constant alertness of the Danes. Another example of a neat translation comes when the coastguard sees the hero approach: 'unless I am mistaken, he is truly noble. This is no mere hanger-on in a hero's armour' (249). Clark Hall, for example, has a less elegant 'that is no retainer dignified by weapons, unless his countenance, his peerless form, belies him.'

The poems within the poem, such as the tragic tale of Finn and Hildeburh, are indicated by italic print and by what he calls 'a quickening of pace', making them stand out as separate lyrics which are nevertheless central 'to the historical and imaginative worlds of the poem as a whole' (p. xiv). The pathos and tragedy of

the helpless Hildeburh is captured in this moving translation by the brief, breath-
less lines that convey the gross understatement and simple sentences of the original, e.g., 'ðæt wæs geomuru ides', 'that was a mournful lady':

> son and brother,
> she lost them both
> on the battlefield.
> She, bereft
> and blameless, they
> foredoomed, cut down
> and spear-gored. She,
> the woman in shock
> waylaid by grief
> (1070–5)

I do wonder, however, why the Sigemund tale is extended to line 915, thus
including the Heremod section, and why the Ingeld and Freawaru episode is not
also considered a separate tale worthy of this treatment.

Beowulf has a habit of lying dormant for periods, like the dragon guarding
the treasure, only to be awakened from time to time. Grundtvig resurrected the
poem after centuries of neglect, as he realised that it gives 'insights into humanity,
ideals of human fellowship and the reflection of a civilised community striving for
peace'. Heaney almost two hundred years later finds in the poem a similar 'level
of insight that approaches the visionary' and once more revives the public interest
in this great work. By doing so, Heaney has created a fine piece of literature in
its own right, as well as reminding us of the beauty and brilliance of *Beowulf*, the
great English epic.

Jan Čermák

Heaney's Beowulf: Gleaning the Unsaid off the Palpable
Seamus Heaney, *Beowulf*. Faber & Faber.
[*Metre* [Dublin] 9 (2001): 106–9]

For a variety of reasons, *Beowulf* has long enjoyed the reputation of a classic that—like the dragon in it—is best left undisturbed in the depths of literary time. Some twenty modern English translations of the poem, full or partial, by scholars and poets alike, have not redeemed the epic for a late twentieth-century reading public. With the latest translation—by Seamus Heaney, perhaps the most distinct and authoritative of recent poetic voices in the lands of *Beowulf* and a Nobel Prize–winner—we may, however, have a breakthrough. The Anglo-Saxonists, who "put a sheen" by research and commentary on the verses of the poem like ancient burnishers, should be particularly pleased by the act of this new translation: a better *edwenden*, or change, could hardly have come to the cause of the earliest literature in English. And yet, when the distinguished Anglo-Saxonist, Tom Shippey, writes in a review of the translation, "Like it or not, Heaney's *Beowulf* is the poem now, for probably two generations", we feel a joy mingled with sadness, even apprehension: that Heaney's rendering may eclipse not only the efforts of his predecessors but also, quite possibly, the Anonymous Creator of the original epic; that a son has, for a long time to come, displaced the father.

But the fact that Heaney gave voice to *Beowulf* could equally be considered an act of loyalty—a thegnly tribute to one of the foundation works of poetry in English and to language seen as a mode of existence that, for poets and philologists alike, is of mythical importance because it gives us our origin. It is in this "unpartitioned linguistic country", as Heaney says in his Introduction, a space *somewhere behind*, in "a region where one's language would not be simply a badge of ethnicity or a matter of cultural preference or an official imposition, but an entry into further language" that poets, Heaney as much as the author of *Beowulf*, have always found the words—"symptoms of memory", as Heaney wrote in "Englands of the Mind", wells of wisdom, anchors of experience. "I prefer to let the natural 'sound of sense' prevail over the demands of the convention: I have been reluctant to force an artificial shape or an unusual word choice just for the sake of correctness", Heaney states in defining the prime rule of his translation. Most often, the sound of sense rings in perfect accord with what the Old English line requires and the two poets share, like Beowulf and Breca once, the same wave length: consider, for example, the image of the boat awaiting the load of Scyld's dead body and treasures before its venture into the unknown:

> A ring-whorled prow rode in the harbour,
> ice-clad, outbound, a craft for a prince.

Where there would be a danger of a correct but limp line, the poet, following the paths of auditory imagination, returns to the original, unpartitioned realm of linguistic signs and brings something back: in describing the last stages of the hero's first duel, the *Beowulf*-poet focuses more on the atmosphere of terror and Grendel's dismay at his physical and spiritual defeat, than on everybody's where-abouts at just that moment. Heaney saves the prepositional phrase "from the wall" in 1. 785, which is puzzling to some critics of the poem (*Where were the Danes?*) while a mere expletive to others, by filling out the half-line with a richly sounding imaginative detail:

> ... and bewildering fear
> came over the Danes. Everyone felt it
> who heard that cry as it *echoed off the wall*,
> ....
> the howl of the loser, the lament of the hell-serf
> keening his wound.

No less revealing are moments when "poetic truth" prevails over "correctness" without artificiality or a strained word choice being the risk. It is in the latter instances that Heaney's translation of *Beowulf*, despite its overall confidence and cogency, can be shown—using the chivalrous idiom of medieval romance—"to lack a little".

Let's consider the very first lines of the poem after the initial address, introduced by the silence-breaking *so* (ll. 4–11):

> There was Shield Sheafson, scourge of many tribes,
> a wrecker of mead-benches, rampaging among foes.
> This terror of the hall-troops had come far.
> A foundling to start with, he would flourish later on
> as his powers waxed and his worth was proved.
> In the end each clan on the outlying coasts
> beyond the whale-road had to yield to him
> and begin to pay tribute. That was one good king.

This paragraph illustrates several of the important differences between the original and Heaney's rendering. They are both semantic and structural and recur with a consistence that turns what was begun as a translation into a highly imaginative rewriting. Of Scyld the "rampaging wrecker" the original text merely says that he "took mead-benches away from enemy bands, from many tribes". The characteristically subdued diction of the two Old English half-lines is here, just as in numerous other places, converted into a forceful, expressive language of heroic conflict with all its violence and clamour. While Grendel in the good old days "sought his dwelling, proud of plunder", Heaney has him rushing to his lair, "flushed up and inflamed from the raid". When the Old English Hrothgar "feels sorry for his (dead) thanes", the Modern English king is made to feel "humiliated by the loss of his guard". The Unferth of the translation is "sick with envy" at Beowulf's arrival even though what he experiences in the original is merely "great vexation"; Unferth's account of Beowulf's swimming match with Breca by Heaney contains an extra lashing remark "the sea-test obsessed you", missing from the original. The translator sees actions and feelings in the poem through a magnifying glass and there is a characteristic bodily quality about his poem: of Grendel in his opponent's grip the *Beowulf*-poet says no more than that "in mind he became frightened, in his spirit", whereas Heaney translates "every bone in his body / quailed and recoiled". We shall never know precisely what the Anglo-Saxon poet's choices and constraints were but his sophisticated, often abstract diction and his reticent style have long been understood to be sure components of his voice. The colour and sensuous power of Heaney's translation is reminiscent of such Old English poems as *The Exodus*, with its abiding terror and vehement heroism.

Another telling instance in the first paragraph above is "he would flourish later on". E. Talbot Donaldson's "he lived to find comfort (for being found helpless)" translates a clause containing two word-emblems of Anglo-Saxon spirituality: *frofor*, "consolation, solace, relief", and *gebidan*, "to await; wait for" and (though combined with a different case of the noun) "to live to see, experience, live through". Phrases like this restore in *Beowulf* a balance between two of its most central themes: courage and endurance. Neither of the concepts is preserved by Heaney who favours courage and with it the foursquare, confident, performative language of active voice and indicative mood: the self-assured heroes of *his Beowulf* go out in the world along the path to power to prove their worth and earn admiration.

A problem on a different level of the text occurs in "(each clan) had to yield to him and begin to pay tribute" above when compared to the Old English "had to obey him, pay him tribute". Heaney's wording breaks the asyndetic unity of the two phrases and the simultaneity of their reference. Seeking explicitness and steady progression, he establishes a temporal sequence of the two acts of subjection. The *Beowulf*-poet's strategy is a contrary one: by uniting the two phrases in the figure of variation, he works with the implicit. By refusing to spell out the links, temporal or other, he chooses to meditate, however briefly, on the nature of obeisance. The contemplative order, with its chains of variations, thus naturally assumes a different pace and structuring of the verse paragraph. This difference of approach, though negligible with regard to one phrase, becomes vastly important when applied consistently throughout the text. The relative prevalence in Heaney's *Beowulf* of the narrative over meditative element neatly dovetails with his predilection for the magnifying glass of the heroic and the forthright, "big-voiced" language.

These are, very briefly, some of the important shifts distinguishing *Beowulf* from this *Beowulfing*, the father from a son, the poem for ever from its most recent and wonderfully imaginative translation into an idiom of extraordinary lexico-stylistic breadth. In assessing this idiom in relation to Heaney's own verse as well as placing this translation in the context of its predecessors we must admit the union of great poets that is embodied in Seamus Heaney's *Beowulf*.

Howell Chickering

Beowulf and 'Heaneywulf'

Beowulf, translated by Seamus Heaney. In *The Norton Anthology of English Literature*, 7th edition. New York and London: W. W. Norton & Company, 2000. *Beowulf*. Translated by Seamus Heaney. London: Faber and Faber, 1999. *Beowulf: A New Verse Translation*. By Seamus Heaney. Bilingual edition. New York: Farrar, Straus and Giroux, 2000. [*Kenyon Review* 24.1 (2002): 160–78]

Over the last two years Seamus Heaney's long-awaited translation of *Beowulf* has been issued by three separate publishing houses to overwhelming critical acclaim. It won the 1999 Whitbread Book of the Year Award and reached the best-seller lists in both the United States and the United Kingdom. Its reception was quite a phenomenon.

Heaney was initially commissioned by Norton to represent the Old English poem to undergraduates in a free-standing and relatively faithful translation, to appear in their anthology. When the translation was published separately, with a couple of notable exceptions (Tom Shippey in the *Times Literary Supplement*, Nicholas Howe in *New Republic*), the reviewers had little or no knowledge of Old English and responded to it as a new poem by the 1995 Nobel Prize winner. Some even praised his translation for the strength of its narrative design, as if he had invented the final conflict between the hero and the dragon. Heaney's own assessment, as reported by Mel Gussow in an interview in the *New York Times*, is that the translation is "about one-third Heaney, two-thirds 'duty to the text.'" (B4). On the other hand, professional Anglo-Saxonists early on derogated it with the name "Heaneywulf" since to them it was "just not *Beowulf*." It isn't, of course. No translation follows its exemplar exactly, no matter how "faithful." The nickname stuck, in academic circles anyway, but has now lost its pejorative sense and instead signals Heaney's efforts to mark the translation as his own poem.

Someone is always translating *Beowulf*, it seems. Since 1900, amazingly enough, there has been one new translation every two years on average. In the short time since Heaney's first appeared, three more have been published or promised.[1] This is in marked contrast to English translations of Homer or Dante, where one poetic translation will hold the field for decades before a new attempt appears. Why this steady stream? Perhaps one answer is that many university students on both sides of the Atlantic learn Old English, often painfully, and they wish to turn their pain into pleasure. Another reason is that the poem is mercifully short

(3,182 lines) in comparison to Homer, and hence apparently less daunting. A more important factor is the persistent genetic fallacy that mistakes the remote historical continuity between Old English and Modern English as an indication of their essential identity, when in reality a whole millennium separates the two culturally and linguistically.

Yet even if conscientious translators treat Old and Modern English as separate source and target languages, they don't seem to "get it right" in others' eyes. Disagreement over what constitutes fidelity to the original has prevented general acceptance of a standard Modern English *Beowulf*. This is as it should be, whether we mean fidelity to the letter or to the literary qualities of the original. It's not only that it is impossible to bring *any* poem's full literary effect across in translation. There also is a special problem in going from Old to Modern English because we cannot help but see prominent features of Old English poetry—alliteration, parataxis, and nominal compounding—as properties of Modern English poetry, when they actually create very different literary effects in Old English. The unavoidable temptation for the poetic translator is to try to transpose these literary effects by using the same linguistic features in Modern English. The results never satisfy everyone, and so translations continue to appear.

Twentieth-century poetic versions of *Beowulf* have mainly been paraphrases, to use Dryden's term, translating sense for sense rather than word for word. Since the Scottish poet Edwin Morgan's 1952 rendition, based on his eloquent plea for a chastened modern diction instead of archaisms and literal compounds, a kind of stylistic consensus can be seen in the more successful poetic paraphrases. They tend to be literal rather than to introduce new metaphors, and they try to mute the effect of the features shared by Old and Modern English poetry. Thus they use a four- or five-stress poetic line, only light alliteration, and what the translator considers a restrained modern diction. (Dictional equivalents in Modern English for the kenning-heavy compounding of *Beowulf* have remained an area of disagreement.) Those versions that also reproduce the syntactical and rhetorical designs of the original come closest to representing at least a faint ghost of their grand exemplar. They remain honorable failures, since Modern English poetry simply cannot match the clangorous magnificence of the Old English, but they show how the poem's thoughts and images develop. Among them I count Kevin Crossley-Holland's 1968 version, my own in 1977, Marc Hudson's in 1990, and Roy Michael Liuzza's 2000 translation. The successful aspects of Heaney's translation place it in this group of poetic paraphrases, although he frequently departs from the Old English syntax and often mixes dictional registers so as to mar his own literary decorum. For fidelity to both the letter and spirit of the original, it is a resounding but mixed success, with some awkward missteps amid many fine poetic achievements.

The very finest passages in Heaney's rendering are the dramatic speeches, which make up about forty percent of the poem. The speeches are freshly faithful to the point of ventriloquism (Nicholas Howe's term). To a reader who knows the original well, passage after passage delivers the sense and tone of the Old English with effortless grace. It doesn't matter which character is speaking, nor whether with enthusiasm or stoic irony: Heaney captures their verbal gestures just about perfectly. When Unferth, Hrothgar's sour-minded retainer, challenges Beowulf upon his arrival at Heorot, Heaney makes his voice modulate from a sneering reproach into a stately catalogue of verbs implicitly acknowledging heroic action. The original moves exactly this way. Similarly, in the close of Beowulf's thoroughly devastating reply to Unferth, Heaney gets the pulse of feeling exactly right:

> "The fact is, Unferth, if you were truly
> as keen or courageous as you claim to be
> Grendel would never have got away with
> such unchecked atrocity, attacks on your king,
> havoc in Heorot and horrors everywhere.
> But he knows he need never be in dread
> of your blade making a mizzle of his blood
> or of vengeance arriving ever from this quarter—
> from the Victory-Shieldings, the shoulderers of the spear.
> He knows he can trample down you Danes
> to his heart's content, humiliate and murder
> without fear of reprisal. But he will find me different.
> I will show him how Geats shape to kill
> in the heat of battle. Then whoever wants to
> may go bravely to mead, when morning light,
> scarfed in sun-dazzle, shines forth from the south
> and brings another daybreak to the world." (590–606)

This passage also shows the translator as tactful interpreter. Here "you Danes" are more sharply contrasted with the Geats than in the Old English text, but most critics read Beowulf's boast as thinly veiled aggression and Heaney simply makes it overt. The brilliant image of the morning light "scarfed in sun-dazzle" is Heaney's own, resting on good textual warrant, and lends subtle symbolic force to what gives "another daybreak to the world," namely Beowulf's proposed salvation of the Danes.

Heaney's final verbs here mirror the confident future indicative of the original. However, there are uncertain touches of diction in the passage as well. "Heart's content" and "fear of reprisal" are shopworn phrases. "[S]uch unchecked atrocity" smacks of journalese, and "need never be in dread . . . of vengeance arriving ever from this quarter" sounds like a back-bencher in Parliament. American readers are unlikely to know, even from context, that "mizzle" is dialectal for "drizzle." In fact it seems selected not only as a countryman's word but also to alliterate with "making," and therefore feels slightly forced.

That line—"of your blade making a mizzle of his blood"—exhibits one of Heaney's favorite rhetorical enrichments, chiasmus, here played out across the *bl-m-m-bl* alliteration. Generally his poetic form is more lightly alliterated, sometimes on unstressed syllables, sometimes only twice in a line, and on rare occasions not at all. Sometimes we hear a strong medial caesura, sometimes only the lightest pause. He has tried, as he says in his Introduction, for "the sound of sense" (xxix) in Frost's famous phrase, and this flexible-form allows him to stay focused on it. His translation can thus keep pace with the original nearly line by line.

Heaney says that he sought to recreate "a kind of foursquareness about the utterance" (xxviii) which he encountered when he first read the Old English poem. He acknowledges that his own prejudice in favor of "forthright delivery" has led him to scant, to some degree, the extended appositions of the poem's syntactical variations and some of its ornate compound-making. This is true: we sorely miss the craggy, bejeweled difficulty of the original in Heaney's flattened-out "directness of utterance." I myself certainly wouldn't call the style of the original Old English "foursquare." It is both restrained and exuberant, often ironic, oblique, ceremonial, sometimes sententious.

Nonetheless, Heaney's mode of translation often works exceptionally well in narrative passages. Here, for instance, is a famous description of nonheroic action, when Beowulf and his men first cross the ocean to Denmark:

> Time went by, the boat was on water,
> in close under the cliffs.
> Men climbed eagerly up the gangplank,
> sand churned in surf, warriors loaded
> a cargo of weapons, shining war-gear
> in the vessel's hold, then heaved out,
> away with a will in their wood-wreathed ship.
> Over the waves, with the wind behind her
> and foam at her neck, she flew like a bird
> until her curved prow had covered the distance
> and on the following day, at the due hours
> those seafarers sighted land,
> sunlit cliffs, sheer crags
> and looming headlands, the landfall they sought.
> It was the end of their voyage and the Geats vaulted
> over the side, out on to the sand,
> and moored their ship. There was a clash of mail
> and a thresh of gear. They thanked God
> for that easy crossing on a calm sea. (210–28)

This is a brilliant rendering of what is already a brilliant passage in the original. Heaney has successfully spread out the ship-as-bird simile over more lines than it takes in the Old English and he has resegmented some of the sentences, but everything works to create an effect equivalent to the Old English. This kind of clear vigor is typical of his best narrative passages. So is his arrival at the translation "It was the end of their voyage," an adroit negotiation of the crux at line 224a, *ēoletes æt ende*, discussion of which takes up nearly seven inches of small print in Dobbie's variorum edition. To my mind, Heaney has made sensible, or at least defensible, decisions about translating all the major cruces in the poem.

In other passages Heaney is less responsive to the text. When he comes upon the most surprising periodic delay in the entire poem, he does not preserve it in his translation. After Grendel's Dam attacks, the Danes and the Geats track her to the mere, and the sentence at 1417b–21 reads literally (to use Roy Liuzza's very exact translation):

> To all of the Danes
> the men of the Scyldings, many a thane,
> it was a sore pain at heart to suffer,
> a grief to every earl, when on the seacliff
> they came upon the head of Æschere.

In the Old English the "when" clause delays the discovery of the head (hafelan) of Hrothgar's beloved counselor until the last half-line: "syðþan Æscheres / on þam holm-clife hafelan metton." This delivers a real narrative shock to the reader as well as to the Danes. However, in Heaney's version Æschere's head is displaced from emphatic final position to the "foot" of the cliff, which isn't even in the original:

> It was a sore blow
> to all of the Danes, friends of the Shieldings.
> a hurt to each and every one
> of that noble company when they came upon
> Æschere's head at the foot of the cliff.

"[A] sore blow" and "a hurt to each and every one" are flaccid phrases compared to the pained literal sense of the Old English. It's notable, too, that Heaney doesn't seek the emphasis of alliteration when he reaches this climax.

Heaney's fidelity to "the sound of sense" may also be tested by his treatment of Grendel's approach to Heorot, much admired by generations of readers. I will cite only lines 710–11, which have a horrifying sound in Old English, like a tolling bell:

> Ða cōm of mōre   under mist-hleoþum
> Grendel gongan,   Godes yrre baer.

The double *g*'s of "gongan" extend the growl in "Grendel" and then become more portentous as they contrast with the even heavier weight of the *g* sound that he must bear, "Godes yrre," God's wrath. In my dual-language edition, with this astonishing texture of sounds on view across the page, I could afford to render the lines quite literally:

> Then up from the marsh,   under misty cliffs,
> Grendel came walking;   he bore God's wrath.

Roy Liuzza, with different nuances in his diction, is also literal:

> Then from the moor, in a blanket of mist,
> Grendel came stalking—he bore God's anger.

Both of us are careful to mimic the grammar and rhythm of the Old English, and hope against hope that the effect will speak for itself. Heaney, on the other hand, has:

> In off the moors, down through the mist-bands
> God-cursed Grendel came greedily loping.

By changing the verbal construction, Heaney loses the sound of slow-marching menace and turns Grendel into a sort of hyena. The *gr* alliteration of his second line no longer sets the monster against his Maker but instead links him to animal appetite. That Grendel has aplenty, and he soon gobbles up a sleeping Geat, but the eerie ritual dignity of his horrid visit has vanished. Of course it is also true that neither my nor Liuzza's version recreates the *sound* of that eerieness. In that sense, none of us "gets it right." Whether or not a young reader of "Heaneywulf" will like Grendel as a greedy loper is another matter.

   The most daunting literary task facing every translator of *Beowulf* is to find an equivalent for the dominant voice of the poem, which moves back and forth between pell-mell narrative and lingering reflection even at the most exciting moments. The Old English achieves this duality of mode in part through its ornate diction and elaborated syntax, aspects that Heaney means to eschew. His solution is, as he says, to establish a firm, level tone with his "foursquare" line and language. This tone has its gains and its costs. Usually it has clarity and force. It helps Heaney to avoid an overblown and compound-clogged Modern English, but not always. Sometimes it merely leaves us with dull stretches. Furthermore, in his attempt to keep on an even keel, he frequently recasts the shape of sentences in startling and distracting ways. On the whole, the chief virtue of his style—apart from the clarity and force of the dramatic speeches—is that it establishes a *decorum* of language that accords well with the heroic dignity of the Old English.

Such decorum is no mean poetic achievement. I therefore find it ironic that he often unintentionally breaks his own decorum. This happens in three ways: by overwrought images derived from already strong metaphors in the Old English; by clunky over-alliterations not required by his form; and by wildly varying dictional choices. At such moments he becomes so enthusiastic about the sense and sound of the original, and about his command over it, that he has to exercise the full range of his poetic talents. He breaks into florid song, as it were, and it clashes with his own levelness.

For instance, when Beowulf tells Hrothgar he has vanquished Grendel, Heaney has him conclude by saying:

> And now he won't be long for this world.
> He has done his worst but the wound will end him.
> He is hasped and trooped and hirpling with pain,
> limping and looped in it. Like a man outlawed
> for wickedness, he must await
> the mighty judgement of God in majesty. (974–79)

The first line is colloquial to the point of flipness. The *h* alliteration of the "hirpling" line is showy overkill, which is carried over into the internal rhyming of "limping and looped." "Hirpling" is a recondite dialectal word for "hobbling" and was not known to several British friends when I tried it out on them. It might as well be a word from "Jabberwocky." Heaney's exuberant performance is more in evidence here than the subject of the passage itself, Grendel's death-wound.

An example of both over-alliteration and overwrought imagery is Heaney's identification of Yrse, the queen of Swedish king Onela, in an early lineage. In line 64 she is literally called "the neck [hence 'close, dear'] bed-companion of the Battle-Scylfing [i.e., Battle-Swede]," a compound name which suggests both the stately and the intimate, but Heaney renders her as "A balm in bed for the battle-scarred Swede." This seems a thumpingly gratuitous foregrounding of the erotic, even though one can admire it as interpretive translation.

Alliteration by itself, especially on *b* sounds, often distracts the reader from the sense. Lines 81b–84a:

> The hall towered,
> its gables wide and high and awaiting
> a barbarous burning. That doom abided,

but in time it would come: the killer instinct
unleashed among in-laws, the blood-lust rampant.

"Barbarous burning"—is there any other kind? "Abided" might have come from any one of a dozen earlier translations. The over-connection of "and . . . and" (not in the original) also flattens out the sense. When Grendel first attacks Heorot, he rushes back to his lair in lines 124–25,

> flushed up and inflamed from the raid,
> blundering back with the butchered corpses.

That second line itself seems to blunder. There are a number of other instances of verbal overkill that break decorum, and do not create the "forthright delivery" the poet says he sought. It is worth noting that they are mainly confined, for whatever reason, to the Grendel's Dam episode and the early part of the dragon fight.

One could argue, I suppose, that the overcooked imagery and the bumping alliteration are deliberate adornments that extend, rather than break, Heaney's basic decorum of style. Certainly such imagery has been cited admiringly in various reviews. However, the more serious problem is his extravagant use of disparate registers of diction, since the disparities cause his normally level tone to dip or knot up. I see three different kinds of dictional shifts that break his own decorum. First, part of Heaney's "foursquareness" is a man-to-man informality with flourishes of emphasis of the sort we love to hear in oral storytelling. The gain is a conversational "readable" quality in the translation. But his sudden drops into the chummily colloquial can be unsettling when the rest of the sentence is not informal. Second, there are what I can only call clichés of speech, which you simply don't expect in a poet of Heaney's stature. Third, there are the deliberate Ulsterisms.

All of these can be seen in the opening lines of "Heaneywulf," which is far and away the most frequently cited passage in the sheaf of reviews I've collected.

> So. The Spear-Danes in days gone by
> and the kings who ruled them had courage and greatness.
> We have heard of those princes' heroic campaigns.
>
> There was Shield Sheafson, scourge of many tribes,
> a wrecker of mead-benches, rampaging among foes.
> This terror of the hall-troops had come far.
> A foundling to start with, he would flourish later on
> as his powers waxed and his worth was proved.
> In the end each clan on the outlying coasts
> beyond the whale-road had to yield to him
> and begin to pay tribute. That was one good king.

> Afterwards a boy-child was born to Shield,
> a cub in the yard, a comfort sent
> by God to that nation. He knew what they had tholed,
> the long times and troubles they'd come through
> without a leader; so the Lord of Life,
> the glorious Almighty, made this man renowned.
> Shield had fathered a famous son:
> Beow's name was known through the north.
> And a young prince must be prudent like that,
> giving freely while his father lives
> so that afterwards in age when fighting starts
> steadfast companions will stand by him
> and hold the line. Behaviour that's admired
> is the path to power among people everywhere. (1–25)

In the first three lines Heaney alters the syntax unnecessarily, losing the original shape of the sentence, and ends up with a subdued, rather flat tone. Here are the lines in Old English and a literal gloss:

> Hwæt! Wē Gār-Dena   in geārdagum
> þēodcyninga   þrym gefrūnon,
> hū ðā æþelingas   ellen fremedon.
>
> What! We of the Spear-Danes   in the old days
> of the tribal kings   the strength have heard tell,
> how those noblemen   courage performed.

The grammatical relationships can be sorted out thus:

> Listen! We have heard tell   of the strength of the tribal kings
> of the Spear-Danes   in the old days,
> [of] how those noblemen   performed [deeds of] courage!

The first verb in the poem, *gefrignan*, is an epic formula of poetic authority that means "to hear tell of," and its first object is the "þrym" of the ancient Danish kings, a word that means "power" or "military troop," and by extension "glory." I punctuate the sentence with an exclamation point because the verb's second object, the "how" clause expanding upon "þrym," is uttered with great warmth of feeling, with the heavy nouns *æþelingas* ("noblemen") and *ellen* ("courage") receiving full metrical emphasis. Despite his announced commitment to the living voices of tellers, Heaney suppresses the initial indication of oral reception and recitation in "wē . . . gefrūnon" and dilutes the syntactic force of line 2 by introducing the two "ands." Then he makes line 3 a separate sentence, which cools its warmth considerably, as does its oddly high-toned propaganda-like diction: "those princes' heroic campaigns." These are uncertain first steps into the poem.

The last sentence of this opening passage is also askew. Literally it reads "in every tribe a man must prosper by deeds of praise," a maxim of conduct that clinches not only the Anglo-Saxon value of a lord's generosity to his men but also their reciprocal loyalty under duress. Heaney's version suggests nothing so much as a modern political climber's recipe for success: "Behaviour that is admired / is the path to power among people everywhere." Perhaps the excesses of the last American presidential election have given me a tin ear. But consider a different tone, in line 11b: "That was one good king." By simply adding "one" for colloquial emphasis to an otherwise exact translation of "þæt wæs gōd cyning," he has deflected our attention from the object of praise to the sound of the praising voice. Perhaps this deflection is always part of the project of a modern poet, but in this case it trivializes when it should emphasize. The colloquial note in line 20, "And a young prince must be prudent like that," doesn't work either; it loses the dignity and decorum of the Old English in head-wagging sententiousness.

Then there are the clichés, some of which I have already cited. "Hold the line" at the end of this passage was originally "bear the brunt" in a version that circulated prior to publication, so I know it's intended as an improvement. A few lines past this quotation we get "laid down the law" for when Scyld literally "ruled by words." These phrases are legitimate interpretive translations. The problem lies in their jazzy tone, as though the words were too easily found. The sense that they are *ad hoc* affects my response to the choice of "boy-child" (for *eafera*, 'son, offspring') and also "cub" (for the adjective *geong* 'young'); those words seem chosen mainly for alliteration.

But the most controversial single word in this opening passage is its first: "So." The Old English opens with the interjection "Hwæt!" which is literally "What!" but can be translated as "Listen" or "Hear me!" or, as some wags have recently suggested on the Anglo-Saxon electronic network, "Hey!" or "Yo!" Older translations had "Hark!" and one even had "What ho!" While there is some controversy over whether "Hwæt" is part of the first complete sentence or a free-standing call for attention, what really matters, as these modern alternatives suggest, is that the Modern English choice for this first word will boldly declare the tonal landscape of any translation. Probably "Hwæt" functioned the same way in the Old English, but we don't know its precise tone or social occasion.

Heaney slices through this Gordian knot by the confident substitution of his own sensibility as a modern Irish poet. To my ear, "So." sounds either tight-lipped and almost grim, or else like a buddy-to-buddy acknowledgment. To other American ears (Nicholas Howe, the members of ANSAXNET) it has implied a continuation of some prior speech, or has sounded like a Yiddish greeting, or like urban guy talk ("So. What's up with the Danes of yore?") To Heaney, however, it comes out of his rural family history. "So." is the first declaration of his desire to appropriate the act of translation to his own complicated cultural heritage. The second indication in this passage is his use of the Ulsterism "tholed" for "suffered," which derives from the Old English verb *þolian*.

In his Introduction he sketches a history of his personal relationship to the Old English. After the translation was first commissioned in the mid-1980s, Heaney says he bogged down after getting part way through.

> Even so, I had an instinct that it should not be let go. An understanding I had worked out for myself concerning my own linguistic and literary origins made me reluctant to abandon the task. I had noticed, for example, that without any conscious intent on my part certain lines in the first poem in my first book conformed to the requirements of Anglo-Saxon metrics. These lines were made up of two balancing halves, each half containing two stressed syllables—"'The spade sinks into gravelly ground: / My father digging. I look down . . .'"—and in the case of the second line there was alliteration linking "digging" and "down" across the caesura. Part of me, in other words, had been writing Anglo-Saxon from the start. . . . I suppose all I am saying is that I consider *Beowulf* to be part of my voice-right. (*New Verse* xxiii)

This goes down very smoothly, and one needs to stop and reflect on how metaphorical it is to say, "Part of me . . . had been writing Anglo-Saxon from the start." This claim and the slippery coinage of "voice-right," playing off "birth-right," show his desire to appropriate *Beowulf* for his own poetic voice. Of course Heaney also knew Irish and "For a long time . . . I tended to conceive of English and Irish as adversarial tongues, as either/or conditions rather than both/and." He had inklings of "the possibility of release from this kind of cultural determination early on" during his first year at Queen's University, Belfast, where through a lecture on the Irish etymology of the English word "whiskey" he glimpsed "some unpartitioned linguistic country, a region where one's language would not be simply a badge of ethnicity or a matter of cultural preference or an official imposition, but an entry into further language" (xxv). Then he discovered *þolian* in the Glossary to Wrenn's edition of *Beowulf* and realized it was:

> the word that older and less educated people would have used in the country where I grew up. "They'll just have to learn to thole," my aunt would say about some family who had suffered an unforeseen bereavement. And now suddenly here was "thole" in the official textual world, mediated through the apparatus of a a scholarly edition, a little bleeper to remind me that my aunt's language was not just a self-enclosed family possession but an historical heritage. . . . (xxv)

But if "þolian had opened my right of way," he still had to find "the note and pitch for the overall music of the work." And that he found close to home:

a familiar local voice, one that had belonged to relatives of my father, people whom I had once described (punning on their surname) as "big-voiced Scullions" [in the poem "The Stand at Lough Beg"].

I called them "big-voiced" because when the men of the family spoke, the words they uttered came across with a weighty distinctness, phonetic units as separate and defined as delph platters displayed on a dresser shelf. A simple sentence such as "We cut the corn today" took on immense dignity when one of the Scullions spoke it. . . . when I came to ask myself how I wanted *Beowulf* to sound in my version, I realized I wanted it to be speakable by one of those relatives. I therefore tried to frame the famous opening lines in cadences that would have suited their voices, but that still echoed with the sound and sense of the Anglo-Saxon. . . . in Hiberno-English Scullionspeak, the particle "so" came naturally to the rescue, because in that idiom "so" operated as an expression that obliterates all previous discourse and narrative, and at the same time functions as an exclamation calling for immediate attention. So, "so" it was. (xxvii)

The way I read this account, Heaney's reasoning for arriving at this choice is emphatically not "a release from cultural determination" but instead a reinstatement of it. He says he used his Ulsterisms sparingly and only when one "presented itself uncontradictably" (the case in point was "keshes" for *frēcne fen-gelād* 1359a). It is true that there are only about a dozen Ulsterisms in "Heaneywulf." In addition to "hirpling," "keshes," and "tholed," they include "wean" (as a noun), "hoked," "stook," "brehon," "session" (from Irish *seissiún*), "reavers," "bothies," "graith," and "bawn" (a word I will return to). To readers who are not speakers of Irish English, which must be the overwhelming majority of Heaney's audience, these Ulsterisms, occurring as they do throughout the translation, are a signal of cultural difference. They act as little bleepers, to use his own term, reminding you that you are not part of the Ulster English-language community. That's if you have read his writing explaining his intentions for "Heaneywulf." Most readers of the *Norton Anthology* will not have done so, since his Introduction is not printed there. For them, these are incomprehensible words that need to be translated into standard English to be understood, and in fact Heaney has had to gloss most of them in explanatory notes in the anthology.

In his 1999 Saint Jerome Lecture, "The Drag of the Golden Chain," he goes out of his way to approve of that peculiar procedure, giving an intensely personal reason:

What keeps the translator in a state of near (but never quite complete) fulfillment is this tension between the impulse to use the work in its first language as a stimulus and the obligations to give it a fair hearing in the second. . . . there could be no better illustration of the fact of the tension itself than the footnotes in the new volume. At certain points, it is the very translation that has to be translated for the benefit of the worldwide audience of English-speakers to whom the anthology is directed. (16)

One can only sympathize with the poet's desire to be at once original and faithful, but this is also a self-serving apologia that makes no concessions to the target audience of the translation. It seems that once he decided to push on with his translation he found that he was really writing for himself, and not for the audience of the *Norton Anthology*. A poet *should* write for himself, without a doubt, and to do so may make "Heaneywulf" more his own work. But this strange dictional coloration does not accurately represent the language of *Beowulf*. There are no Irish words in the Old English poem, and it does a disservice to students to make it look like there is an amalgam of Irish and English in the original poem.

There is yet a deeper difficulty in Heaney's deliberate blending of these different Englishes: it is bad cultural and linguistic history. It does not acknowledge that the varieties of English are shaped by social forces. In his other writings Heaney knows this quite well, and has even noted how the name "Seamus" immediately identified him as a Catholic in Ulster. But in the Saint Jerome Lecture, he would like his posited connections between Old English and the Ulster dialect to work so that when successful "the flash of the right word choice should create a tremor that makes readers feel they exist as 'full strength' members of the language-group" (16). The problem for the majority of his audience is, which language-group is it, Irish or English? It can't be both, given the history of Northern Ireland.

Which brings me back to "bawn." At the end of his Introduction, Heaney says:

> . . . for reasons of historical suggestiveness, I have in several instances used the word "bawn" to refer to Hrothgar's hall. In Elizabethan English, bawn (from the Irish *bó-dhún*, a fort for cattle) referred specifically to the fortified dwellings that the English planters built in Ireland to keep the dispossessed natives at bay, so it seemed the proper term to apply to the embattled keep where Hrothgar waits and watches. Indeed, every time I read the lovely interlude that tells of the minstrel singing in Heorot just before the first attacks of Grendel, I cannot help thinking of Edmund Spenser in Kilcolman Castle, reading the early cantos of *The Faerie Queene* to Sir Walter Raleigh, just before the Irish would burn the castle and drive Spenser out of Munster back to the Elizabethan court. Putting a bawn into *Beowulf* seems one way for an Irish poet to come to terms with that complex history of conquest and colony, absorption and resistance, integrity and antagonism, a history that has to be clearly acknowledged by all concerned in order to render it ever more "willable forward / again and again and again." (xxx)

(The last lines are from his own poem "The Settle Bed," which he uses as the epi-graph to his translation.) This pleasantly fanciful picture of Spenser in his bawn is deeply confused as an analogy to Hrothgar in Heorot. It makes the histori-cal equation read: the oppressed Irish = Grendel, and the colonizing English = Hrothgar. Surely Heaney can't mean that he takes his Elizabethan Irish forebears to have been monsters from the race of Cain, nor the exploitative English plant-ers to have been wise rulers like Hrothgar. Yet that's the way the analogy works. Putting a "bawn" into his translation is *not* a way "to come to terms" with Irish-English history. Ulsterisms like "bawn" operate polemically in "Heaneywulf." They drive home a sense of difference, if not conflict, between Irish English and other varieties of English. Although he doesn't *mean* them to subvert the Englishness of the poem, that is what they must do, as terms coming from a particular history and geography. Heaney can't avoid history, as much as he might wish, in his Christian pacifism, to "will it forward." To use "bawn" in this context is like using the word "intifada" when translating the Old Testament.

How could a poet whose other work is so alive to political and linguistic tensions in the United Kingdom so badly mistake the effect of using his own local dialect in a different cultural context? How, to ask a related question, can his translation often be quite faithful to the sense, and yet at points be so quirky and overheated? I couldn't find an answer to these questions until I realized that before and since publication he has been working hard to induce readers to accept "Heaneywulf" as actually having realized his own personal intentions. He wants it to be seen as a poem by Seamus Heaney—as a poem *said* by Seamus Heaney— more than as a translation from the Old English, despite his assertions to the con-trary. This seems confirmed by the availability of audio cassettes and now a CD, and by the many public readings he has given, where the audience not only hears the story of the Introduction once again but also experiences firsthand a seamless continuity of accent and intonation between his poetic art and his talk about it. When he turns to excerpts from his *Beowulf* after an hour of his other work, they sound very like his own poems.

To put it another way, he is now actively engaged in his own canon forma-tion. He wants to be sure, or so it seems to me, that this big hit, his *Beowulf*, has a place in the already well-developed arc of his career, a place that will, with only a little more hindsight smartly applied to it, come to seem inevitable. No poet writ-ing mainly for himself, after all, would want a new volume to be seen as a wild side step in mid-career, or merely an exercise for the left hand. Especially not after the 1995 Nobel Prize. His writing about the genesis of "Heaneywulf" is therefore an example of that kind of fictional myth-making we call autobiography.

The myth begins from a premise of fact: Norton approached him, he agreed to the project, and got started. After that, the hero of the story (the poet as translator is always a potentially doomed hero) enters the Dark Wood of Despair, gets stuck, loses interest. He is ready to abandon the project and hence, by implication, to turn his back on tawdry Academic Commercialism. But then he has an epiphany: he encounters the word *polian* and connects it with "thole," and a newly green hedge-lane of opportunities and connections opens up before him, or, more accurately, within him. As he writes in the first of his "Glanmore Sonnets":

> Vowels plough the other: opened ground. (*Opened Ground* 156)

Pulling the Ulsterism "thole" from his memory is like pulling the Sword from the Stone (the genre of the myth is ultimately Romance). Now he sees the analogies between Old English poetry and Ulster dialect, and, more important, between heroism and familial manners in these two violent worlds, and he is ready to go onward and upward. The final completion of the translation is the capstone of the narrative. Upon its publication and astounding success, the myth enters the realm of public discourse where it now has an active life as a sanctioned explanation of his intentions. The sanction of the myth is so strong that some readers see the intentions as actual effects.

There is one final segment of the narrative yet to come, like the prediction of Arthur's Return. It is the realization of "an entry into further language." In his Nobel lecture "Crediting Poetry," Heaney sketches out his heartfelt belief that there is a "wholeness" of language which poetry can confer upon "partition." In that essay, in contrast to his remarks about his translation, he acknowledges the pain of division in Northern Ireland, and he looks to "the local" to energize the future. His great example is Yeats's poetry, which "does what the necessary poetry always does, which is to touch the base of our sympathetic nature while taking in at the same time the unsympathetic reality of the world to which that nature is constantly exposed" (*Opened Ground* 430). In his 1997 *Paris Review* interview, Heaney was asked if he was now trying "to go back to, not a Wordsworthian innocence, but a place pre-language, pre-nationalism, pre-Catholicism." He replied that he had "a definite desire to write a kind of poem that cannot immediately be ensnared in what they call the 'cultural debate.' This has become one of the binds as well as one of the bonuses for poets in Ireland. Every poem is either enlisted or unmasked for its clandestine political affiliations" (106). Thus, if we could only see his *Beowulf* as he does, it would provide a vision of the prelapsarian *Urlage*, a place where poetry tells the truth about both the harshness and the sweetness of reality, a place of wholeness beneath and beyond the brutal Irish-English political conflict and its concomitant linguistic division.

This myth of Heaney's is not new. Many elements of it are present in his earlier writing. In his essay "Feeling into Words" (1974), he approvingly connects, through a poem of W. R. Rodgers, the craggy Anglo-Saxonisms of Hopkins, his own first empowering poetic model, with the harsh consonants of the Ulster accent. And in the 1972 essay "Belfast," he places himself symbolically between the two components of the name of his family's farm, Mossbawn. In 1999 he returned to this name in a poem in the *New Yorker* titled "Mossbawn." His affection for and idealized conceptualization of the "bawn," as we see it justified in the *Beowulf* Introduction, have been with him for a long time.

If it is his larger project to inscribe upon English literary culture a poem of his own that is newly "willable forward," I do not believe that he has achieved his intention. However, "Heaneywulf" certainly stands up as one of the better poetic paraphrases of the original, even as it calls attention to itself as his own poem. I predict that, after its day in the sun as a publishing phenomenon, future critics of contemporary poetry will treat it as part of his own corpus, just as he hopes. As a translation of *Beowulf*, it will be assigned out of the *Norton Anthology* by foot-soldiering non-specialists teaching required survey courses. At the same time, other translations of *Beowulf* will continue to appear as the 2000s roll along, and among them English teachers will find equally good translations, of mixed success, to choose from. In turn, those translations will annoy students who have learned Old English and have read the poem in the original. Some few of them will always have the chutzpah to think they have enough poetic talent to render the original into Modern English verse. And *Beowulf* will go on being newly translated for the foreseeable future.

Note

1. Roy Michael Liuzza, *Beowulf: A New Verse Translation* (Peterborough, Ontario: Broadview Press, 2000); Alan Sullivan and Timothy Murphy, *Beowulf*, to be published by Story Line Press; and, still in process at this writing, Timothy Romano's online translation of *Beowulf* at members.dca.net/tim/beowulf_trans.htm.

Works Cited

Chickering, Howell D., Jr. *Beowulf: A Dual-Language Edition*. New York: Anchor Books, 1977.

Crossley-Holland, Kevin. *Beowulf*. New York: Farrar, Straus & Giroux, 1968.

Dobbie, Elliot van Kirk, ed. *Beowulf and Judith*. The Anglo-Saxon Poetic Records, vol. iv. New York: Columbia UP, 1953.

Gussow, Mel. "An Anglo-Saxon Chiller (With an Irish Touch): Seamus Heaney Adds His Voice to 'Beowulf,'" *New York Times*, Mar. 29, 2000: B4.

Heaney, Seamus. "Feeling into Words" and "Belfast," in *Preoccupations: Selected Prose 1968–1978*. New York: Farrar, Straus & Giroux, 1980.

————. Interview by Henri Cole, "The Art of Poetry LXXV," *Paris Review*, No. 144 (1997): 106.

————. *Opened Ground: Selected Poems 1966–1996*. New York: Farrar, Straus & Giroux, 1998.

————. "The Drag of the Golden Chain," *Times Literary Supplement*, November 12, 1999: 16.

Howe, Nicholas. "Scullionspeak," *New Republic* 222.9 (Feb. 2000): 32–37.

Hudson, Marc. *Beowulf: A Translation and Commentary*. Lewisburg: Bucknell UP, 1990.

Klaeber, Friedrich, ed. *Beowulf and the Fight at Finnsburg*. 3rd ed. Boston: D. C. Heath, 1950.

Leonard, William Ellery. *Beowulf: A New Verse Translation for Fireside and Classroom*. New York: Century, 1923.

Liuzza, Roy Michael. *Beowulf: A New Verse Translation*. Peterborough, Ontario: Broadview Press, 2000.

Morgan, Edwin. *Beowulf: A Verse Translation into Modern English*. Aldington: Hand and Flower Press, 1952.

Shippey, Tom. "*Beowulf* for the Big-voiced Scullions," *Times Literary Supplement*, Oct. 1, 1999: 9–10.

Wrenn, Charles Leslie, ed. *Beowulf, with the Finnesburg Fragment*. 3rd ed., revised W. F. Bolton. London: Harrap, 1973.

Daniel Donoghue

The Philologer Poet: Seamus Heaney and the Translation of *Beowulf*
[*Harvard Review* 19 (2000): 12–21]

That every translation is also an act of interpretation has been a commonplace at least since Cicero, Horace, and Augustine of Hippo. It arises in response to the notion that the word-for-word and sense-for-sense task that aims for "faithfulness" provides at best only a partial description of all that a good translation entails. Even the most literal effort, according to this commonplace, sets up a tension between the mechanical and the creative as when, for example, one metaphor substitutes for another. Such moments can become the despair of the philologist who detects a net loss when the changes are extensive, especially if the original is a literary masterpiece. But in most cases readers remain unaware of the specific changes. Presumably, they turn to the translation in the first place because they do not know the original language, and they trust that the rhetorical embellishments will not obscure the essential continuity with the source text. But when a poet like Seamus Heaney turns his attention to translating *Beowulf*, readers pay special attention to the signs of his interpretive touches. What is presumed to be "literal" is taken in stride, perhaps necessary to understanding the narrative but inherently less interesting.

Some strands of literary criticism respond with another commonplace, which rejects the logic behind the mechanical/creative dualism. It questions whether literal accuracy is possible at all. The Old English *cyning*, for example, becomes *king* in Modern English and is always translated so, but what a male monarch meant to the Anglo-Saxons is necessarily different from our notions, which have been colored by later developments such as the divine right of succession, charismatic kingship, constitutional monarchies, and the like. In this case the superficial resemblance between *cyning* and *king* masks a semantic change over the centuries. And such subtle, perhaps imperceptible differences add up in a work of any length. This critical commonplace thus spreads the act of interpretation from a local effect to a universal condition, even in those places where translation seems most mechanical, because the literal meaning is always chimerical.

Without taking up the merits of the critical commonplace, this essay questions the mechanical/creative dualism from an opposite direction. Instead of dissolving the philological pole, it provisionally accepts the possibility of literal accuracy and asks whether "faithfulness" can be as innovative as the most radical reinterpretation. Heaney circles around the same idea in a poem from his 1975 collection *North*, in which he teases out traditional connotations of an Old English kenning for the human body, a compound literally meaning "bone-house":

> In the coffered
> riches of grammar
> and declensions
> I found *bān-hūs*,
>
> its fire, benches,
> wattle and rafters,
> where the soul
> fluttered a while
>
> in the roofspace.[1]

The word's meaning is something to be "found" in philology, and while the sense of distance between then and now prompts the search, it does not open a gap of despair. The search extends beyond the coffers of grammars and glossaries to the airier halls of culture if one follows the allusion of the fluttering soul to its source, the Anglo-Saxon historian Bede (d. 735). The second book of his *History of the English Church and People* tells how Edwin, king of Northumbria about a century before Bede, was deliberating whether to accept Christianity. He turns to his advisors for their opinion. One of them compares human life to "the swift flight of a single sparrow through the banquetting-hall where you are sitting at dinner on a winter's day with your thanes and counsellors. In the midst there is a comforting fire to warm the hall; outside, the storms of winter rain or snow are raging. This sparrow flies swiftly in through one door of the hall, and out through another."[2] He goes on to compare the bird's brief interval inside the hall to their old religion's conception of human existence: Christianity promises something better than a winter storm when the bird flies out.

Heaney turns the moral of Bede's metaphor from religion to language. The "soul" of a living culture animates *bān-hūs* with meaning for only a short time before it passes into the oblivion of time. Death hovers in the not-too-distant background: the coffer could turn at any moment from a treasure chest into a coffin holding the lifeless "bone-house," and winter's darkness threatens just outside the wattle walls. Yet to make poetry about the word's transience is in a way to reverse the process, to breathe life back into the body of language. Heaney's lines gesture toward a model of translation that is optimistic even if it is precarious.

It says that literal accuracy does not arrive by a mechanical process but through the translator's imaginative engagement with tradition. "Faithfulness" is capacious enough to include the interpretive moments that every translation demands. Philology and poetry in this case inform one another.

What applies in a local way for *bān-hūs* applies *in extenso* for Heaney's translation of *Beowulf,* where the length and complexity of the poem help generate its own cultural context. His "Introduction" speaks of the poem's "mythic potency" in terms of a movement similar to Bede's sparrow. "Like Shield Sheafson," the eponymous founder of a line of kings, who arrived as a foundling washed up on Denmark's shores aboard an abandoned ship, *Beowulf* "arrives from somewhere beyond the known bourne of our experience, and having fulfilled its purpose (again like Shield), it passes once more into the beyond."[3] Two funeral scenes frame the plot of the poem; it ends with Beowulf's, of course, but Shield's magnificent burial dominates the first fifty lines. After his death the Danes pile treasures onto his funeral ship and push him back into the sea:

> They decked his body no less bountifully
> with offerings than those first ones did
> who cast him away when he was a child
> and launched him alone out over the waves.
>   (lines 43–6)

Shield earns such a lavish send-off because of his spectacular success as king, but the "life cycle" of his mysterious arrival, later triumphs, and mysterious departure sets a model for the poem itself. *Beowulf* comes to us from an unknown author, written in an unfamiliar language from an uncertain date. Like Shield's career or the sparrow's flight through the hall, the poem makes its mark on the reader in the interval between its mysterious arrival and departure.

Heaney makes an oblique allusion to Shield's funeral ship in "The Settle Bed," from his 1991 collection *Seeing Things*. It would call to mind an Anglo-Saxon clinker-built ship even if Heaney did not tip us off by including lines from it as an epigraph to his introduction to *Beowulf*:

> And now this is "an inheritance"—
> Upright, rudimentary, unshiftably planked
> In the long ago, yet willable forward
>
> Again and again and again.[4]

The settle bed arrives as an unlooked for bequest: clumsy and heavy and bearing a history that can be heard in the "old sombre tide awash in the headboard." It is handed over to the new owner, becomes "an inheritance," and finally is willed away in a cycle that repeats itself "again and again and again." But what matters more than its four-square presence is the lesson that "whatever is given / Can always be reimagined." It is reimagined not "cargoed with / Its own dumb, tongue-and-groove worthiness / And un-get-roundable weight," but as "unkindled boards of a funeral ship" carrying Shield Sheafson piled over with gold. Or it can be reimagined as metaphor for the poem *Beowulf*, as Heaney's epigraph suggests, or more generally as any vehicle for the poet embarking on another exercise of *translatio*.

The vocabulary of "The Settle Bed" gives another hint that *Beowulf*'s Old English is part of the imaginative structure of the poem. The first tercet alone has five compound words, four of which are invented for the occasion: "Trunk-hasped," "cart-heavy," "pew-strait," and "bin-deep." They are hammer-blows of metaphors, announcing the categories "domestic," "rural," "religious," and "mercantile" almost with the force of allegorical figures assigned to the bed's four corners. The English language has always augmented its lexicon by generating compounds, although the preferred way to do so since the later Middle Ages has been through borrowing. But in lines such as these, Heaney's inventiveness rivals that of Gerard Manley Hopkins and the *Beowulf*-poet, the most prolific compounder of all. Responding to the interpretive engagement that compounds demand, readers expand elements like "bin" and "deep" into an image of, say, an ample bin holding flour or nuts or nails in a shop. "Pew-strait," for example, calls to mind the upright wooden back of the pew (where "strait" meets "straight") as well as the narrowness of religious doctrine, so its meaning hovers between carpentry and catechism even though it appears within a catalogue of physical features. The inferred meaning of such compounds can be slippery because the relation between the elements is not always self-evident. From their constituent parts "firewall" and "fireplace" might seem to be similar in meaning, yet one stops a fire and the other allows it to burn. When explaining a compound we instinctively expand it into a phrase or a clause ("a wall designed to stop the spread of fire in a building"), but "pew-strait" is not so easy. Does it mean that the settle bed's headboard is "straight and confining like a pew" and therefore physically uncomfortable when one sits against it? Or is "pew" a metonymy for "religion" so that the compound means "doctrinally narrow," thus more a commentary on the previous owners than the physical features? Few readers of "The Settle Bed" are likely to tease out the various possibilities for "pew-strait" because we are used to the interplay within compounds, and the context does not force a choice between the physical and the doctrinal. "Pew-strait" is in some essential way both.

"The Settle Bed" is by no means Heaney's only effort to exploit the vivid parallels, syntactic openness, and strong rhythm of compounds. He uses them in many other poems, even those inspired by Greek hexameters, for example: "That killing-fest, the life-warp and world-wrong / It brought to pass."[5] He admires their use by

poets like Hopkins, Shakespeare and Philip Larkin.[6] So when he turns to *Beowulf*
part of the translator's philological "faithfulness" shows itself through an inventiveness. Some passages restrict themselves to compounds already found in the English
lexicon, as for example in the scene when Grendel attacks Beowulf in the hall:

> he was bearing in
> with open claw when the alert hero's
> comeback and armlock forestalled him utterly.
>   (lines 746–8)

Some, like "hall-thane" and "neck-torque," are calques from Old English compounds. Just as often, though, newly-minted creations glint here and there in the
lines. An aging Swedish king dies when his "feud-calloused hand / could not stave
off the fatal stroke." An arrow is "feather-fledged." Grendel is a "guilt-steeped,
God-cursed fiend." The dragon coils his "snake-folds." Other compounds that may
seem to be nonce inventions in *Beowulf* have been used by Heaney in earlier poems.
Beowulf comes "first-footing" early in the morning, but so does "Servant Boy" in
Wintering Out (1972). The dragon emerges from his home "underearth," but "the
shut-eyed blank of underearth" also threatens St. Kevin in *The Spirit Level* (1996).[7]

    Just as he reimagines the settle bed as a funeral ship, Heaney reanimates
the *Beowulf*-poet's skillful use of compounds. Their potential as poetic devices
has always been present in English literature, although the *Beowulf*-poet had at
his command a wealth of traditional poetic elements to combine. The example of
bān-hūs is illustrative again. One of the two times it appears in *Beowulf* is near
the end of the poem, when the Geats have lit Beowulf's funeral pyre. The fire
swells, hot to its core, *oðþæt hē ðā bān-hūs gebrocen hæfde*.[8] Heaney translates, "and
flames wrought havoc in the hot bone-house." To liken Beowulf's body to a house
consumed by flames is more than a passing metaphoric touch. Earlier the poem
alludes to the fate of the Dane's great hall Heorot, which was destined to burn to
the ground as a result of the treachery of King Hrothgar's nephew. Just as Heaney
reimagines the wooden "benches, / wattle and rafters" of *bān-hūs*, the metaphor
of a house consumed by fire links the disastrous events suffered by the Danes and
the Geats: both the burning of Heorot and the death of Beowulf contribute to
a deeper theme concerning the limits of heroic action which dominates the end
of the poem. However formidable the hero, however magnificent the hall, the
depredations of time and human weakness will bring them down. To aspire to
the *Beowulf*-poet's allusiveness in compounding becomes another measure of the
translator's philological faithfulness, whether in preserving the elements of *bān-
hūs* or in forging analogous compounds.

    The simple placement of elements side by side in compounds like *bān-hūs*
is mirrored in larger syntactic structures using parallel phrases and clauses. The

half-line structure of the verse seems to have encouraged a mode of expression where ideas are repeated incrementally. Sometimes the effect is simply cumulative; at other times the repetition allows shifting perspectives to examine the same idea. For example, at the crucial moment in Beowulf's fight with Grendel's mother, when his sword has failed him and he despairs for his life, he spots a weapon that may help him:

> Geseah ðā on searwum   sigeēadig bil
> ealdsweord eotenisc   ecgum þȳhtig
> wigena weorðmynd
> > (lines 1557–9)

A literal translation: "Then he saw among the war-gear a victory-blessed sword, an ancient sword made by giants, strong in its edges, the glory of warriors." The three phrases for "sword" do not exactly repeat one another: one hints that it will bring Beowulf success, the second is more than a comment on its enormous size because giants were thought to have superior metal-working skills, and the third draws a correlation between splendid arms and the worthiness of the warrior. The most searching discussion of such constructions is Fred C. Robinson's *Beowulf and the Appositive Style*, which demonstrates how apposition informs much of the poem's theme and structure. Despite the apparent simplicity of the "proximate and parallel status" of the elements in apposition, the rhetorical effect can become complex.[9] The three epithets for sword, for example, have the same referent within a sentence and are not linked syntactically by a function word such as a conjunction. Such appositive constructions are not only ubiquitous in Old English poetry, they are its defining rhetorical trope, much like the long-tailed simile in classical epic. But more to the point they demand inferential judgment on the part of the reader to make connections, and at times those connections are more various than conjunctions alone can indicate.

Translating appositive constructions can be especially challenging, because Modern English prefers the disambiguating touches of grammatical function words and punctuation. A passage like that describing the gigantic sword, for example, might make use of separate clauses in Modern English, e.g., " . . . the victory blessed sword, which was the ancient work of giants . . . " Adding to the difficulty of translation is the common practice of scattering the apposed elements about the sentence rather than lining them up one after the other as in the "sword" passage. The sentence just before it (1550–56) has five separate elements of apposition, including a triplet for God (as a nod to the doctrine of the trinity). Such constructions are no longer idiomatic in Modern English. The closest parallels are simple catalogues, as (famously) in Shakespeare's sonnet

> Th' expense of spirit in a waste of shame
> Is lust in action; and till action, lust
> Is perjured, murd'rous, bloody, full of blame,
> Savage, extreme, rude, cruel, not to trust . . . [10]

And so on. The catalogue is also a favorite device of Heaney, and it shares some of the "parallel and proximate" qualities of *Beowulfian* apposition. In "The Pitchfork," for example, an entire stanza sacrifices syntax for a list:

> Riveted steel, turned timber, burnish, grain,
> Smoothness, straightness, roundness, length and sheen.
> Sweat-cured, sharpened, balanced, tested, fitted.
> The springiness, the clip and dart of it.[11]

What could give a better description than the accumulation of modifiers flowing together without the help of syntax? In other instances the bare juxtaposition of words can deliver a sudden shock. In "The Strand at Lough Beg," some spent shotgun shells discovered on the ground are "Acrid, brassy, genital, ejected." The cumulative effect has less to do with description than evoking the feeling of revulsion at the moment of discovery—almost a sense of violation. The effect of apposition is completely different a few lines later in "The Strand at Lough Beg," in a passage introducing some of Heaney's relatives on his father's side, who (he reveals in his "Introduction") supplied him with the imaginative voice for his translation of *Beowulf*:

> Big-voiced scullions, herders, feelers round
> Haycocks and hindquarters, talkers in byres,
> Slow arbitrators of the burial ground.[12]

In their formal and slightly old-fashioned way, these epithets come closest to *Beowulfian* apposition. It is intriguing to think that *Beowulf* may have supplied the appositive syntax of these lines years before Heaney returned to the Scullions to find a language for his translation that could be "speakable by one of those relatives." In any case Heaney's parallel phrases in these lines find a point of congruence with Old English syntax. An even more extensive example where Heaney's English strains contemporary idiom is "An Artist:"

> I love the thought of his anger.
> His obstinacy against the rock, his coercion
> of the substance from green apples.
>
> The way he was a dog barking
> at the image of himself barking.

> And his hatred of his own embrace
> of working as the only thing that worked –
> the vulgarity of expecting ever
> gratitude or admiration, which
> would mean a stealing from him.
> The way his fortitude held and hardened
> because he did what he knew.
> His forehead like a hurled boule
> travelling unpainted space
> behind the apple and behind the mountain.[13]

Yet this poem may not be an instance of apposition after all, because there is a fundamental difference between a list describing the various things "I love" and the deliberate turning over of a single idea to examine it from different perspectives. It all depends on whether the lists consist of variants of the same thing or an enumeration of one item after another. In either case, Heaney's lists and apposition mark another point of congruence with the language of *Beowulf*.

When translators of *Beowulf* do not retain appositive constructions, they usually smooth out the idiom by incorporating them into separate clauses or merging some together. Grendel, for example, is introduced into the narrative with the apposed epithets *grimma gǣst* (grim creature) and *mǣre mearcstapa* (notorious border-prowler), who held *mōras . . . fen ond fǣsten* (the moors, fen and fastness). Heaney's translation removes the apposition by means of a participial phrase and a conjunction:

> Grendel was the name of this grim demon
> haunting the marches, marauding round the heath
> and the desolate fens
>   (lines 102–4)

In at least one case, however, Heaney makes a passage more appositive than the Old English:

> Afterwards a boy-child was born to Shield,
> a cub in the yard, a comfort sent
> by God to that nation.
>   (lines 12–14)

Here "boy-child," "cub," and "comfort" are parallel nominals, where in the Old English they are part of different constructions:

> Ðǣm eafera wæs   æfter cenned
> geong in geardum   þone god sende

folce tō frōfre

(lines 12–14)

The Old English *geong* ("young") can be taken as a modifier for *eafera* ("son") rather than as a substantive like "cub." A literal translation preserving the word order of Old English would be: "To that one [Shield] a son was later born young in the yards whom God sent to the people as a comfort." The strong impression throughout the poem, however, is that Heaney preserves the rich layering of apposition in the poem without doing violence to his idiom. And as Robinson convincingly points out, apposition extends beyond the sentence boundary to characterization, episodes, and even theology. For example, just after introducing Hygd, the queen of the Geats, the poem plunges into the story of Thryth, a queen who was famous for her vicious retribution. The implicit lesson is that Hygd is virtuous unlike Thryth, although there is no narrative instruction to that effect. Even images can be apposed. After Wiglaf has helped Beowulf kill the dragon, he helplessly watches him die from the dragon's venom:

> It was hard then on the young hero,
> having to watch the one he held so dear
> there on the ground, going through
> his death agony. The dragon from underearth,
> his nightmarish destroyer, lay destroyed as well,
> utterly without life.
>
> (lines 2821–26)

The narrative makes Wiglaf the focal point between the dying hero and the dead dragon, who lie near each other. Following the Old English Heaney links the parallel images across the caesura and across a sentence boundary by alliterating Beowulf's "death agony" with "dragon." The aural link goes even deeper because of the repeating syllables *agon* in each half. But the narrative is reticent about the lesson to be drawn from this juxtaposition: are Beowulf and the dragon somehow equivalent in death? Beowulf fights on the side of good, certainly, but what does his death at the hands of evil mean? It is a tribute to Heaney's understanding of *Beowulf*'s poetic art that his translation here and elsewhere preserves the richness of apposition on many levels.

But in a way his instinct for it is hardly surprising. Apposition is as much Heaney's "voiceright" as Hibernicisms like "kesh" and English archaisms like "thole."[14] It is as familiar as the alliteration, stressed lines and compounding in his verse, because it is as familiar as T. S. Eliot's *Wasteland*, Yeat's hollow moon in "Adam's Curse," and Wallace Stevens's jar in Tennessee. Apposition is as much a master-trope of twentieth century poetry as it is of Old English. Heaney's "Flight

Path" from *The Spirit Level* (1996), for example, combines chronology and travel as its organizing principle, but its immediate structure consists of six numbered segments with no overt indication about their relation to one another. Among other things, the use of apposition allows the poem to explore the volatile subject of Heaney's political affiliations in Northern Ireland. The fourth part begins with language that withholds personal judgment in the most familiar official jargon:

> The following for the record, in the light
> Of everything before and since:
> One bright May morning . . .

From this apparently neutral beginning, it slips into the language of the innocence and exhilaration of home-coming. But the idyll is shattered by a blunt-spoken sectarian who finds him on the train back to Belfast:

> So he enters and sits down
> Opposite and goes for me head on.
> "When, for fuck's sake, are you going to write
> Something for us?"

The poem's immediate answer is equivocal; the deeper response waits for the next stanza, which apposes a haunting reference to the protest in Long Kesh and a quotation from Heaney's "Ugolino." Dante's journey through *Inferno* thus comments on Heaney's journey, but just how the apposed segments comment on one another is left up to the reader. Every part of "The Flight Path," not just the segments outlined here, requires the reader to make the kind of inferential judgments that *Beowulf* does.

There are even more such correspondences. "The Settle Bed," for example, has a series of modifiers—"unkindled," "unwilling," "unbeaten," "unshiftably," "un-get-roundable"—which work by negating an attribute so that the resulting image calls to mind the absence of something that might otherwise be present. It is hard to say what "unkindled" means except as something that is not ignited, but it cannot do so without suggesting fire in the first place. Such negative modifiers are, again, a favorite device of the *Beowulf*-poet. When Grendel attacks Heorot at night, *lēoht unfǣger* or "unbeautiful light" shines from his eyes. Because a person's eyes and light itself are traditionally associated with beauty, to deny it categorically makes the light from Grendel's eyes worse than ugly. When Wiglaf gazes on his dying king he is described as *unfrōd*—meaning both "un-aged" and "unwise"—which makes a brief but telling comparison with Beowulf, who after fifty years as king has become *frōd*. It is probably pointless to ask whether the many levels of affinity between Heaney's poetic voice and *Beowulf* are the result of his study of

Old English, or somehow gathered indirectly through other poets like Hopkins and W. H. Auden, or by a more anonymous transmission of prosodic devices that have survived the centuries. Most of what has been written about Heaney's translation of *Beowulf*, including his own essays, dwell on the foreignness of Old English, the labor of translation, the difficulty of finding the right voice or the right turn of phrase. What this essay shows is that the many affinities already existing between his poetry and *Beowulf* enables Heaney to enter the old clinker-built ship as familiarly as an inherited settle bed, so that his interpretation is measured not merely by the changes imposed from the outside but also by shaping and reshaping the tradition from within.

Notes

1. "Bone Dreams," quoted from *Opened Ground: Selected Poems 1966-1996* (New York: Farrar, Straus and Giroux), p. 105.

2. *A History of the English Church and People*, trans. Leo Sherley-Price, revised by R. E. Latham (Harmondsworth: Penguin, 1968), p. 127.

3. *Beowulf: A New Verse Translation* (New York: Farrar, Straus and Giroux, 2000), p. xii.

4. *Seeing Things* (New York: Farrar, Straus and Giroux, 1991), p. 30; reprinted with small changes in *Opened Ground*, p. 321.

5. "The Watchman's War" from "Mycenae Lookout," quoted from *Opened Ground*, p. 387.

6. See, for example, "Englands of the Mind" in *Preoccupations: Selected Prose 1968-1978* (New York: Farrar, Straus and Giroux, 1980), p. 166.

7. "Servant Boy," *Opened Ground*, p. 48 and "St. Kevin and the Blackbird," *The Spirit Level* (London and Boston: Faber and Faber, 1996), pp. 20-1.

8. Bruce Mitchell and Fred C. Robinson, ed., *Beowulf: An Edition with Relevant Shorter Texts* (Oxford: Blackwell, 1998), line 3147. All quotations from Old English come from this edition.

9. Fred C. Robinson, *Beowulf and the Appositive Style* (Knoxville: U of Tennessee P, 1985), p. 3.

10. Sonnet 129, quoted from Helen Vendler, *The Art of Shakespeare's Sonnets* (Cambridge, Mass: Harvard U P, 1997), p. 549.

11. *Opened Ground*, p. 320.

12. From *Field Work* (1979), quoted from *Opened Ground*, p. 145; "Introduction," p. xxvii.

13. *Opened Ground*, p. 259.

14. "Introduction."

Daniel Donoghue

Translating 'Beowulf'
[*Times Literary Supplement*, 29 October 1999, p. 17]

Sir, —In his review of Seamus Heaney's translation of *Beowulf* (October 1), Tom Shippey's larger point about the nuance and sophistication of the poem's language is well taken, but the specific instances of the subjunctive mood are even more slippery than he allows. In the kinds of Old English clauses cited, the subjunctive mood is determined primarily by syntax, not obliqueness of meaning. So where the *Beowulf* poet had little choice in the mood of the verb, the modern English translator must decide between subjunctive and indicative on the basis of context. I for one do not find that Heaney's choices conform to the "academic folk narrative" that Old English was "just plain primitive". Just the opposite. What I miss in Professor Shippey's review is some assessment of the poetic qualities of Seamus Heaney's translation beyond its literal accuracy.

DANIEL DONOGHUE
Department of English, Harvard University,
Cambridge, Massachusetts 02138.

333

Randi Eldevik

Translating 'Beowulf'
[*Times Literary Supplement*, 5 November 1999, p. 19]

Sir,—Without entering into a debate about the merits or demerits of Seamus Heaney's new translation of *Beowulf* (see Daniel Donoghue's letter, October 29), I should like to point out that its inclusion in the *Norton Anthology* does not have quite as much significance for higher education in North America as it would appear to have from Tom Shippey's remarks (October 1). In the first place, it is not true that all American undergraduates, no matter what their major, take a course in early English literature; many universities require only that undergraduates take some sort of literature course, and often that may turn out to be a course involving only modern English and/or American literature. Certainly, all English majors do take a survey of English literature encompassing the Old and Middle English periods along with later periods. But even for that sort of course, there are alternatives to the *Norton Anthology*. From Longman, for example, there is available an anthology which has many advantages over the Norton; not least of those advantages is that it liberates the study of *Beowulf* from the shackles imposed by Heaney's dominance.

Readers of the *TLS* may be interested to know that Norton, running scared because of American professors' resistance to Heaney's *Beowulf*, is offering a "package deal", in which professors can order the new *Norton Anthology* together with a separate, non-Heaney, *Beowulf* paperback at no extra cost to their students. Does this sound as though Seamus Heaney's *Beowulf* inevitably "is the poem now, for probably two generations"?

RANDI ELDEVIK
Department of English, Oklahoma State
University, Stillwater, Oklahoma 74078.

Loren C. Gruber

"So." So What? It's a Culture War. That's Hwæt![1]
Seamus Heaney's verse translation of *Beowulf*, Bilingual and Critical Editions
[*In Geardagum* XXIII (2002): 67–84]

Those familiar with Seamus Heaney know that he informs his poetry with history and politics. Some Anglo-Saxonists are dismayed and others are pleased that his translation of *Beowulf* is no different. The non-specialist, on the other hand, is often less concerned with such matters, neither knowing—nor caring—if the translator is true to the original provided the modern rendering of an ancient poem is readable and graceful.

Perhaps unaware of its Irish subtext, those high school teachers and literature professors who are unfamiliar with Old English praise the accessibility of Heaney's *Beowulf* in both the dual language edition and the newer Norton Critical Edition. A page-turner, Heaney's poetic translation will be read by new generations of students with greater pleasure than those who have plowed through E. Talbot Donaldson's prose translation since 1966.[2]

Anglo-Saxonists find themselves at a disadvantage, however, since Heaney has essentially re-told *Beowulf* using the Ulster dialect of his relatives.[3] When, for good reason, they fault Heaney's translation, they open themselves to the charge of being elitist. When, for equally good reasons, they acknowledge that Heaney has opened the epic to a wider audience, such Anglo-Saxonists open themselves to the charge of treason by their fellows.

Its popularity and readability notwithstanding, the translation suffers on three counts. Heaney's Irish diction politicizes *Beowulf*; his grammatical renderings sometimes lose the subtlety of the original; and his English diction is sometimes off, issues that will be addressed presently. For the time being, suffice it to say that students, teachers, and professors deserve a translation that is readable *and* faithful to the original; but, in spite of its artistry, Heaney's appears questionable because he chose to filter *Beowulf* through his Ulster experience. Ultimately, he has written a personal reaction to ancient Scandinavian events.

Admittedly, readers and translators in any age encounter texts on their own terms. If such were not the case, we would have had neither the ardency for various translations of the Bible nor the fragmentation of religious denominations and sects, much less the scholarly debates about the Christian and pagan elements within *Beowulf*.[4] Just as it was the custom of the *Beowulf* manuscript's redactor to overlay its pagan elements with Christian images centuries ago, Heaney has imposed Irish views upon the Scandinavian landscape, as is his custom. Occasionally, then, his audience sees the epic as if it were viewed through a slightly out-of-focus stereoscope.

Indeed, we must keep in mind that a poet's nature is that of a transformer. Seeing new relationships among individuals, their societies, their histories—personal and national—and nature itself, the poet creates the world anew. Heaney is no exception. While characterizing individual poems as having "the aura and authenticity of archaeological finds"[5] he sees "poetry as divination, as a restoration of the culture to itself" by defining and interpreting "the present by bringing it into significant relationship with the past."[6] Because poetry is the touchstone for Heaney, he becomes an alchemist *cum* archeologist who creates a new, non-linear historical continuity by invoking the present to metamorphose past treasures.

Those treasures are of two sorts: artifacts yielded by bogs and ancient wordhoards whose coinages are today's currency in Ulster. Significantly, Heaney calls the Irish bog "our national consciousness."[7] As a repository for memories, it is much like its Danish counterpart where, as an apparent sacrifice to Nerthus,[8] the Tollund Man lay until discovered and his head removed to Silkeburg's museum. Like those severed human heads common to the Celtic pagan religion, the Tollund Man's—and possibly Grendel's[9]—became an objective correlative to religious and political martyrdom for Heaney.[10]

As important as these severed heads are, words are even more important to Heaney. "Words themselves," he writes, "are doors; Janus is to a certain extent their deity, looking back to a ramification of roots and associations and forward to a clarification of sense and meaning."[11] Although Heaney's *Beowulf* now contains a word-hoard of Anglo-Saxon, Irish, and English currency, the doors of Irish were for a time closed to him. He felt "robbed of" them.[12]

Robbed, that is, until the outer door to the treasury was opened at a Northern Irish Catholic school: he discovered that Irish words were still in use.[13] Then, the inner door swung wide when he realized that the Anglo-Saxon *polian*, "to suffer," had currency as the Ulster *thole*, spoken by the "older and less educated people" he listened to as a child. As he put it, "*polian* had opened my right of way,"[14] namely an ancient passageway that led Heaney to a deeper understanding of the present and the discovery of his poetic, Ulster voice.[15]

Entering, he likely discovered that *thole* was reminted with the new valuation of Irish political suffering because the passageway echoes of politics, rather than scholarship. Heaney openly admits that he did not follow the advice of

W. W. Norton-appointed Alfred David. Instead, Heaney writes, "I [...] persisted many times in what we both knew were erroneous ways," and—using his term—"skewed" the translation.[16] Irish words such as *bawn* and *bothy* slant towards a politicized subtext.

After explaining that "a local Ulster word seemed either poetically or historically right," Heaney goes on to justify his choice of *bawn*:

> Then, for reasons of historical suggestiveness, I have in several instances used the word 'bawn' to refer to Hrothgar's hall. In Elizabethan English, bawn (from the Irish *bó-dhún*, a fort for cattle) referred specifically to the fortified dwelling which the English planters built in Ireland to keep the dispossessed natives at bay, so it seemed the proper term to apply to the embattled keep where Hrothgar waits and watches. Indeed, every time I read the lovely interlude that tells of the minstrel singing in Heorot just before the first attacks of Grendel, I cannot help thinking of Edmund Spenser in Kilcolman Castle, reading the early cantos of *The Faerie Queene* to Sir Walter Raleigh, just before the Irish burned the castle and drove Spenser out of Munster back to the Elizabethan court. Putting a bawn into *Beowulf* seems one way for an Irish poet to come to terms with that complex history of conquest and colony, absorption and resistance, integrity and antagonism, a history which has to be clearly acknowledged by all concerned in order to render it ever more 'willable forward / Again and again and again.'[17]

Heaney thus opens the door to the room of victims. By anachronistically substituting *bawn* for *hall*, Heaney implies that Grendel, like the Irish, was dispossessed. It is one thing to say the Irish are victims of English conquest and colonialism; it is quite another to imply that Grendel and his mother are victims of Danish hall-sprawl and Geatish invaders. After all, the sixth-century Danes and Geats, fearful of man-eating trolls,[18] are not sixteenth-century Elizabethan English fearful of Irish cattle rustlers. Nor are the Irish Grendel-kin.

Heaney's overlaying the epic's narrative with Anglo-Irish history is therefore problematic, given the *Beowulf* poet's lumping of historical personages with the legendary. Readers and translators must keep in mind Klaeber's caveat, "facts easily give way to fiction,"[19] and Wealhtheow, whose name is a compound of *wealh* ("Celtic" or "foreign"), and *þeow* ("captive" or "carried off in war"), is a case in point. Assuming Klaeber's gloss is accurate, Heaney could assert that Wealhtheow's capture presages Ireland's occupation by the English a thousand years later, but her actions are more legendary than historical.

First, she plays a major, though brief, role in the epic. William A. Schweiker, III, has argued that Wealhtheow "charges Beowulf with the restoration and maintenance of order."[20] Second, Helen Damico, arguing along similar lines,[21] has

convincingly demonstrated that all of Wealhtheow's attributes stem from literature and legend, one of them being the motif of "the bondmaid raised to the status
of a queen."[22] Not all slaves of the Anglo-Saxons remained so. Those with talent
were freed and assimilated into the society, and, if an actual person, Wealhtheow
would be no exception. If won in war by Hrothgar, as her name suggests, she
would have immediately become his queen. Neither Celtic victim nor Elizabethan
noble keeping the Irish at bay, she is a *legendary* character who is at once peace-
weaver and cup-bearing valkyrie.[23] She is Queen Wealhtheow—the true power in
Heorot who recognizes Beowulf as one of her own.[24]

Turning to matters of diction and grammar in Heaney, it is important to
mention *bur*, or *bower*. Beowulf is summoned to Hrothgar's *bure* in line 1310a,
which Heaney translates as *chamber*. In the same vein, a father gazes mournfully at
his son's *bure* in line 2455b, which Heaney translates as *dwelling*. In these examples, Heaney's rendering of *bower* as *quarters*, *chamber*, and *dwelling* seems reasonable enough.

However, while E. Talbot Donaldson rendered *burum* as the neutral "outlying buildings,"[25] Heaney's rendering of *burum* in line 140a as *bothies*, rather than
"bowers," is again anachronistic and political. From "the Irish word *bóthog* that
means 'hut' or 'shanty,'" often for unmarried workers on a farm,"[26] *bothy* is not likely
the type of building associated with a king's hall. Bachelors and farm animals both
bed down in a *bothy*.[27] Perhaps Heaney makes a class distinction when he uses
synonyms for *bur*: thanes sleep in *bothies* while royals sleep in women's quarters,
chambers, and dwellings. Nevertheless, he seems to mutter behind his Ulster door
that the Danes are little better than animals.[28] Once through that Irish portal,
Hrothgar's sepia-toned steeds become Heaney's horses of another color—emerald.

In addition to retelling *Beowulf* with his personal word-hoard, Heaney
alters some passages grammatically. For example, in line 921a, he renders the
dative singular *brydbure*, "from the wife's quarters," as a dative plural, "from the
women's quarters." His translation is misleading because Hrothgar is exiting his
wife's bower, not the women's dormitory. Such lapsed attention to grammar and
diction recasts the drama of the poem, and that gives Anglo-Saxonists pause.

One is Tom Shippey. He takes exception to Heaney's insistent use of the
indicative rather than the subjunctive.[29] Shippey observes, regarding the Danish
coastguard's challenge to Beowulf: "Catching the tone of the subjunctive is hard in
modern English, but it is a major part of the careful, prickly dignity of armed men
in the heroic world."[30] Shippey also notes the marked contrast between the gnomic observation that "a man must thrive [...] by deeds of [...] praise" and Heaney's
flaccid rendering of lines 24b-25, "Behaviour that's admired / is the path to power
among people everywhere."[31] Translations like these capture neither the sound nor
the sense of the original, as I have also argued regarding Burton Raffel's version.[32]

Moreover, Heaney's preference for his childhood idiom over Klaeber's or other standard glossaries[33] creates furrowed brows and footnotes. Two examples will suffice. The epic-opening *Hwæt*[34] is usually translated as "what," "lo," "behold," or "well." Heaney, however, opens with "So" because "in Hiberno-English Scullion-speak [. . .] 'so' operates as an expression which obliterates all previous discourse and narrative, and at the same time functions as an exclamation calling for immediate attention."[35] Likewise, his translation of *gryregeatwum* (324a) as "war-graith" is also from his idiolect. In terms of readability, either "grim gear" or "gruesome gear," would be preferable substitutes for either Klaeber's "terrible armor" or Heaney's "war-graith."[36] In short, Heaney's self-conscious use of "so" and "graith" in his childhood idiom is as alien to American readers as the Anglo-Saxon, and forces readers of the *Critical Edition* to the footnotes. Many students today, however, are not only reluctant readers but are also disinclined to use either footnotes or dictionaries. Encountering an unfamiliar word, they skip it or close the book.[37]

One would thus think that contemporary English, rather than Celtic diction, would always bring non-specialists to the sense of the Anglo-Saxon. Not always, even when the word is a Germanic cousin to the deed. Heaney's decision to translate *scriðan* in line 703a not as "glide" but as "lope,"[38] for example, is as unfortunate as it is inaccurate. Friendly creatures—horses, dogs, hares, deer—lope.[39] Grendel-kin do not. In truth, if we compound Klaeber's glosses, *sceadu* and *gengan*, Grendel, as *sceadugenga*, becomes the "shadow-rider" who glides, grabs, and gulps. Grendel and the dragon glide quickly, silently like spiders. That is what makes them horrific.[40]

Heaney's overlaying Geatish-Danish history with the Elizabethan and contemporary English treatment of the Irish, his use of Ulster rather than standard English diction, his ignoring the text's grammar, and his mismatched word choice are of concern to Anglo-Saxonists. On the other hand, Heaney's translation in the *Bilingual Edition* has won general readers. The translation and the rich supplementary material in the *Critical Edition* excite students, high school teachers, and professors. Despite his Celticisms, Heaney's translation is one that may inspire readers to pursue *Beowulf* studies further and translators to refine their work.[41]

Thus, as an Anglo-Saxonist and professor, I am torn between accuracy and accessibility. Thirty years ago, my Simpson College survey of English literature students who went on to study *Beowulf* with me did so because I taught them Anglo-Saxon first, not because of the Donaldson translation. Recently, my Missouri Valley College survey of world literature students, enthralled with the Raffel translation, nevertheless, appreciated my observations on its departures from the original. They came to realize that translators of ancient texts, guided by their own subjective relationships to the ancient and modern word-hoards, write poems about a poem. Heaney's will likely follow suit: students and teachers will enjoy it; professors will discuss its inaccuracies. Accuracy wins scholars' minds; readability wins students' hearts.

In conclusion, I resent what appears to be Heaney's co-opting the poem to reflect his war with the English. Seamus Heaney is a wonderful poet. He is not a faithful translator (see following appendix for comparative examples). John Leyerle suggested that Beowulf suffered hubris when he desired to view the dragon-guarded treasures.[42] Perhaps the same could be said of Heaney and his recreation of *Beowulf*.

Appendix

Four Versions of "The Father's Lament" in *Beowulf*:

Edward L. Risden, Raymond P. Tripp, Jr., and Stephen O. Glosecki utilize standard glosses in their translations. By avoiding the usual glosses, Heaney's *Beowulf* drifts toward a post-modern translation. Like it or not, our glossaries are our standard until we find a Gandalf who can open the door to Beowulf's world. Heaney 2444–62, from *Bilingual Edition* 165–67 and *Critical Edition* 62:

> It was like the misery felt by an old man
> who has lived to see his son's body
> swing on the gallows. He begins to keen
> and weep for his boy, watching the raven
> gloat where he hangs: he can be of no help.
> The wisdom of age is worthless to him.
> Morning after morning he wakes to remember
> that his child is gone; he has no interest
> in living on until another heir
> is born in the hall, now that his first-born
> has entered death's dominion forever.
> He gazes sorrowfully at his son's dwelling,
> the banquet hall bereft of all delight,
> the windswept hearthstone; the horsemen are sleeping,
> the warriors under ground; what was is no more.
> No tunes from the harp, no cheer raised in the yard.
> Alone with his longing, he lies down on his bed
> And sings a lament; everything seems too large,
> the steadings and the fields.

Raymond P. Tripp, Jr., 2444–62, from his work in progress, *Beowulf: An Edition and Literary Translation in Progress* (n. p., 1990):

> So sad it is for an aging man to let
> Any one of his sons go riding young
> On the gallows. Then he'd sing a sad tale,
> A sorry song indeed, should his other son
> Hang, ruin for the happy raven, and he
> Old and impotent, could not help—nothing!
> Memory is served up each morning fresh,
> Of a son gone elsewhere. He has no room
> To live to see inside his town his heirs
> From his other son, when the first one has
> On death's demand done the last of his deeds.
> Sad he sighs and looks into his son's room,
> A hall wasted of bliss—windswept bedding,
> Ravished of joy's voice. Riding players sleep,
> Those warriors in the dark. No harp sounds,
> No games in the yards, as once there were.
> He stoops chanting to bed, sings sad psalms,
> Slow, one after another. All too roomy now,
> His field-like floors and dwelling plots.

Edward L. Risden 2445–62a, from *Beowulf: A Student's Edition* (Troy, NY: Whitston, 1994):

> Likewise it is sad   for an old man
> to live to see   his son swing,
> young on the gallows;   then he may recite a tale,
> a sorrowful song,   when his son hangs,
> a joy to the raven,   and he cannot help him,
> old and knowing,   or do anything.
> Always it is remembered,   each morning,
> his son's journey elsewhere.   He is not intent
> to see another [heir]   inside the dwellings,
> a guardian of inheritance,   when the one has
> experienced through deeds   death's insistence.
> He looks sorrowfully   on his son's bower,
> at the deserted wine-hall,   the windy resting-place,
> reft of joy. The riders sleep,
> heroes in the hiding-place; nor is there the harp-sound,
> of pleasure in the courtyards,   such as there was
> before.
> He departs then to bed,   sings a sorrowful lay,
> one after another;   it seems to him entirely too large,
> fields and dwelling place.

Stephen O. Glosecki 2444–62a, from "Skalded Epic (Make It Old)," *PN Review* 133.26.5 (May–June 2000): 55. In a newer e-mailed version to the author,

20 Feb. 2002, Glosecki states that his alliterative work in progress (modeled after skaldic verse) is meant to be chanted: "After all, we have as the English national epic the outlandish story of a Swede killing trolls in Denmark. Migration-age stuff, that. Drench it with holy water if you like, but the folk elements of *Beowulf* remain primeval, much older than literacy, England, Christianity." Note how Glosecki remains faithful to the sense of the following passage, while capturing the synesthesia of the father's rubbed, teary eyes and the raven-pecked eyes of his son's corpse:

> No father could find   a fate more mournful—
> no life more wrecked   than the ride of a son
> strung from gallows: in grief he'll wilt
> to a cruel dirge.   The corpse spins slack.
> The ravens clack.   How raw the eyes
> of the old and wise   under wheeling skies.
> His boy looms back   through blue-gray dawning—
> he recalls his son   each crusted morning:
> and his heart rings hollow   to hear the other—
> a new heir at home—   the hanged son's brother.
> How bleak the town   when your boy has died!
> Haggard father,   you'll haunt his room—
> empty chamber   chilled by the wind
> and filled with gloom.   Gone the glad rider,
> he raced to the grave!   And the rippling harp,
> strummed in sunshine,   lies lost in the past.
> So he sinks to couch   to croon a song,
> lonesome, longing: land so empty—
> plains and farmstead.

Notes

1. A version of this review was presented as "Hwæt! So What? Heaney v. Anglo-Saxonists" at the Mid-America Medieval Association, Kansas State University, Manhattan, KS, 23 Feb. 2002. I am indebted to Stephen O. Glosecki, Edward L. Risden, and Raymond P. Tripp, Jr. who provided me with their thoughts on, and translations of, *Beowulf*; to James E. Anderson who provided me with his thoughts and a copy of Tom Shippey's "*Beowulf* for the Big-Voiced Scullions"; to my Missouri Valley College colleague Virginia Kugel-Zank who presented me with Seamus Heaney's *Beowulf: A New Verse Translation, Bilingual Edition*, and alerted me to his essay, "Feeling into Words," and continues to share her wisdom about how we read and how that affects teaching; to Peter J. Fields for encouraging me with, and offering suggestions for, this article; and to Scott J. Berzon, of W. W. Norton, who presented me with Seamus Heaney's *Opened Ground: Selected Poems 1966–1996*, as well as the Donaldson and Heaney Norton Critical Editions of *Beowulf* for this article. Any errors herein are mine.

2. Both the Donaldson and Heaney translations have been issued as Norton Critical Editions. E. Talbot Donaldson, trans., *Beowulf: A Prose Translation*, ed. Nicholas Howe (New York: Norton, 2002), replaces Joseph Tuso, ed., *Beowulf: The Donaldson Translation, Background and Sources, Criticism* (New York: Norton, 1975). Howe's contains illustrations, excellent background material by Donaldson and Robert C. Hughes, as well as important critical essays by Helen Bennett, Roberta Frank, Joyce Hill, Nicholas Howe, Michael Lapidge, John D. Niles, and Fred C. Robinson. Subsequent references to this edition will be cited as "Donaldson." Positioned to become the new classroom classic, Seamus Heaney, trans., *Beowulf: A Verse Translation*, ed. Daniel Donoghue (New York: Norton, 2002), contains a useful bibliography, three-dozen illustrations, a summary of the Swedish-Geatish wars, genealogical tables, and a list of kingdoms and tribes. Selections from Genesis 4.1–16, *Maxims I*, the Grettir analogue, Alcuin, Gregory of Tours, and William of Malmesbury help establish the epic's cultural context. Major critical essays by Jane Chance, Daniel Donaghue, Roberta Frank, R. D. Fulk and Joseph Harris (co-authors), Thomas D. Hill, John Leyerle, Bruce Mitchell and Fred C. Robinson (co-authors), Fred C. Robinson (single author), J. R. R. Tolkien, and Leslie Webster round out the edition. Explanatory footnotes abound. Subsequent references to this edition will be cited as *Critical Edition*. *Beowulf: A New Verse Translation, Bilingual Edition* (New York: Farrar, 2000), affords readers the opportunity of easily checking Heaney against the *Beowulf* manuscript. Subsequent references to this trade book will be cited as *Bilingual Edition*.

3. As Daniel Donoghue explains in his preface to the *Critical Edition*, "It was a bold choice, but it enables him to make a clean break with the scholarly glossaries, which have a way of insinuating their formal, literary, and slightly archaic language into most *Beowulf* translations [...]. Of more immediate concern is the odd fact that the translation requires footnotes to gloss its language, even for the intended audience" (ix), a matter discussed later.

4. Thomas D. Hill, "The Christian Language and Theme of Beowulf" in the *Critical Edition*, 197–211, discusses the issue. C. M. Adderley, "The Role of Wyrd in *Beowulf*," unpublished essay, 2002, says, "When writing did finally come to the Anglo-Saxons, it came hand-in-hand with Christianity, so any pre-Christian philosophy is naturally seen through a glass that would distort it somewhat." Adderley concludes, "If the poet had been asked, 'Is *Beowulf* a Christian or a pagan poem?' he would probably have replied, 'Yes.'" Similarly, if Heaney were asked if his translation of *Beowulf* is an Irish, Anglo-Saxon, Christian, or pagan poem, he likewise might reply, "Yes," since he sees it through his life's experience, just as all translators are influenced by their epistemologies.

5. "Feeling into Words," *The Longman Anthology of British Literature*, ed. David Damrosh, *et al.*, vol. 2 (New York: Longman, 1999) 2844. "Feeling into Words" was delivered before the Royal Society of Literature in October 1974.

6. "Feeling into Words," 2857. Cf. Margo Jefferson, "Myth, Magic and Us Mortals," *New York Times on the Web* 26 May 2002. Although Jefferson refers to playwrights, her comments are transferable to artists in other genres who want "art that matters." She says, "We are looking for treasure in the form of cultural continuity; old griefs and pleasures felt again and more clearly; revelations about who we are and whether we can (or cannot) change." Cf. also Kathryn Harrison, "When Inspiration Stared Stoically from an Old Photograph," *New York Times on the Web* 20 May 2002.

7. "Feeling into Words," 2853.

8. "Feeling into Words," 2855. Heaney cites P. V. Glob, *The Bog People*, trans. Rupert L. Bruce-Mitford (Ithaca: Cornell UP, 1969), who believes the Tollund Man was

sacrificed to Nerthus. His picture is in H. R. Ellis Davidson, *Scandinavian Mythology* (London: Hamlyn, 1969) 42.

9. Cf. my "Grendel Was a Welshman; John Was a Thief: Peers and Possessions, from Epic to Charter." MO Phil. Assoc. Convention. Point Lookout, MO, 12 Apr. 1991. The Magna Carta is explicit regarding the treatment of felons. Once a hue and cry is raised and the posse comitatus is assembled, it pursues and locates the felon, often in a desert place—the mere in Grendel's case; the forest in Robin Hood's. If the felon cannot produce the stolen goods, then the posse is permitted to take the criminal's head and return it to the wronged party. It therefore seems that an Anglo-Saxon custom was precedential for the Magna Carta: Grendel could not restore the devoured thanes, so Beowulf and his men had the right to take the troll's head.

10. "Feeling into Words," 2855–56. Heaney cites Anne Ross, "The Religion of the Pagan Celts," *Pagan Celtic Britain: Studies in Iconography and Tradition* (New York: Columbia UP, 1967), who says that the severed head is "a kind of shorthand symbol for the entire religious outlook of the pagan Celts" (2856). Heaney writes of archaeological artifacts and mythic correspondences throughout *Opened Ground: Selected Poems, 1966–1996* (New York: Farrar, 1998). In "Crediting Poetry: The Nobel Lecture" (1995), Heaney concludes that "poetry's power" is "to remind us that we are hunters and gatherers of values" (430). "Digging" commemorates the skill of his father and his father's father, while observing, "But I've no spade to follow man like them. / Between my finger and my thumb / The squat pen rests. / I'll dig with it," 3–4. And dig he does. See, for example, "Undine," 24; "Tollund Man," 62–63; and "Kinship," 115–19.

11. "Feeling into Words," 2851–52. Heaney also explains, "When I called my second book *Door into the Dark* I intended to gesture towards this idea of poetry as a point of entry into the buried life of the feelings or as a point of exit for it" (2851). Short wave radio broadcasts put young Heaney on the "journey into the wideness of language where each point of arrival—whether in one's poetry or one's life—turned out to be a stepping stone rather than a destination [...]" (416). Heaney believes "poetry can make an order as true to the impact of external reality and as sensitive to the inner laws of the poet's being as the ripples that rippled in and rippled out across the water in that scullery bucket fifty years ago" (417).

12. *Bilingual Edition* xxiv; *Critical Edition* xxxiv.

13. *Bilingual Edition*. Heaney writes that he was thrilled to discover *lachtar* in his Irish-English dictionary, a word still used by his aunt "when speaking of a flock of chicks" (xxiv). *Critical Edition* xxxiv.

14. *Bilingual Edition* xxv–xxvi; *Critical Edition* xxxv.

15. The utterance of words to open figurative and literal doors is universal in tales, from *shibboleth* to *sesame*. Compare Gandalf uttering *mellon*, "friend" in the Elven tongue, to open the Dwarf-door to the mines of Moria in J. R. R. Tolkien, *The Fellowship of the Ring*, 1st ed. (New York: Ballantine, 1965) 401; 2nd ed. (Boston: Houghton, 2001) 300.

16. *Bilingual Edition*, "Acknowledgements," 219. This admission is not in the *Critical Edition*.

17. *Bilingual Edition* xxx; *Critical Edition* xxxviii. Daniel Donoghue points out in his preface to the *Critical Edition* that: "Most of the words in question are Hibernicisms, that is, usages characteristic of the English in Ireland—or more specifically the English Heaney recalls from his Ulster relatives. Not all of the words are Irish in origin; some go back to Scandinavian languages and others to Old English. Perhaps the overriding lesson to be learned from the language that Heaney fashions is that all dialects have an equal claim

on the remote origins of English because they all have a parallel history" (ix–x). Heaney deliberately imposes Ulster words that neither match the architectural, nor capture the metaphorical, senses of the Anglo-Saxon words. See Donoghue's comment, n. 3 above, that Heaney purposefully avoided standard glosses.

18. Fr. Klaeber, ed., *Beowulf and the Fight at Finnsburg*, 3rd ed. (Boston: Heath, 1950). The genealogical table of the Danish royal line gives Hrothgar's dates as approximately AD 473–525 (cf. xxxi).

19. Klaeber xxix.

20. "A Wise and Faithful Defender: The Anglo-Saxon Concept of the Hero," honors thesis, Simpson Coll., 1976, 65. Bolstered by Erich Neumann, *The Origins and History of Consciousness* (Princeton: Princeton UP, 1970) 40, and Edward B. Irving, Jr., *A Reading of Beowulf* (New Haven: Yale UP, 1968) 140.

21. *Beowulf's Wealhtheow and the Valkyrie Tradition* (Madison: U of Wisconsin P, 1984). Damico associates Wealhtheow with *friðusibb*, "a state of peace marked by vigilant activity and a security brought about by action that has been armed and may again become armed" (85).

22. Damico 180.

23. According to Damico, "The queen's very name—*Wealhþeow*—aligns her with Odin's *oskmeyjar* 'chosen maids' who welcome the *einherjar* to Valhalla, with cup or horn outstretched" (179).

24. Cf. my "Forethought: The New Weapon in *Beowulf*," *In Geardagum* 12 (1991): 1–14.

25. Donaldson 5.

26. *Critical Edition* n. 1, 6. Footnoted glosses do not appear in the *Bilingual Edition*, although marginal summaries of the plot do. Heaney's use of *bothies* for *bowers* in line 140 is inaccurate.

27. Tom Shippey, personal conversation at the Mid-America Medieval Association, Kansas State University, Manhattan, KS, 23 Feb. 2002.

28. "English pig dogs," which the French castle guard called King Arthur and his men in *Monty Python and the Holy Grail*, comes to mind.

29. Heaney observes: "I came to the task of translating *Beowulf* with a prejudice in favor of forthright delivery. I remembered the voice of the poem as being attractively direct, even though the diction was ornate and narrative method at times oblique. What I had always loved was a kind of foursquareness about the utterance, a feeling of living inside a constantly indicative mood, in the presence of an understanding that assumes you share an awareness of the perilous nature of life and are yet capable of seeing it steadily and, when necessary, sternly" (*Bilingual Edition* xxviii; *Critical Edition* xxxvi–xxxvii).

30. For an accurate examination of the epic's grammar, see Tom Shippey, "*Beowulf* for the Big-Voiced Scullions," rev. of *Beowulf: A New Translation*, trans. Seamus Heaney, *Times Literary Supplement* 1 Oct. 1999: 9. Shippey points out that after Hrothgar offers to adopt Beowulf, Wealhtheow "tells her husband, five imperatives in a row, to enjoy himself and show appropriate generosity. Then she mentions the adoption, deadpan; and—twice using very careful subjunctives—raises the possibility of her husband's death," (9) implying that he consider who shall be his heirs.

31. "*Beowulf* for the Big-Voiced Scullions," 10.

32. See my "Teaching *Beowulf* to Undergraduates: The Role of Translation," *PMPA* 20 (1995): 1–8.

33. Translation reflects the epistemology of the translator, including the dictionary and the edition used. Many students rely on Klaeber's glossary when learning to read *Beowulf*, rather than J. Bosworth and T. N. Toller, *An Anglo-Saxon Dictionary*, or J. R. Clark Hall and Herbert D. Merritt, *A Concise Anglo-Saxon Dictionary*, or Gregory K. Jember, *English-Old English, Old English-English Dictionary*. Heaney translated from C. L. Wrenn, ed. *Beowulf: With the Finnsburg Fragment*.

34. See Edward L. Risden, *Beowulf: A Student's Edition* (Troy, New York: Whitston, 1994) i–xiv. Risden points out that *hwæt* is similar to modern-day Americans beginning their sentences with "Okay," while the British will capture the listener's attention with "Right" (iii). Heaney wanted to attend "[...] as much to the grain of my original vernacular as to the content of the Anglo-Saxon lines" (*Bilingual Edition* xxviii; *Critical Edition* xxxvii).

35. *Bilingual Edition* xxvii; *Critical Edition* xxxvi.

36. *Bilingual Edition* xxx; *Critical Edition* xxxviii. Klaeber's gloss of *gryregeatwum* as "terrible armor" or "warlike equipment" also seems ineffectual. *The Critical Edition* contains the footnotes that the *Bilingual Edition* lacks.

37. A Day of Whole Language, NCTE Convention, Galt House East, Louisville, KY, 19 Nov. 1992. The mantra of the Whole Language method enumerates four reading steps, but I suspect that students hear only the first commandment, "Skip it." See Diane Stafford, "Age-Related Philosophies Figure in Workplace Loyalty," *Kansas City Star* 23 April 2000, who notes that Carol Kinsey Goman has labeled those born after 1979 "The Twitch-Speed Generation."

38. "Hlaupa," G. T. Zoëga. *A Concise Dictionary of Old Icelandic* (Oxford: Oxford UP, 1910). The ancestor of "lope," *hlaupa* means "leap" or "run," senses current today. Used with prepositions, *hlaupa* can also mean "attack," but, since he does not reference Old Norse, Heaney probably did not have that ancient meaning in mind.

39. Stephen O. Glosecki, in an e-mail to the author, 1 Mar. 2002, observes that "loping sounds like a deer or something (if not a bunny rabbit!)."

40. *Scriðdraca*, "gliding dragon," is the Modern Icelandic term for the tank, a vehicle that, in effect, glides on its treads and belches fire—Michael T. Corgan, *Iceland and Its Alliances: Security for a Small State*, unpublished manuscript, 2002.

41. See James Shapiro, "A Better Beowulf," *New York Times on the Web* 27 Feb. 2000: Heaney's contribution is "simply one more stage in this continuing [translation] process."

42. John Leyerle, "Beowulf the Hero and the King," *Medium Ævum* 34 (1965): 89–102.

Scullionspeak
Beowulf: A New Verse Translation by Seamus Heaney (Farrar, Straus and Giroux)
[*New Republic*, 28 February 2000, pp. 32–37]

I.

For all that it seems to begin English literature, *Beowulf* is a relative new-comer to the canon. First edited by a Danish scholar in 1815, the year of Napo-leon's defeat at Waterloo and Jane Austen's *Emma*, the poem as a whole was not translated into Modern English until 1837. In subsequent years, *Beowulf* has found numerous translators, many of them scholars and few of them possessing any poetic gift. Of the sixty or so translators who have done the complete poem into English, only two have had any larger literary reputation. William Morris published a version in 1892; and C. K. Scott-Moncrieff, the English translator of Proust, published a version in 1921. But their talents lay elsewhere, and neither produced a *Beowulf* that can be read today with pleasure or even much compre-hension.

That the poem made it into the canon, much less into the cliché "from *Beowulf* to Virginia Woolf," is something of a miracle. Unlike most European epics, this poem exists in a single, unadorned manuscript that barely survived a fire in 1731 and today rests, charred edges and all, in the British Library. We know nothing about the manuscript's existence between the early eleventh cen-tury, when it was created, and the sixteenth century, when it re-appeared. Most likely it sat unnoticed in a monastic library for centuries, when nobody could read its Old English or, as it is also called, Anglo-Saxon.

That the manuscript did not circulate during these centuries should make us leery of celebrating the poem as the start of the English literary tradition, and also of demonizing it. *Beowulf* never enjoyed the currency and the prestige that Homer or Virgil had in their respective literary canons. It was not discussed in commentaries, or quoted by later writers, or honored as part of a common culture. Indeed, if the single manuscript of *Beowulf* had disappeared when Henry VIII dissolved the monasteries in England—as might easily have happened, given its physical homeliness and its incomprehensible language—we would not have the faintest suspicion that such a poem had ever existed. No other writer mentions the story of Beowulf, even in passing; nor is any part of it embedded in other works.

The mystery around *Beowulf* extends to such basic matters as who composed it and when. No name attaches itself to the poem, not even one of dubious historical veracity like Homer. Nor is any single date commonly accepted for its composition. Reputable scholars have placed it as early as the middle of the seventh century or as late as the beginning of the eleventh century—a period of 350 years or so, about as long as the period that separates *Paradise Lost* from today. It is hard to know if the undateable poem came at the start of the Old English literary period or at its end. We cannot know, therefore, whether it was composed in a culture that had been (at least in recent memory) oral in form and style, or in an increasingly literate culture that made England into a center of Christian learning.

Having neither an author nor a date for *Beowulf* poses problems for scholars, and temptations for translators. This lack of facts leaves them free to render the poem in the image of their various desires. And so translations of the poem range from effusive bardic performances that bear little relation to the original to scholarly transcriptions that are so close to the original that their Modern English makes sense, paradoxically, only to those who know Old English. It is certainly true that there are features of Old English poetry that contribute to any translator's difficulties in rendering *Beowulf* in Modern English.

For a start, the poetry in the original is heavily alliterative, so that each line marks out three of its four main metrical stresses with the same initial sound: "and find friendship in the Father's embrace," to borrow an example from Seamus Heaney's version. These days alliteration survives most audibly in rap lyrics and advertising jingles, so the translator of *Beowulf* must use it sparingly and knowingly. Nothing kills a translation faster than relentless alliteration; but nothing can help a good one more than the subtle use of alliterative emphasis, especially if the translator avoids ransacking the language for obscure synonyms to fill out the sound pattern.

More difficult to handle in Modern English than alliteration is the pervasive use in Old English poetry of variation or syntactically parallel expressions to describe the same person or object. Thus, a character in *Beowulf* will describe a king as "lord of the Danes," "king of the Scyldings," "giver of rings," and "famous chief" in three and a half lines of poetry. For the modern reader, accustomed to believing that a poet must use the exact word, Old English poetic variation can seem mindless repetition, the piling up of formulaic expressions to pad out a line, a sure sign that the *Beowulf* poet did not really know what he was doing.

As one reads the poetry, however, variation comes to seem evidence not of ineptitude, but of a desire to display a being or an object in all its richness. The more one reads Old English poetry, the more one senses that variation is what stands in the way of its successful journey into Modern English. Either you cut out some of the variants, and thin out the poem; or you render all of them as they appear, and clog the movement of the narrative. The two poetrics seem to find little common ground: the modern is exact and sparing in its inevitability, the early medieval is accretive and multitudinous in its generosity. The closest any twentieth-century poet has come to making Old English variation work in Modern English is Geoffrey Hill, in his Anglo-Saxon-inspired cycle called *Mercian Hymns*, which appeared in 1971.

That Old English and Modern English are not all that different at times, especially at the level of vocabulary, also renders the translation of *Beowulf* tricky. Anyone reading through a translation of *Beowulf* soon encounters some term or phrase that seems archaic, but is in fact perfectly good Old English smuggled in by the translator for lack of an adequate equivalent in Modern English. This usually occurs when the poet offers a rich run of variation for warrior gear—shields, helmets, armor, and so on. Without an equivalent technical vocabulary, the Modern English translator has few choices: either pretend that the Old English word for a piece of armor is still current or else invent some metaphoric rendering. Scholarly translators usually go for the first choice, poetic translators for the second choice. Either way, the original gets distorted. Words that are familiar and specific in Old English—such as words for vehicles are in Modern English—are made quaintly archaic or poetically ornate. Of course, such words are neither archaic nor ornate in *Beowulf*. They are as specific to their language, and circulate as easily in it, as do "minivan" or "sport-utility vehicle" in ours.

The markedly episodic shape of the narrative also raises problems for translators. The first two-thirds of *Beowulf*, a little more than two thousand lines, tells of the young Beowulf's journey from his home in Geatland (perhaps modern Sweden) to the court of Hrothgar, king of the Danes. There he vanquishes the monster Grendel, who has raided Hrothgar's hall and eaten his men for years. That victory is followed, the next night, by the appearance of Grendel's Mother, who raids the hall for the first time to avenge her son. In turn, Beowulf tracks her to the underwater cave where she lives, and kills her. These feats accomplished, Beowulf returns home to Geatland where, after a series of events, he becomes king and rules his people well for fifty years.

The poet effects the transition from the young Beowulf to the old Beowulf in ten lines or so, because the intervening years are of little interest compared to the appearance of a dragon that burns Beowulf's hall and ravages his lands. Beowulf must thus prepare himself for a last fight. And, with his young comrade Wiglaf, he defeats the dragon, but not without receiving a fatal wound. His death leaves the Geats without a leader, and without hope of resisting the onslaught of their traditional enemies. In the absence of Beowulf, the Geats face a future of death and captivity. As a poem about two defining moments in a life, *Beowulf* offers little narrative continuity. It places heavy demands on the audience's attention.

II.

All this said, it is hardly surprising that we have had no translation of *Beowulf* to match those of Homer by Richmond Lattimore, Robert Fitzgerald, Christopher Logue, or Robert Fagles, of Virgil by Fitzgerald, of Horace by David Ferry—to cite only recent renderings of dead white European males. Even Dante's *Divine Comedy*, for all its technical virtuosity, has been better rendered in Modern English than *Beowulf*. Readers who know *Beowulf* through the poetic versions of Burton Raffel, Kevin Crossley-Holland, or Michael Alexander may have some sense of its verbal style but little of its forceful directness; and readers of E. Talbot Donaldson's prose version, usually found in the canon-setting *Norton Anthology of English Literature*, know a *Beowulf* that retains the original's powerful narrative but little of its poetic inventiveness.

Now comes, like an "interloper from the Celtic realms," Seamus Heaney and his poetic version of *Beowulf*, intended for use in that same *Norton Anthology* but also appearing in a separate volume with a facing-page Old English text. For the first time, a major poet has taken on *Beowulf*. Heaney is an "interloper" in much the same sense as he meant when he applied the epithet to Yeats. Both are Irish by birth and cultural affinity; both write and read in English; both occupy an uneasy ground.

This crossing of historical and linguistic allegiances has its value for translating *Beowulf*, because the poem shows an analogous kind of crossing. It is written in Old English and was recited to an English audience, but its narrative is set entirely in north Germanic regions of the European continent in the years before the Anglo-Saxons made their migration to the island of Britain. Reading through it, you will never learn that there is in fact such a place as England or such a people as the Anglo-Saxons. Its religious and cultural landscape is pagan or at least pre-Christian, its geography is Scandinavian, and its ethos is distinctly military. It portrays not the Anglo-Saxons in England, as one might expect from an epic poem, but the world of their fathers in the fifth and early sixth centuries.

From the start of his career in the 1960s, Heaney has shown an affinity for Old English poetry. Having studied the language at Queen's University in Belfast, he could shape some of his lines by Old English metrical practices, as in "Digging," one of the poems that announced his arrival as a significant voice. In a fine lecture of 1976 on "Englands of the Mind," he located the poetry of Ted Hughes, Philip Larkin, and Geoffrey Hill in the English landscape and poetic tradition. When he spoke of these poets and their desire "to keep open the imagination's supply lines to the past, to receive from the stations of Anglo-Saxon confirmations of ancestry," he was also describing one strand in his own work.

Still, there is some surprise in reading Heaney's *Beowulf*, because it reverses the process that he described in "Englands of the Mind." In very forthright ways, Heaney's version demands to be read as his connection back to the stations of his Ulster ancestry. And it does so from the very first word of the poem, the Old English interjection "Hwæt." This word has no fixed semantic meaning but serves instead as a call to attention, a signal that something important is about to be said. Our equivalent in a loud or colloquial setting might be "Yo!"; but that would hardly do for the opening of a canonical poem. Recent translators have used "Attend" or "Indeed" or "Yes" or "Hear" for it; older translators used "Lo" or "Hark."

Heaney offers the less literary "So"; and he notes that in his Ulster colloquial, what he lovingly calls "Hiberno-English Scullionspeak," this word "came naturally to the rescue, because in that idiom 'so' operates as an expression which obliterates all previous discourse and narrative, and at the same time functions as an exclamation calling for immediate attention." His rationale for using "So" is precise, even plausible; but one wonders if it holds for those who use other varieties of English. To my ear, "So" sounds too under-stated, too domestic for the start of a poem such as *Beowulf*. I also hear it with a bit of a Yiddish intonation, an ironic questioning that does not match the poem at all—an inappropriate response, I know, but one that the word carries in my variety of Scullionspeak.

In his translation of the poem's opening, Heaney seems intent to downplay its assertion of epic temporality and heroic achievement: "So. The Spear-Danes in days gone by / and the kings who ruled them had courage and greatness. / We have heard of those princes' heroic campaigns." As he levels the diction of these lines and flattens their claims on the audience, Heaney writes two sentences where the original has one grammatical unit. In the original, the subject and the verb of Heaney's second sentence govern the first sentence as well. A recent version of the passage by the scholar Roy Michael Liuzza goes: "Listen! We have heard of the glory in bygone days / of the folk-kings of the Spear-Danes, / how those noble lords did lofty deeds." The original stresses from the start, as does Liuzza's version, that the "we" of the audience knows all the matter of the poem because poets have recited it so others can hear and learn it. Perhaps Heaney thought that splitting the single Old English sentence into two would make for an easier entry. What gets diminished, though, is the ceremonial opening claim, the reminder to the audience that all they know and can know about the past comes from poets.

That opening assertion matters for the understanding of *Beowulf* and for the appreciation of its style. The poem makes allusive use of the past in ways that speak to the circulation of stories and legends in a traditional culture. Similarly, the poem employs maxims and other terse statements of culturally shared belief. The narrator of the poem and its characters show a gift for the tight laconic expression that speaks to a common sense of how the world works and how one is to live in it. Heaney rightly praises "the cadence and force of earned wisdom" in such passages. To a modern reader, they can seem platitudinous, even trivial, if they are not translated with epigrammatic force. (And some seem so even when they are translated well.) The danger is that the narrator or the characters will seem pompous and verbose in Modern English when, in Old English, they are forceful and direct.

Consider a few examples, taken from high points in the poem. When Beowulf and his band of retainers land in Denmark on their way to help King Hrothgar fight the monster Grendel, they are greeted by a coastguardsman who challenges them. After hearing Beowulf speak, the coastguardsman recognizes that his intentions are honorable and that his status is aristocratic. He adds that learning to judge a man by his words and his works is a survival skill in a warrior culture. In E. Talbot Donaldson's prose version, he says: "A sharp-witted shield-warrior who thinks well must be able to judge each of the two things, words and works." The sentiment is not original to the coastguardsman, and thus its expression can be tight and understated. And that is why it carries conviction in the poem. In Heaney's version, however, the coastguardsman sounds folksy and long-winded: "Anyone with gumption / and a sharp mind will take the measure / of two things: what's said and what's done." This is accurate enough, but it misses the original's proverbial tone, which is at once a stylistic feature of the poem and the coastguardsman's compliment to Beowulf, who is smart enough to get the point even when it is made in a highly elliptical form.

Later in the poem, Grendel's mother comes out of the darkness to avenge the death of her son at Beowulf's hands by killing one of King Hrothgar's beloved comrades. As he tries to encourage Hrothgar after this calamity, Beowulf tells him tersely: "It is better for a man to avenge his friend than to mourn much." The young hero's admonition to the old king risks being disrespectful, and thus it seems to violate protocol, but it is allowed because it is maxim-like in expression. He is saying what anyone in the culture must know, and so he says it as simply as possible. Heaney gets the sentiment right, but in ways that make it seem platitudinous and thus offensive in context: "It is always better / to avenge dear ones than to indulge in mourning." This misses the force of Beowulf's words: that the old king, for all that he mourns, needs only a glancing reminder that his duty is to seek revenge. To say "indulge in mourning" makes the point obvious to the modern reader, but it also makes Beowulf less hard-bitten than he must be at this moment.

Heaney seems throughout to resist the tight, compressed style of *Beowulf*. It is not that his version has more lines or even more words than the original, though the latter is almost unavoidable, but that it seems looser and less edgy as it moves forward line by line. Yet there is one extended section in Heaney's *Beowulf* in which he brilliantly captures this poetic style. As he renders the so-called "Finnsburg Episode," a poem within the poem told by a performer in Hrothgar's court, Heaney moves powerfully and accurately from Old to Modern English, as in these lines:

> Wind and water
> raged with storms,
> wave and shingle
> were shackled in ice
> until another year
> appeared in the yard
> as it does to this day,
> the seasons constant,
> the wonder of light
> coming over us.

Heaney rightly notes that his version of this passage is marked "by a slight quickening of pace and a shortening of metrical rein." Perhaps a translation of all 3,182 lines of *Beowulf* in this style would prove unreadable. Still, these lines do sound truer to the original than other parts of Heaney's translation, precisely because they avoid being tediously explicit or drawn out. Here we are not burdened with an overly long line that uses more language than it needs to render the original.

The overly long line is especially evident in passages in which Heaney has to translate the original's use of variation or apposition. In his introduction, he admits to slighting this aspect of the poem's style. His frankness is winning, but it cannot obscure the fact that some of the dullest lines in his rendering are the consequence of this slighting of variation, as here: "Then he saw a blade that boded well, / a sword in her armoury, an ancient heirloom / from the days of the giants, an ideal weapon, / one that any warrior would envy. . . ." This kind of passage may not sound like poetry to us, but passages like it appear throughout *Beowulf*. To make them work in Modern English, the translator needs to do more than dutifully fill out the list of synonyms. There needs to be also a sense of why the poet clusters so many synonyms at that particular moment in the poem.

Writing about any translation means judging it for its faithfulness to the original as well as for the quality of its own expression. It also means looking at local moments and large passages. As Heaney once remarked, in an essay on John Clare: "I am reminded of a remark made once by an Irish diplomat with regard to the wording of a certain document. 'This,' he said, 'is a minor point of major importance.'" In the judgment of translation, certainly, minor points have major importance; and to my ear Heaney's translation tends to flatten or to elongate the Old English line, to make it seem heavy with words rather than direct and flowing with alliterative stress and verbal energy. His *Beowulf* sounds at times more like some poetry of medieval Ireland than it does like that of Anglo-Saxon England, and this is not unrelated to Heaney's objective as a translator.

III.

There is one thing that Heaney's *Beowulf* does better than any other translation of the poem that I know. The most moving and powerful moments of his translation appear in the speeches delivered by characters during the last third of the poem. This section takes place fifty years into the reign of Beowulf. His triumphs over Grendel and Grendel's mother are in the distant past; all that remains is the final contest. In these speeches, which are addressed at least as much to the audience as to other characters, we hear a wise and weary Beowulf, a man who knows that his time on earth is nearing its end. But first he must fight and defeat the dragon who has burned his hall and ravaged his land, even though that fight will likely end in his death and thus, because he leaves no heir, in a new peril for his people.

After killing the dragon and receiving a mortal wound in exchange, the king takes the measure of his life:

> No king
> of any neighbouring clan would dare
> face me with troops, none had the power
> to intimidate me. I stood my ground
> and took what came, cared for things in my keeping,
> never fomented quarrels, never
> swore to a lie.

The note here is exact: the voice of the old Beowulf seems not so much translated by Heaney into Modern English as ventriloquized into it. The record of a life is finely caught in the dignified, modest assertions of half-lines such as "I stood my ground" or "and took what came." These are almost uncannily accurate renderings of Old English poetic form, especially of direct speech. In such passages, when Heaney seems to enter characters such as the old Beowulf, he finds the right melody for translating Old English.

To expect that Heaney would work at this level throughout would be unfair. And here it may also matter that his translation originated as a commission for the *Norton Anthology of English Literature*. A translation meant for students encountering *Beowulf* for the first time probably should prefer the clear and the accurate over the brilliant and the allusive. Some of the passages that I have criticized for being overly explicit can also be read as attempts to explain the poem to first-time readers. Yet the rationale for the translation is not that simple, despite Heaney's gracious acknowledgement of assistance from various medievalists. What complicates Heaney's translation, and in many ways makes it deeply interesting as a contemporary statement on literature and politics, as a redress of poetry, is that he sets out to make the poem Irish.

At the most immediate level, this means that Heaney is willing to use various words that are current in the English of Ulster but do not circulate widely if at all in the standard English of either England or North America. Some of these words are survivals from Old English that have lasted in Ulster but not elsewhere, such as the verb "thole," meaning "to suffer." Others are forms current in Ulster English that Heaney sets into his translation carefully and sparingly, but also polemically: "bothies," "war-graith," "bawn," "keens," "brehon," "wean," and "hoked." Even if you know Old English, many of these words are puzzling and intrusive, for they introduce an element of what one might call political dialect into the Modern English version that is not in the Old English version. The original does not use words from one specific dialect to make a larger political and poetic claim. What Heaney does with words such as "bawn," "brehon," and "hoked" is his own remaking of the poem. That they are mystifying, at least at the immediate level, is admitted by the practice of the *Norton Anthology* in glossing these words with notes, some written by Heaney.

Adding words that need glossing to a translation when there are reasonably usable words at hand is a provocative thing to do. I think that the method would have been far more successful if Heaney had gone all the way and written a fully Ulsterized version of *Beowulf*, instead of a version that stands at times awkwardly between a textbook version for undergraduates and a remaking of the poem to gather in his own heritage. Heaney's *Beowulf* would have been far more exciting if it had followed the practice of Derek Walcott's *Omeros*, and traveled the full and exhilarating distance from translation to poetic remaking.

Why didn't Heaney do so? It is hard for a reader to say. What can be usefully explored is how this version of *Beowulf* relates to other aspects of Heaney's career. Over the last several years, Heaney has located his fascination with Old English poetry in the figure of the Anglo-Saxon poet Caedmon. Lamenting the death of Ted Hughes, he wrote: "This modern poet from Yorkshire who published in the 1960s a poem called 'The Bull Moses' would have had no difficulty hitting it off with Caedmon, the first English poet, who began life as a farmhand in Northumbria, a fellow northerner with a harp under one arm and a bundle of fodder under the other." It is a lovely image of the poet: a harp and a bundle of fodder. It reminds one vividly of some of Heaney's early poems about his youth in rural Ulster where, as a Catholic in a Protestant region, he sometimes seemed to be more at home with the countryside and its creatures than with most of his fellow citizens. It is a fine image, this poet with harp and fodder; but it is not an accurate image of Caedmon and it may not be fair to Hughes either, who was a learned poet in his terrifying way.

Heaney's retelling of the Caedmon story matters a great deal to his intentions as a translator of *Beowulf* and, more radically, to his use of the poem to graft himself onto the English literary tradition. It also matters to some of his most obvious moves as a translator, especially his use of Ulster vocabulary. The story of Caedmon first appears in 731 in Bede's *Ecclesiastical History of the English Church and People*, and this fact alone should make one hesitate to treat him simply as a bucolic harper. Bede records that Caedmon was a cowherd at the monastery at Whitby, who would withdraw from the drinking when the harp circulated and his turn to sing came round. One night, after slipping away and tending to his animals, Caedmon fell asleep and dreamed that a mysterious figure ordered him to sing a song. Puzzled but awestruck, Caedmon asked of what he should sing, and was told to sing of God and His Creation. The result, spontaneous but technically perfect, is known today as "Caedmon's Hymn."

Bede also tells us that once the cowherd's gifts were recognized, the abbess of the monastery ordered the learned monks to read the Bible to him so he could meditate on these readings like (in Bede's image) a cow chewing its cud and then retell them in traditional vernacular verse.

At that moment, Caedmon ceased to be a cowherd. He matters as the first English poet because he put the oral bard out of business when he became the mouthpiece for a highly literate tradition of Scripture. But Heaney prefers to read Caedmon as the bard who stands "as a reminder of the daemonic strengths of the art, its covenant with the singing voice of Orpheus, the sheer spellbinding power of rhythmic speech," as he recently wrote in *The Threepenny Review*. His preeminent recent example of such a poet is Dylan Thomas.

Perhaps so, but to make the comparison work, to invent a lineage from Caedmon to Dylan Thomas and Ted Hughes and, implicitly but no less firmly to himself and to his translation of *Beowulf*, Heaney has to forget that Caedmon matters because he composed thoroughly orthodox poems in English to persuade pagan Anglo-Saxons to renounce their faith and their culture in order to become good and dutiful Christians. Caedmon is an agent of conversion, of Christian conversion, which means that he is an agent of cultural betrayal. Whichever way one reads him, he is the figure who makes poetry the vehicle for a written scriptural tradition that has little place, or no place at all, for the bardic Orpheus.

Heaney loves his version of Caedmon, so fervently that he makes me want to believe and love it, too. One of his strongest recent poems begins: "Caedmon too I was lucky to have known." This Caedmon is the bard who beneath the

learned poet remains unspoiled and earthy: "And all that time he'd been poet-
ing with the harp / His real gift was the big ignorant roar / He could still let out
of him, just bogging in / As if the sacred subjects were a herd / That had broken
out and needed rounding up." Heaney ends on a note of vernacular praise: "Oh,
Caedmon was the real thing all right." This evocation of the Old English poet
is alluring, and it is designed to advance Heaney's own ends as a poet. For this
particular poem is called "Whitby-sur-Moyola," the first name being the site of
Caedmon's monastery in the north of England and the second being a river that
flows near Heaney's childhood home in the north of Ireland. The French preposition between the place-names looks forward and backward to the arrival of the
Normans in 1066, another part of Heaney's heritage.

Whitby-sur-Moyola belongs on the most beautiful of maps, in the atlas
of imaginary places, because it is a fictive setting for the tension that has driven
Heaney's poetry from the start. And this tension can also be felt in his *Beowulf*, as
he acknowledged proudly in his lecture on translating the poem, "The Drag of the
Golden Chain." Irish by birth, English by language, a partisan of neither side in
the religious troubles of Ireland, Heaney can find no spot in the real atlas to fix his
poetic home. And so Whitby-sur-Moyola is a place deeply attractive in its gesture
toward political, cultural, linguistic, and religious harmony.

Yet Whitby-sur-Moyola is a curious place to work from as a translator of
Beowulf. One might even argue that someone writing from there is not really a
translator of the poem at all. He is, rather, a reinventor of the poem, who turns
Old English into Modern English to remake the literary and cultural history of
the British Isles. And there is an argument in this remaking. The argument is
that there is a deep affinity between the Anglo-Saxon and the Celtic, between
two peoples and traditions that have rarely been at peace with each other from
the time when the Germanic tribes arrived on the island of Britain in the fifth
century A.D.

One can only roar like Heaney's Caedmon at the irony of a revisionist
Beowulf appearing in that most canonical of textbooks, the *Norton Anthology*; but
for Heaney's purposes, where better than a textbook that will assure his *Beowulf*
of several generations of readers? Or one would roar at this irony if Heaney had
really rewritten *Beowulf* to be the poem of Whitby-sur-Moyola. As it is, he had
added some Celtic echoes to an Old English poem because that can be, in his
words, "one way for an Irish poet to come to terms with that complex history of
conquest and colony, absorption and resistance, integrity and antagonism" that has
characterized Anglo-Irish relations since the time when the Irish burned the poet
Edmund Spenser out of Ireland and back to Elizabeth's court.

As a translator, Heaney does not work forward from the start of a literary
tradition, as a scholar might. He looks back from his moment in that tradition, as

a poet seeking out connections, trying to refashion the Old English in ways that can disturb a scholar, but always locating his poetry and his history on his own grounds. The result is a *Beowulf* that is sometimes deeply exciting to read for its energy, for its allegiance to the colloquial and idiomatic rather than the academic and official, for its sometimes astonishing acts of ventriloquism in rendering some of the characters' speeches into Modern English. Whether this makes it as well into a good translation is a more complicated matter, because Heaney sometimes seems at a loss to render some of the poem's most essential stylistic features.

For reasons that have as much to do with its virtues as with poetic reputation and publishing houses, Heaney's *Beowulf* is likely to be the most commonly read version of the poem over the next few years. In its thrilling passages, it reads better than any other translation that we have; and in its dullest passages, it is no worse than many others. Does it belong with the best recent translations from Latin and Greek? Probably not. For that *Beowulf*, we await a translator who has worked deeply through Old English poetic style and who has thus, in Geoffrey Hill's words, "exchanged gifts with the Muse of History."

Heather O'Donoghue

Beowulf: A New Translation. By Seamus Heaney. London: Faber, 1999.
[*Translation and Literature* 9 (2000): 231–36]

Readers of Seamus Heaney's *Beowulf* will be, broadly, of two very different kinds—
that is, they will be approaching the translation from very different angles. Much
the larger group will be Heaney fans; their interest will lie primarily with what
effect this encounter with a strange Old English classic has had on a familiar and
much admired poet. For them, Heaney's *Beowulf* will be read less as a translation than an original poem in its own right. They may not know the poem in its
original Old English, and may even be coming to it for the first time, intrigued
by the potential of an epic meeting between two great poets from the most recent
and the most distant ends of the canon of 'English Literature'. A smaller group
of readers will comprise those who know the poem well, in the original, and who
want to know, straightforwardly enough, what Heaney has done with it (the earliest reviews of Heaney's *Beowulf*, and media articles in which various *litterati*
were quizzed on what happens at the end of *Beowulf*, suggest that this group
may be very small indeed). Proprietorial, even a little defensive about the poem,
their concern will be with such matters as the literalness and accuracy of Heaney's
translation, disguising, perhaps, anxiety about appropriation. But with Heaney,
distinctions between the roles of scholar, critic, and poet dissolve; he combines the
strengths of all three in this new text.

    The first twenty-nine lines of poem—that is, one modern page's worth—
are printed in parallel translation, Old English on the left, Heaney on the right.
After this first page, Heaney is on his own. The parallel translation has a double
effect: it dramatically highlights the impenetrability of Old English to modern
readers, but it also suggests a comforting physical closeness between the two texts,
for the line lengths are the same, the verse paragraphs are made to correspond
precisely, and each of the twenty-nine lines in the original has its counterpart on
the facing page. This ostensible similarity is an illusion (the layout of the poem,
the punctuation, and of course the typeface, are all modern) but reflects an actual
formal correspondence. The visible caesura between the two half-lines in each

full Old English line, unmarked on the page in Heaney's translation, is in fact elegantly evident when the modern English is read, without the least effect of paratactic monotony. So it is with the alliteration in each text: it's so pronounced in the Old English that one can actually see it on the page, whilst Heaney's text doesn't look alliterative, and one is surprised by how insidiously the alliteration is worked into the line; particularly attractive (and indeed authentic) is Heaney's tendency to alliterate on stressed second syllables, so that 'behind' alliterates with 'housed', or 'beyond' with 'yield'. Modern English is still naturally alliterative; significantly, only Latinate words draw unwanted attention to it, as in 'the privilege of purifying Heorot'.

In the original, these alliterating, two-stress half-lines are paratactically juxtaposed in implicit grammatical relation to one another; one of Heaney's major achievements is to translate this loose variation into modern syntax without losing the metrical effects of the original. Thus, the poem's opening three lines, 'Hwæt we Gar-Dena in geardagum / þeodcyninga þrym gefrunon / hu ða æþelingas ellen fremedon', are rendered:

> So. The Spear-Danes in days gone by
> and the kings who ruled them had courage and greatness.
> We have heard of those princes' heroic campaigns.

The intricate sound-play of 'Gar-Dena' and 'geardagum' is echoed but not imitated in Heaney's 'Danes'/'days'; the caesura is intact but unobtrusive; and the alliteration preserved. But the great thing is the syntactical rearrangement. Instead of the ambiguous and heavy double genitive of the Old English—the glory *of* the people-kings *of* or *and of* the Spear-Danes', a construction which can really only work in an inflected language—and the double but grammatically dissimilar objects of 'we have heard' ('glory' and 'how princes performed valour'), Heaney produces two separate sentences, the solemn approbatory truth of the first underlined by its simple status as statement of fact, and both governed by the authority of the first-person speaker in the second.

The very first word in the poem—'Hwaet'—has been the downfall of all too many early translations (the religious 'Lo'; the bathetic 'Well then'; the risible if cognate 'What Ho!'); Heaney's grave monosyllable 'So' seems to me as near perfect as possible. It's interesting, then, that in his introduction Heaney acknowledges a debt here to the colloquial Ulster language he grew up with. Irishisms abound in this translation. Most often, they work unexpected miracles. Thus, for example, the Old English poet uses the compound word 'ealuscerwen'—'a drink of bitter ale', perhaps, though it's still a notorious crux—to convey the transformation of the warriors' experience in Heorot from celebratory feasting to the terror of Grendel's attack. Heaney uses another metaphor for the transformation of cel-ebration into terror: the hall timbers 'sing' as Beowulf and Grendel fight, such that their encounter is a 'hall-session'. The terminology of Irish music is also wonder-fully appropriate to convey the recitations in Heorot, where the barely imaginable 'scop' is vividly realized as 'a traditional singer deeply schooled / in the lore of the past'. Sometimes, an Irishism is misleading: only those familiar with Hiberno-English will recognize the polite, formal greeting in Wealhtheow's 'salute' to the warriors in the hall. Some words—'bawn', 'kesh', 'bolter', 'thole'—may be as unin-telligible as the Old English. But to reject such dialect words as anomalous is to miss the point; they are coded signals to remind the reader of the shared, but very different, marginality of two linguistic departures from Standard English: Ulster English and Anglo-Saxon.

This takes us to the first unexpected point of similarity between two poets separated by such an enormous cultural and chronological gap: though both are unarguably major figures, their relation to what is commonly called 'English Lit-erature' is controversial and problematic. The simple paraphrase 'Literature in English' is enough to accommodate Heaney's work, though without in the least effacing its linguistic and political differences from the English tradition. The sta-tus of *Beowulf* is much trickier.

Beowulf is an Anglo-Saxon poem set in sixth-century Scandinavia. Whether or not it is representative of the literary tradition of its own time we can't tell—it has resisted being dated, even to within almost five centuries, and nothing else at all like it has come down to us from the Old English period. And yet it exudes centrality, authority, a profoundly wide-ranging and reliable humanity. Its language (apart from a few dialectal forms which might locate its origin no more precisely than somewhere in the extensive Anglian provinces of Anglo-Saxon England) is the poetic *koine* which some scholars have argued had developed as a standard literary language amongst Anglo-Saxon poets. Nowadays fluency in Standard English, even its Shakespearean or Chaucerian forms, is not enough to unlock *Beowulf*. Its present-day marginality, then, even though an historical acci-dent—or inevitability—and by no means a feature of the original poem, is assured. Heaney's own position is a precise mirror-image of this. Though conscious himself of writing and speaking for and from what is perceived by literary London as a lin-guistic and political margin, he has himself centralized that margin, foregrounding the language, politics, and troubled history of Ulster.

Heaney's use of viking themes as a metaphor for the Ulster Troubles—most obviously in *North*—has been well documented. But to write about violence is always to risk being accused of condoning it, the most notorious example in Heaney's work being the poem 'Punishment' from *North*, in which it is suggested that beneath the veneer of 'civilized outrage' over a tarring and feathering there may lurk a darker sense of what Heaney calls 'tribal, intimate revenge'. Some have mis-read this as insufficient condemnation, particularly of Republican violence; inevi-tably, Heaney has also been criticized for not making an explicit case for nationalist ideals. The poet of *Beowulf* may well also have used Scandinavian subject-matter to make a political point to his Anglo-Saxon audience, and he too treads a narrow but acutely poised path, in his case between celebrating the achievements of his pagan ancestors while, as a Christian, deploring them as benighted. His attitude to violence has also been persistently misrepresented. Though it's true that the poem is full of violent action—violence long past, and violence still to come, as well as the violence of the poem's present—nonetheless the poet is very far from condoning, still less celebrating it. To depict in less than full detail its far-reaching workings deep in the heart of society is to underestimate its power, and to fail to pay due respect to real heroism: the unremitting struggle by people of good will to slow its inexorable progress.

There are three kinds of violence in *Beowulf*: amongst family members; between warring tribes; and between men and monsters. It is the interrelationship between these sets which preoccupies the *Beowulf*-poet and establishes the funda-mental structure of the whole poem, and it illustrates a theme repeatedly stressed in Heaney's own work: the mirroring of the personal in the political, which civil war always exposes. The Danes have a glorious past—this is the very first thing the poet tells us—but while their present is threatened by the depredations of the monster Grendel, the real horror facing the Danish royal house is yet to come, and cannot be averted by the action of any visiting superhero: the next generation after this present king, Hrothgar, is to be wiped out by dynastic infighting, a terrible phase in Danish history well known in Norse legend and history, and periodi-cally alluded to by the poet himself. Setting his poem on the brink of the Danes' troubles emphasizes the poignancy and precariousness of Heorot's splendour, and offers the grim, voyeuristic thrill of hindsight. But it also allows the poet to play with the possibility that the course of history might have been different: Hroth-gar's queen Wealhtheow dissuades him from making Beowulf his heir, but with a strong non-Danish leader the Danes' dynastic integrity might, paradoxically, have been defended. This powerful 'if only' moment is compelling evidence of the *Beowulf*-poet's deploring of violence.

Internecine warfare is inextricably linked with inter-tribal feuding. In the complex sets of wars between the Swedes and the Geats there are two constant factors: the defeated party will be always on the alert for signs of weaknesses in their enemy, the signal that the tables may be turned; and any one act of hostil-ity will eventually be repaid, for violence begets more violence. And finally, the three monsters—Grendel, his avenging mother, and the magnificent dragon—are surreal manifestations of the spirit of familiar, squalid human violence. Grendel is part of the legacy of Cain, who initiated the most intimate familial violence, fratricide—the mythic equivalent of what Heaney himself has called 'neighbourly murder'. His mother, avenging Grendel's death at Beowulf's hands, exemplifies the truism that violence begets violence, a fact disturbingly elevated to the status of an ideal—vengeance—in heroic life. And the dragon represents a sort of solitary isolationism, nursing gold rather than sharing it out; inward-looking rather than productively interactive; possessive, defensive, and dug-in, but given to sudden provocative and flamboyant displays of its power. By contrast, Hrothgar and Beowulf are peacemaking statesmen: nurturing neighbourly affection, they repay debts of gratitude and look to future co-operation. But peacemaking is a perilous business: Hrothgar's daughter, Freawaru, is to be married to the leader of the Danes' old enemies, the Heathobards, in a predictably doomed attempt; the Danes themselves ought to have recognized that it would fail, for one of the stories told in Heorot laments the fate of Hildeburh, caught up in a conflict between brothers on the one side, and husband and son on the other, the fragile peace-pledge holding both sides together at the cost of bringing them into fatally close proximity.

It will be clear that there are any number of resonant correspondences with the recent history of the North of Ireland. Though it may be true that human conflict unfolds in similar ways in different times and places, nonetheless those words and phrases we associate with the troubles—tit-for-tat killings, the peace process, mixed marriages, the legacy of history—are the ones we reach for in trying to recount the events of *Beowulf*. But Heaney never uses them in his translation. Remarkably, he manages to preserve the cultural and literary alterity of his original: he has not reduced the poem to a costume-drama allegory of the Ulster situation. His great service to the poem is to relay to the disinterested reader its difficult mix of grandeur and humanity, its poetic dignity, and why it deserves its central place in literary history. Even the most proprietorial of medievalists must celebrate this.

Tom Shippey

Beowulf for the big-voiced Scullions
Seamus Heaney, *Beowulf: A new translation*. Faber.
[*Times Literary Supplement*, 1 October 1999, pp. 9–10]

In the 1997 *Beowulf Handbook* edited by Robert Bjork and John Niles, Marijane Osborn lists some twenty full or partial English translations of *Beowulf*, and that is by no means a complete list. Some have been produced by distinguished scholars (J. R. Clark Hall and C. L. Wrenn, E. T. Donaldson, Constance Hieatt), some by rated poets (Edwin Morgan, Burton Raffel, Kevin Crossley-Holland, Michael Alexander). And all this is now immaterial. Seamus Heaney is a Nobel Prize–winner; his translation of the poem was commissioned for and is going straight into *The Norton Anthology of English Literature*; set for virtually every introductory course in English on the North American continent (and all undergraduates have to take them, not just English majors); and he is a Northern Irish Catholic, one of the excluded, a poet in internal exile. All this, within the power poker of American academe, gives him something like a straight flush, ace high; to which any reviewer must feel he can oppose no more than two pairs, and aces and eights at that, the Dead Man's Hand. Like it or not, Heaney's *Beowulf* is the poem now, for probably two generations.

So. This is the way Heaney starts the poem, quelling instantly the long (and tedious) academic debate about how to translate its opening word, *Hwæt*. He gets "so", Heaney explains, from his Irish relations, whom he calls, in a previous poem and in the "introduction" to this one, "big voiced Scullions". Why "big voiced"? Because, "when the men of the family spoke, the words they uttered came across with a weighty distinctness, phonetic units as separate and defined as the delph platters displayed on a dresser shelf". In their mouths, a sentence like "we cut the corn today", says Heaney, "took on immense dignity"; when they opened a statement with "So", the idiom operated "as an expression that obliterates all previous discourse and narrative, and at the same time functions as an exclamation calling for immediate attention". Heaney wanted, then, to make *Beowulf* speakable by one of his Scullion relatives; what he loved about the poem was "a kind of foursquareness about the utterance, a feeling of living inside a constantly indicative mood".

Right, then (for as Edward Risden pointed out in his 1994 translation of the poem, "right" is the English English for *Hwaet*); maybe the first thing to say is that we seem here to be in the presence of two folk narratives, a personal one and an academic one. On the personal side, no one can grouch at Heaney relating a poem to his own experience and hearing his own history in it. He was much struck, he says, when he first read the poem at university, to realize that the strange verb *þolian* in the glossary, with its weird runic initial letter, was also the dialect word "thole" which he was used to hearing in completely non-academic surroundings. The word and its history (Old English to Scottish to Ulster planters to native Irish) gave him "illumination by philology", it "opened my right of way", it made *Beowulf* "part of my voice-right".

Fair enough, and no one wants to take the voice-right away. But Heaney's illumination is, or ought to be, pretty widespread. Ever since William Morris (at the very least), it has been noted that many Old English words, and many Beowulfian words, are unfamiliar only to educated English, with its self-imposed burden of French and Latin. From the first few lines I pull "settle", "wax", "dree", "ere", "barm", "bairn"—Heaney has replaced *drugon* (= "dreed") with "tholed", so making one point but rejecting another. If he is under the impression that "Scullion-speak", as he calls it, somehow preserves a native purity which other and more effete dialects of English do not, then that is a delusion: an amiable delusion, maybe, for ancestral piety is to be admired, but a dangerous one too. A hundred years ago, foolish philologists, who should have known better, were claiming that standard English was intrinsically superior to dialects because it had nicer vowels; reversing the statement makes it no wiser.

As for the academic folk narrative, that crops up perhaps in the remark about the indicative mood. Heaney is fond of indicatives. In his poem "From the Canton of Expectations" (first published in the *TLS*, January 24, 1986), he sees the history of his people as moving from optative to imperative, and wishes for someone "who stood his ground in the indicative; / whose boat will lift when the cloudburst happens". But is *Beowulf* an especially indicative poem? If one is talking real grammar, not the folk-grammar of John Major and most English-department introductory courses, then the poet of *Beowulf* might be thought to be distinguished by his handling (among much else) of subjunctives. How does Heaney take these?

A test case is Beowulf's early confrontation, before we even know his name, with the Danish coastguard. As Beowulf's crew, heavily armed, stream over the *bolca* (the baulk, the gangplank), the Danish warden, Hrothgar's thane, rides down to meet them. Is he going to start shooting? Is he going to wave them through? What he does is offer a long speech, almost agonizingly balanced between threat and conciliation. Twice, for sure—you cannot always tell—he uses subjunctive verbs, switching the first time from a very plain compliment, *nis þæt seldguma* ("that's no hanger-on") to an immediately doubtful half-retraction, *næfne him his wlite leoge* ("unless his looks should happen to belie him"); moving the second time from the peremptory modal *ic sceal* ("I shall, I must") and the definitely uncomplimentary *leassceaweras* ("false seers, spies") to another retractive subjunctive, *ær ge . . . furþur feran* ("before you should happen to go any further"). Catching the tone of the subjunctive is hard in modern English, but it is a major part of the careful, prickly dignity of armed men in the heroic world.

How does Heaney catch it? His translation of the latter part of the speech runs as follows:

> Nor have I seen
> a mightier man-at-arms on this earth
> than the one standing here: unless I am mistaken,
> he is truly noble. This is no mere
> hanger-on in a hero's armour.
> So now, before you fare inland
> as interlopers, I have to be informed
> about who you are and where you hail from.

Heaney has switched the "unless" clause to precede the compliment, and added the bit about "truly noble". Also, the "unless" now governs the coastguard being mistaken (which is deprecatory), not the stranger's looks being lies (which is suspicious). "Before you fare" is pretty good, keeping the characteristic Old English "pararhyme", but to my ear "I have to be informed" sounds apologetic. The Old English is both flatter, more uncompromising, "bigger-voiced" indeed, and at the same time more subjunctive, more open-optioned, than Heaney can get across. *Beowulf* is a highly aggressive poem, of course, and in the folk narrative of modern academe this translates out as "butch". But maybe real warriors, as opposed to thugs or gangsters, had to learn complex social skills. "Foursquare" does not always seem to be the right description of how they talk.

Try another scene, a speech so oblique, though riddled with imperatives, that no reader in the early modern period understood it for sixty years and the interpretation was ignored for another forty and resisted into my own student days by scholars like Kenneth Sisam, who just did not believe that Anglo-Saxon housecarls, "men not chosen primarily for their intellectual qualities", to use his polite formulation, could possibly have taken it in. Hrothgar's queen Wealhtheow is speaking, after Beowulf has got rid of Grendel, and after her husband has made a perhaps rash offer to adopt Beowulf into his own family. She tells her husband, five imperatives in a row, to enjoy himself and show appropriate generosity. Then she mentions the adoption, deadpan; and—twice using very careful subjunctives—

raises the possibility of her husband's death. She never at all says the words, "who is going to succeed you, who is going to inherit?", let alone rebukes her husband for gratuitously importing a competitor to his and her sons. But it is there (and much else is there, for the speech is not over) in the gaps, in the contrasts between grammatical moods.

Heaney again:

> The queen spoke:
> "Enjoy this drink, my most generous lord,
> raise you your goblet, entertain the Geats
> duly and gently, discourse with them,
> be open-handed, happy and fond.
> Relish their company, but recollect as well
> all of the boons that have been bestowed on you.
> The bright court of Heorot has been cleansed
> and now the word is that you want to adopt
> this warrior as a son. So, while you may,
> bask in your fortune, and then bequeath
> kingdom and nation to your kith and kin,
> before your decease."

Wealhtheow said neither "before" nor "decease", she said something like (and this is E. T. Donaldson), "when you must go forth", though the "must" was subjunctive—"when you may perhaps have to". She didn't say the "but" in line 6 above either, and I think the "boons" she is telling her husband to "recollect" are the ones he should be giving, not the ones he has received. The Anglo-Saxon speech treads much more delicately than the modern one. Maybe we have got more four-square (or ruder), not less; though, of course, in academic folk narrative it is well known that Anglo-Saxons were just plain primitive, a distinguished professor of literature recently calling them the Falkland Islanders of the first millennium, which is rude on several levels.

How does Heaney handle, then, the most plainly indicative statements in the poem, its many gnomic sayings and maxims? It has to be said that he gets off to a bold but shaky start. Very early in the poem, the son of Scyld Sceafing arrives, and the poet comments, for no apparent reason, that this is how sons should behave: they should give gifts and buy loyalty while their fathers are alive, so as to have willing support in war when they grow up. The poet ends with an uncompromisingly universal statement, *lofdædum sceal / in mægþa gehwære / man gepeon*. This means, translating very literally, "in each one of the tribes a man must thrive (is bound to thrive?) by deeds of *lof*"—what is *lof*? "Praise", say the dictionaries—so, "by deeds of praise". Heaney, claiming to be "attending as much to the grain of my original vernacular as to the content of the Anglo-

Saxon lines", translates "Behaviour that's admired / is the path to power among people everywhere".

This is universal enough, and the echo of *gehwære* in "everywhere" is good. But who in the world could begin to go about believing it? The people of power now are financiers and politicians. Are they remarkable for "behaviour that's admired"? Does the maxim survive contact with mention of Robert Maxwell and Bill Clinton? Were the Anglo-Saxons (or the Scullions whom Heaney cites once again as models for those lines) really as starry-eyed as that? I do not think *lof* means "praise" here, I think it means the other half of the exchange relationship, "generosity". The poet is saying that men rise to the top everywhere through judicious payoffs: in his culture with its hatred of stinginess, that is a virtue without cynical suggestion. But it has stayed true even in a quite different political culture, which is one mark of a good saying.

Heaney does not always guess wrong, or shy away from the unwelcome. I appreciate his demotic "That was one good king" for Scyld Sceafing, as also "That is no good place" for the monsters' mere, and "They were a right people" for the sleeping Danes. His "voice-right" has helped him out in another respect, too, in his dealings with what he calls, in careful awareness of modern commentary, the poem's "appositional" syntax. The bane of translators of Old English poetry from the lowest levels upwards is its use of variation, saying the same thing in different ways. In Old English, with its ability to indicate syntactic connections through word endings, this is a flexible and often climactic technique, but in modern English, where word-order rules, the unspoken instruction to get everything in and not leave any phrases out often leads to sentences which feel like someone pushing a line of supermarket trolleys.

Heaney deals with this sometimes (not often) by judicious cutting; more often by skilful permutation of the syntactic resources modern English still allows, mixing adverbial phrases with relative clauses, using non-finite constructions (something his own poetry has always exploited). Compare, for instance, Clark Hall and Wrenn, a self-proclaimed students' crib, with Heaney on Hrothgar getting up. The crib is resolutely uninteresting: "the king, too, guardian of ring-hoards, came from his bed-chamber; he, famed for noble qualities, advanced majestically with a great company, and his queen with him passed over the path to the mead-hall with a company of maidens." Compare Heaney:

> the king himself,
> guardian of the ring-hoard, goodness in person,
> walked in majesty from the women's quarters
> with a numerous train, attended by his queen
> and her crowd of maidens, across to the mead-hall.

The vocabulary is not much different, but the syntax is. One finite verb, not three; an appositional pronoun cut out; a couple of adverbial phrases relocated, a co-ordinate clause subordinated: and the trolley effect, thankfully, has disappeared. It does make the poem much easier to read at length, for which many successive cohorts of students and tutors will be grateful.

More importantly, though, can Heaney hit the heights? I do not know if it is because the poem gets sadder towards the end, but I formed the impression that he was becoming more comfortable with his mode as time went by. There are many moments of pathos, usually understated, in the last third of *Beowulf*, and Heaney singles some of them out for comment in his introduction. His "Lay of the Last Survivor" is excellent, plain, like the original full of unexplained transitions and unstated regrets:

> Now, earth, hold what earls once held
> and heroes can no more; it was mined from you first
> by honourable men. My own people
> have been ruined in war; one by one
> they went down to death, looked their last
> on sweet life in the hall. I am left with nobody.

I am not so sure about Beowulf's part-weary, part-proud, reminiscence. How can one go wrong with *Ic wæs syfanwintra, þa mec sinca baldor / freawine folca æt minum fæder genam*? "I was seven winters, when the prince of treasures, / friend and lord of peoples, took me from my father": the honorifics contrast with the little boy taken into service, a service he now means to complete in loyalty to men long dead. Heaney has, "At seven, I was fostered out by my father, / left in the charge of my people's lord"; the little boy has become the subject of the fostering, not the object taken away. Often, it seems to me, the plain flat phrase is ducked, as in the tragedy of line 2439, when Beowulf's uncle *miste mercelses ond his mæg ofscet*, "missed the mark and shot his brother"; in Heaney, "shot wide and buried a shaft / in the flesh and blood of his own brother".

On the other hand, Beowulf's three last dying speeches to Wiglaf are good—"You are the last of us, the only one left . . . "—as are Wiglaf's own, and in particular his speech to the shirkers, where long and complex sentences are kept rolling through the appositions to the crunch lines, "now the day has come / when this lord we serve needs sound men". Thirteen monosyllables in a row; if this is "Scullion-speak", we need more of it.

How, finally, should one deal with the last three lines, the end of a poem sometimes described not as an epic but as a long, long dirge? In the Old English, they are both plain and complex, the last two lines being the only ones in the poem which follow each other identically in the rhythm (trochaic stress, two central

stresses, trochaic stress, two central stresses) and, apart from a genitive changing to a dative, in grammar. I translate them as near as I can word for word and
sound for sound. The Geats, mourning their lord, "said that he were [subjunctive],
of world-kings, / of-men mildest and most loyal / to-men kindest and praise-
yearnest", "Mildest" and "kindest" (*mildost, lindost*) are surprising words to use of
the dead hero; the fourth superlative seems (but is it?) out of line with the others.
Heaney gives:

> They said that of all the kings upon the earth
> he was the man most gracious and fair-minded,
> kindest to his people and keenest to win fame.

Tom Shippey is co-editor of *Beowulf: The Critical Heritage* (1998).

E. G. Stanley

Seamus Heaney (trans.), *Beowulf.* London: Faber and Faber, 1999.
[*Notes and Queries* 47 [2000]: 346–48]

That those teaching and learning Anglo-Saxon now have so good a verse transla-tion of *Beowulf* into Modern English is a great gain and we have every reason to be grateful to Seamus Heaney. Its only rival is Edwin Morgan's of 1952, with its long and brilliant introduction on translating the poem. He too succeeded in translating it well in spite of the problems he described. Heaney's introduction is shorter and differently excellent, also in discussing some of the problems, and presenting the reader with his solutions. To set forth a scholarly understanding of the problems proves mastery of the gentle craft of Anglo-Saxon studies, less useful than shoemaking but in its way as demanding of practicalities; to present satisfying solutions proves mastery of the art of poetry. The usual bibliographies list many other translations into verse and prose;[1] and till Morgan and Heaney no translator of real distinction had undertaken the task, except Nik. Fred. Sev. Grundtvig, whose *Bjowulfs Drape. Et Gothisk Helte-Digt fra forrige Aar-Tusinde* (Copenhagen, 1820) is highly important for its annotations, but, alas, my Danish is too poor for me to be able to evaluate its literary excellence.

Heaney's translation will probably be used as a substitute for the poem, though the fact that he prints the first twenty-nine lines of the original may indi-cate that he does not intend it as that. His replacement at line 9 of MS *para* (often omitted altogether by editors following Sievers) by *pær* following John C. Pope's *Speculum* article of 1988 (accepted by George Jack in his edition, an edition Heaney says he follows for the Anglo-Saxon text) and, more significantly, his sen-sitive omission of any editorial mark of punctuation after the initial *Hwæt* (Jack has *Hwæt, we*) show that if he had edited the whole of *Beowulf* he might well have been among the best editors. Heaney records his thanks to Professor Alfred David (Indiana University, Bloomington) and several other scholars, at Harvard and Berkeley and Dublin for help given, and the published version is a highly scholarly work as well as a good poem.

The lack of a point after *Hwæt* is no misprint; that is clear from the identical

371

lack of punctuation *Hwæt we* in the otherwise slightly differently punctuated and more hyphenated printing of lines 1–3 in the introduction, where he discusses the sense of the first word. The reader should not be misled by some of Heaney's modest statements; thus on the subject of the initial *Hwæt* he brings in what he describes as the particle *so* in 'Hiberno-English Scullion-speak', and elsewhere he describes himself as if a scullion, or, at least, his sympathies as with the scullions of Ireland. Dialect diction is now probably more often felt to be low in social class, when not archaic within literary artificiality. But there is nothing of Scullion-speak in Heaney's translation, and nothing artificial either. There are a few words that survive in Hiberno-English but not in standard Modern English and he uses them to good effect, as may be seen in lines 3021–7:

> Forðon sceall gar wesan
> monig morgenceald   mundum bewunden,
> hæfen on handa,   nalles hearpan sweg
> wigend weccean,   ac se wonna hrefn
> fus ofer fægum   fela reordian,
> earne secgan,   hu him æt æte speow,
> þenden he wið wulf   wæl reafode.

In E. Talbot Donaldson's prose rendering[2] these lines are:

> Therefore many a spear, cold in the morning, shall be grasped with fingers, raised by hands; no sound of harp shall waken the warriors, but the dark raven, low over the doomed, shall tell many tales, say to the eagle how he fared at the feast when with the wolf he spoiled the slain bodies.

Seamus Heaney turns these lines into:

> Many a spear
> dawn-cold to the touch will be taken down
> and waved on high; the swept harp
> won't waken warriors, but the raven winging
> darkly over the doomed will have news,
> tidings for the eagle of how he hoked and ate,
> how he and the wolf made short work of the dead.

In Old English this is the poet at his best. The art of the translator shows best by doing justice to the excellence of the original. I did not know *to hoke* (in the dictionaries, those of England and Scotland, most often spelt *hówk*, more rarely *holk*); it appears to mean 'to grub up', also, in Older Scottish, 'to pluck out (the eyes)'—as ravens do on the field of battle, I have been told by a French scholar who in the First World War saw action in the trenches. The horror of the beasts of battle has been brought out to the full in Heaney's translation of these lines. A clue to his success is to be found in his note of how he has always understood the poem:

> I came to the task of translating *Beowulf* with a prejudice in favour of forthright delivery. I remembered the voice of the poem as attractively direct, even though the diction was ornate and the narrative method at times oblique.

The recognition of the poet's art of obliqueness leads Heaney to see the 'Finn Episode' thus:

> the most famous of what were once called the 'digressions' in the poem, the one dealing with the fight between Danes and Frisians at the stronghold of Finn, the Frisian king—the song the minstrel sings has a less obvious bearing on the immediate situation of the hero, but its import is nevertheless central to both the historical and imaginative worlds of the poem.

In his translation this episode, lines 1071–1159a, is printed in half-lines set out differently from the arrangement of lines in the rest of the poem. That too was a good idea.

Seamus Heaney has captured the directness as well as the ornateness of the original, to the extent to which that is acceptable in Modern English. His introduction deserves to stand beside J. R. R. Tolkien's famous British Academy lecture of 1936 (to which he pays tribute), if not now above it, not scullion-speak, but 2000-speak. An excellent translation is useful to awaken pre-university readers to the poetic art of *Beowulf*, and it may usefully remind ageing readers of the story-line. Glenda Cooper and Jane Kelly, celebrating in the *Daily Mail* of 27 January 2000, p. 13—a contribution not to be overlooked by the annual bibliographers—how 'Seamus Heaney's Beowulf wins the £21,000 Whitbread award', quote 'Prof Malcolm Bradbury [t]he novelist who was shortlisted for the 1982 Booker Price'; he recalls the end of the poem thus: 'It ends with Grendel's mother killing our hero . . .'.

Notes

1. I have discussed a number of them in 'Translation from Old English: "The Garbaging War-Hawk", or, The Literal Materials from Which the Reader Can Re-create the Poem', in M. I. Carruthers and E. D. Kirk (eds), *Acts of Interpretation . . . in Honor of E. Talbot Donaldson* (Norman, Oklahoma, 1982), 67–101; rptd in E. G. Stanley, *A Collection of Papers with Emphasis on Old English Literature* (Toronto, 1987), 83–114.

2. First published by W. W. Norton & Co. in 1966; they were the first publishers also of Seamus Heaney's *Beowulf*.

G. Storms

Beowulf. A New Translation. Translated by Seamus Heaney.
London: Faber & Faber, 1999.
[*English Studies* 83.2 (2002): 176–77]

When I first received this work I began by reading it through in its entirety with-out looking at the original Anglo-Saxon text. It had been praised extensively in England and America by critics who were writing their reviews for newspapers and popular periodicals. These critics were not Anglo-Saxon scholars and they awarded a literary prize from a modern point of view. These prizes are sometimes deserved and sometimes meant for advertising purposes. In this case the prize and praise are deserved, for the translation is pleasing and the metre attractive. I read the work through from the beginning to the end and I was not disappointed. To modern Englishmen and Americans, who are naturally proud that theirs is the earliest Germanic work in existence and who are told that *Beowulf* has great liter-ary merit, Seamus Heaney's rendering has great appeal. The blurb of my edition contains the nonsensical statement that the poem was composed towards the end of the first millennium and that it is one of the great Northern epics. As if the date of a manuscript and the contents of *Romeo and Juliet* make it into an Italian work. Mr Heaney slightly improves upon this in the first sentence of his introduction by remarking that it was composed some time between the middle of the seventh and the end of the tenth century. A reading of Klaeber's masterful introduction could have informed him better.

On the whole Heaney has preserved the four stresses to the line of the origi-nal text, but there is nothing of the fivefold variety of each stress, nothing of the balance of the two half-lines, nothing of the first stress of the second half-line as the one that sets the alliteration, nothing of the clear and striking caesura that sepa-rates the two half-lines, nothing of the fact that the consonantal alliterative force of *sp, st* and *sk* (*sc*) only applies to these sounds, never to other *s* sounds (see line 30 or 41 of his translation). He says nothing of the importance of the oral singer, nor of the harp whose music emphasized the two half-lines and also binds them together. In other words his metre is not the Beowulfian metre in spite of his general reten-tion of the four stresses and the general use of a weak modern alliteration.

A good example of my partial admiration and great disappointment is provided by lines 102ff:

> Wæs se grimma gæst   Grendel haten
> mære mearcstapan,   se þe moras heold
> fen ond fæsten

> Grendel was the name of this grim demon
> haunting the marshes, marauding round the heath
> and the desolate fens.

(Desolate) fens is excellent, but where is the *mære mearcstapan* and the (impregnable) fortress he inhabits? *Mære* means 'well-known', here with the connotation 'feared', in other contexts 'illustrious, famous'. *Mearc* denotes the borderline region between the Danes (in this case) and the habitation of the monster.

The metre and the alliteration cannot compare with the strict and fixed metrical alliteration of the original text, nor with the full Anglo-Saxon meaning. In line 202 for instance we find the word *siðfæt*, 'journey, far voyage', suggesting a dangerous, worrisome journey, for in the poem we see that *sið* is most frequently accompanied by words like *cear-*, *ellor-*, *gryre-*, *sæ-*, *wræc-*, so that *sið* itself seems to assume an unfortunate connotation.

'(Even) wise men did not dissuade him from undertaking a far voyage, though he was dear to them'. Heaney merely translates:

> Nobody tried to keep him from going,
> no elder denied him, dear as he was to them.

Heaney's *Beowulf* is a retelling of an Anglo-Saxon poem, it is by no means a satisfactory translation. In my opinion no translation of the value of the poem is possible, only a literary commentary would do it justice.

In an earlier article[1] I explained how the Danes and the Geats found a foothold in East Anglia and then in *Beowulf*. The poem is an East Anglian work, not a Northern or Danish one, belonging to the sixth and seventh centuries and it sets England in the context of the struggle for power between the Franks and the Ostrogoths in the time of the 'Völkerwanderung', the time of the migration of the nations. As such it is a curious illustration that in England, too, people were aware of the struggle of two strong and dangerous rivals on the continent.

Notes

1. *English Studies*, Vol. 80, no. 1, pp. 46-49. My remark on p. 47 that the Hetware were mentioned in the *Carta Peutingeriana* was untrue.

Julian Wasserman

Still Epic After All These Years
[*New Orleans Review* 26/3–4 (2000): 179–81]

A thousand years after its Initial Public Offering, *Beowulf*'s stock has soared in a year that has included the big screen release of *The 13th Warrior*, Michael Crichton's retelling of the Anglo-Saxon epic, in addition to Tulane medievalist Roy Liuzza's excellent academic translation of the poem. Yet the most surprising sign of life in this first millennium classic about a hero's battles against two monsters and a dragon has been Seamus Heaney's new verse translation of the poem edging out the high-flying Harry Potter for the Whitbread Award.

Translating *Beowulf* has always been a tricky business. In the original, the poem reflects the Anglo-Saxon love of indirection, of leisurely renaming, of poetic elaboration at the expense of directness and verbal economy, qualities that are difficult to appreciate by modern readers bound by constraints of time and deadlines. Old English, which relies heavily on case endings as opposed to word order, provides a syntax difficult to capture in modern English. Above all there is the imagery. Sure, Old English has the word "swerd" (sword). But no self-respecting hero carries one. Instead, they wield the "foe-hammer" or "lightning-slasher." Beowulf doesn't "speak," he deals treasure from his "word-hoard." It's easy to lose the narrative thread in the midst of such creative compounding. At heart has been a choice between capturing one of two elements, the smooth flow of narrative or the looping indirectness of the poem's seventh to tenth century poetics and the idiosyncrasies of heroic speech.

Part of the reason that Heaney has captured imaginations is that he steers a middle ground, avoiding both options in order to highlight what will come as a surprise to many who think of the poem solely as a work about the slaying of monsters. If each translator has brought a different gift to the task of rendering the epic, Heaney's is a recognition of the poem's inherent, but often overlooked, lyricism. Indeed, *Beowulf* is, foremost, a product of an oral culture, one that finds the ability to speak well as important as strength of arm.

That means that there's far more speaking than fighting in this poem, including melancholy laments about human nature, the Grendels inside all beings and our heroic struggle to overcome them. There's the sorrowful wisdom of the once-strong Hrothgar, the lament over gold once held by earls but now the decayed hoard of the dragon. Then there's the last battle boast of the doomed hero, and Wiglaf's scornful reproach of those who desert the now aged Beowulf in his final hour of need against the dragon. For what Heaney understands is that *Beowulf* is not simply a heroic tale. It is also a meditation on the human condition, on life in a mutable world that sets snares for human weakness and creates opportunities for greatness.

To capture the elegiac music of the poem, Heaney has, however, refused to surrender the heroic. Even in the battle scenes, there is unusual lyricism. The rendering of Grendel's attack hints at the internal dimension of attack on the feast-hall from which he is eternally excluded:

> Then his rage boiled over, he ripped open
> the mouth of the building, maddening for blood,
> pacing the length of the patterned floor
> with his loathsome tread, while a baleful light,
> flame more than light, flared from his eyes.

There is awe and poetry in details often minimized in translation, such as when the giant's sword used to slay Grendel's mother,

> began to wilt into gory icicles,
> to slather and thaw. It was a wonderful thing,
> the way it all melted as ice melts
> when the Father eases the fetters off the frost
> and unravels the water-ropes.

The unnatural melting of the sword into the gory, prosaic "icicles" stands in counterpoint to the Father's natural melting of the "water-rope," icicles made over by poetic compounding.

Is such poetry the result of Heaney's poetic gifts, or the unlocking of what was there all along in the original? No doubt even the non-specialist might want to take a quick look at the original Old English. The edition reviewed here is a bilingual one, but one that is curiously impractical. Without a glossary, there is of course very little of the original, other than the proper names, that an untrained reader might follow. Even more curious is that, despite a splendid introduction by Heaney and a brief note on names by Alfred David, the volume does not contain even a hint as to the pronunciation of the Old English, so readers are denied the opportunity to read/hear the poem's cadences aloud. Even more curious is the fact that there is no note or explanation of the two runic letters (both of which are pronounced "th") that appear regularly in the text.

In short, the Old English original seems to present an assurance, largely unnecessary here, that the translation is faithfully anchored to the original text. In translating *Beowulf*'s "word hoard" for the modern reader, Heaney does indeed show why the poem—unlike the dragon's ancient, moldering gold—is a lasting treasure.

Hideki Watanabe

Seamus Heaney (trans.), *Beowulf: A New Translation*.
London: Faber and Faber, 1999.
[*Studies in English Literature. English number* 43.2 (2002): 65–72]

So, once again, Seamus Heaney has 'unlocked his word-hoard.' This is the last translation of *Beowulf* in the twentieth century and by a Nobel laureate. Even without his name, this translation would undoubtedly be rated as one of the highest achievements in Beowulfiana of the last decade.

Heaney visited Japan and delivered a series of lectures in 1997. He was recently featured in *The Rising Generation* (1997, Vol. 142, No. 11). His collections of poems and essays, including *The Spirit Level* and *Preoccupations*, have been translated into Japanese. In line with a boom in and the revaluation of Irish Literature, this latest translation of the Old English epic is the cynosure of Japanese philologists. It is not merely in the academic spotlight; general readers of the literature also note that Heaney's *Beowulf* is a '*Harry Potter* destroyer,' as one reviewer puts it, and it clawed and stomped its way to the Whitbread Poetry Award in 1999.

For Japanese readers of *Beowulf*, in Old or Modern English, or in Japanese, the name of Nagase Kiyoko is memorable. She started her career as a poet with *Grendel's Mother* (1930), the title of which apparently alludes to the epic. The anthology was followed two years later by the first full Japanese translation made by Kuriyagawa Fumio (*English Literature and Philology*, Vol. III, Tokyo; Maruzen Co., 1931–2). Based on this earlier version he published a revised edition in 1941. His was a version molded on older Japanese literature, with a touch of *Kojiki*, an ancient history of Japan orally inherited, written and compiled during the seventh and eighth centuries. This first Japanese translation of the epic appeared in Iwanami's Classical Library, thereby having long provided an easy access to the great work and exerted a great influence, too, on the readers. After Kuriyagawa there appeared four versions of *Beowulf* in Japan: Nagano Sakari (1965), Oba Keizo (revised, 1985), Hazome Takekazu (1978; reprinted, 1985), and Oshitari Kinshiro (1990). Oshitari's version replaced the long out-of-print Kuriyagawa's in Iwanami's Library. It is to be noted here that in that library of classical literature only few, truly great foreign literary works, are reprinted or reissued. In this sense *Beowulf* should be compared to *Aeneis*, which was translated into Japanese first by Tanaka Hidenaka and Kimura Mitsuzo in 1940 and later by Izui Hisanosuke in 1976 or possibly to Milton's *Paradise Lost*, which was translated into Japanese first by Fujii Takeshi in 1938, and later by Hirai Masao in 1981 for the Library. Apart from these five versions there is a bilingual edition with critical apparatus published in the *Bulletins of Niigata University* by Karibe Tsunenori, who is the first reviewer of Heaney's *Beowulf*.[1] Thus in modern Japan, chronologically and geographically remote from the Anglo-Saxon world, there is at least a seventy-year tradition of general and critical acceptance of the epic. It is rather remarkable that the Japanese started to read it even before J. R. R. Tolkien delivered his famous lecture.

It is a common view among the medievalists that the lecture by Tolkien, later published as *Beowulf: The Monsters and the Critics* (1936)[2] changed the course of Old English scholarship. Heaney's Introduction to the translation is compared by many reviewers to this epoch-making lecture. Heaney has acknowledged his debt to Tolkien.[3] In the Introduction Heaney explains why he adopted words of his local origin and he terms 'Scullion-speak.' Heaney's adoption of such words has led to much dispute. Observing that 'dialect diction is now probably more often felt to be low in social class, when not archaic within literary artificiality,' E. G. Stanley allows, ' . . . there is nothing of Scullion-speak in Heaney's translation, and nothing artificial either.'[4] This is perhaps a reply to another eminent Old English scholar's denunciation of the poet's use of 'Hiberno-English.' Nicholas Howe is puzzled to see sporadic appearances of such words as 'bawn,' 'hawked,' or 'wean' and concluded that the translation would have been more successful 'if Heaney had gone all the way and written a fully Ulsterized version of *Beowulf*, instead of a version that stands at times awkwardly between a textbook version for undergraduates and a remaking of the poem to gather in his own heritage.'[5] Contrastively there is a view that his use of common rural words clearly shows, in the words of Tom Shippey, that 'many Old English words and many Beowulfian words are unfamiliar only to educated English, with its self-imposed burden of French and Latin.'[6]

Critics, however, admire Heaney's restructuring of the context. Terry Eagleton in his very political review observes, that "the canny colloquialisms" resulted in "a marvelously sturdy, intricate reinvention" of the original.'[7] Most reviewers also praise his handling of alliteration, especially when realized in the two-beat rhythm, and note that 'Heaney has shown an affinity for Old English poetry.'[8] Influenced by his mentor, Gerald Manley Hopkins, Heaney paved his way to *Beowulf* in a series of earlier works of short lines, whetting his verbal knife to carve strong alliterative staves. I would like to add a few cases to those already mentioned in the previous reviews.

Here is a further example of his treatment of varieties of rhythm and alliteration (513–8), where Unferth describes, and enviously distorts, Beowulf's swimming match with Breca:

> You waded in, embracing water,
> taking its measure, mastering currents,
> riding on the swell. The ocean swayed,
> winter went wild in the waves, but you vied
> for seven nights; and then he outswam you,
> came ashore the stronger contender.

The two-beat half lines, stopped mercilessly by each caesura, ring in the rhythm of heartbeat, here the heartbeats of the two contenders at rough sea. They are followed and taken over by the two longer lines, as if to assume the modern counterparts of what are called hypermetric lines in Old English verse.

In the passage preceding Beowulf's fight with Grendel at Heorot (653–668) he boldly dismisses the alliterative schemes on h's and w's in the original, thereby creating a new resonance among the verbs and noun phrases in the initial g sounds instead.

> Hrothgar wished Beowulf health and good luck,
> named him *hall-warden* and announced as follows:
> 'Never, since my hand could hold a shield
> have I entrusted or given control
> of the Danes' hall to anyone but you.
> *Ward and guard* it, for it is the greatest of houses.
> . . .
> Hrothgar departed then with his *house-guard*.
> The lord of the Shieldings, their shelter in war,
> left the mead-hall to lie with Wealhtheow,
> his queen and bedmate. The King of Glory
> (as people learned) had posted a lookout
> who was a match for Grendel, *a guard against monsters*,
> special protection to the Danish prince.

Here *eoton-weard* (literally 'giant-ward') in line 668 is expanded to 'a guard against monsters' and the verbs *hafa* and *geheald* are rephrased with a pair of imperative doublets, *ward* and *guard*. Even assonance and consonance is achieved in the rendering of line 662 where *house-guard* follows *Hrothgar*.

As for assonance and consonance his artistry is perhaps best shown in the description of Heorot, which awaits the fearful doom of 'the killer instinct / unleashed among in-laws, the blood-lust rampant.' (85–6) This lionhearted line, roaring along with initial and internal l sounds, symbolizes a fitful fire and ambition in the bosom of Hrothulf, Hrothgar's nephew. The two compounds, 'in-laws' and 'blood-lust,' employed to render *aþum-swerian* and *ecg-hete*, are fine examples of Heaney's reconstruction and renovation in the original context. The meaning is made clearer, and the alliteration schemes are transferred from vowels and w sounds in Old English to k and l sounds in Heaney's version. In this way, the Irish poet interprets the merits and demerits of poetic compounds or kennings. He sometimes inks over the original drawings if they look nice in Modern English, too. But more often, he unwaveringly cuts apart, and often discards the elements of those compounds whenever they would not make sense or sound impressive. At the same time he effectively creates or employs elements which are not in the original. This is what James Wood remarks on in one of the earliest reviews of the translation saying '[t]he Anglo-Saxon poet was a great discoverer of analogies and formulaic compounds, and this in turn is one of the strongest beauties of Heaney's version.'[9]

It might be interesting to compare treatments of compounds in previous translations of *Beowulf*. Here, for instance, are William Morris's version of the compounds to render those in some sixty lines at the turn of Fits seven and eight: *wan-heed, man-lord, hand-grip, war-hall, lone-goer, blood-mark, war-shrouds, hand-work, hand-bane, war-dread, South-Danes, Dane-folk, youth-tide, hoard-burg, hate-wiles, hall-floor, war-heap, ale-stoup, beer-hall, mead-hall, warrior-hall, gore-stain'd, sword-gore,* and *war-fame.* In striking contrast with Morris, who retains here twenty-four compounds, Heaney appropriates only seven out of thirty in the original. In exchange he newly coins three compounds in order to reinterpret and restructure the original context with the movement contained in the modifiers. What is gained in this way surpasses what might be lost otherwise.

A century ago, the editors of the *New English Dictionary* adopted as many as nine instances from Morris's translation and four from Benjamin Thorpe's to enrich their quotation columns. Most of them are artlessly, if not slavishly, modernized and queer-sounding compounds (e.g. *hoard-burg, hate-wiles*). Heaney's vivid renditions such as *heather-stepper* (1368)[10] 'deer' or *sword-play* (682) 'battle' are more colloquial and transparent. They will no doubt appear in the quotation columns in the *Oxford English Dictionary* third edition in ten years' time. It is very probable that Heaney's *heather-stepper* with its precursor in the original (*hæð-stapa*) will form a new subordinate headword under *heather*. Contrastively under the headword *sword-play* the *OED* registers *Waldere* 13 as the only instance of the metaphoric use (a kenning); Heaney's would revive the sense division I. †a. (Fight, battle. OE.) just as Tennyson's *shield-wall* (1880, *Brunanburh*) alludes to and revives *scieldweall* in 3118 of *Beowulf*. The second edition of the *OED* has already registered seven quotations from his early poems.[11]

It is well known among *Beowulf* scholars that there are discernible verbal and thematic resonance and repetitions in the poem. A golden banner (*segen gylden(ne)*) first appears very significantly at Scyld's ship-funeral (47), then as one item of the gift to victorious Beowulf by king Hrothgar (1021), and once again as among the dragon's hoard (2767) with an emphatic *eall-*. Heaney renders the first two instances as 'a gold standard' and the third one as 'a standard, entirely of gold,' well matched to the strength intended in the original. Heaney sometimes maintains this kind of resonance in his renderings, but more often discards them. See, for example, the alliterative eulogy 'æþeling ær-god,' which is distinctively bestowed on Hrothgar (130), Æschere, his favorite vassal (1329), and Beowulf (2342). While Heaney follows or expands this phrase and its variation for the first two as 'Their mighty prince, / the storied leader' and as 'Æschere was everything / the world admires in a wise man and a friend', he just throws away everything to give 'he' for the third, though this alliterative phrase is the subject without variational phrase in the original. In *Beowulf* Grendel and his mother are, in a sense, assimilated to and classed into dragon's kin, for they writhe themselves to creep and glide, as is particularly shown by the poet's use of the verb *scriðan*. In Old English it typically denotes the movement of reptiles, ships, or heavenly objects.

With this verb he first introduces Grendel in 163, suggesting later with its plural form in 650 that Grendel has his kin, sets the man-eating monster hovering under the black night, and finally describes the fire-dragon in 2569. Most translators have, in some way or another, tried to relate these monsters with each other, and Crossley-Holland unifies them to render *shrithe* for the four instances.[12] Its adoption by Crossley-Holland might have been twofold purposeful: to describe and unify the monster's walk onomatopoeically in association with such verbs as *slither* and *writhe*, and to have a great impact and keep the modern readers in suspense with the very strange word.[13] Contrastively in Heaney the association is lost with the varied renderings of the same verb: *roam* (163), (*came*) *stealing forth* (650), (*came*) *stealthy and swift* (703), and (*came*) *gliding* (*and flexing*) (2569).

We also notice such intentional repetitions in the form of a half-line in *Beowulf* as an exclamation 'Þæt wæs god cyning.' It is used to summarize the achievements of the three good kings: Scyld (11), Hrothgar (863), and Beowulf (2390).[14] Heaney retains an emphatic *that* for the first as 'That was one good king' but prefers a personal pronoun to give 'he was a good king' for the last two. As David Tandy clearly points out,[15] 'Þæt wæs god cyning' is carefully positioned so as to signify the resemblance among the three eminent men, singling them out of many kings. Crossley-Holland renders the first and the third as 'he was a noble king!' but changes the adjectives and misses the exclamation in the second as 'he was a great king.' Stanley Greenfield does not unify the forms of the renderings, either, but instead, has smelled and kept a touch of exclamation: 'a good king indeed!' 'he was a good king!' and 'that was a good king.'[16] It is clear that eminent poets and scholars have neglected this kind of verbal or thematic resonance in the poem. Nevertheless, this is the loss, found elsewhere, too, and is what I regret in Heaney's otherwise magnificent translation.

We should perhaps note the fact that some passages are reworded in the American edition. This is not mentioned in any of the reviews that I have read so far. One example will suffice to show this. Nicholas Howe quotes the following passage and praises its grip of emotions described in the original (*Beowulf* 2733–39):

> No king
> of any neighbouring clan would dare
> face me with troops, none had the power
> to intimidate me. I stood my ground
> and took what came, cared for things in my keeping,
> never fomented quarrels, never
> swore to a lie.

Observing, '[t]he record of a life is finely caught in the dignified, modest assertions of half-lines such as "I stood my ground" or "and took what came,"' he goes on to say that '[t]hese are almost uncannily accurate renderings of Old English poetic form, especially of direct speech.' Strangely enough, however, Howe quotes the passage from the English edition and to his surprise, Heaney rewrote and changed the order of the three verbs in the past tense, *stood, took*, and *cared* to have discarded the half-line, which is praised by the influential critic. In the American edition the middle of the passage runs as 'I took what came, / cared for and stood by things in my keeping.'

'Heaney,' as James Wood aptly summarizes, 'is a poet, not a scholar, and he excites our interest as a translator not through marital fidelity but through amorous commitment.'[17] To put it otherwise, Heaney's *Beowulf* is not a faithful reproduction but a fine recreation. However, his journey through the Anglo-Saxon world is not only a fascinating read for people who first encounter *Beowulf* in his modern version. His findings or interpretations, reshaped into dexterously manipulated verse, will also hold researchers in the curious spell, and refreshing rediscovery, of the original.

In this century of increasing social anomie, where there is need of "a set of myths and archetypes" which might remind us of the long-neglected questions of hierarchy and tradition, Heaney's *Beowulf* will surely "provide an alternative symbolic universe,"[18] which once was and continues to be an invisible undercurrent of our too material and ephemeral world. This new translation, with its extraordinary rhythms and drive, makes us look back to those millennium-old world view and values, and, for that merit, will establish itself as a new classic in the English Literature for the new century. As the *Beowulf* poet might have put it, *Þæt is god boc.*

Notes

1. *Studies in Medieval English Language and Literature*, 16. 2001, The Japan Society For Medieval English Studies.

2. *Publications of British Academy* 22, 245–95.

3. See xi.

4. *Notes and Queries*, September, 2000.

5. *The New Republic*, February 28, 2000.

6. *Times Literary Supplement*, October 1, 1999, p. 9.

7. *London Review of Books*, November 11, 1999, p. 16.

8. Nicholas Howe, *The New Republic*, February 28, 2000.

9. *The Guardian*, October 16, 1999.

10. Heaney does not like 'march-stepper' for *mearcstappa* in 103, and expands the compound into a phrase 'haunting the marches.' (p. 6)

11. See the headwords *Lambeg*, *ramrod*, *slap* v., *sledge*, *sogged*, *tell*, and *truck* n.

12. Kevin Crossley-Holland, ed. and tr. 1984, *The Anglo-Saxon World*. Oxford University Press.

13. Hideki Watanabe, 1988, 'Monsters Creep?: the Meaning of the Verb *scriðan* in *Beowulf*,' *Studies in Language and Culture*, Osaka University, 14, 107–20

14. Hideki Watanabe, 1999, 'A Reconsideration on *þæt was god cyning* Type Sentences in Old English Poems—Exclamation, Parenthetical Explanation, or Ending Remark?' *Studies in Language and Culture*, 25, 91– 103.

15. David Tandy, 1984, 'The Evidence for Editing in *Beowulf*,' *Neuphilologische Mitteilungen*, 85, 289–98.

16. Stanley B. Greenfield, tr. 1982, *A Readable Beowulf*, Southern Illinois University Press.

17. *The Guardian*, October 16, 1999.

18. Terry Eagleton, *London Review of Books*, November 11, 1999, p. 15.

Works Consulted (Excluding reviews and translations in the footnotes)

David Tandy, 1984, 'The Evidence for Editing in *Beowulf*,' *Neuphilologische Mitteilungen*, 85, 289–98.

Tomoaki Mizuno, 1999, "The Magical Necklace and the Fatal Corslet in *Beowulf*,' *English Studies*, 80, 377–97.

Hideki Watanabe, 1988, 'Monsters Creep?: the Meaning of the Verb scriðan in *Beowulf*,' *Studies in Language and Culture*, Osaka University, 14, 107– 20.

Hideki Watanabe, 1999, 'A Reconsideration on *Þæt was god cyning* Type Sentences in Old English Poems.—Exclamation, Parenthetical Explanation, or Ending Remark?' *Studies in Language and Culture*, Osaka University, 25, 91– 103.

Hideki Watanabe, 2000, 'Final Words on *Beowulf* 1020b: *brand Healfdenes*,' *Neuphilologische Mitteilungen*, 101, 61–7.

Hideki Watanabe, 2000, 'The Quotations from *Beowulf* and Other Old English Poems in the *Oxford English Dictionary*,' *Lexicographica* Series Maior, 103, Max Niemeyer, 264–9.

R. M. Liuzza, *Beowulf: A New Verse Translation*. Peterborough:
Broadview Press, 2000.
Seamus Heaney, *Beowulf: A New Verse Translation*. New York and London:
W. W. Norton & Company, 2000.
[*Arthuriana* 11.3 (2001): 134–37]

These two verse translations, despite their claim in the title, are no longer 'new', but have been critically acclaimed, Liuzza's by fellow Anglo-Saxonists, and Heaney's by a formidable array of prestigious newspapers. Heaney's translation, moreover, has won the Whitbread Award. Consequently there seems to be little to do for this reviewer but to join in the chorus of praise for these two eminently readable verse translations. I shall do so summarily here at the beginning of my review: yes, both translations are reliable, accurate, accessible, fluent, excellent, direct, and sophisticated, to use the adjectives employed by previous critics. This litany of laudatory adjectives is applied to both translations and thus raises the question whether and how they differ from each other. It is this latter question this review attempts to answer.

The cover illustrations provide a first clue to the differences between these two translations. Heaney has chosen the back of the head and the shoulders of a warrior armed in silvery chain mail, while Liuzza opted for a landscape in sepia tones depicting craggy sea cliffs overhung by a few stunted trees. Heaney thus foregrounds the hero, the warrior ethos, the interlinked complexities of reward and revenge, while Liuzza concentrates on the windswept headlands that are home to Grendel, Grendel's mother, *mutatis mutandis* to the dragon, and finally to Beowulf's beacon. Heaney's depiction of the warrior from behind demonstrates that the hero is ultimately unknowable, and the many lines and surfaces of Liuzza's illustration point to the complexities of the poem as a whole. The illustrations suggest that Heaney will take an individualistic approach to the individual Beowulf, while Liuzza will attempt a holistic approach to the entire poem.

Some of the sentiments the two translators express in their introductions bear out this surface impression. Liuzza is careful to take into account all of the latest scholarship on *Beowulf* when he speaks about the poem's manuscript, about the interpretation of the poem, about its position between myth and history, between orality and literacy, and between court and cloister. He digresses—unnecessarily so in a translation—on Old English pronunciation and word order and admits to his translational creed which places fluency and precision before sound-for-sound equivalence. Heaney, though clearly informed of the latest scholarship, describes his personal relationship to the poem. The poem comes to life for him when he discovers words in it which his Dublin forebears had used in living speech. Heaney's own poetry, before *Beowulf*, that is, had been shaped by the rhythms of Gerard Manley Hopkins whom he considers 'a chip off the Old English block' (p. xxiii). Neither vocabulary nor rhythm of *Beowulf* was thus a stranger to him. It is the kinship, however distant, which he felt to the poem's language that made him translate it. His is a personal, not a scholarly, approach to the poem.

The two different approaches imply different audiences: Heaney's translation is addressed more to the general reader for whom the poem will come alive, while Liuzza's concerns itself more with an audience of fellow scholars and graduate students. Liuzza, for instance, is careful to gloss the word 'ealu-scerwen' of line 769: 'The general sense . . . is "panic" or "terror," but its precise meaning . . . is unclear,' and he translates the word as a 'wild ale-sharing,' thus keeping the Old English components of the word and simultaneously communicating its putative meaning. Heaney has no such compunctions; he translates 'a hall-session that harrowed every Dane,' ignoring the semantic process that might have transformed an 'ale-sharing' into 'harrowing.' Heaney, of course, had been asked by Norton to create a translation for their anthology, and thus had the general student in mind, while Liuzza wanted to provide 'an account of [his] sense of [*Beowulf*'s] context and meaning,' and as a scholar he presents to other scholars his understanding of the cruces and multiple interpretations the poem contains.

Both authors use alliteration in their translations. Heaney begins Beowulf's riposte to Unferth with these words:

> Well, friend Unferth, you have had your say
> about Breca and me. But it was mostly beer
> that was doing the talking. The truth is this.

Liuzza translates the same lines thus:

> What a great deal, Unferth my friend,
> drunk with beer, you have said about Breca,
> told his adventures! I will tell the truth.

Neither has any alliteration in the first of these lines; both reproduce the 'b' alliteration of the second line, which rests on the Old English original; and both, by chance, alliterate on 't' in the third line, though the Old English line alliterates on 's.' Liuzza's translation remains closer to the Old English 'beore druncen' with his 'drunk with beer,' while Heaney retains the Old English sense but uses a decidedly modern idiom 'But it was mostly the beer / that was doing the talking.' The two translators clearly differ on the level of language. Liuzza says: 'To mimic the formal diction of the poem I have used a slightly more multisyllabic vocabulary and Latinate syntax at certain points' (p. 48). Heaney has no such ambitions. What attracts him to *Beowulf* is 'a kind of foursquareness about the utterance, a feeling of living inside a constantly indicative mood' (p. xxviii). He feels that the only appropriate modern English equivalent would be the rhythms and the tone of what he calls the 'big voiced Scullions,' who, when they spoke, 'had a kind of Native American solemnity of utterance, as if they were announcing verdicts rather than making small talk' (p. xxvii). Heaney's poetic intuition here seems to come closer to the mark than Liuzza's scholarly sophistication.

All readers of *Beowulf* have their own favourite lines that they find difficult or impossible to translate, and that challenge the translator's ingenuity. One of my favourites occurs early in the poem, when Scyld Scefing 'ofteah' the 'meodosetla' from the neighbouring tribes. Neither Liuzza's 'seized the meadbenches' nor Heaney's 'a wrecker of meadbenches' in my opinion conveys the chutzpah of Scyld who walks into a meadhall and pulls the benches out from under the infuriated, but impotent, enemy warriors. The Old English phrase encapsulates Scyld's superiority as well as his mischievousness while the translations dwell only on his superiority. Grendel, in my opinion, gets worse press by the translators than the poet gave him. In line 748, for instance, the Old English poet calls Grendel a 'feond'—'an enemy.' Heaney at this point makes of him a 'captain of evil' and Liuzza a 'monster,' whereas 'enemy, adversary, opponent' would suffice. And the 'man-scaða' of line 737 is one who causes injury ('sceaðe') on account of his evil ('man' with a long 'a'), so a 'criminal' or 'evil-doer,' but not a 'maneater,' as Liuzza has it, or a 'monster,' as Heaney translates. Poetic licence of course excuses these excessive translations, but in instances such as these the modern reader will imagine a Grendel who is more demonic, bestial, monstrous, and repulsive than the Old English poet paints him. At these points translation shades into interpretation, and does so at the cost of the original.

Translations, however, are not to be read side by side with the original, as I felt I had to do as reviewer, but as independent works in themselves. And once one does that, one gets swept away by the power of Heaney's 'big-voiced Scullions,' and enmeshed in Liuzza's subtle verbal interlace. The two translations clearly address themselves to different audiences, have different tones, and approach their subject matter differently, with Liuzza's being the more scholarly and Heaney's the more poetic version. If it is poetry you want, buy Heaney's translation; if it is scholarship, buy Liuzza's. If you want a wonderful translation of *Beowulf*, buy both.

Jonathan Wilcox

Seamus Heaney, *Beowulf: A New Translation*. London: Faber and Faber, New York: Farrar, Straus & Giroux, 1999. Also in *The Norton Anthology of English Literature*, New York: Norton, 2000. R M Liuzza, *Beowulf: A New Verse Translation*. Peterborough, Ontario: Broadview Press, 2000.
[*Modern Poetry in Translation* n.s. 18 (2001): 259–73]

Seamus Heaney has long displayed sympathy for the language and poetry of Anglo-Saxon times. He strips bare the layers in 'Bone Dreams' in his collection *North* (1975):

> Bone-house:
> a skeleton
> in the tongue's
> old dungeons.
>
> I push back
> through dictions,
> Elizabethan canopies,
> Norman devices,
>
> the erotic mayflowers
> of Provence
> and the ivied latins
> of churchmen
>
> to the scop's
> twang, the iron
> flash of consonants
> cleaving the line.
>
> In the coffered
> riches of grammar
> and declensions
> I found *ban-hus*,
>
> its fire, benches,
> wattle and rafters,
> where the soul
> fluttered a while
>
> in the roofspace.

Here an Old English kenning for the body sparks new life, stirred by Bede's famous sparrow, while the whole collection brims with modern-day kennings, i.e. compound words containing a compressed image, like the *skull-ware* of the Bog Queen, or the *oak-bone*, *brain-firkin* of the garrotted bog woman, or Hercules as the *sky-born*, *snake-choker*, *dung-heaver*. In that collection, Heaney demonstrated how northern mythology and turbulent northern history could resonate with a contemporary landscape of violence. Throughout his poetry, a sparseness of line, a concrete quality, and a love of heavy-consonanted monosyllables ('the iron / flash of consonants / cleaving the line') have made Heaney's poems resonate with Anglo-Saxon poetic technique. In such ways, he has long been borrowing from the Old English tradition; now he returns the favour by translating the most famous of Old English poems, *Beowulf*, and the pay-back is handsome.

Heaney's sureness of touch is evident from the very opening:

> So. The Spear-Danes in days gone by
> and the kings who ruled them had courage and greatness.
> We have heard of those princes' heroic campaigns.
>
> There was Shield Sheafson, scourge of many tribes,
> a wrecker of mead-benches, rampaging among foes.
> This terror of the hall-troops had come far.
> A foundling to start with, he would flourish later on
> as his powers waxed and his worth was proved.
> In the end each clan on the outlying coasts
> beyond the whale-road had to yield to him
> and begin to pay tribute. That was one good king.

Heaney's choice of a four-stress line unified through alliteration and with the hint of a caesura clearly conjures the form of the Old English verse line without holding closely to its stricter conventions. Such a choice is broadly characteristic of many *Beowulf* translations. What is most distinctive here is the freedom Heaney gives himself in tackling Old English syntax, which is so heavily accretive and appositional that it has led many translators to bog down in a mire of grammar words and dangling clauses as they chase the will o' the wisp of closeness to the original.

Take another recently published translation of the poem, this one by R M Liuzza. Liuzza is an academic Anglo-Saxonist with years of teaching *Beowulf* and numerous essays on the poem to his credit. His translation provides a perfect counter-example to Heaney's, even in this opening:

> Listen! We have heard of the glory in bygone days
> of the folk-kings of the spear-Danes,
> how those noble lords did lofty deeds.

> Often Scyld Scefing seized the mead-benches
> from many tribes, troops of enemies,
> struck fear into earls. Though he first was
> found a waif, he awaited solace for that—
> he grew under heaven and prospered in honor
> until every one of the encircling nations
> over the whale's-riding had to obey him,
> grant him tribute. That was a good king!

Liuzza has adopted the same formal constraints as Heaney: a four-stress line, a caesura, and (mild) alliteration. His version is much closer to the Old English, particularly in syntax, but therein lies the problem. In the original, the first three lines read:

> Hwæt! We Gar-Dena   in geardagum
> þeodcyninga   þrym gefrunon,
> hu ða æþelingas   ellen fremedon.

As an inflected language, Old English signals clearly that *þrym*, 'glory', is the object of the opening verb, *gefrunon*, while *þeodcyninga* is a genitive dependent on *þrym*, and *Gar-dena* is either a further dependent noun in apposition or qualifies *þeodcyninga*. Liuzza's translation retains this perfectly, even replicating the mild ambiguity ('glory of the folk-kings from among the spear-Danes' or 'glory of both the folk-kings and the spear-Danes'). Yet the Old English does all this with economy and punch. Liuzza's repeated 'of the' sounds ponderous by comparison, no matter how accurate. His semantic closeness is also a problem: *fremedon* in the third line means *did*, but it probably did not sound as enervated as the modern verb does. And the things we have heard that they did, *þrym* and *ellen*, are reasonably glossed by Liuzza's 'glory' and 'lofty deeds', except that the Old English words packed a far heftier punch with none of the hint of embarrassment that accrues to 'glory' in the world of poetry after Wilfred Owen or the stiffness of 'lofty deeds'.

How, then, might that more forceful effect be conveyed? Heaney uses two words to do the work of *ellen*—'courage and greatness'—which between them give a straightforward and unironized sense of assertiveness. *Þrym* becomes 'heroic campaigns', again more assertive, this time because more specific. The *þeodcyninga* have become 'the kings who ruled them', a more comprehensible relation than the literal 'folk-kings'. Heaney switches round the verbs and alters the syntax, saving the 'we have heard' to act as main verb in a second sentence, thereby staying true to Modern English's imperative to signal relationships with a subject-verb-object word order. Liuzza translates the 14 words of the Old English sentence with 25 words, Heaney with 26, yet Heaney's two sentences and avoidance of a concatenation of grammatical words makes for the more vigorous and economical-sounding translation. Heaney's relative freedom produces something more powerfully compelling and therefore, paradoxically, closer to the effect of the Old English.

The same is true for the treatment of variation in the next lines. Again, Liuzza's version stays very close to the movement of the Old English: 'from many tribes, troops of enemies' reproduces precisely the Old English technique of variation in these lines (*sceapena preatum / monegum mægpum*). Heaney reproduces the effect rather than the specifics, varying a sequence of parallel descriptive epithets which get across the idea of the Old English while remaining natural to a Modern English ear ('scourge of many tribes, a wrecker of mead-benches' was 'rampaging among foes'). Heaney stays close to the content of the lines but not so close to the wording as to falsify the voice of his own verse.

Of course, such choices reflect an age-old conundrum for translators, articulated in English as early as King Alfred (reigned 871–899), who claimed that his translations from Latin proceeded 'hwilum word be worde, hwilum andgit of andgiete', 'sometimes word for word, sometimes sense by sense'. It is surprising to what extent an attempt at word for word translation, i.e. closeness to syntax and to detail, has been the tradition in translations of *Beowulf* for most of the last century. Charles W. Kennedy's translation from 1940, kept alive through its reproduction in the Oxford Anthology of English literature (*Medieval English Literature*, ed. J B Trapp), opens:

> Lo! we have listened to many a lay
> Of the Spear-Danes' fame, their splendor of old,
> Their mighty princes, and martial deeds!

Variation is in full play, encouraged by the single main verb, creating a listing effect that results in anticlimax. Michael Alexander (*Beowulf: A Verse Translation*, Penguin, 1973) begins:

> Attend!
> We have heard of the thriving of the throne of Denmark,
> how the folk-kings flourished in former days,
> how those royal athelings earned that glory,

for a translation that manages to take liberties, use archaisms and overly-close glosses ('folk-kings', 'athelings') and still sound tiresomely grammatical. S A J Bradley's prose translation from 1982, common in Old English courses because of the scope of the volume in which it is published (Everyman's *Anglo-Saxon Poetry* contains almost the whole corpus in translation), opens:

> Listen! We have heard report of the majesty of the people's kings of
> the spear-wielding Danes in days of old: truly, those princes accom-
> plished deeds of courage!

The turgid triple 'of the' phrases, with two more *of*s lurking later in the sentence, introduce immediately the slough of grammatical detail within which this translation will remain enmired.

Such close translations have been standard perhaps because of the apparent closeness of Old English to Modern English, although the differences in syntax and semantic resonance have already been suggested. The result, to my ear, has been a tradition of unreadable or of lame *Beowulf* translations that, for all their closeness to the poem, always fail to capture any of the excitement of the original or hint why it might be interesting to read the Old English version. This is a tradition I am delighted to see bucked in such style by Heaney.

Not that Heaney chooses to make his language entirely and straightforwardly accessible to the average reader. He eschews archaisms that spring from over-close translation, but includes a striking array of unfamiliar words: *bawn* (a fortified enclosure), *brehon* (judge), *bothies* (huts), and *wean* (*wee ane*, a young child) all derive from Celtic originals. Another cluster of unfamiliar words derive from Old English and became obsolete in standard English but survived in dialectal usage, particularly in the north, such as *tholed* (suffered), *graith* (war-gear), *reek* (smoke). Still others are dialect words of obscure origin, such as *stook* (bundle), *keshes* (crags?), and *hoked* (hollowed out). It is striking how many of these words are heavy-consonanted monosyllables ('the iron / flash of consonants / cleaving the line' again). The effect of such vocabulary on most readers, I suspect, is to keep the reader conscious that the work is, indeed, something old and strange. For a particular locality such words are apparently familiar: Heaney talks in his introduction about how his acquaintance with the verb *thole* in the Ulster dialect of his family gave him a point of entry to the language of the Anglo-Saxons (which might otherwise be thought Anglo-Saxon in the more restricted sense of White Anglo-Saxon Protestant). He also talks of how his own writing consciously broke away from seeing a clashing nationalist opposition between Irish and Anglo-Saxon into a more creative synthesis, 'into some unpartitioned linguistic country, a region where one's language would not be simply a badge of ethnicity or a matter of cultural preference or an official imposition, but an entry into further language'. His use of Ulster dialect words in an Anglo-Saxon epic is part of that rapprochement.

The opening word of the poem encapsulates the challenge of translation in miniature. *Hwæt!* is a traditional opening of Old English poems and a conjurer of attention in Old English prose. It is hard to translate because interjections have become so quaint in Modern English as to sound either farcical or maudlin (or both): Lo! Ah! Oh! Indeed! Liuzza's 'Listen!' is probably as close as uncolloquial English comes to the effect. Heaney's 'So' is so much more forceful because it conjures his story-telling voice, suggesting in his Ulster dialect that a story is about to begin so you'd better pay attention and that there'll be consequences in that story—all things implied by Old English *hwæt*. This particular translation choice is also discussed by Heaney in his introduction. He explains that he has adopted for the poem the 'big-voiced' language of his Ulster Catholic family: 'in that idiom "so" operates as an expression that obliterates all previous discourse and narrative, and at the same time functions as an exclamation calling for immediate attention. So, "so" it was.'

So, Heaney has a voice for translating the epic, but how does he do with the story? *Beowulf* is, at core, an account of action, of a hero fighting three monsters— a fact that any interpretation ignores at its peril ever since Tolkien's famous essay from 1936—and Heaney is good with this action. The *Beowulf*-poet gives considerable space to each of the fights, describing them in attentive detail, as when the hero and the audience first view Grendel in action. The scene is translated closely by Liuzza:

> he seized at once at his first pass
> a sleeping man, slit him open suddenly,
> bit into his joints, drank the blood from his veins,
> gobbled his flesh in gobbets, and soon
> had completely devoured that dead man,
> feet and fingertips (740–45a).

This is a heightened moment of terror in the original (nicely and emphatically paced in Benjamin Bagby's oral performance of the poem), with the unusual use of rhyme ('slat unwearnum, / bat banlocan, blod edrum dranc', 741b–742) and that rapacious rhythm is captured by Liuzza's 'gobbled his flesh in gobbets'. Heaney maintains a more measured pace, albeit with an onomatopœically shaved-down penultimate line:

> he grabbed and mauled a man on his bench,
> bit into his bone-lappings, bolted down his blood
> and gorged on him in lumps, leaving the body
> utterly lifeless, eaten up
> hand and foot.

Here the vocabulary is appropriately revolting, with a particularly striking kenning for *banlocan* (glossed by Mitchell and Robinson as 'bone-lock, (i.e. joint)'), namely 'bone-lappings'. The heavily-consonanted monosyllables work to good purpose and join the strong alliteration to replicate the *Beowulf*-poet's *tour de force*. Characteristically, Heaney does not just achieve the occasional good phrase but maintains his effect consistently over the sentence.

Some of the lustre of Heaney's translation comes from his handling of weapons, where the Old English word-hoard was clearly more expansive than what is available to a modern translator. Heaney explicitly begs off close translation of terms for weapons or battles in his introduction, claiming that he cannot match the multitude of words in the poem: 'Old English abounds in vigorous, evocative and specifically poetic words for these things, but I have tended to follow modern usage and in the main have called a sword a sword'. Nevertheless, weapons are given the heft they deserve. Hrunting, the important sword given by Unferth which is not up to the business of Grendel's Mother, is a 'wave-patterned sword, / hard-edged, splendid' in Liuzza's close rendering, but a 'sharp-honed, wave-sheened wonderblade' in Heaney, which gets across the (sharpened) point. In the Finnsburh Episode, Heaney brings to life the word for the sword that at a crucial moment passes from the son of Hunlaf to Hengest, 'hildeleoman / billa selest' (1143b–44a), 'a glinting sword, / the best of battle-flames' in Liuzza's perfectly reasonable translation, '*Dazzle-the-Duel, the best sword of all*' in Heaney's bold reanimation of the kenning as sword name.

In speaking of kennings in his introduction, Heaney remarks 'I try to match the poet's analogy-seeking habit at its most original' and he is predictably good at this throughout. The *fægne flæschoman* of Grendel's Mother (literally 'the doomed flesh-garment') becomes 'the doomed / house of her flesh'. The *banhus* of Heaney's reflections in 'Bone Dreams' is rendered simply as 'bone-house', while *bancofa* (glossed by Mitchell and Robinson as 'bone chamber (i.e. body)') becomes 'the bone-cage of his body'.

But there is more to *Beowulf* than the series of fights undertaken by its hero. For a start, there is a lot more fighting beyond the central action, which helps create the dark tone that pervades most of the poem, a tone often called elegiac. For example, when Beowulf has disposed of Grendel and all would appear happy in Denmark, a poet tells a story at the celebratory feast about an earlier Danish engagement among the Frisians in which nobody looks very glorious. This story, known as the *Finnsburh Episode*, is introduced by the Old English poet through the doomed figure of Hildeburh, wife of the Frisian leader Finn and sister of the Danish visitor Hnæf, who cannot turn out a winner since both her brother and her son have died fighting, but on opposite sides. Heaney's verse becomes heightened here through a depressing spareness of line:

> *Hildeburh*
>> *had little cause*

> *to credit the Jutes:*
>   *son and brother,*
> *she lost them both*
>   *on the battlefield.*
> *She, bereft*
>   *and blameless, they*
> *foredoomed, cut down*
>   *and spear-gored. She,*
> *the woman in shock,*
>   *waylaid by grief,*
> *Hoc's daughter—*
>   *how could she not*
> *lament her fate*
>   *when morning came*
> *and the light broke*
>   *on her murdered dears?* (34–35)

The fractured lines emphasize the lament and pained non-understanding. Heaney's telling of the whole story matches the bleakness of the original.

This elegiac tone becomes particularly prominent in the last third of the poem. Two famous moments play such sadness to the full—the lament of the last survivor of his race who buries the treasure now useless to him that will become the dragon's hoard (2247–66) and the lament of a father for a dead son judicially hanged (2444–62a)—and both are *tours de force* in Heaney's translation. The last survivor laments the absence of the joys of the heroic life:

> 'No trembling harp,
> no tuned timber, no tumbling hawk
> swerving through the hall, no swift horse
> pawing the courtyard. Pillage and slaughter
> have emptied the earth of entire peoples.'

Here, unusually, Heaney makes his emotive point through a series of qualifiers—trembling, tuned, tumbling, swift—and through forceful verbs suggesting action now denied—the swerving of the hawk, the pawing of the horse. The right tone is established for the last survivor's demise ('death's flood / brimmed up in his heart') and a bleakness is associated with that treasure hoard.

Even when things are going well in this poem there is a spirit of doom lurking. *Beowulf*'s most characteristic movement is an insistence on *edwenden*, 'reversal', usually figured as an awareness of impending doom that will undercut even the most celebratory moments of the narrative. So, when Hrothgar is on the rise and has the glorious hall Heorot built, the poet cannot resist inscribing within its building a hint of the hall's impending destruction:

> The hall towered,
> its gables wide and high and awaiting
> a barbarous burning. That doom abided,
> but in time it would come: the killer instinct
> unleashed among in-laws, the blood-lust rampant.

Blood-lust rampant is very much the point: even if the precise details of this encounter are murky (Beowulf predicts a conflict between Hrothgar and his son-in-law Ingeld in his report-back to Hygelac), the moral of the interruption lies in that killer instinct, the blood-lust rampant, an idea the Old English poet can convey with the compounds *ecghete*, '[sword-]edge hatred' and *wælniðe*, 'slaughter-hostility', more literally but less informatively translated in Liuzza's

> The hall towered
> high and horn-gabled—it awaited hostile fires,
> the surges of war; it was not yet long
> before the sword-hate of sworn in-laws
> should arise after ruthless violence. (82–85)

Liuzza's close translation of the temporal markers for the shift in fortunes makes for an awkwardness overcome by Heaney's explicit rearrangement: 'That doom abided, / but in time it would come'.

The Old English poet is fond of expressing this pattern of reversal with an economy that can't be matched in Modern English. Heaney anticipates the ever-present doom, the suggestion that something is rotten in the state of Denmark, with pleasing simplicity in his use of adverbs.

> The Shielding nation
> was not yet familiar with feud and betrayal,

the poet observes, where the word *yet* does plentiful work; or, at a moment of Wealhtheow's exercise of *realpolitik*,

> and Wealhtheow came to sit
> in her gold crown between two good men,
> uncle and nephew, each one of whom
> still trusted the other,

in which that *still* hangs in the air over any accommodation the queen can suggest. Again, in Hrothgar's so-called sermon, Hrothgar holds up his own case as a moral for the young Beowulf, calling attention with that problematic *hwæt*:

> Hwæt, me þæs on eþle   edwenden cwom,
> gyrn æfter gomene (1774–75)

translated emphatically if not quite idiomatically by Liuzza:

> Look! Turnabout came in my own homeland,
> grief after gladness

and more quietly but effectively by Heaney:

> Still, what happened was a hard reversal
> from bliss to grief.

In *Beowulf*, the movement 'from bliss to grief' is very much the point.

While the poem may be doom-ridden in its implications, it is not consistently decorous in its bleak tone. Indeed, the original includes a strand of (mostly dark) humour, that is a challenge for the translator to match. For example, part of the horror of Grendel's ravaging of Heorot is his disregard of the feuding system and the poet grimly jokes on the retainers' inability to receive *wergild*, the appropriate compensation in place of revenge:

> nor did any of the counselors need to expect
> bright compensation from the killer's hands,

as Liuzza suggests, with a note about the *wergild* system. Heaney offers:

> No counsellor could ever expect
> fair reparation from those rabid hands,

where the shift from description of monstrous action to the counsellors' expectation for normalcy hints at the joke without needing a footnote, and where the decorum of *reparation* is clearly incongruous beside the lack of control suggested by *rabid*. Subsequently, as Beowulf makes his defiant speech in front of Hrothgar, he briefly engages the possibility of losing and being carried off by Grendel, an unsettling possibility that he allays through macabre humour nicely retained by Heaney:

> 'Then my face won't be there
> to be covered in death . . .
>   No need then
> to lament for long or lay out my body;'

no need, indeed, since the body won't be there.

> 'Fate goes ever as fate must'

concludes the hero with gnomic pithiness appropriately captured by Heaney and rather ducked by Liuzza's '*Wyrd* always goes as it must!'

Heaney does not rise to all the comic moments, though. In a particularly clear-cut case, when the retainers reach the terrible mere of the Grendels, one of the Geats kills a water-monster with an arrow. The Old English poet provides a laboured joke, captured by Liuzza:

> he was a slower swimmer
> on the waves, when death took him away. (1435–36)

An Old English tradition of understatement allows a listener no doubt what is at stake in such tardiness of motion, yet the literal sense creates a comic incongruity, a joke in keeping with the laboured death of a creature defined in a nearby kenning in relation to his motion as a *wǣgbora* (1440, Liuzza gives 'wave-roamer'). Heaney presumably finds the joke distracting and its underpinnings untranslatable and so gives a straight version:

> his freedom in the water
> got less and less. It was his last swim.

This spells out the point even as it refrains from attempting the tone of the original.

A more serious moment of comedy is also underplayed by Heaney. When Grendel's Mother surprises the Danes with her revenge attack, Beowulf knows nothing of the calamity when he is summoned by a newly-grieving Hrothgar. As he breezes in, his enquiry about how Hrothgar slept is a *faux pas* in the newly-serious circumstances, picked up by a distraught Hrothgar. Beowulf

> asked him whether
> the night had been agreeable, after his urgent summons.
>> Hrothgar spoke, protector of the Scyldings:
> 'Ask not of joys! Sorrow is renewed
> for the Danish people. Æschere is dead' (1318–23)

in Liuzza's translation. The humour depends on realizing the incongruity of *agreeable* beside *urgent summons*, as does the Old English in contrasting *getǣse* with *neodlaðu*, a unique compound presumably coined for the occasion. Heaney makes the exchange more forceful by playing a single word across Beowulf's blunder and Hrothgar's grief. Beowulf enters:

> asking if he'd rested,
> since the urgent summons had come as a surprise.
>
> Then Hrothgar, the Shieldings' helmet, spoke:
> 'Rest? What is rest? Sorrow has returned.
> Alas for the Danes! Æschere is dead.' (44)

As often, Heaney provides more clarity than the original with that explanatory conjunction ('since') and makes explicit the echo across the speeches ('rested' / 'rest'). The effect here is to make Beowulf sound a little more in control than the Old English poet allows him to be. Heaney's statement of the grief of Hrothgar (strikingly named 'the Shieldings' helmet' as in the Old English 'helm Scyldinga') is forceful in its pithiness and in that way matches the original. In other words, Heaney is being as effective as ever here in getting across the poet's main thrust but, since Old and Modern English have different ways, he is forced to sacrifice the comic nuances that the Old English poet can play even in a predominantly serious scene.

The balance within *Beowulf* of a celebratory but elegiac world is matched by the balance with which the poet places his characters in a pagan world viewed from a Christian perspective, an apparent dichotomy about which the poet seems to worry very little. In summing up the fate of Beowulf, the poet observes:

> Famous for his deeds
> a warrior may be, but it remains a mystery
> where his life will end, when he may no longer
> dwell in the mead-hall among his own,

suggesting a pagan viewpoint, which is kept in balance by Wiglaf's anachronistic-sounding memorial that Beowulf will lodge 'for a long time in the care of the Almighty'. Such a balance is retained in the famous final lines, which Heaney renders:

> They said that of all the kings upon the earth
> he was the man most gracious and fair-minded,
> kindest to his people and keenest to win fame,

where public opinion mostly reflects neutral or Christian values (gracious, fair and kind) until that final word, *lofgeornost*, turns back to an economy of heroism where the lasting memorial depends upon the story-telling potential achieved through a life's reputation.

Beowulf himself makes a strong statement of heroic values earlier in the poem. After he has committed his little gaffe in asking about Hrothgar's night's sleep, and after Hrothgar has expressed his sorrow, Beowulf reestablishes verbal control with a strong assertion:

> 'Ne sorga, snotor guma.   Selre bið æghwæm
> þæt he his freond wrece   þonne he fela murne', (1383–4)

which is rendered by Liuzza:

> 'Sorrow not, wise one! It is always better
> to avenge one's friend than to mourn overmuch.'

The Old English here is particularly forceful and concise. Part of the effect is achieved by the parallel yet contrasting verbs in the second line which are balanced through placement and through grammatical rhyme and yet are antithetical in content ('he ... wrece / he ... murne'); part is achieved through the appeal to a gnomic voice expressed through an impersonal generalizing ('selre bið æghwæm') which, nevertheless, keeps an active agent in the following clause ('he ... he')—literally 'Do not sorrow, wise man. It is better for each one that he avenge his friend than that he mourn much'. Heaney gives:

> Wise sir, do not grieve. It is always better
> to avenge dear ones than to indulge in mourning.

where the slight assonance of *avenge/indulge* matches the balanced grammatical rhyme of *wrece/murne*, and where the lexical choice 'dear ones' for 'his freond' avoids the pitfall of a false cognate and extends the generalized wisdom. Still the utterance is not as forceful as in Old English and the impersonal voice does not allow an active agent in the second line. Heancy continues building effects as the speech continues:

> For every one of us, living in this world
> means waiting for our end. Let whoever can
> win glory before death. When a warrior is gone,
> that will be his best and only bulwark.

'Glory before death' has much of the climactic weight of the forcefully straightforward original, 'domes ær deaþe'. On the other hand, 'bulwark' may represent a heavy-consonant too many, suggesting a solidity not apparent in the original.

So, Heaney's translation presents a dazzling success, yet even Heaney's version lacks some of the poetic force and misses some of the tone of the original—inevitably, of course, since Old English and Modern English have different ways.

Heaney's is the best translation available and as such deserves its place in the Norton Anthology. Here is a translation that makes for a coherent and exciting reading in Modern English and that achieves a music of its own. If a reader is tempted to turn from this to the Old English poem itself, Liuzza's volume might serve well as a bridge. Heaney includes a judicious and very readable introduction to the poem (in the Faber volume), but this is inevitably quite brief. Liuzza provides a more extensive if still concise introduction, which will bring a reader up to speed on the major critical issues surrounding the poem. Liuzza also provides a number of useful appendices including, most valuably, a wonderful collection of analogues to the poem, many newly translated. Gathered together here are the remaining Old English heroic fragments, such as *The Fight at Finnsburg* and *Widsith*; the obvious Norse analogues for the major action of the poem, including the parallel monster fight from *Grettissaga*; and a number of Latin and Old English contexts for understanding the balance between Christianity and paganism or Old English attitudes towards Danes, including a generous selection from the leading churchmen of the time of the *Beowulf*-manuscript, Ælfric and Wulfstan. Liuzza's translation, if somewhat heavy-going as an independent work, would serve well as a crib to the original poem. And the serious student of the poem can now approach that original with relative ease in the newly-standard edition by Bruce Mitchell and Fred C. Robinson, *Beowulf: An Edition* (Blackwell, 1998).

Still, while I may hope (as a professional Anglo-Saxonist) that Heaney's translation will bring enthusiasts flocking to read Old English in the original and to discover the rest of the Old English wordhoard, its most important function will be to give readers with no knowledge of Old English a taste of the vitality and complexity and music of the poem *Beowulf*. To do that, it was necessary to create a gripping epic that, while as true as possible to the original, works in the modern language to entertain, to challenge, and to amaze modern readers. Heaney has done that and it is an accomplishment well worthy of the Whitbread Prize. Once again, as is narrated once in the poem:

> a carrier of tales,
> a traditional singer deeply schooled
> in the lore of the past, linked a new theme
> to a strict metre. The man started
> to recite with skill, rehearsing Beowulf's
> triumphs and feats in well-fashioned lines,
> entwining his words.

Bibliography

Translations and Editions of *Beowulf*

Alexander, Michael, trans. *Beowulf: A Verse Translation*. Harmondsworth: Penguin, 1973.

Alfred, William, trans. *Beowulf*. In *Medieval Epics*, edited by William Alfred, W. S. Merwin, and Helen Mustard, pp. 3–83. New York: Modern Library, 1963.

Arnold, Thomas, trans. *Beowulf: A Heroic Poem of the Eighth Century*. London: Longmans, Green, 1876.

Baugh, A. C., trans. *Beowulf*. In *English Literature: A Period Anthology*, edited by Albert Baugh and George McClelland, pp. 18–53. New York: Appleton-Century-Crofts, 1954.

Benedetti, Anna, trans. *La canzone di "Beowulf," poema epico anglosassone del VI secolo: Versione italiana, con introduzione e note*. Palermo: Travi, 1915.

Beowulf. In *Traduzioni dalla poesia anglo-sassone*, edited by Federico Olivero, pp. 73–119. Bari: Laterza, 1915.

Björnsson, Halldóra B., trans. *Bjólfskviða*. Edited by Pétur Knútsson Ridgewell. Reykjavík: Fjölvi, 1983.

Borges, Jorge Luis, and María Kodama. "Fragmento de la Gesta de Beowulf." In *Breve antología anglosajona*, pp. 789–90. 3rd ed. Madrid: Alianza, 1978.

Bradley, S. A. J., trans. *Beowulf*. In *Anglo-Saxon Poetry*, pp. 408–94, edited by S. A. J. Bradley. London: Dent, 1982.

Bravo, Antonio, trans. *Beowulf: Estudio y traducción*. Oviedo: Servicio de Publicaciones de la Universidad de Oviedo, 1981.

———. *Beowulf*. In *Literatura anglosajona y antología bilingüe del antiguo inglés*, pp. 77–110. Oviedo: Servicio de Publicaciones de la Universidad de Oviedo, 1982.

Brown, J. L., trans. *Beowulf*. Campbell, CA: Academy, 1973.

Brunetti, Giuseppe, trans. *Beowulf*. Rome: Carocci, 2003.

Campos Vilanova, Xavier, trans. *Beowulf*. Castelló: Societat Castellonenca de Cultura, 1998.

Cano, María Fernanda, and Óscar Rojas, trans. *Beowulf: La leyenda de las dos criaturas*. Buenos Aires: Ediciones del Eclipse, 1994.

Cañete Álvarez-Torrijos, Ángel, trans. *Beowulf*. Málaga: Servicio de Publicaciones de la Universidad de Málaga, 1991.

Cecioni, Cesare, trans. *Beowulf: Poema eroico anglosassone*. Bologna: Malipiero, 1959.

Čermák, Jan, ed. and trans. *Béowulf*. Prague: Torst, 2003.

Chambers, R. W., trans. *Beowulf with the Finnsburg Fragment*. Cambridge: University Press, 1914.

Chickering, Howell D., ed. and trans. *Beowulf: A Dual-Language Edition*. Garden City, NY: Anchor Books, 1977.

Child, Clarence, trans. *Beowulf and the Finnesburg Fragment*. Boston: Houghton Mifflin, 1904.

Ciuferri, Caterina, and David Murray, trans. *Beowulf e il Frammento di Finnsburh*. Rimini: Il Cerchio, 2000.

Clark Hall, John R., trans. *Beowulf and the Fight at Finnsburg*. London: Swan Sonnenschein, 1901.

———. *Beowulf and the Finnsburg Fragment: A Translation into Modern English Prose*. London: Swan Sonnenschein, 1911. Reprint, London: Allen & Unwin, 1958.

———. *Beowulf: A Metrical Translation into Modern English*. Cambridge: Cambridge University Press, 1914.

Conybeare, J. J., trans. *Illustrations of Anglo-Saxon Poetry*. London: Harding and Lepard, 1826.

Crawford, D. H., trans. *Beowulf*. London: Chatto & Windus, 1926.

Crossley-Holland, Kevin, trans. *Beowulf*. New York: Farrar, Straus and Giroux, 1968.

———. *Beowulf*. London: Macmillan, 1968.

Dobbie, Elliot Van Kirk, ed. *Beowulf and Judith*. Anglo-Saxon Poetic Records 4. New York: Columbia University Press, 1953.

Donaldson, E. Talbot, trans. *Beowulf*. New York: Norton, 1966.

———. *Beowulf: A Prose Translation; Backgrounds and Contexts, Criticism*, edited by Nicholas Howe. New York: Norton, 2002.

Earle, John, trans. *The Deeds of Beowulf*. Oxford: Clarendon Press, 1892.

Fulk, R. D., ed. and trans. *The Beowulf Manuscript: Complete Texts and the Fight at Finnsburg*. Dumbarton Oaks Medieval Library. Cambridge, MA: Harvard University Press, 2010.

Fulk, R. D., Robert E. Bjork, and John D. Niles, eds. *Klaeber's Beowulf and the Fight at Finnsburg*. 4th ed. Toronto Old English Series 21. Toronto: University of Toronto Press, 2008.

García de Diego, Vicente, trans. *Beowulf*. In *Antología de las leyendas de la literatura universal*, pp. 1077–87. Barcelona: Labor, 1953.

Garmonsway, George, and Jacqueline Simpson, trans. *Beowulf and Its Analogues*. London: Dent, 1968.

Garnett, James, trans. *Beowulf*. Boston: Ginn, 1882.

Gerould, Gordon H., trans. *Beowulf and Sir Gawain and the Green Knight*. New York: Ronald, 1929.

Gordon, R. K., trans. *The Song of Beowulf*. London: Dent, 1923.

Green, A. Wigfall, trans. *Beowulf*. Boston: Humphries, 1935.

Greenfield, Stanley B., trans. *A Readable Beowulf*. Carbondale: Southern Illinois University Press, 1982.

Grion, Giusto, trans. "*Beowulf*: Poema epico anglosassone del VII secolo." *Atti della Real Accademia lucchese di scienze, lettere e arti* 22 (1883): 197–379.

Grundtvig, Nicolai F. S., trans. *Bjowulfs drape: Et gothisk helte-digt*. Copenhagen: Seidelin, 1820.

Gummere, Francis B., trans. *The Oldest English Epic: Beowulf*. New York: Macmillan, 1909.

———. *The Oldest English Epic: Beowulf.* New York: Macmillan, 1922.

Haley, Albert, Jr., trans. *Beowulf.* Boston: Branden, 1978.

Hall, John Lesslie, trans. *Beowulf, an Anglo-Saxon Epic Poem.* Boston: D. C. Heath, 1892.

Harrison, James, trans. *Beowulf.* Boston: Ginn, 1883.

Heaney, Seamus, trans. *Beowulf.* London: Faber & Faber, 1999.

———. *Beowulf: A New Verse Translation.* New York: Farrar, Straus and Giroux, 1999.

———. *Beowulf: A New Verse Translation.* New York: Farrar, Straus and Giroux, 2000.

———. *Beowulf.* In *The Norton Anthology of English Literature*, edited by M. H. Abrams et al., pp. 29–99. 7th ed. New York: Norton, 2000.

———. *Beowulf: A Verse Translation; Authoritative Text, Contexts, Criticism*, edited by Daniel Donoghue. New York: Norton, 2002.

Herrera, J. L., and Julio Castro, trans. *Beowulfo.* Madrid: Aguilar, 1965.

Hieatt, Constance B., trans. *Beowulf and Other Old English Poems.* Indianapolis: Odyssey, 1967.

Hudson, Marc, trans. *Beowulf.* Lewisburg, PA: Bucknell University Press, 1990.

Hull, William H., trans. *The Hull Alliterative Beowulf.* Lake Gardens, Calcutta: Lal, 1984.

Huppé, Bernard, trans. *Beowulf.* Binghamton, NY: Medieval and Renaissance Texts & Studies, 1987.

Huyshe, Wentworth, trans. *Beowulf: An Old English Epic.* London: Routledge, 1907.

Jack, George, ed. *Beowulf: A Student Edition.* Oxford: Clarendon Press, 1994.

———. *Beowulf: A Student Edition.* 2nd ed. Oxford: Clarendon Press, 1995.

Kemble, John, ed. *The Anglo-Saxon Poem of Beowulf.* London: Pickering, 1833.

———, trans. *The Anglo-Saxon Poem of Beowulf.* London: Pickering, 1837.

Kennedy, Charles W., trans. *Beowulf: The Oldest English Epic.* New York: Oxford University Press, 1940.

Kennedy, Thomas C., trans. *Beowulf.* Overland Park, KS: Leathers, 2001.

Kiernan, Kevin, ed. *Electronic Beowulf.* 2 CDs. London and Ann Arbor: The British Library and University of Michigan Press, 1999.

Kirtlan, Ernest, trans. *Story of Beowulf.* New York: Crowell, 1913.

Klaeber, Friedrich, ed. *Beowulf and the Fight at Finnsburg.* Lexington, MA: D. C. Heath, 1922.

———. *Beowulf and the Fight at Finnsburg.* 3rd ed. Boston: D. C. Heath, 1950.

Koch, Ludovica, trans. *Beowulf.* Turin: Einaudi, 1987.

Lehman, Ruth, trans. *Beowulf.* Austin: University of Texas Press, 1988.

Leonard, William E., trans. *Beowulf.* New York: Century, 1923.

———. *Beowulf.* Illustrations by Lynd Ward. New York: Heritage, 1939.

Lerate, Luis, trans. *Beowulf y otros poemas épicos antiguo germánicos.* Barcelona: Seix Barral, 1974.

———. *Beowulf y otros poemas anglosajones: Siglos VII–X.* Madrid: Alianza, 1986.

Liuzza, R. M., trans. *Beowulf: A New Verse Translation.* Peterborough, ON: Broadview, 2000.

Lumsden, H. W., trans. *Beowulf: An Old English Poem.* London: Kegan Paul, Trench, 1881.

Magoun, Francis P., Jr., ed. *Béowulf and Judith.* Cambridge, MA: Harvard University Press, 1959.

Manent, Marià, trans. *Beowulf.* In *La poesía inglesa*, pp. 34–39. Barcelona: Janés, 1958.

McLeod, Thomas J., trans. *Beowulf: An Interlinear Translation.* Hillsboro, TX: Medical School of the Southwest Foundation, 1970.

McNamara, John, trans. *Beowulf.* New York: Barnes & Noble Classics, 2005.

Mitchell, Bruce, and Fred C. Robinson, eds. *Beowulf: An Edition with Relevant Shorter Texts.* Oxford: Blackwell, 1998.

Monnet, Camille, trans. *Beowulf.* Turin: Lattes, 1937.

Morgan, Edwin, trans. *Beowulf.* Aldington, Kent: Hand and Flower, 1952.

————. *Beowulf: A Verse Translation into Modern English.* Berkeley and Los Angeles: University of California Press, 1952, 1962, and 1964.

————. *Beowulf: A Verse Translation into Modern English.* Aldington, Kent: Hand and Flower, 1952. Reprint, Manchester: Carcanet, 2002.

Morris, William, and A. J. Wyatt, trans. *The Tale of Beowulf.* London: Longmans, Green, 1895.

————. *The Tale of Beowulf.* London: Longmans, Green, 1910.

Munn, James B., trans. *Beowulf.* In *Ideas and Forms in English and American Literature,* edited by Homer A. Watt and James B. Munn, pp. 11–51. New York: Scott, Foresman, 1925.

O Monstro de Caim. Epopéia 33 (1955): 3–20.

Olivero, Federico, trans. *Beowulf.* Turin: Edizioni dell' "Erma," 1934.

Osborn, Marijane, trans. *Beowulf.* Berkeley and Los Angeles: University of California Press, 1983.

Pearson, Lucien, trans. *Beowulf.* Bloomington: Indiana University Press, 1965.

Porter, John, trans. *Beowulf.* London: Pirate, 1975.

Puhvel, Martin, trans. *Beowulf. A Verse Translation and Introduction.* Lanham, MD: University Press of America, 2006.

Raffel, Burton, trans. *Beowulf.* New York: New American Library, 1963.

Rebsamen, Frederick, trans. *Beowulf: A Verse Translation.* New York: Icon, 1991.

————. *Beowulf Is My Name.* San Francisco: Rinehart, 1971.

Ringler, Dick, trans. *Beowulf: A New Translation for Oral Delivery.* Indianapolis: Hackett, 2007.

Roa Vial, Armando, trans. *Beowulf, el cantar del hierro.* Santiago de Chile and Bogotá: Norma, 2006. Reissued as *Beowulf.* Barcelona: Belacqua, 2007.

Roberts, Gildas, trans. *Beowulf: A New Translation into Modern English Verse.* Saint John's, NL: Breakwater, 1984.

Rodrigues, Louis J., trans. *Beowulf.* London: Runetree, 2002.

Rogers, Bertha, trans. *Beowulf.* Delhi, NY: Birch, 2000.

Sanesi, Roberto, trans. *Poemi anglosassoni, VI–X secolo,* pp. 3–23. 2nd ed. Milan: Guanda, 1975.

Schuhmann, Giuseppe, trans. *"Beovulf,* antichissimo poema epico de' popoli germanici." *Giornale napoletano di filosofia e lettere, scienze morali e politiche* 7 (1882): 25–36, 175–90.

Scott Moncrieff, Charles, trans. *Widsith, Beowulf, Finnsburgh, Waldere, Deor: Done into Common English after the Old Manner.* London: Chapman & Hall, 1921.

Sedgefield, W., ed. *Beowulf.* Manchester: Manchester University Press, 1910.

Strong, Archibald, trans. *Beowulf.* London: Constable, 1925.

Sullivan, Alan, and Timothy Murphy, trans. *Beowulf.* Vol. 1 of *The Longman Anthology of British Literature,* edited by David Damrosch et al. 2nd ed. New York: Longman, 2003.

————. *Beowulf: A Longman Cultural Edition.* Edited by Sarah Anderson. New York: Longman, 2004.

Swanton, Michael, trans. *Beowulf.* Manchester: Manchester University Press, 1978.

————. *Beowulf.* New York: St. Martin's, 1997.

————. *Beowulf: Revised Edition.* Manchester: Manchester University Press, 1997.

Swearer, Randolph, Raymond Oliver, and Marijane Osborn. *Beowulf: A Likeness.* New Haven, CT: Yale University Press, 1990.

Szegő, György, trans., and Katalin Halácsy, ed. *Beowulf.* Budapest: Eötvös Loránd Tudományegyetem Anglisztika Tanszék, 1994.

Teresi, Loredana, ed. *Poesia medievale.* In *Antologia della poesia inglese.* Part 1, *Dalle origini al Romanticismo*, edited by Franco Marucci, pp. 86–103. Rome: Gruppo Editoriale L'Espresso, 2004.

Tharaud, Barry, trans. *Beowulf.* Niwot: University Press of Colorado, 1990.

Thorkelin, Grímur Jónsson. *De Danorum rebus gestis secul. III & IV: Poëma danicum dialecto anglo-saxonico.* Copenhagen: Seidelin, 1815.

Thorpe, Benjamin, trans. *The Anglo-Saxon Poems of Beowulf, The Scop or Gleeman's Tale, and The Fight at Finnesburg.* Oxford: James Wright, 1855.

Tinker, Chauncey, trans. *Beowulf.* New York: Newson, 1902.

Trask, Richard M., trans. *Beowulf and Judith.* Lanham, MD: University Press of America, 1998.

Tuso, Joseph F., ed. *Beowulf: The Donaldson Translation, Backgrounds and Sources, Criticism.* New York: Norton, 1975.

Urrutia Raspall, Antonio, trans. "El poema de Beowulf." In *Leyendas nórdicas*, 3rd ed., pp. 123–61. Barcelona: Ediciones AFHA Internacional, 1974.

Vallvé, Manuel, trans. *Beowulf.* Barcelona: Araluce, 1934.

Vera Pérez, Orestes, trans. *Beowulf.* Madrid: Aguilar, 1962.

Wackerbarth, A. Diedrich, trans. *Beowulf: An Epic Poem.* London: Pickering, 1849.

Waterhouse, Mary E., trans. *Beowulf in Modern English: A Translation in Blank Verse.* Cambridge: Bowes and Bowes, 1949.

Whiting, B. J., trans. *Beowulf.* In *The College Survey of English Literature*, edited by B. J. Whiting et al., pp. 16–50. New York: Harcourt, 1942.

Wrenn, Charles L., ed. *Beowulf with the Finnsburg Fragment.* London: Harrap, 1953.

———. *Beowulf with the Finnsburgh Fragment.* Rev. ed. London: Harrap, 1958.

———. *Beowulf with the Finnesburg Fragment.* 3rd ed. Revised by Whitney F. Bolton. London: Harrap, 1973.

Wrenn, C. L., and W. F. Bolton, eds. *Beowulf with the Finnesburg Fragment.* 5th ed. Exeter: University of Exeter Press, 1996.

Wright, David, trans. *Beowulf.* London: Penguin, 1957.

Wyatt, A. J., ed. *Beowulf.* Cambridge: Cambridge University Press, 1894.

———. *Beowulf: Edited with Textual Footnotes, Index of Proper Names, and Alphabetical Glossary.* Revised by Raymond W. Chambers. Cambridge: Cambridge University Press, 1914.

Secondary Sources

Alexander, Michael J. *The Poetic Achievement of Ezra Pound.* London: Faber and Faber, 1979.

Alexander, Ronelle. "South Slavic Traditions." In Foley, *Teaching Oral Traditions*, pp. 273–79.

Alfano, Christine. "The Issue of Female Monstrosity: A Reevaluation of Grendel's Mother." *Comitatus: A Journal of Medieval and Renaissance Studies* 23 (1993): 1–16.

Alpāmish: Ozbek xalq qahramānlik eposi [Alpāmish: An Uzbek heroic folk epic]. Edited by T. Mirzaer. Translated by M. Abdurakhimov. Tashkent: Fan, 1999.

Amodio, Mark C. *Writing the Oral Tradition: Oral Poetics and Literate Culture in Medieval England.* Notre Dame: University of Notre Dame Press, 2004.

Anderson, Carolyn. "Gæst, Gender, and Kin in *Beowulf*: Consumption of the Boundaries." *Heroic Age* 5 (Summer/Autumn 2001), http://www.mun.ca/mst/heroicage/issues/5/toc.html.

Andrew, S. O. *Syntax and Style in Old English.* Cambridge: Cambridge University Press, 1940.

Azaustre Galiana, Antonio, and Juan Casas Rigall. *Manual de retórica española.* Barcelona: Ariel, 1997.

Basa, Enikő Molnár. *Hungarian Literature.* New York: Griffin House. 1993.

Basari, Enrico. "*Beowulf*: Leggenda cristiana dell'antica Danimarca, cineepopea eroica." *Il Vittorioso* 5 (1941).

Başgöz, İ. "The Epic Tradition among Turkic Peoples." In Oinas, *Heroic Epic and Saga*, pp. 310–35.

Bauman, Richard. *Verbal Art as Performance.* Long Grove, IL: Waveland, 1984.

Beliaev, V. M. *Central Asian Music: Essays in the History of the Music of the Peoples of the U.S.S.R.* Edited and translated by M. and G. Slobin. Middletown, CT: Wesleyan University Press, 1975.

Benjamin, Walter. "The Task of the Translator." Translated by James Hynd and E. M. Valk. *Delos* 2 (1968): 76–99.

Benkő, Loránd, and Imre Samu. *The Hungarian Language.* Budapest: Akadémiai Kiadó, 1972.

Bertau, K. H. "Epenrezitation im deutschen Mittelalter." *Études Germaniques* 20 (1965): 1–17.

Bertone, Giorgio. "Allitterazione." In *Dizionario di linguistica e di filologia, metrica, retorica*, edited by Gian Luigi Beccaria, p. 40. 2nd ed. Turin: Einaudi, 2004.

Bessinger, Jess B., Jr., ed. *A Concordance to the Anglo-Saxon Poetic Records.* Programmed by Philip H. Smith, Jr. Ithaca, NY: Cornell University Press, 1978.

Bjork, Robert E. "Digressions and Episodes." In Bjork and Niles, *Beowulf Handbook*, pp. 193–212.

Bjork, Robert E., and John Niles, eds. *A Beowulf Handbook.* Lincoln: University of Nebraska Press, 1997.

Björnsson, Halldóra B. *Eitt er það land* [There is a land]. Reykjavík: Hlaðbúð, 1955.

———. *Jarðljóð* [Earth poems]. Reykjavík: Helgafell, 1968.

———. *Jörð í álögum: þættir úr byggðum Hvalfjarðar* [Spell-bound earth: Stories from Borgarfjörður]. Reykjavík: Iðunn, 1969.

———. *Ljóð* [Poems]. Reykjavík: Helgafell, 1949.

———, ed. *Pennaslóðir: Ellefu stuttar sögur eftir ellefu höfunda.* [Pen-Trails: Eleven short stories by eleven writers]. Reykjavík: Hlaðbúð, 1959.

———. *Trumban og lútan* [The drum and the lute]. Reykjavík: Menningarsjóður, 1959.

———. *Þyrill vakir.* [Mount Thyrill watches]. Akranes: Hörpuútgáfan, 1986.

———. *Við sanda* [On the sands]. Reykjavík: Helgafell, 1968.

Björnsson, Halldóra B., et al. *Raddir dalsins.* [Voices of the valley]. Edited by Jón Magnússon. Akranes: Hörpuútgáfan, 1993.

Bloomfield, Josephine. "Benevolent Authoritarianism in Klaeber's *Beowulf*: An Editorial Translation of Kingship." *Modern Language Quarterly* 60 (1999): 129–59.

———. "The Bourgeois Family in *Beowulf*: Frederick Klaeber and Sentimental Kinship." *Nineteenth-Century Contexts* 17 (1993): 63–81.

———. "Diminished by Kindness: Frederick Klaeber's Rewriting of Wealhtheow." *Journal of English and Germanic Philology* 93 (1994): 183–203.

Bonjour, Adrien. *The Digressions in "Beowulf."* Oxford: Blackwell. 1950.

———. "Grendel's Dam and the Composition of *Beowulf*." *English Studies* 30 (1949): 113–24.

Booth, Wayne. *A Rhetoric of Irony*. Chicago: University of Chicago Press, 1974.

Børdahl, Vibeke, and Jette Ross. *Chinese Storytellers: Life and Art in the Yangzhou Tradition*. Boston: Cheng & Tsui, 2002.

Borges, Jorge Luis. "Composición escrita en un ejemplar de la 'Gesta de Beowulf.'" In *El otro, el mismo*, p. 139.

———. *El otro, el mismo*. Buenos Aires: Emecé, 1969.

———. "Fragmento." In *El otro, el mismo*, p. 143.

———. *Las Kénningar*. Buenos Aires: Colombo, 1933. Reprinted in *Historia de la Eternidad*. Buenos Aires: Viau y Zona, 1936, pp. 43–68. Translated by Norman Thomas Di Giovanni. "The Kenning." *New Yorker* (26 January 1976), 35–36.

Borges, Jorge Luis, and Delia Igenieros. *Antiguas literaturas germánicas*. 1st ed. Mexico City: Fondo de Cultura Económica, 1951.

Bosworth, Joseph. *An Anglo-Saxon Dictionary Based on the Manuscript Collections of the Late Joseph Bosworth*, edited by T. Northcote Toller. Oxford: Oxford University Press, 1898.

Bowra, C. M. *Heroic Poetry*. London: Macmillan, 1952.

Bradbury, Nancy Mason. "Traditional Referentiality: The Aesthetic Power of Oral Traditional Structures." In Foley, *Teaching Oral Traditions*, pp. 136–45.

Brandl, Alois. "Henry Sweet." *Archiv für das Studium der Neueren Sprache und Literaturen*, n.s., 30 (1913): 8–10.

Bravo, Antonio, and María José Mora. "Anglo-Saxon Studies in Spain." *Old English Newsletter* 29, no. 1 (1995): 23–27.

Brinton, Laurel J. "A Linguistic Approach to Certain Old English Stylistic Devices." *Studia Neophilologica* 59 (1987): 177–85.

Brodeur, Arthur G. *The Art of "Beowulf."* Berkeley and Los Angeles: University of California Press, 1959.

Brooks, Cleanth. "Irony as a Principle of Structure." In *Literary Opinion in America: Essays Illustrating the Status, Methods, and Problems of Criticism in the United States in the Twentieth Century*, edited by Morton Dawen Zabel, 2:729–41. 2nd rev. ed. 2 vols. 1951. Reprint, New York: Harper and Row, 1962.

———. *The Well-Wrought Urn: Studies in the Structure of Poetry*. New York: Harcourt, Brace, 1947.

Brunetti, Giuseppe. "Tradurre Beowulf." In *Tradurre testi medievali: Obiettivi, pubblico, strategie*, edited by Maria G. Cammarota and Maria V. Molinari, pp. 67–72. Bergamo: Bergamo University Press, 2002.

———. "Ritradurre il *Beowulf*." In Dolcetti and Gendre, *Lettura di "Beowulf,"* pp. 205–21.

Buber, Martin, and Franz Rosenzweig. *Scripture and Translation*. Translated by Lawrence Rosenwald. Bloomington: Indiana University Press, 1994.

Bueno, Jorge L. "De Frisia a Fisterra, ou como facer unha tradució aliteratirva á lingua galega do poema épico anglosaxón *Beowulf*." *Viceversa* 11 (2005): 77–93.

Bullough, Donald A. "What Has Ingeld to Do with Lindisfarne?" *Anglo-Saxon England* 22 (1993): 93–125.

Byliny Pechory [The *bylinas* from the [region of the river] Pechora]. Edited by A. A. Gorelov et al. Svod russkogo fol'klora [Collection of Russian folklore]. 2 vols. St. Petersburg: Nauka; Moscow: Izd. Centr "Klassika," 2001.

Bynum, David E. "The Collection and Analysis of Oral Epic Tradition in South Slavic: An Instance." *Oral Tradition* 1 (1986): 302–43.

Cable, Thomas. *The Meter and Melody of "Beowulf."* Illinois Studies in Language and Literature 64. Urbana: University of Illinois Press, 1974.

———. "The Meter and Musical Implications of Old English Poetry." In *The Union of Words and Music in Medieval Poetry*, edited by Rebecca A. Baltzer, Thomas Cable, and James I. Wimsatt, pp. 49–71. Austin: University of Texas Press, 1991.

Campbell, Jackson J. "Adaptation of Classical Rhetoric in Old English Literature." In *Medieval Eloquence: Studies in the Theory and Practice of Medieval Rhetoric*, edited by James J. Murphy, pp. 173–97. Berkeley and Los Angeles: University of California Press, 1978.

Carlson, Signe. "The Monsters of *Beowulf*: Creations of Literary Scholars." *Journal of American Folklore* 80 (1967): 357–64.

Cassidy, Frederic G. "How Free Was the Anglo-Saxon Scop?" In *Franciplegius: Medieval and Linguistic Studies in Honour of Francis Peabody Magoun, Jr.*, edited by Jess B. Bessinger, Jr., and Robert P. Creed, pp. 75–85. London: Allen & Unwin, 1965.

Čermák, Jan. "'A Prow in Foam': The Old English Bahuvrihi Compound as a Poetic Device." *Acta Universitatis Carolinae, Philologica 5, Prague Studies in English* 22 (1997): 13–31.

———. "Vilém Mathesius (1882–1945), the *Ærfæder* of Czech Anglo-Saxon Studies." *Old English Newsletter* 28, no. 1 (1994): B-6–B-8.

Chadwick, H. M., *The Heroic Age*. Cambridge: Cambridge University Press, 1912.

Chadwick, H. M., and N. K. Chadwick. *The Growth of Literature*. 3 vols. Cambridge: Cambridge University Press, 1932–40.

Chadwick, N. K., and V. Zhirmunsky. *Oral Epics of Central Asia*. Cambridge: Cambridge University Press, 1969.

Chailley, Jacques. "Autour de la chanson de geste." *Acta Musicologica* 27 (1955): 1–12.

Chance, Jane. *Woman as Hero in Old English Literature*. Syracuse, NY: University of Syracuse Press, 1986.

Chickering, Howell. "*Beowulf* and 'Heaneywulf.'" *Kenyon Review* 24 (2002): 160–78.

Clark Hall, John R., ed. *A Concise Anglo-Saxon Dictionary*. 3rd ed. Cambridge: University Press, 1931.

Cleasby, Richard, and Gudbrand Vigfússon, eds. *An Icelandic-English Dictionary*. Oxford: Clarendon Press, 1975.

Clemoes, Peter. "Action in *Beowulf* and Our Perception of It." In *Old English Poetry: Essays in Style*, edited by Daniel G. Calder, pp. 147–68. Berkeley and Los Angeles: University of California Press, 1979.

———. *Interactions of Thought and Language in Old English Poetry*. Cambridge Studies in Anglo-Saxon England 12. Cambridge: Cambridge University Press, 1995.

Cohen, Jeffrey Jerome. "Monster Culture (Seven Theses)." In *Monster Theory*, edited by Jeffrey Jerome Cohen, pp. 2–25. Minneapolis: University of Minnesota Press, 1996.

Colgrave, Bertram, and R. A. B. Mynors, eds. and trans. *Bede's Ecclesiastical History of the English People*. Oxford: Clarendon Press, 1969.

Coote, Mary Putney. "Serbo-Croatian Heroic Songs." In Oinas, *Heroic Epic and Saga*, pp. 257–85.

Coupez, A., and T. Kamanzi. *Littérature de Cour au Rwanda*. Oxford: Clarendon Press, 1970.

Creed, Robert. "On the Possibility of Criticising Old English Poetry." *Texas Studies in Literature and Language* 3 (1961): 97–106.

Czigány, Lóránt. *The Oxford History of Hungarian Literature: From the Earliest Times to the Present*. Oxford: Clarendon Press, 1984.

Czigány, Magda. *Hungarian Literature in English Translation Published in Great Britain 1830–1968: A Bibliography.* London: Szepsi Csombor Literary Circle, 1969.

Damico, Helen. *"Beowulf"'s Wealhtheow and the Valkyrie Tradition.* Madison: University of Wisconsin Press, 1984.

Dane, Joseph A. *The Critical Mythology of Irony.* Athens: University of Georgia Press, 1991.

Dante Alighieri. *Divina Commedia.* Ed. Giorgio Petrocchi. *La Commedia secondo l'antica vulgata.* Florence: Le Letterre, 1994.

Dary krásných stromů [Gifts of beautiful trees]. Edited by Mariana Housková, Miloš Komanec, and Jan Čermák. Prague: Modern Language Association, 2001.

DeGregorio, Scott. "Theorizing Irony in *Beowulf*: The Case of Hrothgar." *Exemplaria* 11 (1999): 309–43.

Del Real Montes, Juan Alonso. *Beowulf, el sudor de la guerra.* Alzira: UNED/Centro Francisco Tomás y Valiente, 2002.

Deleuze, Giles, and Félix Guattari. *On the Line.* Translated by John Johnston. New York: Columbia University Semiotext(e), 1983.

———. *A Thousand Plateaus: Capitalism and Schizophrenia.* Translated by Brian Massumi. Minneapolis: University of Minneapolis Press, 1987.

Derrida, Jacques. "Living On: Border Lines." Translated by J. Hulbert. In *Deconstruction and Criticism*, edited by H. Bloom, pp. 75–176. New York: Seabury, 1979.

DeWeese, Devin. *Islamization and Native Religion in the Golden Horde: Baba Tükles and Conversion to Islam in Historical and Epic Tradition.* University Park: Pennsylvania State University Press, 1994.

Di Sciacca, Claudia. "Sweorcan: Una nota ai vv. 1737–1802a del *Beowulf* e alle relative traduzioni italiane." In Dolcetti and Gendre, *Lettura di "Beowulf,"* pp. 291–329.

Dictionary of Old English. Published for the Dictionary of Old English Project, Centre for Medieval Studies, University of Toronto. Toronto: Pontifical Institute of Mediaeval Studies, 1986–.

Dmitriev, P. N., et al., eds. and trans. *Yakutskiy geroicheskiy èpos "Kyys Dèbiliyè"* [The Yakut heroic epic *Qïïs Debiliye*]. Novosibirsk: Nauka, 1993.

Doane, A. N. "Oral Texts, Intertexts, and Intratexts: Editing Old English." In *Influence and Intertextuality in Literary History*, edited by Jay Clayton and Eric Rothstein, pp. 75–113. Madison: University of Wisconsin Press, 1991.

———. "Performance as a Constitutive Category in the Editing of Anglo-Saxon Poetic Texts." *Oral Tradition* 9 (1994): 420–39.

Dobrovol'skij, B. M., and V. V. Korguzalov, eds. *Byliny: Russkiy muzykal'nyi èpos* [Bylina: The Russian musical epic]. Moscow: Sovetskiy Kompozitor, 1981.

Dolcetti Corazza, Vittoria, and Renato Gendre, eds. *Lettura di "Beowulf": Atti del V Seminario di Filologia Germanica.* Alessandria: dell'Orso, 2005.

Domínguez Caparrós, José. *Métrica española.* Madrid: Síntesis, 2000.

Duch můj byl živ [Hæfde ferð cwicu]. Edited by Jan Čermák. Prague: Modern Language Association, 1999.

Dyushaliev, K. *Pesennaya kul'tura kyrgyzskogo naroda* [The song tradition of the Kirghiz people]. Bishkek: Institut literaturovedeniya i isskustvovedeniya AN Respubliki Kyrgyzstan, 1993.

Eagleton, Terry. "Hasped and Hooped and Hirpling." *London Review of Books* 21, no. 22 (11 November 1999): 15–16.

Egilsson, Sveinbjörn. *Lexicon poëticum antiquae septentrionalis*. Copenhagen: Kongelige Nordiske oldskrift selskab, 1860.

Einars, Sigríður, et al. "Minning: Halldóra B. Björnsson skáldkona" [A remembrance: Halldóra B. Björnsson, poetess, by Sigríður Einars frá Munaðarnesi, Þorsteinn frá Hamri, and María Þorsteinsdóttir]. *Þjóðviljinn* 4, no. 10 (1968): 4.

Einarsson, Stefán. "Wídsíð = Víðförull." *Skírnir* 110 (1936): 164–90.

Eliot, T. S. *The Sacred Wood: Essays on Poetry and Criticism*. London: Methuen, 1948.

Fish, Stanley. "Short People Got No Reason to Live: Reading Irony." *Daedalus* 112 (1983): 175–91.

Fjalldal, Magnús. *The Long Arm of Coincidence: The Frustrated Connection between "Beowulf" and "Grettis saga."* Toronto: University of Toronto Press, 1998.

Foley, John Miles. *Homer's Traditional Art*. University Park: Pennsylvania State University Press, 1999.

———. *How to Read an Oral Poem*. Urbana: University of Illinois Press, 2002. With e-companion available at http://www.oraltradition.org/hrop.

———. *Immanent Art: From Structure to Meaning in Traditional Oral Epic*. Bloomington: Indiana University Press, 1991.

———. *Oral-Formulaic Theory and Research: An Introduction and Annotated Bibliography*. New York: Garland, 1985.

———. *The Singer of Tales in Performance*. Bloomington: Indiana University Press, 1995.

———. "Texts That Speak to Readers That Hear." In *Speaking Two Languages: Traditional Disciplines and Contemporary Theory in Medieval Studies*, edited by Allen Frantzen, pp. 141–56. Albany: State University of New York Press, 1991.

———. "Textualization as Mediation: The Case of Traditional Oral Epic." In *Voice, Text, and Hypertext: Emerging Practices in Textual Studies*, edited by Raimonda Modiano, Leroy Searle, and Peter Shillingsburg, pp. 101–20. Seattle: University of Washington Press, 2004.

———. *Traditional Oral Epic: The "Odyssey," "Beowulf," and the Serbo-Croatian Return Song*. 1990. Reprint, Berkeley and Los Angeles: University of California Press, 1993.

———, ed. *Teaching Oral Traditions*. 1998. Reprint, New York: Modern Language Association, 2002.

———, ed. and trans. *The Wedding of Mustajbey's Son Bećirbey as Performed by Halil Bajgorić*. Folklore Fellows Communications, 283. Helsinki: Academia Scientiarum Fennica, 2004. With eEdition available at http://www.oraltradition.org/zbm.

Foster, H. Wakefield. "The Role of Music." In Foley, *Wedding*, pp. 223–60.

Foucault, Michel. "What Is an Author?" In *The Foucault Reader*, edited by Paul Rabinow, pp. 101–20. New York: Pantheon Books, 1984.

Frantzen, Allen J. *Desire for Origins: New Language, Old English, and Teaching the Tradition*. New Brunswick, NJ: Rutgers University Press, 1990.

Fry, Donald K. *"Beowulf" and "The Fight at Finnsburh": A Bibliography*. Charlottesville: University Press of Virginia, 1969.

Galván, Fernando. "Rewriting Anglo-Saxon." *Journal of the Spanish Society for Medieval English Language and Literature* 2 (1992): 70–90.

Gardner, Thomas. "The Application of the Term 'Kenning.'" *Neophilologus* 56 (1972): 464–68.

———. "The OE Kenning: A Characteristic Feature of Germanic Poetical Diction?" *Modern Philology* 67 (1969–70): 109–17.

Garnett, George. "Conquered England, 1066–1215." In *The Oxford Illustrated History of Medieval England*, edited by Nigel Saul, pp. 61–101. Oxford: Oxford University Press, 1997.

Gendre, Renato. "Coppie di opposti nel *Beowulf*: I. 'Bene' e 'male.'" In Dolcetti and Gendre, *Lettura di "Beowulf,"* pp. 29–126.

———. "Tradurre e altro." In *Traduzione: Dalla letteratura alla macchina*, edited by Sergio Zoppi, pp. 11–24. Rome: Bulzoni, 1996.

Gennrich, Friedrich. *Der musikalische Vortrag der altfranzösischen Chansons de geste: Eine literarhistorisch-musikwissenschaftliche Studie*. Halle: Niemeyer, 1923.

Gillam, Doreen. "The Use of the Term 'æglæca' in *Beowulf* at Lines 813 and 2592." *Studia Germanica Gandensia* 3 (1961): 145–69.

Glatzer, Nahum N. *Franz Rosenzweig: His Life and Thought*. New York: Schocken, 1953.

Goethe, Johann Wolfgang von. "Überseztungen." In Goethe, *West-östlicher Divan*. Vol. 2 of *Werke* (Berlin: Grote, 1819). Translated as "Translations." In Schulte and Biguenet, *Theories of Translation*, pp. 60–62.

Goldsmith, Margaret E. "The Christian Perspective in *Beowulf*." *Comparative Literature* 14 (1962): 71–80. Reprinted in Nicholson, *An Anthology of "Beowulf" Criticism*, pp. 373–86.

Gould, David. "*Beowulf*: A Formulaic Translation with a Critical Introduction." PhD diss., University of Connecticut, 1993.

Grebnev, L. V. *Tuvinskij geroicheskij èpos* [The Tuvan heroic epic]. Moscow: Izd. Vostochnoj literatury, 1960.

Greenfield, Stanley B., and Fred C. Robinson. *A Bibliography of Publications on Old English Literature to the End of 1972*. Manchester and Toronto: Manchester University Press and University of Toronto Press, 1980.

Gull-Þóris saga. Edited by Grímur M. Helgason and Vésteinn Ólason. Íslenzkar fornsögur 3. Akranes: Skuggsjá, 1969.

Hatto, A. T., ed. and trans. *The Memorial Feast for Kökötöy-Khan (Kökötöydün aši): A Kirghiz Epic Poem*. London Oriental Series 33. London: Oxford University Press, 1977.

Heaney, Seamus. "The Drag of the Golden Chain." *Times Literary Supplement*, 12 November, 1999, 14–16.

———. "The Impact of Translation." In *The Government of the Tongue: Selected Prose*, pp. 36–44. New York: Farrar, Straus and Giroux, 1988.

———. "The Irish Poet and Britain." In *Finders Keepers: Selected Prose*, pp. 396–415. New York: Farrar, Straus and Giroux, 2002.

———. "Translator's Introduction." In Donoghue, *Beowulf: A Verse Translation*, xxiii–xxxviii.

———. "Ugolino." In *Opened Ground: Selected Poems, 1966–1996*. New York: Farrar, Straus and Giroux, 1998.

Heinemann, Fredrik J. "*Beowulf* 665b–738: A Mock Approach-to-Battle Type Scene." In *Perspectives on Language in Performance: To Honor Werner Hüllen on the Occasion of His 60th Birthday*, edited by W. Lörscher and R. Schulze, pp. 677–94. Tübingen Beiträge zur Linguistik 317. Tübingen: Narr, 1987.

Henderson, Eugénie J. A. *The Indispensable Foundation: A Selection from the Writings of Henry Sweet*. London: Oxford University Press, 1971.

Heusler, Andreas. "Heusler über Meißner, Die Kenningar der Skalden." *Anzeiger für deutsches Altertum und deutsche Literatur* 41 (1922): 127–34.

Hill, Geoffrey. *Somewhere Is Such a Kingdom: Poems, 1952–71*. Introduction by Harold Bloom. Boston: Houghton Mifflin, 1975.

Hill, John M. *The Cultural World in "Beowulf."* Toronto: University of Toronto Press, 1995.
———. "Hrothgar's Noble Rule: Love and the Great Legislator." In *Social Approaches to Viking Studies*, edited by Ross Samson, pp. 161–78. Glasgow: Cruithne, 1991.
———. "Translating Social Speech and Gesture in *Beowulf.*" In Ramsey, *"Beowulf" in Our Time*, pp. 67–79.
Hirsch, E. D. *Validity in Interpretation.* New Haven, CT: Yale University Press, 1967.
Hofmann, D. "Die Frage des musikalischen Vortrags der altgermanischen Stabreimdichtung in philologischer Sicht." *Zeitschrift für deutsches Altertum* 92 (1963): 83–121.
Hofmann, D., and E. Jammers. "Zur Frage des Vortrags der altgermanischen Stabreimdichtung." *Zeitschrift für deutsches Altertum* 94 (1965): 185–95.
Hoppin, Richard H. *Medieval Music.* New York: Norton, 1978.
Household Words: A Weekly Journal, 1850–1859; Conducted by Charles Dickens. Compiled by Anne Lohrli. Toronto: University of Toronto Press, 1973.
Howe, Nicholas. "*Beowulf* in the House of Dickens." In *Latin Learning and English Lore: Studies in Anglo-Saxon Literature for Michael Lapidge*, edited by Katherine O'Brien O'Keeffe, and Andy Orchard, pp. 421–39. Toronto: University of Toronto Press, 2005.
———. "Praise and Lament: The Afterlife of Anglo-Saxon Poetry in Auden, Hill and Gunn." In *Words and Works: Studies in Medieval English Language and Literature in Honour of Fred C. Robinson*, edited by Peter S. Baker and Nicholas Howe, pp. 293–310. Toronto: University of Toronto Press, 1998.
———. "Scullionspeak: On Seamus Heaney's *Beowulf.*" *New Republic*, 28 February 2000, 32–37.
Hu, Djen Hua, and R. Dor. "*Manas* chez les Kirghiz du Xinjiang: Bref Aperçu." *Turcica: Revue d'Études Turques* 16 (1984): 29–50.
Huffines, Marion Lois. "OE *āglǣce*: Magic and Moral Decline of Monsters and Men." *Semasia: Beitrage zur germanisch-romanischen Sprachforschung* 1 (1974): 71–82.
Hutcheon, Linda. *Irony's Edge: The Theory and Politics of Irony.* New York: Routledge, 1995.
Index Translationum. http://www.unesco.org/culture/xtrans/.
Irving, Edward B., Jr. *Rereading "Beowulf."* Philadelphia: University of Pennsylvania Press, 1989 [1992].
———. "What to Do with Old Kings." In *Comparative Research on Oral Traditions: A Memorial for Milman Parry*, edited by John Miles Foley, pp. 259–68. Columbus: Slavica, 1987.
István, Király, et al., eds. *Világirodalmi lexikon* [Encyclopedia of world literature]. 3rd ed. Budapest: Akadémiai Kiadó, 1992.
Jammers, E. "Das mittelalterliche deutsche Epos und die Musik." *Heidelberger Jahrbücher* 1 (1957): 31–90.
Jantzen, H. Review of Sweet's *First Steps in Anglo-Saxon. Englische Studien* 26 (1899): 60–62.
John of Salisbury. *The Metalogicon of John of Salisbury: A Twelfth-Century Defense of the Verbal and Logical Arts of the Trivium.* Translated by Daniel D. McGarry. Gloucester, MA: P. Smith, 1971.
Jonson, Ben. *Timber; or, Discoveries.* Ed. Ralph S. Walker. Syracuse, NY: Syracuse University Press, 1953.
Kalevala. Translated by Josef Holeček. 2nd ed. Prague: SNKLHU, 1953.
The Kalevala Heritage. CD. Helsinki: Ondine, 1995. ODE 849-2.

Karāmatli, Fayzulla M. "O muzyke uzbekskikh dastanov i osobennostyakh eë proyavleniya v 'Alpamyshe'" [On the music of Uzbek epics and its characteristic traits as found in "Alpamysh"]. In *Alpāmish*, pp. 50–63, musical illustrations after p. 816.

Kartschoke, D. *Bibeldichtung: Studien zur Geschichte der epischen Bibelparaphrase von Juvencus bis Otfrid von Weißenburg*. Munich: Fink, 1975.

Kaske, Robert E. "*Sapientia et Fortitudo* as the Controlling Theme in *Beowulf*." *Studies in Philology* 55 (1958): 423–56. Reprinted in Nicholson, *An Anthology of "Beowulf" Criticism*, pp. 269–310.

Kavros, Harry E. "The Feast-Sleep Theme in *Beowulf*." *Neophilologus* 65 (1981): 120–28.

Kay, Matthew. *The Index of the Milman Parry Collection, 1933–35: Heroic Songs, Conversations, and Stories*. New York: Garland, 1995.

Kecskés, András, and Andrew Kerek. "Directions in Hungarian Metric Research." In *Linguistic and Literary Studies in Eastern Europe, Language, Literature and Meaning II: Current Trends in Literary Research*, edited by John Odmark, pp. 319–59. Amsterdam: Benjamins, 1980.

Keenoy, Ray. *The Babel Guide to Hungarian Literature in English Translation*. Oxford: Boulevard, 2001.

Kendon, Adam. "Gesture." In *Folklore, Cultural Performances, and Popular Entertainments: A Communications-Centered Handbook*, edited by Richard Bauman, pp. 179–90. New York: Oxford University Press, 1992.

Ker, W. P. *The Dark Ages*. London: Blackwood, 1904.

Kiernan, Kevin. "Grendel's Heroic Mother." *In Geardagum: Essays on Old and Middle English Language and Literature* 6 (1984): 13–33.

Klaeber, Friedrich. Review of Sweet's *First Steps in Anglo-Saxon*. *Modern Language Notes* 13 (1898): 93–94.

Klaniczay, Tibor, ed. *A History of Hungarian Literature*. Budapest: Corvina, 1983.

Klasszikus angol költők a középkortól a XX. századig [Classics of English poetry from the Middle Ages to the twentieth century]. Budapest: Európa Könyvkiadó, 1986.

Knútsson, Pétur. "Intertextual Quanta in Formula and Translation." *Language and Literature* 4, no. 2 (1995): 102–25.

———. "Intimations of the Third Text: An Enquiry into Translation and Tertiary Textuality." PhD diss., Copenhagen, 2004.

———. "Learned and Popular Etymology: Prescription vs. Intertextual Paronomasia." *Íslenskt mál* 15 (1993): 99–120.

Kondrat'eva, S. N. *Karel'skaya narodnaya pesnya* [Karelian folk song]. Moscow: Sovetskiy Kompozitor, 1977.

Körting, Gustav. *Grundriss der Geschichte der englischen Literatur von ihren Anfängen bis zur Gegenwart*. Münster: [n.p.], 1887.

Kovács, Sándor Iván. *Szenczi Molnár Redivivus*. Budapest: Ister, 2000.

Kuhn, Sherman. "Old English *aglǣca*—Middle Irish *oclach*." In *Linguistic Method: Essays in Honor of Herbert Penzl*, edited by Irmengard Rauch and Gerald F. Carr, pp. 213–30. Mouton: The Hague, 1979.

Lanham, Richard. *A Handlist of Rhetorical Terms*. Berkeley and Los Angeles: University of California Press, 1991.

Lapidge, Michael. "The Archetype of *Beowulf*." *Anglo-Saxon England* 29 (2000): 5–41.

Lattimore, Richmond, trans. *The Iliad of Homer*. Chicago: University of Chicago Press, 1951.

————. *The Stride of Time: New Poems and Translations.* Ann Arbor: University of Michigan Press, 1966.

Leicester, H. Marshall, Jr. "The Art of Impersonation: A General Prologue to the *Canterbury Tales,*" *PMLA* 95 (1980): 213–24.

Lewis, Richard W. "*Beowulf* 992a: Ironic Use of the Formulaic." *Philological Quarterly* 61 (1975): 663–64.

Leyerle, John. "The Interlace Structure of *Beowulf.*" *University of Toronto Quarterly* 37 (1967): 1–17. Reprinted in *Interpretations of "Beowulf": A Critical Anthology,* edited by R. D. Fulk, 145–67. Bloomington: University of Indiana Press, 1991.

Liggens, Elizabeth. "Irony and Understatement in *Beowulf.*" *Parergon* 29 (1981): 3–7.

Liuzza, R. M. "*Beowulf* in Translation: Problems and Possibilities." In Ramsey, *"Beowulf" in Our Time,* pp. 23–40.

————. "Lost in Translation: Some Versions of *Beowulf* in the Nineteenth Century." *English Studies* 83 (2002): 281–95.

Lock, Charles. "Double Voicing, Sharing Words: Bakhtin's Dialogism and the History of the Theory of Free Indirect Discourse." In *The Novelness of Bakhtin,* edited by Jörgen Bruhn and Jan Lundquist, pp. 71–87. Copenhagen: Museum Tusculanum Press, 2001.

Lord, A. B. *The Singer of Tales.* 2nd ed. Cambridge, MA: Harvard University Press, 2000.

Lotman, Yuri. *Universe of the Mind.* Translated by Ann Shukman. London: Tauris, 2001.

Lye, Edward. *Dictionarium saxonico et gothico-latinum.* Edited by Owen Manning. London: B. White, 1772.

MacMahon, Michael K. C. "Henry Sweet." In *Medieval Scholarship: Biographical Studies on the Formation of a Discipline.* Vol. 2, *Literature and Philology,* edited by Helen Damico, Donald Fennema, and Karmen Lenz, pp. 167–75. New York: Garland, 1998.

Madariaga, Salvador de. *Ensayos Anglo-Españoles.* Madrid: Atenea, 1922.

Magnússon, Ásgeir Blöndal. *Íslensk orðsifjabók.* [Icelandic etymological dictionary]. Reykjavík: Orðabók Háskólans, 1989.

Magoun, Francis P., Jr. "Béowulf in Denmark: An Italo-Brazilian Variant." In *Mélanges de Linguistique et Philologie: Fernand Mossé in Memoriam,* pp. 247–55. Paris: Didier, 1959.

————. "The Oral-Formulaic Character of Anglo-Saxon Poetry." *Speculum* 28 (1953): 446–67.

————. "The Theme of the Beasts of Battle in Anglo-Saxon Poetry." *Neuphilologische Mitteilungen* 56 (1955): 81–90.

Makkai, Adam, ed. *In Quest of the "Miracle Stag": The Poetry of Hungary; An Anthology of Hungarian Poetry from the Thirteenth Century to the Present in English Translation.* Chicago: Atlantis-Centaur; Budapest: Szivárvány and Corvina, 1996.

Maksetov, K. M., ed. *Ocherki po istorii karakalpakskogo fol'klora* [Essays on the history of Karakalpak folklore]. Tashkent: Fan, 1977.

Mamay, Jüsüp. *Manas.* Edited by A. Matïlï et al. 2 vols. Ürümchi: Shinjang el basmasï, 1984.

Marquardt, Hertha. *Die ae Kenningar: Ein Beitrag zur Stilkunde altgermanischer Dichtung.* Halle: Niemeyer, 1938.

Mathesius, Vilém. *Dějiny literatury anglické, Část první: Doba anglosaská* [A history of English literature, Part 1: The Anglo-Saxon period]. Prague: [n.p.], 1910.

Meißner, Rudolf. *Die Kenningar der Skalden: Ein Beitrag zur skaldischen Poetik.* Bonn: Schroeder, 1921.

Menzer, Melinda J. "*Aglæcwif* (*Beowulf* 1259a): Implications for -wif Compounds, Grendel's Mother, and Other *Aglæcan.*" *English Language Notes* 34, no.1 (1996): 1–6.

Mitchell, Bruce. "'Apo koinou' in Old English Poetry?" *Neuphilologische Mitteilungen* 100 (1999): 477–97.

———. *Old English Syntax.* 2 vols. Oxford: Clarendon Press, 1985.

Mitchell, Bruce, and Susan Irvine. *"Beowulf" Repunctuated*, Old English Newsletter, Subsidia 29. Kalamazoo: Western Michigan University, 2000.

Mitchell, Bruce, and Fred C. Robinson. *A Guide to Old English.* 6th ed. Oxford: Blackwell: 2001.

Morris, William. *The Collected Works of William Morris.* 24 vols. London: Longman, Green, 1910–15.

Mourek, Václav E. *Přehled dějin literatury anglické* [A Survey of the history of English literature]. Prague: Otto, 1890.

Muecke, D. C. *The Compass of Irony.* London: Methuen, 1969.

Navarro Tomás, Tomás. *Métrica española.* Barcelona: Labor, 1991.

A New Latin Dictionary. Revised by Charlton Lewis and Charles Short. New York: American Book Company, 1907.

Nicholson, Lewis, ed. *An Anthology of "Beowulf" Criticism.* Notre Dame: University of Notre Dame Press, 1963.

Nida, Eugene A. "Translation." *Current Trends in Linguistics* 12 (1974): 1045–68.

Nida, Eugene A., and Charles Taber. *The Theory and Practice of Translation.* 1969. Reprint, Leiden: Brill, 1974.

Niles, John D. "Rewriting *Beowulf:* The Task of Translation." *College English* 55 (1993): 858–78.

Norris, Robin. "From Beowulf to 'Heaneywulf': Bookending the British Literature Survey." In *The Future of the Past: Anglo-Saxon Studies in the Classroom*, edited by Glenn Davis and Robin Norris [= *Studies in Medieval and Renaissance Teaching* 14, no. 2 (2007): 57–69].

O'Brien O'Keeffe, Katherine. "*Beowulf*, Lines 702b–836: Transformations and the Limits of the Human." *Texas Studies in Literature and Language* 23 (1981): 484–94.

———. *Visible Song: Transitional Literacy in Old English Verse.* Cambridge: Cambridge University Press, 1990.

Oinas, F. J., ed. *Heroic Epic and Saga: An Introduction to the World's Great Folk Epics.* Bloomington: Indiana University Press, 1978.

Olsen, Alexandra Hennessey. "The *Aglæca* and the Law." *American Notes & Queries* 20, no. 5–6 (1982): 66–68.

———. "Oral-Formulaic Research in Old English Studies." *Oral Tradition* 1 (1986): 548–606 and 3 (1988): 138–90.

Ong, Walter. *Orality and Literacy: The Technologizing of the Word.* London: Methuen, 1982.

Opland, Jeff. *Anglo-Saxon Oral Poetry: A Study of the Traditions.* New Haven, CT: Yale University Press, 1980.

Orchard, Andy. *A Critical Companion to "Beowulf."* Rochester, NY: Brewer, 2003.

———. "Oral Tradition." In *Reading Old English Texts*, edited by Katherine O'Brien O'Keeffe, pp. 101–23. Cambridge: Cambridge University Press, 1997.

———. *Pride and Prodigies: Studies in the Monsters of the "Beowulf"-Manuscript.* Toronto: University of Toronto Press, 1995.

Osborn, Marijane. "Annotated List of Beowulf Translations." ACMRS Online Resources Annotated Beowulf Bibliography, http://www.asu. du/clas/acmrs/web_pages/online _resources/online_resources_ annotated _beowulf_bib.html.

———. "Foreign Studies of *Beowulf*: A Critical Survey of Beowulf Scholarship outside English-Speaking Countries and Germany, with Bibliographies." PhD. diss., Stanford University, 1968.

———. "Translations, Versions, Illustrations." In Bjork and Niles, *Beowulf Handbook*, pp. 341–72.

Overing, Gillian R. *Language, Sign and Gender in "Beowulf."* Carbondale: Southern Illinois University Press, 1990.

Pecchio, Giuseppe. *Storia critica della poesia inglese.* 4 vols. Lugano: Ruggia, 1833–35.

Pound, Ezra. *Translations.* With an introduction by Hugh Kenner. New York: New Directions, 1963.

Psalterium Ungaricum. Herborn: [n.p.], 1607.

Quilis, Antonio. *Métrica española.* 6th ed. Barcelona: Ariel, 1991.

Radloff, Wilhelm, ed. and trans. *Proben der Volkslitteratur der nördlichen türkischen Stämme,* Vol. 5, *Der Dialect der Kara-Kirgisen.* St. Petersburg: Kaiserliche Akademie, 1885.

Ramsey, Mary K., ed. *"Beowulf" in Our Time: Teaching "Beowulf" in Translation.* Old English Newsletter, Subsidia 31. Kalamazoo: Western Michigan University, 2002.

Reichl, Karl, ed. and trans. *Edige: A Karakalpak Heroic Epic as Performed by Jumabay Bazarov.* FF Communications 293. Helsinki: Academia Scientiarum Fennica, 2007.

———. "The Mixture of Verse and Prose in Turkic Oral Epic Poetry." In *Prosimetrum: Crosscultural Perspectives on Narrative in Prose and Verse,* edited by Joseph Harris and Karl Reichl, pp. 321–48. Cambridge: Brewer, 1997.

———, ed. *The Oral Epic: Performance and Music.* Intercultural Music Studies 12. Berlin: Verlag für Wissenschaft und Bildung, 2000.

———. "Oral Tradition and Performance of the Uzbek and Karakalpak Epic Singers." In *Fragen der mongolischen Heldendichtung. III,* edited by Walther Heissig, pp. 613–43. Asiatische Forschungen 91. Wiesbaden: Harrassowitz, 1985.

———. "The Performance of the Karakalpak *Zhyrau*." In Reichl, *Oral Epic,* pp. 129–50.

———. *Singing the Past: Turkic and Medieval Heroic Poetry.* Ithaca, NY: Cornell University Press, 2000.

———. *Turkic Oral Epic Poetry: Traditions, Forms, Poetic Structure.* New York: Garland, 1992.

———. *Das usbekische Heldenepos Alpomish: Einführung, Text, Übersetzung.* Turcologica 48. Wiesbaden: Harrassowitz, 2001.

———. "Uzbek Epic Poetry: Tradition and Poetic Diction." In *Traditions of Heroic Epic Poetry.* Vol. 2, *Characteristics and Techniques,* edited by J. B. Hainsworth and A. T. Hatto, pp. 94–120. London: Modern Humanities Association, 1989.

Renoir, Alain. *A Key to Old Poems: The Oral-Formulaic Approach to the Interpretation of West-Germanic Verse.* University Park: Pennsylvania State University Press, 1988.

———. "Point of View and Design for Terror in *Beowulf*." *Neuphilologische Mitteilungen* 63 (1962): 154–67.

Review of Sweet's *First Steps in Anglo-Saxon. Athenaeum* (1897): 670.

Ringler, Richard. *"Him sēo wēn gelēah*: The Design for Irony in Grendel's Last Visit to Heorot." *Speculum* 41 (1966): 49–67.

Roberts, Jane. "Hrothgar's Admirable Courage." In *Unlocking the Wordhord: Anglo-Saxon Studies in Memory of Edward B. Irving, Jr.,* edited by Mark C. Amodio and Katherine O'Brien O'Keeffe, pp. 240–51. Toronto: University of Toronto Press, 2003.

Robinson, Fred C. *"Beowulf" and the Appositive Style.* Knoxville: University of Tennessee Press, 1985.

————. "*Beowulf* in the Twentieth Century." *Proceedings of the British Academy* 94 (1997): 45–62.

————. "Did Grendel's Mother Sit on Beowulf?" In *From Anglo-Saxon to Early Middle English: Studies Presented to E. G. Stanley*, edited by Malcolm Godden, Douglas Gray, Terry Hoad, pp. 1–8. Oxford: Clarendon Press, 1994.

————. "Two Aspects of Variation in Old English Poetry." In *Old English Poetry: Essays on Style*, edited by Daniel G. Calder, pp. 127–45. Berkeley and Los Angeles: University of California Press, 1979.

Sadykov, A. S., et al, eds. and trans. *Manas: Kirgizskiy geroicheskiy èpos* [Manas: A Kirghiz heroic epic]. 4 vols. Moscow: Nauka, 1984–95.

Sauer, Hans, Inge B. Milfull, and Diana Rumrich. "Translations, Paraphrases and Adaptations of *Beowulf*, 1805–2005: A Preliminary Bibliography." In *Recent Trends in Medieval English Language and Literature in Honour of Young-Bae Park*, edited by Jacek Fisiak and Hye-Kyung Kang, pp. 377–431. Seoul: Thaehaksa, 2005.

Schaefer, Ursula. "The Medial Approach: A Paradigm Shift in the Philologies?" In *Written Voices, Spoken Signs: Tradition, Performance, and the Epic Text*, edited by Egbert J. Bakker and Ahuvia Kahane, pp. 215–31, 260–64. Cambridge, MA: Harvard University Press, 1997.

————. "Rhetoric and Style." In Bjork and Niles, *Beowulf Handbook*, pp. 105–24.

————. *Vokalität: Altenglische Dichtung zwischen Mündlichkeit und Schriftlichkeit.* Script Oralia 39. Tübingen: Narr, 1992.

Scheub, Harold. "Body and Image in Oral Narrative Performance." *New Literary History* 8 (1976–77): 345–67.

Schmitz, Andrea. *Die Erzählung von Edige: Gehalt, Genese und Wirkung einer heroischen Tradition.* Turcologica 27. Wiesbaden: Harrassowitz, 1996.

Schopenhauer, Arthur. "On Language and Words." In Schulte and Biguenet, *Theories of Translation*, pp. 32–35. Translated by Peter Mollenhauer, "Über Sprache und Wörte." In *Parerga und Paralipomena*, by Arthur Schopenhauer, 2:460–68. 2 vols. Berlin: Hayn, 1851.

Schücking, Levin. "Wann Entstand der *Beowulf*: Glossen, Zweifel und Fragen." *Beiträge zur Geschichte der deutschen Sprache und Literatur* 42 (1917): 347–410.

Schulman, Jana K. "Translating *Beowulf*: Translators Crouched and Dangers Rampant." *Medieval and Early Modern English Studies* 12, no. 1 (2004): 5–41.

Schulte, Rainer, and John Biguenet, eds. *Theories of Translation: An Anthology of Essays from Dryden to Derrida.* Chicago: University of Chicago Press, 1992.

Schwab, Ute. "Caedmons *carmen*—'Deo suavis laudatio.'" In *Philologische Untersuchungen gewidmet Elfriede Stutz zum 65. Geburtstag*, edited by Alfred Ebenbauer, pp. 408–61. Philologica Germanica 7. Vienna: Braumüller, 1984.

Sen o kříži [The dream of the rood]. Edited and translated by Jan Čermák. Prague: Jitro, 2005.

Serbo-Croatian Heroic Songs (Srpskohrvatske junačke pjesme) [*SCHS*]. Collected, edited, and translated by Milman Parry, Albert B. Lord, and David E. Bynum. Cambridge, MA: Harvard University Press, 1953–. (Vols. 1–2 co-published with the Serbian Academy of Sciences, Belgrade.)

Shaw, George Bernard. "Preface to *Pygmalion*: A Professor of Phonetics." In *George Bernard Shaw on Language*, edited by Abraham Tauber, with a foreword by Sir James Pitman, pp. 47–53. London: Opwen, 1963.

Shippey, T. A. "*Beowulf* for the Big-Voiced Scullions." *Times Literary Supplement*, 1 October 1999, 9–10.

Shippey, T. A., and Andreas Haarder, eds. *"Beowulf": The Critical Heritage*. London: Routledge, 1998.

Simonis de Keza. *Gesta Hungarorum*—Simon of Kéza, *The Deeds of Hungarians*. Edited and translated by László Veszprémy and Frank Schaer. Budapest: Central European University Press, 1999.

Stäblein, Bruno. *Schriftbild der einstimmigen Musik*. Musikgeschichte in Bildern 3.4. Leipzig: VEB Deutscher Verlag für Musik, 1975.

Stanley, Eric G. "'Apo Koinou' Chiefly in *Beowulf*." In *Anglo-Saxonica: Beiträge zur Vor- und Frühgeschichte der englischen Sprache und zur altenglischen Literatur; Festschrift für Hans Schabram*, edited by Klaus R. Grinda and Claus-Dieter Wetzel, pp. 181–207. Munich: Fink, 1993.

Stevens, John. *Words and Music in the Middle Ages: Song, Narrative, Dance and Drama, 1050–1350*. Cambridge: Cambridge University Press, 1986.

Stewart, Ann Harleman. "Kenning and Riddle in Old English." *Papers on Language and Literature* 15 (1979): 115–36.

Stoll, Béla, ed. *Szenci Molnár Albert költői művei* [The poetical works of Albert Szenci Molnár]. Régi magyar költők tára 17, század, 6. Budapest: Akadémiai Kiadó, 1971.

Sudby lidí, stezky spásy [Fates of men, paths of salvation]. Edited by Jan Čermák. Prague: Department of English and American Studies, Faculty of Arts, Charles University, and Modern Language Association, 2004.

Sutton, John William. *Beowulfiana: Modern Adaptations of "Beowulf,"* http://www.library.rochester.edu/camelot/BeowulfBooklet.htm.

Sweet, Henry. *First Steps in Anglo-Saxon*. Oxford: Clarendon Press, 1897.

———, ed. *King Alfred's Version of Gregory's "Pastoral Care."* 2 vols. Early English Text Society, o.s., 45–50. London: Trübner, 1871–72.

———. *The Practical Study of Languages: A Guide for Teachers and Learners*. 1899. Reprint, Oxford: Oxford University Press, 1972.

———. *Student's Dictionary of Anglo-Saxon*. 1896. Reprint, Oxford: Clarendon Press, 1997.

Sweet's Anglo-Saxon Primer. Revised by Norman Davis. Oxford: Clarendon Press, 1965.

Szabó, András. *Szenci Molnár Albert és a Magyar időmértékes vers* [Albert Szenci Molnár and the quantitative meter]. Budapest: Irodalomtörténeti Közlemények, 1996.

Szepes, Erika, and István Szerdahelyi. *Verstan* [Metrics]. Budapest: Gondolat, 1981.

Taeger, B. "Ein vergessener handschriftlicher Befund: Die Neumen im Münchener 'Heliand.'" *Zeitschrift für deutsches Altertum* 107 (1978): 184–93.

Taylor, Keith. "*Beowulf* 1259a: The Inherent Nobility of Grendel's Mother." *English Language Notes* 31, no. 3 (1994): 13–25.

Taylor, Paul Beekman. "The Epithetical Style in *Beowulf*." *Neuphilologische Mitteilungen* 91 (1990): 195–206.

Tezla, Albert. *An Introductory Bibliography to the Study of Hungarian Literature*, http://www.mek.iif.hu/porta/szint/egyeb/katalog/hunlit/html.

Tinker, Chauncey Brewster. *The Translations of "Beowulf": A Critical Bibliography*. With updated bibliography by Marijane Osborn and a new foreword by Fred C. Robinson. Hamden, CT: Archon Books, 1974.

Tolkien, J. R. R. *"Beowulf": The Monsters and the Critics*. Proceedings of the British Academy, Sir Israel Gollancy Memorial Lecture 22. London: Milford, 1936.

———. "Prefatory Remarks." In *Beowulf*, translated by John R. Clark Hall, pp. ix–xliii. London: Allen & Unwin, 1940.

Tóth, István. "Balassi Bálint és az Árgírus-széphistória szerzősége" [Bálint Balassi and the authorship of the Árgírus romance]. *Filológiai Közlöny* 2 (1978): 155–94.

Tripp, Raymond P., Jr. "Bad Breath at the Barrow (*Beowulf* 2288a: Stonc ða æfter stane): The Implications of a Homiletic Perspective." *In Geardagum* 20 (1999): 7–26.

———. "The Homiletic Sense of Time in *Beowulf*." *In Geardagum* 21 (2000): 23–40.

———. "No Rest for the Wicked: A New Homiletic Reading of Grendel's Attack." *Publications of the Medieval Association of the Midwest* 6 (1999): 1–24.

———. "Summing Up the Dragon Episode: An Apophatic Reading of *Beowulf* 3058–75." *In Geardagum* 22 (2001): 57–75.

Trnka, Bohumil. "The *Beowulf* Poem and Virgil's *Aeneid*." *Poetica* (Tokyo) 12 (1981): 150–56.

———. "Dnešní stav bádání o *Beowulfovi*." [Current research on *Beowulf*] *Časopis pro moderní filologii* 12 (1926): 35–51, 124–29, 247–54.

Turner, Sharon. *The History of the Manners, Landed Property, Government, Laws, Poetry, Literature, Religion, and Language of the Anglo-Saxons.* Vol. 4 of *The History of the Anglo-Saxons: From Their First Appearance above the Elbe, to the Death of Egbert.* London: Longman, Hurst, Rees, and Orme, 1807.

Þrymskviða. In *Edda: Die Lieder des Codex Regius.* Vol. 1, *Text*, edited by Gustav Neckel, revised by Hans Kuhn, pp. 111–15. 5th ed. Heidelberg: Carl Winter Universitätsverlag, 1983.

Usmanov, M. "O tragedii èposa i tragediyakh lyudskikh" [On the tragedy of the epic and the human tragedies]. In *Idegey: Tatarskiy narodny èpos* [Idegey: A Tatar folk epic], translated by Semyon Lipkin, pp. 247–54. Kazan: Tatarskoe knizhnoe izd., 1990.

van der Merwe-Scholtz, Hendrik. *The Kenning in Anglo-Saxon and Old Norse Poetry.* Utrecht: Dekker, Van de Vegt en Van Leeuwen, 1927.

Vergilius összes művei [The complete works of Virgil], translated by István Lakatos. Budapest: Európa, 1984.

Vikár, Béla. "Hangsúly és ritmus" [Stress and rhythm]. *Magyar Csillag* 16 (1943): 681–85.

Vinogradov, V. *Kirgizskaya narodnaya muzyka* [Kirghiz folk music]. Funze: Kirgizskoe gosudarstvennoe izd., 1958.

———. "Napevy 'Manasa'" [The melodies of *Manas*]. In Sadykov et al., *Manas*, 1:492–509.

Watts, Ann. C. *The Lyre and the Harp: A Comparative Reconsideration of Oral Tradition in Homer and Old English Epic Poetry.* New Haven, CT: Yale University Press, 1969.

Wéber, Antal, trans. *Érzékeny utazások* [Sentimental journey], by Laurence Sterne. Budapest: Magyar Helikon, 1976.

Weil, Simone. *The Iliad, or, The Poem of Force.* 1940. Reprint, Wallingford, PA: Pendle Hill, 1957.

Whallon, William. "The Diction of *Beowulf*." *PMLA* 76 (1961): 309–19.

Whitelock, Dorothy, ed. *Sweet's Anglo-Saxon Reader in Prose and Verse.* 15th rev. ed. Oxford: Clarendon Press, 1967.

Wilde, Alan. *Horizons of Assent: Modernism, Postmodernism, and the Ironic Imagination.* Baltimore: John Hopkins University Press, 1981.

Williams, David. *Cain and Beowulf: A Study in Secular Allegory.* Toronto: University of Toronto Press, 1982.

———. *Deformed Discourse: The Function of the Monster in Medieval Thought and Literature.* Montreal: McGill-Queen's University Press, 1996.

Wiora, Walter. *European Folk Song: Common Forms in Characteristic Modifications.* Anthology of Music 4. Cologne: Volk, 1966.

Wrenn, C. L. Presidential Address Delivered to the Philological Society, Friday, 10 May 1946. *Transactions of the Philological Society, 1946*, pp. 177–201. London: David Nutt [A. G. Berry], 1947.

Wyld, H. C. "Henry Sweet." *Modern Language Quarterly* 4 (1901): 73–79.

———. "Henry Sweet." *Archiv für das Studium der Neueren Sprache und Literaturen*, n.s., 30 (1913): 1–8.

———, comp. *Collected Papers of Henry Sweet*. Oxford: Clarendon Press, 1913.

Zhirmunsky, V. M. "The Epic of 'Alpamysh' and the Return of Odysseus." *Proceedings of the British Academy* 52 (1966): 267–86.

———. *Skazanie ob Alpamyshe i bogatyrskaya skazka* [The legend of Alpamysh and the heroic tale]. Moscow: Izd. Vostochnoy literatury, 1960.

———. "Vvedenie v izuchenie èposa 'Manas'" [Introduction to the study of "Manas"]. In *Tyurkskiy geroicheskiy èpos* [The Turkic heroic epic], pp. 23–116. Leningrad: Nauka, 1974.

Zhirmunsky, V. M., and H. Zarifov. *Uzbekskiy narodny geroicheskiy èpos* [The Uzbek heroic folk epic]. Moscow: Gos. izd. Khudozhestvennoy literatury, 1947.

Zrínyi, Miklós. *Adriai tengernek Syrenaia* [The Syren of the Adriatic Sea]. Vienna, 1651. Facsimile of the first edition, with a supplement by Sándor Iván Kovács. Budapest: Akadémiai Kiadó; Magyar Helikon, 1980.

Zumthor, Paul. *Oral Poetry: An Introduction*. Translated by Kathryn Murphy-Judy. Minneapolis: University of Minnesota Press, 1990.

Contributors

Mark Amodio is Professor of English at Vassar College, where he teaches early British literature. He is the author of *Writing the Oral Tradition: Oral Poetics and Literate Culture in Medieval England* (Notre Dame) and of the forthcoming *Blackwell Guide to Anglo-Saxon Literature*. His current project focuses on embodied performances in and of *Beowulf*.

Benjamin Bagby is a performer and scholar of medieval musical performance. He directs the Sequentia ensemble for medieval music, which is based in Paris (www.sequentia.org). In addition to the research and ensemble work of Sequentia, Mr. Bagby performs Anglo-Saxon and Germanic oral poetry; his performance of the *Beowulf* epic has been given worldwide since 1990, with a DVD production released in 2007 (www.BagbyBeowulf.com). He writes extensively on performance practice and teaches performance courses in Europe and North America. In 2005 he joined the faculty of the Université de Paris Sorbonne–Paris IV, where he teaches in the masters program for medieval music performance.

Jan Čermák is Associate Professor of English at Charles University in Prague. His research is focused on the history of English, with particular interests in Old and Early Middle English morphology, word-formation and literary language, and Old and Middle English literature, with particular interests in heroic poetry, romance, and the Alliterative Revival, and on the history of Finnish, with particular interests in the *Kalevala*. His translations into Czech include *Beowulf*, the *Old English Exodus*, the *Dream of the Rood*, the *Rune Poem*, and a selection of the Anglo-Saxon laws.

Claudia Di Sciacca is Associate Professor of Germanic Philology at the University of Udine, Italy. Her research activity has mainly concerned Old English language and literature, with a focus on source studies. Her interests also pertain to

423

the lexicon of Old English and other Germanic languages, including the OE verb *sweorcan*, its compounds and derivatives, of which she has investigated the occurrences in *Beowulf* and relevant translations in Italian. Her publications include "*Sweorcan*: una nota ai vv. 1737–1832a del *Beowulf* e alle relative traduzioni italiane," in *Lettura di "Beowulf,"* ed. V. Dolcetti Corazza and R. Gendre (Alessandria: dell'Orso, 2005), pp. 291–329, and *Finding the Right Words: Isidore's "Synonyma" in Anglo-Saxon England* (Toronto: UTP, 2008).

DANIEL DONOGHUE is the John P. Marquand Professor of English at Harvard University, where he has taught a wide range of medieval literature since 1986. Among his books are *Lady Godiva: A Literary History of the Legend* (2003) and *Old English Literature: A Short Introduction* (2004). He has also edited the Norton Critical Edition of Seamus Heaney's translation of *Beowulf* (2002). He currently edits the *Year's Work in Old English Studies* and is editor of the Old English series in the Dumbarton Oaks Medieval Library published by Harvard University Press.

JOHN MILES FOLEY (http://johnmilesfoley.org/portal/Welcome.html) specializes in the world's oral traditions, especially the ancient Greek, medieval English, and contemporary South Slavic traditions. He serves as W. H. Byler and Curators' Professor of Classical Studies and English, and as Founding Director of the Center for Studies in Oral Tradition (www.oraltradition.org, 1986–) at the University of Missouri-Columbia, where he edits the journal *Oral Tradition* (now online and open-access at http://journal.oraltradition.org). Recent major publications include *How To Read an Oral Poem* (2002), complemented by the website www.oraltradition .org/hrop; an edition-translation of *The Wedding of Mustajbey's Son Bećirbey* (2004, eEdition at http://oraltradition.org/zbm); and *A Companion to Ancient Epic* (2005). His *Oral Tradition and the Internet: Pathways of the Mind* is forthcoming in 2012, with a partner website at http://pathwaysproject.org.

MARÍA JOSÉ GÓMEZ-CALDERÓN is lecturer at Universidad de Sevilla, Spain, where she currently teaches English literature in the School of Philology. She specializes in Old English literature, cultural studies, and medievalism; her research interests focus on the reception of the history and literature of Anglo-Saxon England in different cultural traditions, the popular genres, and the media. Among her latest publications are "My Name Is Beowulf: An Anglo-Saxon Hero on the Internet," *Journal of Popular Culture* 43.5 (2010): 988–1003; and "*Beowulf* and the Comic: Contemporary Readings," *Revista Canaria de Estudios Ingleses* 55 (2007): 107–30.

NICHOLAS HOWE, who died in September 2006, was Professor of English at the University of California, Berkeley. Prior to his move to Berkeley, he was director of the Center for Medieval and Renaissance Studies at Ohio State University. While there, he edited several essay collections on medieval culture. In addition, he became a Fellow of the Medieval Academy of America in 2005. His publications include *Writing the Map of Anglo-Saxon England: Essays in Cultural Geography* (Yale, 2007), *Migration and Mythmaking in Anglo-Saxon England* (Notre Dame, 2001), and *The Old English Catalogue Poems* (Copenhagen, 1985).

Pétur Knútsson is Senior Lecturer, English Language, School of Humanities, at the University of Iceland, where he teaches Old English, the history of English, and oral and literate textuality. His research focuses on translation between closely related languages; the archaeology of semantics in medieval and modern Icelandic; the dialogism of topography in the sagas; the textuality of landscape; and on centers, horizons, indices (pointing fingers), and pollices (pointing thumbs). Among his latest publications are "Thumbing through the Index," *Milli mála, Yearbook of the Vigdís Finnbogadóttir Institute of Foreign Languages* (University of Iceland Press, 2010); and "Náin kynni, nýtt líf. Þýðingar milli náskyldra tungumála" [Intimate relationships, new life. translations between closely related languages], *Frændafundur 6* (2008): 65–73.

R. M. Liuzza is Professor of English at the University of Tennessee–Knoxville where he specializes in Old English language, literature, and culture. He is the author of *Beowulf: A New Verse Translation* (2nd edition, Broadview Press, 2011) and *Anglo-Saxon Prognostics* (Boydell and Brewer, 2011), and is a General Editor of the *Broadview Anthology of British Literature*.

Karl Reichl is Professor Emeritus at the University of Bonn, Germany. As a medievalist he has been teaching in the English Department of the University of Bonn but as visiting professor also in departments of comparative literature and Oriental/Near Eastern studies (Harvard University, the Hebrew University of Jerusalem, École Pratique des Hautes Études, Paris, the University of Wisconsin–Madison). His main research interests lie in medieval oral literature and in contemporary (or near contemporary) oral epic poetry in Turkey and the Turkic-speaking areas of Central Asia. His publications include *Turkic Oral Epic Poetry: Traditions, Forms, Poetic Structure* (New York, 1992), *Singing the Past: Turkic and Medieval Heroic Poetry* (Ithaca, NY, 2000), and *Edige: A Karakalpak Oral Epic as Performed by Jumabay Bazarov* (Helsinki, 2007). Forthcoming is a handbook, *Medieval Oral Literature*, ed. K. Reichl (Berlin: de Gruyter).

Jana K. Schulman is Professor of English at Western Michigan University. Her research and teaching interests include Old English and Old Norse languages, literatures, and cultures. She is the author of "Retelling Old Tales: Germanic Myth and Language in Christopher Paolini's *Eragon,*" *Year's Work in Medievalism* 25 (2010): 33–41; "An Anglo-Saxonist at Oxford and Cambridge: Dorothy Whitelock 1901–1982," in *Women Medievalists and the Academy,* ed. Jane Chance (Madison, WI, 2005), 553–64; and "Translating *Beowulf*: Translators Crouched and Dragons Rampant," *Medieval and Early Modern English Studies* 12.1 (2004): 5–41.

KATALIN HALÁCZY SCHOLZ is Senior Lecturer at the Department of English Studies at Eötvös Loránd University in Budapest. Her research interest is Anglo-Saxon poetry, the shorter poems and the Advent Lyrics in particular.

PAUL E. SZARMACH is Emeritus Professor of English and Medieval Studies at Western Michigan University, where for thirteen years he served as Director of the Medieval Institute. Retiring from Western Michigan in 2007, he became Executive Director of the Medieval Academy of America and Editor of *Speculum.* Currently Szarmach is the President of the International Boethius Society. Szarmach's major field of study is Old English prose with special reference to Latin backgrounds and to Alfredian translations. In 2004 he received the Officer's Cross of the Legion of Merit from the Republic of Poland. Szarmach was elected Fellow of the Medieval Academy in 2006, when he also received the Robert L. Kindrick Service Award from Centers and Regional Associations, a standing committee of the Academy.

LOREDANA TERESI is Associate Professor of Germanic Philology at the University of Palermo, Italy. Her research work focuses on many aspects of Old English language and literature. Recent essays on translations and related topics include: "The Old English Term *Heoru* Reconsidered," in *Studies in Anglo-Saxon England,* ed. K. Powell and D. G. Scragg, *Bulletin of the John Rylands University Library of Manchester* 86.2 (2004): 127–78 and "'Mangiatori di uomini' e 'mangiatori d'erba' nell'*Andreas*: due modalità 'mostruose' dell'alto medioevo anglosassone," in *Fabelwesen, mostri e portenti nell'immaginario occidentale: Medioevo germanico e altro,* ed. C. Rizzo (Turin, 2004), pp. 303–25.

Index

Adaptations of *Beowulf*, 1, 11n4, 103, 128, 154

Æschere, 23, 79, 99, 288, 289, 295, 309, 383, 399, 400

Alliteration: in Czech, 106, 110; in Hungarian, 138, 142–44, 146–50; in Icelandic, 191, 195; in Italian, 6, 155–56, 157, 159, 162, 164, 165, 167, 184n86; in *Manas*, 260; in Old English, 34–35, 37, 40, 146, 163–64, 168, 181n36, 184n86, 191, 195, 287, 299, 348, 374–75, 383. *See also* Heaney

Ambiguity, 59–60, 63, 67n46, 69, 70, 74, 77, 81–82, 97, 111, 145, 170, 360, 391

Ambivalence, 52, 60, 62, 75, 170, 284, 294

Andreas, 76, 90, 91, 194, 201, 205, 244, 245, 246, 252

Apposition: in Old English, 21, 61, 174, 327, 391. *See also* Heaney

Appropriation of poem (for national culture), 129, 130, 359

Archaisms: in Czech, 112–13; in English translations, 29n14, 39, 46, 306, 349, 392; in Hungarian, 144; in Italian, 6, 169, 174; in South Slavic, 236; in Spanish, 133n33; in Turkic singing, 258, 262. *See also* Heaney

Assonance: in Italian, 6, 159, 162, 164–65, 168–69; in *Manas*, 260. *See also* Heaney

Audience: academic, 98, 129, 227, 387–88; Anglo-Saxon, 8, 50, 57–58, 62, 66n19, 80–81, 97, 144, 170, 203, 247, 255, 289, 290, 350, 354, 362, 394; general, 15, 17, 227, 387; knowledgeable, 220, 242, 244. *See also* Performance—performer—audience; Poet—audience collective

—, modern: for Bagby's performance, 8, 221, 229–30; for *Beowulf*, 40, 102, 219, 239, 249; for epic singers, 269, 270; for *Wedding of Mustajbey's Son*, 241, 252n23; Italian, 173; Spanish, 117–18, 120–21, 128. *See also* Heaney

Bagby, Benjamin, 7–8, 104n21, 209, 214, 217, 219–21, 226, 228, 251n12, 253, 394

Battle of Maldon, 199, 201, 247

Beowulf as character: as monster-slayer, 128; death of, 38–39, 63, 248, 326, 330, 354; fight with dragon, 177; fight with Grendel, 100–101, 102, 311, 381; fight with Grendel's mother, 100, 194–97, 327; *flyting* with Unferth, 228–29, 307, 387; in Spanish-language adaptation, 126; in Sweet's version, 96; verbal skill of, 57–59; mentioned, 41, 79, 82, 162, 246, 289, 290, 295, 352

Beowulf: poem as simple, primitive, rude, unsophisticated, 3, 17–19, 51, 65n3, 292

—, characters in. *See* Æschere; Beowulf as character; Dragon; Grendel; Grendel's mother; Hrothgar; Scyld Scefing; Unferth; Wealhtheow; Wiglaf

—, date of, 50, 123, 124, 154–55, 324, 348, 361

Typeset in 10/13 Adobe Caslon Pro
Composed by Tom Krol
Manufactured by McNaughton & Gunn, Inc.

Medieval Institute Publications
College of Arts and Sciences
Western Michigan University
1903 W. Michigan Avenue
Kalamazoo, MI 49008-5432
http:/ /www.wmich.edu/medieval/mip

 WESTERN MICHIGAN UNIVERSITY